Cisco CCNA Security
Simplified

*Your Complete Guide to Passing
the IINS Exam*

Paul Browning (LLB Hons) CCNA MCSE

Farai Tafa dual CCIE

ISBN: 978-0-9557815-4-4

Published by:
Reality Press Ltd.
Midsummer Court
314 Midsummer Blvd.
Milton Keynes
MK9 2UB
help@reality-press.com

LEGAL NOTICE

The advice in this book is designed to assist you in reaching the required standard for the CCNA Security (IINS) exam. The labs are designed to illustrate various learning points and are not suggested configurations to apply to a production network. Please check all your configurations with a qualified Cisco professional.

These labs are designed to be used on your own private home labs or rental racks and NOT on production networks. Many of the commands including debug commands can cause serious performance issues on live networks.

Introduction

Congratulations on your decision to study for the prestigious Cisco CCNA Security (aka Implementing Cisco IOS Network Security or IINS) exam. Today's Cisco engineer is expected not only to have a good grasp of network fundamentals, routing protocols, VLANs and spanning tree but also a good working knowledge of security and voice.

Life as a Cisco engineer means a life dedicated to continual learning and self improvement. What you were expected to know just a few years ago pales in comparison to what today's CCNA level engineer must digest and demonstrate during the exam an on a live network.

Cisco CCNA Security Simplified has been written to help you achieve two goals. Firstly, to get you to and beyond the level required to pass your IINS exam. Secondly, and most important, to enable you to become a confident and competent security engineer so you can either be the security engineer for your company or as a freelance consultant.

In order to complete the hands-on labs you will require at least two routers running a late release of IOS (we used c2600-advsecurityk9-mz.124-15.T9.bin) and a copy of Cisco Security Device Manager which is a free download via Cisco.com. You can also use our live racks at http://racks.howtonetwork.net which all members (see below) have free access to.

Although this book contains everything we feel you need to know there are further study resources such as exams, flash study cards and videos of all the labs on our Cisco certification membership site www.howtonetwork.net. We also have a CCNA Security forum moderated by our very own dual CCIE—Farai Tafa.

As a very rough guide I would allow 60 days studying at around 2 hours per day before you take your IINS exam. This estimate is based upon the fact that you should already have passed your CCNA exam before you can take the IINS and that you have only a CCNA level knowledge of network security.

Lastly, this book comes with free updates for life. Please register your copy at the below link so we can contact you when updates become available. http://www.howtonetwork.net/public/1835.cfm

If you have any questions at all, please drop me us line to help@howtonetwork.net
All the best with your studies.

Paul Browning & Farai Tafa (CCIE RS & SP #14811)—January 2010
www.howtonetwork.net

About the Authors

Paul Browning

Paul Browning is the author of CCNA Simplified which is one of the industry's leading CCNA study guides. Paul used to work for Cisco TAC but left in 2002 to start his own Cisco training company in the UK. Paul has taught over 2000 Cisco engineer with both his classroom courses and online Cisco training site www.howtonetwork.net

Paul lives in the UK with his wife and daughter.

Farai Tafa

Farai is a dual CCIE in both Routing and Switching and Service Provider. He currently works for one of the worlds largest telecoms companies as a network engineer. He has written work books for the CCNA, CCNP and Cisco Security exams.

He lives in Washington DC with his wife and daughter.

Table of Contents

PART 1

Theory

CHAPTER 1

An Introduction to Network Security

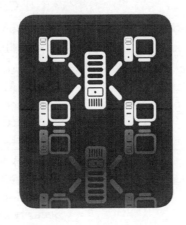

The rapid emergence of the Internet, as well as integrated network infrastructure, has resulted in complex, mission-critical networks that introduce a plethora of security concerns. The IINS exam objectives covered in this chapter are as follows:

- Describe and list mitigation methods for common network attacks
- Describe and list mitigation methods for worm, virus, and Trojan horse attacks
- Describe the Cisco Self-Defending Network architecture

This chapter is broken up into the following sections:

- Network Security Threats
- The CIA Triad
- Vulnerabilities, Exploits, and Risks
- Denial-of-Service Attacks
- Distributed Denial-of-Service Attacks
- Malicious Code Attacks
- Other Common Attacks
- Attack Categories
- Responding to Security Threats

- The Cisco SAFE Blueprint
- Cisco SAFE Security Solutions
- The Cisco PPDIOO Model
- The Cisco Self-Defending Network
- Network Admission Control (NAC)
- Operations Security
- Security Documentation
- The Security Wheel
- Network Security Best Practices

IINS Exam Objective	Section(s) Covered
Describe and list mitigation methods for common network attacks	• Vulnerabilities, Exploits, and Risks • Denial-of-Service Attacks • Distributed Denial-of-Service Attacks • Other Common Attacks • Attack Categories
Describe and list mitigation methods for worm, virus, and Trojan horse attacks	• Malicious Code Attacks • Responding to Security Threats
Describe the Cisco Self-Defending Network architecture	• The Cisco SAFE Blueprint • Cisco SAFE Security Solutions • The Cisco PPDIOO Model • The Cisco Self-Defending Network • Network Admission Control (NAC)
Other Related Topics	• Network Security Threats • The CIA Triad • Operations Security • Security Documentation • The Security Wheel • Network Security Best Practices

Network Security Threats

IP networks are susceptible to security breaches by intruders using a number of different methods. Through the campus network, by dialup, and, most commonly, through the Internet, attackers can view IP data and attack vulnerable network devices and hosts. The OSI Model enables different Layers to work independently of each other. Each Layer of the OSI Model is responsible for a specific function within the stack, with information flowing upwards or downwards to the next Layer as data is processed.

In terms of network security, this means that if one of the Layers of the OSI Model is compromised, then communications are compromised without the other Layers knowing about it. For example, if the Physical Layer is compromised, then all other Layers could also be compromised in succession. Security should cover all Layers of the OSI Model, because, when it comes to networking, security is only as strong as the weakest link.

Every IP network infrastructure should be based on a sound security policy, which will be described in detail later in this chapter. This security policy should be designed to address all of these potential weaknesses and threats. In addition to this, network vulnerabilities must be constantly monitored, found, and addressed because they define points in the network that are potential security weak points that can be exploited by attackers. These vulnerabilities can be discovered by performing a network evaluation, which can include the following:

1. Scanning a network for active IP addresses and open ports on those IP addresses
2. Scanning identified hosts for known vulnerabilities
3. Using password cracking utilities
4. Reviewing system and security logs
5. Performing virus scans
6. Performing penetration testing to see if specific systems (e.g. servers) can be compromised
7. Scanning for unsecured wireless networks

There are two broad categories of network security threats: internal and external.

Internal Threats

Internal security threats originate within the network. That is, these threats are from authorized users of the network, for example, employees, vendors, and possibly even business partners. According to the Computer Security Institute (CSI), approximately 60 to 80 per cent of network security incidents originate from within the network. The reasons internal threats are so common include the following:

- Internal users have knowledge of the network and its resources. For example, users know the IP addresses of servers and network devices (e.g. routers and switches) as well as the location of documentation (e.g. network shares). Armed with this knowledge, users can attempt to connect to these resources and gain unauthorized access.

- Internal users typically have some level of access granted to them because of their position requirements. For example, network and security administrators have access to network devices and servers because of their requirements. However, these users can also use this access for malicious purposes, such as to cover up audit trails of their activities by deleting logs of their activities from certain systems, etc.

- Traditional network security mechanisms are typically deployed on external-facing networks (e.g. the Internet) to prevent external users from unauthorized access. However, this means that they offer no protection from internal users on the trusted network.

External Threats

External threats are those that originate from external attackers who do not yet have intimate knowledge of the network. The majority of these attackers are not very skilled; however, there are some that do possess considerable skill. Some common types of attackers are listed and described in Table 1.1:

Table 1.1. Common Attacker Types

Attacker Type	Description
White Hat Hacker	While White Hat Hackers possess the skill and knowledge to break into computer systems and do damage, they use their skills to help protect organizations from other malicious attackers.
Black Hat Hacker	Black Hat Hackers are also referred to as Crackers, and they use their skill and knowledge for unethical reasons, such as stealing classified information, etc.
Gray Hat Hacker	Gray Hat Hackers are somewhere in-between White Hat Hackers and Black Hat Hackers. These hackers may work for a legitimate organization, as is the case with White Hat Hackers, but may stray and use their skills for unethical reasons, as is the case with Black Hat Hackers.
Phreaker	Phreakers are simply telecommunications hackers who use their skills to hack into telecommunications networks for their own personal gain, e.g. free long distance service.
Script Kiddy	Script Kiddies are users that do not have the skill to write their own hacking programs and therefore use materials and programs downloaded from the Internet to launch attacks.
Hacktivist	Hacktivists are hackers with political motivations. For example, a Hacktivist may deface the website of the rival of their political candidate during a campaign.
Computer Security Hacker	Computer Security Hackers are people who have significant knowledge on computer and network security systems, and they leverage that knowledge to break firewalls, intrusion prevention systems, etc.

Academic Hacker	Academic Hackers are typically students at higher learning institutions who use the institutions computing programs to write their own hacking programs.
Hobby Hacker	Hobby Hackers focus on personal computing, e.g. unlocking iPhones so they can be used on any carrier network instead of just AT&T.

The CIA Triad

One of the most widely accepted security models is the Confidentiality, Integrity, and Availability (CIA) triad. The CIA triad is generally accepted as defining the primary goals of network security, and these three principles should guide all secure systems. Additionally, the CIA triad provides a measurement tool for security implementations.

The CIA principles are applicable across the entire spectrum of security analysis and should be correlated with an implemented security model. A security model is the symbolic portrayal of the security policy, which will be described in detail later in this chapter. Security models integrate the security policies that should be enforced in the system by mapping the security policy requirements into a set of rules and regulations that should be followed by a computer or network system. The simplest way to remember the difference between security models and security policies is that security policies are a set of conceptual goals and high-level requirements, while the security model is the actual dos and don'ts that make this happen. Figure 1.1 illustrates the CIA triad and its correlation security models:

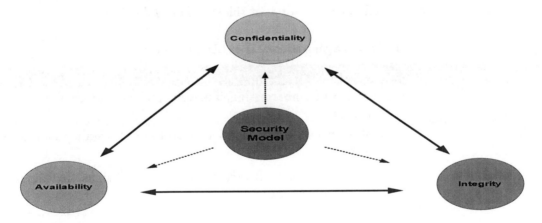

Figure 1.1. The CIA Triad

Confidentiality

Confidentiality prevents the unauthorized disclosure of sensitive information. While encryption and other cryptography methods can be used to safeguard confidential information, it is also important that people understand their roles when it comes to the protection of sensitive data. Networks that ensure confidentiality typically implement the following policies:

- They employ network security mechanisms, such as firewalls, to prevent unauthorized network resource access;
- They require the use of proper credentials to access specific network resources, such as email, servers, and file shares; and
- They encrypt data so that unauthorized users are unable to view the contents contained therein, even if they were to capture the data packets using a network sniffer.

In order to ensure some level of confidentiality, documents are typically classified and document owners are the people that initially determine the level of classification. There are different levels and types of classification used by the civilian world (the majority of us) and by the military that determine who or what groups have access to what data. The data classification levels used in the military are illustrated in Table 1.2:

Table 1.2. Military Data Classifications

Document Category	Description
Confidential	Data that has a reasonable probability of causing damage if disclosed to an unauthorized party.
Secret	Data that has a reasonable probability of causing serious damage if disclosed to an unauthorized party.
Top-Secret	Data that has a reasonable probability of causing exceptionally grave damage if disclosed to an unauthorized party.

The data classification levels used by organizations are illustrated in Table 1.3:

Table 1.3. Organizationial Data Classifications

Document Category	Description
Sensitive	Data that may be embarrassing, if revealed, but will not cause a security threat.
Private	Information that should be kept secret, and whose accuracy should be maintained.
Confidential	Sensitive information, such as customer network designs, that should be protected with great care.

Once the data has been classified by the owners, custodians, who are given the responsibility of protecting the data by the document owners, verify the integrity of the data and keep up-to-date backup copies of the same. The data is then provided to users, who are expected to access and use the data in accordance with an established security policy. Users should also take measures to ensure the data they are using is in safe hands because confidentiality is susceptible to attacks, such as packet captures and dumpster diving.

Integrity

Integrity prevents the unauthorized modification of data, systems, and information. In addition to this, integrity ensures that information is not altered, intentionally or accidentally, without authorization or while en route to the authorized receiver.

There are numerous integrity attacks. The most common of these are salami attacks, which are a series of minor attacks that together result in a larger attack; data diddling, which entails modifying data before it is stored; trust relationship exploitation, which exploits the trust relationship between devices within an organization; and password attacks, botnets, and session hijacking – all of which will be described in detail later in this chapter.

To ensure data integrity, checksum or hash values from protocols such as Message Digest 5 (MD5) and Secure Hash Algorithm (SHA), which will be described in detail later in this guide, can be used to validate the integrity of received information.

Availability

Availability is the prevention of loss of access to resources and information to ensure that information is available for use when it is needed. This can be performed using numerous methods, such as design redundancy, firewall failover, data backups, spare parts, uninterruptible power supplies (UPS), and security architectures. The most common availability attacks are DoS and DDoS attacks, such as TCP SYN flooding and smurf attacks, which are used to prevent access to legitimate resources and information. These attacks will be described in detail later in this chapter.

Vulnerabilities, Exploits, and Risks

It is important that as a network security administrator you understand the differences between vulnerabilities, exploits, and risks.

Vulnerabilities

Vulnerabilities are weaknesses in computing systems, such as routers, switches, and workstations, that attackers use to gain unauthorized access to the system or the data contained within the system. There are numerous types of vulnerabilities that network security administrators should take into consideration. These vulnerabilities include:

- **Physical vulnerabilities**—These include earthquakes and other natural disasters, as well as physical security, and all should be taken into consideration. To avoid a possible security breach, network devices should be stored in physically safe locations, such as locked cabinets with restricted access control. Without such security, networks may be vulnerable to attacks; for example, an attacker may gain access to the Console port of the device and perform a password recovery procedure. From there, the attacker can breach other devices in the network.

- **Operating System vulnerabilities**—These vulnerabilities are based on a system's design. For example, a recently discovered issue in Windows-based Operating Systems is the Windows Registry Editor Utility String concealment weakness, which makes it possible for malware (which will be described later in this guide) to hide strings in the registry.

- **Protocol vulnerabilities**—These vulnerabilities are based on the protocols used by a system. For example, the EIGRP implementation in all versions of IOS is vulnerable to a denial-of-service (DoS) attack if it receives a flood of neighbor announcements.

- **System code vulnerabilities**—These vulnerabilities are based on the code that is executed by a system. For example, programming languages commonly associated with buffer overflows (which will be described in detail in this chapter) include C and C++, which provide no built-in protection against accessing or overwriting data in any part of the memory and do not automatically check that data written to an array (the built-in buffer type) is within the boundaries of that array.

- **Poor system configuration vulnerabilities**—These vulnerabilities are based on poor system configuration. For example, the password hashed on Cisco IOS routers using the enable password command can easily be decrypted using tools that are easily and readily available online; therefore the enable secret command, which uses Message Digest 5 (MD5) encryption (which will be described in detail later in this guide) is recommended instead.

- **Malicious software vulnerabilities**—These vulnerabilities are originated by malicious code that includes viruses and Trojan horses, both of which are explained in detail later in this chapter. For example, Back Orifice is a common Trojan horse that provides the attacker a backdoor in which to bypass normal authentication, secure remote access to a computer, obtain access to plaintext, and so on while attempting to remain undetected.

- **Human vulnerabilities**—These vulnerabilities may or may not be intentional; however, they are vulnerabilities all the same. For example, human trust is a vulnerability from a network security point-of-view. By using social engineering, which is nothing more than creative lying, would-be attackers can gain the trust of employees and use that to obtain valuable information from those employees. This information can then be used to attack and breach the network.

Exploits

Once an attacker has indentified vulnerability, he or she will typically write or use programs designed to take advantage of that vulnerability. These malicious programs are referred to as exploits. Some of the most common exploits take advantage of the following:

- **Default passwords**—For example, on newer Cisco IOS routers, when the router is first shipped the default username and password pair to log in is cisco/cisco. This default username and password pair could be exploited by attackers and should be removed.

- **IP spoofing**—In IP spoofing, the attacker fakes the source IP addresses of packets to gain access to a network and access resources in the same manner as legitimate network hosts. Spoofing is easy to accomplish because there are no real checks in TCP/IP to validate that a packet is really coming from the IP address indicated in the IP header.

- **Application weaknesses**—These exploits occur when attackers find faults in desktop and workstation applications, such as email clients, and execute arbitrary code, implant Trojan horses for future compromise, or crash systems. Further exploitation can occur if the compromised workstation has administrative privileges on the rest of the network.

- **Protocol weaknesses**—These exploits work mostly with plain text transmission protocols such as Telnet, FTP, and HTTP transfers. For example, using a simple network sniffer, attackers can acquire username and password information from Telnet because the protocol sends this information across the network in clear text.

Risks

Information security risk assessment is the process used to identify and understand risks to the confidentiality, integrity, and availability of information and information systems. A risk assessment consists of the identification and valuation of assets and an analysis of those assets in relation to potential threats and vulnerabilities, resulting in a ranking of risks to mitigate. This information should be used to develop strategies to mitigate those risks. The risk analysis can be performed using either quantitative or qualitative analysis.

A quantitative analysis uses a mathematical formula to model the probability and severity of risk. This method is used to calculate the Annualized Loss Expectancy (ALE), which produces a monetary value that can be used to help justify the expense of security solutions.

A qualitative analysis, on the other hand, uses a scenario model in which scenarios of risk occurrence are identified. This can then be used to help justify the expense of security solutions. Qualitative analysis is more commonly used than quantitative analysis. Most qualitative risk analysis methodologies make use of a number of interrelated elements, including:

- **Threats**—things that can go wrong or that can attack the system. Examples might include fire or fraud. Threats are ever-present for every system.

- **Vulnerabilities**—makes a system more prone to attack by a threat or make an attack more likely to have some success or impact. Examples could include system code weaknesses or protocol weaknesses.

- **Controls**—the countermeasures for vulnerabilities. There are four types:
  1. Deterrent controls reduce the likelihood of a deliberate attack.
  2. Preventative controls protect vulnerabilities and make an attack unsuccessful.
  3. Corrective controls reduce the effect of an attack.
  4. Detective controls discover attacks and trigger preventative or corrective controls.

The correlation of these elements is illustrated in Figure 1.2:

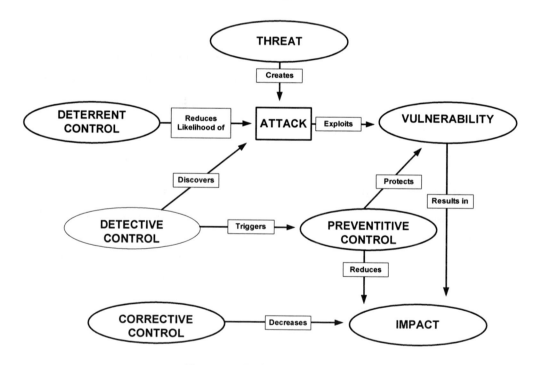

Figure 1.2. Risk Analysis Model

Denial of Service Attacks

A denial-of-service (DoS) or distributed denial-of-service (DDoS) attack is used to restrict or outright deny service from a legitimate network resource or service, such as a public web server, for example. These attacks reduce the ability to service legitimate clients by overloading the intended target or sending traffic that causes these targets to behave unpredictably, which typically results in the targets locking up or crashing completely.

DoS attacks typically do not pose a significant threat to confidential or sensitive data, but they do deny service from legitimate hosts and are difficult to detect and repel. Furthermore, these attacks may also be used to mask other malicious intrusive activities happening elsewhere in the network. For example, a perpetrator could use a DoS or DDoS attack as a diversion to capture the attention of administrators and officials and then proceed to breach or break into other parts of the network while the administrators are reacting to and trying to repel the attacks.

Although these attacks typically occur from a remote location, which makes them more difficult to isolate and identify, they can also be initiated from within an organization, i.e. within the internal network. However, local DoS attacks are typically much easier to identify and isolate and are much less common than remote DoS attacks. The five basic goals of DoS attacks are:

1. The consumption of computational resources, such as bandwidth, disk space, or CPU time;
2. The disruption of configuration information, such as routing information;
3. The disruption of state information, such as unsolicited resetting of TCP sessions;
4. The disruption of physical network components; and
5. The obstruction of communication media between the intended users and the victim.

There have been numerous DoS attacks that have caused massive damage. For example, Morris Worm, written by Robert Morris, a Cornell University CS graduate student, and launched on 2 November 1988, was the first DoS attack of significance. It was said that this worm caused some 5000 machines to be taken out of commission for several hours.

Another classic case occurred in 2000, when CNN, Yahoo, E-Bay, and Datek were taken down for several hours due to traffic flooding from a Stacheldraht-distributed DoS attack. And, finally, in 2002, a Ping Flood DDoS attack briefly interrupted web traffic on nine of the 13 DNS 'root' servers that control the Internet.

While there are numerous types of DoS attacks, the following section describes the most common types, and it is expected that you are familiar with each as part of the IINS requirements. These attacks are as follows:

- Smurf Attacks
- ARP Poison Attacks
- Teardrop Attacks
- Permanent Denial-of-Service Attacks
- UDP Storm Attacks
- Mail Bomb Attacks
- SSH Process Table Attacks
- SYN Attacks

Smurf Attacks

Smurf attacks are also commonly referred to as a ping flood or ICMP flood attacks. These attacks send large amounts of ICMP packets to a machine in order to attempt to crash the TCP/IP stack on the machine and cause it to stop responding to TCP/IP requests. In smurf attacks, the victim is flooded with ICMP echo-reply packets via a reflector or an amplifier.

The attacker sends numerous ICMP echo-request packets to the broadcast address of the reflector subnet. These packets contain the victim's address as the source IP address. Every targeted machine that belongs to any of these subnets responds by sending ICMP 'echo-reply' packets to the victim, as illustrated in Figure 1.3:

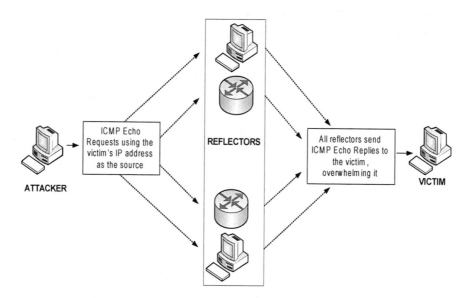

Figure 1.3. Smurf Attacks

To mitigate this problem, Cisco recommends using Committed Access Rate (CAR) to limit the throughput of ICMP echo-request and echo-reply packets. In addition to this, ICMP packets can also be rate limited using the Modular QoS Command Line (MQC) in later Cisco IOS software versions.

To prevent Cisco routers from being used as reflectors in smurf attacks, the routers should be configured not to forward packets directed to broadcast addresses by using the `no ip directed-broadcast` interface configuration command. At Layer 2, IP Source Guard, used in conjunction with DHCP Snooping, can also be used to prevent such attacks. These two techniques will be described in detail later in this guide.

ARP Poison Attacks

An Address Resolution Protocol (ARP) Poison attack requires the attacker to have access to the victim's LAN. The attacker deludes the hosts of a specific LAN by providing them with wrong MAC addresses for hosts with already-known IP addresses, as illustrated in Figure 1.4:

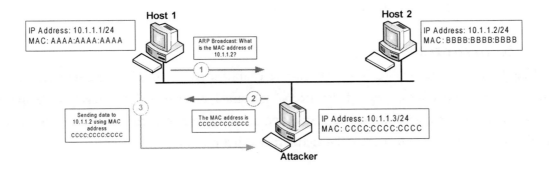

Figure 1.4. ARP Poison Attacks

In the diagram illustrated above, Host 1 and Host 2 reside on the same LAN. In addition to this, an attacker has also managed to infiltrate the same LAN as these two hosts. In order for Host 1 to send frames to Host 2, it must first send out an ARP broadcast asking for who is the MAC address of 10.1.1.2, as illustrated in step 1. The attacker sees this broadcast and before Host 2 can respond, the attacker replies to Host 1 providing it with his machine's MAC address, as illustrated in step 2. In step 3, Host 1 receives this information and begins forwarding data to the attacker's machine, assuming it to be Host 2.

To protect against such attacks, Cisco recommends the use of Dynamic ARP Inspection (DAI) in conjunction with DHCP snooping. These concepts will be described in detail later in this guide.

Teardrop Attacks

A teardrop attack involves sending malformed IP fragments with overlapping, over-sized, payloads to the target machine, i.e. a stream of IP fragments with their offset field overloaded. The Internet Protocol allows IP fragmentation so that datagrams can be broken up into pieces small enough to pass over a link with a smaller MTU than the original datagram size; however, these fragments should not be malformed and should never be the initial packets in a data stream. The destination host that tries to reassemble these malformed fragments eventually crashes or reboots. Cisco recommends the use of IP Access Control Lists that allow only non-initial fragments to protect against such attacks.

Permanent Denial-of-Service Attacks

A permanent denial-of-service (PDoS), or phlashing, attack is one that damages a system so badly that it requires replacement or reinstallation of hardware. Unlike the DDoS attack (which will be described later in this section), a PDoS attack exploits security flaws in the remote management interfaces of the victim's hardware, be it routers, printers, or other devices.

These flaws leave the door open for an attacker to 'update' remotely the device firmware to a modified, corrupt, or defective firmware image, therefore 'bricking' the device and making it permanently unusable for its original purpose. The PDoS is a pure hardware-targeted attack. While there is no single solution to prevent against PDoS attacks, it is important to keep current with updates on security vulnerabilities posted on vendor websites.

UDP Storm Attacks

In a User Datagram Protocol (UDP) connection, a character generation (commonly referred to as chargen) service generates a series of characters each time it receives a UDP packet, while an echo service echoes any character it receives. Exploiting these two services, the attacker sends a packet with the source spoofed to be that of the victim to another machine.

Next, the echo service of the former machine echoes the data of that packet back to the victim's machine and the victim's machine, in turn, responds in the same way. Hence, a constant stream of useless load is created that burdens the network. Such attacks can be mitigated by disabling these and other unnecessary services, such as TCP and UDP small servers, in Cisco IOS.

Mail Bomb Attacks

In a mail bomb attack, the victim's mail queue is flooded by an abundance of messages, causing system failure. There are two methods of perpetrating a mail bomb attack. These methods are mass mailing and list linking. Mass mailing consists of sending numerous duplicate mails to the same email address. While these types of mail bombs are simple to design and are very common, they can also be easily detected by spam filters, which reduce their overall threat.

In addition to this, there is also a variant of mail bomb attacks referred to as Zip bombing. After most commercial mail servers began checking mail with anti-virus software and filtering certain malicious file types, attackers tried to send Trojan horse viruses compressed into archives, such as ZIP, RAR, or 7-Zip. While these attacks affected legacy mail servers, modern mail servers usually have sufficient intelligence to recognize such attacks, as well as sufficient processing power and memory to process malicious attachments without interruption of service, though some are still susceptible if the ZIP bomb is mass-mailed.

SSH Process Table Attacks

This attack makes hundreds of connections to the intended target device(s) with the Secure Shell (SSH) Protocol without completing the login process. In this way, the SSH daemon on the victim's system is obliged to start so many SSH processes that it is eventually exhausted and legitimate users are unable to access the service, or device. In Cisco IOS software, such attacks can be mitigated by using restrictive ACLs that permit only legitimate users and subnets SSH to devices. In addition to this, features such as TCP Intercept can also be used.

SYN Attacks

SYN attacks are a type of DoS attack and are also referred to as SYN flood attacks. These attacks occur during the three-way handshake that is used to establish a TCP connection. This handshake is illustrated in Figure 1.5:

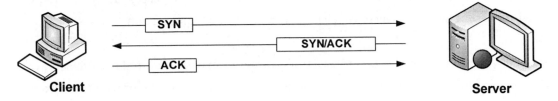

Figure 1.5. SYN Attacks

In the three-way handshake, a client requests a new connection by sending a TCP SYN packet to a server. The server sends a TCP SYN/ACK packet back to the client and places the connection request in a queue. Finally, the client acknowledges the TCP SYN/ACK packet received from the server with a TCP ACK packet.

During a TCP SYN flood, the attacker sends an abundance of TCP SYN packets to the victim, obliging it both to open a lot of TCP connections and to respond to them; however, the attacker does not execute the third step of the three-way handshake that follows, rendering the victim unable to accept any new incoming connections because its queue is full of half-open TCP connections, as illustrated in Figure 1.6:

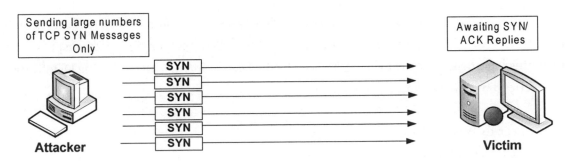

Figure 1.6. SYN Flood Disabled Victim

TCP SYN floods are relatively easy to mitigate and to protect against. In addition to using ACLs to rate limit TCP SYN packets, Cisco also recommends the use of the TCP Intercept feature to protect against TCP-based DoS attacks. TCP Intercept will be described in detail later in this guide.

In addition to the DoS attacks described in this section, there are other DoS attacks pertaining exclusively to operating systems (OS) that you should be aware of. A particularly dangerous OS DoS attack is the Land, or Land.C, attack. In this attack, the perpetrator sends the victim a TCP SYN packet that contains the same IP address as the source and destination addresses. The reason a Land attack works is because it causes the machine to reply to itself continuously, which eventually completely locks the system. This attack can be used against the majority of operating systems used in today's networks.

A banana attack is another particular type of DoS. This attack involves redirecting outgoing messages from the client back onto the client, thereby preventing outside access as well as flooding the client with the sent packets, which will eventually lock up the target system.

Additionally, an attacker with access to a victim's computer may slow it until it is unusable or crash it by using a fork bomb. A fork bomb works by creating a large number of processes very quickly in order to saturate the available space in the list of processes kept by the computer's OS. If the process table becomes saturated, no new programs can start until another process terminates. Even if that happens, it is not likely that a useful program will be started since the instances of the bomb program will each attempt to take any newly available slot themselves.

Distributed Denial of Service Attacks

As bad as DoS attacks may be, DDoS attacks do even more damage. These attacks are generally executed in two phases. In the first phase, the perpetrator compromises computers scattered on the Internet and installs specialized software on these hosts to assist in the attack. In the second phase, the compromised hosts—commonly referred to as zombies—are then instructed (through masters) to begin the attack.

Using control software, each of these zombies can then be used to mount its own DoS attack on the intended target(s). The cumulative effect is to overwhelm the target, or simply exhaust resources, preventing legitimate users from being serviced by the DDoS target(s). The following DDoS attacks are described in this section:

1. Peer-to-Peer Attacks
2. Reflected Attacks
3. Distributed Attacks

Peer-to-Peer Attacks

Attackers have found a way to exploit a number of bugs in peer-to-peer servers to initiate DDoS attacks. Unlike regular botnet (which is a collection of software robots, or bots, that run autonomously and automatically) attacks, with peer-to-peer there is no botnet and the attacker does not have to communicate with the clients it subverts. Instead, the attacker acts as a 'puppet master', instructing clients of large peer-to-peer file sharing hubs to disconnect from their peer-to-peer network and to connect to the victim's website instead. The targeted web server will be plugged up by the incoming connections.

While peer-to-peer attacks are easy to identify with signatures, the large number of IP addresses that need to be blocked means that this type of attack can overwhelm mitigation defenses. Once the connection is opened to the server, the identifying signature can be sent and detected, and the connection subsequently torn down, which takes server resources and can harm the server. This method of attack can be prevented by specifying, in the peer-to-peer protocol, which ports are and are not allowed. If port 80 is not allowed, then the possibilities for attacks on websites can be very limited. In most cases, it is recommended that peer-to-peer protocols are filtered and blocked entirely.

Reflected Attacks

A distributed reflected denial-of-service (DRDoS) attack involves sending forged requests of some type to a very large number of computers that will reply to the requests. Using Internet protocol spoofing, the source address is set to that of the targeted victim, which means all the replies will go to (and flood) the target.

Smurf attacks can be considered a form of reflected attack, as the flooding host sends echo- request packets to the broadcast address of a network or networks, thereby enticing many hosts to send echo-reply packets to the victim. Many services can be exploited to act as reflectors, with some harder to block than others.

Distributed Attacks

A distributed denial-of-service (DDoS) attack occurs when multiple systems are used to flood the bandwidth or resources of a targeted system, usually one or more web servers. These systems may be compromised by attackers using a variety of methods. Malware can carry DDoS attack mechanisms, as was the case with MyDoom. This attack mechanism was triggered on a specific date and time and involved hard-coding the target IP address prior to release of the malware.

A system may also be compromised with a Trojan—which is a term used to describe malware that appears, to the user, to perform a desirable function but, in fact, facilitates unauthorized access to the user's computer system—allowing the attacker to download a zombie agent. Attackers can also break into systems using automated tools that exploit flaws in programs that listen for connections from remote hosts.

Stacheldraht is a classic example of a DDoS tool. It utilizes a layered structure where the attacker uses a client program to connect to handlers, which are compromised systems that issue commands to the zombie agents, which in turn facilitate the DDoS attack.

Agents are compromised by the attacker via the handlers, using automated routines to exploit vulnerabilities in programs that accept remote connections running on the targeted remote hosts. Each handler can control up to a thousand agents. These collections of systems compromisers are known as botnets. This concept is illustrated in Figure 1.7:

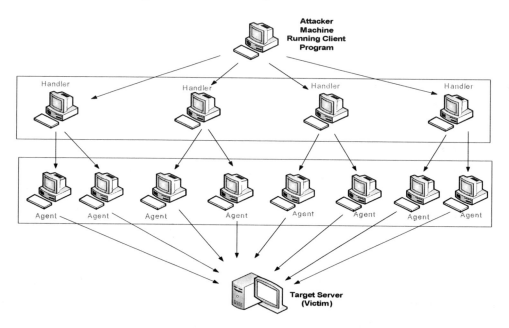

Figure 1.7. DDoS Attack

DDoS tools such as Stacheldraht still use classic DoS attack methods centered on IP spoofing and amplification, such as smurf attacks and fraggle attacks. A fraggle attack occurs when the perpetrator sends a large amount of UDP echo traffic to IP broadcast addresses, all of it having a fake source address. This attack is simply a rewrite of the smurf attack code, which uses UDP echo packets instead of ICMP.

It is important to note the difference between a DDoS and DoS attack. If an attacker mounts a smurf attack from a single host, this would be classified as a DoS attack; in fact, any attack against availability would be classed as a DoS attack. On the other hand, if an attacker uses a thousand zombie systems to simultaneously launch smurf attacks against a remote host, this would be classified as a DDoS attack.

SECTION 1: AN INTRODUCTION TO NETWORK SECURITY

To an attacker, the major advantages of using a DDoS attack are that multiple machines can generate more attack traffic than one machine; multiple attack machines are harder to turn off than a single attack machine; and the behaviour of each attack machine can be stealthier, making it harder to track and shut down. These attacker advantages can cause challenges for some defense mechanisms.

Malicious Code Attacks

Malicious code attacks use programs that are written by attackers and are designed to do damage. Trojan horses, viruses, and malicious software (malware) are all examples of malicious code attacks. These programs typically do not require that the attacker be present for them to do damage, and they are among the most dangerous types of attacks. The following are the six types of malicious code attacks:

1. Malware
2. Viruses
3. Trojan Horses
4. Logic Bombs
5. Worms
6. Backdoor

Malware

Two types of malware are viruses and Trojan horses. Viruses are programs that self-replicate, i.e. reproduce themselves without user intervention. In addition to this, some viruses can actually modify themselves to prevent detection, making such attacks very difficult to repel.

A Trojan horse (sometimes referred to simply as a Trojan) is a program that masquerades as one thing but actually does something else instead of, or even in addition to, its intended use. These programs are typically packaged as attractive programs that offer potential victims great benefits, such as a faster computer or spyware removal, for example.

Infamous examples of data-stealing malware include: Bancos, an information stealer that waits for the user to access banking websites then spoofs pages of the bank website to steal sensitive information; Gator, spyware that covertly monitors web-surfing habits, uploads data to a server for analysis, and then serves targeted pop-up ads; LegMir, spyware that steals personal information such as account names and passwords related to online games; and Qhost, a Trojan that modifies the Hosts file to point to a different DNS server when banking sites are accessed and then opens a spoofed login page to steal login credentials for those financial institutions.

27

UXBRIDGE COLLEGE
LEARNING CENTRE

Viruses

A computer virus is a computer program that can copy itself and infect a computer without the permission or knowledge of the owner. The word virus is also often, but erroneously, used to refer to other types of malware, adware, and spyware, which cannot self-reproduce.

Adware is software that automatically plays, displays, or downloads advertisements to a computer after the software is installed on it or while the application is being used, while spyware is a type of malware that is installed secretly on computers to collect information about users, their computers, or their browsing habits without their informed consent. There are several examples of infamous viruses.

The Melissa virus, for example, attacked computers in March 1999, infecting machines when users opened a Word document attachment. Though the effect the virus had on individuals' computers was minimal, users of Outlook Express unintentionally sent the virus on to the first 50 people in their Global Address Book. For companies, however, the virus had a larger impact. More than a million users were affected, and the virus caused $80 million in damage. This was also the first virus to travel through email.

Another classic example is that of the 911 virus. In April 2000, the National Infrastructure Protection Center (NIPC) released an alert about the 911 virus, which erased hard drives and programmed computers to dial 911. In spite of efforts to protect against it, a version of the attack resurfaced in July 2002 with a more alarming result. In that case, the virus targeted WebTV user-group boards; reports say that once the infected attachment was opened, the WebTV device shut down, rebooted, and dialed 911.

Like any other computer program, viruses must be executed in order to function and then the computer must follow the viruses' instructions, which are referred to as virus payloads. This is not to say that a virus will not run if the user does not explicitly execute it. In most cases, a virus typically has some written code that will trick the computer's OS into running it, most likely without the user being aware of this.

Once executed, the virus payload can then disrupt or change data files, display erroneous messages, or cause the OS to malfunction. Viruses spread when the payload is transferred from one computer to another, via infected files, for example.

Trojan Horses

While Trojan horses somewhat resemble viruses, they are actually in a category of their own. These programs are often disguised as something else, such as a program designed to make your computer run faster, for example. However, they contain a malicious program and when the program the user installed is called to perform its function, the malicious program can cause all sorts of problems, such as ruining a hard disk.

The most famous Trojan horse to date is probably Back Orifice, which was developed by the hacker group known as Cult of the Dead Cow. Once installed, this program gives the attacker access and control over any computer running a Windows 95/98 or later operating system.

Logic Bombs

Logic bombs are a type of malware that are designed to do damage after a certain condition is met, such as the passing of a certain date, for example. In addition to this, logic bombs may also be left behind after an attack, so that the attacker can destroy any evidence of the attack that the system administrators may find.

One of the most well-known logic bombs was the Chernobyl virus, which spread via infected floppy disks or through infected files and replicated itself by writing to an area of the boot sector of a disk. This virus was set to activate on a certain date and, on that date, it caused severe issues for infected users as it attempted to rewrite the BIOS (Basic Input/Output System) and erase the hard drives of the victims' computers. The damage was so severe that those who were affected required new BIOS chips from manufactures to repair the damage caused by the virus.

Worms

Worms are self-replicating programs that do not alter files but reside in the active memory on the infected devices and duplicate themselves via the network. Worms use the automated functionality found in operating systems and are invisible to the user. In addition to this, some worms also contain a malicious payload and are noticed only after the network resources are completely consumed or the victim's computer has been degraded to unusable levels. There have been numerous cases of worms causing severe amounts of damage; however, perhaps the most infamous two worms ever are Code Red and the Love Bug.

The Code Red worm operated in three stages—scanning, flooding, and sleeping. During the scanning phase, the worm searched for vulnerable computers and ran damaging computer code on them. Next, in the flooding phase, the worm sent bogus data packets to the White House website. At its peak, the worm infected 2,000 machines every minute, infecting 359,000 machines in total, and cost $1.2 billion worth of damage. The worm could have affected more computers, but because of a Code Red warning, many people were able to protect their machines. Originally, 35 per cent of the 3.5 million sites that used Microsoft IIS software were vulnerable, but that number dropped to 15 per cent following the warning.

The Love Bug worm flooded the Internet with emails in May 2000 with the subject ILOVEYOU. The body of the deceptive email read, "Kindly check the attached love letter coming from me." When opened, the email wreaked havoc on computers, replicating it automatically, sending copies to everyone in the user's address book, and damaging computer files, such as MP3s. Although it was first detected in Asia, this worm spread across the world, infecting US government computers at Congress, the White House, and the Pentagon. Officials estimated that the worm affected 80 per cent of businesses in Australia and a similar percentage in the US.

As we have learned, worms can cause massive amounts of damage and pose one of the most significant threats to networks in general. Because of the potential damage that worms can cause, there is a specific model that is recommended for worm attack mitigation. Worm attacks can be prevented via containment, planning, tools, and techniques.

The first stage of the reaction process is to contain the spread of the worm inside the network. Compartmentalization, which is a core principle of the SAFE Blueprint (which will be described later in this chapter), allows isolation of parts of the network that are not yet infected. Containment may be performed using one of two actions, as illustrated in Figure 1.8:

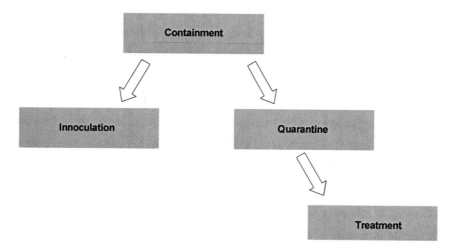

Figure 1.8. Containment in Action

The inoculation phase involves patching all systems. If the appropriate signature files or plug-ins are available for tools, it is worthwhile to start scanning the network for vulnerable systems. This activity might allow operations staff to find vulnerable systems before they become infected. It is important to remember that during a worm crisis, there are three types of systems in your network: patched systems, unpatched systems, and infected systems.

The quarantine phase involves finding each infected machine and disconnecting, removing, or blocking them from the network to prevent them from infecting other unpatched machines on the network. To achieve this goal, the infected systems need to be isolated and quarantined. The treatment phase involves the cleaning and the patching of each infected system. Some worm attacks might require complete reinstallations of the core system to ensure that the machine is clean.

The second phase is planning. When these events occur, reaction time is critical, and these processes need to be in place. It is strongly recommended that every organization plan the reaction methodology ahead of the next crisis. This may include contacts, escalation procedures, conference calls, etc. and it should be clearly understood by everyone.

Finally, tools and techniques should be used in the third phase of worm prevention. Because of their nature, it is important to know and understand that there is currently no single guaranteed solution for dealing with worm attacks; however, some of the tools that can be used to defend against worm attacks are as follows:

1. Access Control Lists (ACLs)
2. Unicast Reverse Path Forwarding (uRPF)
3. NetFlow and NetFlow export
4. Routing protocols such as remote-triggered black hole filtering (RTBH)

Access Control Lists (ACLs) serve a dual purpose as security tools. They provide a mechanism to permit or deny traffic as well as a mechanism to detect certain traffic types. The use of ACLs to permit or deny traffic is a well-understood and well-documented security feature. For worm mitigation, it is important to know that ACLs can play a key role in preventing the spread of a worm by blocking its attack vector, which is usually a TCP or UDP port.

The Unicast RPF (uRPF) feature helps to mitigate problems that are caused by the introduction of malformed or forged (spoofed) IP source addresses into a network by discarding IP packets that lack a verifiable IP source address. For Internet Service Providers (ISPs) that provide public access, uRPF deflects such attacks by forwarding only packets that have source addresses that are valid and consistent with the IP routing table. This action protects the network of the ISP, its customers, and the rest of the Internet.

NetFlow is used as the foundational technology for obtaining traffic flow information across a network. A flow is defined by seven unique keys: source IP address, destination IP address, source port, destination port, Layer 3 protocol type, Type of Service (ToS) byte, and input logical interface. By observing traffic flows across the network, it is possible to see events that might be malicious. Some events might cause high traffic volumes, such as a DoS attack; others might be more subtle. In any case, observing the flow of information can detect these events.

While going into the details of **RTBH** is beyond the scope of this course, you should have a basic understanding of how it works. In essence, a sinkhole is a multifaceted security tool and a portion of the network that is designed to accept and analyze attack traffic. Sinkholes were originally used by ISPs to engulf attack traffic, in many cases drawing attacks away from a customer or other target. In more recent times, sinkholes have been used in enterprise environments to monitor attacks, detect scanning activity from infected machines, and generally monitor for other malicious activity. You are not required to go into specifics on sinkholes and/or their configuration for the IINS course requirements.

In addition to internal preparation and groups, it is also important to realize and understand the importance of external support groups. Entities that are helpful are the Computer Emergency Response Team Coordination Center (CERT/CC), the Cisco Product Security Incident Response Team (PSIRT), and the various newsgroups that enable administrators to share valuable security information.

The CERT/CC is a US federally funded research and development center that works with the Internet community to facilitate responses to incidents involving the Internet and the hosts that are attacked. CERT/CC is also designed to take proactive steps to ensure that future vulnerabilities and attacks are communicated to the entire Internet community. In addition to this, CERT/CC also conducts research aimed at improving the security of existing systems.

For Cisco customers, the Cisco Product Security Incident Response Team (PSIRT) is available for customers to report any security concerns regarding flaws in Cisco IOS products. The Cisco PSIRT investigates all reports regardless of the Cisco software code version or product lifecycle status. Issues will be prioritized on the potential severity of the vulnerability and other environmental factors. The ultimate resolution of the reported incident may require upgrades to products that are under active support from Cisco.

For vulnerabilities reported to Cisco that may impact multiple vendors (i.e. a generic protocol issue), the PSIRT works with third-party coordination centers, such as CERT/CC, to manage a coordinated industry disclosure. In those situations, the PSIRT will either assist the vulnerability reporter in contacting the coordination center, or may do so on their behalf. For vulnerabilities reported to PSIRT involving another vendor's product(s), the PSIRT will notify the vendor directly, coordinate with the reporter, or engage a third-party coordination center.

Newsgroups are mailing list type forums that can be used to share ideas and past incidents to keep current with the latest security concerns and protection policies. While there are numerous newsgroups on the Internet, the CERT/CC recommends (along with several others) the **alt.security** newsgroup, which lists computer and other security issues; the **comp.virus** newsgroup, which lists computer viruses and related topics; and **comp.security.announce**, which provides computer security announcements, including new CERT/CC advisories, summaries, and vendor-initiated bulletins.

Backdoor

There are several types of back doors, or backdoors, which are simply programs or deliberate configurations that allow for unauthenticated access to systems, a notorious example being Back Orifice. Legitimate programs such as Virtual Network Computing (VNC) and PC Anywhere, as well as malicious programs, can all provide backdoor access to systems.

In addition, attackers can also use a rootkit, which is a collection of programs that attackers can use to mask their presence, instead of using backdoors. Rootkits are much more difficult to detect than the average backdoor.

For the most part, a good majority of malicious code attacks can be detected by using up-to-date anti-virus software to secure network hosts. In addition to this, Intrusion Prevent Systems, such as the Cisco IPS Sensor, can also be used to detect viruses and other anomalies based on signatures, thus providing an additional layer of network security.

Password Attacks

Password attacks are fairly common and are easy to perform, and often result in successful intrusion. Because of this, it is recommended that a strict password policy be enforced. There are two types of password attacks that can be performed. The first method is brute force password attacks and the second is dictionary-based attacks.

Brute Force Attacks

A brute force attack is the simple act of guessing keys and passwords until the correct one is found. These attacks are typically successful because key lengths used to secure passwords are always finite. For example, 56-bit Data Encryption Standard (DES), which will be described in detail later in this guide, is relatively easy to crack by trying every key combination from 56 zeros to 56 ones. While this may seem daunting for a novice, a skilled attacker can perform this in a matter of minutes. Increasing the key lengths, for example, using 3DES (Triple DES) instead, will significantly reduce the probability that a brute force attack will be successful.

Brute force attacks typically attempt to discover passwords by stealing a copy of the username and hashed (encrypted) password and then methodically encrypting different possible passwords using the same hashing function until a match is found. If a match is found, the password is considered cracked.

Simple hashing functions can be cracked in very little time and offer no real security. The most effective method to secure passwords is to use advanced hashing functions, such as RSA and other public key encryption techniques, all of which will be described in detail later in this guide.

Dictionary-based Attacks

In this type of attack, long lists of words of a particular language, called dictionary files, are searched to find a match to the encrypted password. These attacks are fairly successful on passwords that contain common letters; however, more complex passwords that incorporate letters, numbers, and symbols (such as the password c(n@s3cur!ty, for example) require a different brute force technique and generally take much longer to run and crack.

Other Common Attacks

In addition to the attacks already explained, there are several other common attacks that you are expected to be familiar with. This section describes the following attacks:

1. Spoofing Attacks
2. Man-in-the-Middle Attacks
3. Replay Attacks
4. TCP/IP Hijacking Attacks
5. War Dialing Attacks
6. Vulnerability Scanning
7. Sniffing
8. Privilege Escalation
9. Footprint Analysis
10. Buffer Overflows

Spoofing Attacks

Spoofing attacks involve providing false information about your identity, i.e. pretending to be someone that you are not, in order to gain unauthorized access to systems. The most common type of spoofing is IP spoofing, where the attacker fakes the source IP address of packets to gain access to a network and access resources in the same manner as legitimate network hosts. There are two types of spoofing attacks: blind spoofing attacks, where the attacker can only send and has to make assumptions about replies; and informed (non-blind) spoofing attacks, where the attacker can actually monitor, and therefore participate in, bi-directional communications.

Spoofing is easy to perform because there are no real checks in TCP/IP to validate that a packet is really coming from the IP address indicated in the IP header. Although spoofing is very common, it can be mitigated fairly easily. In Cisco IOS software, for example, Unicast Reverse Path Forwarding (uRPF), which will be described later in this guide, and Access Control Lists (ACLs) can be used to prevent IP spoofing.

In addition to this, firewalls (e.g. the Cisco Adaptive Security Appliance (ASA)), other techniques (e.g. disabling and preventing features such as source routing, which allow users to control the path a packet takes), and using cryptographic algorithms (which will be described in detail later in this guide) can also be used to prevent spoofing attacks.

Man-in-the-Middle Attacks

Man-in-the-middle (MIM or MITM) attacks, also known as bucket-brigade or Janus attacks, are a form of active eavesdropping in which the attacker makes independent connections with the victims and relays messages between them, making them believe that they are talking directly to each other over a private connection when in fact the entire conversation is controlled by the attacker. The attacker must be able to intercept all messages going between the two victims and inject new ones.

Figure 1.9 illustrates the establishment of a simple Telnet session from the client computer to the network router:

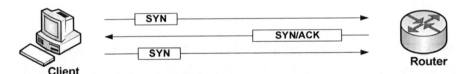

Figure 1.9. Telnet Session

Because Telnet is TCP-based, the three-way handshake is used to establish the connection between the client and the router (which is acting as the TCP server in this case). In MITM attacks, the attacker monitors the packets moving between the client and the router and analyzes them in order to manipulate the data. This is possible by using tools to predict the correct sequence number in the packet exchanges between the client and the router.

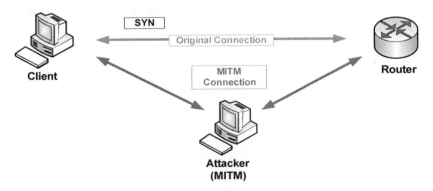

Figure 1.10. MITM Attack

As illustrated in Figure 1.10 above, once the TCP connection is intercepted, the attacker acts as a proxy, being able to read, insert, and modify the data in the intercepted communication. MITM attacks are very difficult to prevent. This is because of the fact that there are plenty of tools that can be used to predict TCP sequence numbers available to attackers.

As a safeguard, however, it is recommended that secure TCP-based services such as HTTPS and SSH be used in place of clear text services such as HTTP and Telnet. While these may not completely deter MITM attacks, the added security employed by HTTPS and SSH ensures that the data is not easily viewable as would be if clear text methods were used.

Replay Attacks

Replay attacks are performed by capturing sensitive data and then replaying it back to the host in order to replicate the transaction. Replay attacks can be used to gain unauthorized access to systems by attackers. For example, legitimate users use their credentials to log in to a server housing sensitive information. However, an attacker captures the session information and when the legitimate user logs off, the attacker logs on using the captured session information. The attacker then accesses the file server masquerading as the authorized user and gains access to sensitive files and other information.

These attacks can be reduced by using session tokens and timestamps. A session token is a unique identifier (usually in the form of a hash generated by a hash function) that is generated and sent from a server to a client to identify the current interaction session, while a timestamp is a sequence of characters, denoting the date and time at which a certain event occurred.

TCP/IP Hijacking

TCP/IP hijacking is also referred to as session hijacking. In order to hijack a TCP/IP session, attackers must first intercept a legitimate user's data and then insert themselves into the session. This is not the same as MITM attacks where the attacker simply changes the packets between the client and the server, because the actual session is hijacked by the attacker in this attack, as illustrated in Figure 1.11:

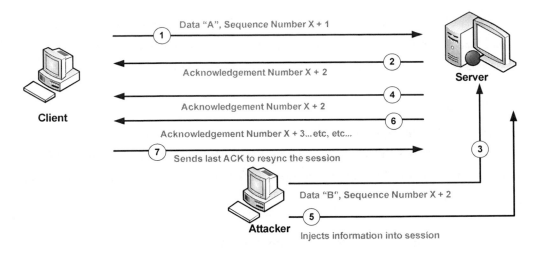

Figure 1.11. TCP/IP Hijack

Based on the diagram above, in step 1, the client sends the server data (A) with a TCP sequence number of X + 1. The server acknowledges this data, in step 2, with an ACK number X + 2. The attacker, who has been watching the TCP session between the client and the server, then quickly sends the server a data packet (B) with a TCP sequence number of X + 2, as illustrated in step 3. The server responds to the client with an ACK number X + 2, as illustrated in step 4.

Meanwhile, the attacker injects information into the session, as illustrated in step 5. The server acknowledges the data being sent by the attacker by sending ACK packets to the client, as illustrated in step 6. The client receives these ACK packets for data that he or she has not sent and then becomes confused. The client then attempts to send the last ACK sent back to the server to try to resync the session, as shown in step 7. This continues as the attacker continues to send data to the server, and eventually the client terminates the session and the attacker continues to inject information as desired.

Online tools are readily available and can be used to monitor and hijack basic Telnet and File Transfer Protocol (FTP) sessions quite easily. In addition to this, attackers can also hijack session cookies, which are normally used to store login credentials and other sensitive information, and then use those cookies to access the user's session. The legitimate user, in this case, receives a 'session expired' or 'login failed' message and is most likely unaware that anything suspicious even occurred.

Attackers can also hijack sessions during periods of inactivity and before the server terminates the connection based on pre-configured inactivity timeouts. For example, a user logs in to his or her bank account and then locks the computer and walks away to take a break. During this period of inactivity, the server begins to count down to the termination of the session because there is no activity from the user. However, depending on how long the session expiration timer is, it is possible for an attacker to hijack the session before it expires. Again, the user is most likely unaware of this event.

These attacks can be prevented by using encryption (which will be described in detail later in this guide). In addition to this, web servers should also be configured to use unique and pseudo-random session IDs and cookies, along with Secure Sockets Layer (SSL) encryption.

War Dialing Attacks

War dialing entails dialing large blocks of telephone numbers, via modem, with the objective being to locate a computer to which to connect. Because of advances such as Caller ID and Call tracing, war dialing is now a relatively risky method of attack because the attacker can be located fairly quickly.

However, war dialing can also be used as a means of validating security within a company. For example, a company can use war dialing to dial all known company numbers to check for modems that may be connected without their knowledge. These systems may then be secured, or removed if they are not supposed to be there, as they may present an attacker with a back door into the network, which is referred to as Out-of-Band access, or OOB access.

Vulnerability Scanning

Vulnerability scanning refers to the act of probing a host in order to find an exploitable service or process. This is one of the most common attacks because there are a plethora of tools available on the Internet that can be used to perform these attacks.

Using the information gained from vulnerability scanning, attackers can then have a better idea of what type of attack they can launch against that particular host. To prevent against such attacks, security personnel should also perform their own vulnerability scanning and ensure that discovered vulnerable services or ports that should not be open are secured or disabled.

It is also important to keep in mind that while vulnerability scanning tools, such as Network Mapper (Nmap), may be used by attackers, they can also be used by security administrators to ensure that all ports or services that are not being used and could be potential security threats are identified and closed. In fact, Nmap is a great tool for security administrators. Make sure that you familiarize yourself with this tool because unlike most tools Nmap is a free and open source (license) utility for network exploration or security auditing. Figure 1.12 illustrates a typical vulnerability scan using Nmap on a web server:

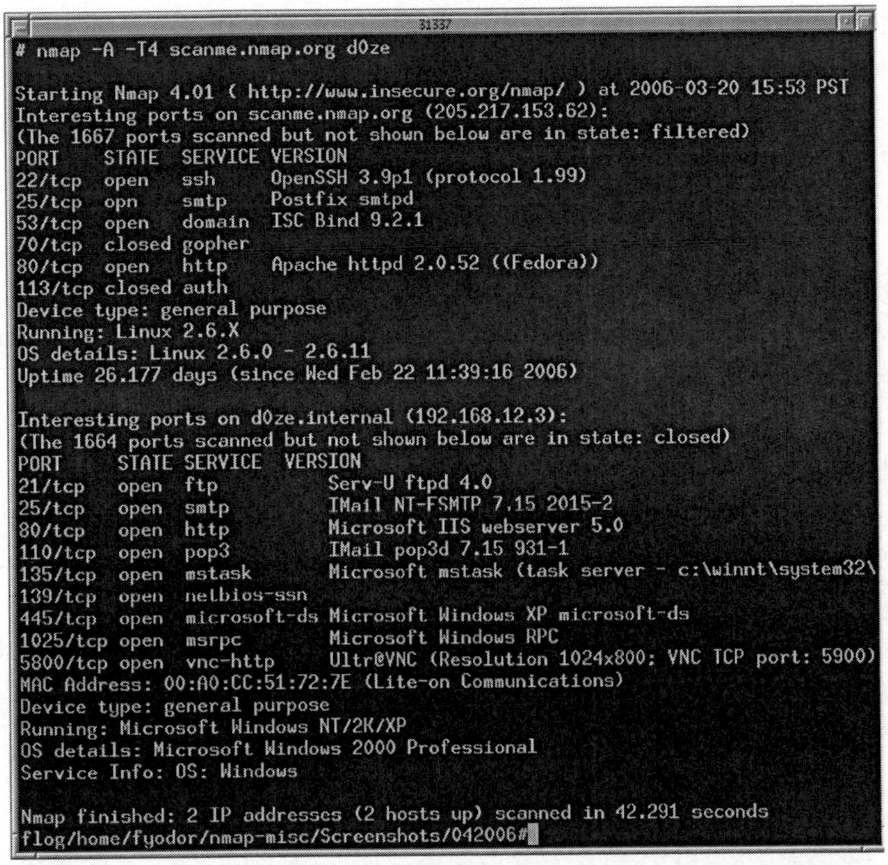

```
# nmap -A -T4 scanme.nmap.org d0ze

Starting Nmap 4.01 ( http://www.insecure.org/nmap/ ) at 2006-03-20 15:53 PST
Interesting ports on scanme.nmap.org (205.217.153.62):
(The 1667 ports scanned but not shown below are in state: filtered)
PORT     STATE  SERVICE VERSION
22/tcp   open   ssh     OpenSSH 3.9p1 (protocol 1.99)
25/tcp   opn    smtp    Postfix smtpd
53/tcp   open   domain  ISC Bind 9.2.1
70/tcp   closed gopher
80/tcp   open   http    Apache httpd 2.0.52 ((Fedora))
113/tcp  closed auth
Device type: general purpose
Running: Linux 2.6.X
OS details: Linux 2.6.0 - 2.6.11
Uptime 26.177 days (since Wed Feb 22 11:39:16 2006)

Interesting ports on d0ze.internal (192.168.12.3):
(The 1664 ports scanned but not shown below are in state: closed)
PORT      STATE SERVICE     VERSION
21/tcp    open  ftp         Serv-U ftpd 4.0
25/tcp    open  smtp        IMail NT-FSMTP 7.15 2015-2
80/tcp    open  http        Microsoft IIS webserver 5.0
110/tcp   open  pop3        IMail pop3d 7.15 931-1
135/tcp   open  mstask      Microsoft mstask (task server - c:\winnt\system32\
139/tcp   open  netbios-ssn
445/tcp   open  microsoft-ds Microsoft Windows XP microsoft-ds
1025/tcp  open  msrpc       Microsoft Windows RPC
5800/tcp  open  vnc-http    Ultr@VNC (Resolution 1024x800; VNC TCP port: 5900)
MAC Address: 00:A0:CC:51:72:7E (Lite-on Communications)
Device type: general purpose
Running: Microsoft Windows NT/2K/XP
OS details: Microsoft Windows 2000 Professional
Service Info: OS: Windows

Nmap finished: 2 IP addresses (2 hosts up) scanned in 42.291 seconds
flog/home/fyodor/nmap-misc/Screenshots/042006#
```

Figure 1.12. Nmap Vulnerability

Sniffing

Sniffing is eavesdropping on a network. Sniffers, which are tools that enable machines to see all of the packets that are traversing the wire, can be used by attackers to eavesdrop on networks and gain valuable information, such as usernames and passwords, if unsecure services such as Telnet are being used, for example.

Common tools that may be used by network administrators, such as TCPDUMP (Unix) and Snoop (Solaris), and more popular tools such as Wireshark and Ethereal, are also used by attackers to view packets on the wire and acquire valuable information, which the attacker can then use to reassemble viewed web pages, downloaded files, or even emails sent.

While sniffing network traffic typically requires some form of manual configuration—for example, Switched Port Analyzer (SPAN) in Cisco Catalyst switches, which allows administrators to monitor traffic on a port other their own—it is also good security practice to utilize encryption and secure services (e.g. SSH instead of Telnet) where possible to ensure that data being transferred across the wire is safe and secure.

Privilege Escalation

Privilege escalation is the act of exploiting a design flaw in a software application to gain access to resources that normally would have been protected from an application or user. The result is that the application performs actions with more privileges than intended by the application developer or system administrator.

Privilege escalation occurs when an application with elevated privileges has a flaw that allows security to be bypassed or, alternatively, flawed assumptions about how it will be used. Privilege escalation occurs in two forms:

- Vertical privilege escalation, also known as privilege elevation, occurs when a lower privilege user accesses functions or content reserved for higher privilege users. An example of vertical privilege escalation would be a user getting administrator rights to a server that he or she is authorized to use.
- Horizontal privilege escalation, where a normal user accesses functions or content reserved for other normal users. A typical example of horizontal privilege escalation would be a user being able to access the email account of another user.

Footprint Analysis

A footprint analysis is used by an attacker to gather as much information as possible about the intended target through publicly available sources such as the local library or the Internet. This analysis is used by the attacker to provide information on how large the targets may be, the number of potential entry points, and what security mechanisms, if any, are employed to prevent attacks.

When performing a footprint analysis, attackers may use port scanners to determine which hosts are alive on the Internet, which TCP and UDP ports are open on each system, and which operating system is installed on each host. Additionally, attackers may perform a Traceroute to identify the relationship of each host to every other host and network device, as well as to identify potential security mechanisms between the attacker and the target, such as firewalls and any other security devices.

After the port scanning and Traceroute is finished, attackers create a network map that represents their understanding of the target's Internet footprint. It is important to understand that a footprint analysis is not an actual attack in itself; instead, it is part of a larger process used by attackers to gain unauthorized access to systems.

While going into detail on all the steps in this process is beyond the requirements of the IINS course, the footprint analysis is the first step in a systematic method used by advanced attackers. This systematic method generally covers these seven steps:

1. Perform a footprint analysis
2. Enumerate information
3. Obtain access through user manipulation
4. Escalate privileges
5. Gather additional passwords and secrets
6. Install backdoors
7. Leverage the compromised system

Although some of the steps have been included in earlier sections, you are not required to demonstrate any advanced knowledge of these steps.

Buffer Overflows

Buffers are simply areas of memory that are used to store data or instructions. Buffer overflow attacks involve writing too much data to that particular area of memory, overwriting its contents. This new information may be meaningless and may simply be used to cause an interruption with the server or it could be malicious and contain new instructions that the victim's computer runs. These instructions can contain information that installs software on the target computer, which allows the intruder unauthorized access to the computer.

Programming languages commonly associated with buffer overflows include C and C++, which provide no built-in protection against accessing or overwriting data in any part of the memory and do not automatically check that data written to an array (the built-in buffer type) is within the boundaries of that array. However, other programs, such as Visual Basic and Java, use bounds checking to prevent against such attacks. Bounds checking is any method of detecting whether a variable is within some bounds before its use. A failed bounds check usually results in the generation of some sort of exception signal.

Attack Categories

The ever-changing nature of attacks is a major challenge facing network administrators. The attackers of today are typically well organized, extremely knowledgeable, and well trained. In addition to this, the size of the Internet provides very easy targets and provides lower risk to attackers, who can use this to launch any number of threats. These threats fall into one of the following categories:

1. Active Attacks
2. Passive Attacks
3. Malicious Code Attacks
4. Password Attacks

5. Insider Attacks
6. Close-in Attacks
7. Distribution Attacks

Active Attacks

Active attacks can be described as attacks where the perpetrator is actively attempting to cause harm to a network or system. In other words, the perpetrator is actively attempting to breach or shut down a particular service, or services. Because the damage from these attacks is very noticeable, these attacks are typically highly visible. Examples of active attacks include DoS and DDoS attacks.

Passive Attacks

During passive attacks, the attacker is not directly affecting the victim's network. In other words, these attacks are the exact opposite of active attacks. Passive attacks are analogous to eavesdropping on a conversation or using a telescope to spy on someone. Some examples of passive attacks include sniffing and vulnerability scanning.

Malicious Code Attacks

Malicious code attacks are programs that are written by attackers and are designed to do damage. Trojan horses and viruses are examples of malicious code attacks. These attacks typically do not require that the attacker be present for them to do damage, and they are one of the most dangerous types of attacks.

Password Attacks

Password attacks are fairly common, are easy to perform, and often result in successful intrusion. Because of this, it is recommended that a strict password policy be enforced. There are two types of password attacks: brute force and dictionary-based.

Insider Attacks

Insider attacks, as the name implies, are performed by insiders (e.g. employees) who use their legitimate credentials for illegitimate access to network resources. These are the most common types of attacks in present-day networks.

Close-in Attacks

Close-in attacks occur when the attacker is in close proximity to the intended target system. For example, an attacker can initiate an attack if he or she gains physical access to a network device, such as a router, switch, or firewall, for example.

Distribution Attacks

Distribution attacks intentionally introduce backdoors, which will be described in detail later in this chapter, to hardware or software systems during the manufacturing process. Once the flawed systems are distributed to customers, the attacker can use their knowledge of the implanted backdoor to gain unauthorized access to these systems.

Responding to Security Threats

An organization's internal operational processes are a critical aspect of dealing with any kind of security incident. Although sophisticated software can isolate possible security incidents, there is still a significant degree of human intervention required, making the establishment of reliable incident response procedures vital. The overall framework and process to respond to network threats and breaches is depicted in Figure 1.13:

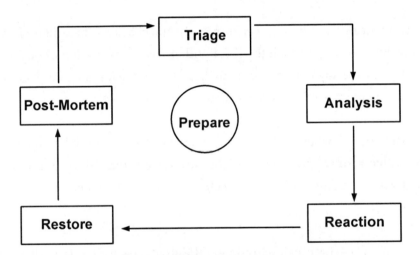

Figure 1.13. Responding to Network Threats

The following section describes the steps and procedures that are recommended during each phase of the general incident response model.

Triage

The first phase of incident response is to verify that the event is an actual security incident, such as an attack or worm event. In some cases, an incident could be the result of scheduled maintenance; therefore, it is important that this be validated to prevent raising a false alarm.

After the event is confirmed, take quick action to limit the damage. Doing so might entail steps such as turning off a device or removing a device from the network. However, any actions taken need to be in line with maintaining business continuity. For example, if a web-based company notes an attack on their server, simply removing those servers or turning them off in the event of a possible security incident might actually cost the company more money and have long-lasting ramifications. For this reason, it is important to communicate with other relevant parties within the organization.

Analysis

The second phase is the analysis phase. A key part of this process is incident classification, which involves understanding the type of attack and the damage it is causing. It is important to perform the analysis with as little impact as possible on business functions.

Next, determine the scope of the incident, i.e. the number of devices, data, and other resources affected. It is important to look beyond the initially identified target because the event might be more widespread than initially thought.

In some cases, it might be necessary to perform an IP traceback to the origin of the attack; this activity might involve working through the ISP. In other cases, restoration of business operations might require priority over any IP traceback activities. IP traceback is a name given to any method that can reliably determine the origin of a packet on the Internet.

Measure the impact and ask what the resulting effects of the incident on the organization are. Did it cause a minor problem, or was the impact on the business greater? The results of this analysis will help determine the most appropriate reaction techniques for the incident.

Reaction

The reaction phase involves some action to counter the attack. Each situation will dictate the action to be taken, such as widely deploying ACLs in a worm event; restoring a device to normal operation by reloading the OS from the original media and restoring data from backups in a server compromise; or changing any static passwords because they might have been compromised. In addition to this, it is important to understand that in some situations an entirely reasonable response might be to do nothing at all.

Generally speaking, the highest priority is to regain full business operations. In many cases, it is often less important to spend time finding the perpetrator of the attack.

Restore

This phase entails restoring systems and operations back to pre-attack levels. This may entail rebooting devices, restarting applications, or other similar activities.

Post-Mortem

A post-mortem involves a full, in-depth analysis of the event and the response to the event. The goal is to determine what can be done to build resistance and prevent this type of attack from happening again. Essentially, it is learning from the experience. As a simple example, if a network penetration occurred, it would be prudent to identify what vulnerability was used to obtain access, and then fix all occurrences of that vulnerability. Additionally, it should be determined whether the incident was detected in an acceptable amount of time; if not, measures should be deployed to speed detection in the event of further incidents. The post-mortem is a step that is often ignored. It is critical that it is not forgotten.

The Cisco SAFE Blueprint

Before delving into the specifics of the Cisco SAFE Blueprint, we are going to learn about one of its core elements, which is defense in depth. Defense in depth is simply a security philosophy that uses a layered security approach to eliminate a single point of failure and provide overlapping protection.

In a defense in depth deployment, each layer of security should have some kind of redundancy, and all layers should provide a variety of defense strategies for protecting multiple areas of the network. The defense in depth includes the following recommendations:

- Defend multiple attack targets in the network by protecting the network infrastructure, as well as critical host machines, such as corporate email and web servers, via a Host-based Intrusion Prevention System (HIPS). HIPS will be described in detail later in this guide.

- Create overlapping defenses, such as using both Intrusion Detection Systems (IDS) and Intrusion Prevention Systems (IPS). Cisco IDS and IPS systems will be described in detail later in this guide.

- Allow the value of the protected device to mandate the level of security implemented. For example, a server, such as an email server or Active Directory server, or a core network router or switch should be afforded more security than an end-user workstation.

- Use strong encryption mechanisms to ensure data confidentiality. While there are numerous encryption mechanisms available, it is important to keep in mind that some are significantly stronger than others, as will be described in detail later in this guide.

Figure 1.14 illustrates the defense in depth philosophy, which illustrates the implementation of a firewall, two Intrusion Prevention System (IPS) devices, and an Intrusion Detection System (IDS) device:

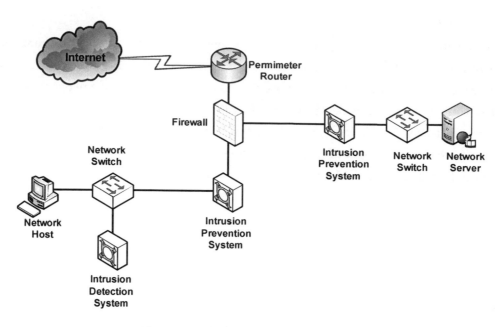

Figure 1.14. Defense in Depth Philosophy

Cisco SAFE delivers defense in depth by strategically positioning Cisco products and capabilities throughout the network and by using the collaborative capabilities between the platforms. A wide range of security technologies are deployed in multiple layers, under a common strategy and administration. Cisco SAFE is delivered in two forms:

- Design blueprints
- Security solutions

Cisco SAFE design blueprints are simply Cisco Validated Designs (CVDs) and security best practice guides. CVDs provide prescriptive design guidance, which cover the various places in the network (PINs) present in an enterprise network, such as campus, WAN edge, branches, and data center. Design guidance is also provided for technologies such as Unified Communications, network virtualization, and network foundation protection, which are present in multiple places in the network. The selection of platforms and capabilities within those designs is driven by the application of the Cisco Security Control Framework (SCF).

The Cisco SCF is a security framework aimed at ensuring network and service availability, as well as business continuity. The SCF is designed to address current key threats, as well as track new and evolving threats, through the use of best common practices and comprehensive solutions. Cisco SAFE uses SCF to create network designs that ensure network and service availability and business continuity. Cisco SCF drives the selection of the security products and capabilities, and guides their deployment throughout the network where they best enhance visibility and control.

The SCF assumes the existence of security policies developed as a result of threat and risk assessments, and in alignment with business goals and objectives. The security policies and guidelines are expected to define the acceptable and secure use of each service, device, and system in the environment. The security policies should also determine the processes and procedures needed to achieve the business goals and objectives. The collection of processes and procedures defines security operations. It is crucial to business success that security policies, guidelines, and operations do not prevent but rather empower the organization to achieve its goals and objectives.

The success of the security policies ultimately depends on the degree they enhance visibility and control. Simply put, security can be defined as a function of visibility and control. Without any visibility, there is no control; and without any control, there is no security. Therefore, the SCF's main focus is enhancing visibility and control. In the context of SAFE, SCF drives the selection and deployment of platforms and capabilities to achieve a desirable degree of visibility and control.

SCF defines six security actions that help enforce the security policies and improve visibility and control. Visibility is enhanced through the actions of identify, monitor, and correlate. Control is improved through the actions of harden, isolate, and enforce. These six security actions are illustrated in Figure 1.15:

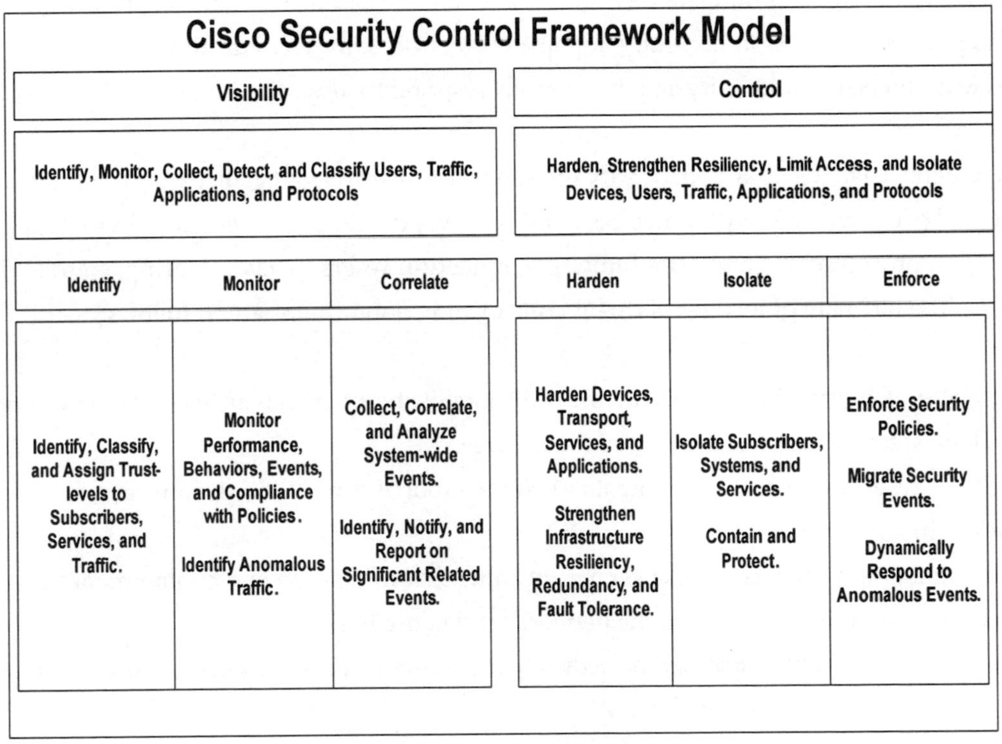

Cisco Security Control Framework Model

Visibility			Control		
Identify, Monitor, Collect, Detect, and Classify Users, Traffic, Applications, and Protocols			Harden, Strengthen Resiliency, Limit Access, and Isolate Devices, Users, Traffic, Applications, and Protocols		
Identify	Monitor	Correlate	Harden	Isolate	Enforce
Identify, Classify, and Assign Trust-levels to Subscribers, Services, and Traffic.	Monitor Performance, Behaviors, Events, and Compliance with Policies. Identify Anomalous Traffic.	Collect, Correlate, and Analyze System-wide Events. Identify, Notify, and Report on Significant Related Events.	Harden Devices, Transport, Services, and Applications. Strengthen Infrastructure Resiliency, Redundancy, and Fault Tolerance.	Isolate Subscribers, Systems, and Services. Contain and Protect.	Enforce Security Policies. Migrate Security Events. Dynamically Respond to Anomalous Events.

Figure 1.15. Cisco Security Control Framework Model

Cisco SAFE uses various forms of network telemetry present on most networking equipment, security appliances, and endpoints to achieve consistent and accurate visibility into network activity. Logging and event information generated by routers, switches, firewalls, intrusion prevention systems, and endpoint protection software are collected, trended, and correlated. By delivering infrastructure-wide security intelligence and collaboration, the architecture can:

- Identify threats by collecting, trending, and correlating logging, flow, and event information, and help identify the presence of security threats, compromises, and data leaks;
- Confirm compromises by tracking an attack as it transits the network, and by having visibility out to the endpoints, allowing the architecture to confirm whether or not the attack was successful;
- Reduce false positives (which will be described in detail later in this guide) and use endpoint and system visibility to help identify whether a target is vulnerable to a given attack;
- Reduce volume of event information via event correlation, which dramatically reduces the number of events, saving security operators precious time to allow them to focus on what is important; and
- Dynamically adjust the severity level of an incident via enhanced visibility.

Cisco SAFE uses the infrastructure-wide intelligence and collaboration capabilities provided by Cisco products to control and mitigate well-known and day-zero attacks. Intrusion protection systems, firewalls, network admission control, endpoint protection software, and monitoring and analysis systems work together to identify and dynamically respond to attacks.

The architecture has the ability to identify the source of the threat, visualize the attack path, and to suggest, and even dynamically enforce, response actions. Possible response actions include the isolation of compromised systems, rate limiting, connection resets, packet filtering, source filtering, and more. The ultimate objectives of threat control and containment are as follows:

- Complete visibility, where infrastructure-wide intelligence provides an accurate view of network topologies, attack paths, and extent of the damage.
- Adaptive response to real-time threats, such that source threats are dynamically identified and blocked in real-time.
- Consistent policy enforcement coverage, meaning that mitigation and containment actions may be enforced at different places in the network for defense in depth.
- Minimizing effects of attacks by immediately triggering response actions as soon as an attack is detected, thereby minimizing damage.
- A common policy and security management platform that simplifies control and administration, and reduces operational expense.

Cisco SAFE Security Solutions

The SCF and the design blueprints provide the foundation for industry security solutions that address the requirements of specific industries, such as retail, financial, healthcare, and manufacturing. Best practices and design recommendations are provided for the following:

1. Infrastructure Device Access
2. Device Resiliency and Survivability
3. Routing Infrastructure
4. Switching Infrastructure
5. Network Policy Enforcement
6. Network Telemetry

Infrastructure Device Access

Key steps to securing both interactive and management access to an infrastructure device are as follows:

- Restrict device accessibility by limiting the accessible ports and restricting the permitted communicators and the permitted methods of access.
- Present legal notification by displaying a legal notice developed in conjunction with company legal counsel for interactive sessions. For example, use an MOTD banner.
- Authenticate access and ensure access is granted only to authenticated users, groups, and services. For example, RADIUS can be used for user, group, and service authentication.
- Authorize actions and restrict the actions and views permitted by any particular user, group, or service. This can be performed after security protocols such as TACACS+. Both RADIUS and TACACS+ security protocols will be described in detail later in this guide.
- Ensure the confidentiality of data and protect locally stored sensitive data from viewing and copying. Evaluate the vulnerability of data in transit over a communication channel to sniffing, session hijacking, and MITM or MIM attacks.
- Log and account for all access, and record who accessed the device, what occurred, and when for auditing purposes.

Device Resiliency and Survivability

The architecture designs use the following best practices to ensure resiliency and survivability of routers and switches:

- Disable unnecessary services by disabling default-enabled services that are not required.
- Restrict access to the infrastructure address space and deploy ACLs at the network edges to shield the infrastructure from unauthorized access, DoS, and other network attacks.

- Protect the control plane and filter, and rate limit traffic destined to the control plane of routers and switches. The control plane manages control traffic such as routing protocols.
- Control switch Content Addressable Memory (CAM) usage and restrict the MAC addresses that are allowed to send traffic on a particular port.
- Implement redundancy and eliminate single points of failure using redundant interfaces, standby devices, and topological redundancy.

Routing Infrastructure

The architecture designs make use of the following measures to secure the routing plane:

- Restrict routing protocol membership and limit routing sessions to trusted peers, and validate origin and integrity of routing updates.
- Control route propagation and enforce route filters to ensure only valid routing information is propagated. Control routing information exchange between routing peers and between redistributing processes.
- Log status changes and the status changes of adjacency or neighbor sessions.

Switching Infrastructure

Baseline switching security is concerned with ensuring the availability of the Layer 2 switching network. To that end, the architecture designs implement the following:

- Design the Layer-2 infrastructure, limiting the size of the broadcast domains.
- Use existing features to secure Spanning Tree Protocol (STP).
- Implement VLAN best common practices, for example, restricting VLANs on Trunk links.

Network Policy Enforcement

The architecture designs implement the following measures:

- Control traffic destined to the infrastructure space by using ACLs.
- Implement ACLs and other mechanisms to block packets with spoofed IP addresses.

Network Telemetry

This section highlights the baseline forms of telemetry recommended for network devices as follows:

- Implement Network Time Protocol (NTP) to ensure that the dates and times in logs and alarms are synchronized.
- Maintain local device traffic statistics by using device global and interface traffic statistics.
- Maintain system status information by using memory, CPU, and process status information.

- Log and collect system status, traffic statistics, and device access information.
- Log and account for all access, and record who accessed the device, what occurred, and when for auditing purposes.
- Establish the mechanisms to allow the capture of packets in transit for analysis and correlation purposes, SPAN, for example.

The Cisco PPDIOO Model

Cisco also offers an integrated security solution, which goes above and beyond the 'one size fits all' model. In addition to this, Cisco products are designed to deliver value throughout the entire network lifecycle, which includes the stages of Prepare, Plan, Design, Implement, Operate, and Optimize, commonly referred to as PPDIOO.

The Cisco PPDIOO model encompasses all steps from network vision to optimization, which enables Cisco to provide a broader portfolio of support and end-to-end solutions to its customers. The PPDIOO model is illustrated in Figure 1.16:

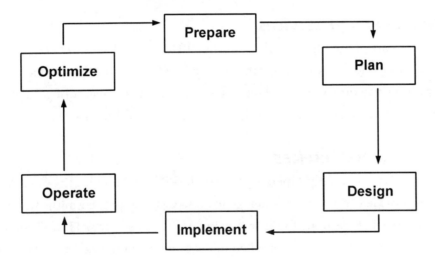

Figure 1.16. Cisco PPDIOO Model

In conjunction with the PPDIOO model, Cisco also offers the Cisco Lifecycle Security Services, which has five distinct services. These services include the following:

1. Strategy and Assessment Services
2. Deployment and Migration Services
3. Remote Management Services
4. Security Intelligence Services
5. Security Optimization Services

Strategy and Assessments Services

Strategy and assessments are part of the Prepare and Plan phases of the PPDIOO model. Cisco offers a comprehensive set of assessment services based on a structured IT governance, risk management, and compliance approach to information security.

These services help the customer to understand the needs and gaps, and recommend remediation based on industry and international best practices, as well as help the customer strategically to plan the evolution of an information security program, including updates to security policy, processes, and technology.

Deployment and Migration Services

These services are part of the Design and Implement phases of the PPDIOO model. Cisco offers deployment services to support the customer in planning, designing, and implementing Cisco security products and solutions. In addition, Cisco has services to support the customer in evolving its security policy and process-based controls to make people and the security architecture more effective.

Remote Management Services

These services are part of the Operate phase of the PPDIOO model. Cisco Remote Management Services engineers become an extension of the customer's IT staff, proactively monitoring the security technology infrastructure and providing incident, problem, change, configuration, and release management, as well as management reporting 24 hours a day, 365 days a year.

Security Intelligence Services

These services are also a part of the Operate phase of the PPDIOO model. The Cisco Security Intelligence Services provide early warning intelligence, analysis, and proven mitigation techniques to help security professionals respond to the latest threats. The customer's IT staff can use the latest threat alerts, vulnerability analysis, and applied mitigation techniques developed by Cisco experts, who use in-depth knowledge and sophisticated tools to verify anomalies and develop techniques that help ensure timely, accurate, and quick resolution to potential vulnerabilities and attacks.

Security Optimization Services

These services are part of the Optimize phase of the PPDIOO model. Cisco Security Optimization Services is an integrated service offering designed to assess, develop, and optimize the customer's security infrastructure on an ongoing basis. Through quarterly site visits and continual analysis and tuning, the Cisco security team becomes an extension of the customer's security staff, supporting them in long-term business security and risk management, as well as near-term tactical solutions to evolving security threats.

The Cisco Self-Defending Network

The Cisco Self-Defending Network integrates a collection of security solutions to identify, prevent and adapt to threats. The ultimate goal of the Cisco Self-Defending Network is that the network has the ability and the intelligence to protect itself from threats. However, this can only happen if the components of the network are working together to ensure this level of security, intelligence, and adaptability.

In addition to this, it is also important to understand that because network devices must work together and be integrated in order for the Cisco Self-Defending Network to do its job, it is very probable that there will be no third-party network components on the organization's network participating in the Cisco Self-Defending Network.

While it is important to know that the Cisco Self-Defending Network is a large, complex roadmap made up of many Cisco components, it is also important to understand that an organization is not required to have all the components. However, you should be familiar with the suite of security products and components that make up the Cisco Self-Defending Network. The following section provides a list of some of the most common components that can be found within the Cisco Self-Defending Network:

Anomaly Detection and Mitigation

- The Cisco Traffic Anomaly Detector XT 5600 delivers multi-Gigabit performance to protect the largest enterprise environments by rapidly detecting and alerting users to potential distributed denial-of-service (DDoS), worms, and other attacks. Detection is based on sophisticated anomaly detection capabilities that compare current activity to profiles of known 'normal' behaviour, enabling the Traffic Anomaly Detector XT to identify even day-zero attacks that have never been seen before.

- The Cisco Guard XT 5650 delivers multi-Gigabit performance to protect the largest enterprises from DDoS attacks by performing per-flow-level attack analysis, identification, and mitigation to block specific attack traffic.

Email Security

- Cisco IronPort Email Security Appliances are easy-to-deploy solutions that defend email systems against spam, viruses, phishing, and a wide variety of other threats.

- The Cisco Spam and Virus Blocker is a dedicated anti-spam, anti-virus, and anti-phishing security appliance, designed specifically for small businesses, that virtually eliminates email threats right out of the box. It blocks spam, requires minimal administration, and connects to one of the largest databases of email security threats to bolster its accuracy.

Endpoint Security

• Cisco NAC Appliance (formerly Cisco Clean Access) is an easily deployed Network Admission Control (NAC) product that uses the network infrastructure to enforce security policy compliance on all devices seeking to access network computing resources. With NAC Appliance, network administrators can authenticate, authorize, evaluate, and remediate wired, wireless, and remote users and their machines prior to network access. It identifies whether networked devices such as laptops, IP phones, or game consoles are compliant with the network's security policies and repairs any vulnerability before permitting the device access to the network.

• Cisco Security Agent is the first endpoint security solution that combines zero-update attack protection, data loss prevention, and signature-based antivirus in a single agent. This unique blend of capabilities defends servers and desktops against sophisticated day-zero attacks and enforces acceptable-use and compliance policies within a simple management infrastructure.

• Cisco Trust Agent is a core component of the NAC solution. This client software must be installed on hosts whose host policy state is to be validated before permitting network access. Cisco Trust Agent allows NAC to determine if the Cisco Security Agent or antivirus software is installed and current, and can determine current operating systems and patch levels.

Firewall

• The Cisco ASA 5500 provides advanced application-aware firewall services with identity-based access control, DoS attack protection, and much more.

• Cisco Firewall Services Module (FWSM)—a high-speed, integrated firewall module for Cisco Catalyst 6500 switches and Cisco 7600 Series routers—provides the fastest firewall data rates in the industry: 5-Gbps throughput, 100,000 CPS, and 1M concurrent connections.

• Cisco IOS Firewall helps ensure the network's availability and the security of company resources by protecting the network infrastructure against network- and application-layer attacks, viruses, and worms. It protects unified communications by guarding Session Initiation Protocol (SIP) endpoints and call-control resources. Cisco IOS Firewall is a stateful firewall solution, certified by Common Criteria (EAL4).

Identity Management

• Cisco Security Monitoring, Analysis, and Response System (MARS) provides security monitoring for network devices and host applications supporting both Cisco and other vendors. Security monitoring with MARS greatly reduces false positives by providing an end-to-end topological view of the network, which helps improve threat identification, mitigation responses, and compliance.

- Cisco Secure Access Control Server (ACS) is an access policy control platform that helps organizations to comply with growing regulatory and corporate requirements. By integrating with other access control systems, it helps improve productivity and contain costs. It supports multiple scenarios simultaneously, including device administration (i.e. it authenticates administrators, authorizes commands, and provides an audit trail); remote access (i.e. it works with VPN and other remote network access devices to enforce access policies); wireless (i.e. it authenticates and authorizes wireless users and hosts and enforces wireless-specific policies); and Network Admission Control, by communicating with posture and audit servers to enforce admission control policies.

Intrusion Prevention System

- Cisco IPS 4200 Series Sensors detect threats to intellectual property and customer data, with modular inspection throughout the network stack; stop sophisticated attackers by detecting behavioural anomalies, evasion, and attacks against vulnerabilities; prevent threats with confidence using the industry's most comprehensive set of threat prevention actions; focus response with dynamic threat ratings and detailed logging; and provide protection from the latest threats and vulnerabilities.

- The second-generation Cisco IDSM-2 protects switched environments by integrating full-featured IPS functions directly into the network infrastructure through the widely deployed Cisco Catalyst chassis. This integration allows the user to monitor traffic directly off the switch backplane—a logical platform for additional services such as firewall, VPN, and IPS. The Cisco IDSM-2 with Cisco IPS Sensor Software v6.0 helps users stop more threats with greater confidence through multi-vector threat identification and accurate prevention.

Security Management

- Cisco Adaptive Security Device Manager (ASDM) is a powerful yet easy-to-use application that delivers integrated security management. It accelerates security policy creation while reducing management overhead and human error with wizards, debugging tools, and monitoring services. Its secure design enables anytime, anywhere management access to Cisco ASA 5500 Series Adaptive Security Appliances, Cisco PIX security appliances, and Cisco Catalyst 6500 Series Firewall Services Module (FWSM).

- Cisco Router and Security Device Manager (SDM) is a web-based device-management tool for Cisco routers that can improve the productivity of network managers, simplify router deployments, and help troubleshoot complex network and VPN connectivity issues. Network and security administrators and channel partners can use Cisco SDM for faster and easier deployment of Cisco routers for integrated services such as dynamic routing, WAN access, WLAN, firewall, VPN, SSL VPN, IPS, and QoS.

- Cisco IronPort M-Series security management appliances offer complete security control and flexible management at the network gateway. By delivering top performance for all application security gateways, these appliances provide a single location for organizations to manage, store, and monitor all corporate policy settings and audit information.

Virtual Private Networks (VPN)

- The Cisco Easy VPN solution helps integrate VPN remote devices within a single deployment and with a consistent policy and key management method, which simplifies remote site administration. Cisco Easy VPN consists of two components: the Easy VPN Remote feature and the Easy VPN Server feature.

- Simple to deploy and operate, the Cisco VPN Client allows organizations to establish end-to-end, encrypted VPN tunnels for secure connectivity for mobile employees or teleworkers. This thin design, IP security (IPSec) implementation is compatible with all Cisco virtual private network (VPN) products.

Web Security

- The Cisco-IronPort S-Series web security appliance is the industry's first and only secure web gateway to combine traditional URL filtering, reputation filtering, malware filtering, and data security on a single platform to address these risks. By combining innovative technologies, the Cisco IronPort S-Series helps organizations address the growing challenges of both securing and controlling web traffic.

It is important to remember that the products listed above are not the entire suite of products available. However, these are common products that you should be familiar with. The three core characteristics of the Cisco Self-Defending Network are that it is integrated, collaborative, and adaptive. These characteristics are defined in the following section:

Integrated Security

This is the first phase of the Self-Defending Network. Security is built into the existing network, as opposed to being added to an existing network. In other words, security is incorporated into network devices, such as routers and switches, thus providing for an integrated security infrastructure within the components, rather than as an add-on. This allows all components in the network to act as a point of defense.

Collaborative Security Systems

This is the second phase of the Self-Defending Network. IT personnel focusing on security collaborate with IT personnel focusing on network operations. This phase allows for a security system that collaborates amongst all network and security components. In addition to this, the system also has the capability to collaborate with policy-enforcement endpoints.

Adaptive Threat Defense

This is the third and final phase of the Self-Defending Network. In the Cisco Self-Defending Network, security solutions have the flexibility to adapt to threats. This phase provides the capability for networks to evolve dynamically and intelligently to adapt and respond proactively to emerging threats at multiple layers of the network based on a new set of Anti-x (i.e. Anti-Virus, Anti-Spyware, etc.) technologies. The Cisco Threat Defense System offers security solutions and intelligent networking technologies to identify and prevent both known and unknown threats from internal and external network environments.

To begin creating the Cisco Self-Defending Network, the network platforms used must have integrated security features. Then, additional security features—depending on business objectives—are integrated and layered on top of the secure foundation. These features are divided into three categories: Threat Containment, Protected Communications, and Management, which are illustrated in Figure 1.17:

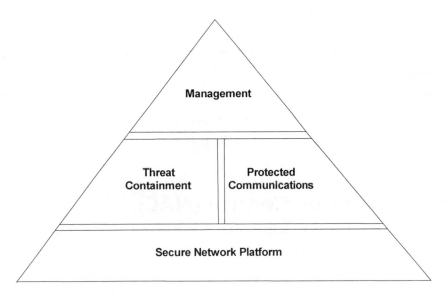

Figure 1.17. Adaptive Threat Defense

Threat containment

Threat containment includes strategies to contain and control threats. These strategies include, but are not limited to, the following:

1. Endpoint threat control, which is used to defend endpoints against threats such as viruses, spyware, adware, and other malicious attacks.

2. Infrastructure threat control, which is used to protect servers and shared applications from both internal and external threats.

3. Email threat control, which is used to protect against threats from emails; for example, malicious attachments or links received via email.

Protected Communications

Protected communications includes methodologies and technologies used to provide confidential and authenticated communications channels. The Cisco Secure Communications offers a set of products that can be categorized into one of two broad categories:

*   Remote access communications security secures data transmission from remote users accessing the corporate network and resources via secure tunnels.
*   Site-to-site communications security secures data transmission between different sites within an organization.

Management

Management includes products that allow for a system-wide control of policies and configuration. These solutions facilitate the following:

*   Efficiency in rolling out new policies to multiple devices, while maintaining configuration consistency amongst these devices
*   A comprehensive view of the Cisco Self-Defending Networks end-to-end security status
*   The ability to respond quickly and efficiently to attacks
*   Synchronization with an organizational security policy

Network Admission Control (NAC)

A network admission control (NAC) solution is required to ensure that endpoints are complying with predetermined security policies. These policies, which may include the latest anti-virus and operating system patches, are used to prevent vulnerable and noncompliant hosts from obtaining network access.

NAC uses the Network Access Devices (NADs) to protect the infrastructure from any endpoint seeking network access. Only trusted endpoints that are in compliance with security policy are granted access to the network. Noncompliant devices, on the other hand, are denied access and are quarantined for remediation. This policy compliance limits the potential damage from known and unknown threats alike.

It is important to remember that NAC is a part of the Cisco Self-Defending Network that enables the network to automatically identify, detect, and prevent emerging security threats. NAC is focused on proactive, not reactive, security solutions and is offered in two forms:

1. Cisco NAC Appliance
2. Cisco NAC Framework

Cisco NAC Appliance

Cisco NAC Appliance, formerly known as Cisco Clean Access, is the most widely used NAC solution from Cisco. This solution is based on the dedicated NAC Appliance and does not rely on partners and vendors because it offers self-containment endpoint assessment, policy management, and remediation services. The NAC Appliance solution accommodates LAN, WAN, Wireless, and Remote Access scenarios, amongst others. The Cisco NAC Appliance solution consists of the following three options:

1. Clean Access Server
2. Clean Access Agent
3. Clean Access Manager

The Clean Access Server is a network device that triggers assessment when users attempt network access, and it can enforce network access privileges based on endpoint compliance. The Clean Access Server is primarily used as an enforcement device that can block users at the port level, effectively restricting access to the trusted network until they pass the inspection. The Clean Access Server can be implemented either in-band or out-of-band in Layer 2 or Layer 3 mode, and as a virtual or real IP gateway for endpoints.

The Clean Access Manager is a web-based GUI application that is used to create security policies, establish roles, perform compliance checks, manage users, and define remediation rules. The Clean Access Manager communicates with the Clean Access Server, which is the primary component used for enforcement in the NAC Appliance architecture.

The Clean Access Agent (CAA) is an optional component (i.e. read-only agent software) that runs on a client's endpoint to provide posture information and streamline remediation functions. CAA can also inspect the local host and provide information by analyzing the registry, services, and other files. In addition to this, CAA can determine whether or not the endpoint has the required patches, anti-virus, and other security software, such as Cisco Security Agent (CSA). Unlike the Clean Access Manager and Server, which users must purchase, CAA is distributed freely by Cisco.

Figure 1.18 illustrates Cisco NAC Appliance in-band deployment:

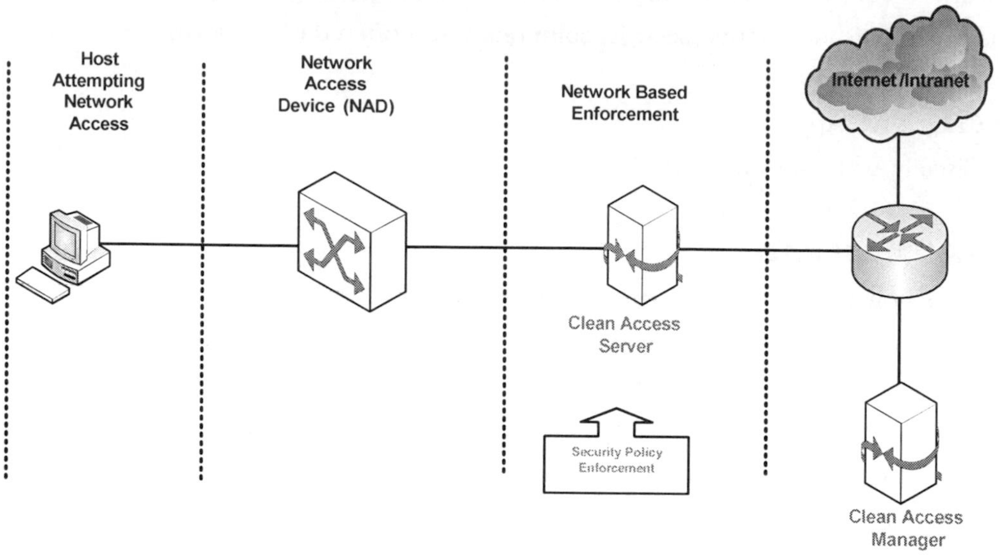

Figure 1.18. Cisco NAC Framework

Cisco NAC Framework

The Cisco NAC Framework solution uses the existing network infrastructure and third-party vendor solutions to enforce security policy compliance on all endpoints. This solution is designed for highly specialized network environments. The NAC framework can be implemented on NAC-enabled Network Access Devices (NADs), such as Cisco routers, switches, Wireless Access Points, and firewalls, to grant access to compliant endpoints that are attempting to access the network, while placing noncompliant endpoints into quarantine.

It is import to remember that the NAC Framework solution does not require investment in new devices because it utilizes existing NADs. Therefore, an overlay system is not required to perform admission control. The four primary components of the NAC framework solution include the following:

1. Endpoint Software
2. Network Access Devices (NADs)
3. Access Control and Policy Server
4. Management System

Endpoint security software includes products such as anti-virus software, Cisco Security Agent, Cisco Trust Agent, and other personal firewalls, such as the Windows Firewall. Policy enforcement and admission control decisions are made on the basis of application and OS status. Cisco and NAC program partners integrate CTA with their security software clients.

NADs are Layer 2 or Layer 3 Cisco devices (e.g. routers and switches) that are used for policy enforcement and admission control based on endpoint compliance. NADs are primarily used as enforcement devices and can block users at Layer 2 or Layer 3, allowing access only to trusted endpoints and restricting or quarantining noncompliant endpoints. NADs relay credential information to the access control and policy server(s), where the admission decisions are made. Based on the various policies defined, the NAD will enforce the appropriate posture states: permit, deny, quarantine, or restrict.

Access control and policy servers, such as the Cisco Secure Access Control System (ACS), as well as third-party vendor servers, are responsible for evaluating the endpoint security information that is relayed from the NAD and determining the proper access to be applied. Typically, Cisco Secure ACS is used as the AAA (Authentication, Authorization, and Accounting) server, in conjunction with the RADIUS protocol. Both AAA and RADIUS will be described in greater detail later in this guide.

Cisco security management systems provide monitoring and reporting tools for the NAC Framework solution. These tools include CiscoWorks VPN and Security Management Solution (CiscoWorks VMS), CiscoWorks Security Information Manager Solution (CiscoWorks SIMS), and, most commonly, the Cisco Security Manager, which you are expected to be familiar with.

The Cisco Security Manager (CSM) is a tool that is used to centrally provision all aspects of device configuration and policies for Cisco Firewalls (e.g. ASA and Firewall Switch Module), Virtual Private Networks (VPNs), and Intrusion Prevention System (IPS) services. CSM can be used to provision networks with less than 10 devices or scale to configure networks with 1000 devices or more. CSM provides a powerful and user-friendly, easy-to-use interface, by incorporating three simple-use views into the management system for users to manage devices and policies, which are the device-centric, policy-centric, and topology-centric views.

The device-centric view (DCV) enables users to view the properties of devices being managed, add/delete devices from the CSM inventory, and centrally manage all device policies, properties, interfaces, and other related device parameters.

The policy-centric view (PCV) enables users to create and manage shared, reusable policies at the system level that can be shared amongst multiple devices. With PCV, users can also view all shared policies that are defined for a particular type, as well as create, view, and edit policies, and modify their device assignments.

Finally, the topology-centric view (TCV), also referred to as the Map view, enables users to create customized topology-based visual maps of the network, allowing users to manage policies directly from the topology view. TCV also allows users to view network connections between devices, link topologies, and configure VPN and other access control settings directly from the view maps.

While going into further detail on the NAC Framework is beyond the scope of the IINS course requirements, Table 1.4 shows the differences between the Cisco NAC Appliance and the Cisco NAC Framework:

Table 1.4. Cisco NAC Appliance and Framework

Cisco NAC Appliance	Cisco NAC Framework
Based on dedicated appliance-leveraging CCA products. NAC Appliance is self-sufficient.	An embedded approach implemented in NAC-enabled NADs.
Can identify, authentication, scan, and remediate endpoints without requiring other products.	Can identify, authenticate, and scan endpoints via Cisco-enabled NADs, while remediation is performed by Cisco ACS server or other third-party partner products, such as Trend Micro, for example.
Includes preconfigured checks for Microsoft from Windows Update, and most major anti-virus software packages are sent regularly to the Clean Access Server.	Vendors in the NAC Framework solution are required to implement an Application Programming Interface (API) to perform these functions.
Uses a Simple Network Management Protocol (SNMP) trap to pre-assign incoming users to a quarantined authentication VLAN. SNMP will be described in detail later in this guide.	Uses 802.1x and Extensible Authentication Protocol (EAP) to perform verification prior to VLAN assignment. These technologies will be described in detail later in this guide.
Forwards authentication requests to a back-end server, such as a RADUIS or Active Directory server.	Requires the use of Cisco Secure ACS as the AAA authentication server.
CCA is used to provide posture information, whereas CSA provides protection.	Third-party plug-ins provide posture information to the CTA, and CSA provides protection.

Operations Security

Operations security is used to secure hardware, software, and various media while investigating anomalies in the network. Recommendations for operations security are divided into four broad categories:

1. Separation of Duties
2. Rotation of Duties
3. Trusted Recovery
4. Configuration and Change Control

Separation of Duties

This recommendation proposes that information systems personnel (e.g. network security administrators, etc.) be assigned responsibilities in such a way that no one single employee can compromise a system's security. The separation of duties can be accomplished by using a dual-operator system in which specific tasks require two people, a good example being opening the safe in a bank. Additionally, organizations can employ a two-person control system in which two employees have to approve one another's work.

Rotation of Duties

The rotation of duties recommendation proposes that multiple employees periodically rotate duties, with the basis that the potential of a single employee to cause an ongoing security breach is lessened if duties are rotated between employees. Whilst this is not feasible in most corporations (e.g. banks, or service providers) it may work very well for companies that offer security guard or armored truck services, for example.

Trusted Recovery

This recommendation is centered on ensuring that recovery procedures are in place and that sensitive and critical data can be restored in the event of a system failure. It is imperative that the data that is recovered is restored to its original form. This includes privileges, restrictions, and any other related attributes.

Configuration and Change Control

Change control is one of the most widely adopted recommendations. Most organizations have some form of change control process, be it automated or manual, where proposed changes to systems, network devices, or polices are reviewed by other personnel before being approved. The primary goals of change control are to minimize system or network disruptions, back out of changes quickly and in a structured manner, and use resources more efficiently and effectively.

Security Documentation

This section provides details on the necessary documentation that you should be familiar with regarding security, which includes security policies, standards, procedures, baselines, and guidelines. All of these documents work together to provide a security system that complies with industry best practices and regulations. Security policies are used to describe the 'whats' of information security, while standards, procedures, baselines, and guidelines describe the 'hows' for the implementation of the security policy.

Security Policies

Security policies are a set of rules, practices, and procedures that dictate how sensitive information is managed, protected, and distributed. In addition to this, security policies state exactly what the security level should be by setting the goals of what the security mechanisms are going to, or supposed to, accomplish.

Security policies are typically written by higher management and describe information security. The main reason for security policies is to ensure that everyone complies with the same set of rules. A security policy should state the level of control users must observe and balance that with productivity goals. In other words, security policies should not be so restrictive that they impede the productivity and operation of users. However, a security policy should also not be so loose that no one has any accountability. There are three broad categories of security policies. These are regulatory policies, advisory policies, and informative policies.

1. Regulatory policies are mandatory enforcements of compliance with industry regulations and legislations (laws). These policies ensure that the organization is following the industry standards as regulated by the law.

2. Advisory policies drive confidentiality and the integrity of information systems. These policies are also used to outline the ramifications of noncompliance.

3. Finally, informative policies are non-enforceable policies that provide generic guidelines for best practices and acceptable behaviour. Within these categories, several different types of security policies can be created.

Some common examples of security policies are:
*   Acceptable Use Policies
*   Ethics Policies
*   Information Sensitivity Policies
*   Email Policies
*   Password Policies
*   Risk Assessment Policies

Acceptable use policies outline the acceptable use of computer equipment, such as PCs, laptops, and other electronic devices. The rules in this policy are intended to protect both the employer and the employee. Inappropriate use may expose the company to risks, such as viruses, the compromising of network systems and services, and even legal issues.

Ethics policies emphasize the employee and consumer's expectations to be subject to fair business practices, thus establishing a culture of trust, openness, and integrity. Such policies typically guide business behaviour to ensure ethical conduct.

Information sensitivity policies are used to assist employees in understanding what information can be disclosed to nonemployees, partners, customers, or other parties, such as news agencies. In addition to this, these policies typically provide information on who is authorized to provide such information, which may include electronic information and information on paper.

Email policies cover the use of any email sent from an organization's email address and apply to all employees, vendors, and agents that are acting on behalf of that organization. Such policies may also include acceptable email address use and disclosure. For example, the policy may prevent employees, vendors, and agents from using their company email address to register on social networking sites such as Facebook and MySpace.

Password policies are used to establish a standard for the creation of string passwords, the protection of those passwords, and the frequency of change for the passwords. For example, a company password policy may state that passwords should be at least eight characters in length and must contain letters (both uppercase and lowercase), numbers, and special characters.

Risk assessment policies are used to empower the information security group(s) to perform information security risk analysis periodically, in order to determine the areas of vulnerability and to initiate the proper remediation.

Standards

Standards are industry-recognized best practices, frameworks, agreed principles, concepts, and designs, which are designed to implement, achieve, and maintain the required levels of processes and procedures. These documents define systems' parameters and processes and typically vary by industry. However, it is important to know that in the context of security information management and regulatory compliance, there are two notable standards: the ISO 17799/20002 and COBIT.

The International Organization for Standardization 17799/20002 is an internationally recognized and accepted standard for implementing IT security and best practices for information security management. This standard focuses on the security of information systems and addresses related control objectives.

The Control Objectives for Information and related Technology (COBIT) is a recognized set of best practices framework and an open standard for IT controls and security developed by the Information Systems Audit and Control Association (ISACA) and the IT Governance Institute (ITGI). COBIT is used mainly by the IT audit community to demonstrate risk mitigation and avoidance mechanisms. In addition to this, COBIT focuses on information system processes and addresses information security management process requirements.

Procedures

Procedures are low-level documents that provide instructions on how the security policy and standards will be implemented. These documents are very detailed in order to provide users with all necessary information required to implement and enforce the security policy, as well as apply the standards and guidelines of the security program as a whole.

Baselines

Baselines are the minimal level of security required in a system; for example, ensuring that all routers in a network are running a specific version of Cisco IOS software, or that all computers are running a specific service pack for their operating system. The baseline document would also provide instructions on where to download this software and how it should be installed.

The Security Wheel

The security wheel is used to show the process of striving towards achieving a secured network infrastructure. This model contains five steps:

1. Developing a Security Policy
2. Securing the Network
3. Monitoring and Responding
4. Testing
5. Managing and Improving

Developing a Security Policy

It is important to have a security policy. Such a policy should be well defined, implemented, and documented, but at the same time it should be simple and straightforward enough so that employees, etc. can still conduct business within the defined parameters.

Securing the Network

Security solutions should be implemented to secure the network. Such solutions include, but are not limited to, authentication, encryption, firewalls, and intrusion prevention. These solutions should prevent unauthorized access and protect information and information systems.

Monitoring and Responding

Monitoring and responding involves system auditing and real-time intrusion detection and prevention systems. Monitoring is used to detect violations of the security policy, and responding is used to take action against these violations.

Testing

Testing is used to validate the effectiveness of the security policy through practices such as system auditing and vulnerability scanning using products such as Nmap, for example. Nmap is a security scanner used to discover computers and services on a computer network in order to create a map of the network.

In addition to this, Nmap can also perform host discovery (i.e. identifying computers on a network), port scanning (i.e. listing the open ports on one or more target computers), version detection (i.e. determining the application name and version number on remote devices), and operating system detection (i.e. determining the operating system and some hardware characteristics of network devices).

Managing and Improving

Using information from the monitoring and testing phases, improvements can, and may need to, be made to the current security implementation. In such cases, the security policy should be modified when new vulnerabilities and risks are identified.

The different phases of the security wheel are illustrated in Figure 1.19:

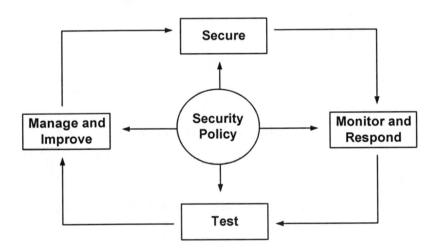

Figure 1.19. The Security Wheel

Guidelines and Best Practices

The final section of this chapter will address general security guidelines and will conclude with Cisco-recommended best practices.

Guidelines

Guidelines are recommended actions and operational guides for users. Unlike standards, which are mandatory, guidelines are simply used as reference material. When addressing security policies, standards, procedures, baselines, and guidelines, it is important to know that security policies are strategic in nature, while standards, procedures, baselines, and guidelines are all tactical documents. These documents are all intertwined and work together, as illustrated in Figure 1.20:

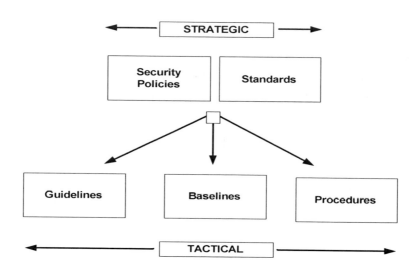

Figure 1.20. Cisco Security Guidelines

Best Practices

When dealing with network security, Cisco recommends the following best practices to guide you in your role as a network security administrator:

1. Routinely apply patches to operating systems and applications. Keep in mind that this does not have to be a manual process. For example, Windows-based machines have the capability to automatically download patches and updates. Ensure that such features are enabled and that users are aware of how to use them.

2. Disable unneeded services and ports on hosts. Unneeded services can be potential security holes. For example, on Cisco IOS routers, unnecessary services that should be disabled include TCP and UDP small servers, as well as the finger service—which is used to provide information about a device.

3. Require strong passwords and enable password expiration. In other words, ensure passwords are not indefinite and have some kind of expiration so that users change them periodically. Also, specify a minimum length for passwords and enforce a policy where passwords must contain numbers, letters, and special characters.

4. Protect physical access to computing and networking equipment. Lock or restrict access to cabinets or rooms that contain network devices, such as routers, switches, and firewalls.

5. Enforce secure programming practices, such as limiting valid characters that can be entered into an applications dialog box. For example, users should not be able to type in and execute **.exe** commands or files on a production server.

6. Train users on good security practices and educate them about social engineering tactics. Keep in mind that most people are very trusting. Attackers often take advantage of this; therefore, ensure that users are aware of what information they can and cannot give out.

7. Use strong encryption for sensitive data. Some encryption algorithms are stronger than others. Ensure that the most suitable (i.e. in line with business objectives) methods are used.

8. Defend against technical attacks by deploying both hardware and software-based security solutions, for example, firewalls (hardware) and anti-virus (software) solutions.

9. Create a documented security policy for company-wide use. It is important that this document is easily understood by everyone but, at the same time, it is not too vague.

Chapter Summary

The following section is a summary of the major points you should be aware of in this chapter:

Network Security Threats

- Every IP network infrastructure should be based on a sound security policy
- Network vulnerabilities must be constantly monitored, found, and addressed
- These vulnerabilities via a network evaluation, which includes:
    1. Scanning a network for active IP addresses and open ports on those IP addresses
    2. Scanning identified hosts for known vulnerabilities
    3. Using password cracking utilities
    4. Reviewing system and security logs
    5. Performing virus scans
    6. Performing penetration testing to see if specific systems (e.g. servers) can be compromised
    7. Scanning for unsecured wireless networks

- There are two broad categories of network security threats: internal and external threats
- Internal security threats originate within the network
- External threats are those that originate from external attackers

The CIA Triad

- The CIA triad is generally accepted as defining the primary goals of network security
- Confidentiality prevents the unauthorized disclosure of sensitive information
- Integrity prevents the unauthorized modification of data, systems and information
- Availability is the prevention of loss of access to resources and information

Vulnerabilities, Exploits and Risks

- Vulnerabilities are weaknesses in computing systems
- Examples of vulnerabilities include:
    1. Physical vulnerabilities
    2. Operating System vulnerabilities
    3. Protocol vulnerabilities
    4. System code vulnerabilities
    5. Poor system configuration vulnerabilities
    6. Malicious software vulnerabilities
    7. Human vulnerabilities

- Exploits are malicious programs that take advantage of vulnerabilities
- Common exploits take advantage of the following:

1. Default Passwords
2. IP Spoofing
3. Application weaknesses
4. Protocol weaknesses

- Information security risk assessment is the process used to identify and understand risks
- Risk analysis can be performed using either quantitative or qualitative analysis
- A quantitative analysis uses a mathematical formula
- A qualitative analysis, on the other hand, uses a scenario model

Denial of Service Attacks

- A DoS or DDoS attack is used to deny service from a legitimate resource or service
- DoS attacks typically do not pose a significant threat to sensitive data
- The five basic goals of DoS attacks are:
  1. The consumption of computational resources, such as bandwidth, disk space, or CPU time
  2. The disruption of configuration information, such as routing information
  3. The disruption of state information, such as unsolicited resetting of TCP sessions
  4. The disruption of physical network components
  5. The obstruction of communication media between the intended users and the victim

- Common examples of Denial of Service attacks are:
  1. Smurf Attacks
  2. ARP Poison Attacks
  3. Teardrop Attacks
  4. Permanent Denial of Service Attacks
  5. UDP Storm Attacks
  6. Mailbomb Attacks
  7. SSH Process Table Attacks
  8. SYN Attacks

Distributed Denial of Service Attacks

- Distributed Denial of Service attacks are generally executed in two phases
- In the first phase, the perpetrator compromises computers
- In the second phase, the compromised hosts begin the attack
- Common examples of DDoS attacks are:
  1. Peer-to-peer attacks
  2. Reflected attacks
  3. Distributed attacks

Malicious Code Attacks

- Malicious code attacks use programs that are written by attackers to do damage
- Most programs do not require that the attacker be present for them to do damage
- There are six types of malicious code attacks, and these are:
  1. Malware
  2. Viruses
  3. Trojan Horses
  4. Logic Bombs
  5. Worms
  6. Backdoor

- Worm attacks can be prevented by via containment, planning, tools and techniques
- Some of the tools that can be used to defend against worm attacks are:
  1. Access Control Lists (ACLs)
  2. Unicast Reverse Path Forwarding (uRPF)
  3. NetFlow and NetFlow export
  4. Routing protocols such as remote-triggered black hole filtering (RTBH)

Password Attacks

- Password attacks are fairly common and are easy to perform and often result in success
- There two types of password attacks are brute force dictionary-based attacks
- A brute force attack is the simple act of guessing keys and passwords
- Dictionary-based attacks search dictionary files to find a match to the encrypted password

Other Common Attacks

- Other common network security attacks include:
  1. Spoofing Attacks
  2. Man-in-the-Middle Attacks
  3. Replay Attacks
  4. TCP/IP Hijacking Attacks
  5. WarDialing Attacks
  6. Vulnerability Scanning
  7. Sniffing
  8. Privilege Escalation
  9. Footprint Analysis
  10. Buffer Overflows

Attack Categories

Network security threats fall into one of the following categories:

1. Active Attacks
2. Passive Attacks
3. Malicious Code Attacks
4. Password Attacks
5. Insider Attacks
6. Close-in Attacks
7. Distribution Attacks

Responding to Security Threats

- The overall framework and process to respond to threats includes the following steps:
  1. Triage
  2. Analysis
  3. Reaction
  4. Restore
  5. Post-Mortem

The Cisco SAFE Blueprint

- Defense in depth is a security philosophy that that uses a layered security approach
- In a defense in depth deployment, each layer of security should have redundancy
- The defense in depth includes the following recommendations:
  1. Defend multiple attack targets in the network
  2. Create overlapping defenses
  3. Allow the value of the protected device to mandate the level of security implemented.
  4. Use strong encryption mechanisms to ensure data confidentiality

- Cisco SAFE delivers defense in depth by strategically via Cisco products and capabilities
- Cisco SAFE is delivered in two forms:
  1. Design blueprints
  2. Security solutions

- Cisco SAFE design blueprints are simply CVDs and security best practice guides
- The selection of platforms and capabilities in CVDs is driven by the SCF
- The SCF is aimed at ensuring network and service availability and business continuity

Cisco SAFE Security Solutions

- Best practices and design recommendations are provided for the following:
  1. Infrastructure device access
  2. Device resiliency and survivability
  3. Routing infrastructure
  4. Switching infrastructure
  5. Network policy enforcement
  6. Network telemetry

The Cisco PPDIOO Model

- The Cisco PPDIOO model encompasses all steps from network vision to optimization
- PPDIOO stands for prepare, plan, design, implement, operate, and optimize
- The Cisco Lifecycle Security Services, which has five distinct services, which are:
  1. Strategy and Assessments Services
  2. Deployment and Migration Services
  3. Remote Management Services
  4. Security Intelligence Services
  5. Security Optimization Services

The Cisco Self Defending Network

- SDN integrates a collection of security solutions to identify, prevent and adapt to threats
- The three core characteristics of the Cisco Self Defending Network are:
  1. Integrated Security
  2. Collaborative Security Systems
  3. Adaptive Threat Defense

- To begin creating the SDN, the platforms used must have integrated security features
- These features are divided into three categories:
  1. Threat Containment
  2. Protected Communications
  3. Management

Network Admission Control (NAC)

- NAC uses NADs to protect the infrastructure from any endpoint seeking network access
- NAC is a part of the Cisco Self Defending Network
- NAC is focused on proactive security solutions and is offered in two forms:
  1. Cisco NAC Appliance
  2. Cisco NAC Framework

- The Cisco NAC appliance solution consists of the following three options:
  1. Clean Access Server
  2. Clean Access Agent
  3. Clean Access Manager

- The four primary components of the NAC framework solution are:
  1. Endpoint software
  2. Network Access Devices (NADs)
  3. Access Control and Policy Server
  4. Management System

Operations Security

- Operations security is used to secure hardware, software and various media
- Recommendations for operations security are divided into four categories:
  1. Separation of Duties
  2. Rotation of Duties
  3. Trusted Recovery
  4. Configuration and Change Control

Security Documentation

- Security policies are used to describe the 'whats' of information security
- Standards, procedures, baselines and guidelines describe the 'hows' of the security policy
- Security policies are a set of rules, practices, and procedures
- Security policies are typically written by higher manageme
- Some common examples of security policies are:
  1. Acceptable Use Policies
  2. Ethics Policies
  3. Information Sensitivity Policies
  4. Email Policies
  5. Password Policies
  6. Risk Assessment Policies

- Standards are industry-recognized best practices, frameworks, and agreed principles
- Standard define systems parameters and processes and typically vary by industry
- Procedures are low-level documents
- Procedures provide instructions on security policy and standard implementation
- Baselines are the minimal level of security required in a system

The Security Wheel

- The security wheel shows the process of striving towards achieving a secured network
- The security wheel contains five steps, which are:
    1. Developing a security policy
    2. Securing the network
    3. Monitoring and Responding
    4. Testing
    5. Managing and Improving

Guidelines and Best Practices

- Guidelines are recommended actions and operational guides for users
- Guidelines are simply used as reference material
- Cisco recommends the following best:
    1. Routinely apply patches to operating systems and applications.
    2. Disable unneeded services and ports on hosts.
    3. Require strong passwords and enable password expiration.
    4. Protect physical access to computing and networking equipment.
    5. Enforce secure programming practices
    6. Train users on good security practices and educate them about social engineering tactics
    7. Use strong encryption for sensitive data
    8. Defend against attacks by deploying both hardware and software-based security solutions
    9. Create a documented security policy for company-wide use.

CHAPTER 2

Securing Cisco IOS Routers

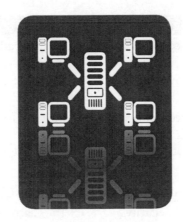

On most networks, routers are typically used as perimeter devices that connect internal networks to public networks, such as the Internet. For outside users, which include legitimate users and potential attackers, such deployments make routers the first point of entry into the network. It is therefore important to understand the methods available in Cisco IOS to protect routers and their related components. The IINS exam objectives covered in this chapter are as follows:

- Secure administrative access to Cisco routers by setting strong encrypted passwords, exec timeout, and login failure rate and by using IOS login enhancements
- Secure administrative access to Cisco routers by configuring multiple privilege levels
- Secure administrative access to Cisco routers by configuring role-based CLI
- Secure the Cisco IOS image and configuration file
- Secure Cisco routers using the SDM Security Audit feature
- Use the One-Step Lockdown feature in SDM to secure a Cisco router

This chapter is broken up into the following sections:

- Securing administrative access to IOS routers
- Usernames, user passwords, and privilege levels
- Cisco IOS Login Block
- Cisco IOS Role-based Command Line Interface
- Securing Cisco IOS router files and images
- Cisco IOS AutoSecure
- The Cisco SDM Security Audit feature
- The Cisco SDM One-Step Lockdown feature

IINS Exam Objective	Section(s) Covered
Secure administrative access to Cisco routers by setting strong encrypted passwords, exec timeout, and login failure rate and by using IOS login enhancements	• Securing administrative access to IOS routers • Cisco IOS Login Block
Secure administrative access to Cisco routers by configuring multiple privilege levels	• Usernames, passwords, and privilege levels
Secure administrative access to Cisco routers by configuring role-based CLI	• Cisco IOS Role-based Command Line Interface
Secure the Cisco IOS image and configuration file	• Securing Cisco IOS router files and images
Secure Cisco routers using the SDM Security Audit feature	• The Cisco SDM Security Audit feature
Use the One-Step Lockdown feature in SDM to secure a Cisco router	• The Cisco SDM One-Step Lockdown feature
Other related topics	• Cisco IOS AutoSecure

Securing Administrative Access to IOS Routers

Because routers form an integral part of the network and security infrastructure, it is imperative that these devices are not overlooked in the overall security solution implementation. Cisco IOS devices provide several features that can be used to implement basic security for Command Line Interface (CLI) sessions.

The Cisco IOS CLI is divided into different command modes. Each command mode has its own set of commands available for the configuration, maintenance, and monitoring of router and network operations. The commands available to you at any given time depend on the mode you are in. Entering a question mark (?) at the system prompt, for a particular mode, allows you to obtain a list of commands available within that mode.

The standard order in which a user would access the modes would be user EXEC mode, privileged EXEC mode, global configuration mode, specific configuration modes, configuration submodes, and configuration sub-submodes. In order to gain access to router configuration mode, a user must first gain access to privileged EXEC mode by using the enable [privilege level] command in EXEC mode as illustrated in the following output:

```
R1>enable ?
 <0-15>  Enable level
 view    Set into the existing view
 <cr>
```

By default, the Cisco IOS software command-line interface (CLI) has two levels of access to commands: user EXEC mode (level 1) and privileged EXEC mode (level 15). However, you can configure additional levels of access to commands, called privilege levels, to meet the needs of your users while protecting the system from unauthorized access. Up to 16 privilege levels can be configured, from level 0, which is the most restricted level, to level 15, which is the least restricted level. Access to each privilege level is enabled through separate passwords, which you specify when configuring the privilege level.

In addition to configuring the privilege levels locally on the Cisco networking device, these command privileges can also be implemented using AAA with TACACS+ and RADIUS. For example, TACACS+ provides two ways to control the authorization of router commands on a per-user or per-group basis. The first way is to assign privilege levels to commands and have the router verify with the TACACS+ server whether the user is authorized at the specified privilege level. The second way is explicitly to specify in the TACACS+ server, on a per-user or per-group basis, the commands that are allowed. AAA, TACACS+, and RADIUS are all described in detail in the next chapter.

If you do not include a specific privilege level at the end of the enable command, Cisco IOS automatically assumes access using a privilege level of 15; therefore, the Level 15 must be used, otherwise authentication will not succeed. The local password for different privilege levels can be set via the enable password level [level] [password], or, more preferably, the enable secret level [level] [password] command.

> NOTE: It is important to remember that while the enable password command is a valid command, it uses a weak hashing algorithm and can be cracked with relative ease, and is therefore not recommended. In addition to this, by default, the password is stored in unencrypted form in the router configuration, unless the service password-encryption configuration command is used. This command should not be used if the enable secret command is available. It is retained in Cisco IOS software for the purposes of maintaining backward compatibility with older Cisco IOS software versions.
>
> However, in recent Cisco IOS versions (i.e. Cisco IOS 12.3 and later), whenever the enable password level [level] [password] command is used, the router will automatically change this command to the enable secret level [level] [password] command, will automatically encrypt the password (using the MD5 hash algorithm), and will print the password in encrypted form without the need for any additional configuration, as illustrated in the following:

```
R1(config)#enable password level 1 cisco123
% Converting to a secret. Please use "enable secret" in the future.

R1(config)#end
R1#
R1#show running-config | include enable
enable secret level 1 5 $1$g1ul$LOSsygicl1C02.8xCOnjO1
R1#
R1#
```

Referring back to the use of the enable secret command, the following example illustrates the steps required to configure an enable password for Level 15 access on a Cisco IOS device. The privilege level can then be validated by using the show privilege command:

```
R1(config)#enable secret level 15 security456
R1(config)#exit
R1#disable
R1>
R1>enable 15
Password:
R1#
R1#show privilege
Current privilege level is 15
R1#
```

The use of different enable passwords for different CLI privilege levels typically goes hand-in-hand with the restriction of command execution at certain privilege levels via the privilege exec [all|level] [level] [command] command. It is important to keep in mind that before Cisco IOS Releases 12.0(22)S and 12.2(13)T, each command in a privilege level had to be specified with a separate privilege command. However, in Cisco IOS Releases 12.0(22)S, 12.2(13)T and later releases, a wildcard option, specified by the keyword all, was introduced. This keyword allows administrators to configure access to multiple commands with only one privilege command.

By using the all keyword, you can specify a privilege level for all commands that begin with the string you enter. In other words, the all keyword allows you to grant access to all command-line options and sub-options for a specified command. For example, if you wanted to create a privilege level to allow users to configure all dynamic routing protocols (i.e. via the use of the router command), the following configuration would be implemented on the router:

```
R1(config)#privilege exec all level 15 router
R1(config)#
```

The use of the wildcard all in the output illustrated above negates the need to have to configure a privilege command for all routing protocols, for example, privilege exec level 15 router ospf, privilege exec level 15 router eigrp, and privilege exec level 15 router rip, to set a privilege level of 15 for OSPF, EIGRP, and RIP configuration.

If the command specified in the privilege command used with the all keyword contains a configuration sub-mode, all commands in the sub-mode of that command will also be set to the specified privilege level. An example of sub-mode configuration would be the configuration of a sub-interface off a main router interface, such as an Ethernet or Frame Relay interface.

When privilege levels are used for commands, users must use the appropriate password (and level) in order to be allowed to execute restricted commands. For example, in the following configuration, all show commands are assigned a privilege level of 7, while all debug * commands are assigned a privilege level of 9. These two levels are assigned two different passwords: security7 and security9, respectively.

```
R1(config)#privilege exec all level 7 show
R1(config)#privilege exec all level 9 debug
R1(config)#enable secret level 7 security7
R1(config)#enable secret level 9 security9
R1(config)#exit
R1#
```

Based on this configuration, the Level 7 password will enable the user to execute any show commands, as well as their options. However, no debug commands will be allowed. On the other hand, logging in with the Level 9 password automatically grants access to the Level 7 show commands (because they are of a lower privilege Level), as well as any debug commands and their options, as illustrated in the following output:

```
R1>enable 7
Password:
R1#
R1#show ip interface brief
Interface          IP-Address      OK?     Method         Status
Protocol
FastEthernet0/0    172.16.1.1      YES     NVRAM          up
up
Serial0/0          10.1.1.1        YES     NVRAM          down
down
R1#
R1#
R1#debug ip packet
   ^
% Invalid input detected at '^' marker.

R1#
R1#disable
R1>
R1>
R1>enable 9
Password:
R1#
R1#show ip interface brief
Interface          IP-Address      OK?     Method         Status
Protocol
FastEthernet0/0    172.16.1.1      YES     NVRAM          up
up
Serial0/0          10.1.1.1        YES     NVRAM          down
down
R1#
R1#debug ip packet
IP packet debugging is on
R1#
```

Although the privilege command is typically used to restrict access to the Cisco IOS EXEC, it is important to know that it can also be used to restrict access to configuration commands as well. The same configuration logic is applicable to the restriction of configuration commands, as that which applies to EXEC commands. For example, to allow a user with a privilege level of 7 to access configuration mode, but restrict them to only routing protocol configuration, the following configuration would be implemented on the router:

```
R1(config)#enable secret level 7 mypassword
R1(config)#privilege exec level 7 configure terminal
R1(config)#privilege configure all level 7 router
R1(config)#line vty 0 4
R1(config-line)#login local
R1(config-line)#exit
R1(config)#exit
R1#
```

This configuration can then be tested by accessing the router and logging in using the Level 7 secret, as illustrated in the following output:

```
R1>enable 7
Password:
R1#
R1#show privilege
Current privilege level is 7
R1#
R1#configure terminal
Enter configuration commands, one per line.  End with CNTL/Z.
R1(config)#router ospf 1
R1(config-router)#exit
R1(config)#ip route 10.0.0.0 255.255.255.0 fastethernet0/0
         ^
% Invalid input detected at '^' marker.

R1(config)#hostname r1
         ^
% Invalid input detected at '^' marker.
```

As illustrated in the output above, the Level 7 user is able to log in to the router and is immediately put into privileged mode, which allows the user to enter the configure terminal command that has been manually configured as a level 7 command. Additionally, the user is successfully able to enable OSPF routing on R1, using a process ID of 1 because all configuration commands that begin with router are permitted for users with a privilege Level of 7.

However, as can also be seen, the user is unable to configure a static route, or even change the hostname of the router, because these commands still default to Level 15 access, which is the default privilege level for all configuration commands in Cisco IOS software, and are therefore unavailable to or invalid for a Level 7 user.

While using the enable secret and privilege exec commands provide security for local CLI access, consideration must also be given to remote CLI access. Remote CLI sessions are created between a host (e.g. a PC) and a networking device (e.g. a router) over a network using a remote terminal access application, such as Telnet and Secure Shell (SSH). Local CLI sessions start in user EXEC mode. It is important to remember that terminal lines, such as the Console and VTY lines, can be used for both local and remote CLI sessions.

These lines can be secured using passwords, which is performed via the use of the password command. Unlike the password used to enter EXEC mode, all passwords specified on terminal lines are Level 1 passwords, and this cannot be changed. This means that once the password has been entered, the user is placed into EXEC mode and must use the enable command and specify the correct password to gain access to privileged EXEC mode. The configuration for both the Console and VTY lines is similar and is performed as follows:

```
R1(config)#line con 0
R1(config-line)#password security
R1(config-line)#exit
R1(config)#line vty 0 4
R1(config-line)#password security
R1(config-line)#exit
R1(config)#exit
R1#
```

When configuring terminal-line passwords, these passwords are treated in the privileged EXEC password configured using the enable password command and are not encrypted by default. This means that these passwords are viewable in plain text in the running configuration of a router, as illustrated in the following output:

```
R1#show running-config | begin line
line con 0
 password security
line aux 0
line vty 0 4
 password security
 login
!
!
end
```

In order to change this default behaviour, the router must be configured with the service password-encryption global configuration command, as follows:

```
R1#config t
Enter configuration commands, one per line.  End with CNTL/Z.
R1(config)#service password-encryption
R1(config)#exit
```

```
R1#show running-config | begin line
line con 0
 password 7 111A1C06020002181D
line aux 0
line vty 0 4
 password 7 03175E08131D285857
 login
!
!
end
```

Even though the passwords are now encrypted, it is important to remember that the encryption algorithm used is the same as that used for the enable password command and is very weak.

In addition to simply setting passwords, the exec-timeout command can also be used for remote CLI sessions inbound on terminal lines. This command is used to set the interval that the EXEC command interpreter waits until user input is detected.

By default, this value is ten minutes, which means that if a user is connected via the Console, for example, the EXEC process will remain idle for up to ten minutes before the user must log in again. Naturally, this is a relatively excessive amount of time; therefore, it is recommended that this value be lowered to enhance security to the device, as illustrated in the following example where the EXEC process timeout is reduced to one and a half minutes for VTY 0:

```
R1(config)#line vty 0
R1(config-line)#exec-timeout 1 30
R1(config-line)#exit
R1(config)#exit
R1#
R1#
R1#show line vty 0
```

Tty Typ	Tx/Rx	A Modem	Roty	AccO	AccI	Uses	Noise	Overruns
Int								
66 VTY	- -		-	-	-	0	0	0/0
-								

```
Line 66, Location: "", Type: ""
Length: 24 lines, Width: 80 columns
Baud rate (TX/RX) is 9600/9600
Status: No Exit Banner
Capabilities: none
Modem state: Idle
```

Special Chars: Escape	Hold	Stop	Start	Disconnect	Activation
^^x	none	-	-	none	

Timeouts:	**Idle EXEC** **00:01:30**	Idle Session never	Modem	Answer	Session none	Dispatch not set

Idle Session Disconnect Warning
never

Login-sequence User Response
00:00:30

Autoselect Initial Wait
not set

Modem type is unknown.
Session limit is not set.
Time since activation: never
Editing is enabled.
History is enabled, history size is 20.
DNS resolution in show commands is enabled
Full user help is disabled
Allowed input transports are pad telnet rlogin mop v120 ssh.
Allowed output transports are pad telnet rlogin mop v120 ssh.
Preferred transport is telnet.
No output characters are padded
No special data dispatching characters

In the same manner that user workstations can and should be locked if active programs are running, the terminal lines in Cisco IOS routers can also be locked by using the lockable line configuration command. This command requires a valid password to lock and unlock the terminal line and provides an additional layer of security, as follows:

```
R1(config)#line vty 0 4
R1(config-line)#lockable
R1(config-line)#exit
R1(config)#exit
R1#
R1#lock
Password:
Again:


        Locked



Password:
R1#
R1#show line vty 0
```

Tty Typ	Tx/Rx	A Modem	Roty	AccO	Accl	Uses	Noise	Overruns
Int								
66 VTY	- -		-	-	-	0	0	0/0
-								

```
Line 66, Location: "", Type: ""
Length: 24 lines, Width: 80 columns
Baud rate (TX/RX) is 9600/9600
Status: No Exit Banner
Capabilities: Lockable
Modem state: Idle
Special Chars: Escape      Hold    Stop    Start    Disconnect      Activation
               ^^x         none    -       -        none
Timeouts:    Idle EXEC  Idle Session     Modem    Answer    Session    Dispatch
             never      never                               none       not set
                        Idle Session Disconnect Warning
                        never
                        Login-sequence User Response
                        00:00:30
                        Autoselect Initial Wait
                        not set
Modem type is unknown.
Session limit is not set.
Time since activation: never
Editing is enabled.
History is enabled, history size is 20.
DNS resolution in show commands is enabled
Full user help is disabled
Allowed input transports are pad telnet rlogin mop v120 ssh.
Allowed output transports are pad telnet rlogin mop v120 ssh.
Preferred transport is telnet.
No output characters are padded
No special data dispatching characters
```

In addition to setting different passwords for different privilege levels, Cisco IOS software also provides additional commands that can be used (and should be used) to further secure the router. These commands are the security passwords min-length <length> and the security authentication failure rate <threshold-rate> log commands.

The security passwords min-length <length> command is a global command that sets the minimum password length for user, enable, and terminal line passwords. This command is used to specify the minimum length of a configured password, which is six characters by default. As stated in Chapter 1, it is good practice to ensure that all passwords are no less than eight characters and contain letters, numbers, and symbols.

This best practice rule can be put into practice on Cisco IOS routers via the use of this command. For example, if this command is used to specify that passwords must be no less than ten characters in length and the user attempts to create a password shorter than that, the following error message will be received:

```
R1(config)#security passwords min-length 10
R1(config)#enable secret ccnapass
% Password too short—must be at least 10 characters. Password configuration failed
R1(config)#
```

The security authentication failure rate <threshold-rate> log command is used to configure the number of allowable unsuccessful login attempts, which is ten by default. This default value should generally be shortened to ensure that no one has up to ten attempts to crack the router password. For example, setting a threshold of two or three is generally good practice.

When the threshold is exceeded (before a 15-second delay) this command generates a log message indicating the failure, thus quickly allowing administrators to be aware of any possible attempts to gain unauthorized access into the router without the correct credentials, which could very well be a type of password attack, for example.

When using the security authentication failure rate <threshold-rate> log command, it is important to remember that logging must be enabled on the router, either locally or to a remote Syslog server. Syslog is a standard for forwarding log messages across an IP network to a remote server running a Syslog daemon. These log messages are sent via UDP, using a destination port of 514. Syslog is explained in detail later in this guide.

For example, to specify that a log message must be generated and sent to Syslog server 192.168.1.254, in the event of two unsuccessful attempts to access the router before a 15-second delay, the following configuration would be implemented:

```
R1(config)#logging on
R1(config)#logging host 192.168.1.254
R1(config)#security authentication failure rate 2 log
R1(config)#exit
R1#
```

Usernames, User Passwords, and Privilege Levels

In Cisco IOS software, in addition to configuring passwords and setting different privilege levels for commands, administrators also have the capability to create local user accounts, assign those accounts specific privilege levels, which can be used in conjunction with the command restrictions configured using the privilege command, and create passwords for those users. Cisco IOS devices can then be configured so that local and remote sessions to the router are granted access based on configured username and password pairs.

Although the use of the username command is introduced and explained in the CCNA course, it is important to remember that before Cisco IOS Releases 12.0(18)S and 12.2(8)T, there were two types of passwords that were associated with usernames: Type 0, a clear text password visible to any user who has access to privileged mode on the router; and Type 7, a password encrypted by the service password-encryption command.

However, in Cisco IOS Releases 12.0(18)S, 12.2(8)T, and later releases, the new secret keyword for the username command allows you to configure Message Digest 5 (MD5) encryption for user passwords. This is the same encryption algorithm used by the enable secret command. This provides greater security than the algorithm used by the enable password command, which was also used to generate the password hash for user accounts in older IOS versions.

Configuring usernames, their passwords, and privileges in Cisco IOS software is a straightforward task that is performed using the username [name] privilege [level] secret [password] global configuration command. In order to allow terminal lines to authenticate users based on configured usernames, the login local configuration command is required under the terminal lines (i.e. under line con 0, for example).

The following example illustrates how three usernames are configured on a Cisco IOS router. The first user (BASIC) is assigned a privilege level of 1; the second user (INTERMEDIATE) is assigned a privilege level of 7; and the final user (EXPERT) is assigned a privilege level of 15:

```
R2(config)#username BASIC privilege 1 secret basic
R2(config)#username INTERMEDIATE privilege 7 secret intermediate
R2(config)#username EXPERT privilege 15 secret expert
R2(config)#exit
R2#
R2#show running-config | include username
username BASIC secret 5 $1$49Tu$Wi3WXbLGNOM1pl2MEgiig0
username INTERMEDIATE privilege 7 secret 5 $1$jjnj$tpZzs1l7RpxRwAmN1eLSR/
username EXPERT privilege 15 secret 5 $1$giSy$qLsRy0r4Kfpi427CeiiT61
```

In addition to the configured usernames, administrators can also use the privilege command to set restrictions on the commands the users can enter. For example, to restrict the user BASIC (Level 1) to only the ping and traceroute commands, and the user INTERMEDIATE (Level 7) to all show commands, the following configuration would be implemented on the router:

```
R2(config)#privilege exec all level 1 ping
R2(config)#privilege exec all level 1 traceroute
R2(config)#privilege exec all level 7 show
R2(config)#exit
```

```
R2#
User Access Verification

Username: BASIC
Password:
R2>show version
     ^
% Invalid input detected at '^' marker.

R2>ping 172.16.1.2

Type escape sequence to abort.
Sending 5, 100-byte ICMP Echos to 172.16.1.2, timeout is 2 seconds:
!!!!!
Success rate is 100 percent (5/5), round-trip min/avg/max = 1/2/4 ms
R2>exit


User Access Verification

Username: INTERMEDIATE
Password:
R2#
R2#show ip interface brief
Interface          IP-Address      OK?    Method      Status      Protocol
FastEthernet0/0    172.16.1.2      YES    NVRAM       up          up
Serial0/0          10.1.1.2        YES    NVRAM       up          up
R2#debug ip packet
        ^
% Invalid input detected at '^' marker.

R2#
```

In addition to setting privilege levels, the username [name] secret [password] autocommand [command] command can also be used to further restrict users by immediately executing a specified command for a particular user and then logging the user off automatically. When using the autocommand feature, it is important to remember that the user must have the appropriate privilege level in order to execute the command specified in the command string; otherwise, this feature will simply not work. For example, to configure a router to automatically execute the show ip interface brief command for a user (AUTO) and then automatically log the user off, the following configuration would be implemented on the router:

```
R2(config)#username AUTO secret autosecret
R2(config)#username AUTO autocommand show ip interface brief
R2(config)#exit
R2#
```

In the configuration illustrated above, it is important to remember that, by default, all show commands are available for Level 1 users. Therefore, the privilege command does not need to be used and the user's privilege level can also remain the same. The autocommand feature can then be validated by logging in as AUTO. The router simply prints the specified output and automatically terminates the session, as illustrated in the following output:

```
R2>login
Username: AUTO
Password:
Interface          IP-Address     OK?    Method     Status        Protocol
FastEthernet0/0    172.16.1.2     YES    NVRAM      up            up
Serial0/0          10.1.1.2       YES    NVRAM      up            up

R2 con0 is now available

Press RETURN to get started.
```

Cisco IOS Login Block

The Cisco IOS Login Block feature, which is a part of the Cisco IOS Login Enhancements feature set, allows administrators to enhance the security of a router by configuring options to automatically block further login attempts when a possible DoS or password attack is detected.

By enabling the Cisco IOS Login Block feature, DoS attacks, such as TCP SYN floods or SSH Process Table attacks, that can be used to prevent legitimate administrators from logging in to the device, or that floods the device so that it ceases to route or forward packets as expected, can be mitigated. Additionally, this feature can also be used to slow down dictionary attacks. The prevention of these types of attacks is performed by enforcing a quiet period during which the router will not accept any incoming connection requests if multiple failed connection attempts to the router are detected, which effectively protects the router from an attack.

The login block and login delay options introduced by this feature can be configured for Telnet, SSH, or HTTP connections. This feature provides enhanced security over the security authentication failure rate <threshold-rate> log functionality, which can only send a log message in the event of unsuccessful login attempts within a specified interval, but does not automatically 'lock down' the router to prevent any further login attempts.

It is important to keep in mind, however, that even though the router denies connection requests during the quiet period, it is possible to use an ACL (with the addresses that you know to be associated with system administrators) to allow connections only from those addresses. This ensures that administrators have the ability to manage devices during the quiet period.

In order to implement successfully the Cisco IOS Login Block feature, it is important to have a solid understanding of the new CLI options available to enable this feature correctly. The commands associated with this feature are as follows:

- The login block-for [seconds] attempts [tries] within [seconds] command
- The login quiet-mode access-class [ACL] command
- The login delay [seconds] command
- The login on-failure log every [number] command
- The login on-success log every [number] command

The login block-for [seconds] attempts [tries] within [seconds] command is the very first command that must be issued before any other login command can be used! This command is used to configure the router for login parameters and specifies the amount of time the router should remain in the quiet period if the administrator-specified number of failed attempts is exceeded within the specific period of time.

For example, to configure the router to enter quiet mode for five minutes if three unsuccessful login attempts are received within two minutes, the following configuration would be implemented:

```
R1(config)#login block-for 300 attempts 3 within 120
R1(config)#exit
R1#
R1#show login
    A default login delay of 1 seconds is applied.
    No Quiet-Mode access list has been configured.

    Router enabled to watch for login Attacks.
    If more than 3 login failures occur in 120 seconds or less,
    logins will be disabled for 300 seconds.

    Router presently in Normal-Mode.
    Current Watch Window
        Time remaining: 107 seconds.
        Login failures for current window: 0.
    Total login failures: 0.
```

The login quiet-mode access-class [ACL] command specifies an ACL (named or numbered) that is to be applied to the router when it switches to quiet mode to allow access to the subnets or addresses specified in the ACL. Even though this is an optional command, it is important to keep in mind that if this command is not enabled then all login requests, legitimate and otherwise, will be denied during quiet mode.

Therefore, it is good practice to ensure that an ACL is configured and this command is used so administrators still have access to the device during the quiet period. For example, to configure the router to allow administrators from the 172.16.1.0/24 subnet access to the router during the quiet period, the following configuration would be implemented:

```
R1(config)#login quiet-mode access-class 100
R1(config)#access-list 100 permit ip 172.16.1.0 0.0.0.255 any
R1(config)#exit
R1#
R1#show login
    A default login delay of 1 seconds is applied.
    Quiet-Mode access list 100 is applied.

    Router enabled to watch for login Attacks.
    If more than 3 login failures occur in 120 seconds or less,
    logins will be disabled for 300 seconds.

    Router presently in Normal-Mode.
    Current Watch Window
        Time remaining: 15 seconds.
        Login failures for current window: 0.
    Total login failures: 0.
```

The login delay [seconds] command is used to configure a delay between successive login attempts. This is an optional command because, by default, the router uses a default login delay of one second, as illustrated in the output of the show login command:

```
R1#show login
    A default login delay of 1 seconds is applied.
    Quiet-Mode access list 100 is applied.

    Router enabled to watch for login Attacks.
    If more than 3 login failures occur in 120 seconds or less,
    logins will be disabled for 300 seconds.

    Router presently in Normal-Mode.
    Current Watch Window
        Time remaining: 113 seconds.
        Login failures for current window: 0.
    Total login failures: 0.
```

This command can be used to change this value to any other value that the administrator so desires.

For example, to change the delay interval between successive login attempts to five seconds, the following configuration would be implemented on the router:

```
R1(config)#login delay 5
R1(config)#end
R1#
R1#show login
    A login delay of 5 seconds is applied.
    Quiet-Mode access list 100 is applied.

    Router enabled to watch for login Attacks.
    If more than 3 login failures occur in 120 seconds or less,
    logins will be disabled for 300 seconds.

    Router presently in Normal-Mode.
    Current Watch Window
        Time remaining: 27 seconds.
        Login failures for current window: 0.
    Total login failures: 0.
```

The login on-failure log every [number] command is used to generate Syslog messages for failed login attempts. The [number] option generates a log message for the specified number of failed login attempts. When this optional command is configured, it is important to enable logging capabilities on the router, using either the local buffer or a remote Syslog server.

For example, to configure a router to generate a Syslog message for every two (2) failed login attempts, to both the local buffer and a remote Syslog server with the IP address 172.16.1.254, the router would be configured as follows:

```
R1(config)#login on-failure log every 2
R1(config)#logging on
R1(config)#logging buffered informational
R1(config)#logging trap informational
R1(config)#logging host 172.16.1.254
R1(config)#exit
R1#
R1#show login
    A login delay of 5 seconds is applied.
    Quiet-Mode access list 100 is applied.
    Every 2 failed login is logged.

    Router enabled to watch for login Attacks.
    If more than 3 login failures occur in 120 seconds or less,
    logins will be disabled for 300 seconds.

    Router presently in Normal-Mode.
```

```
Current Watch Window
    Time remaining: 91 seconds.
    Login failures for current window: 0.
Total login failures: 0.
```

The login on-success log every [number] command performs the same functions as the login on-failure log every [number] command, with the exception that it provides logging for successful login attempts.

For example, to configure a router to generate a Syslog message for every successful login attempt, to both the local buffer and a remote Syslog server with the IP address 172.16.1.254, the router would be configured as follows:

```
R1(config)#login on-success log every 1
R1(config)#logging on
R1(config)#logging buffered informational
R1(config)#logging trap informational
R1(config)#logging host 172.16.1.254
R1#
R1#show login
    A login delay of 5 seconds is applied.
    Quiet-Mode access list 100 is applied.
    All successful login is logged.
    Every 2 failed login is logged.

    Router enabled to watch for login Attacks.
    If more than 3 login failures occur in 120 seconds or less,
    logins will be disabled for 300 seconds.

    Router presently in Normal-Mode.
    Current Watch Window
        Time remaining: 72 seconds.
        Login failures for current window: 0.
    Total login failures: 0.
```

To validate Login Block configuration and parameters, the show login command—which has already been illustrated above—is used. This command can also be used with the failures keyword, which is used to display information related only to failed login attempts, as follows.

```
R1#show login ?
  failures  Display Login failures in the current watch period
  |         Output modifiers
  <cr>

R1#show login failures
*** No logged failed login attempts with the device.***
```

It is important to remember that logging information should also be contained in the local router buffer (log). The show logging command can be used to view any information pertaining to the Cisco IOS Login Block feature (depending on feature configuration) as follows:

R1#**show logging**
Syslog logging: enabled (1 messages dropped, 0 messages rate-limited,
      0 flushes, 0 overruns, xml disabled, filtering disabled)

No Active Message Discriminator.

No Inactive Message Discriminator.

    Console logging: disabled
    Monitor logging: level debugging, 0 messages logged, xml disabled,
        filtering disabled
    Buffer logging: level informational, 8 messages logged, xml disabled,
        filtering disabled
    Logging Exception size (4096 bytes)
    Count and timestamp logging messages: disabled
    Persistent logging: disabled
    Trap logging: level informational, 37 message lines logged
      Logging to 172.16.1.254 (udp port 514, audit disabled,
        authentication disabled, encryption disabled, link up),
        10 message lines logged,
        0 message lines rate-limited,
        0 message lines dropped-by-MD,
        xml disabled, sequence number disabled
        filtering disabled

Log Buffer (4096 bytes):

*Mar 1 01:32:37.456: %SYS-5-CONFIG_I: Configured from console by console
*Mar 1 01:33:52.515: %SYS-5-CONFIG_I: Configured from console by console
*Mar 1 01:34:11.863: %SYS-5-CONFIG_I: Configured from console by console
*Mar 1 01:36:36.127: %SYS-5-CONFIG_I: Configured from console by console
*Mar 1 01:36:52.318: %SEC_LOGIN-5-LOGIN_SUCCESS: Login Success [user: cisco]
[Source: 0.0.0.0] [localport: 0] at 01:36:52 UTC Fri Mar 1 2002
*Mar 1 01:37:32.031: %SEC_LOGIN-5-LOGIN_SUCCESS: Login Success [user: cisco]
[Source: 0.0.0.0] [localport: 0] at 01:37:32 UTC Fri Mar 1 2002

Cisco IOS Role-based Command Line Interface

The Cisco IOS role-based CLI access feature allows an administrator to define views, which are a set of operational commands and configuration capabilities that provide selective or partial access to Cisco IOS EXEC and configuration (Config) mode commands.

Views restrict user access to Cisco IOS command-line interface (CLI) and configuration information. In other words, a view can define what commands are accepted and what configuration information is visible. The role-based CLI access feature provides greater administrative control of commands than the use of the username and the privilege commands to accomplish the same goal.

Therefore, if the router platform you are working on supports CLI views, this is the recommended method to ensure detailed access control capability for administrators, which improves the overall security and accountability of Cisco IOS software.

In order to configure the role-based CLI access feature, two prerequisites must be met. The first prerequisite is that AAA (Authentication, Authorization, and Accounting—which will be described in detail later in this guide) must be enabled in order to use the role-based CLI access feature. This is performed by using the aaa new-model global configuration command, as illustrated in the following output:

```
R2#config t
Enter configuration commands, one per line.  End with CNTL/Z.
R2(config)#aaa new-model
R2(config)#exit
R2#
```

The second prerequisite is that the system must be in root view. Root view is a special view mode that has all of the access privileges as a user who has Level 15 privileges in Cisco IOS software. However, the difference between a user who has Level 15 privileges and a root view user is that a root view user can configure a new view and add or remove commands from the view. It is also important to remember that while users assigned a certain privilege level have access to all commands at and below that privilege level (e.g. a user with a privilege level of 10 has access to all commands assigned privilege levels 1–10), users in CLI views are restricted only to the commands available in that view.

In addition to this, when users are in a CLI view, they will only have access to the commands that have been added to that view by the root view user. Enabling the root view is accomplished by using the enable view EXEC command and entering the Level 15 secret command if prompted, as illustrated in the following output:

```
R2#disable
R2>
R2>enable view
Password:

R2#show privilege
Currently in View Context with view 'root'
```

Once these two prerequisites have been met, administrators can begin to configure views using the parser view [name] global configuration command. This command allows you to create the name of a parser view to be used. Once the name is created, the router then goes into view configuration mode, which allows the router to specify a password for the configured view, as well as the commands that are available within that view.

The password for a particular view is set by using the secret command within view configuration mode. It is important to remember that you must associate a password with a view. If you do not associate a password, and you attempt to add commands to the view, a system message such as the following will be displayed:

%Password not set for view BASIC

Commands are added to views via the commands [mode] (include | include-exclusive | exclude) [all] [interface (name) | command] command. In order to understand the correct use of this command, it is important to understand the options presented and what they mean. These options are described in Table 2.1:

Table 2.1. IOS Command Options

Option	Description
mode	This option is used to specify the router mode in which the command that will be specified exists. For example, the show command would exist in EXEC mode, while the router command would exist in CONFIGURE mode.
include	This option adds a command or an interface to the view and allows the same command or interface to be added to another view.
include-exclusive	This option adds a command or an interface to the view and excludes the same command or interface from being added to all other views.
exclude	This option excludes a command or an interface from the view. In other words, users cannot access a command or an interface excluded by this option for the particular view they are in.
all	This option is a wildcard that allows every command in a specified configuration mode that begins with the same keyword or every subinterface for a specified interface to be part of the view. In essence, this performs the same function as the all keyword in the privilege command that we learned about earlier.
interface (name)	This option is used to specify the interface that is added to the view.
command	This option is used to specify the command that is added to the view.

To reinforce the configuration of views, we will go through the required steps using a practical example, as follows, where four (4) different views will be created: Level-1, Level-2, Level-3, and Level-4. The Level-1 view will be restricted to only ping and traceroute commands; the Level-2 view will be restricted to only show commands; the Level-3 view will be restricted to only static and dynamic routing configuration commands, as well as all interface configuration commands; and, finally, the Level-4 view will be restricted to only debug and undebug commands. In addition to this, the include-exclusive option is used in all configured view configuration to ensure that commands are restricted only to those views, as illustrated in the following output:

```
R2(config)#parser view Level-1
R2(config-view)#secret level1
R2(config-view)#commands exec include-exclusive all ping
R2(config-view)#commands exec include-exclusive all traceroute
R2(config-view)#exit
R2(config)#parser view Level-2
R2(config-view)#secret level2
R2(config-view)#commands exec include-exclusive all show
R2(config-view)#exit
R2(config)#parser view Level-3
R2(config-view)#secret level3
R2(config-view)#commands exec include-exclusive all configure
R2(config-view)#commands configure include-exclusive all router
R2(config-view)#commands configure include-exclusive all ip route
R2(config-view)#commands configure include-exclusive all interface
R2(config-view)#exit
R2(config)#parser view Level-4
R2(config-view)#secret level4
R2(config-view)#commands exec include-exclusive all debug
R2(config-view)#commands exec include-exclusive all undebug
R2(config-view)#exit
R2(config)#exit
R2#
```

The view configuration can be validated by the administrator via the use of the enable view [name] command and by entering the correct password for the specified view. Once successfully logged in to a particular view, the question mark can be used to view the commands available within that view, as illustrated in the following output for the Level-1 and Level-4 views:

```
R2>enable view Level-1
Password:

R2#?
Exec commands:
  enable    Turn on privileged commands
  exit      Exit from the EXEC
```

```
  ping         Send echo messages
  show         Show running system information
  traceroute   Trace route to destination
```

R2#**show ?**
parser Show parser commands

R2#**show parser view**
Current view is 'Level-1'

R2#**show ip interface brief**
```
        ^
```
% Invalid input detected at '^' marker.

R2#**ping 172.16.1.2**

```
Type escape sequence to abort.
Sending 5, 100-byte ICMP Echos to 172.16.1.2, timeout is 2 seconds:
!!!!!
Success rate is 100 percent (5/5), round-trip min/avg/max = 1/2/4 ms
R2#exit
```

Press RETURN to get started.

```
R2>
R2>
R2>enable view Level-4
Password:
```

R2#**?**
Exec commands:
```
  debug     Debugging functions (see also 'undebug')
  enable    Turn on privileged commands
  exit      Exit from the EXEC
  show      Show running system information
  undebug   Disable debugging functions (see also 'debug')
```

R2#**show parser view**
Current view is 'Level-4'
R2#
R2#**show ip interface brief**
```
     ^
```
% Invalid input detected at '^' marker.

R2#**debug ip packet**
IP packet debugging is on
R2#
R2#**undebug all**
All possible debugging has been turned off

In addition to creating standard views, it is also possible to create a superview. A superview consists of one or more already configured CLI views, which allow users to define what commands are accepted and what configuration information is visible. Superviews easily allow a network administrator to assign all users within configured CLI views to a superview instead of having to assign multiple CLI views to a group of users. Superviews contain the following characteristics:

- A CLI view can be shared among multiple superviews. In other words, standard CLI views can belong to more than one superview.
- Commands cannot be configured for a superview. Therefore, administrators must add commands to a CLI view and add that CLI view to the superview.
- Users who are logged in to a superview can access all of the commands that are configured for any of the CLI views that are part of the superview.
- Each superview has a password that is used to switch between superviews or from a CLI view to a superview.
- Deleting a superview will not also delete all CLI views associated with that superview. In order words, deleting a superview does not delete the standard views that are associated with that superview. If CLI views need to be deleted, the administrator must manually delete them while logged in to the root view.

When configuring superviews, the secret command is used to configure the password for the superview, in the same manner as in standard views. However, unlike standard CLI views, there is no commands option in superviews. The only command available is the view command, which allows administrators to add standard CLI views to the superview.

Adding to the view configuration performed earlier, the following configuration creates three (3) superviews. The first superview (LEVEL-1-2) will include all commands available from the Level-1 and Level-2 standard CLI views, which were previously configured. The second superview (LEVEL-3-4) will include all commands available from the Level-3 and Level-4 standard CLI views, which were also previously configured. And, finally, the third superview (LEVEL-ALL) will contain commands available in all four standard views:

```
R2>enable view
Password:

R2#config t
Enter configuration commands, one per line.  End with CNTL/Z.
R2(config)#parser view LEVEL-1-2 superview
R2(config-view)#?
View commands:
  default    Set a command to its defaults
```

```
exit      Exit from view configuration mode
no        Negate a command or set its defaults
secret    Set a secret for the current view
view      View to be added to SuperView

R2(config-view)#secret level12
R2(config-view)#view Level-1
R2(config-view)#view Level-2
R2(config-view)#exit
R2(config)#parser view LEVEL-3-4 superview
R2(config-view)#secret level34
R2(config-view)#view Level-3
R2(config-view)#view Level-4
R2(config-view)#exit
R2(config)#parser view LEVEL-ALL superview
R2(config-view)#secret levelall
R2(config-view)#view Level-1
R2(config-view)#view Level-2
R2(config-view)#view Level-3
R2(config-view)#view Level-4
R2(config-view)#exit
R2(config)#exit
R2#
R2#show parser view
Current view is 'root'
R2#
R2#show parser view all
Views/SuperViews Present in System:
 Level-1
 Level-2
 Level-3
 Level-4
 LEVEL-1-2 *
 LEVEL-3-4 *
 LEVEL-ALL *
-------(*) represent superview-------
```

As is the case with standard CLI views, the enable view [name] command followed by the password is used to log in to superviews. Again, a question mark can be used to validate the command options available to that particular view, as illustrated in the following output:

```
R2 con0 is now available

Press RETURN to get started.

R2>enable view LEVEL-1-2
Password:
```

```
R2#?
Exec commands:
  enable      Turn on privileged commands
  exit        Exit from the EXEC
  ping        Send echo messages
  show        Show running system information
  traceroute  Trace route to destination
R2#
R2#exit

R2 con0 is now available

Press RETURN to get started.

R2>
R2>enable view LEVEL-3-4
Password:

R2#?
Exec commands:
  configure Enter configuration mode
  debug     Debugging functions (see also 'undebug')
  enable    Turn on privileged commands
  exit      Exit from the EXEC
  show      Show running system information
  undebug   Disable debugging functions (see also 'debug')
R2#
R2#exit

R2 con0 is now available

Press RETURN to get started.
R2>
R2>
R2>
R2>enable view LEVEL-ALL
Password:

R2#?
Exec commands:
  configure   Enter configuration mode
  debug       Debugging functions (see also 'undebug')
  enable      Turn on privileged commands
  exit        Exit from the EXEC
  ping        Send echo messages
  show        Show running system information
  traceroute  Trace route to destination
  undebug     Disable debugging functions (see also 'debug')
```

Securing Cisco IOS Router Files and Images

The Cisco IOS resilient configuration feature, available in Cisco IOS 12.2SX and 12.4, enables a router to secure and maintain a working copy of the running image and configuration so that those files can withstand malicious attempts to erase the contents of persistent storage, which include NVRAM and flash memory.

This feature is intended to speed up the recovery process in the event that a router has been compromised and its operating software and configuration data have been erased from its persistent storage. This is possible because the Cisco IOS resilient configuration feature maintains a secure working copy of the router image and the startup configuration (NVRAM) at all times and the user cannot remove these secure files. This set of image and router running configuration is referred to as the primary bootset. The resilient configuration feature has the following characteristics:

- The copy of the running configuration that was in the router when the feature was first enabled is used as the configuration file in the primary bootset.
- The feature secures the smallest working set of files to preserve persistent storage space. No extra space is required to secure the primary Cisco IOS image file.
- The feature automatically detects Cisco IOS image or configuration version mismatch.
- Only local storage (i.e. on the router itself) is used for securing files, eliminating scalability maintenance challenges from storing multiple images and configurations on TFTP servers.
- The feature can be disabled only through a console session, which means that the administrator must have physical access to the router to perform this, enhancing security.

The Cisco IOS resilient configuration feature is very straightforward to implement. In order to save a primary bootset to a secure archive in persistent storage, only two configuration commands are required. The first configuration command, the secure boot-image command, is used to enable Cisco IOS image resilience. The second configuration command, the secure boot-config command, is used to store a secure copy of the primary bootset in persistent storage.

Although the IOS resilient configuration feature provides enhanced security for Cisco IOS routers, it is important to understand that it has several restrictions. The first major restriction is that this feature is available only on platforms that support a Personal Computer Memory Card International Association (PCMCIA) Advanced Technology Attachment (ATA) disk. In addition to this, even on these devices, there must be enough space on the storage device to accommodate at least one Cisco IOS image (two for upgrades) and a copy of the running configuration, and it is required that IOS Files System (IFS) support for secure file systems is also supported by the software. This reduces the platforms that this feature can be implemented on.

Another restriction is that it may be possible to force removal of secured files using an older version of Cisco IOS software that does not contain file system support for hidden files. In other words, booting up the router using an older image that does not support the IOS resilient configuration feature effectively negates the security afforded by this feature.

In addition, as previously mentioned, you cannot secure a bootset with an image loaded from the network—i.e. from a TFTP or FTP server residing on the network. The running image must be loaded from persistent storage to be secured as primary.

Finally, it is important to remember that secured files will not appear on the output of a dir command issued from the EXEC shell because the IFS prevents secure files in a directory from being listed. Additionally, it is important to remember that the Cisco IOS image will not be visible in the output of the show flash command. Instead, use the show secure bootset command to verify archive existence. However, ROM monitor (ROMMON) mode does not have any such restriction and can be used to list and boot secured files.

In addition to the Cisco IOS resilient configuration feature, administrators can also leverage the IOS image verification. This feature automatically allows administrators to verify the integrity of Cisco IOS images, thus ensuring that the image is protected from corruption (accidental or otherwise), which can occur at any time during transit, starting from the moment the files are generated by Cisco until they reach the user.

This negates the need for administrators to validate manually the IOS image MD5 hash printed on the Cisco download website with one generated on their own server before verifying that an image has not been corrupted, because the MD5 hashes are the same.

To enable this feature, the file verify auto global configuration command must be configured on the router. Next, after issuing the file verify auto command, each image that is copied or reloaded (i.e. when the router reboots) will automatically be verified. This is illustrated in the following output on a router that has been configured to verify automatically the Cisco IOS image and is then reloaded (rebooted):

```
R2#config t
Enter configuration commands, one per line.  End with CNTL/Z.
R2(config)#file verify auto
R2(config)#end
R2#
R2#copy system:running-config nvram:startup-config
Destination filename [startup-config]?
Building configuration...
```

```
[OK]
R2#
R2#
R2#reload
Verifying file integrity of flash:/c2600-advsecurityk9-mz.124-15.T9.bin...........................
.........................................................................................................................................
.........................................................................................................................................
...........................................................................................................Done!
Embedded Hash    MD5 : 7F57E6DA1A57A0EC80AF4215F80967B8
Computed Hash    MD5 : 7F57E6DA1A57A0EC80AF4215F80967B8
CCO Hash         MD5 : ABCA61DDB615FB5722CEC3303B9A8DDC
Signature Verified

Proceed with reload? [confirm]
```

If the file verify auto configuration command has not been applied globally onto the router, it is still possible to verify the Cisco IOS image when copying it from its location or when the router is rebooted (reloaded). To verify the Cisco IOS image when copying it, the copy /verify command is used. It is important to keep in mind that the basic functionality and options of the copy /verify command still remain the same, as illustrated in the following output:

```
R2#copy /verify ?
  /erase          Erase destination file system.
  archive:        Copy from archive: file system
  cns:            Copy from cns: file system
  flash:          Copy from flash: file system
  ftp:            Copy from ftp: file system
  http:           Copy from http: file system
  https:          Copy from https: file system
  null:           Copy from null: file system
  nvram:          Copy from nvram: file system
  rcp:            Copy from rcp: file system
  running-config  Copy from current system configuration
  scp:            Copy from scp: file system
  startup-config  Copy from startup configuration
  system:         Copy from system: file system
  tar:            Copy from tar: file system
  tftp:           Copy from tftp: file system
  tmpsys:         Copy from tmpsys: file system
  xmodem:         Copy from xmodem: file system
  ymodem:         Copy from ymodem: file system
```

To verify an image when the router boots (assuming the file verify auto command has not been used), the reload /verify command is used. As is the case with the copy /verify command, the reload /verify command still performs the same basic function and still presents the same options, as illustrated in the following output:

```
R2#reload /verify ?
  LINE      Reason for reload
  at        Reload at a specific time/date
  cancel    Cancel pending reload
  in        Reload after a time interval
  <cr>
```

The final topic we are going to learn about in this section is the Secure Copy (SCP) feature that is available in Cisco IOS routers. SCP provides a secure and authenticated method for copying router configuration or image files. SCP relies on Secure Shell (SSH).

Before SCP can be used, the administrator must correctly configure SSH, Authentication, and Authorization on the router (both Authentication and Authorization are described in detail later in this guide). In addition to this, the router must have a Rivest, Shamir, and Adelman (RSA) key pair. These two requirements pertain to SSH configuration, which is a necessity due to the fact that SCP relies on SSH.

Because SSH and Authentication, Authorization, and Accounting (AAA) are described in detail later in this guide, the emphasis in this section is centered on the SCP feature. Therefore, do not worry if the SSH or AAA configuration presented here seems confusing at first glance, as it is provided simply for the sake of being thorough. You will learn about SSH and AAA theory and configuration in detail later in this guide.

The only SCP-related configuration command required in order to allow a router to support SCP server functionality is the ip scp server enable global configuration command. The other commands required for the SCP feature pertain to SSH and AAA configuration. In order to understand SCP, Figure 2.1 will be used as an example, illustrating the configuration commands required to enable SCP server functionality on a Cisco IOS router:

Figure 2.1. Network Ready for SCP Configuration

Based on Figure 2.1 illustrated above, R1 will be configured as an SCP server. In addition to this, R1 will also be configured as a TFTP server. The TFTP file that R1 will allow clients to download is named TEST, and this file will be stored on R1's flash memory. Users wishing to download this file via must log in using the username SCPUSER with a password SCPPASSWORD. The configuration on R1 to perform this is implemented as follows:

NOTE: Do not focus on the SSH or AAA configuration. This is provided for the purposes of being thorough and is described later in this guide:

```
R1(config)#ip domain-name howtonetwork.net
R1(config)#crypto key generate rsa
The name for the keys will be: R1.howtonetwork.net
Choose the size of the key modulus in the range of 360 to 2048 for your
  General Purpose Keys. Choosing a key modulus greater than 512 may take
  a few minutes.

How many bits in the modulus [512]:
% Generating 512 bit RSA keys, keys will be non-exportable...[OK]

R1(config)#aaa new-model
R1(config)#aaa authentication login default group local
R1(config)#aaa authorization exec default local
R1(config)#username SCPUSER privilege 15 secret SCPPASSWORD
R1(config)#ip scp server enable
R1(config)#tftp-server flash:TEST
R1(config)#exit
R1#
```

Next, R2 can then be configured to copy the file named TEST from R1 using SCP. This is performed by using the copy scp command, as illustrated in the following output:

```
R2#copy scp: flash:
Address or name of remote host []? 172.16.1.1
Source username [R2]? SCPUSER
Source filename []? TEST
Destination filename [TEST]? TEST
Erase flash: before copying? [confirm]n
Password:
!
Verifying checksum...  OK (0x6C6)
2766 bytes copied in 9.295 secs (298 bytes/sec)
R2#
R2#show flash:

System flash directory:
File  Length       Name/status
  1   19615064     c2600-advsecurityk9-mz.124-15.T9.bin
  2   1038         home.shtml
  3   2754         sdmconfig-26xx.cfg
  4   112640       home.tar
```

```
5   1505280        common.tar
6   6389760        sdm.tar
7   931840         es.tar
8   2766           TEST
[28567324 bytes used, 4462816 available, 33030140 total]
32768K bytes of processor board System flash (Read/Write)
```

Cisco IOS AutoSecure

The Cisco IOS AutoSecure feature eliminates the complexity of securing a router by creating a new CLI that automates the configuration of security features and disables certain features, which are typically enabled by default but could be exploited for security holes. AutoSecure provides the following mechanisms to enhance security access to the router:

- Simplified Router Security Configuration
- Enhanced Password Security
- Roll-back and System Logging Message Support

Simplified Router Security Configuration

AutoSecure is valuable to customers without special Security Operations Applications because it quickly allows them to secure their network without thorough knowledge of all the Cisco IOS features and commands.

This feature eliminates the complexity of securing a router by creating a new CLI that automates the configuration of security features and disables certain features, which are typically enabled by default but could be exploited for security holes.

Enhanced Password Security

AutoSecure provides two mechanisms to enhance password security on the router. The first mechanism is the ability to configure a required minimum password length, which can eliminate common passwords, such as 'cisco', for example.

The second mechanism is the ability to generate Syslog messages after the number of unsuccessful attempts exceeds the configured threshold.

Roll-back and System Logging Message Support

AutoSecure also provides support for the roll-back of the AutoSecure configuration. Roll-back enables a router to revert back to its pre-AutoSecure configuration state if the AutoSecure configuration fails or does not work as expected.

The two main focuses of the AutoSecure feature are to secure the Management plane and the Forwarding plane. The Management plane is the logical path of all traffic related to the management of a router. The Management plane performs management functions for a network and is used to manage a device through its connection to the network. Some examples of protocols that are processed in the Management plane are Simple Network Management Protocol (SNMP), Telnet, HTTP, Secure HTTP (HTTPS), and SSH. These management protocols are used for monitoring and for CLI access.

The Forwarding plane refers to a router's forwarding path involved in processing transit traffic or traffic that is destined to the router. The Forwarding plane constitutes the packet-forwarding, switching, and queuing components involved in the packet flow. Examples of features covered in Forwarding plane security are ACLs and Unicast Reverse Path Forwarding (uRPF).

Securing the Management Plane

Cisco IOS AutoSecure secures the Management plane by disabling certain global and interface services that can potentially be exploited for security attacks and, at the same time, enabling global services that help mitigate the threat of attacks. In addition to this, AutoSecure configures secure access and secure logging for the router. After enabling this feature, via the auto secure command, the following global services will be disabled on the router without prompting the user:

- **Finger**—which can be used to collect information about the system before an attack. If enabled, the information can leave your device vulnerable to attacks. This is disabled by issuing the no service finger command.

- **PAD**—which enables all packet assembler and disassembler (PAD) commands and connections between PAD devices and access servers. If enabled, it can leave your device vulnerable to attacks. This is disabled by issuing the no service pad command.

- **Small Servers**—these can allow for TCP and User Datagram Protocol (UDP) diagnostic port attacks, where a sender transmits a volume of fake requests for UDP diagnostic services on the router, consuming all CPU resources. These are disabled by issuing the no service tcp-small-servers and the no service udp-small-servers commands.

- **BOOTP Server**—BOOTP is an unsecure protocol that can be exploited for an attack. This feature is disabled by issuing the no ip bootp server command.

- **HTTP Server**—without Secure HTTP (HTTPS) or authentication embedded in the HTTP server with an associated ACL, the HTTP server is unsecure and can be exploited for an attack. The

HTTP server is disabled by issuing the no ip http server command. However, if you must enable the HTTP server, you will be prompted for authentication or an ACL.

- **Identification Service**—this is an unsecure protocol, defined in RFC 1413, that allows one to query a TCP port for identification. An attacker can access private information about the user from the ID server. This is disabled by issuing the no ip identd command.

- **CDP**—while CDP is generally a useful and desirable service, it is important to know that if a large number of Cisco Discovery Protocol (CDP) packets are sent to the router, the available memory of the router can be consumed, causing the router to crash. CDP is disabled by issuing the no cdp run command.

- **NTP**—without authentication or access-control, Network Time Protocol (NTP) is unsecure and can be used by an attacker to send NTP packets to overload or crash the router. NTP is disabled by issuing the no ntp command. However, if you want to enable NTP, you must configure NTP authentication using MD5, as well as an ACL, to filter NTP sources. If NTP is enabled globally, disable it on all interfaces on which it is not needed.

- **Source Routing**— this allows users to control (to some extent) the path a packet will take from source to destination. This may be used by attackers to bypass firewalls or other mechanisms and is therefore disabled by using the no ip source-route command.

In addition to the global services that are disabled by AutoSecure, the following interface services are also disabled by the AutoSecure feature:

- **ICMP redirects**—these allow for hosts to be redirected by other gateways with better paths to the intended destination but do not add a useful functionality to a correctly configured network. These are disabled on interfaces via the no ip redirects command, as this feature could be used by attackers to exploit security holes.

- **ICMP unreachables**—ICMP unreachables are a known cause for some ICMP-based DoS attacks and are sent when a service or port is unreachable. These are disabled on interfaces via the no ip unreachables command.

- **ICMP mask reply messages**—these messages can give an attacker the subnet mask for a particular subnet in the internetwork and are therefore disabled via the no ip mask-reply interface configuration command.

- **Proxy-Arp**—this allows a router to respond on behalf of another device. Proxy-Arp requests are a known cause for DoS attacks because the available bandwidth and resources of the router can be consumed in an attempt to respond to the repeated requests that are sent by an attacker. Proxy-ARP is disabled via the no ip proxy-arp command.

- **Directed broadcast**—this feature allows routers to forward directed broadcasts, which can potentially be used for DoS smurf attacks. This feature is disabled by issuing the no ip directed-broadcast command.

- **Maintenance Operations Protocol (MOP) service**—MOP is used for utility services such as uploading and downloading system software, remote testing, and problem diagnosis. Because of this, it is possible to be used for malicious activities by an attacker. MOP is disabled by issuing the no mop enabled command.

Finally, AutoSecure enables several global services, further secures the router, and enables logging and. AutoSecure performs the following:

- Enables the service password-encryption command, which prevents passwords from being visible in the configuration.

- Enables the service tcp-keepalives-in and service tcp-keepalives-out commands, which ensure that abnormally terminated TCP sessions are removed.

- If a text banner does not exist, users will be prompted to add a banner.

- The login and secret commands are configured on the CON, AUX, VTY, and TTY lines. The transport input [telnet|ssh] and transport output [telnet|ssh] commands are configured on all of these lines. Also, the exec-timeout 10 command is configured on the CON and AUX.

- When the image on the device is a crypto image, AutoSecure enables SSH and SCP for access and file transfer to and from the router. The ip ssh timeout [seconds] and ip ssh authentication-retries [number] options for SSH are configured to a minimum number. Telnet and FTP are not affected by this operation and remain operational.

- If the AutoSecure user specifies that his or her device does not use Simple Network Management Protocol (SNMP) in interactive mode, the user is asked whether to disable SNMP, regardless of the values of the community strings, which act like passwords to regulate access to the agent on the router; however, in non-interact mode, SNMP will be disabled if the community string is 'public' or 'private.'

- AutoSecure enables sequence numbers and time stamps for all debug and log messages via the service sequence-numbers and service timestamps [options] commands. This is useful when auditing logging messages.

Securing the Forwarding Plane

Unlike the Management plane, there are considerably fewer recommendations that can be implemented to secure the Forwarding plane, as follows:

- Cisco Express Forwarding
- TCP Intercept
- Unicast Reverse Path Forwarding
- Context-Based Access Control

Cisco Express Forwarding (CEF) is used to increase packet switching speed, reducing the overhead and delays introduced by other routing techniques, and to increase overall router performance. While going into detail on CEF is beyond the scope of the IINS course requirements, it is important to know that routers configured for CEF perform better under SYN attacks than routers using the traditional cache. CEF is enabled by issuing the ip cef command.

The TCP Intercept feature implements software to protect TCP servers from TCP SYN flooding attacks, which are a type of DoS attack. This feature helps prevent SYN flooding attacks by intercepting and validating TCP connection requests. As is the case with CEF, going into detail on the TCP Intercept feature is beyond the scope of the IINS course requirements. However, if the TCP Intercept feature is available, it can be configured on the router for connection timeout. TCP Intercept is enabled by using the ip tcp intercept [options] command.

Unicast Reverse Path Forwarding (uRPF) was described in Chapter 1. The uRPF feature helps to mitigate problems that are caused by the introduction of malformed or forged (spoofed) IP source addresses into a network by discarding IP packets that lack a verifiable IP source address. This feature is enabled by the ip verify unicast reverse-path [options] interface configuration command.

Context-Based Access Control (CBAC) is an integral part of the Cisco IOS Firewall. CBAC intelligently filters TCP and UDP packets based on Application Layer protocol session information. This feature, which is described in detail later in this guide, is enabled by using the ip inspect [options] command.

Enabling and Using AutoSecure

Now that we have an understanding of the AutoSecure feature, the next logical step is how to use or implement this feature. AutoSecure is enabled by using the auto secure [options] privileged EXEC command. The options available with this command are as follows:

```
R2#auto secure ?
  firewall        AutoSecure Firewall
  forwarding      Secure Forwarding Plane
  full            Interactive full session of AutoSecure
  login           AutoSecure Login
  management      Secure Management Plane
  no-interact     Non-interactive session of AutoSecure
  ntp             AutoSecure NTP
  ssh             AutoSecure SSH
  <cr>
```

Because this command provides numerous options, it is important to discuss the options that pertain to the IINS course requirements. These options are firewall, forwarding, management, and no-interact.

The firewall option is used to enable CBAC, which is a feature of the overall Cisco IOS Firewall solution. The forwarding option secures only the router Forwarding plane. The management option is used to secure only the Management plane. And, finally, if the no-interact option is selected, the AutoSecure feature does not prompt the user for any interactive configurations. However, if no options are specified, the user will be prompted for all interactive options, which is the equivalent of the auto secure full command.

Figure 2.2 demonstrates how to enable the AutoSecure feature to secure an Internet-facing router by using the auto secure firewall command:

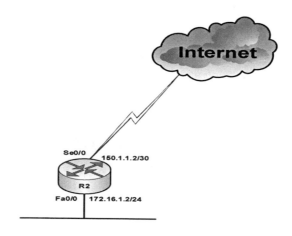

Figure 2.2. Enabling AutoSecure

The steps to perform this configuration are illustrated in the following output:

R2#auto secure firewall
         --- AutoSecure Configuration ---

*** AutoSecure configuration enhances the security of
the router, but it will not make it absolutely resistant
to all security attacks ***

AutoSecure will modify the configuration of your device.
All configuration changes will be shown. For a detailed
explanation of how the configuration changes enhance security
and any possible side effects, please refer to Cisco.com for
AutoSecure documentation.
At any prompt you may enter '?' for help.
Use ctrl-c to abort this session at any prompt.

Gathering information about the router for AutoSecure

Is this router connected to internet? [no]: **yes**
Enter the number of interfaces facing the internet [1]: **1**

Interface	IP-Address	OK?	Method	Status	Protocol
FastEthernet0/0	172.16.1.2	YES	NVRAM	up	up
Serial0/0	150.1.1.2	YES	manual	up	up

Enter the interface name that is facing the internet: **Serial0/0**

Configure CBAC Firewall feature? [yes/no]: **yes**

This is the configuration generated:

ip inspect audit-trail
ip inspect dns-timeout 7
ip inspect tcp idle-time 14400
ip inspect udp idle-time 1800
ip inspect name autosec_inspect cuseeme timeout 3600
ip inspect name autosec_inspect ftp timeout 3600
ip inspect name autosec_inspect http timeout 3600
ip inspect name autosec_inspect rcmd timeout 3600
ip inspect name autosec_inspect realaudio timeout 3600
ip inspect name autosec_inspect smtp timeout 3600
ip inspect name autosec_inspect tftp timeout 30
ip inspect name autosec_inspect udp timeout 15
ip inspect name autosec_inspect tcp timeout 3600
ip access-list extended autosec_firewall_acl
 permit udp any any eq bootpc
 deny ip any any
interface Serial0/0

```
ip inspect autosec_inspect out
ip access-group autosec_firewall_acl in
!
end

Apply this configuration to running-config? [yes]: yes

Applying the config generated to running-config

R2#
R2#
```

Once the configuration has been applied to the running-config, do not forget to save it to NVRAM (startup-config); otherwise, all changes and implementations will be lost if the router is rebooted or reloaded. The current configuration can be saved to NVRAM using either the copy running-config startup-config command or the copy system:running-config nvram:startup-config command.

The Cisco SDM Security Audit Feature

Cisco SDM provides an intuitive router security audit feature with one-step security audit capability that validates router configurations against a list of common security vulnerabilities and Cisco-recommended settings and provides a summary of recommended best practices.

The audit report highlights the potential security problems identified in the router configuration and can generate corresponding configurations to correct the shortfalls. The SDM Security Audit feature operates in one of two modes—the Security Audit wizard, which lets you choose which potential security-related configuration changes to implement on your router, and One-Step Lockdown, which automatically makes all recommended security-related configuration changes. This section focuses exclusively on the Security Audit wizard; the One-Step Lockdown mode is described in the next section.

To begin the Cisco SDM Security Audit feature, select **Security Audit** in the left frame of the configuration page, as illustrated by the arrow in Figure 2.3:

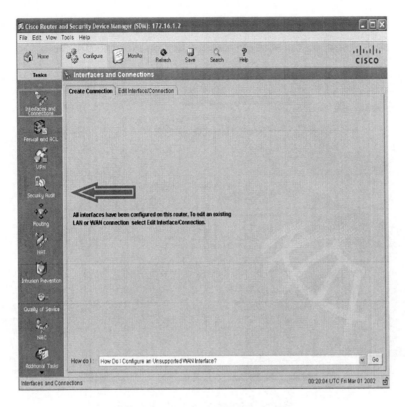

Figure 2.3. Select Security Audit

On the following screen, click on the **Perform security audit** button, as illustrated by the arrow in the Figure 2.4:

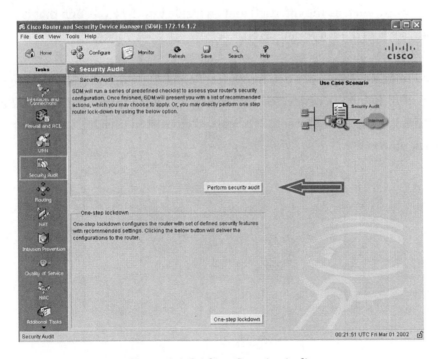

Figure 2.4. Perform Security Audit

This action launches the Security audit wizard. The following page provides an overview of the actions that will be performed via the security audit. Click on **Next** to proceed:

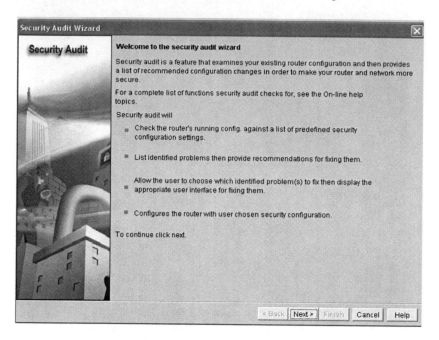

Figure 2.5. Security Audit Wizard

The previous action brings you to the Security audit interface configuration page. Depending on the interfaces on your router, you need to select an outside interface (i.e. one that is connected to an untrusted network, such as the Internet) and an inside interface (i.e. one that is connected to a trusted network, such as the corporate LAN).

The router used in this example has two interfaces: Serial0/0 (which is connected to the Internet) and FastEthernet0/0 (which is connected to the trusted LAN); therefore, Serial0/0 is marked as untrusted (outside), while FastEthernet0/0 is marked as trusted (inside). Once your selection has been made, click on **Next**:

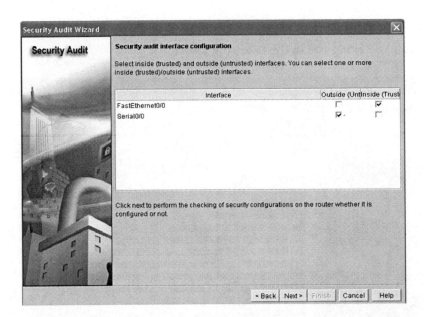

Figure 2.6. Designate Inside and Outside Interfaces

Once you click on **Next**, the Security Audit is performed, and you will be brought to the Security audit screen. A screen showing the progress of this action appears, listing all of the configuration options being tested for and whether the current router configuration passes those tests.

You can use the scroll bar on the right to scroll down and look at the status of the entire report. If you want to save this report to a file for later viewing and consideration, simply click the **Save Report** button illustrated in Figure 2.7:

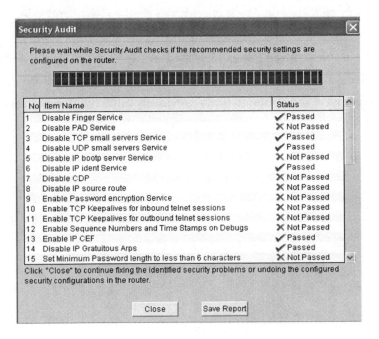

Figure 2.7. Security Audit is Performed

However, if you want to implement the recommendations of the Security Audit, simply click on the **Close** button. This will bring you to the following screen:

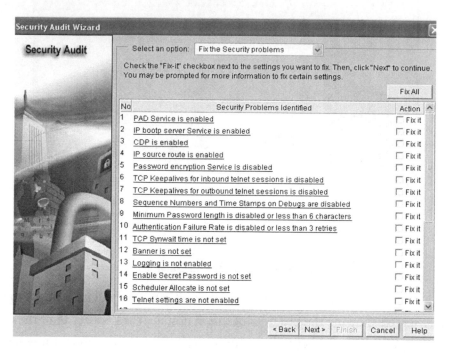

Figure 2.8. Options to Fix Issues

As illustrated in Figure 2.8 above, an administrator can select the **Fix All** button to fix all issues identified in the Security Audit or individually select the features he or she would like fixed or implemented by simply checking the **Fix it** checkboxes on the right-hand side.

In addition to fixing implementing issues identified in the Security Audit, SDM is also capable of undoing changes identified in the Security Audit. If the **Select an option:** drop-down menu is clicked, administrators have the option to undo previously implemented security changes:

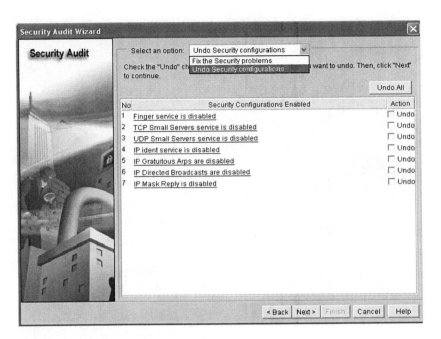

Figure 2.9. Changes Can Be Undone

As is the case with the **Fix the Security problems** options, administrators can choose to undo all configurations by clicking on the **Undo All** button or they can individually select which security configurations to undo by checking the **Undo** check boxes on the right-hand side.

Depending on the option selected and the boxes checked for that option, the next step is to click on the **Next** button. In our example, only a few select services have been selected to be fixed, as illustrated in Figure 2.10:

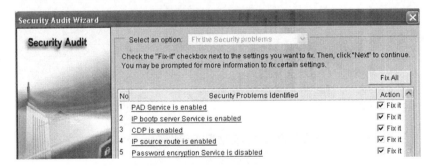

Figure 2.10. Click 'Next' to Confirm Changes

After clicking **Next**, SDM prints a summary of the changes the administrator specified:

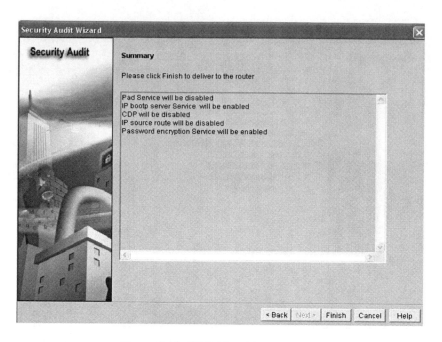

Figure 2.11. Click 'Finish' to Progress

The next step is to click on the **Finish** button. Once clicked, the SDM prepares the commands that it will deliver to the router and implements them. The final screen provides a summary of the number of commands delivered to the router. To complete the implementation, click on the **OK** button, as illustrated in Figure 2.12:

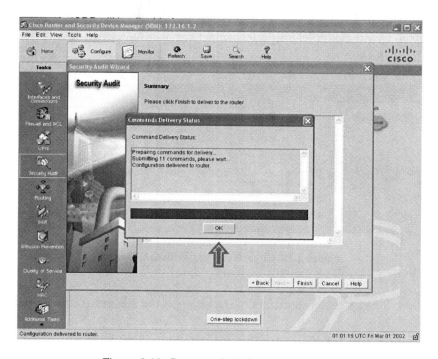

Figure 2.12. Commands Delivered to Router

An often forgotten step is saving the configuration to NVRAM. It is important that you do not forget this step; otherwise, all applied configuration will be lost if the router is reloaded. To save the running configuration to NVRAM using SDM, simply click on the **Save** button illustrated by the arrow in Figure 2.13, and then click on the **Yes** button to copy the running-config to the startup-config:

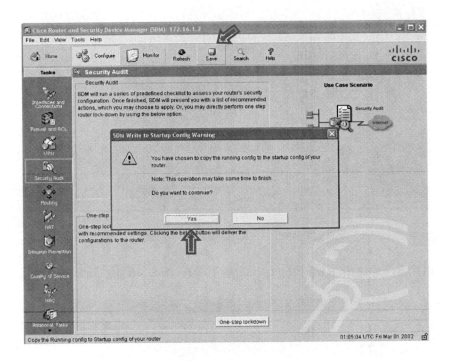

Figure 2.13. Copy Run Start

The Cisco SDM One-Step Lockdown Feature

In addition to the Security Audit feature, Cisco SDM can also perform a one-step lockdown function to configure the router for recommended best practices security configuration. The One-Step Lockdown feature performs numerous tasks, which are basically the same tasks performed by the Cisco IOS AutoSecure feature via the auto secure full command.

To enable the One-Step Lockdown feature, click on the **One-step lockdown** button on the **Security Audit** page, right below the **Perform security audit** section, as illustrated by the arrow in Figure 2.14:

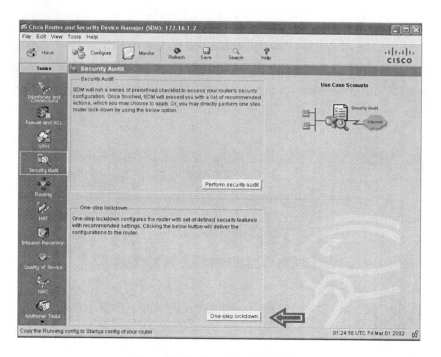

Figure 2.14. One Step Lockdown

Cisco SDM will then bring up a warning message. To proceed, simply click on **Yes**:

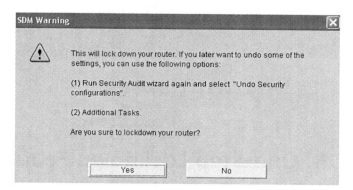

Figure 2.15. Warning Message Displayed

Once you have clicked on **Yes**, SDM prepares the commands that it will deliver to the router and the following screen appears, presenting a summary of the recommended actions. To allow SDM to proceed, and implement these settings on the router, click on the **Deliver** button:

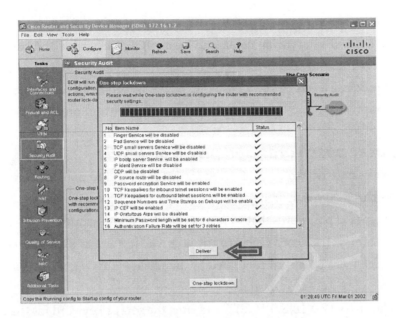

Figure 2.16. Commands Delivered to Router

Once the configuration has been delivered to the router, i.e. the router has been configured by SDM, do not forget to save the configuration to NVRAM; otherwise, all changes will be lost in the event that the router is rebooted. The router is locked down and the SDM one-step lockdown process is complete. As you can see, it is a very straightforward and easy process.

Chapter Summary

The following section is a summary of the major points you should be aware of in this chapter:

Securing administrative access to IOS routers

- The Cisco IOS CLI is divided into different command modes, all of which are unique.
- The standard order in which a user would access the modes would be:
  1. User EXEC mode
  2. Privileged EXEC mode (enabled mode)
  3. Global configuration mode
  4. Specific configuration modes
  5. Configuration submodes
  6. Configuration sub-submodes

- The enable [privilege level] command is used to move to privileged EXEC mode.
- Privilege levels range from 1 to 15, with 1 being the lowest and 15 being the highest.
- It is not recommend using the enable password command due to the weak hash algorithm.

- The enable password command stores the password in plain text format.
- The service password-encryption command hashes the plain enable and line passwords.
- The enable secret command provides an MD5 has and should be used to set passwords.
- All command privilege levels can be adjusted by using the privilege command.
- The security passwords min-length command specifies the minimum password lengths.

Usernames, user passwords and privilege levels

- Cisco IOS devices can then to be configured so that local and remote sessions to the router are granted access based on configured username and password pairs.
- There are two types of passwords that were associated with usernames:
  1. Type 0, a clear text password visible to any user who has access to privileged mode.
  2. Type 7, which has a password encrypted by the service password-encryption command

- In Cisco IOS Releases 12.0(18)S, 12.2(8)T, and later, the secret keyword for the username command allows you to configure MD5 encryption for user passwords.
- In order to allow terminal lines to authenticate users based on configured usernames, the login local configuration command is required under the terminal lines.
- The username [name] secret [password] autocommand [command] command can also be used to further restrict users by immediately executing a specified command for a particular user and then logging the user off automatically.

Cisco IOS Login Block

- The Cisco IOS Login Block feature (a part of the Cisco IOS Login Enhancements feature set), allows administrators to enhance the security of a router by configuring options to automatically block login attempts when a possible DoS or password attack is detected.
- The login block and login delay options introduced by this feature can be configured for Telnet, SSH or HTTP connections.
- This feature provides enhanced security over the security authentication failure rate <threshold-rate> log functionality.

Cisco IOS Role-based Command Line Interface

- The Cisco IOS role-based CLI access feature allows administrator to define views, which are a set of operational commands and configuration capabilities that provide selective or partial access to Cisco IOS EXEC and configuration (Config) mode commands.
- Views restrict user access to Cisco IOS command-line interface (CLI) and configuration information, i.e. a view can define what commands are accepted and what configuration information is visible.
- In order to configure the role-based CLI access feature, two prerequisites must be met:

1. First, AAA must be enabled on the router via the `aaa new-model` command.
2. Second, the system must be in root view. This is done via the `enable view` command.

- All views MUST have a password (secret) configured, otherwise they will not be enabled.
- In addition to basic (normal) views, it is also possible to configure a superview.
- A superview consists of one or more already configured CLI views
- A CLI view can be shared among multiple superviews and has the following characteristics:
    1. A CLI view can be shared among multiple superviews.
    2. Commands cannot be configured for a superview.
    3. Superview users can access all commands for any CLI views that are part of the superview.
    4. Each superview has a password that is used to switch between superviews.
    5. If a superview is deleted, all CLI views associated with that superview will not be deleted.

Securing Cisco IOS router files and images

- The Cisco IOS resilient configuration feature enables a router to secure and maintain a working copy of the running image and configuration so that those files can withstand malicious attempts to erase the contents of persistent storage (NVRAM and flash).
- The resilient configuration feature has the following characteristics:
    1. The copy of the running configuration that was in the router when the feature was first enabled is used as the configuration file in the primary bootset.
    2. The feature secures the smallest working set of files to preserve persistent storage space. No extra space is required to secure the primary Cisco IOS image file.
    3. The feature automatically detects Cisco IOS image or configuration version mismatch.
    4. Only local storage (i.e. on the router itself) is used for securing files, eliminating scalability maintenance challenges from storing multiple images and configurations on TFTP servers.
    5. The feature can be disabled only through a console session, which means that the administrator must have physical access to the router to perform this; enhancing security.

- In addition to the Cisco IOS resilient configuration feature, administrators can also leverage the IOS image verification.
- IOS image verification allows administrators to automatically verify the integrity of Cisco IOS images, thus ensuring that the image is protected from corruption.
- SCP provides a secure and authenticated method for copying configuration or image files.
- SCP relies on Secure Shell (SSH) and Authentication, Authorization and Accounting (AAA).

Cisco IOS AutoSecure

- AutoSecure provides the following mechanisms to enhance security access to the router:
    1. Simplified Router Security Configuration

2. Enhanced Password Security
3. Roll-Back and System Logging Message Support

• Cisco IOS AutoSecure secures the Management and Forwarding planes by disabling certain global and interface services that can be potentially exploited for security attacks and, at the same time, enabling global services that help mitigate the threat of attacks.

The Cisco SDM Security Audit Feature

• SDM provides an intuitive router security audit feature with one-step security audit capability that validates router configurations against a list of common security vulnerabilities and Cisco recommended settings, and provides a summary of recommended best practices.

• The SDM Security Audit feature operates in one of two modes—the Security Audit wizard, which lets you choose which potential security-related configuration changes to implement on your router, and One-Step Lockdown, which automatically makes all recommended security-related configuration changes.

• The audit report highlights the potential security problems identified in the router configuration and can generate corresponding configurations to correct the shortfalls.

• The Security Audit Feature is launched from the Security page as illustrated below:

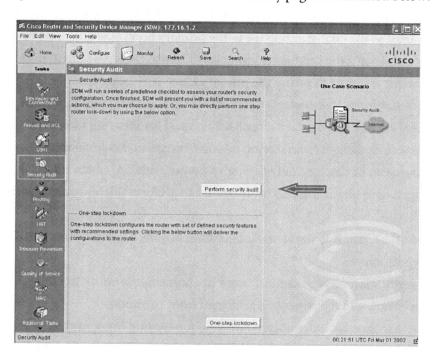

The Cisco SDM One-Step Lockdown Feature

- Cisco SDM can also perform a one-step lockdown function to configure the router for recommended best practices security configuration.

- The one-step Lockdown feature performs numerous tasks, which are basically the same tasks performed by the Cisco IOS AutoSecure feature via the auto secure full command.

- One-step Lockdown is launched from the Security page as illustrated below:

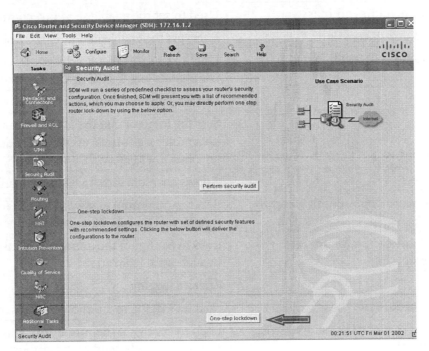

Commands Used in this Chapter

The following section is a summary of the commands used in this chapter:

Command	Description
enable [privilege level]	Used to navigate to privileged EXEC mode
enable password level [level] [password]	Used to set the enable password (not safe)
enable secret level [level] [password]	Used to set the enable secret (recommended)
service password-encryption	Encrypts the enable and line passwords
privilege [mode] [all|level] [level] [command]	Used to specify default privilege levels for commands (e.g. EXEC or Config commands)
password	Used to specify terminal line passwords
exec-timeout	Sets the interval that the EXEC command interpreter waits until user input is detected on terminal lines (e.g. VTY and CON)
lockable	Allows terminal lines to be locked/unlocked
security passwords min-length <length>	Sets the minimum password length for user, enable, and terminal line passwords
security authentication failure rate <threshold-rate> log	used to configure the number of allowable unsuccessful login attempts
logging on	Enables logging
logging host <address>	Enables logging to a remote Syslog server
login block-for [seconds] attempts [tries] within [seconds]	Used to configure the router for login parameters and specifies the amount of time the router should remain in the quiet period if the administrator specified number of failed attempts is exceeded within the specific period of time
login quiet-mode access-class [ACL]	Specifies an ACL that is to be applied to the router when it switches to quiet mode to allow access to the subnets specified in the ACL
login delay [seconds]	Used to configures a delay between successive login attempts
login on-failure log every [number]	Used to generate Syslog messages for failed login attempts
login on-success log every [number]	Used to generate Syslog messages for successful login attempts
logging buffered [severity]	Enables logging to the local router buffer
logging trap [severity]	Specifies the severity of logs to send to a remote Syslog server
show login [failures]	Used to view Login Block information

Command	Description
show logging	Used to view logging information
aaa new-model	Enables AAA on the router
enable view [name]	Used to access the root (or any other) view
show privilege	Used to view the current user privilege level
parser view [name]	Used to configure a view
commands [mode] (include | include-exclusive | exclude) [all] [interface (name) | command]	Used to specify the commands that are included, or excluded from the view being configured
view	Used to add CLI views to a superview
secure boot-image	Used to enable Cisco IOS image resilience
secure boot-config	Used to store a secure copy of the primary bootset in persistent storage.
dir	Used to view directories (e.g. in Flash)
show secure bootset	Used to verify archive existence
file verify auto	Enables IOS image validation
copy system:running-config nvram: startup-config	Saves the running-config (RAM) to the startup-config (NVRAM)
Reload [options]	Reloads the device (i.e. router)
copy [options]	Used to copy files to and from the router
ip scp server enable	Enables SCP server functionality
ip domain-name [name]	Configures a Domain for the router
crypto key generate rsa	Generates RSA key pair
aaa authentication [options]	Configures AAA Authentication
aaa authorization [options]	Configures AAA Authorization
tftp-server [options]	Enables TFTP server functionality
copy scp	Used to perform SCP copying
no service finger	Disables Finger
no service pad	Disables PAD
no service tcp-small-servers	Disables TCP small servers
no service udp-small-servers	Disables UDP small servers
no ip bootp server	Disables BOOTP server
no ip http server	Disables HTTP server
no ip identd	Disables the Identification service
no cdp run	Disables CDP
no ntp	Disables NTP
no ip source-route	Disables source-routing

Command	Description
no ip redirects	Disables ICMP redirects
no ip unreachables	Disables ICMP unreachables
no ip mask-reply	Disables ICMP mask reply messages
no ip proxy-arp	Disables Proxy-ARP
no ip directed-broadcast	Disables directed Broadcast forwarding
no mop enabled	Disables MOP
service tcp-keepalives-in	Enables keepalives for inbound TCP sessions
service tcp-keepalives-out	Enables keepalives for outbound TCP sessions
transport input [telnet|ssh]	Enables Telnet or SSH for terminal lines
ip ssh timeout [seconds]	Specifies the idle timeout for SSH sessions
ip ssh authentication-retries [number]	Specifies the number of times SSH users are allowed to attempt to authenticate successfully
service sequence-numbers	Enables sequence numbers for logs and debugs
service timestamps [options]	Enables timestamps for logs and debugs
ip cef	Enables CEF
ip tcp intercept [options]	Enables TCP intercept and sets desired options
ip verify unicast reverse-path [options]	Enables uRPF
ip inspect [options]	Enables CBAC
auto secure [options]	Enables AutoSecure functionality

CHAPTER 3

Authentication, Authorization, and Accounting

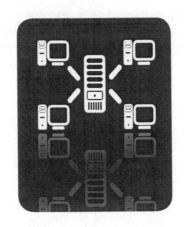

As identity security and access management become more complex, networks and network resources require safeguarding from unauthorized access. Authentication, Authorization, and Accounting, referred to as AAA (Triple-A), provide the framework that controls and monitors network access. The IINS exam objectives that will be covered in this chapter are as follows:

- Explain the functions and importance of AAA
- Describe the features of RADIUS and TACACS+ AAA protocols
- Configure AAA authentication
- Configure AAA authorization
- Configure AAA accounting

This chapter is broken up into the following sections:

- AAA Overview
- The AAA Model
- AAA Operation
- RADIUS
- TACACS+
- Implementing AAA Services
- Configuring AAA Servers and Groups
- Configuring AAA Authentication
- Configuring AAA Authorization
- Configuring AAA Accounting
- Kerberos Basics

IINS Exam Objective	Section(s) Covered
Explain the functions and importance of AAA	• AAA Overview • The AAA Model • AAA Operation
Describe the features of RADIUS and TACACS+ AAA protocols	• RADIUS • TACACS+
Configure AAA authentication	• Configuring AAA Servers and Groups • Configuring AAA Authentication
Configure AAA authorization	• Configuring AAA Servers and Groups • Configuring AAA Authorization
Configure AAA accounting	• Configuring AAA Servers and Groups • Configuring AAA Accounting
Other related topics	• Kerberos Basics

AAA Overview

Authentication is used to validate identity, i.e. who the user is. Authorization is used to determine what that particular user can do, i.e. the services available to the user. And Accounting is used to allow for an audit trail, i.e. what that user did.

AAA provides a flexible, modular solution for controlling access to the network. It provides the primary framework through which access control is set up on a network device, such as a router, switch, or firewall. In such devices, AAA services can be used to control administrative access, such as via Telnet and Console login, which is referred to as character mode access. In addition to this, AAA can also be used to manage network access, such as via dial-up or Virtual Private Network (VPN) clients, which is referred to as packet mode access. The primary advantages of using AAA are as follows:

- Standard authentication methods
- Scalability
- Greater flexibility and control
- Multiple backup systems

AAA uses standard authentication methods, which include Remote Authentication Dial-In User Service (RADIUS), Terminal Access Controller Access Control System Plus (TACACS+), and Kerberos. These authentication methods will be described in detail later in this chapter.

AAA scales to networks of all sizes. Multiple security servers can be implemented allowing access control to be added easily. This allows AAA to scale from small networks with very few devices to very large networks that may contain hundreds of devices.

In addition to scalability, AAA provides great flexibility and control. For example, in small networks, AAA services can be administered by using local databases that are stored on the network devices instead of using a security server. Username and password credentials can be stored on the local database of the device and referenced by the AAA services. AAA services can also be configured for per-user, per-group, or per-service control.

AAA allows devices to point to multiple security servers, often referred to as server groups. User, device, and services information can be replicated between multiple servers, which provide redundancy in large networks.

The AAA Model

The AAA framework uses a set of three independent security functions in a modular format to offer secure access control. The AAA model is used to control access to network devices (Authentication), enforce policies (Authorization), and audit usage (Accounting). AAA uses RADIUS, TACACS+, and Kerberos as authentication protocols to administer the AAA security functions. Using the AAA engine, network devices establish communications with the security server(s) using these protocols. The three independent security functions that offer secure access control and are provided by AAA are as follows:

- Authentication
- Authorization
- Accounting

Authentication

Authentication is used to validate user identity before allowing access to network resources. It occurs when a client passes the appropriate credentials to a security server for validation. This validation is based on verifying user credentials, which can be any of the following:

- **Something the user knows**—which is referred to as Authentication by knowledge. This method verifies identity by something known only to the user, such as a username and password, for example.
- **Something the user possesses**—which is referred to as Authentication by possession. This method verifies identity by something possessed only by the user. Examples of this type of authentication include ATM cards or tokens (such as RSA Secure ID tokens).
- **Something the user is**—which is referred to as user characteristics or biometrics. This is the strongest authentication method because it avoids the problems that are associated with other authentication methods, for example, the password being cracked or the ATM card being stolen. Examples of biometrics include finger prints, face recognition, and DNA.

Once the security server has received the credentials, it will respond with a pass (accept) or fail (deny) message. Authentication also offers additional services, such as challenge and response, messaging support, and even encryption, depending on the security protocol implemented.

Authorization

Authorization provides the capability to enforce policies for network resources after the user has been successfully authenticated. In other words, Authorization is used to determine the actions a user, group, system, or server is allowed to perform. Attribute-value (AV) pairs—which are described in the next section—that define user rights are associated with the user to determine the specific rights of the user.

Clients query the AAA server to determine what actions a user is authorized to perform, and the server provides AV pairs that define user authorization. The client is then responsible for enforcing user access control based on those AV pairs.

Accounting

Accounting provides the means to capture resource utilization by collecting and sending information that can be used for billing, auditing, and reporting to the security server. This information can include user identities (who logged in), session start and stop times, the command(s) executed, and traffic information such as bytes or packets transmitted.

Accounting records are also made up of accounting AV pairs. Accounting methods must be defined through AAA. The client then sends the Accounting records, with the relevant AV pairs, to the AAA server for storage.

Now that we are familiar with the three independent security functions within the AAA framework, it is important to understand what their correlation is, as follows:

1. **Authentication is valid without Authorization.** This means that you can enable and authenticate users without enabling and authorizing those same users.
2. **Authentication is valid without Accounting.** This means that you can enable and authenticate users without enabling accounting for the actions performed by those users.
3. **Authorization is not valid without Authentication.** This means that you must authenticate users before you can authorize them. You cannot authorize anyone who has not been authenticated.
4. **Accounting is not valid without Authentication.** This means that you must authenticate users before you enable accounting for them. You do not need to enable authorization because authentication is valid without authorization.

AAA Operation

In order for AAA to work, the Network Access Server (NAS), which is any device—such as a router, switch, or firewall—must be able to access security information for a specific user before providing AAA services. This information may be stored locally, i.e. on the NAS itself, or remotely, i.e. on a RADUIS, TACACS+, or Kerberos server.

Although both methods are valid, it is important to keep in mind that the local user database supports only a limited number of Cisco-specific security attribute-values, but server-based AAA provides more capabilities and security information is stored on the server, not the network device. An AV pair is simply a secured network object. It is comprised of an attribute, such as the username or password, and a value for that particular attribute.

To reinforce the concept of AV pairs, Figure 3.1 illustrates their use in AAA services when the security information is stored locally on the NAS:

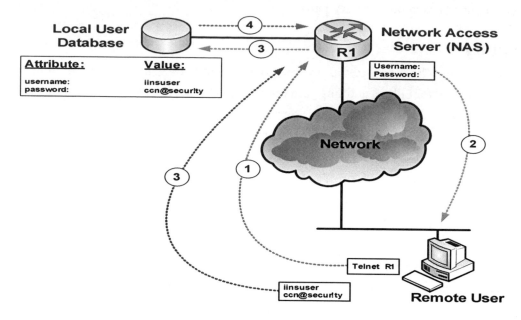

Figure 3.1. AV Pairs with NAS

Based on the diagram illustrated above, in step 1, the remote user attempts to connect to R1 (NAS) via Telnet. Assuming that the NAS has been configured for AAA services, using its local database for Authentication, the NAS presents the remote user with the username and password prompt, as illustrated in step 2.

The remote user then enters his or her credentials, providing the username **iinsuser** (which is the ATTRIBUTE) and password **ccn@secur!ty** (which is the VALUE for that ATTRIBUTE), as illustrated in step 3. The NAS then checks the information against its local database:

Attribute	Value
Username	iinsuser
Password	ccn@secur!ty

Assuming that the NAS has been configured with the username iinsuser secret ccn@secur!ty global configuration command, each AV is on file and the AV pair is found. The request is accepted and a pass message is returned (as illustrated in step 4), which enables the connection from the remote user to be made. The same logic would apply if AAA services were authenticating against a remote server, such as TACACS+ or RADIUS, for example.

Taking this example a step further, this time depicting the use of an external AAA server, Figure 3.2 illustrates the use of AV pairs for Authorization:

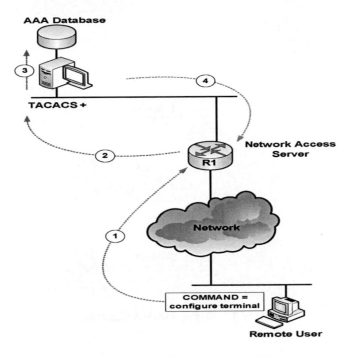

Figure 3.2. AV Pairs with External AAA Server

In the diagram above, assume that the remote user has been successfully authenticated. Once logged in to R1 (NAS), the remote user attempts to issue the configure terminal command, as illustrated in step 1. The NAS has been configured to use AAA services for Authorization, and so the request is sent to the TACACS+ server, as illustrated in step 2. The TACACS+ server then checks the following information against its local database:

Attribute	Value
command	configure terminal

In step 3, the server finds that the attribute and value are on file, and an AV pair is found. The request is accepted and the configure terminal command is successfully authorized on R1, as illustrated in step 4. The remote user successfully enters configuration mode. Again, the same concept would be applicable if Authorization was being performed using the local database.

Unlike Authentication and Authorization, there is no search for AV pairs in any kind of database for Accounting. Instead, information is simply received with AV pairs and is stored in the database. Accounting is illustrated in Figure 3.3:

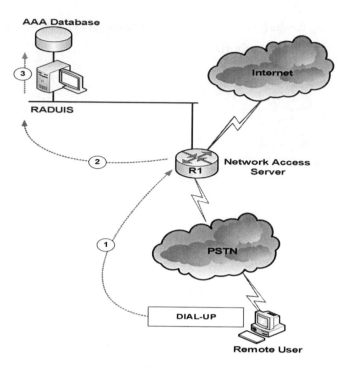

Figure 3.3. AV Pairs with Accounting

Based on Figure 3.1 above, in step 1, the remote user dials in to the NAS for access to the network resources and services. We will assume that R1 belongs to an ISP providing its customers with Internet service via dial-up modems.

We will also assume that the remote user has authenticated successfully and is authorized to use this service. The NAS has been configured for Accounting so that the ISP can bill customers based on usage, etc. Based on this, in step 2, the NAS sends the following Accounting AV pair information to the AAA server:

Attribute	Value
start time	02:30:00
stop time	04:30:00
elapsed time	02:00:00
packets sent	1234567
packets received	9876543

The AAA server simply receives this information and performs no AV pair searches. Instead, the information is stored in the local database, as illustrated in step 3, where it can later be retrieved and the remote user billed for the amount of time spent on the ISP network.

Now that we have an understanding of AAA and how it works, we are going to move along and learn about the two main security server protocols: RADIUS and TACACS+.

Radius

RADIUS stands for Remote Authentication Dial-In User Service. RADIUS is a client/server protocol that is used to secure networks against intruders. RADIUS was created by Livingston Enterprises but is now defined in RFC 2138 and RFC 2139. The RADIUS protocol Authentication and Accounting services are documented separately in RFC 2865 and RFC 2866, respectively. These two RFCs replace RFC 2138 and RFC 2139.

A RADIUS server is a device that has the RADIUS daemon or application installed. Unlike TACACS+, which is described in detail in the following section, RADIUS is an open-standard protocol that is distributed in C source code format. This allows for interoperability and flexibility between RADIUS-based products from different vendors; however, as will be explained later in this chapter, this is also one of the main problems with using RADIUS.

Before delving into the specifics pertaining to RADIUS, it is important to have a solid understanding of the RADIUS packet format and the fields contained therein. Figure 3.4 illustrates the header format of the RADIUS packet:

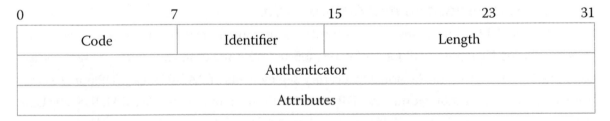

0	7	15	23	31

Code	Identifier	Length
Authenticator		
Attributes		

Figure 3.4. RADIUS Header

The information contained in each field is as follows:
- **Code**

This 1-byte field contains the message type of the RADIUS packet. Valid codes are:
1. Code 1 = Access-Request
2. Code 2 = Access-Accept
3. Code 3 = Access-Reject
4. Code 4 = Accounting-Request
5. Code 5 = Accounting-Response
6. Code 11 = Access-Challenge

- **Identifier**

  This 1-byte field matches request and reply packets. The identifier is a message sequence number that allows the RADIUS client to match a RADIUS response with the correct outstanding request, i.e. the value in reply is equal to the value in request.

- **Length**

  This 2-byte field includes the message length and the header.

- **Authenticator**

  This 16-byte field is used to authenticate the reply from the RADIUS server. The value in the request packet is randomly generated, whereas the value in the reply packet is an MD5 hash of the reply message data appended with a shared secret using a vector from the request packet.

- **Attributes**

  RADIUS attributes carry the specific Authentication, Authorization, and Accounting details for the request and response. Some attributes may be included more than once. These attributes are stored in Type/Length/Value (or TLV) notation. The Type specifies the attribute type and is 8-bits in length. The Length is 8-bits long and is used to indicate the length of the attribute. And, finally, the Value is a variable-length field that contains the information specific to the attribute.

RADIUS Authentication and Authorization

RADIUS uses UDP as the Transport layer protocol for communications between the client and the server, using UDP port 1812 for Authentication and Authorization and UDP port 1813 for Accounting. However, it should be noted that earlier deployments of RADIUS use UDP port 1645 for Authentication and Authorization and UDP port 1646 for Accounting. Because RADIUS uses UDP as a transport protocol, there is no offer of guaranteed delivery of RADIUS packets. Therefore, any issues related to server availability, the retransmission of packets, and timeouts, for example, are handled by the RADIUS-enabled devices.

RADIUS communication is triggered by a user login that consists of a query. Figure 3.5 illustrates the sequence of messages that are exchanged:

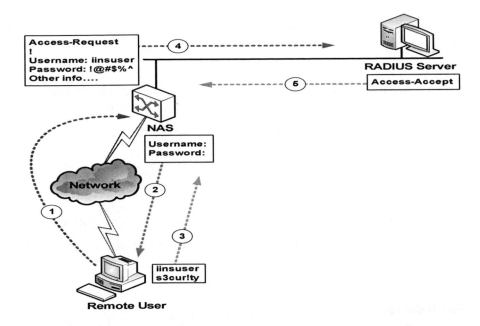

Figure 3.5. RADIUS Sequence

Following Figure 3.5 above, in step 1, the remote user dials in to the NAS. The NAS proceeds and asks the remote user for a username and password, as illustrated in step 2.The user then proceeds and inputs his or her assigned, valid credentials, which are the username **iinsuser** and the password **s3cur!ty**. This process is illustrated in step 3.

This received username and encrypted password, as well as the NAS IP address and NAS port information, is sent as an Access-Request packet from the NAS to the RADIUS server, as illustrated in step 4. The Access-Request packet will also contain other information on the type of session that the user wants to initiate. For example, if the query is presented in character mode (e.g. Telnet), the packet will include **Service-Type=Shell**; however, if the packet is presented in PPP mode, for example, it will include **Service-Type=Framed-User**, as well as **Framed-Type=PPP**.

When the RADIUS server receives the Access-Request packet from the NAS, the first thing it will check for is the shared secret key for the client that is sending the request. This step is performed to ensure that only authorized clients are able to communicate with the server. In the event that the shared secret key is not configured or is incorrect, the server will silently discard the request packet without sending back a response.

However, if the username is found in the database and the password is validated, the server returns an Access-Accept response back to the client, as illustrated in step 5. The Access-Accept carries a list of AV pairs that describe the parameters to be used for this session. In addition to the standard set of attributes, RADIUS also specifies the vendor-specific attribute (Attribute 26) that allows vendors to support their own extended attributes, which may be specifically tailored to their particular application and are not for general use.

Although the diagram used in the example depicts the Access-Accept packet being sent from the RADIUS server to the NAS in step 5, it is important to know that this is simply one of many possible responses that the server may provide. In this step, the RADIUS server may also send one of the following messages:

1. Access-Reject

The Access-Reject response is returned to the client when the username is not found in the database or if the password entered is incorrect. This packet may also be sent when Authorization fails.

2. Access-Challenge

The Access-Challenge response is typically issued when the RADIUS server wants more information from the user. Depending on the information requested, the client then sends that in another Access-Request packet. When the server receives the additional requested information, it responds back to the client with either an Access-Accept or Access-Reject.

3. Change-Password

The Change-Password response is sent from the RADIUS server to the client when asking the user to select a new password. This may be because the password has expired or this is a new account with a default password and the user must create a new password.

Although RADIUS is a security protocol, its own operation is not entirely secure. When the Access-Request packet is sent from the NAS to the RADIUS server, only the password is encrypted by a shared secret but the remainder of the packet is sent in clear text, making it vulnerable to various exploits and attacks, such as MITM attacks. It is important to take this into consideration when deploying and using RADIUS for AAA services in production networks.

RADIUS Accounting

The RADIUS Accounting function is designed for data to be transmitted at the beginning and at the end of a session. This data can indicate resource utilization, such as bandwidth and time used, and may be used for billing and/or security purposes.

There are two types of messages that are exchanged during RADUIS Accounting sessions: Accounting-Request and Accounting-Response messages. Figure 3.6 illustrates the exchange of messages between the NAS (AAA client) and the RADIUS server:

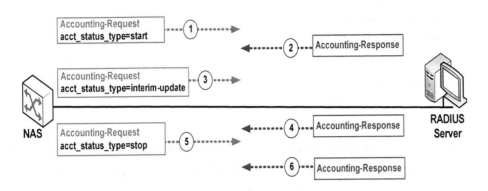

Figure 3.6. NAS and RADIUS Exchange

As illustrated in Figure 3.6 above, after the user has been Authenticated and Authorized (which is considered a single process in RADIUS), the NAS sends an Accounting Start packet, which is simply a RADIUS Accounting-Request packet that contains the attribute **acct-status-type** and the value **start**. This AV pair is used to signal the start of the user's network access and typically contains the user's identification, network address, point of attachment, and a unique session identifier. This is illustrated in step 1.

When the RADIUS server receives this packet, it responds with an Accounting-Response packet, which is used as an acknowledgement that the Accounting information was received. This process is illustrated in step 2.

As the user session progresses, the NAS periodically sends interim update records. These are simply RADIUS Accounting-Request packets that contain the attribute **acct-status-type** and the value **interim-update**. This AV pair is used to communicate the current duration of the session and other information (e.g. bandwidth, bytes used, etc.) that pertain to data usage by the user for this session. This is illustrated in step 3. The RADIUS server acknowledges this packet again by sending the Accounting-Response packet, as illustrated in step 4.

When the user's network access is closed, the NAS issues an Accounting Stop record to the RADIUS server. This packet is simply an Accounting-Request packet with the attribute **acct-status-type** and the value **stop**. This packet is used to provide information on the final usage of network resources and may include time, packets transferred, data transferred, disconnect reason, and any other information related to the user's activities during the session. This is illustrated in step 5. When the RADIUS server receives this packet, it acknowledges it by sending an Accounting-Response packet, as illustrated in step 6.

Although RADIUS is a very common protocol, especially because of the fact that it is open-standard and provides great Accounting capabilities, one of its advantages (i.e. the fact that it is distributed in C source code format, which allows for interoperability and flexibility between RADIUS-based products from different vendors) has become a disadvantage as individual organizations extend RADIUS to meet their specific needs. This has resulted in RADIUS compatibility issues amongst different vendors; for example, the RADIUS implementation by Vendor X may be incompatible with that of Vendor Y, due to proprietary enhancements, etc.

To address this issue, a new open-standard security protocol, called DIAMETER, has been proposed to replace RADIUS. While DIAMETER will work in the same basic manner as RADIUS (i.e. as a client/server security protocol), it also aims to improve on some of the weaknesses of RADIUS by offering greater AAA capabilities and using the connection-oriented TCP as the Transport Layer protocol, instead of UDP.

In addition, DIAMETER also provides an improved method of encrypting message exchanges that offer more security than that provided by RADIUS. Going into detail and the specifics of DIAMETER is beyond the scope of the IINS course requirements; however, as a future security administrator, ensure that you are aware of this upcoming protocol. It may very well be something you are called on to consider, speak on, or even deploy, at some point in your career.

RADIUS Attributes

RADIUS supports numerous attributes that can be exchanged between client and server. These attributes carry specific information about Authentication and are defined in RFC 2138. Although going into detail and knowing every one of these attributes is beyond the scope of the IINS course requirements, Table 3.1 contains a list of some of the more common RADIUS attributes:

Table 3.1. RADIUS Attributes

Attribute	Description/Purpose
Type 1	Username—used to define usernames, e.g. ASCII characters or SMTP addresses
Type 2	Password—used to define the password, which is encrypted using MD5
Type 3	CHAP Password—used only in Access-Request packets
Type 4	NAS IP Address—defines the NAS IP address; used in Access-Request packets
Type 5	NAS Port—used to indicate the physical port of the NAS (ranging from 0 to 65,535)
Type 6	Service-Type—used to indicate the Type of Service; not supported by Cisco
Type 7	Protocol—used to define the required framing, e.g. PPP
Type 8	IP Address—used to define the IP address to be used by the remote user
Type 9	IP Subnet Mask—used to define the subnet mask to be used by the remote user
Type 10	Routing—used to define routing options
Type 13	Compression—used to define data compression

Type 19	Callback ID—used to specify the number or address for callback
Type 26	Vendor-specific—used to define the vendor-specific attribute
Type 61	NAS Port Type—used to specify the type of port on the NAS

NOTE: Attribute 26 is particularly important to remember, as it is of particular importance in the Cisco security world. Cisco, vendor ID 9, uses a single defined option, which is vendor type 1 named the Cisco-AV Pair. This attribute is used to transmit TACACS+ AV pairs. TACACS+ is a Cisco-proprietary security protocol, which is described in the next section.

TACACS+

TACACS+ stands for Terminal Access Controller Access Control System Plus. Unlike RADIUS, which is an open-standard protocol, TACACS+ is a Cisco-proprietary protocol that is used in the AAA framework to provide centralized authentication of users who are attempting to gain access to network resources.

There are several notable differences between TACACS+ and RADIUS. One of the most notable differences is that TACACS+ uses TCP as a Transport Layer protocol, using TCP port 49. In addition to this, TACACS+ separates the three AAA architectures, unlike RADIUS, which groups Authentication and Authorization together and separates Accounting. TACACS+ also encrypts the data between the user and the server, unlike RADUIS, which encrypts only the password. Finally, TACACS+ supports multiple protocols, such as IP, IPX, AppleTalk, and X.25, whereas RADIUS has limited protocol support. The TACACS+ packet header is illustrated in Figure 3.7:

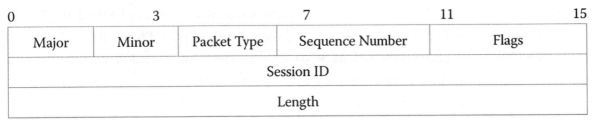

0	3	7	11	15

Major	Minor	Packet Type	Sequence Number	Flags
Session ID				
Length				

Figure 3.7. TACACS+ Header

The information contained in each field is as follows:

- **Major**

  This 4-bit field indicates the major TACACS+ version number. This value appears in the header as TAC_PLUS_MAJOR_VER=0xc.

- **Minor**

  This 4-bit field indicates the minor TACACS+ version number, which is the revision number.

This value allows for revisions to the TACACS+ protocol while maintaining backward compatibility. Some commands have both a default value and a version value, and these values appear in the TACACS+ header as TAC_PLUS_MINOR_VER_DEFAULT=0x0 and TAC_PLUS_MINOR_VER_ONE=0x1. If a TACACS+ server receives a TACACS+ packet other than the two just listed, it sends an error status back and sets the Minor Version field to the closest version that is supported.

- **Packet Type**

  This 1-byte field defines whether the packet is used for Authentication, Authorization, or Accounting. The possible values that this field may contain are as follows:
  1. TAC_PLUS_AUTHEN=0x01 (Authentication)
  2. TAC_PLUS_AUTHOR=0x02 (Authorization)
  3. TAC_PLUS_ACCT=0x03 (Accounting)

- **Sequence Number**

  This 1-byte field contains the sequence number for the current session. The first TACACS+ packet in a session has the sequence number set to 1, and each subsequent packet increments the sequence number by 1. Thus, clients send only packets that contain ODD numbers (e.g. 1, 3, 5, and 7) because they send the first packet, and TACACS+ servers send only EVEN numbers (e.g. 2, 4, 6, and 8) in response to the packets from the client. The highest sequence number that can be reached during a session is 2^8-1. If this limit is reached, the current session between the client and the TACACS+ server is reset and a new session is established.

- **Flags**

  This 1-byte field contains various flags in the form of bitmaps, which can be the TAC_PLUS_UNENCRYPTED_FLAG and the TAC_PLUS_SINGLE_CONNECT_FLAG. The TAC_PLUS_UNENCRYPTED_FLAG is the TACACS+ packet that is being encrypted. If this flag is set to a value of 1, it means that no encryption is being performed; however, if the flag is set to 0, then the packet is being encrypted. Keep in mind that only the packet payload is encrypted; the packet header is always sent in clear text. The TAC_PLUS_SINGLE_CONNECT_FLAG flag determines whether multiplexing (joining) multiple TACACS+ sessions over one TCP session is supported, which is determined in the first two TACACS+ messages of a session, and once determined, this will not change during the course of the session.

It is important to understand that the encryption of the TACACS+ packet is not the same as that of traditional user data. Instead, it relies on a combination of a hashing function and an XOR or EOR algorithm, which is an algorithm that basically means either one or the other, but not both. This process is performed as follows:

1. Information is taken from the packet header and the pre-shared key calculates a series of hashes. The first is a hash that is calculated on a concatenation of the Session ID, the version, the Sequence Number, and the pre-shared key value. Each hash that is created also includes the previous hash, and this is performed on a number of times, depending on the particular implementation of TACACS+.

2. The calculated data is linked together and then shortened to the length of the data that is being encrypted. Each hash has the previous hash linked into its input values, and the end result is referred to as the pseudo pad.

3. The cipher text is produced by doing a byte-wise XOR or EOR algorithm on the pseudo pad with the data that is being encrypted.

4. The receiving device uses its pre-shared key to calculate the pseudo pad, and then an XOR algorithm of the newly created pseudo pad results in the original data in clear text, i.e. unencrypted text.

- **Session ID**
  This 4-byte field contains the ID for the TACACS+ session. This random value remains the same during the course of the session.

- **Length**
  This 4-byte field contains the total length of the TACACS+ packet, excluding the header.

TACACS+ Authentication

TACACS+ Authentication is typically initiated when a user attempts an ASCII login by authenticating to a server running the TACACS+ daemon. The TACACS+ Authentication phase uses three distinct packet types, as follows:

1. START packets—which are used initially when the user attempts to connect.
2. REPLY or RESPONSE packets—which are sent by the AAA server during Authentication.
3. CONTINUE packets—which are used by AAA clients to return username and password information to the TACACS+ server.

The TACACS+ Authentication communication process is illustrated in Figure 3.8:

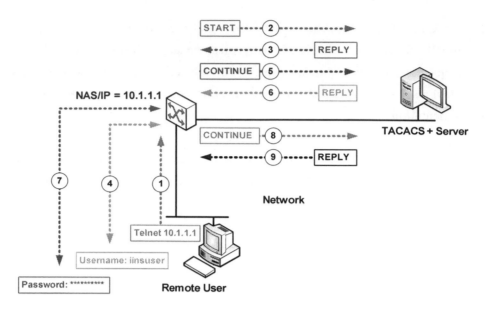

Figure 3.8. TACACS+ Authentication Process

Figure 3.8 illustrated above, in step 1, the remote user initiates a connection to the NAS, which is configured for AAA services using TACACS+.

The NAS then contacts the TACACS+ server (START) to get a username prompt, as illustrated in step 2. The TACACS+ server responds (REPLY) with username prompt, illustrated in step 3, and this is then displayed to the user, in step 4.

The user types in his or her username, also illustrated in step 4, and the NAS sends this information (CONTINUE packet) to the TACACS+ server, as illustrated in step 5.

The TACACS+ server receives the username and checks its local or external database for the username. The name is found and the TACACS+ server sends a request for a password (REPLY), as illustrated in step 6. The NAS relays this information to the remote user, who inputs the password, as illustrated in step 7.

The NAS relays the password (CONTINUE) to the TACACS+ sever, in step 8, and the TACACS+ server checks its local or external database for the correct password. Depending on the result, the TACACS+ server responds, as illustrated in step 9, with the result (REPLY), which could be any one of the following messages:

1. ACCEPT

This response indicates that the user has been successfully authenticated and service may begin. If the NAS is required to perform Authorization, that begins at this time as well.

2. REJECT

This response states that Authentication has failed. This could be due to incorrect credentials and could result in the user being denied further access at that point.

3. ERROR

This response is usually received when a communication problem exists between the NAS and the AAA server. The error can be on either the client-side or the server-side. Some of the reasons that could cause this response to be received include an incorrect secret key, an incorrect NAS IP address, or even a latency (delay) issue in the network. When the NAS receives this message from the server, it typically attempts to use an alternate method to continue the Authentication process.

4. CONTINUE

This response states that the server is expecting additional information and, as such, the user is prompted for further input variables.

TACACS+ Authorization

The TACACS+ Authorization process is performed using two distinct message types: REQUEST and RESPONSE. The Authorization process is performed using a session that consists of this pair of messages.

REQUEST messages are sent by clients and they contain information pertaining to the authenticity of the user or service (Authentication information), as well as a list of the services or options for which Authorization is being requested.

When the TACACS+ server receives the REQUEST message, it replies with a RESPONSE message. This message contains one of the following replies:

1. FAIL

This message indicates that the services or options requested for Authorization are denied.

2. PASS_ADD

This message indicates that request is authorized and the information returned in the RESPONSE packet is used in addition to the requested information. If no additional arguments are returned in the RESPONSE, the request is authorized.

3. PASS_REPL

This message is sent by the AAA server when it ignores the request and, instead, replaces it with the information placed in the RESPONSE packet.

4. FOLLOW

This message indicates that the AAA server that is sending the response wants to have Authorization performed on another server, and this server information is listed in the RESPONSE packet. The NAS can either follow this response or view it as a FAIL.

5. ERROR

This message is used to indicate an error on the AAA server, such as a pre-shared key mismatch, for example.

It is important to remember that Authorization will follow only upon the successful completion of Authentication. You cannot have Authorization before Authentication. In Authentication and Authorization, attribute-value (AV) pairs are used to enforce various services and functions, as well as to determine the user access for network resources. Some of the more common AV pairs used by TACACS+ are provided later in this chapter. Figure 3.9 provides a basic illustration of TACACS+ Authorization communication:

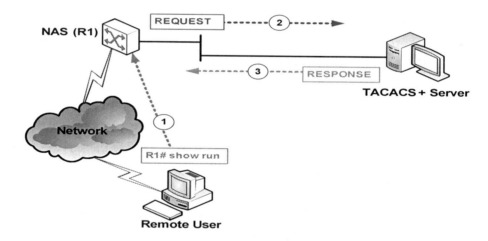

Figure 3.9. TACACS+ Authorization Process

In Figure 3.9 illustrated above, the remote user (who has been successfully authenticated), issues the show run command on the NAS (R1), as illustrated in step 1.

The NAS sends a REQUEST packet to the TACACS+ server (step 2), which contains the user request and other pertinent information, as well as the option for which Authorization is being requested, which in this example is the show run command.

The TACACS+ server receives this REQUEST and replies back with a RESPONSE message, illustrated in step 3. For the sake of simplicity, the RESPONSE is a pass and the command is successfully executed, and the running configuration is provided by the router.

TACACS+ Accounting

TACACS+ Accounting is similar to Authorization in that it uses the same two messages that Authorization uses, i.e. REQUEST and RESPONSE. However, the information contained in the Accounting RESPONSE message may either be a SUCCESS message, which indicates that the server received the Accounting record from the AAA client; an ERROR message, which indicates that the AAA server was unable to commit the Accounting record to its database; or a FOLLOW message, which is similar to the FOLLOW message used in Authorization.

TACACS+ Accounting takes place by sending a record to the AAA server. Each record includes an AV pair for Accounting and one of three types of record may be sent:

1. START

The START record indicates when a service begins. This record also includes information that was included in the Authorization process and other specific information pertaining to the user account.

2. STOP

The STOP record indicates when a service is about to stop or when a service is stopped. This record also includes information that was included in the Authorization process and other specific information pertaining to the user account.

3. CONTINUE

The CONTINUE, or WATCHDOG, record is sent when a service is still in progress and allows the AAA client (NAS) to provide updated information to the AAA server. As with the previous two records, this record also includes information that was included in the Authorization process and other specific information pertaining to the user account. A CONTINUE record can also be sent with a START record. When this happens, it means that the CONTINUE record is a duplicate of the START record.

TACACS+ Attributes

Table 3.2 provides a brief list of some of the attributes used by the TACACS+ security protocol. Please note that this is not a complete list of all attributes, as knowledge of those is beyond the requirement of the IINS course; however, this provides some common attributes that you should be familiar with:

Table 3.2. TACACS+ Attributes

AAA Function	Attribute	Description
Authentication	user=	Specifies the user ID
	authen_type=	Specifies the Authentication type, e.g. CHAP
	service=	Specifies the service type, e.g. PPP
	list=	Specifies the Authentication Method List
	action=	Specifies the action being performed, e.g. login
	method=	Specifies the Authentication method, e.g. TACACS+
	priv=	Specifies the user privilege level
Authorization	nas-password=	Specifies the NAS password
	protocol=	A protocol is a subset of a service; e.g. IPCP for PPP
	ip-addresses=	IP addresses(s) for the tunnel endpoint, e.g. for PPP
	dns-servers=	Specifies the IP address(es) of the DNS server(s)
	port-type=	Specifies the physical port of the NAS
	priv-lvl=	Specifies the EXEC privilege level
Accounting	timezone=	Specifies the Time Zone, e.g. UTC/GMT, EST, etc.
	bytes_in=	The received number of bytes from the session
	bytes_out=	The sent number of bytes from the session
	paks_in=	The received number of packets from the session
	paks_out=	The sent number of packets from the session
	elapsed_time=	The duration of the session
	service=	The type of service, e.g. the router EXEC
	protocol=	The type of protocol, e.g. Telnet
	cmd=	The command(s) entered

Now that we have a solid understanding of the RADIUS and TACACS+ security protocols, we will move on to the next section, which addresses AAA implementation.

Implementing AAA Services

All major Cisco devices, including router, switches, and firewalls, support AAA services. Although firewall (e.g. Cisco ASA and PIX) configuration is beyond the scope of the IINS course requirements, you are required to know how to implement AAA services on Cisco IOS devices. Following are three ways in which AAA services can be implemented:

1. AAA can be implemented as a self-contained AAA local security database containing usernames and passwords, which are typically configured via the username [name] privilege [level] secret [password] global configuration command, directly on the NAS device, such as a router, for example. This implementation is suitable for a small network with a small amount of users.

2. AAA can be implemented as a Cisco Access Control Server (ACS) application server. This can be an external server that operates well. Cisco ACS can be installed onto both Windows and Unix-based platforms. This implementation is suitable for medium to large networks.

3. Finally, AAA can be implemented using the Cisco Secure ACS Solutions Engine appliance. This is a dedicated external platform offered by Cisco that scales very well and is suitable for very large networks.

AAA services are based on method lists, which contain sequenced AAA entries and are configured to define which of the three AAA services will be performed and the sequence in which they will be performed. The method argument refers to the actual method the Authentication algorithm tries. Therefore, when a user attempts to authenticate, the NAS contacts each of the entries in sequence to validate the user.

Method lists allow control of one or more security protocols and security servers to be used to offer fault tolerance and backup of Authentication databases. The AAA engine will use the first method listed in the method list, and if that is unavailable, it will fall back to the next method list. However, it is important that this works only if the message received from the first method listed is not a FAIL message of any kind.

In other words, even though multiple methods may be listed, if a FAIL (i.e. deny) message is received from the first method tried, the Authentication process stops and no further Authentication methods are attempted in the list. In addition to this, it is also important to know that if all entries are processed without receiving a PASS message, access is denied.

In AAA implementation, there are two basic types of method lists:

1. Named Method

A named method list can be configured for any AAA service, such as Authentication or Authorization, for example. These methods are applied to specific interfaces or even terminal lines (e.g. Console and VTY) as required by the administrator.

2. Default Method

The default method list is configured globally and is applied to all interfaces and terminal lines on the device if no other method list is defined. However, if a defined (named) method list is configured, that list will take precedence over the default method list.

The following is an example of an Authentication method list configured on a Cisco IOS router:

R1(config)#aaa authentication login default group tacacs+ local none

To reinforce the concepts we have just been learning, we will dissect this command and highlight the various facets we have learned about, as illustrated in Figure 3.10:

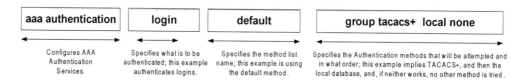

Figure 3.10. AAA Method List Options

Based on Figure 3.10 above, the aaa authentication command enables AAA Authentication services. Next, the login command tells the router to use AAA Authentication for all logins into the router. The keyword, or option, default specifies the AAA method. Because no named methods are used, the administrator is opting to use the default method list.

The group tacacs+ local none command lists the methods that will be used for Authentication of all logins. First, the AAA engine will attempt to contact the TACACS+ server group (group tacacs+), which may be a single server or a group of servers. If there is no response from the server(s), the AAA engine will attempt to use the local database (local) to authenticate all logins. If there is no entry in the local database, then the third option (none) will be attempted. This option tells the AAA engine not to attempt any other Authentication methods, meaning that the Authentication process ceases at this point. If at this point the user has not received a PASS, he or she will be denied access.

In order to configure AAA services, the following general steps should be taken:

1. Globally enable AAA services using the aaa new-model global configuration command.

2. Configure the security protocol parameters, such as the IP address and shared key of the TACACS+ and RADIUS server via the aaa group server [radius|tacacs+][group_name] global configuration command for TACACS+ or RADIUS server groups. Alternatively, you can configure individual TACACS+ or RADIUS servers by using the tacacs-server host [address|hostname] key [shared_key] or the radius-server host [address|hostname] key [shared_key] global configuration commands, respectively.

3. Define the Authentication service and the method lists by using the aaa authentication global configuration command. Keep in mind that named method lists must be configured on the AAA server; they are simply applied (as configured on the server) to the NAS.

4. Apply the Authentication named method list(s) to interfaces or terminal lines by using the login authentication interface or line configuration command.

5. Define the Authorization method list(s) using the aaa authorization global configuration command. As is the case with Authentication, named (defined) method lists must be configured on the server; they are simply applied (as configured on the server) to the NAS.

6. Apply the Authorization method list(s) to terminal lines via the authorization line configuration command. Authorization can also be enabled for WAN interfaces using protocols such as PPP by using the ppp authorization interface configuration command.

7. Define the Accounting service and method lists by using the aaa accounting global configuration command.

8. Apply the Accounting method list(s) to terminal lines via the accounting line configuration command. Accounting can also be enabled for WAN interfaces using protocols such as PPP by using the ppp accounting interface configuration command.

Configuring AAA Servers and Groups

In this section, we are going to be learning about configuring AAA servers and server groups in Cisco IOS software. The first part of this section focuses on RADIUS server configuration and the second part will focus on TACACS+ server configuration.

RADIUS server parameters are configured by using the radius-server host [address|hostname] global configuration command. However, before you can configure AAA servers, it is important that you enable AAA services via the aaa new-model global configuration command. RADIUS server configuration has the following options:

```
R1(config)#aaa new-model
R1(config)#radius-server host 10.1.1.254 ?
  acct-port       UDP port for RADIUS accounting server (default is 1646)
  alias           1-8 aliases for this server (max. 8)
  auth-port       UDP port for RADIUS authentication server (default is 1645)
  backoff         Retry backoff pattern (Default is retransmits with constant delay)
  key             per-server encryption key (overrides default)
  non-standard    Parse attributes that violate the RADIUS standard
  retransmit      Specify the number of retries to active server (overrides default)
  test            Configure server automated testing.
  timeout         Time to wait for this RADIUS server to reply (overrides default)
  <cr>
```

Before we progress any further, we are going to look at the options provided by this command and what they are used for; however, because some of the options are beyond the scope of the IINS course requirements, we will be looking at only those that are applicable at this level. These options are described in Table 3.3:

Table 3.3. AAA Options

Keyword	Description
acct-port	This keyword is used to specify the UDP port that RADIUS will use for Accounting. By default, the Cisco IOS will use UDP port 1646, which is the port defined in RFC 2138. However, it is recommended that the UDP port number be set to 1813.
auth-port	This keyword specifies the UDP port that RADIUS will use for Authentication and Authorization. By default, the Cisco IOS will use UDP port 1645, which is the port defined in RFC 2138. However, it is recommended that the UDP port number be set to 1812.
key	This keyword is used to configure the pre-shared key that RADIUS will use.
timeout	This keyword is used to specify the duration that the NAS will wait for the RADIUS server to respond before moving on to the next method specified.

To reinforce these concepts, we will go through an example of RADIUS server configuration. In the following example, a RADIUS server with the IP address 10.1.1.254 is configured. This server will use the pre-shared key h0w2n3tw0rk.

The RADIUS server will be configured to use UDP port 1812 for Authentication and Authorization, and the UDP port 1813 for Account communication. Finally, the NAS will be configured to wait 30 seconds for the server to reply before attempting the next method specified in the method list:

```
R1(config)#aaa new-model
R1(config)#radius-server host 10.1.1.254 key h0w2n3tw0rk
R1(config)#radius-server host 10.1.1.254 auth-port 1812 acct-port 1813
R1(config)#radius-server host 10.1.1.254 timeout 30
R1(config)#end
R1#
```

It is important to remember that, depending on the Cisco IOS version your NAS is running, these commands can be performed on a single line or they may need to be implemented on a line-by-line basis. Either method is acceptable and produces the same end result.

Next, we are going to learn about TACACS+ server configuration, which is performed by using the tacacs-server host [address|hostname] global configuration command. This command provides the following options:

```
R1(config)#tacacs-server host 10.1.1.254 ?
key                 per-server encryption key (overrides default)
nat                 To send client's post NAT address to tacacs+ server
port                TCP port for TACACS+ server (default is 49)
single-connection   Multiplex all packets over a single tcp connection to server (CiscoS-
ecure)
timeout             Time to wait for this TACACS+ server to reply (overrides default)
<cr>
```

As was performed with RADIUS, we are going to describe the keywords that are relevant to the IINS course requirements, as applicable to TACACS+. These are described in Table 3.4:

Table 3.4. TACACS+ Options

Keyword	Description
key	This keyword is used to configure the pre-shared key that TACACS+ will use.
port	This keyword is used to utilize a TCP port other than 49 for TACACS+.
timeout	This keyword is used to specify the duration that the NAS will wait for the TACACS+ server to respond before moving on to the next method specified.

The following example illustrates the configuration of a TACACS+ server using the IP address 10.1.1.254, with a pre-shared key of h0w2n3tw0rk and a timeout value of 15 seconds. As with RADUIS configuration, this can all be performed on a single line or on multiple lines. The net effect of using either method is the same as long as the configured options are correct:

```
R1(config)#aaa new-model
R1(config)#tacacs-server host 10.1.1.254
R1(config)#tacacs-server key h0w2n3tw0rk
R1(config)#tacacs-server timeout 15
R1(config)#exit
R1#
```

Now that we have an understanding of the configuration commands required to configure individual RADIUS and TACACS+ servers, we will move on and look at the configuration commands required to configure AAA server groups, starting with RADIUS. AAA server groups are configured by using the aaa group server [radius|tacacs+][name] global configuration command. Once in server group configuration mode, the same basic concepts apply for the configuration of RADIUS or TACACS+ servers.

When configuring a RADIUS server group, the aaa group server radius [name] global configuration command is used. The options available with this command are as follows:

```
R1(config)#aaa group server radius MY-RADIUS-GROUP
R1(config-sg-radius)#?
RADIUS Server-group commands:
  accounting      Specify a RADIUS attribute filter for accounting
  attribute       Customize selected radius attributes
  authorization   Specify a RADIUS attribute filter for authorization
  backoff         Retry backoff pattern (Default is retransmits with constant delay)
  deadtime        Specify time in minutes to ignore an unresponsive server
  default         Set a command to its defaults
  exit            Exit from RADIUS server-group configuration mode
  ip              Internet Protocol config commands
  load-balance    Server group load-balancing options.
  no              Negate a command or set its defaults
  server          Specify a RADIUS server
  server-private  Define a private RADIUS server (per group)
```

Before we move forward, we need to understand the meaning of the keywords used and what function they serve. As before, the majority of these options are beyond the scope of the IINS course requirements; therefore, only applicable keywords are described. This is provided in Table 3.5:

Table 3.5. RADIUS Options

Keyword	Description
deadtime	This is the same as the timeout command when configuring individual servers. It is used to specify the duration that the NAS will wait for a RADIUS server to respond before moving on to the next server in the group. This value, however, is in minutes.
ip	This keyword is used to specify RADIUS IP parameters. The only applicable option (for IINS) is using this keyword to specify the source interface RADIUS packets will be sent from.
load-balance	This keyword is used to perform load balancing between the RADIUS servers in the group.
server	This keyword is used to specify the IP address of the hostname of a server in the group. This option also allows the administrator to specify the AAA ports that the RADIUS server will use.

The following example illustrates how to configure a RADIUS server group named IINS-RADIUS. This group will contain servers with IP addresses 10.1.1.1, 10.1.1.2, and 10.1.1.3. The RADIUS servers will be configured to use ports 1812 and 1813 for AAA services. Finally, all RADIUS packets will be sourced from the FastEthernet0/0 interface of the NAS:

```
R1(config)#aaa new-model
R1(config)#aaa group server radius IINS-RADIUS
R1(config-sg-radius)#server 10.1.1.1 auth-port 1812 acct-port 1813
R1(config-sg-radius)#server 10.1.1.2 auth-port 1812 acct-port 1813
R1(config-sg-radius)#server 10.1.1.3 auth-port 1812 acct-port 1813
R1(config-sg-radius)#ip radius source-interface fastethernet0/0
R1(config-sg-radius)#exit
R1(config)#exit
R1#
```

TACACS+ server groups are configured via the aaa group server tacacs+ [name] global configuration command. The options available with this command are:

```
R1(config)#aaa group server tacacs+ MY-TACACS-GROUP
R1(config-sg-tacacs+)#?
TACACS+ Server-group commands:
  accounting       Accounting specific command
  default          Set a command to its defaults
  exit             Exit from TACACS+ server-group configuration mode
  ip               Internet Protocol config commands
  no               Negate a command or set its defaults
  server           Specify a TACACS+ server
  server-private   Define a private TACACS+ server (per group)
```

The keywords that fall within the scope of the IINS course requirements are described in Table 3.6:

Table 3.6. TACACS+ Server Group Options

Keyword	Description
ip	This keyword is used to specify TACACS+ IP parameters. The only applicable option (for IINS) is using this keyword to specify the source interface TACACS+ packets will be sent from.
server	This keyword is used to specify the IP address of the hostname of a server in the group.

The following example illustrates how to configure a TACACS+ server group named IINS-TACACS. This TACACS+ server group will contain servers with IP addresses 10.1.1.254, 172.31.1.254, and 192.168.1.254. All TACACS+ packets will be sourced from the Loopback0 interface of the NAS:

```
R1(config)#aaa new-model
R1(config)#aaa group server tacacs+ IINS-TACACS
R1(config-sg-tacacs+)#server 10.1.1.254
R1(config-sg-tacacs+)#server 172.31.1.254
R1(config-sg-tacacs+)#server 192.168.1.254
R1(config-sg-tacacs+)#ip tacacs source-interface loopback0
R1(config-sg-tacacs+)#exit
R1(config)#exit
R1#
R1#show running-config
Building configuration...

Current configuration : 2679 bytes
!
version 12.4
service timestamps debug datetime msec
service timestamps log datetime msec
no service password-encryption
!
hostname R1
!
boot-start-marker
boot-end-marker
!
no logging console
!
aaa new-model
!
!
```

```
!
aaa group server tacacs+ IINS-TACACS
 server 172.31.1.254
 server 192.168.1.254
 server 10.1.1.254
 ip tacacs source-interface Loopback0
!
!
!
aaa session-id common
!
---- [Truncated Output] ----
```

Now that we have a solid understanding of the configuration requirements for AAA servers and server groups, we will move on to the configuration of AAA services, beginning with Authentication.

Configuring AAA Authentication

Authentication can also be configured for interfaces or terminal lines by using the login authentication interface or line configuration command. The options available with Authentication are configured via the aaa authentication global configuration command, as follows:

```
R1(config)#aaa authentication ?
  arap              Set authentication lists for arap.
  attempts          Set the maximum number of authentication attempts
  banner            Message to use when starting login/authentication.
  dot1x             Set authentication lists for IEEE 802.1x.
  enable            Set authentication list for enable.
  eou               Set authentication lists for EAPoUDP
  fail-message      Message to use for failed login/authentication.
  login             Set authentication lists for logins.
  password-prompt   Text to use when prompting for a password
  ppp               Set authentication lists for ppp.
  sgbp              Set authentication lists for sgbp.
  username-prompt   Text to use when prompting for a username
```

Table 3.7 describes the keywords that you must be familiar with for the purposes of satisfying the IINS requirements:

Table 3.7. AAA Authentication Options

Keyword	Description
attempts	This keyword is used to specify the maximum number of login attempts allowed. Possible values range from 1 to 255.
banner	This keyword is used to configure a banner for login Authentication.
dot1x	This keyword is used to enable Authentication for 802.1x—which will be described in detail later in this guide.
enable	This keyword is used to enable Authentication for enable access.
fail-message	This keyword is used to specify a message that is printed when Authentication fails.
login	This keyword is used to enable Authentication for all logins.
password-prompt	This keyword is used to specify the password prompt that users will see when authenticating.
username-prompt	This keyword is used to specify the username prompt that users will see when authenticating.

Once you have selected the service you would like to authenticate (e.g. logins), you must then specify the method list that will be used for Authentication. You can either use a named (defined) method list or select the default method list, as illustrated in the following output:

```
R1(config)#aaa authentication login ?
  WORD      Named authentication list.
  default   The default authentication list.
```

Once the method lists have been selected, the next step is to define an ordered list of methods, which will be attempted by the AAA engine in the order in which they are configured:

```
R1(config)#aaa authentication login default ?
  enable         Use enable password for authentication.
  group          Use Server-group
  krb5           Use Kerberos 5 authentication.
  krb5-telnet    Allow logins only if already authenticated via Kerberos V Telnet.
  line           Use line password for authentication.
  local          Use local username authentication.
  local-case     Use case-sensitive local username authentication.
  none           NO authentication.
  passwd-expiry  enable the login list to provide password aging support
```

Before we move forward, it is imperative to understand the options presented here. Therefore, they are described in detail in Table 3.8:

Table 3.8. AAA Authentication Login Options

Keyword	Description
enable	This keyword specifies that the enable password/secret should be used for Authentication.
group	This keyword specifies that TACACS+ or RADIUS servers, or server groups, should be used for Authentication.
line	This keyword specifies that the line password (e.g. VTY) should be used for Authentication.
local	This keyword specifies that the username—configured via the username command—be used for Authentication.
local-case	This keyword specifies that the username—configured via the username command—be used for Authentication; however, the username is case-sensitive.
none	This method is effectively a deny all. It should be specified at the end of the list of methods configured because it prevents any further Authentication attempts once reached.

To reinforce Authentication configuration, we will go through a few examples, illustrating the different ways in which Authentication can be configured in Cisco IOS software.

In the first example, Authentication will be configured on the router for all logins using the default method list. The sequential methods used in Authentication will be via:

1. TACACS+, using a server with the IP address 10.1.1.254 and a pre-shared key of 11nsc3rt;
2. The enable password; and
3. The line password.

In addition, all terminal lines will be configured so that they are authenticated using AAA. This configuration is performed as follows:

```
R1(config)#aaa new-model
R1(config)#aaa authentication login default group tacacs+ enable line none
R1(config)#tacacs-server host 10.1.1.254 key 11nsc3rt
R1(config)#line con 0
R1(config-line)#login authentication default
R1(config-line)#exit
R1(config)#line vty 0 4
R1(config-line)#login authentication default
R1(config-line)#exit
R1(config)#exit
R1#
```

In the second example, Authentication will be enabled for 802.1x using a method list named RADIUS-DOT1X. The sequential methods used in Authentication will be via:

1. RADIUS server 10.1.1.254, using default ports for AAA and a pre-shared key of dot1x;
2. The local database; and
3. The enable password.

This configuration is performed as follows:

```
R1(config)#aaa new-model
R1(config)#aaa authentication dot1x RADIUS-DOT1X group radius local enable none
R1(config)#radius-server host 10.1.1.254 key dot1x
R1(config)#exit
R1#
```

The third, and final, example demonstrates how to configure Authentication for all logins using a method list named LOGIN-LIST. The sequential methods used in Authentication will be via:

1. A TACACS+ server group named TAC-GRP, which contains servers 10.0.0.1 and 10.0.0.2;
2. A RADIUS server group named RAD-GRP, which contains servers 11.0.0.1 and 11.0.0.2; and
3. The enable secret.

This configuration is performed as follows:

```
R1(config)#aaa new-model
R1(config)#aaa authentication login LOGIN-LIST group TAC-GRP group RAD-GRP enable none
R1(config)#aaa group server tacacs+ TAC-GRP
R1(config-sg-tacacs+)#server 10.0.0.1
R1(config-sg-tacacs+)#server 10.0.0.2
R1(config-sg-tacacs+)#exit
R1(config)#aaa group server radius RAD-GRP
R1(config-sg-radius)#server 11.0.0.1
R1(config-sg-radius)#server 11.0.0.2
R1(config-sg-radius)#exit
R1(config)#line con 0
R1(config-line)#login authentication LOGIN-LIST
R1(config-line)#exit
R1(config)#line vty 0 4
R1(config-line)#login authentication LOGIN-LIST
R1(config-line)#exit
R1(config)#exit
R1#
```

Although the configuration options may seem confusing at first glance, remember that practice makes perfect. Take your time to understand the manner in which these commands are executed and the logic behind method lists, and in no time, it will all make perfect sense. Having stated that, we will now move on to the second part of the AAA framework: Authorization.

Configuring AAA Authorization

Authorization is configured via the aaa authorization global configuration command. In addition to this, Authorization can be applied to terminal lines (e.g. VTY) via the authorization line configuration command. In order for Authorization to work, Authentication must be configured and the AAA client must have successfully authenticated. The options available for Authorization in the Cisco IOS software are as follows:

```
R2(config)#aaa authorization ?
  auth-proxy       For Authentication Proxy Services
  cache            For AAA cache configuration
  commands         For exec (shell) commands.
  config-commands  For configuration mode commands.
  configuration    For downloading configurations from AAA server
  console          For enabling console authorization
  exec             For starting an exec (shell).
  multicast        For downloading Multicast configurations from an AAA server
  network          For network services. (PPP, SLIP, ARAP)
  reverse-access   For reverse access connections
  template         Enable template authorization
```

Table 3.9 describes the keywords that you are expected to be familiar with when configuring Authorization:

Table 3.9. AAA Authorization Options

Keyword	Description
commands	This keyword is used to enable Authorization for EXEC commands.
config-commands	This keyword is used to enable Authorization for configuration (Config) commands, e.g. router ospf 1.
console	This keyword is used to enable Authorization for Console access.
exec	This keyword is used to enable Authorization for beginning an EXEC shell on the selected lines.
network	This keyword is used to enable Authorization for network services, such as PPP.

Once you have selected the service you want to authorize, you must then select the method list to use for Authorization. As is the case for Authentication, you can select either a named (defined) method list that is configured on a AAA server or use the default method list, as illustrated in the following output:

```
R2(config)#aaa authorization network ?
  WORD      Named authorization list.
  default   The default authorization list.
```

The final step is specifying the methods used after the method list has been defined. This step follows the same logic as that used in Authentication. In a manner similar to Authentication, we will go through a few examples on Authorization to ensure that you are comfortable with the Authorization CLI in Cisco IOS software.

The first example illustrates how to configure Authorization for PPP (network) using the method list PPP-AUTHOR. PPP will be enabled and authorized via the same method list on the Serial0/0 interface of the router. The sequential methods to be used will be the local user database. This is performed as follows:

```
R2(config)#aaa authorization network PPP-AUTHOR local none
R2(config)#interface serial0/0
R2(config-if)#encapsulation ppp
R2(config-if)#ppp authorization PPP-AUTHOR
R2(config-if)#exit
R2(config)#exit
R2#
```

The second Authorization example illustrates how to authorize level 15 commands if the user has been successfully authenticated via the method list COMND-AUTHOR. This method list is also applied to all terminal lines on the router (this example assumes that Authentication has been configured and, thus, focuses only on Authorization commands), as follows:

```
R2(config)#aaa authorization commands 15 COMND-AUTHOR if-authenticated
R2(config)#line con 0
R2(config-line)#authorization commands 15 COMND-AUTHOR
R2(config-line)#exit
R2(config)#line vty 0 4
R2(config-line)#authorization commands 15 COMND-AUTHOR
R2(config-line)#exit
R2(config)#exit
R2#
```

The final example in this section illustrates how to enable Authorization for configuration commands. Authorization is also configured so that users attempting to begin an EXEC shell on any terminal lines should be authorized using the method list TAC-AUTHOR. TACACS+ is configured to authorize EXEC shell access and a TACACS+ server group named TAC-GROUP, which contains servers 10.1.1.1 and 11.1.1.1, is used for Authorization:

```
R2(config)#aaa authorization config-commands
    R2(config)#aaa authorization exec TAC-AUTHOR group TAC-GROUP
    R2(config)#aaa group server tacacs+ TAC-GROUP
    R2(config-sg-tacacs+)#server 10.1.1.1
    R2(config-sg-tacacs+)#server 11.1.1.1
    R2(config-sg-tacacs+)#exit
    R2(config)#line con 0
    R2(config-line)#authorization exec TAC-AUTHOR
    R2(config-line)#exit
    R2(config)#line vty 0 4
    R2(config-line)#authorization exec TAC-AUTHOR
    R2(config-line)#exit
    R2(config)#exit
    R2#
```

Configuring AAA Accounting

As we learned earlier in this chapter, Accounting is configured via the aaa accounting global configuration command. Accounting is enabled for terminal lines via the accounting line configuration command and can also be enabled for certain WAN protocols (e.g. PPP) via the ppp accounting interface configuration command. The options available for Accounting in Cisco IOS software are as follows:

```
R1(config)#aaa accounting ?
   delay-start        Delay PPP Network start record until peer IP address is known.
   nested             When starting PPP from EXEC, generate NETWORK records before EXEC-STOP
   send               Send records to accounting server.
   session-duration   Set the preference for calculating session durations
   suppress           Do not generate accounting records for a specific type of user record.
   auth-proxy         For authentication proxy events.
   commands           For exec (shell) commands.
   connection         For outbound connections. (telnet, rlogin)
   dot1x              For dot1x sessions.
   exec               For starting an exec (shell).
   gigawords          64 bit interface counters to support Radius attributes 52 & 53.
   multicast          For multicast accounting.
   network            For network services. (PPP, SLIP, ARAP)
   resource           For resource events.
   system             For system events.
   update             Enable accounting update records.
```

As is the case with Authentication and Authorization, some of the keywords presented are beyond the scope of the IINS course requirements. However, Table 3.10 lists and describes the Accounting keywords that you are expected to be familiar with:

Table 3.10. AAA Accounting Options

Keyword	Description
send	This keyword configures Accounting to send stop records for authenticated users (or failures) to the AAA server.
commands	This keyword configures Accounting to send records for EXEC commands to the AAA server.
connection	This keyword configures Accounting to send records for all outbound connections to the AAA server.
exec	This keyword configures Accounting for EXEC sessions (user shells).
network	This keyword configures Accounting for network-related services, such as PPP.
system	This keyword configures Accounting for all system-level events.

Once the service for which you want Accounting enabled has been selected, you then have the option of specifying either the default method list or a named (defined) method list to be used for Accounting. In addition to these two options, a third option is also available for Accounting. This option, guarantee-first, guarantees that the first AAA packet sent will be the Accounting-On packet. This is not a desirable trait (due to reasons beyond the scope of the IINS course requirements); therefore, we will not be discussing this keyword in any further detail. Accounting options are as follows:

```
R1(config)#aaa accounting commands 15 ?
  WORD            Named Accounting list.
  default         The default accounting list.
  guarantee-first Guarantee system accounting as first record.
```

Now that we have an understanding of the command logic required to successfully configure Accounting, we will conclude this section with a few configuration examples to reinforce the concepts and steps we have learned. The first example illustrates how to enable Accounting to send start and stop records for EXEC sessions using a method list named ACCT-LIST. Accounting information will be sent to the RADIUS server 192.168.1.254 using port 1813:

```
R1(config)#aaa accounting exec ACCT-LIST start-stop group radius
R1(config)#radius-server host 192.168.1.254 auth-port 1812 acct-port 1813
R1(config)#line con 0
R1(config-line)#accounting exec ACCT-LIST
R1(config-line)#exit
R1(config)#line vty 0 4
R1(config-line)#accounting exec ACCT-LIST
R1(config-line)#exit
R1(config)#exit
R1#
```

The second example illustrates how to enable only stop records Accounting for all Level 15 commands using the CMD-ACC method list. This Accounting information will be sent to a TACACS+ server group named TAC-ACC, which contains servers 10.1.1.254 and 10.2.2.254:

```
R1(config)#aaa accounting commands 15 CMD-ACC stop-only group TAC-ACC
R1(config)#aaa group server tacacs+ TAC-ACC
R1(config-sg-tacacs+)#server 10.1.1.254
R1(config-sg-tacacs+)#server 10.2.2.254
R1(config-sg-tacacs+)#exit
R1(config)#line con 0
R1(config-line)#accounting commands 15 CMD-ACC
R1(config-line)#exit
R1(config)#line vty 0 4
R1(config-line)#accounting commands 15 CMD-ACC
R1(config-line)#exit
R1(config)#exit
R1#
```

The final example illustrates how to enable Accounting for network services (PPP) using the default method list. Start and stop records will be sent to RADIUS server 172.16.1.254 using the default Accounting port 1646 and a pre-shared key **accntkey**. PPP is enabled on the Serial0/0 interface of the router and configured for Accounting services:

```
R1(config)#aaa accounting network default start-stop group radius
R1(config)#radius-server host 172.16.1.254 key accntkey
R1(config)#interface serial0/0
R1(config-if)#encapsulation ppp
R1(config-if)#ppp accounting default
R1(config-if)#exit
R1(config)#exit
R1#
```

As with any other new concept, practice makes perfect. Therefore, if you are able to get your hands on a personal router, practice configuring AAA as much as possible. If you do not have your own personal router(s), then leverage the labs available on www.howtonetwork.net to practice your configurations and reinforce these concepts.

The last section in this chapter deals with Kerberos. Although not explicitly stated in the IINS exam objectives, Kerberos is a security protocol that falls under the AAA umbrella. Going through this section will provide you with a basic understanding of the Kerberos protocol.

Kerberos Basics

Kerberos is a trusted third-party Authentication Layer 7 (Application Layer) service. Kerberos is a secret-key network authentication protocol developed at the Massachusetts Institute of Technology (MIT) that uses the Data Encryption Standard (DES) cryptographic algorithm for encryption and authentication services. DES is described in detail later in this guide. In the Kerberos protocol, the trusted third party is the Key Distribution Center (KDC). Figure 3.11 illustrates the basic operation of Kerberos:

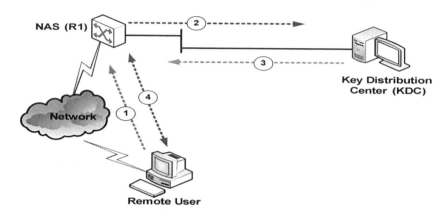

Figure 3.11. Kerberos in Operation

In the diagram illustrated above, the Kerberos Authentication process begins when the remote user initiates a connection to the NAS, as illustrated in step 1. When the NAS receives this connection, it builds a service credential request and sends it to the Key Distribution Center (KDC), as illustrated in step 2.

In step 3, the KDC decrypts the request from the NAS and builds a service credential, which is then sent back to the remote user. When the service credential from the NAS is sent, both the NAS and the remote user decrypt the credential. Once decrypted, the remote user is then able to exchange data with the NAS, as illustrated in step 4.

Unlike RADIUS and TACACS+, Kerberos authenticates users by issuing tickets. These tickets have a limited lifespan and are stored in a user's credential cache. These tickets can then be used in place of the standard username/password Authentication scheme.

The Kerberos credential scheme uses a concept called single logon. This process allows for a user to be authenticated once and then allows a user access to network resources whenever the user's credentials are accepted. To enhance security, Kerberos also uses timestamps, which are simply numbers that represent the date and time, to assist in the detection of replay attacks.

Unlike RADIUS and TACACS+, Kerberos uses both TCP and UDP ports. TCP/UDP ports 88, 543, and 749 and TCP ports 754, 2105, and 444 are all used for packet delivery in Kerberos. In addition to this, Kerberos supports username/password encryption and allows for Telnet sessions to be encrypted. While we will not be going into any further technical details on Kerberos, Table 3.11 provides a brief description of common Kerberos terminology:

Table 3.11. Kerberos Terminology

Kerberos Term	Definition
Credential	This is a general term that refers to authentication tickets, such as ticket granting tickets (TGTs) and service credentials. Credentials are used to verify the identity of a user or service. If a network service trusts the Kerberos server that issued a ticket, it can be used in place of retyping in a username and password. Credentials have a default lifespan of 8 hours.
Instance	This is an authorization level label for Kerberos principals. Most Kerberos principals are in the form user@REALM, for example, paul@HOWTONETWORK.NET. In Kerberos, the realm name MUST be in uppercase letters.
Kerberized	Applications and services that have been modified to support the Kerberos credential infrastructure are said to be Kerberized.
Kerberos realm	A domain consisting of users, hosts, and network services that are registered to a Kerberos server. Kerberos realms are always in uppercase letters. The Kerberos realm is also used to map a DNS domain to a Kerberos realm.
Kerberos server	A daemon running on a network host. Users and network services register their identities with the Kerberos server. Network services query the Kerberos server to authenticate to other network services. It is sometimes referred to as the Master Kerberos server.
Key Distribution Center (KDC)	A Kerberos server and database program that runs on a network host. It is used to issue TGTs.
Principal	Also known as a Kerberos identity, this is who you are or what a service is according to the Kerberos server.
Service credential	A credential for a network service. When issued from the KDC, service credentials are encrypted with the password shared by the network service and the KDC, and also with the user's TGT.
SRVTAB	A password that a network service shares with the KDC. The network service authenticates an encrypted service credential using the SRVTAB to decrypt it. The SRVTAB is also referred to as the KEYTAB.
Ticket Granting Ticket (TGT)	A credential issued by the KDC to authenticated users. When users receive a TGT, they can authenticate to network services within the Kerberos realm represented by the KDC.

Chapter Summary

The following section is a summary of the major points you should be aware of in this chapter:

AAA Overview

- AAA stands for Authentication, Authorization and Accounting
- Authentication is used to validate identity
- Authorization is used to determine what that particular user can do
- Accounting is used to allow for an audit trail
- The primary advantages of using AAA are:
    1. Standard Authentication methods
    2. Scalability
    3. Greater Flexibility and Control
    4. Multiple Backup Systems

- AAA uses the TACACS+, Kerberos, and RADIUS authentication methods

The AAA Model

- The AAA model is used to control access to devices, enforce policies and audit usage
- The AAA framework uses a set of three independent function which are:
    1. Authentication
    2. Authorization
    3. Accounting

- Authentication is based on verifying user credentials, which can be any of the following:
    1. Something the user knows—which is referred to as Authentication by knowledge
    2. Something the user possesses—which is referred to as Authentication by possession
    3. Something the user is—which is referred to as user characteristic or, biometrics.

- Authorization uses AV pairs to determine the actions a user, etc is allowed to perform
- AAA clients are responsible for enforcing user access control based on AV pairs
- Accounting records are made up of accounting AV pairs
- The AAA client then sends Accounting records to the AAA server for storage
- AAA services are correlated as follows:
    1. Authentication is valid without authorization
    2. Authentication is valid without accounting
    3. Authorization is not valid without authentication
    4. Accounting is not valid without authentication

AAA Operation

- In order for AAA to work, the NAS must be able to access security information for a specific user to provide AAA services. This information may be stored locally, i.e. on the NAS itself, or remotely, on a RADUIS, TACACS+ or Kerberos server
- Unlike authentication and Authorization, there is no search for AV pairs in Accounting

RADIUS

- RADIUS stands for Remote Authentication Dial-In User Service
- The original specification for RADIUS is defined in RFC 2138 and 2139
- Updates to RADIUS are included in newer RFCS 2865 and 2866
- A RADIUS server is a device that has the RADIUS daemon or application installed
- RADIUS is an open-standard protocol that is distributed in C source code format
- RADIUS only encrypts the password, the rest of the packet is sent in clear text
- RADIUS uses UDP as the Transport layer protocol
- RADIUS uses UDP port 1812 for Authentication and Authorization
- RADIUS uses UDP port 1813 for Accounting
- Legacy applications use 1645 for Authentication and Authorization and 1646 for Accounting
- RADIUS has limited protocol support, and does not support protocols like IPX, for example
- RADIUS packet message types are:
  1. Access-Request (username/password and other information is sent to the AAA server)
  2. Access-Accept (the username is found in the database, and the password is validated)
  3. Access-Reject (username is not found in the database, or the password is incorrect)
  4. Accounting-Request (used by the NAS to start, send updates, or stop Accounting)
  5. Accounting Response (sent by the AAA server to acknowledge Accounting-Requests)
  6. Access-Challenge (the RADIUS server wants more information from the user)

TACACS+

- TACACS+ is a Cisco-proprietary protocol that is used in the AAA framework
- TACACS+ uses TCP as a Transport Layer protocol, using TCP port 49
- TACACS+ separates the three AAA architectures
- TACACS+ encrypts the data between the user and the server
- TACACS+ supports multiple protocols, e.g. IP, IPX, AppleTalk and X.25
- The TACACS+ Authentication phase uses three distinct packet types:
  1. START packets (used initially when the user attempts to connect)
  2. REPLY / RESPONSE packets (sent by the AAA server during)
  3. CONTINUE packets (used by AAA clients to return username/password information)

- Valid TACACS+ REPLY / RESPONSE packets could be any one of the following messages:

1. ACCEPT (user has been successfully authenticated)
2. REJECT (Authentication has failed)
3. ERROR (a communication problem exists between the NAS and the AAA server)
4. CONTINUE (that the server is expecting additional information)

- TACACS+ Authorization uses REQUEST and RESPONSE messages
- TACACS+ REQUEST messages are sent by the NAS
- TACACS+ RESPONSE messages are sent by the server and contain one of the following:
  1. PASS_ADD (indicates that request is authorized)
  2. PASS_REPL (sent by the AAA server when it ignores the request)
  3. FOLLOW (the AAA wants to have Authorization performed on another server)
  4. ERROR (indicates indicate an error on the AAA server)

- TACACS+ Accounting also uses REQUEST and the RESPONSE messages
- TACACS+ Accounting takes place by sending a record to the AAA server
- Each record includes an AV pair for Accounting and one of three types may be sent:
  1. START (indicates when a service begins)
  2. STOP (indicates when a service is about to stop, or when a service is stopped)
  3. CONTINUE (is sent when a service is still in progress)

Implementing AAA Services

- There are three ways in which AAA services can be implemented:
  1. AAA can be implemented as a self-contained AAA local security database
  2. AAA can be implemented as a Cisco Access Control Server (ACS) application server
  3. AAA can be implemented using the Cisco Secure ACS Solutions Engine appliance

- AAA services are based on method lists
- Methods lists contain sequenced AAA entries
- Method lists allow control of one or more security protocols and servers to be used
- There are two basic types of method lists:
  1. Named Method
  2. Default Method

- In order to configure AAA services, the following general steps should be taken:
  1. Enable AAA via the aaa new-model global configuration command.
  2. Configure the security protocol parameters, such as the IP address and shared key
  3. Define the Authentication service and the method lists
  4. Apply the Authentication named method list(s) to interfaces or terminal lines

5. Define the Authorization method list(s)
6. Apply the Authorization method list(s) to terminal lines
7. Define the Accounting service and method lists
8. Apply the Accounting method list(s) to terminal lines

Configuring AAA Servers and Groups

- RADIUS server parameters are configured by using the radius-server host [address|hostname] global configuration command
- TACACS+ server parameters are configured by using the tacacs-server host [address|hostname] global configuration command
- AAA server groups are configured by using the aaa group server [radius|tacacs+][name] global configuration command

Configuring AAA Authentication

- Authentication is configured via the aaa authentication global configuration command

Configuring AAA Authorization

- Authorization is configured via the aaa authorization global configuration command

Configuring AAA Accounting

- Accounting is configured via the aaa accounting global configuration command

Kerberos Basics

- Kerberos is a trusted third-party Authentication Layer 7 service
- In the Kerberos protocol, the trusted third-party is the KDC
- The Kerberos credential scheme uses a concept called single logon
- Kerberos uses both TCP and UDP ports
- Kerberos uses TCP/UDP ports 88, 543, 749 and TCP ports 754, 2105, and 444

Commands Used in this Chapter

The following section is a summary of the commands used in this chapter:

Command	Description
username [name] privilege [level] secret [password]	Used to configure a username, assign privileges and set the user password
aaa new-model	Globally enables AAA
aaa group server [radius|tacacs+][group_name]	Used to configure AAA RADIUS or TACACS+ server groups
tacacs-server host [address|hostname] key [shared_key]	Used to configure TACACS+ server and specify parameters
radius-server host [address|hostname] key [shared_key]	Used to configure RADIUS server and specify parameters
aaa authentication [attempts|banner|dot1x|enable|fail-message|login|password-prompt|username-prompt]	Used to configure AAA Authentication globally
login authentication	Used to configure AAA Authentication for interfaces and terminal lines
aaa authorization [commands|config-commands|console|exec|network]	Used to configure AAA Authorization globally
authorization	Used to configure AAA Authorization for interfaces and terminal lines
aaa accounting [send|commands|connection|exec|network|system]	Used to configure AAA Accounting globally
accounting	Used to configure AAA Accounting for interfaces and terminal lines

CHAPTER 4

Access Control via Cisco IOS Access Control Lists

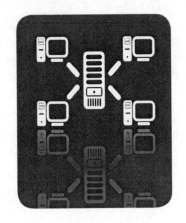

Cisco IOS software provides traffic-filtering capabilities for Access Control Lists (ACLs) with the capability to prevent traffic from entering or exiting the network. ACLs provide filtering in Cisco IOS software because they can be used to control traffic by allowing or denying network access. The IINS exam objectives that will be covered in this chapter are as follows:

- Explain the functionality of standard, extended, and named IP ACLs used by routers to filter packets
- Configure and verify IP ACLs to mitigate given threats (filter IP traffic destined for Telnet, SNMP, and DoS attacks) in a network using CLI
- Configure IP ACLs to prevent IP address spoofing using CLI
- Discuss the caveats to be considered when building ACLs

This chapter is broken up into the following sections:

- Access Control List Overview
- Access Control List Types
- ACL Processing and Packet Flow Rules
- Implementing ACLs
- Using ACLs to Mitigate Network Layer Attacks
- Using ACLs to Secure Telnet Access
- Using ACLs to Secure SNMP Access

IINS Exam Objective	Section(s) Covered
Explain the functionality of standard, extended, and named IP ACLs used by routers to filter packets	<ul><li>Access Control List Overview</li><li>Access Control List Types</li><li>ACL Processing and Packet Flow Rules</li></ul>
Configure and verify IP ACLs to mitigate given threats (filter IP traffic destined for Telnet, SNMP, and oS attacks) in a network using CLI	<ul><li>Implementing ACLs</li><li>Using Access Lists to Mitigate Network Layer Attacks</li><li>Using ACLs to Secure Telnet Access</li><li>Using ACLs to Secure SNMP Access</li></ul>
Configure IP ACLs to prevent IP address spoofing using CLI	<ul><li>Using Access Lists to Mitigate Network Layer Attacks</li></ul>
Discuss the caveats to be considered when building ACLs	<ul><li>ACL Processing and Packet Flow Rules</li><li>Implementing ACLs</li></ul>

Access Control List Overview

An Access Control List (ACL) is a list of permit and deny statements that controls network access to enforce a security policy. Each filter in an ACL, referred to as an Access Control Entry (ACE), permits or denies a packet, or packets, across an interface based on the information contained inside the packets. There are two broad categories for data received by a router:

1. It is traffic that passes through the router via the forwarding path; or
2. It is traffic destined for the router for route processor handling.

In normal operations, the vast majority of traffic simply flows through a router en route to its ultimate destination. Therefore, if ACLs are not configured and implemented, all packets passing through the router can also be allowed onto all parts of the network—which is very undesirable in terms of network security. Administrators can use ACLs to prevent such behavior and restrict traffic between networks so as to comply with security policy. In addition to this, administrators can also use ACLs in numerous other ways, such as to:

*   Filter routing information received from or sent to adjacent neighbors;
*   Control access to networks by permitting or denying particular types of traffic;
*   Control interactive access to the router itself, e.g. Telnet, HTTPS, and SSH;
*   Define interesting traffic that can be used to initiate ISDN connections;
*   Define interesting traffic for IPSec Virtual Private Network (VPN) encryption;
*   Define queuing and Quality of Service (QoS) features, allowing traffic to be prioritized;
*   Use in security techniques such as TCP Intercept and the Cisco IOS Firewall;
*   Define traffic for Network Address Translation (NAT); and
*   Mitigate IP spoofing, smurf attacks, and other similar network attacks.

While this list provides some of the most common applications and uses of ACLs, it is important to know that it does not encompass all possible uses of ACLs. However, the list is a good starting point for understanding the flexibility afforded by ACLs.

Access Control List Types

There are many types of ACLs that can be configured in Cisco IOS software. While knowledge of the majority of these ACLs is beyond the scope of the IINS course requirements, as a future network security administrator, you should be familiar with the different ACL configuration options available in Cisco IOS software. Therefore, the following section provides a brief description of the different types of IP ACLs available in Cisco IOS software. The different types of ACLs that are covered in this section are as follows:

- IP Standard ACLs
- IP Extended ACLs
- IP Named ACLs
- Dynamic ACLs
- Reflexive ACLs
- Time-based ACLs
- Turbo ACLs
- Receive ACLs
- Infrastructure Protection ACLs
- Transit ACLs
- Classification ACLs

IP Standard ACLs

IP standard ACLs are one of the most basic types of ACLs that can be configured for matching IP packets. These ACLs inspect traffic based on the source address of the IP packets.

IP standard ACLs filter only the source address. This allows administrators to restrict or allow access to the network for a subnet, group of subnets, or specific hosts based on where they are coming from. Because they filter only the source address, IP standard ACLs should be placed as close as possible to the destination network. This concept is illustrated in Figure 4.1:

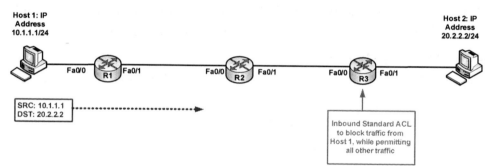

Figure 4.1. Access List Placement

In Figure 4.1 illustrated above, Host 1 sends an IP packet to Host 2. However, based on network security policy, Host 1 should not be allowed to communicate with Host 2. When using IP standard ACLs, an inbound IP ACL should be configured on the FastEthernet0/0 interface of R3.

One of the most common mistakes when using IP standard ACLs is to implement them in the wrong place. For example, if the standard ACL to prevent Host 1 from communicating with Host 2 was placed on the FastEthernet0/0 interface of R1, Host 1 not only would be unable to communicate with Host 2, it also would be unable to communicate with any other host that did not reside on the 10.1.1.0/24 subnet, as illustrated in Figure 4.2:

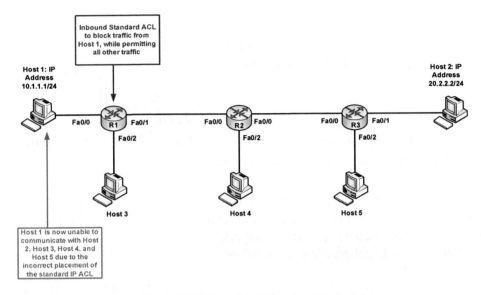

Figure 4.2. Access List Placement Error

In Figure 4.2 above, an IP standard ACL is incorrectly configured on the FastEthernet0/0 interface of R1, in the inbound direction, with the intention of preventing this host from communicating with Host 2. However, because IP standard ACLs match only on source addresses, and not destination addresses, this incorrect placement effectively means that R1 will deny any and all packets from Host 1. This results in Host 1 not only being unable to communicate with Host 2 but also being unable to communicate with Hosts 3, 4, and 5.

IP standard ACL's numbers can be anywhere from 1 to 99 or 1300 to 1999, as illustrated by the bold text in the following output:

```
R1(config)#access-list ?
  <1-99>              IP standard access list
  <100-199>           IP extended access list
  <1100-1199>         Extended 48-bit MAC address access list
  <1300-1999>         IP standard access list (expanded range)
  <200-299>           Protocol type-code access list
  <2000-2699>         IP extended access list (expanded range)
  <700-799>           48-bit MAC address access list
  dynamic-extended    Extend the dynamic ACL absolute timer
  rate-limit          Simple rate-limit specific access list
```

The syntax used to configure IP standard ACLs is:
```
access-list access-list-number {deny | permit} source [source-wildcard] [log [word]]
```

For example, to configure an IP standard ACL to permit traffic from the 172.16.0.0/12 subnet, while denying traffic from host 192.168.1.254, the following configuration would be implemented on the router:

```
R1(config)#access-list 5 permit 172.16.0.0 0.15.255.255
R1(config)#access-list 5 deny host 192.168.1.254
```

The following example illustrates how to configure an IP standard ACL to permit traffic from host 10.1.1.254, deny traffic from all other hosts on the 10.1.1.0/24 subnet, block traffic from host 172.16.1.1, and allow traffic from the 172.16.1.0/24 subnet:

```
R1(config)#access-list 10 permit host 10.1.1.254
R1(config)#access-list 10 deny 10.1.1.0 0.0.0.255
R1(config)#access-list 10 deny host 172.16.1.1
R1(config)#access-list 10 permit 172.16.1.0 0.0.0.255
```

NOTE: When configuring ACLs, the host keyword can be replaced with the 0.0.0.0 address. For example, access-list 10 permit host 10.1.1.254 can be configured as access-list 10 permit 10.1.1.254 0.0.0.0. These two configuration commands produce the same result.

One of the most common mistakes made with ACL configuration is applying the incorrect wildcard mask. A wildcard mask is simply the inverse of a subnet mask and is used to match subnets when configuring ACLs. For example, a network may have the subnet mask 255.255.255.0. In order to configure an ACL to match all hosts on this network, a wildcard mask of 0.0.0.255 must be used. As a second example, if a network has the subnet mask 255.255.255.128, a wildcard mask of 0.0.0.127 must be used to match all hosts on the subnet.

The simplest method to calculate the wildcard masks is to subtract the subnet mask from 255.255.255.255. This concept is illustrated Table 4.1 for the subnet mask 255.255.255.0:

Table 4.1. Wildcards masks 1

All-1s Subnet Mask	255	255	255	255
Minus Subnet Mask	255	255	255	0
Wildcard Mask	0	0	0	255

As a second example, to determine the wildcard mask for the 255.255.255.128 subnet, the same basic calculation would be performed. This is illustrated in Table 4.2:

Table 4.2. Wildcards masks 2

All-1s Subnet Mask	255	255	255	255
Minus Subnet Mask	255	255	255	128
Wildcard Mask	0	0	0	127

Using this as a reference, an ACL to permit the 172.16.1.0/25 and 172.16.1.128/25 subnets would be configured as follows:

```
R1(config)#access-list 50 permit 172.16.1.0 0.0.0.127
R1(config)#access-list 50 permit 172.16.1.128 0.0.0.127
```

Using the same concept, we would calculate the wildcard mask for the 70.7.7.64/26 subnet, as illustrated in Table 4.3:

Table 4.3. Wildcard masks 3

All-1s Subnet Mask	255	255	255	255
Minus Subnet Mask	255	255	255	192
Wildcard Mask	0	0	0	63

The ACL to deny this subnet, for example, would therefore be configured as follows:

```
R1(config)#access-list 25 deny 70.7.7.64 0.0.0.63
```

IP Extended ACLs

IP extended ACLs allow for greater filtering capabilities than IP standard ACLs. IP extended ACLs can be used to filter based on source address, destination address, specific protocols, ports, and flags. IP extended ACLs are configured using a range of 100 to 199 or 2000 to 2699. The syntax used to configure an IP extended ACL is:

```
access-list access-list-number [dynamic dynamic-name [timeout minutes]] {deny | per-
mit} protocol source source-wildcard destination destination-wildcard [precedence pre-
cedence] [tos tos] [time-range time-range-name] [fragments] [log [word] | log-input
[word]]
```

The syntax used to configure an IP extended ACL for ICMP is:

```
access-list access-list-number [dynamic dynamic-name [timeout minutes]] {deny | per-
mit} icmp source source-wildcard destination destination-wildcard [icmp-type [icmp-
code] | icmp-message] [precedence precedence] [tos tos] [time-range time-range-name]
[fragments] [log [word] | log-input [word]]
```

The syntax used to configure an IP extended ACL for TCP is:

access-list access-list-number [dynamic dynamic-name [timeout minutes]] {deny | permit} tcp source source-wildcard [operator [port]] destination destination-wildcard [operator [port]] [established] [precedence precedence] [tos tos] [time-range time-range-name] [fragments] [log [word] | log-input [word]]

And, finally, the syntax used to configure an IP extended ACL for UDP is:

access-list access-list-number [dynamic dynamic-name [timeout minutes]] {deny | permit} udp source source-wildcard [operator [port]] destination destination-wildcard [operator [port]] [precedence precedence] [tos tos] [time-range time-range-name] [fragments] [log [word] | log-input [word]]

As can be seen, IP extended ACLs provide far greater filtering capabilities than those provided by IP standard ACLs. These are the most commonly used ACLs when enforcing network security policy. It is therefore important that you thoroughly understand the options available with IP extended ACLs.

Unlike IP standard ACLs, extended ACLs should be placed closest to the source as possible. This is because IP extended ACLs have the capability to match based on source and destination addresses. This concept is illustrated in Figure 4.3:

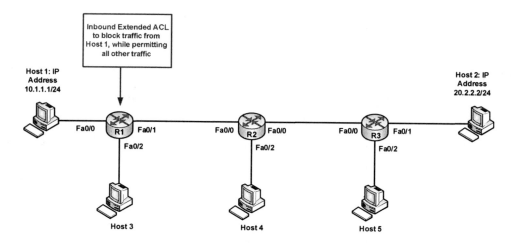

Figure 4.3. Placing Extended Access Lists

As illustrated in Figure 4.3 above, extended IP ACLs should be applied as close to the ingress point (source) as possible because they can filter based on source and destination pairs. Therefore, applying an IP extended ACL inbound on the FastEthernet0/0 interface of R1 would effectively prevent Host 1 from being able to communicate with Host 2, while still allowing the same host to communicate with Hosts 3, 4, and 5.

Although applying the same ACL inbound on the FastEthernet0/0 interface of R3 would produce the same result, it demonstrates a lack of knowledge on extended ACL application. This is because the packet is allowed to traverse R1 and R3 before being blocked, when it actually should be blocked on R1, thus preventing the unnecessary consumption of resources (e.g. memory, route lookups, etc.) on R1 and R2.

The following example illustrates how an IP extended ACL can be configured to permit OSPF traffic, deny all UDP packets that are destined to host 10.1.1.254, deny ICMP ping packets, and, finally, permit WWW traffic from the 192.168.1.0/24 subnet to any subnet:

```
R1(config)#access-list 150 permit ospf any any
R1(config)#access-list 150 deny udp any host 10.1.1.254
R1(config)#access-list 150 deny icmp any any echo
R1(config)#access-list 150 deny icmp any any echo-reply
R1(config)#access-list 150 permit tcp 192.168.1.0 0.0.0.255 any eq www
```

When using IP extended ACLs for security purposes, one of the most important functions or services provided by these ACLs is the ability to provide detailed logging information. While both IP standard and IP extended ACLs provide the administrator the capability to log against matches via the log keyword, only IP extended ACLs provide detailed logging capabilities provided by the log-input keyword.

Logging, which is described in detail in the next chapter, is globally enabled via the logging on global configuration command. Cisco IOS routers have the capability to store logs locally (i.e. on the router itself) and administrators can use the logging buffered [level] global configuration command to enable this functionality. Administrators can check local logs on the router by issuing the show logging command.

Additionally, administrators can also send logs to a remote Syslog server via the logging host [ip address] global configuration command to specify the IP address of the Syslog server, and then the logging trap [level] global configuration command to specify the level of messages to send to the Syslog server. Syslog, and other logging types, are also described in detail in the next chapter.

The log keyword used in IP standard and extended ACLs causes an informational logging message about the packet that matches the entry to be sent to the Console, buffer, or a remote Syslog server, depending on the router configuration.

For IP standard ACLs, the log message includes the ACL number, whether the packet was permitted or denied, the source address, the number of packets, and, if appropriate, the user-defined cookie or router-generated hash value, which is beyond the scope of the IINS course requirements. The message is generated for the first packet that matches and then at 5-minute intervals, including the number of packets permitted or denied in the prior 5-minute interval.

However, for IP extended ACLs, the log message includes the ACL number, whether the packet was permitted or denied, the protocol, whether it was TCP, UDP, ICMP, or a number, and, if appropriate, the source and destination addresses and port numbers, and the user-defined cookie or router-generated hash value. As is the case with IP standard ACLs, the message is generated for the first packet that matches and then at 5-minute intervals, including the number of packets permitted or denied in the prior 5-minute interval.

The log-input keyword includes the input interface and source MAC address or virtual circuit in the logging output. This can provide valuable information during an attack. For example, the following ACL is configured to provide detailed logging for all TCP and UDP packets sourced from the 172.16.1.0/24 subnet:

```
R1(config)#access-list 180 permit tcp 172.16.1.0 0.0.0.255 any log-input
R1(config)#access-list 180 permit udp 172.16.1.0 0.0.0.255 any log-input
```

In the following output, the show ip access-lists command shows some matches against this ACL, based on TCP and UDP packets from the 172.16.1.0/24 subnet:

```
R1#show ip access-lists 180
Extended IP access list 180
    10 permit tcp 172.16.1.0 0.0.0.255 any log-input (20 matches)
    20 permit udp 172.16.1.0 0.0.0.255 any log-input (39 matches)
```

Assuming that extended ACL 180 is applied inbound on an Ethernet interface, because of the log-input keyword, the MAC address of the IP address matching against this ACL, as well as the input interface, will be provided in the log, as follows:

```
R1#show logging
Syslog logging:     enabled (1 messages dropped, 0 messages rate-limited,
                    0 flushes, 0 overruns, xml disabled, filtering disabled)

No Active Message Discriminator.

No Inactive Message Discriminator.

    Console logging: disabled
    Monitor logging: level debugging, 0 messages logged, xml disabled,
```

filtering disabled
Buffer logging: level informational, 4 messages logged, xml disabled,
                   filtering disabled
Logging Exception size (4096 bytes)
Count and timestamp logging messages: disabled
Persistent logging: disabled
Trap logging: level informational, 22 message lines logged

Log Buffer (4096 bytes):

***Mar   1 01:45:30.074: %SEC-6-IPACCESSLOGP: list 180 permitted udp 172.16.1.254(0)
(FastEthernet0/0 001d.09d4.0238) -> 172.16.1.255(0), 1 packet
*Mar   1 01:45:58.405: %SEC-6-IPACCESSLOGP: list 180 permitted tcp 172.16.1.254(0)
(FastEthernet0/0 001d.09d4.0238) -> 172.16.1.1(0), 1 packet**

The subsequent example illustrates how an IP extended ACL can be used to perform the following:

- Disallow Web traffic from network 172.16.1.0/24 to network 192.168.1.0/29
- Allow traffic from network 172.16.1.0/24 to access only FTP on 192.168.1.0/29
- Allow TACACS+ traffic from host 10.1.1.254 to host 192.168.254.1
- Disallow SNMP traffic from any network to server 192.168.254.1

r1(config)#**access-list 100 remark 'Disallow WWW Traffic from 172.16.1.0/24 to 192.168.1.0/29'**
r1(config)#**access-list 100 deny tcp 172.16.1.0 0.0.0.255 eq www 192.168.1.0 0.0.0.7**
r1(config)#**access-list 100 remark 'Allow 172.16.1.0/24 to access FTP on 192.168.1.0/29'**
r1(config)#**access-list 100 permit tcp 172.16.1.0 0.0.0.255 192.168.1.0 0.0.0.7 eq 21**
r1(config)#**access-list 100 remark 'Allow TACACS+ from host 10.1.1.254 to host 192.168.254.1'**
r1(config)#**access-list 100 permit tcp host 10.1.1.254 eq tacacs host 192.168.254.1**
r1(config)#**access-list 100 remark 'Deny SNMP traffic from any to server 192.168.254.1'**
r1(config)#**access-list 100 deny udp any eq snmp host 10.1.1.254**

The following example illustrates how an IP extended ACL can be used to perform the following:

- Allow all OSPF routing protocol traffic
- Disallow all EIGRP routing protocol traffic
- Allow all RIP routing traffic
- Allow all other traffic from any source network to any destination and log it

r1(config)#**access-list 150 remark 'Allow OSPF'**
r1(config)#**access-list 150 permit ospf any any**
r1(config)#**access-list 150 remark 'Deny EIGRP'**
r1(config)#**access-list 150 deny eigrp any any**
r1(config)#**access-list 150 remark 'Allow RIP'**
r1(config)#**access-list 150 permit udp any eq rip any**
r1(config)#**access-list 150 remark 'Allow all IP traffic and log it'**
r1(config)#**access-list 150 permit ip any any log**

IP Named ACLs

IP named ACLs are simply IP standard and IP extended ACLs that are configured using administrator-defined names, instead of the reserved ranges used in Cisco IOS. Their functionality is exactly the same as that of numbered ACLs, and they are applied to both interfaces and terminal lines in the same manner. The main difference, however, is in the configuration. The syntax used to configure standard or extended IP named ACLs is:

```
ip access-list {standard | extended} {access-list-name | access-list-number}
```

If you opt to use a number for the configuration of an IP named ACL, you must adhere to the ranges reserved for both IP standard and extended ACLs. In other words, the Cisco IOS software will not allow you to configure a standard IP named ACL using the number 100, for example, as that is used by numbered IP extended ACLs. If you so attempt, you will receive an error message similar to the following:

```
R1(config)#ip access-list standard 100
%
% Invalid access list name.
```

The same is applicable when configuring IP named extended ACLs; you cannot use a number that is reserved for IP extended ACLs. To avoid such situations, it is simply recommended that if you prefer to use names for ACL configuration, configure IP named ACLs using unique names, instead of numbers; however, if you prefer to use numbers for ACL configuration, then use the IP standard and extended ACLs in your configuration instead.

The following example illustrates how to configure an IP named extended ACL named EXT-ACL and an IP named standard ACL named STA-ACL on a router:

```
R1(config)#ip access-list extended EXT-ACL
R1(config-ext-nacl)#permit tcp any any
R1(config-ext-nacl)#permit udp any any
R1(config-ext-nacl)#exit
R1(config)#ip access-list standard STA-ACL
R1(config-std-nacl)#permit host 10.1.1.1
R1(config-std-nacl)#permit host 10.1.1.2
```

Dynamic ACLs

Dynamic ACLs are also referred to as Lock-and-Key ACLs. These ACLs allow administrators to set up a dynamic access that will allow per-user access control to a particular source or destination using an authentication mechanism. The lock-and-key feature depends on the following items: Telnet, an authentication process, and an IP extended ACL.

Because dynamic ACL configuration is beyond the scope of the IINS course requirements, the configuration commands required to enable this functionality will not be discussed. However, the following example illustrates the output of the show ip access-lists command on a router if a dynamic IP ACL was configured and applied to an interface:

```
R1#show ip access-lists
Extended IP access list DYNAMIC-ACL-EXAMPLE
    10 permit tcp host 172.16.1.254 host 172.16.1.1 eq telnet (60 matches)
    20 Dynamic DACL permit ip any any
      permit ip host 172.16.1.254 any (90 matches) (time left 599)
```

Reflexive ACLs

Reflexive ACLs allow IP packets to be filtered based on upper-layer session information. These ACLs are generally used to allow outbound traffic, while limiting inbound traffic to traffic from sessions originated from the internal network(s), as illustrated in Figure 4.4:

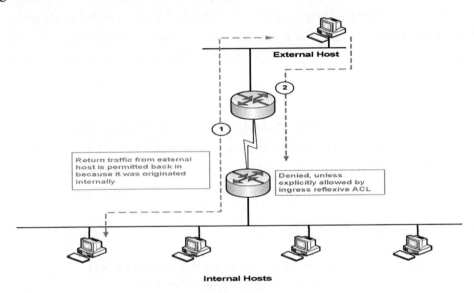

Figure 4.4. Reflexive Access Lists

In Figure 4.4 above, when reflexive ACLs are configured and implemented, the router will only permit inbound traffic from external networks, or hosts, if it was originated by internal hosts, as illustrated in step 1. If external hosts attempt to connect to internal hosts, the packets will be denied, unless explicitly permitted on the inbound ACL on the router, as illustrated in step 2.

Reflexive ACLs can only be used with IP extended ACLs. You cannot configure IP named or standard ACLs as reflexive ACLs; however, reflexive ACLs can be used in conjunction with IP named or numbered ACLs. In other words, reflexive ACLs can be applied on the same interface as other ACLs; however, they can only be defined using IP standard ACLs.

As is the case with dynamic ACLs, the configuration of reflexive ACLs is beyond the scope of the IINS course requirements. However, the following output illustrates how a configured reflexive ACL would look in the output of the show ip access-lists command in Cisco IOS routers:

```
R1#show ip access-lists
Extended IP access list INBOUND
    10 permit tcp any any reflect MY-REFLECT (93 matches)
    20 permit icmp any any reflect MY-REFLECT (24 matches)
Reflexive IP access list MY-REFLECT
    permit icmp host 1.1.1.1 host 172.16.1.254  (10 matches) (time left 297)
    permit icmp host 150.1.1.1 host 172.16.1.254  (10 matches) (time left 289)
    Extended IP access list OUTBOUND
    10 evaluate MY-REFLECT
```

Time-based ACLs

Time-based ACLs are similar to IP extended ACLs; however, they provide an additional capability that controls access based on the time. The time specified in the configuration of time-based ACLs is dependent on the router's system clock. However, the majority of time-based ACL implementations are deployed on routers that have their system clock synchronized to a Network Time Protocol (NTP) server.

NTP is a protocol for synchronizing the clocks of computer systems over IP to network time servers, which may be private or public (i.e. on the Internet). Time-based ACL configuration is beyond the scope of the IINS course requirements; however, the following output illustrates how entries in a time-based ACL would appear on a router configured with a time-based ACL:

```
R1#show ip access-lists
Extended IP access list 100
    10 permit tcp any any time-range MY-TIME (active) (67 matches)
    20 permit icmp any any time-range MY-TIME (active) (12 matches)
```

Turbo ACLs

The turbo ACL feature is designed to process ACLs more efficiently and improve router performance. This feature is available only on high-end Cisco IOS routers, such as the Cisco 7200 and 7500 series routers, which are beyond the requirements of the IINS course.

Traditional ACLs are searched sequentially, in a top-down manner, until a match is found. However, as ACLs grow larger, a significant amount of time and resources, such as memory, will be consumed as the router processes packets. This can add to a delay in the forwarding of packets and result in poor router performance.

The turbo ACL feature compiles ACLs into a group of lookup tables while maintaining the first match requirements. This leads to reduced latency because the time it takes to match packets is fixed and consistent. Turbo ACLs are enabled by using the show access-list compiled global configuration command. The following output illustrates a router with turbo ACLs configured on it:

```
R1#show access-list compiled
Compiled ACL statistics:
12 ACLs loaded, 12 compiled tables
```

ACL	State	Tables	Entries	Config	Fragment	Redundant	Memory
1	Operational	1	2	1	0	0	1Kb
2	Operational	1	3	2	0	0	1Kb
3	Operational	1	4	3	0	0	1Kb
4	Operational	1	3	2	0	0	1Kb
5	Operational	1	5	4	0	0	1Kb
9	Operational	1	3	2	0	0	1Kb
20	Operational	1	9	8	0	0	1Kb
21	Operational	1	5	4	0	0	1Kb
101	Operational	1	15	9	7	2	1Kb
102	Operational	1	13	6	6	0	1Kb
120	Operational	1	2	1	0	0	1Kb
199	Operational	1	4	3	0	0	1Kb

First level lookup tables:

Block	Use	Rows	Columns	Memory used
0	TOS/Protocol	6/16	12/16	66048
1	IP Source (MS)	10/16	12/16	66048
2	IP Source (LS)	27/32	12/16	132096
3	IP Dest (MS)	3/16	12/16	66048
4	IP Dest (LS)	9/16	12/16	66048
5	TCP/UDP Src Port	1/16	12/16	66048
6	TCP/UDP Dest Port	3/16	12/16	66048
7	TCP Flags/Fragment	3/16	12/16	66048

Receive ACLs

Receive ACLs are used to increase security on Cisco 12000 routers by protecting the gigabit route processor (GRP) of the router from unnecessary and potentially nefarious traffic. Cisco 12000 series routers are typically found in Service Provider networks and are beyond the requirements of the IINS course.

Receive ACLs can be configured using the ip receive-access-list {100-199|1300-2699} global configuration command. You are not expected to demonstrate knowledge on the Cisco 12000 series platform or receive ACLs as part of the IINS course requirements.

Infrastructure Protection ACLs

Infrastructure Protection ACLs (iACLs) are a conceptual view and require no special configuration. These ACLs are mainly used to reduce the risk of network infrastructure attacks by explicitly permitting only authorized traffic to the network infrastructure devices, such as routers, switches, and firewalls.

When configuring iACLs, it is important to ensure that when you explicitly deny traffic to infrastructure devices, you allow authorized (legitimate) transit traffic to pass through the router, to ensure uninterrupted traffic flow. Depending on the router platform, network infrastructure protection can be achieved through a variety of techniques, as follows:

- **Receive ACLs (rACLs)**

These are supported on Cisco 12000 and 7500 platforms support. These ACLs are designed to filter all traffic destined to the Route Processor (RP) and do not affect transit traffic. Authorized traffic must be explicitly permitted and the rACL must be deployed on every router. The RP performs route processing services on the router.

- **Hop-by-hop router ACLs**

Routers can also be protected by defining ACLs that permit only authorized traffic to the interfaces of the router, denying all others except for transit traffic, which must be explicitly permitted. This ACL is logically similar to a receive ACL but does affect transit traffic, and therefore can have a negative performance impact on the forwarding rate of a router, if it grows too large—although this can be mitigated by using turbo ACLs, if supported.

- **Edge filtering via infrastructure ACLs**

ACLs can be applied to the edge (i.e. the very beginning) of the network. This ACL explicitly filters traffic destined for infrastructure address space. Deployment of edge infrastructure ACLs requires that you clearly define your infrastructure space and the required and authorized protocols that access this space. The ACL is applied at ingress to your network on all externally facing connections, such as peering connections, customer connections, and so forth.

To clarify further this concept, we will use Figure 4.5 as an example:

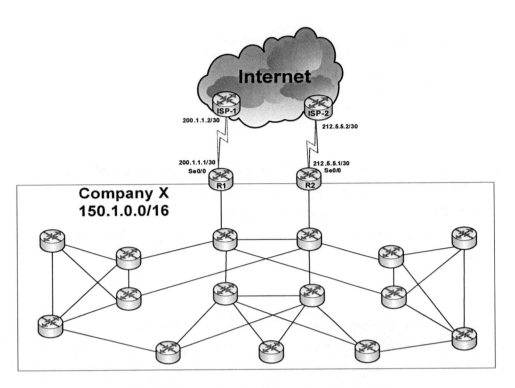

Figure 4.5. Infrastructure Protection Access Lists

In Figure 4.5 above, Company X owns the 150.1.0.0/16 public IP address space. This company has a large network, with many internal devices (i.e. routers, switches, etc.). Company X has therefore decided to dedicate the 150.1.0.0/24 and 150.1.1.0/24 to infrastructure devices; the remainder of the IP address space will be used for network hosts, which will include PCs, laptops, printers, servers, etc.

Company X is also peering to an Internet Service Provider. This peering is via the R1 and R2 routers belonging to Customer X and the ISP-1 and ISP-2 routers belonging to the ISP. The ISP routers are in turn connected to the Internet. Company X and the ISP are using BGP to advertise and exchange routing information.

Following best practices, Company X implements iACLs on its edge routers (R1 and R2). These iACLs will be used to deny external networks access to internal devices, which are all located on the 150.1.0.0/24 and 150.1.1.0/24 subnets.

The following output illustrates the configuration and application of an iACL to protect the infrastructure devices in the Company X network. Although this example depicts configuration on R1, the same concept would be applicable to R2:

```
R1(config)#ip access-list extended iACL-Inbound
R1(config-ext-nacl)#remark 'Deny Access To Internal Infrastructure Devices'
```

```
R1(config-ext-nacl)#deny ip any 150.1.0.0 0.0.1.255
R1(config-ext-nacl)#remark 'Permit All Other Traffic'
R1(config-ext-nacl)#permit ip any any
R1(config-ext-nacl)#exit
R1(config)#interface serial 0/0
R1(config-if)#ip access-group iACL-Inbound in
```

Keep in mind, however, that there is no defined standard for configuring and creating iACLs. This is generally left to the discretion of network administrators, who can utilize best practices defined in RFCs, such as RFC 2827, which is described in the following section. However, it is important to ensure that the IP address range assigned to infrastructure devices is included; otherwise, the ACL cannot be considered a true iACL.

Transit ACLs

Transit ACLs are similar to infrastructure ACLs (iACLs) in two ways:

• Transit ACLs give administrators only a conceptual view; and

• Transit ACLs do not require any special configuration.

Transit ACLs are used to enhance network security by permitting only legitimate traffic into the network. In most cases, the filtering should be performed at the network edge, allowing for the control of inbound traffic into the network and blocking any unauthorized attempts at the edge of the network. Transit ACLs can be developed using the following guidelines:

• Use of anti-spoofing protection based on the following RFCs:
    1. RFC 1918—This RFC defines private IP address space that is not routable on the Internet.
    2. RFC 2827—This RFC provides anti-spoofing guidelines for network ingress filtering.
    3. RFC 3330—This RFC provides special addresses that might require filtering, e.g. 127.0.0.0/8.

• Explicitly permit return traffic from all connections originating from the internal network.

• Explicitly permit externally sourced traffic that is originating from the external network.

• Explicitly use a deny statement at the end of the ACL.

The following output illustrates how one might configure a transit ACL:

```
R1(config)#ip access-list extended TRANSIT-ACL
R1(config-ext-nacl)#remark 'Permit BGP Peer Session'
R1(config-ext-nacl)#permit tcp host 200.1.1.2 host 200.1.1.1 eq bgp
R1(config-ext-nacl)#permit tcp host 200.1.1.2 eq bgp host 200.1.1.1
R1(config-ext-nacl)#remark 'Permit Return Traffic'
R1(config-ext-nacl)#permit icmp any any echo-reply
```

```
R1(config-ext-nacl)#permit icmp any any unreachable
R1(config-ext-nacl)#permit icmp any any time-exceeded
R1(config-ext-nacl)#remark 'Permit Traffic to Our Web Server'
R1(config-ext-nacl)#permit tcp any host 150.1.100.254 eq 80
R1(config-ext-nacl)#remark 'Deny All Other Traffic'
R1(config-ext-nacl)#deny ip any any log
```

As with the iACL example, keep in mind that this is simply an example because there is no single defined standard for configuring transit ACLs. Ensure that you are familiar with the three RFCs mentioned in this section. While going into their specific details is beyond the scope of the IINS course requirements, you should be able to identify RFCs based on their names and usage.

Classification ACLs

Classification ACLs are also referred to as characterization ACLs and are initially composed with all permit statements for various protocols, ports, and other characteristics that the administrator would like to identify. These ACLs are used to classify and categorize denial-of-service (DoS) attacks by identifying the type of traffic and its source.

When configuring classification ACLs, it is good practice to enable logging for the traffic you are trying to classify. In addition to this, it is also important to remember to enable the permit ip any any statement at the end of all classification ACLs so that all other traffic will not be blocked. The following example illustrates the configuration of a classification ACL:

```
R1(config)#show ip access-list extended CLASSIFICATION-ACL
R1(config-ext-nacl)#permit icmp any any echo log-input
R1(config-ext-nacl)#permit tcp any any syn log-input
R1(config-ext-nacl)#permit tcp any any fragment log-input
R1(config-ext-nacl)#permit udp any any fragment log-input
R1(config-ext-nacl)#permit ip any any fragment log-input
R1(config-ext-nacl)#permit ip any any
```

The administrator can then use the show ip access-lists command repeatedly to view the ACL counters and to determine the type of attack that is occurring. The administrator could then view the router logs, via the show logging command, to identify the source(s) of the attack and then create an applicable filter to block the source(s), while allowing legitimate traffic.

For example, an increasing amount of TCP SYN packets may be an indication of a SYN flood attack, while an increasing number of ICMP echo packets may indicate a smurf attack:

```
R1#show ip access-lists CLASSIFICATION-ACL
Extended IP access list CLASSIFICATION-ACL
    10 permit icmp any any echo log-input (12 matches)
```

20 permit tcp any any syn log-input (11 matches)
30 permit tcp any any log-input fragments
40 permit udp any any log-input fragments
50 permit ip any any log-input fragments
60 permit ip any any (401 matches)

Using this information, the administrator can then configure restrictive ACLs to block the source host or subnet. This ACL would include both permit and deny statements and should never end with the permit ip any any statement used in classification ACLs.

ACL Processing and Packet Flow Rules

When a packet enters a router, the destination address of the packet is checked against the entries in the routing table to identify the egress interface. The packet is also checked against any configured ACLs assigned to the interface and will either be permitted or denied accordingly. ACLs can be applied to inbound or outbound directions on router interfaces. Figure 4.6 illustrates the inbound and outbound directions as they apply to LAN and WAN interfaces:

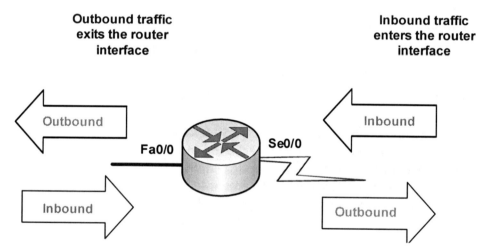

Figure 4.6. Access List Directions

Inbound ACL Processing

When an inbound ACL is applied to an interface, the router checks the received packets against the statements in the ACL, looking for a match. If a match is found, and the ACL action is to permit, then the router continues to process the packet. However, if a match is found, and the action is to deny, the router discards the packet and typically (unless otherwise configured) sends an ICMP Destination Unreachable message, typically using the Administratively Prohibited code, back to the source address. This is illustrated in Figure 4.7 for a simple ping generated from a Windows-based client to a subnet blocked by an Access Control List:

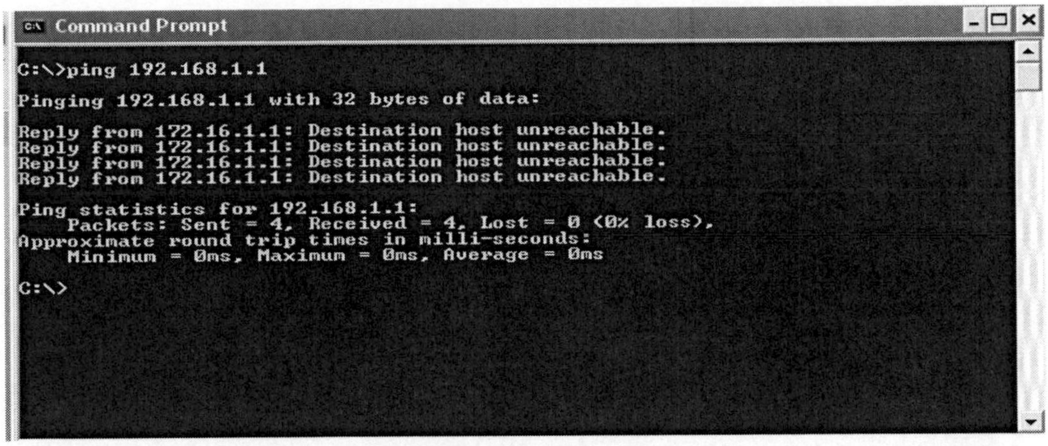

Figure 4.7. ICMP Unreachable

In Figure 4.7 provided above, the Windows-based client is receiving an ICMP Destination Unreachable message from 172.16.1.1. This IP address is the address of the device (router) that has been configured with an ACL preventing traffic from being sent to the 192.168.1.1 host. The configuration of the router is as follows:

R1#**show running-config interface fastethernet 0/0**
Building configuration...

Current configuration : 119 bytes
!
interface FastEthernet0/0
 ip address 172.16.1.1 255.255.255.0
 ip access-group 100 in
 duplex auto
 speed auto
end

R1#**show ip access-lists 100**
Extended IP access list 100
    10 deny ip any host 192.168.1.1 (12 matches)
    20 permit ip any any (186 matches)

In the event that a match is not found, the router applies the default deny all statement at the end of ACLs and discards the packet(s), sending the source an ICMP Destination Unreachable message. ICMP is a core component of Cisco CCNA certification, and ICMP messages are covered in detail in the CCNA study guide.

Inbound ACL Packet Flow Processing in Cisco IOS routers

Figure 4.8 illustrates the processing of an inbound packet:

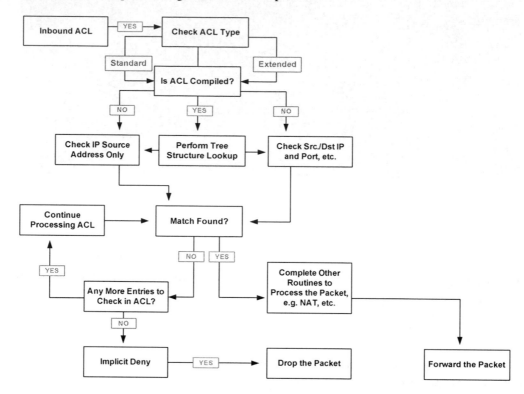

Figure 4.8. Inbound Packet Processing

Outbound ACL Processing

When an outbound ACL is applied to an interface, the router first performs a route lookup for the destination address in the routing table to determine the egress interface via which the packet should be forwarded. If a valid path is found in the routing table and a match is found for the ACL, and the action of the ACL is to permit, then the router continues to process the packet. But if the ACL action is to deny the packet, then the packet is discarded by the router and the router sends an ICMP Destination Unreachable message back to the source host(s).

However, if a match is not found, the implied deny all statement at the end of the ACL is applied and the router discards the packet, sending the source an ICMP Destination Unreachable message. Finally, if a valid path to the intended destination is not found in the routing table, then the router simply discards the packet.

Outbound ACL Packet Flow Processing in Cisco IOS routers

Figure 4.9 illustrates the processing of an outbound packet:

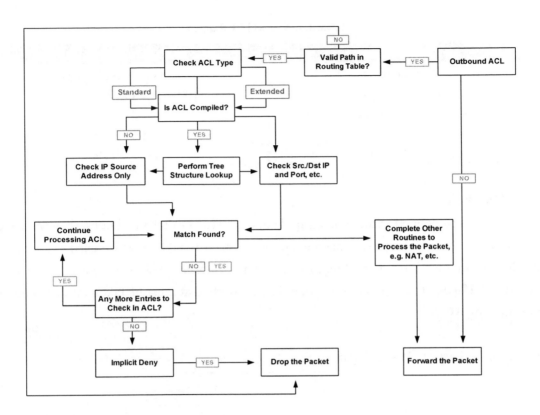

Figure 4.9. Outbound Packet Processing

Implementing ACLs

There are two basic steps required in the implementation of ACLs:

1. Create the ACL
2. Apply the ACL

Create the ACL

To create an ACL in Cisco IOS software, specify the protocol to be filtered by assigning a unique number or name to the ACL and by defining the matching criteria. Each individual rule that is part of an ACL is referred to as an access control entry (ACE). A single ACL can have multiple ACEs, and a group of ACEs forms an ACL.

Each ACL must be uniquely identified by using either a name or a number. Because it is possible to configure multiple ACLs per device, the names or numbers assigned to ACLs allows the device to distinguish one ACL from another. In addition to this, assigning each ACL a unique name or number allows for the ACEs to be bound together. Table 4.4 illustrates the ACL numbers that you should be familiar with:

Table 4.4. Access List Ranges

Protocol	ACL Number Range
IP standard	1 – 99 and 1300 – 1999
IP extended	100 – 199 and 200 – 2699
Protocol type-code	200 – 299
MAC ACL	700 – 799
Extended MAC ACL	1100 – 1199

Apply the ACL

While ACLs can be defined without being applied to interfaces or terminal lines, they will have no effect on the router until they are applied to an interface, terminal line, or are used in conjunction with other techniques, such as routing protocol update filtering. Although ACLs can be applied to various interfaces, etc., there are some functional aspects that must be taken into consideration before applying ACLs.

This concept is illustrated using Figure 4.10:

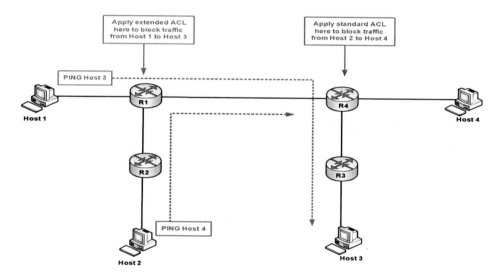

Figure 4.10. Access List Application

Standard ACLs should always be applied as close to the destination as possible. This is because these ACLs have the capability to filter based only on the source address. Using the diagram illustrated above as a reference, a standard ACL to block traffic from Host 2 destined to Host 4 would be applied on R4, because this is the closest router to the destination. Applying the standard ACL on R1 or R2, for example, would block Host 2 entirely. In other words, Host 2 not only would be unable to communicate with Host 4, but also it would be unable to communicate with Host 1, which is undesirable in this case.

Extended ACLs, on the other hand, should be applied as close to the source (ingress point) as possible. Extended ACLs filter based on source and destination IP address and ports and provide more granular filtering than that provided by standard ACLs. Referencing the diagram illustrated above, to block traffic (in this case, ICMP echo packets) from Host 1 to Host 3, the extended ACL would be applied on R1. Although the extended ACL could be implemented on R3, and still provide the same result, it causes unnecessary resource consumption on other routers in the path (i.e. R4), which would still have to process the packet(s).

General Guidelines for Implementing ACLs

The following section provides some general guidelines for implementing ACLs in Cisco IOS routers. Keep in mind that these are not standards but, rather, general guidelines that you should be familiar with as a network security administrator. These guidelines are as follows:

- ACLs can be assigned to multiple interfaces on a device. This refers to either different ACLs or even the same ACL.

- Only one ACL is allowed per protocol per interface per direction; you can have one inbound and one outbound ACL applied using this rule.

- ACLs are processed from the top down; therefore, take care when planning ACEs in ACLs. Entries that are more specific should appear first.

- When creating an ACL, the router appends each ACE to the end of the ACL; however, in newer versions of IOS, beginning with 12.2, administrators have the ability to insert ACEs between current entries in the ACL.

- There is an implicit deny for all traffic that is not explicitly permitted. You will never see any matches or log entries against this implicit deny in an ACL. If an ACL does not have at least one permit statement, all traffic will be blocked.

- Always create an ACL before applying it to an interface. Additionally, when editing an ACL, always remove it from the interface, make the desired modifications, and then reapply it to the interface; otherwise, you may block legitimate traffic or even yourself from the router. This is a very important point to remember.

- Outbound ACLs applied to router interfaces only check for traffic traversing the router; they do not and will not filter traffic that is originated by the router itself.

Understanding the concepts described in this section will greatly assist you in understanding the fundamentals of ACL implementation as well as identifying caveats pertaining to ACLs.

Using ACLs to Mitigate Network Layer Attacks

In this section, we are going to be learning about how to use and apply ACLs to mitigate against Layer 3 (Network Layer) attacks. This section will be broken up into the following sections:

- Established ACLs
- ACLs and Fragmented Packets
- Using ACLs to Characterize Smurf Attacks
- Using ACLs to Characterize SYN Attacks
- Using ACLs to Prevent IP Address Spoofing Attacks
- Unicast Reverse Path Forwarding with ACLs

Established ACLs

The established keyword, used in extended TCP ACLs, is used to validate that a packet belongs to an existing connection from an ongoing TCP session initiated earlier and checks whether the TCP packet has either the ACK or RST bit set. The use of the established keyword in an extended TCP ACL is to allow only internal hosts to initiate a TCP session to an external (outbound) location, while preventing any TCP sessions originated from external networks into the internal network.

In a TCP segment, there are six flag bits, two of which are the ACK (acknowledgement) and the RST (reset). If any one of these two bits is set, a match will be made on an ACL that contains the established keyword. To clarify this concept, Figure 4.11 illustrates the three-way TCP handshake between a client and a server:

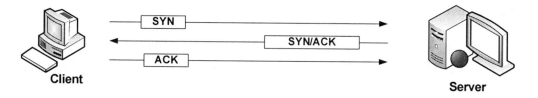

Figure 4.11. Three-Way Handshake

As illustrated in Figure 4.11, during the three-way TCP handshake, the client requests a new connection by sending a SYN packet to a server. The server sends a SYN/ACK packet back to the client and places the connection request in a queue. Finally, the client acknowledges the packet received from the server with an ACK packet.

Now let's look at the same connection being made through a router with an ACL containing the established keyword:

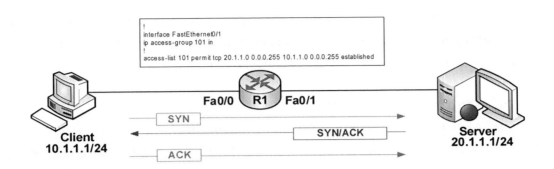

Figure 4.12. Three-Way Handshake Established

In Figure 4.12 above, the client and the server are connected to the FastEthernet0/0 and FastEthernet0/1 interfaces of R1, respectively. The FastEthernet0/1 interface of R1 has been configured with an inbound ACL, which is ACL 101. This ACL has a single statement that reads: access-list 101 permit tcp 20.1.1.0 0.0.0.255 10.1.1.0 0.0.0.255 established.

The client initiates a TCP connection to the server at address 20.1.1.1/24 by sending a SYN packet. The server receives the SYN packet from the client and responds with a SYN/ACK packet. R1 receives this packet from the server on its FastEthernet0/1 interface and looks at the ACL configured and applied on this interface. Because the established keyword is used in the ACL, R1 checks to ensure only packets with either the TCP ACK or RST bit set are allowed.

Given that the packet from the server is a SYN/ACK packet, the condition is satisfied and the packet is permitted. The client then responds to the server's SYN/ACK packet by sending out its own ACK packet, and the TCP session between the client and the server is established. Figure 4.13 illustrates the same basic condition, except for the fact that this time it is the server initiating the TCP connection to the client:

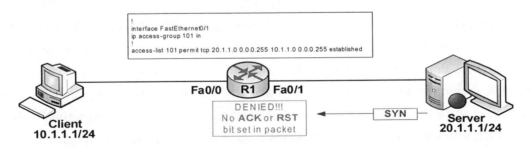

Figure 4.13. Packet Without ACK or RSK Bit Denied

Referencing Figure 4.13 illustrated above, the FastEthernet0/1 interface of R1 is still configured with the ACL statement access-list 101 permit tcp 20.1.1.0 0.0.0.255 10.1.1.0 0.0.0.255 established. Therefore, when the server attempts to establish a connection to the client, it starts off by sending a TCP SYN packet. The router receives this packet and notices that the established keyword is used in the ACL configuration. The router then checks the packet for either the ACK or RST bit and does not see it enabled. The packet is then simply denied.

ACLs and Fragmented Packets

Before we delve into the specifics of how ACLs can be used to filter fragmented packets, it is important to understand what fragmentation means as far as Internet Protocol is concerned. IP implements datagram (packet) fragmentation so that packets may be formed that can pass through a link with a smaller Maximum Transmission Unit (MTU) than the original datagram size. The MTU of a layer of a communications protocol is the size (in bytes) of the largest protocol data unit that it can pass onwards. For example, consider the following scenario:

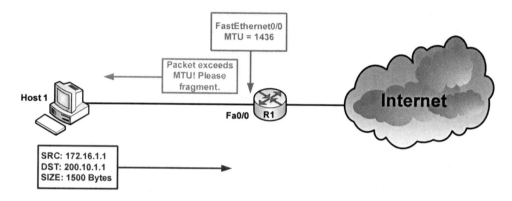

Figure 4.14. Packet Fragmentation

In Figure 4.14 illustrated above, Host 1 is connected to R1, which is connected to the Internet. Host 1 attempts to send a packet to 200.10.1.1 and the packet has a size of 1800 bytes. The MTU configured on the FastEthernet0/0 interface of R1 is 1436 bytes. This means that R1 is only capable of sending and receiving packets with a byte size less than or equal to 1436 bytes.

Because the packet received from Host 1 is 1500 bytes in size, the R1 is unable to accept the entire packet due to an MTU limitation on its FastEthernet0/0 interface. Therefore, when the packet reaches R1, it will discard the packet and send Host 1 an ICMP message stating the packet must be fragmented, i.e. broken up into smaller pieces that will be within the MTU range, in order for R1 to receive and forward the packet to its intended destination. When Host 1 receives this ICMP message from R1, it fragments the packet and sends it again. R1 then accepts the fragmented packets and forwards them to their intended destination, as illustrated in Figure 4.15:

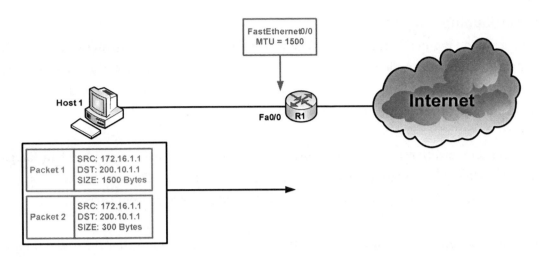

Figure 4.15. Fragmented Packet Forwarded

Once Host 1 is aware of the MTU restrictions on R1, it will not send packets that exceed the MTU value of 1500 bytes (i.e. further fragments), which are commonly referred to as non-initial fragments. While fragmentation has its advantages, attackers can also take advantage of this feature to breach networks.

RFC 1858 covers security considerations for IP fragment filtering and highlights two attacks on hosts that involve IP fragments of TCP packets. These two attacks are:

- The Tiny Fragment Attack; and
- The Overlapping Fragment Attack.

The Tiny Fragment Attack

A Tiny Fragment Attack is a class of attack that takes advantage of the fact that it is possible to impose an unusually small fragment size on outgoing packets. If the fragment size is made small enough to force some of a TCP packet's TCP header fields into the second fragment, filter rules that specify patterns for those fields will not match. If the filtering implementation does not enforce a minimum fragment size, a disallowed packet might be passed because it didn't hit a match in the filter. In essence, every Internet device must be able to forward a datagram of 68 octets without further fragmentation. This is because an Internet header may be up to 60 octets, and the minimum fragment is 8 octets.

RFC 1858 provides two techniques that can be used to prevent the Tiny Fragment Attack: the direct method and the indirect method. In the direct method, initial fragments that are smaller than a minimum length are discarded. The indirect method involves discarding the second fragment of a fragment set, if it starts 8 bytes into the original IP datagram or packet.

The Overlapping Fragment Attack

An Overlapping Fragment Attack is also called IP Fragmentation Attack. In an Overlapping Fragment Attack, the re-assembled packet starts in the middle of another packet. As the OS receives these invalid packets, it allocates memory to hold them. This eventually uses all the memory resources and causes the machine to reboot or hang.

There is no standard that can be used to prevent these attacks. However, vendors can safeguard against such attacks by updating the router's filtering capabilities. In Cisco IOS software, the fragments keyword can be used in conjunction with extended ACLs to prevent such attacks.

Non-initial fragments, which are IP packets that have been fragmented after the initial fragments (as explained earlier) that match the Layer 3 statements, irrespective of the Layer 4 information in an ACL, are affected by the permit or deny statement of the matched entry that includes the fragments keyword. In addition to this, the use of the fragments keyword can force ACLs to either deny or permit non-initial fragments with greater flexibility. Filtering fragments adds an additional layer of protection against a DoS attack, such as the Tiny Fragment Attack, which uses only non-initial fragments.

Going into greater detail on ACL processing of fragments is beyond the scope of the IINS course requirements. In fact, this is a topic that you will most likely run into at the Professional level (e.g. CCNP) and most definitely at the Expert level (e.g. CCIE Security) in Cisco certification programs. However, the following example illustrates how the fragments keyword can be used in an IP extended ACL to deny any non-initial fragment access to the network, while non-fragmented packets or initial fragments pass to the next lines of the ACL unaffected by the deny fragment statements used in the ACL:

```
R1(config)#int s0/0
R1(config-if)#description 'Connected to ISP'
R1(config-if)#ip address 150.1.1.1 255.255.255.252
R1(config-if)#no shutdown
R1(config-if)#exit
R1(config)#int f0/0
R1(config-if)#description 'Connected to LAN with Web Server'
R1(config-if)#ip address 200.1.1.1 255.255.255.0
R1(config-if)#exit
R1(config)#access-list 100 deny ip any host 200.1.1.254 fragments
R1(config)#access-list 100 permit tcp any host 200.1.1.254 eq 80
R1(config)#access-list 100 deny ip any 200.1.1.0 0.0.0.255 fragments
R1(config)#access-list 100 permit ip any 200.1.1.0 0.0.0.255
R1(config)#int s0/0
R1(config-if)#ip access-group 100 in
```

In the example above, non-initial fragments to the web server with the IP address 200.1.1.254 are denied; however, HTTP connections to this server are permitted. In addition to this, non-initial fragments to the 200.1.1.0/24 subnet are denied, while all other IP packets are permitted.

It is important to keep in mind that allowing the non-initial fragments of an IP datagram through is acceptable because the host receiving the fragments is not able to reassemble the original IP datagram without the initial fragment.

Using ACLs to Characterize Smurf Attacks

IP extended ACLs can be used to characterize smurf (ICMP flood) attacks. Smurf attacks, which were described in detail in Chapter 1, have two victims: the target and the reflector, or amplifier. Because ICMP echo and echo-reply packets are typically used as a troubleshooting tool, denying them could hinder network troubleshooting efforts. Therefore, network administrators can use classification ACLs to identify the sources of smurf attacks before creating and applying ACLs to restrict these sources. A typical classification ACL used to identify the source of smurf attacks would be configured as follows:

```
R1(config)#show ip access-list extended CLASSIFY-SMURF
R1(config-ext-nacl)#permit icmp any any echo log-input
R1(config-ext-nacl)#permit icmp any any echo-reply log-input
R1(config-ext-nacl)#permit ip any any
```

By using the show ip access-lists and the show logging commands, administrators can quickly identify the source IP address, and MAC address if the packets are received from a LAN interface, of large numbers of ICMP echo and echo-reply packets. There are several ways an administrator can differentiate between a simple ping flood and a smurf attack.

First, smurf packets are sent to a directed broadcast address, such as 172.16.1.255 for the 172.16.1.0/24 subnet, rather than to a Unicast address, such as 172.16.1.2 for the 172.16.1.0/24 subnet, whereas ordinary ping floods are always sent to a Unicast address.

When the log-input keyword is used in a classification ACL, an administrator can use the captured log information (show logging) to determine the type of attack, as illustrated in the following output:

```
R1#show logging
Syslog logging:    enabled (1 messages dropped, 0 messages rate-limited,
                   0 flushes, 0 overruns, xml disabled, filtering disabled)

No Active Message Discriminator.
```

No Inactive Message Discriminator.

    Console logging: disabled
    Monitor logging: level debugging, 0 messages logged, xml disabled,
            filtering disabled
    Buffer logging: level informational, 5 messages logged, xml disabled,
            filtering disabled
    Logging Exception size (4096 bytes)
    Count and timestamp logging messages: disabled
    Persistent logging: disabled
    Trap logging: level informational, 32 message lines logged

Log Buffer (4096 bytes):

*Mar 1 21:10:10.700: %LINEPROTO-5-UPDOWN: Line protocol on Interface Loopback1, changed state to up
*Mar 1 21:10:16.702: %SYS-5-CONFIG_I: Configured from console by console
*Mar 1 21:10:26.999: %SEC-6-IPACCESSLOGDP: list CLASSIFY-SMURF permitted icmp 172.16.1.254 (FastEthernet0/0 001d.09d4.0238) -> 200.1.1.1 (8/0), 1 packet
*Mar 1 21:10:31.827: %SEC-6-IPACCESSLOGDP: list CLASSIFY-SMURF permitted icmp 172.16.1.254 (FastEthernet0/0 001d.09d4.0238) -> 200.1.1.255 (8/0), 1 packet

In the output illustrated above, the router log shows that two ICMP packets matched the CLASSIFY-SMURF ACL. These packets were sourced from a host with the IP address 172.16.1.254, and the MAC address 001d.09d4.0238. Additionally, this packet was received by the router on the FastEthernet0/0 interface.

Secondly, when experiencing a smurf reflector attack, there are typically a larger number of broadcast packets shown in the output of the show interfaces command. Because simple ping floods target Unicast addresses, the counter would not increase, as no broadcast packets would be sent. A sample output of the show interfaces command is illustrated below. The fields you should be concerned with are provided in bold font:

```
R1#show interfaces fastethernet 0/0
FastEthernet0/0 is up, line protocol is up
  Hardware is AmdFE, address is 0013.1986.0a20 (bia 0013.1986.0a20)
  Description: 'Connected to LAN'
  Internet address is 172.16.1.1/24
  MTU 1500 bytes, BW 100000 Kbit/sec, DLY 100 usec,
    reliability 255/255, txload 1/255, rxload 1/255
  Encapsulation ARPA, loopback not set
  Keepalive set (10 sec)
  Full-duplex, 100Mb/s, 100BaseTX/FX
  ARP type: ARPA, ARP Timeout 04:00:00
```

```
Last input 00:02:42, output 00:00:00, output hang never
Last clearing of "show interface" counters never
Input queue: 0/75/0/0 (size/max/drops/flushes); Total output drops: 0
Queueing strategy: fifo
Output queue: 0/40 (size/max)
5 minute input rate 0 bits/sec, 0 packets/sec
5 minute output rate 0 bits/sec, 0 packets/sec
   318 packets input, 46258 bytes
   Received 185 broadcasts, 0 runts, 0 giants, 0 throttles
   0 input errors, 0 CRC, 0 frame, 0 overrun, 0 ignored
   0 watchdog
   0 input packets with dribble condition detected
   8687 packets output, 879144 bytes, 0 underruns
   0 output errors, 0 collisions, 0 interface resets
   0 unknown protocol drops
   0 babbles, 0 late collision, 0 deferred
   0 lost carrier, 0 no carrier
   0 output buffer failures, 0 output buffers swapped out
```

In addition, the show ip traffic command can also be used to view IP packet statistics. A sample output of the information printed by this command is provided below. The field that you should be looking at to verify whether this is a smurf attack is in bold font:

```
R1#show ip traffic
IP statistics:
  Rcvd:     316 total, 150 local destination
            0 format errors, 0 checksum errors, 0 bad hop count
            0 unknown protocol, 12 not a gateway
            0 security failures, 0 bad options, 0 with options
  Opts:     0 end, 0 nop, 0 basic security, 0 loose source route
            0 timestamp, 0 extended security, 0 record route
            0 stream ID, 0 strict source route, 0 alert, 0 cipso, 0 ump
            0 other
  Frags:    0 reassembled, 0 timeouts, 0 couldn't reassemble
            0 fragmented, 0 fragments, 0 couldn't fragment
  Bcast: 151 received, 24 sent
  Mcast:    0 received, 0 sent
  Sent:     75 generated, 0 forwarded
  Drop:     0 encapsulation failed, 0 unresolved, 0 no adjacency
            107 no route, 0 unicast RPF, 0 forced drop
            0 options denied
  Drop:     0 packets with source IP address zero
  Drop:     0 packets with internal loop back IP address
            36 physical broadcast
-----[Truncated Output]-----
```

Once administrators have identified the source(s) of smurf attacks, they can configure an ACL to deny ICMP echo packets from the source(s). In addition to this, administrators can also use the no ip directed-broadcast command on Cisco router interfaces to prevent Cisco routers from being reflectors in such attacks.

The following output provides a sample configuration that would be applied on a router to prevent ICMP echo packets from the 200.1.1.0/24 subnet, while allowing all IP packets from any other subnet. In addition, the example illustrates how to prevent the router from being used as a reflector in a smurf attack:

```
R1(config)#ip access-list extended NO-ICMP-ECHO-FROM-NET-200
R1(config-ext-nacl)#deny icmp 200.1.1.0 0.0.0.255 any echo
R1(config-ext-nacl)#permit ip any any
R1(config-ext-nacl)#exit
R1(config)#int s0/0
R1(config-if)#ip access-group NO-ICMP-ECHO-FROM-NET-200
R1(config-if)#no ip directed-broadcast
```

Using ACLs to Characterize SYN Attacks

TCP SYN flood attacks occur during the three-way handshake that is used to establish a TCP connection. During a TCP SYN flood, the attacker sends an abundance of TCP SYN packets to the victim, obliging it both to open many TCP connections and to respond to them. However, the attacker does not execute the third step of the three-way handshake that follows, rendering the victim unable to accept any new incoming connections, because its queue is full of half-open TCP connections, as illustrated in Figure 4.16:

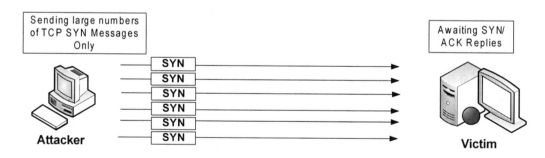

Figure 4.16. TCP SYN Flood

In order for a SYN flood attack to be successful, the attacker must fill and overflow the TCP server's memory so that the oldest received SYN entries are flushed, as well as fill the TCP queue faster than the typical time it takes to send SYN + ACK packets to and receive the corresponding ACK packet from legitimate hosts. In a manner similar to smurf attacks, classification ACLs can be used to characterize a TCP SYN attack, and the administrator can then use the captured information to create and apply a restrictive ACL for the source(s) of these attacks.

The following example illustrates a classification ACL for TCP SYN floods:

```
R1(config)#ip access-list extended TCP-CLASSIFY
R1(config-ext-nacl)#permit tcp any any syn log-input
R1(config-ext-nacl)#permit ip any any
```

Once the source(s) of high TCP SYN packets has been identified by looking at matches against the ACL (by issuing the show ip access-lists command repeatedly), as well as the output contained in the router log (by issuing the show logging command), administrators can configure a restrictive ACL to filter out TCP packets from the source(s), while allowing all other traffic through. For example, to prevent TCP SYN attacks from the 172.16.1.0/24 subnet, while allowing all other TCP traffic from that subnet, as well as all other IP subnets, the following ACL would be configured:

```
R1(config)#ip access-list extended NO-SYN-FROM-172-16-1-0-SUBNET
R1(config-ext-nacl)#permit tcp 172.16.1.0 0.0.0.255 any established
R1(config-ext-nacl)#permit tcp any any
R1(config-ext-nacl)#exit
R1(config)#int s0/0
R1(config-if)#ip access-group NO-SYN-FROM-172-16-1-0-SUBNET in
```

NOTE: Remember, the use of the established keyword permits TCP packets only if the ACK or RST bit is set, which effectively means that it allows internal-to-external TCP session initiation but not external-to-internal TCP session initiation.

In addition to using ACLs to classify and then protect against SYN flood attacks, administrators can also use the TCP Intercept feature available in Cisco IOS routers. Although advanced configuration pertaining to the TCP Intercept feature is beyond the scope of the IINS course requirements, you should be aware of how this feature works and should be familiar with the basic commands required to configure TCP Intercept in Cisco IOS routers.

The TCP Intercept feature works by intercepting and validating all incoming TCP connection requests flowing between a TCP client and a server. TCP Intercept operates in two modes, which are watch mode and intercept mode.

In watch mode, the router allows all connection requests to pass through it while passively watching the connection(s) being established. If a connection fails to establish within a configurable threshold, Cisco IOS software intervenes and terminates the connection attempt.

In intercept mode, Cisco IOS software actively intercepts all incoming connection SYN requests and responds on behalf of the server with a SYN/ACK, while waiting for an ACK from the server. When an ACK is received from the server, the original SYN packet is sent to the server and the software performs a three-way handshake with the server. When this is complete, the two half-sessions are joined and the actual client and server have an established TCP session. This concept is illustrated in Figure 4.17:

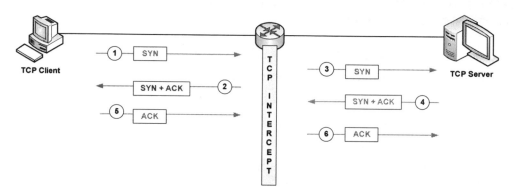

Figure 4.17. Intercept Mode

In Figure 4.17 illustrated above, the TCP Intercept feature is enabled for intercept mode on the router. In step 1, the TCP client initiates a connection to the TCP server. The TCP Intercept feature intercepts this connection and the router sends a proxy SYN/ACK to the TCP client, as illustrated in step 2.

In the meantime, the router sends a SYN packet to the TCP server, as illustrated in step 3, and the TCP server responds to the router with a SYN/ACK packet, accepting the connection, as illustrated in step 4.

If the client returns a valid ACK to complete the three-way TCP handshake, as illustrated in step 5, the TCP Intercept feature passes this to the TCP server and joins the two half-open connections, effectively allowing the establishment of a session between the client and server.

To enable basic TCP intercept, three simple steps must be taken. The first step is defining an IP extended ACL that matches the TCP traffic you want the Cisco IOS software to intercept. The second step is to configure TCP Intercept to watch the traffic specified in the ACL via the ip tcp intercept list [acl] global configuration command. And, finally, the third step is to specify the mode in which you want TCP Intercept to work. This last step is performed by using the ip tcp intercept mode [intercept|watch] global configuration command.

The following example illustrates how to enable TCP Intercept to intercept all incoming TCP connection requests from any IP subnet to a web server with the IP address 150.1.1.254:

R1(config)#**access-list 100 permit tcp any host 150.1.1.254**
R1(config)#**ip tcp intercept list 100**
R1(config)#**ip tcp intercept mode intercept**

Using ACLs to Prevent IP Address Spoofing Attacks

IP address spoofing attacks are those where the attacker fakes the source IP address of packets to gain access to a network and access resources in the same manner as legitimate network hosts and users. Anti-spoofing measures should be implemented at every point in the network where practical but are usually easiest to implement at the network edge.

Anti-spoofing techniques are described in detail in RFC 2827 – Network Ingress Filtering: Defeating Denial of Service Attacks Which Employ IP Source Address Spoofing. This RFC states that no packet should be sent out to the Internet with a source address other than the valid addresses that have been allocated to your network. In summary, anti-spoofing is used to:

1. Deny incoming packets if the source address is allocated to your network; and
2. Deny outgoing packets if the source address is not allocated to your network.

To clarify further this point, we will use Figure 4.18 as an example:

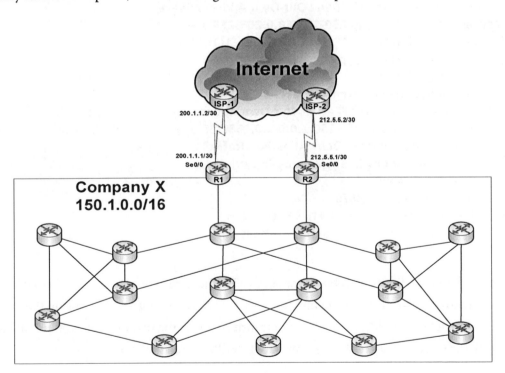

Figure 4.18. Anti-Spoofing

In Figure 4.18 illustrated above, Company X owns the 150.1.0.0/16 public IP address space. Company X is also peering to an Internet Service Provider. This peering is via the R1 and R2 routers belonging to Customer X and the ISP-1 and ISP-2 routers belonging to the ISP. The ISP routers are in turn connected to the Internet. Company X and the ISP are using BGP as the protocol of choice to advertise and exchange routing information.

To adhere to the best practices recommended in RFC 2827, Company X must configure two ACLs, one inbound and the other outbound, which will then be applied to the Serial0/0 interfaces of R1 and R2. The inbound ACL will be configured to prevent any and all packets within the 150.1.0.0/16 subnet from coming into the network. This is because this range has been allocated to Company X. Therefore, there is no reason that packets outside of their network should have an IP address within this range. The inbound ACL will then permit other traffic.

The outbound ACL that will be applied to the Serial0/0 interfaces of R1 and R2 will permit only traffic with an IP address in the 150.1.0.0/16 subnet. This is because there is no valid reason a host or device that resides in the Company X network should use an IP address that is not within this range. As an example, the configuration on the edge routers would be as follows:

```
R1(config)#ip access-list extended ANTI-SPOOF-IN
R1(config-ext-nacl)#remark "Deny Our Own Address Space"
R1(config-ext-nacl)#deny ip 150.1.0.0 0.0.255.255 any
R1(config-ext-nacl)#remark "Permit All Other Traffic"
R1(config-ext-nacl)#permit ip any any
R1(config-ext-nacl)#exit
R1(config)#ip access-list extended ANTI-SPOOF-OUT
R1(config-ext-nacl)#remark "Permit Our Own Address Space"
R1(config-ext-nacl)#permit ip 150.1.0.0 0.0.255.255 any
R1(config-ext-nacl)#remark "Deny All Other Traffic"
R1(config-ext-nacl)#deny ip any any log-input
R1(config-ext-nacl)#exit
R1(config)#interface serial0/0
R1(config-if)#ip access-group ANTI-SPOOF-IN in
R1(config-if)#ip access-group ANTI-SPOOF-OUT out
```

While the configuration illustrated above is applied to R1, the same would be applicable to R2. It is important to remember that there is no defined standard for Network Ingress Filtering, in the same way that there are no defined standards for iACLs or transit ACLs. In the real world, it is common practice to include all three techniques within the same ACL, as illustrated in the following example:

```
R1(config)#ip access-list extended PERIMETER-ACL-IN
R1(config-ext-nacl)#remark 'Deny RFC 1918 Addresses'
```

```
R1(config-ext-nacl)#deny ip 10.0.0.0 0.255.255.255 any
R1(config-ext-nacl)#deny ip 172.16.0.0 0.15.255.255 any
R1(config-ext-nacl)#deny ip 192.168.0.0 0.0.255.255 any
R1(config-ext-nacl)#remark 'Deny RFC 3330 Special Use Addresses'
R1(config-ext-nacl)#deny ip 127.0.0.0 0.255.255.255 any
R1(config-ext-nacl)#deny ip 192.0.2.0 0.0.0.255 any
R1(config-ext-nacl)#deny ip 224.0.0.0 31.255.255.255 any
R1(config-ext-nacl)#deny ip host 255.255.255.255 any
R1(config-ext-nacl)#deny ip host 0.0.0.0 any
R1(config-ext-nacl)#remark 'Allow BGP Peering Session'
R1(config-ext-nacl)#permit tcp host 200.1.1.2 host 200.1.1.1 eq bgp
R1(config-ext-nacl)#permit tcp host 200.1.1.2 eq bgp host 200.1.1.1
R1(config-ext-nacl)#remark 'Deny Our Own Address Space'
R1(config-ext-nacl)#deny ip 150.1.0.0 0.0.255.255 any
R1(config-ext-nacl)#remark 'Permit Only TCP Sessions Initiated Internally'
R1(config-ext-nacl)#permit tcp any any established
R1(config-ext-nacl)#remark 'Prevent Fragment Attacks'
R1(config-ext-nacl)#deny ip any any fragments
R1(config-ext-nacl)#remark 'Explicitly Allow Return Traffic'
R1(config-ext-nacl)#permit icmp any any echo-reply
R1(config-ext-nacl)#permit icmp any any unreachable
R1(config-ext-nacl)#permit icmp any any time-exceeded
R1(config-ext-nacl)#remark 'Explicitly Deny All Other Traffic'
R1(config-ext-nacl)#deny ip any any log-input
```

As illustrated, these ACLs can become very long indeed. It is therefore important to consider the capabilities of the router prior to creating such long ACLs. For example, while the ACL illustrated above may have minimal impact on a high-end router, such as a Cisco 7200 series router, it would definitely have an impact on a lower-end router, such as a Cisco 1700 or 1800 series router. Do not be tempted to create hundreds of permit and deny statements because those are the recommendations in RFC 3330, etc.

Unicast Reverse Path Forwarding with ACLs

Unicast Reverse Path Forwarding (uRPF) is a tool that helps mitigate IP source address spoofing attacks by discarding IP packets that lack a verifiable source address in the routing table. As is the case with Network Ingress Filtering, uRPF should be deployed at the network edge. However, unlike Network Ingress Filtering, it is mandatory that Cisco Express Forwarding (CEF) be enabled in order to implement uRPF.

CEF is used to increase packet switching speed, reducing the overhead and delays introduced by other routing techniques, and to increase overall router performance. While going into detail on CEF is beyond the scope of the IINS course requirements, it is important to enable CEF for uRPF by issuing the ip cef command.

There are two ways in which uRPF can be implemented:

1. Strict Mode—This mode complies with RFC 2827: Network Ingress Filtering; and
2. Loose Mode—This mode is commonly used by ISPs and is beyond the scope of the IINS course requirements.

Figure 4.19 provides a conceptual view of how the uRPF feature works:

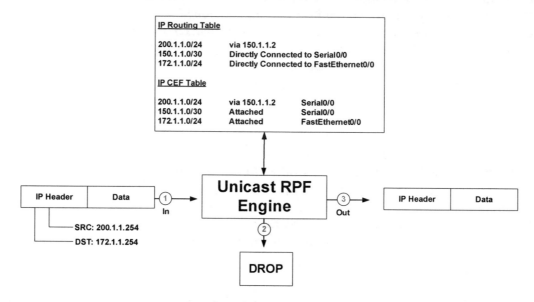

Figure 4.19. uRPF Feature

In Figure 4.19 illustrated above, the uRPF feature is enabled on a Cisco IOS router. This router then receives an IP packet from 200.1.1.254 with a destination IP address of 172.1.1.254, as illustrated in step 1.

When the router receives this packet, it first checks to see if the reverse path, i.e. the path back to the source address, matches the input interface that it has in both its IP routing table and its IP CEF table. If the uRPF check fails, meaning that the packet from 200.1.1.254 arrived on an interface other than Serial0/0, the router will discard the packet, as illustrated in step 2.

However, if the RPF check succeeds, meaning that the packet was in fact received on the Serial0/0 interface of the router, the router would forward the packet on to the destination IP address, which is 172.1.1.254 in this example. This is illustrated in step 3.

The uRPF feature is also typically used with ACLs in what is commonly referred to as pass-through mode. In this mode, all uRPF violations are logged using the log-input keyword that is appended to the referenced ACL. If a packet fails a uRPF check, the ACL is checked to determine what should happen to the packet, i.e. if the packet should be permitted or denied. The ACL logging and match counter statistics are then incremented in such an event and can be referenced by administrators to reflect statistics for packets with spoofed IP addresses. This concept is illustrated in Figure 4.20:

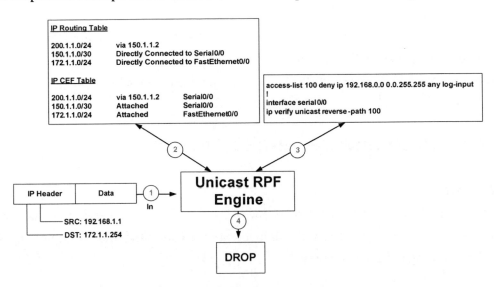

Figure 4.20. uRPF With Access List

Referencing Figure 4.20 illustrated above, a router with uRPF enabled on its Serial0/0 interface receives a packet sourced from 192.168.1.1, with a destination IP address of 172.1.1.254, as illustrated in step 1.

When the router receives this packet, it first checks to see if the reverse path, i.e. the path back to the source address, matches the input interface that it has in both its IP routing table and its IP CEF table. As illustrated in step 2, there is no matching entry for this packet. The router then proceeds and references ACL 100, which has been configured in conjunction with uRPF. This ACL, however, has been configured to deny and log all packets from the 192.168.0.0/16 subnet, which includes 192.168.1.1. This is illustrated in step 3.

In step 4, the router drops the packet due to the deny statement in the ACL. In addition to this, the ACL counter is incremented (i.e. the number of matches against the ACL increments) and a log message is generated due to the use of the log-input keyword appended to the ACL. The following configuration example illustrates the use of uRPF in conjunction with ACLs:

```
R1(config)#ip cef
R1(config)#access-list 150 deny ip 10.0.0.0 0.255.255.255 any log-input
R1(config)#access-list 150 permit ip 172.16.0.0 0.15.255.255 any log-input
R1(config)#access-list 150 deny ip 192.168.0.0 0.0.255.255 any log-input
R1(config)#int se0/0
R1(config-if)#ip verify unicast reverse-path 150
```

In the configuration above, if the router receives a packet from the 10.0.0.0/8 or 192.168.0.0/16 subnets and the packet fails the uRPF check, the router will deny the packet because of the deny statement in the ACL and increment the ACL counters, plus generate a log message.

However, if the same router receives a packet from the 172.16.0.0/12 subnet, even if that packet fails the uRPF check, the packet will be permitted because of the permit statement in the ACL. In addition to this, the router will increment the ACL counter and generate a log message.

Using ACLs to Secure Telnet Access

Telnet Basics

Telnet, which stands for teletype network, is one of the most common network management applications used to access network devices. Telnet is a user command and an underlying TCP/IP protocol for accessing remote computers.

Typically, Telnet provides access to a command-line interface on a remote host via a virtual terminal connection, which consists of an 8-bit byte-oriented data connection over the TCP using port 23 as the destination port. When using Telnet, user data is combined and sent in-band with Telnet control information. In-band signaling is simply the process of sending control information in the same channel as used for data.

As popular as Telnet is, it is important to understand that the protocol itself has very little security and Secure Shell (SSH) should be used for remote login and management of devices, from a security perspective. Secure Shell provides greater security than Telnet and will be described in detail later in this guide. The shortcomings of Telnet, from a security point of view, are listed and described in the following section:

- By default, Telnet does not encrypt any data sent over the connection, which includes password information. This makes it very easy for attackers to steal username and password information from Telnet sessions using readily-available tools such as Wireshark and Ethereal sniffers. However, some comfort can be derived from the fact that security protocols (e.g. Kerberos) have the ability to encrypt Telnet sessions.
- Most implementations of Telnet have no authentication that would ensure communication is carried out between the two desired hosts and not intercepted in the middle. To address this issue, SSH should be used instead of Telnet.
- Commonly used Telnet daemons have several vulnerabilities discovered over the years. The vulnerable systems include Sun Solaris, Linux, and FreeBSD, to name a few.

Although extensions to the Telnet protocol provide Transport Layer Security (TLS) security and Simple Authentication and Security Layer (SASL) authentication that address the above issues, most Telnet implementations do not support these extensions, and there has been relatively little interest in implementing these, as SSH is adequate for most purposes. The main advantage of TLS-Telnet would be the ability to use certificate-authority signed server certificates to authenticate a server host to a client that does not yet have the server key stored. TLS is described in detail later in this guide; SASL is beyond the scope of the IINS course requirements.

Securing Telnet Access to Cisco IOS Routers

By default, Cisco IOS routers will accept incoming Telnet connections without any special configuration. However, even though the routers will accept incoming Telnet connections, if a password is not configured for the Virtual Terminal (VTY) line(s), users will receive the Password required, but none set message before being disconnected by the router.

Prior to implementing ACLs, VTY lines must be configured in order to allow users to log in to the device. This is performed by configuring a password, via the password command, in line configuration mode, and then issuing the login command to allow users to log in to the device. The basic configuration statements to enable Telnet access to Cisco IOS devices are illustrated in the following output:

```
R1(config)#line vty 0 4
R1(config-line)#password c!sc0
R1(config-line)#login
R1(config-line)#exit
R1(config)#exit
R1#
```

From a network security standpoint, it is recommended that Telnet access to routers be restricted to authorized hosts, subnets, or both. Telnet access to Cisco IOS devices can be restricted by configuring an IP standard or extended named or numbered ACL, defining which host(s) or subnet(s) will be permitted or denied and then applying it to the router using the access-class line configuration command. For example, to restrict Telnet access to R1 to any host residing on the 172.16.0.0/12 subnet, the following configuration would be applied:

```
R1(config)#access-list 5 permit 172.16.0.0 0.15.255.255
R1(config)#line vty 0 4
R1(config-line)#access-class 5 in
R1(config-line)#exit
R1(config)#exit
R1#
```

The following example illustrates how to allow Telnet access to a specific IP address configured on the device from a specific host, as well as an authorized subnet:

```
R1(config)#interface loopback0
R1(config-if)#description 'Telnet Management Interface'
R1(config-if)#ip address 1.1.1.1 255.255.255.255
R1(config-if)#exit
R1(config)#ip access-list extended TELNET-TO-MANAGEMENT
R1(config-ext-nacl)#permit tcp host 192.168.1.254 host 1.1.1.1 eq telnet
R1(config-ext-nacl)#permit tcp 10.1.1.0 0.0.0.255 host 1.1.1.1 eq telnet
R1(config-ext-nacl)#exit
R1(config)#line vty 0 4
R1(config-line)#access-class TELNET-TO-MANAGEMENT in
R1(config-line)#exit
R1(config)#exit
R1#
```

Using ACLs to Secure SNMP Access

Although going into detail on SNMP is beyond the scope of the IINS course requirements, it is imperative that you have a solid grasp of the basics pertaining to SNMP. This section provides an overview of SNMP and then concludes with securing SNMP access to Cisco IOS devices via the use of IP Access Control Lists.

SNMP Basics

The Simple Network Management Protocol (SNMP) is a widely used management protocol and defined set of standards for communications with devices connected to an IP network. SNMP provide a means to monitor and control network devices. In addition to this, SNMP is also used to manage device configurations, collect statistics, and monitor device performance such as CPU, memory, and interface utilization, for example.

SNMP is an Application Layer (Layer 7) protocol that facilitates the exchange of management information between network devices using UDP ports 161 and 162. In general terms, an SNMP-managed network consists of a management system, agents, and managed devices.

A management system executes monitoring applications and controls managed devices. The management systems execute most of the management processes and provide the bulk of memory resources used for network management. A network might be managed by one or more management systems. Examples of SNMP management systems include HP OpenView, SolarWinds, and NetCool.

An SNMP agent resides on each managed device and translates local management information data, such as performance information or event and error information caught in software traps, into a readable form for the management system. SNMP agents use get-requests that transport data to the network management software. SNMP agents capture data from Management Information Bases (MIBs), which are device parameter and network data repositories, or from error or change traps.

A managed element, such as a router, computer host, or firewall, is accessed through the SNMP agent. Managed devices collect and store management information, making it available through SNMP to other management systems having the same protocol compatibility. Figure 4.21 illustrates the primary components of an SNMP-managed network:

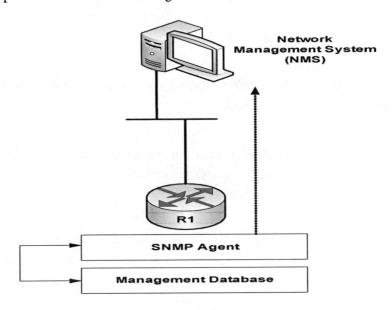

Figure 4.21. An SNMP Managed Network

In Figure 4.21 above, R1 is the SNMP-managed device. Residing on this device (logically) is the SNMP agent. The SNMP agent translates local management information data, stored in the management database of the managed device, into a readable form for the management system, which is also referred to as the Network Management System (NMS).

The main feature of SNMP is the ability to generate notifications from SNMP agents. SNMP notifications can be generated as traps or inform requests. SNMP traps are simply SNMP messages that alert the SNMP manager of a condition on the network. Examples of SNMP traps could include an interface transitioning from an up state to a down state. SNMP informs are SNMP traps that include a confirmation of receipt from the SNMP manager. These messages can be used to indicate failed authentication attempt, or the loss of a connection to a neighbor router, for example. Figure 4.22 illustrates the communication between the SNMP manager and the SNMP agent:

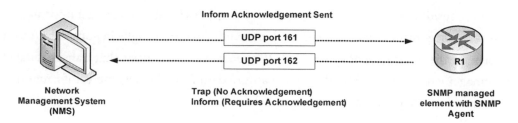

Figure 4.22. SNMP Manager and Agent

The most significant difference between SNMP traps and SNMP informs is that traps require no acknowledgement. Therefore, the SNMP agent never knows if the trap was received by the NMS. However, all inform requests must be acknowledged. The SNMP agent will not stop sending inform requests until an acknowledgement is received.

Currently, there are three versions of SNMP, which are versions 1, 2, and 3. The following section provides a brief overview of these three versions:

NOTE: You are NOT required to demonstrate advanced knowledge of SNMP as a part of the IINS course requirements. However, you are expected to have a basic understanding of SNMP theory, and, most importantly, knowledge of basic SNMP configuration via the CLI.

SNMPv1 is the initial implementation of the SNMP protocol. SNMPv1 operates over protocols such as User Datagram Protocol (UDP), Internet Protocol (IP), and the OSI Connectionless Network Service (CLNS). SNMPv1 is widely used and is the de facto network-management protocol in the Internet community.

SNMPv2 revises SNMPv1 and includes improvements in the areas of performance, security, confidentiality, and manager-to-manager communications. SNMPv2 also defines two new operations: GetBulk and Inform. The GetBulk operation is used to efficiently retrieve large blocks of data. The Inform operation allows one NMS to send trap information to another NMS and then to receive a response. In SNMPv2, if the agent responding to GetBulk operations cannot provide values for all the variables in a list, it provides partial results.

SNMPv3 provides three additional security services that are not available in previous versions of SNMP. The additional security features provided in SNMPv3 are message integrity, authentication, and encryption. SNMPv3 uses message integrity to ensure that a packet has not been tampered with in-transit. SNMPv3 also uses authentication, which is used to determine if the message is from a valid source. And, finally, SNMPv3 provides encryption, which is used to scramble the contents of a packet to prevent it from being seen by unauthorized sources.

When using SNMP, managed devices are monitored and controlled using three common SNMP commands. These three commands are the read, write, and trap commands.

The read command is used by an NMS to monitor managed devices. This is performed by the NMS examining different variables that are maintained by managed devices. The write command is used by an NMS to control managed devices. Using this command, the NMS can change the values of variables stored within managed devices. Finally, the trap command is used by managed devices to report events to the NMS. Cisco IOS routers can be configured to send SNMP traps or informs to an NMS. The traps and informs that are sent are dependent on the version of Cisco IOS software running on the device, as well as the platform, e.g. Cisco 2600, Cisco 3800, Cisco 7200, etc.

Securing SNMP Access to Cisco IOS Routers

Both SNMPv1 and SNMPv2 use a community-based form of security. This community string is used to allow access to the SNMP agent and can also be defined by an IP ACL and password. To configure a community string to permit access to SNMP on Cisco IOS routers, the snmp-server community [string] [view [view-name]] [ro|rw] [acl] global configuration command must be used. The keywords that are used in conjunction with this command are listed and described in Table 4.5:

Table 4.5. SNMP Server Keywords

Keyword	Description
[string]	This keyword is used to specify the case-sensitive community string that acts as a password and permits access to the SNMP protocol.
[view [view-name]]	This keyword is used to specify the name of a previously configured view, and is used in SNMPv3 implementations – which are beyond the scope of the IINS course requirements and will not be described in this chapter. The view is used to define the objects available to the community.
ro	This keyword specifies read-only access. Authorized management stations are only able to retrieve MIB objects.
rw	This keyword specifies read-write access. Authorized management stations are able to retrieve and modify MIB objects.
[acl]	This keyword is used to specify an IP standard numbered ACL (i.e. 1- 99) that includes the IP addresses or subnets that are allowed to use the community string to gain access to the SNMP agent.

To reinforce these concepts, we will go over a couple of configuration examples. The first configuration example illustrates how to enable SNMP on a Cisco IOS device, specify an SNMP community string, and authorize read access from an NMS with the IP address 10.1.1.254:

```
R3(config)#access-list 5 permit host 10.1.1.254
R3(config)#snmp-server community !in5c0urs3 ro 5
R3(config)#exit
R3#
```

In the configuration output above, the access-list 5 permit host 10.1.1.254 command is used to create a standard IP that permits only the IP address of the NMS (10.1.1.254). The snmp-server community !in5c0urs3 ro command enables SNMP on a Cisco IOS router. The SNMP community string, which is in5c0urs3, serves as a password protection mechanism for SNMP. This community string will be sent in every SNMP packet, so an incorrect community string results in no access to the SNMP agent running on the router. The ro keyword means that only read access will be permitted via SNMP, for the host specified by ACL 5.

The second configuration example illustrates how to enable SNMP on a Cisco IOS device, specify a community string that will be used for read/write access, and allow read/write access to any host residing on the 192.168.1.0/24 subnet:

```
R3(config)#snmp-server community !in5wr!t3 rw 10
R3(config)#access-list 10 permit 192.168.1.0 0.0.0.255
R3(config)#exit
R3#
```

Breaking down the configuration commands used in the output above, the snmp-server community !in5wr!t3 rw command enables SNMP on a Cisco IOS router, using the SNMP community string in5c0urs3, which provides read/write access to the SNMP agent, as indicated by the rw keyword. In addition to this, ACL 10 is used to restrict read/write access to the 192.168.1.0/24. No other SNMP managers have access to any objects.

Now that we have an understanding of the configuration commands required to enable SNMP on a Cisco IOS device, to specify community strings, and to restrict SNMP access via ACLs, it is important to also understand how to configure SNMP to send notifications to an NMS. The snmp-server host {hostname | ip-address} [vrf vrf-name] [traps | informs] [version {1 | 2c | 3 [auth | noauth | priv]} [community-string [udp-port port] [notification-type]] command is used in Cisco IOS software to configure a router to send SNMP traps and informs to an NMS.

While most of the options provided by this command are beyond the scope of the IINS course requirements, Table 4.6 lists and describes the options you should be familiar with:

Table 4.6. SNMP Server Host Keywords

Keyword	Description
hostname | ip-address	This keyword is used to specify the hostname (e.g. snmp1.howtonetwork.net) or the IP address of the target NMS.
traps	This keyword is used to send traps to the NMS, which is the default.
informs	This keyword is used to send Inform messages to the NMS.
version	This keyword is used to specify the SNMP version to use. In order to send Inform messages, you must use SNMPv2 or SNMPv3.
community-string	This keyword is used to specify the SNMP community string. It is recommended that this string be configured using the snmp-server community command before it is used with this command.
notification-type	This keyword is used to specify the type of notification to send to the NMS. The options available will vary based on router IOS image, as well as platform. For example, the options for Cisco 7200 series routers will vary from those available for Cisco 2600 series routers.

In addition to the snmp-server host... global configuration command, administrators can also use the snmp-server enable traps [notification-type] global configuration command to enable all traps (default) or specific traps. These are then sent to the NMS specified in the snmp-server host global configuration command.

As was done with community strings, we will go through a few examples demonstrating basic SNMP configuration. Please note that these examples will be based only on SNMPv1 or SNMPv2. SNMPv3 configuration is beyond the scope of the IINS course requirements.

The first configuration example illustrates how to configure a router to send OSPF traps to an NMS with the IP address 10.1.1.254 using the community string !in5s3cur!ty:

```
R3(config)#snmp-server enable traps ospf
R3(config)#snmp-server host 10.1.1.254 !in5s3cur!ty
```

The second configuration example illustrates how to send all configuration informs to an NMS with an IP address of 192.168.1.254 using the community string !in5s3cur!ty:

```
R3(config)#snmp-server enable traps config
R3(config)#snmp-server host 192.168.1.254 informs version 2c !in5s3cur!ty config
```

Chapter Summary

The following section is a summary of the major points you should be aware of in this chapter:

Access Control List Overview

- An ACL is a list of permit and deny statements that controls network access
- There are two broad categories for data received by a router:
    1. It is traffic that passes through the router via the forwarding path; or
    2. It is traffic destined for the router for route processor handling

ACLs provide administrators great flexibility and they can be used for:
1. Filter routing information received from or sent to adjacent neighbors
2. Control access to networks by permitting or denying particular types of traffic
3. Control interactive access to the router itself, e.g. Telnet, HTTPS and SSH
4. Define interesting traffic that can be used to initiate ISDN connections
5. Define interesting traffic for IPSec Virtual Private Network (VPN) encryption
6. Define queuing and Quality of Service (QoS) features, allowing traffic to be prioritized
7. Use in security techniques such as TCP Intercept and the Cisco IOS Firewall
8. Define traffic for Network Address Translation (NAT)
9. Mitigate IP spoofing, SMURF and other similar network attacks

Access Control List Types

- The different types of IP ACLs that are available in Cisco IOS software are:

    1. IP Standard ACLs—Filter based on source IP address or subnet
    2. IP Extended ACLs—Filter based on source and destination IP address, port(s), flag(s)
    3. IP Named ACLs—Can be standard or extended and do the same as numbered ACLs
    4. Dynamic ACLs—Lock-and-Key ACLs; they allow dynamic, per-used access control
    5. Reflexive ACLs—Allow IP packets to be filtered based on upper-layer session information
    6. Time-based ACLs—They are used to control network access based on the time
    7. Turbo ACLs—Designed to process ACLs more efficiently and improve router performance
    8. Receive ACLs—Used to increase security on Cisco 12000 routers by protecting the GRP
    9. Infrastructure Protection ACLs—Used to reduce the risk of network infrastructure attacks
    10. Transit ACLs—Used to permit only legitimate traffic into the network
    11. Classification ACLs—Used to classify and categorize Denial of Service (DoS) attacks

ACL Processing and Packet Flow Rules

- When an inbound ACL is applied to an interface, the router checks the received packets against the statements in the ACL looking for a match

- When an outbound ACL is applied on an interface, the router first performs a route lookup for the destination address in the routing table to determine the egress interface via which the packet should be forwarded

Implementing ACLs

There are two basic steps required in the implementation of ACLs:

1. Create the ACL
2. Apply the ACL

The following table illustrates the most common ACL numbers in Cisco IOS software:

Protocol	ACL Number Range
IP standard	1 – 99 and 1300 – 1999
IP extended	100 – 199 and 200 – 2699
Protocol type-code	200 – 299
MAC ACL	700 – 799
Extended MAC ACL	1100 – 1199

- Standard ACLs should always be applied as close to the destination as possible
- Extended ACLs should be applied as close to the source as possible
- The general guidelines that should be used when implementing ACLs are:
  1. ACLs can be assigned to multiple interfaces on a device. This refers to either different ACLs or even the same ACL.
  2. Only one ACL is allowed per protocol per interface per direction; you can have one inbound and one outbound ACL applied using this rule.
  3. ACLs are processed from the top down; therefore, take care when planning ACEs in ACLs. More specific entries should appear first.
  4. When creating an ACL, the router appends each ACE to the end of the ACL; however, in newer versions of IOS, beginning with 12.2, administrators have the ability to insert ACEs between current entries in the ACL.
  5. There is an implicit deny for all traffic that is not explicitly permitted. You will never see any matches or log entries against this implicit deny in an ACL. If an ACL does not have at least one permit statement, all traffic will be blocked.
  6. Always create an ACL before applying it to an interface. Additionally, when editing an ACL, always remove it from the interface, make the desired modifications, and then reapply it to the interface, otherwise you may block legitimate traffic or even yourself from the router. This is a very important point to remember.
  7. Outbound ACLs applied to router interfaces only check for traffic traversing the router; they do not and will not filter traffic that is originated by the router itself.

Using ACLs to Mitigate Network Layer Attacks

- The following ACLs can be used to mitigate against and identify potential Layer 3 attacks:
  1. Established ACLs—Permit external TCP traffic only if it was originated internally
  2. ACLs and Fragmented Packets—Prevent the Tiny and Overlapping fragment attacks
  3. Using ACLs to characterize SMURF attacks—Match on ICMP echo and echo-reply packets
  4. Using ACLs to characterize SYN attacks—Match on TCP SYN packets
  5. Using ACLs to prevent IP address spoofing attacks—Use recommendations in RFC 2827
  6. Unicast Reverse Path Forwarding with ACLs—ACL permit or deny packets that fail RPF

Using ACLs to secure Telnet Access

- Telnet is one of the most common network management applications
- The shortcomings of Telnet, from a security point of view are:
  1. By default, Telnet does not encrypt any data sent over the connection
  2. Most implementations of Telnet have no authentication
  3. Commonly used Telnet daemons have several vulnerabilities

- The access-class line configuration command is used to secure Telnet in Cisco IOS routers

Using ACLs to secure SNMP Access

- SNMP provide a means to monitor and control network devices
- SNMP is an Application Layer (Layer 7) protocol uses UDP ports 161 and 162
- An SNMP-managed network consists of:
  1. A management system (NMS)
  2. Agents
  3. Managed devices

- Currently, the IETF has defined three versions of SNMP, which are versions 1, 2, and 3
- SNMPv1 is the initial implementation of the SNMP protocol
- SNMPv2 includes improvements in the areas of performance, security, confidentiality
- SNMPv3 message integrity, authentication, and encryption
- The snmp-server community command is used to enable and secure SNMP access
- The snmp-server host command is used to specify a trap or inform destination
- The snmp-server enable traps command is used to generate and send SNMP traps

Commands Used in this Chapter

The following section is a summary of the commands used in this chapter:

Command	Description
access-list [1-99| 1300-1999]	Used to configure IP standard ACLs
access-list [100-199| 2000-2699]	Used to configure IP extended ACLs
log-input	Used to provide detailed logging in extended ACLs
show ip access-lists [name]	Used to view configured ACLs
show logging	Used to view the local router log messages
ip access-list	Used to configure named standard or extended ACLs
access-list compiled	Used to configure turbo ACLs
show access-list compiled	Used to view configured turbo ACLs
ip receive-access-list	Used to configure receive ACLs (rACLs)
ip access-group	Used to apply an ACL to an interface
show interfaces	Used to view interface statistics
show ip traffic	Used to view IP traffic statistics
no ip directed-broadcast	Used to disable directed Broadcast forwarding
ip tcp intercept list	Used to specify the ACL to be used for TCP Intercept
ip tcp intercept mode	Used to specify the mode TCP Intercept operates in
ip verify unicast reverse-path	Used to enable uRPF; can also be used with an ACL
access-class	Used to apply an ACL to VTY lines
snmp-server community	Used to configure the SNMP community string
snmp-server host	Used to configure an NMS to send traps or informs
snmp-server enable traps	Used to enable SNMP traps

CHAPTER 5

Secure Network Management and Reporting

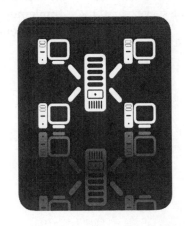

In Chapter 4, we learned about Telnet, which is one of the most common management applications for remote access Cisco IOS routers. However, we also learned about the inherent security flaws in Telnet. This chapter describes the recommended alternative to Telnet—Secure Sockets Shell (SSH)—as well as Command Line Interface (CLI) and Security Device Manager (SDM) configuration tasks required to implement SSH in Cisco IOS routers. In addition to SSH, this chapter also explains reporting via the use of Syslog. The IINS exam objectives covered in this chapter are as follows:

- Use CLI and SDM to configure SSH on Cisco routers to enable secured management access
- Use CLI and SDM to configure Cisco routers to send Syslog messages to a Syslog server

This chapter is broken up into the following sections:

- Secure Sockets Shell Overview
- Implementing SSH via CLI
- Implementing SSH via SDM
- Syslog Overview
- Implementing Syslog via CLI
- Implementing Syslog via SDM

IINS Exam Objective	Section(s) Covered
Use CLI and SDM to configure SSH on Cisco routers to enable secured management access	• Secure Sockets Shell Overview • Implementing SSH via CLI • Implementing SSH via SDM
Use CLI and SDM to configure Cisco routers to send Syslog messages to a Syslog server	• Syslog Overview • Implementing Syslog via CLI • Implementing Syslog via SDM

Secure Sockets Shell Overview

Secure Sockets Shell (SSH) provides a more secure and reliable method for device access and administration than Telnet. SSH is an application and a protocol that provides secure replacement for the suite of Berkeley remote tools such as RSH, RLOGIN, and RCP.

RSH—Remote Shell—is a UNIX command-line utility that allows users to execute commands remotely. RLOGIN—Remote Login—is a software utility for Unix-like computer operating systems that allows users to log in on another host via a network, using TCP port 513. RCP—Remote Copy—is a command on UNIX operating systems that is used to copy one or more files from one computer system to another. RCP, RLOGIN, and RSH are beyond the scope of the IINS course requirements.

SSH secures the sessions using standard cryptographic mechanisms. SSH uses TCP and UDP port 22, although TCP port 22 is the de facto port listed for SSH. Unlike Telnet, SSH ensures that data is encrypted and is therefore untraceable by network sniffers, for example.

There are two versions of SSH available: SSH version 1 and SSH version 2. While SSH version 1 is an improvement over Telnet, which sends username and password information in clear text, some fundamental design flaws exist in SSH version 1. For example, there are numerous tools (which are not named, for ethical reasons) readily available on the Internet that can decrypt SSHv1 traffic on the fly, thus removing most security from encrypting the traffic with SSHv1. Therefore, when implementing SSH, it is highly recommended that SSH version 2 be used.

SSH version 2 is a re-worked and stronger version of SSH. In addition to all the features and functionality in SSH version 1, SSH version 2 brings encrypted File Transport Protocol (FTP), support for digital certificates and Public Key Infrastructure (PKI), and many other features. FTP is beyond the scope of the IINS course requirements; however, digital certificates and PKI are within scope and will be described in detail later in this guide.

Despite the advantages afforded by SSH version 2, it does not support some of the faster ciphers. Ciphers, which provide encryption or decryption, are a requirement in the IINS course and will be described in detail later in this guide. In addition to this, unlike most software that contains revisions, it is important to keep in mind that SSH version 1 and SSH version 2 are not completely compatible. For example, most SSH version 1 clients cannot automatically connect to an SSH version 2 server unless the server is compiled up to support "compatibility" mode.

SSH resides on top of the TCP/IP layers, protecting hosts from unknown devices. The SSH Transport Layer protocol is responsible for securing data by using a strong encryption algorithm. Figure 5.1 illustrates the SSH protocol layers:

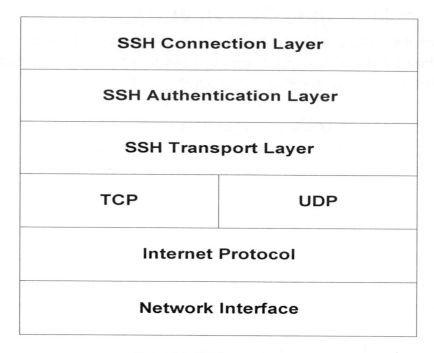

Figure 5.1. SSH Protocol Layers

SSH, coupled with the AAA mechanism using RADUIS or TACACS+, provides the best solution for a secure, scalable access mechanism.

Implementing SSH via CLI

Before we go into the configuration tasks pertaining to SSH implementation on Cisco IOS routers, it is important that you understand the restrictions that apply regarding SSH. The first restriction is that SSH version 1 is supported in Cisco IOS 12.1(1)T and later, while SSH version 2 is supported in Cisco IOS 12.3(4)T and later. Therefore, the version of SSH you are able to configure on the Cisco IOS router will be dependent on the version of software that the router is running.

The second restriction is that SSH is only supported in Cisco IOS images that have cryptographic capabilities. For example, if you are running Cisco IOS 12.4, but the image is a basic Enterprise image, the software will not support SSH configuration. It is therefore imperative to ensure that not only the correct version of software but also the capabilities and type of software on routers within the network are consistent throughout.

Once these two restrictions have been identified and addressed, the following steps are required to implement SSH on Cisco IOS routers:

1. Configure a domain name on the router. This is performed via the ip domain-name [name] global configuration command.

2. Generate the security keys that will be used by SSH. This is performed by using the crypto key generate rsa global configuration command and specifying the desired key size; or, alternatively, via the crypto key generate rsa general-keys and specifying the desired key size. Both of these commands automatically enable SSH when executed, and no further configuration is necessary. The key (modulus) size that is used for SSH can be up to 2048 bits in length. The larger the key size, the more secure the implementation; however, larger keys also take a longer time to generate. When generating a public key, Cisco recommends a minimum key size of 1024 bits.

3. Specify the time that the router waits on the SSH client, in seconds, to input username and password information before disconnecting the session via the ip ssh timeout global configuration command. This is an optional step because, by default, the router will wait for 120 seconds (2 minutes).

4. Specify the number of SSH authentication retries before a session is reset via the ip ssh authentication-retries global configuration command. By default, the Cisco IOS router will allow up to three failed logins before resetting the SSH connection. As is the case with the ip ssh timeout global configuration command, this is an optional step.

5. Allow only SSH sessions to the Cisco IOS router by issuing the transport input ssh line configuration command to allow only SSH. This is performed for all VTY lines.

6. Save your router configuration by using the copy running-config startup-config or the copy system:running-config nvram:startup-config commands, depending on the Cisco IOS version that is running on the device.

The following example illustrates how to enable SSH on a Cisco IOS router using the steps provided. The router will be configured to use the domain name howtonetwork.net, a general key size of 1024 bits for SSH, a 30-second SSH timeout, and will allow two authentication attempts before the SSH session is terminated. Finally, the router is configured to allow only SSH sessions and no Telnet sessions for remote access and management. These configuration steps are performed as follows:

```
R1(config)#ip domain-name howtonetwork.net
R1(config)#crypto key generate rsa
The name for the keys will be: R1.howtonetwork.net
Choose the size of the key modulus in the range of 360 to 2048 for your
```

General Purpose Keys. Choosing a key modulus greater than 512 may take a few minutes.

```
How many bits in the modulus [512]: 1024
% Generating 1024 bit RSA keys, keys will be non-exportable...[OK]

R1(config)#ip ssh time-out 30
R1(config)#ip ssh authentication-retries 2
R1(config)#line vty 0 4
R1(config-line)#transport input ssh
R1(config-line)#exit
R1(config)#exit
R1#copy system:running-config nvram:startup-config
Destination filename [startup-config]?
Building configuration...
[OK]
R1#
```

To verify the local public keys that have been generated on the router, administrators can use the show crypto key mypubkey rsa command. A sample output is provided below:

```
R1#show crypto key mypubkey rsa
% Key pair was generated at: 02:57:45 UTC Mar 1 2002
Key name: R1.howtonetwork.net
 Storage Device: not specified
 Usage: General Purpose Key
 Key is not exportable.
 Key Data:
  30819F30 0D06092A 864886F7 0D010101 05000381 8D003081 89028181 00C98784
  4F358BC6 2A3908F0 CF29F52B CD1BF757 23FF69C0 57A4B129 36F72D22 42CC205C
  8BD5002B 7DC462C5 EBFC4ABE 4D404195 BD883014 19D423BB 6C490174 C27A0009
  EC080C2E 0C23ABFA 7FCB66BD 495BD9D3 84BBC9EA 4951A292 5A8F395B 7BD57145
  F69E83B0 3C76DF8B 8951B88C C033CE5C D8627EE1 5FD1ACA1 1C5DEC91 EB020301
  0001
 % Key pair was generated at: 02:57:51 UTC Mar 1 2002
Key name: R1.howtonetwork.net.server
Temporary key
 Usage: Encryption Key
 Key is not exportable.
 Key Data:
  307C300D 06092A86 4886F70D 01010105 00036B00 30680261 00C0E578 9B223536
  CB3B6F88 25D03C0B B46803A9 1CCD589B 99704A48 0FD75C5E 0AFF9F76 D4DD51D7
  DC8809D0 16A8E4AE D0963662 E2408242 4B33E42E 8CC405EA 233DBF39 E12DFAEE
  D9EB92C8 0D2B0C27 573B8386 BF0B761F 6ED634FC DCFBA622 ED020301 0001
```

In the real world, it is common practice to rotate keys every so often, in accordance with security policies. Therefore, to delete an existing key with the intention of configuring a new one, administrators can used the crypto key zeroize rsa global configuration command, as illustrated in the following output:

```
R1(config)#crypto key zeroize rsa
% All RSA keys will be removed.
% All router certs issued using these keys will also be removed.
Do you really want to remove these keys? [yes/no]: y
R1(config)#
```

Once SSH has been enabled on Cisco IOS routers, administrators can verify that only SSH, and not Telnet, is allowed for inbound remote access sessions to the router by using the show line vty [number] command, as illustrated in the following output:

```
R1#show line vty 0
   Tty Typ    Tx/Rx   A Modem Roty AccO   Accl  Uses  Noise Overruns  Int
   66 VTY              -     -    -    -     -    0     0     0/0       -

Line 66, Location: "", Type: ""
Length: 24 lines, Width: 80 columns
Baud rate (TX/RX) is 9600/9600
Status: No Exit Banner
Capabilities: none
Modem state: Idle
Special Chars:      Escape Hold Stop       Start   Disconnect Activation
                    ^^x    none  -         -       none
Timeouts:           Idle EXEC  Idle Session  Modem   Answer  Session Dispatch
                    00:10:00   never                         none    not set
                    Idle Session Disconnect Warning
                      never
                    Login-sequence User Response
                    00:00:30
                    Autoselect Initial Wait
                      not set
Modem type is unknown.
Session limit is not set.
Time since activation: never
Editing is enabled.
History is enabled, history size is 20.
DNS resolution in show commands is enabled
Full user help is disabled
Allowed input transports are ssh.
Allowed output transports are pad telnet rlogin mop v120 ssh.
Preferred transport is telnet.
```

No output characters are padded
No special data dispatching characters

Additionally, depending on platform capability, administrators can also use the show ip ssh command to ensure that SSH version 2 has been enabled on the router. However, keep in mind that in Cisco IOS software, it will actually show up as SSH version 1.99. This is, in fact, SSH version 2, since there is no such thing as SSH version 1.99. A sample output of this command is illustrated below:

```
R1#show ip ssh
SSH Enabled - version 1.99
Authentication timeout: 30 secs; Authentication retries: 2
R1#
```

Once SSH is enabled, administrators can log in using tools such as SecureCRT, which requires a license and must be purchased, or freeware, such as Putty. From a Windows-based client, administrators can simply telnet to the device and specify port 22 (SSH) as the intended destination port. Figure 5.2 illustrates the use of Putty to access a Cisco IOS router enabled for SSH remotely:

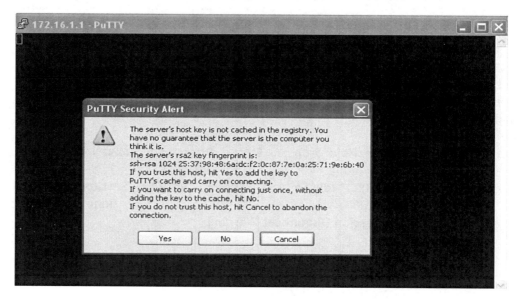

Figure 5.2. Putty Access to SSH Enabled Router

When the warning is displayed by the Putty client, simply click on the **Yes** button to proceed with the connection to the router and then log in using your credentials, as follows:

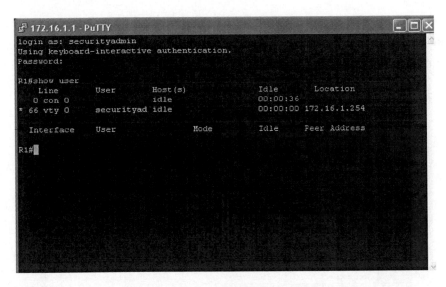

Figure 5.3. Login to SSH Enabled Router

While SSH access to a router is illustrated using the Putty client, it is important to keep in mind that this may be different for other SSH clients.

Implementing SSH via SDM

In addition to configuring SSH via CLI, you are also expected to demonstrate knowledge on SSH configuration via SDM. This is performed by clicking on the **Additional Tasks** button on the main configuration page in Cisco SDM. This is illustrated in Figure 5.4:

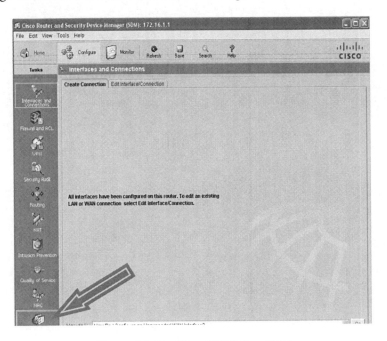

Figure 5.4. Enabling SSH Using SDM

As we learned earlier in this section, before SSH can be enabled on a Cisco IOS router, a domain name must be configured on the router. This is performed by clicking on the + sign next to **Router Properties** menu, as illustrated in Figure 5.5:

Figure 5.5. A Domain Name is Required

To configure a domain name, highlight **Domain Name** and click on the **Edit** button, as illustrated in Figure 5.6:

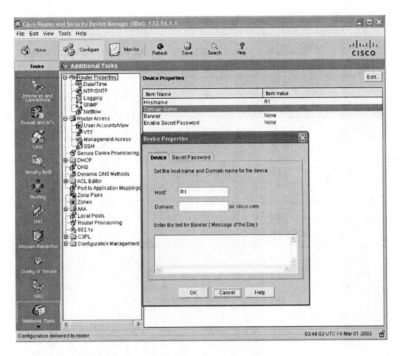

Figure 5.6. Configuring a Domain Name

Next, simply type in the desired domain name and click on the **OK** button, as illustrated in Figure 5.7:

Figure 5.7. Click 'OK' When Done

Once the DNS domain name has been configured, you can proceed and enable SSH access to the Cisco IOS router. This is performed on the **Additional Tasks** page in SDM, under the **Router Access** menu, as illustrated in Figure 5.8:

Figure 5.8. Enable SSH Next

Under the **Router Access** menu, select **SSH** and then click on the **Generate RSA Key**, as illustrated in Figure 5.9:

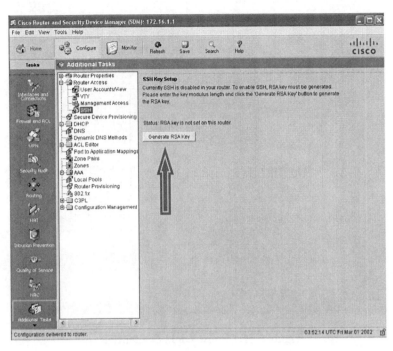

Figure 5.9. Generate RSA Key with SDM

In the following pop-up box, type in the desired RSA key size and then click on the **OK** button, as illustrated in Figure 5.10:

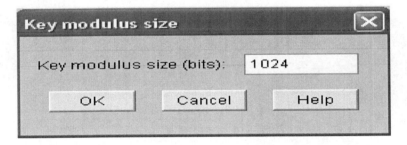

Figure 5.10. Choose Key Size

Next, type in the credentials used to access the device via SDM. This username should have Level 15 access to the device, as required when configuring a router for SDM. Once you have typed in the credentials, click on the **OK** button, as shown in Figure 5.11:

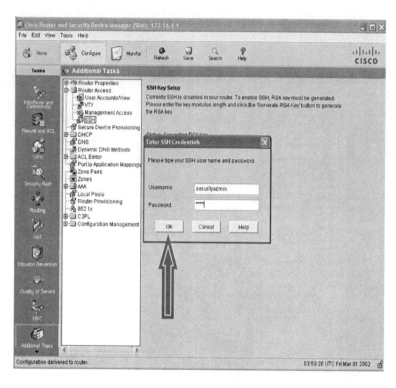

Figure 5.11. Choose Login Credentials

Once complete, SDM delivers the configuration commands to the device and SSH access will be enabled. To validate SSH access, you can use an SSH client (such as Putty) to connect to the router and then log in using your credentials, as illustrated in Figure 5.12 and Figure 5.13:

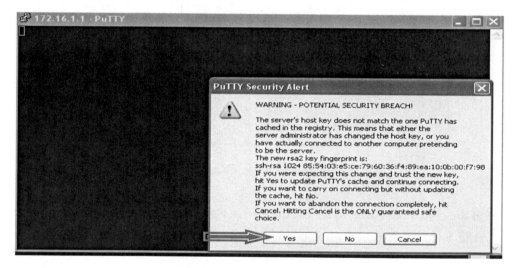

Figure 5.12. Loin Using SSH Client

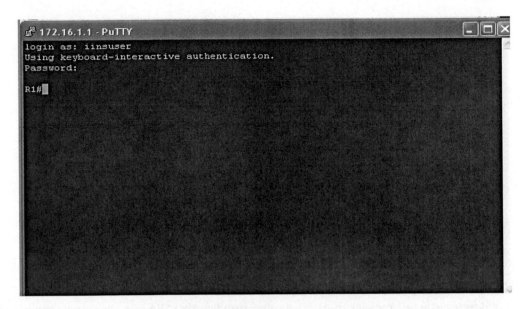

Figure 5.13. Successful Login

Syslog Overview

Syslog is a protocol that allows a host to send event notification messages across IP networks to event message collectors—also known as Syslog Servers or Syslog Daemons. In other words, a host or a device can be configured in such a way that it generates a Syslog Message and forwards it to a specific Syslog Daemon (Server).

A Syslog Daemon or Server is an entity that listens to the Syslog messages that are sent to it. You cannot configure a Syslog Daemon to ask a specific device to send it Syslog Messages. In other words, if a specific device has no ability to generate Syslog Messages, then a Syslog Daemon cannot do anything about it. In the real world, corporations typically use Solarwinds (or similar) software for Syslog capturing. Additionally, freeware such as the Kiwi Syslog Daemon is also available for Syslog capturing.

Syslog uses User Datagram Protocol (UDP) as the underlying transport mechanism, so the data packets are unsequenced and unacknowledged. While UDP does not have the overhead included in TCP, this means that on a heavily used network, some packets may be dropped and therefore logging information will be lost. However, the Cisco IOS allows administrators to configure multiple Syslog servers for redundancy. A Syslog solution is comprised of two main elements: a Syslog server and a Syslog client. These components are illustrated in Figure 5.14:

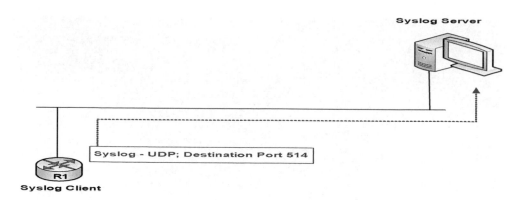

Figure 5.14. Syslog Server and Client

In Figure 5.14 above, the Syslog client (R1) sends Syslog messages to the Syslog sever using UDP as the Transport Layer protocol and specifying a destination port of 514. Syslog messages cannot exceed 1,024 bytes in size; however, there is no minimum length. All Syslog messages contain three distinct parts:

1. Priority
2. Header
3. Message

Priority

The priority of a Syslog message represents both the Facility and Severity of the message. This number is an 8-bit number. The first 3 bits are the least significant and represent the Severity of the message (with 3 bits you can represent eight different Severities) and the other 5 bits represent the Facility of the message. You can use the Facility and the Severity values to apply certain filters on the events in the Syslog Daemon.

It is important to know that these values are generated by the applications on which the event is generated, and not by the Syslog server itself. The values sent by Cisco IOS devices are listed and described in Table 5.1:

Table 5.1. Syslog Levels

Level	Name	Description
0	Emergencies	This level is used for the most severe error conditions that render the system unusable.
1	Alerts	This level is used to indicate conditions that need immediate attention from administrators.

2	Critical	This level is used to indicate critical conditions that are less than Alerts but still require administrator intervention.
3	Errors	This level is used to indicate errors within the system; however, these errors do not render the system unusable.
4	Warnings	This level is used to indicate warning conditions about system operations that did not complete successfully.
5	Notifications	This level is used to indicate state changes within the system, e.g. a routing protocol adjacency transitioning to a down state.
6	Informational	This level is used to indicate informational messages about the normal operation of the system.
7	Debugging	This level is used to indicate real-time (debugging) information that is typically used for troubleshooting purposes.

In Cisco IOS software, the logging facility global configuration command can be used to specify the Syslog facility. The options available with this command are as follows:

```
R1(config)#logging facility ?
  auth     Authorization system
  cron     Cron/at facility
  daemon   System daemons
  kern     Kernel
  local0   Local use
  local1   Local use
  local2   Local use
  local3   Local use
  local4   Local use
  local5   Local use
  local6   Local use
  local7   Local use
  lpr      Line printer system
  mail     Mail system
  news     USENET news
  sys10    System use
  sys11    System use
  sys12    System use
  sys13    System use
  sys14    System use
  sys9     System use
  syslog   Syslog itself
  user     User process
  uucp     Unix-to-Unix copy system
```

NOTE: Going into the specifics of logging facilities is beyond the scope of the IINS course requirements.

In order to specify a logging severity level in Cisco IOS software, you must first select the location to which Syslog messages will be sent. Once selected, an administrator can then select the severity of log messages that will be sent to that location. The options available are illustrated in the following output (which depicts logging to the local router buffer):

```
R1(config)#logging buffered ?
  <0-7>                Logging severity level
  <4096-2147483647>  Logging buffer size
  alerts               Immediate action needed       (severity=1)
  critical             Critical conditions           (severity=2)
  debugging            Debugging messages            (severity=7)
  discriminator        Establish MD-Buffer association
  emergencies          System is unusable            (severity=0)
  errors               Error conditions              (severity=3)
  informational        Informational messages        (severity=6)
  notifications        Normal but significant conditions (severity=5)
  warnings             Warning conditions            (severity=4)
  xml                  Enable logging in XML to XML logging buffer
  <cr>
```

Administrators can use either the Cisco IOS-provided keyword or the number to perform the same action. For example, the logging buffered 7 and the logging buffered debugging commands will both log and send debugging Syslog messages to the specified destination, which is specified by using the logging [destination] global configuration command. In addition to this, it is imperative to remember that the severity level specified includes all other severity levels below it.

For example, if an administrator configures a router with the logging buffered notifications command, the router will log notifications as well as warnings, errors, critical messages, alerts, and emergencies. Similarly, if an administrator configures a router with the logging buffered notifications command, the router will log ALL messages to the local buffer, i.e. Levels 0 through 7 will be included and logged.

The Syslog destination options available in Cisco IOS software are provided, in bold font, in the router output illustrated below:

```
R1(config)#logging ?
  Hostname or A.B.C.D  IP address of the logging host
  buffered             Set buffered logging parameters
  buginf               Enable buginf logging for debugging
  cns-events           Set CNS Event logging level
  console              Set console logging parameters
  count                Count every log message and timestamp last occurrence
  discriminator        Create or modify a message discriminator
```

```
dmvpn              DMVPN Configuration
exception          Limit size of exception flush output
facility           Facility parameter for syslog messages
history            Configure syslog history table
host               Set syslog server IP address and parameters
message-counter    Configure log message to include certain counter value
monitor            Set terminal line (monitor) logging parameters
on                 Enable logging to all enabled destinations
origin-id          Add origin ID to syslog messages
persistent         Set persistent logging parameters
queue-limit        Set logger message queue size
rate-limit         Set messages per second limit
reload             Set reload logging level
server-arp         Enable sending ARP requests for syslog servers when first configured
source-interface   Specify interface for source address in logging transactions
trap               Set syslog server logging level
userinfo           Enable logging of user info on privileged mode enabling
```

Table 5.2 lists and describes the bolded options, which you must be familiar with:

Table 5.2. Logging Options

Keyword	Description
Hostname or A.B.C.D	This option is used to specify the DNS hostname or IP address of the remote Syslog server.
buffered	This option is used to configure the Cisco IOS router to send and store Syslog messages in the local buffer.
console	This option is used to enable logging messages to the Console, which is enabled by default in Cisco IOS software.
host	This option is used to specify the IP address or DNS hostname of the remote Syslog server and specify advanced Syslog options.
source-interface	This option is used to specify the source IP address that will be used for Syslog messages. This is typically set at the Loopback interface.
trap	This option is used to specify the log severity level to send Syslog messages to a remote Syslog server.

Header

The header of a Syslog message contains the timestamp and the hostname or IP address of the device. The timestamp is the date and time at which the message was generated. In Cisco IOS software, routers can be configured to use Network Time Protocol (NTP) to sync their internal clocks or administrators can manually set the clocks on the devices via the clock set hh:mm:ss privileged EXEC command. NTP configuration is beyond the scope of the IINS course requirements.

Message

The message part will fill the remainder of the Syslog packet. This will usually contain some additional information of the process that generated the message, and then the text of the message. This part has two fields: the TAG field and the CONTENT field. The value in the TAG field is the name of the program or process that generated the message. The CONTENT field contains the details of the message.

Figure 5.15 illustrates a typical Syslog message received on a Syslog server. While the Syslog server used in this example is a Kiwi Syslog server, the message format presented will basically be the same in all Syslog servers.

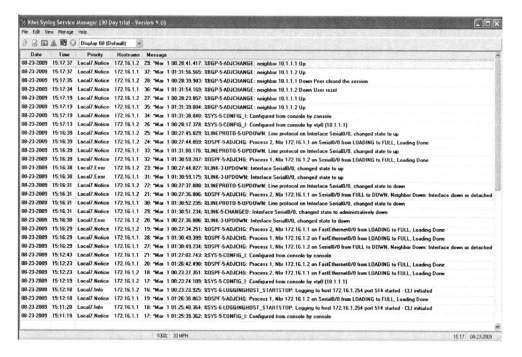

Figure 5.15. Syslog Message

Implementing Syslog via CLI

To implement Syslog using CLI, the following sequence of steps should be taken:

1. Enable logging globally by issuing the logging on global configuration command.

2. Specify the location the router should send the logs using the logging command. For example, to send Syslog messages to the local buffer, the logging buffered command would be used; whereas to send Syslog messages to a Syslog server with the IP address 10.1.1.254, the logging 10.1.1.254 or logging host 10.1.1.254 global configuration commands would be used.

3. Specify the level of log messages to send to the Syslog server. For example, to send Level 7 (debugging logs) to the local buffer, an administrator would use the logging buffered debugging global configuration command; however, to send Level 5 logs to a remote Syslog server, an administrator would use the logging trap notifications global configuration command.

4. Specify the facility for Syslog messages using the logging facility global configuration command. This step is optional and you are not required to implement this as part of the IINS course requirements.

5. Verify logging by issuing the show logging command. This step is also optional.

To reinforce what we have just learned, we will go over a few configuration examples pertaining to Syslog configuration. The following example illustrates how to send all Level 6 Syslog messages to a remote Syslog server with the IP address 172.16.1.254:

```
R1(config)#logging on
R1(config)#logging host 172.16.1.254
R1(config)#logging trap informational
R1(config)#exit
R1#
R1#show logging
Syslog logging:     enabled (1 messages dropped, 0 messages rate-limited,
                    0 flushes, 0 overruns, xml disabled, filtering disabled)

No Active Message Discriminator.

No Inactive Message Discriminator.

    Console logging: disabled
    Monitor logging: level debugging, 0 messages logged, xml disabled,
            filtering disabled
    Buffer logging:  level debugging, 1 messages logged, xml disabled,
            filtering disabled
    Logging Exception size (4096 bytes)
    Count and timestamp logging messages: disabled
    Persistent logging: disabled
    Trap logging: level informational, 38 message lines logged
        Logging to 172.16.1.254 (udp port 514, audit disabled,
            authentication disabled, encryption disabled, link up),
            22 message lines logged,
            0 message lines rate-limited,
            0 message lines dropped-by-MD,
```

The following example illustrates how to log all critical notifications to the local buffer:

```
R2(config)#logging on
R2(config)#logging buffered
R2(config)#logging buffered critical
R2(config)#exit
R2#
R2#show logging
Syslog logging:      enabled (1 messages dropped, 0 messages rate-limited,
                     0 flushes, 0 overruns, xml disabled, filtering disabled)

No Active Message Discriminator.



No Inactive Message Discriminator.


    Console logging: disabled
    Monitor logging: level debugging, 0 messages logged, xml disabled,
            filtering disabled
    Buffer logging:  level critical, 0 messages logged, xml disabled,
            filtering disabled
    Logging Exception size (4096 bytes)
    Count and timestamp logging messages: disabled
    Persistent logging: disabled
    Trap logging: level debugging, 32 message lines logged

Log Buffer (4096 bytes):
```

When logging messages to the buffer, it is important to remember that older logs are deleted as the buffer becomes full. By default, the router buffer size is 4096 bytes. Depending on the level of logging enabled, it is possible that older messages will be flushed within a short period of time as new messages are received.

Therefore, in order to retain messages in the local buffer for a greater period of time, increase the size of the local buffer by issuing the logging buffered [size] global configuration command. This is illustrated and validated in the following router output:

```
R2(config)#logging buffered 10000
R2(config)#exit
R2#
R2#show logging
Syslog logging:      enabled (1 messages dropped, 0 messages rate-limited,
                     0 flushes, 0 overruns, xml disabled, filtering disabled)

No Active Message Discriminator.
```

No Inactive Message Discriminator.


```
      Console logging: disabled
      Monitor logging: level debugging, 0 messages logged, xml disabled,
                       filtering disabled
      Buffer logging:   level debugging, 1 messages logged, xml disabled,
                        filtering disabled
      Logging Exception size (4096 bytes)
      Count and timestamp logging messages: disabled
      Persistent logging: disabled
      Trap logging:     level debugging, 33 message lines logged
```

Log Buffer (10000 bytes):

The following example illustrates how to log all Level 7 messages to a remote Syslog server with the IP address 172.16.1.254, while also logging all Level 6 messages to the local router buffer. In addition to this, all Console level logging is disabled:

```
R2(config)#logging on
R2(config)#logging host 172.16.1.254
R2(config)#logging trap 7
R2(config)#logging buffered
R2(config)#logging buffered 6
R2(config)#no logging console
R2(config)#exit
R2#
R2#show logging
Syslog logging:      enabled (1 messages dropped, 0 messages rate-limited,
                     0 flushes, 0 overruns, xml disabled, filtering disabled)
```

No Active Message Discriminator.

No Inactive Message Discriminator.


```
      Console logging: disabled
      Monitor logging: level debugging, 0 messages logged, xml disabled,
                       filtering disabled
      Buffer logging:  level informational, 2 messages logged, xml disabled,
                       filtering disabled
      Logging Exception size (4096 bytes)
      Count and timestamp logging messages: disabled
      Persistent logging: disabled
      Trap logging: level debugging, 35 message lines logged
```

Logging to 172.16.1.254 (udp port 514, audit disabled,
authentication disabled, encryption disabled, link up),
2 message lines logged,
0 message lines rate-limited,
0 message lines dropped-by-MD,
xml disabled, sequence number disabled
filtering disabled

Log Buffer (4096 bytes):

*Mar 1 00:56:16.486: %SYS-5-CONFIG_I: Configured from console by vty0 (172.16.1.1)
*Mar 1 00:56:17.488: %SYS-6-LOGGINGHOST_STARTSTOP: Logging to host 172.16.1.254
port 514 started—CLI initiated

Implementing Syslog via SDM

In Cisco SDM, administrators can configure Syslog parameters by clicking on the **Additional Tasks** tab and then selecting **Router Properties,** as illustrated in Figure 5.16:

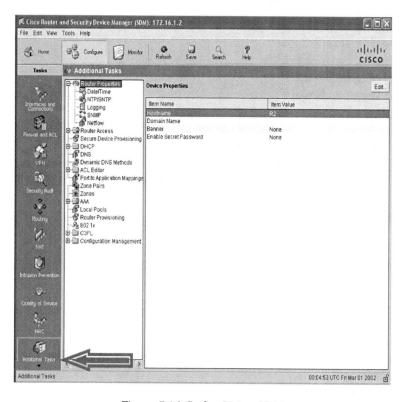

Figure 5.16. Syslog Using SDM

Next, under **Router Properties**, click on **Logging** to bring you to the following screen:

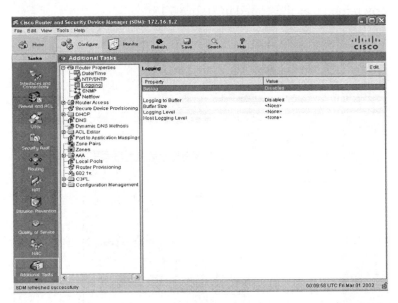

Figure 5.17. Select 'Syslog Property'

As illustrated in Figure 5.17 above, all logging capabilities are currently disabled on the device. To enable Syslog logging, highlight the **Syslog** property and then click on the **Edit** button, as illustrated in Figure 5.18:

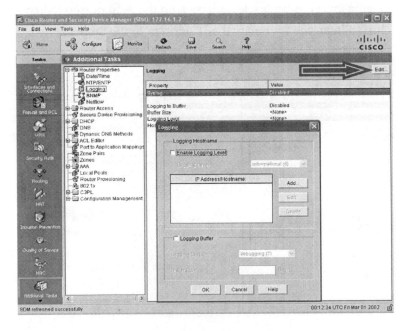

Figure 5.18. Select 'Edit'

Next, check the **Enable Logging Level** checkbox and select the desired logging level from the **Logging Level** drop-down menu, as illustrated in Figure 5.19:

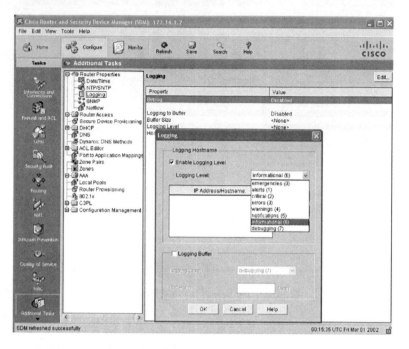

Figure 5.19. Choose the Logging level

Once the desired logging level has been selected, click on the **Add** button to bring up the following pop-up window, which allows you to specify the IP address of the Syslog server:

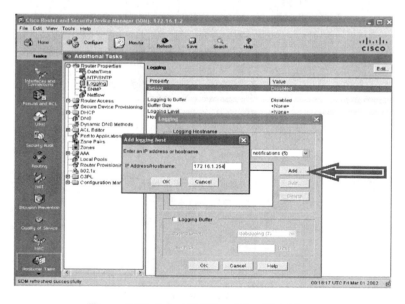

Figure 5.20. Select 'Add' and the IP Address

Once you have entered the IP address of the server, click on the **OK** button. Next, click on the **Logging Buffer** checkbox to configure local buffer parameters, as illustrated in Figure 5.21:

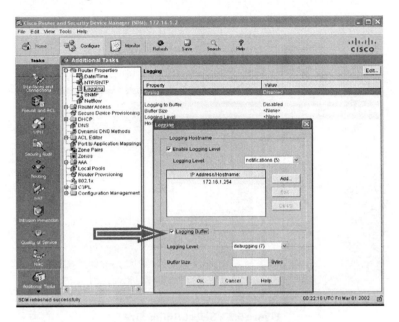

Figure 5.21. Select 'Logging Buffer'

Next, select the desired level of logging from the **Logging Level** drop-down menu, as illustrated in Figure 5.22:

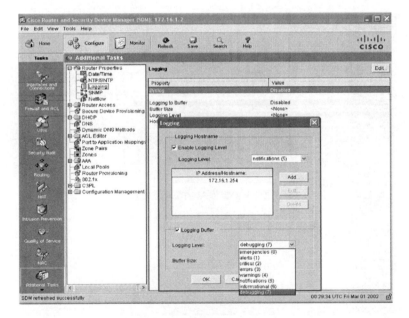

Figure 5.22. Select the Logging Level

Optionally, you can also set the size of the local buffer by typing in the desired size in the **Buffer Size** option, as illustrated in Figure 5.23:

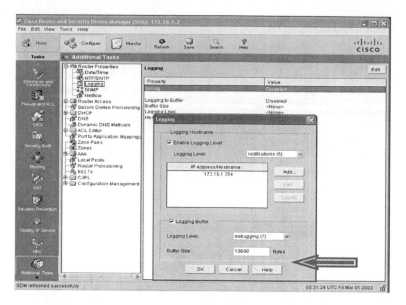

Figure 5.23. Select Buffer Size

Once complete with your desired input and configuration, click on the **OK** button at the very bottom. SDM then configures the router, as illustrated in Figure 5.24:

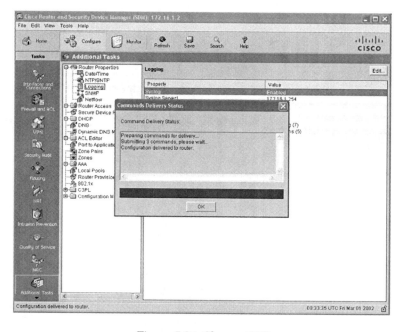

Figure 5.24. Choose 'OK'

Click on **OK** and SDM shows the configured options as illustrated in Figure 5.25:

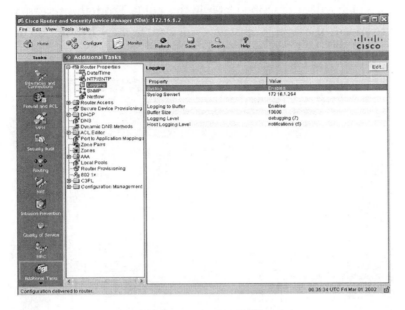

Figure 5.25. View Your Selections

To view logging via SDM, click on **Monitor**—next to the **Configure** main tab—at the very top, and then click on **Logging,** as illustrated in Figure 5.26:

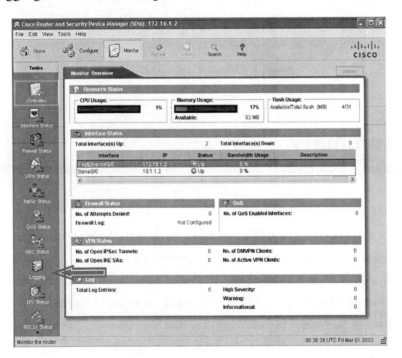

Figure 5.26. Logging Screenshot

SDM then brings you to the following screen, which allows you to view Syslog messages—as well as other log messages, which will be described later in this guide. From this screen, you can select the drop-down menu to specify the level of messages you want to view. In addition to this, administrators can also clear the buffer or search through the logs:

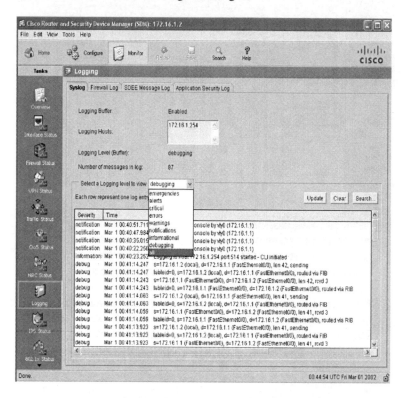

Figure 5.27. View Logging Messages

Chapter Summary

The following section is a summary of the major points you should be aware of in this chapter:

Secure Sockets Shell Overview

- SSH provides a more secure and reliable method for device administration than Telnet
- SSH secures the sessions using standard cryptographic mechanisms
- SSH uses TCP and UDP port 22, although TCP port 22 is the de-facto port listed for SSH
- There are two versions of SSH available: SSH version 1 and SSH version 2
- SSH version 1 is not safe and it is recommended that SSH version 2 be used
- SSH version 1 and SSH version 2 are not completely compatible

Implementing SSH via the CLI

- SSH version 1 is supported in Cisco IOS 12.1(1)T and later versions
- SSH version 2 is supported in Cisco IOS 12.3(4)T and later versions
- SSH is only supported in Cisco IOS images that have cryptographic capabilities
- The following steps are required to implement SSH on Cisco IOS routers:

1. Configure a domain name on the router. This is performed via the ip domain-name [name] global configuration command.

2. Generate the security keys that will be used by SSH. This can be performed by using the crypto key generate rsa global configuration command and specifying the desired key size; or, alternatively, via the crypto key generate rsa general-keys and specifying the desired key size. The key size, which is used for SSH, can be up to 2048 bits in size. The larger the key size, the more secure the implementation. However, keep in mind that larger keys also take a longer time to generate. Typically, a key size of 1024 is used.

3. Specify the time that the router waits on the SSH client, in seconds, to input username and password information before disconnecting the session via the ip ssh timeout global configuration command. This is an optional step because, by default, the router will wait for 120 seconds (2 minutes).

4. Specify the number of SSH authentication retries before a session is reset via the ip ssh authentication-retries global configuration command. By default, the Cisco IOS router will allow up to three failed logins before resetting the SSH connection. As is the case with the ip ssh timeout global configuration command, this is an optional step.

5. Allow only SSH sessions to the Cisco IOS router by issuing the transport input ssh line configuration command to allow only SSH. This is performed for all VTY lines.

6. Save your router configuration by using the copy running-config startup-config or the copy system:running-config nvram:startup-config commands, which depend on the Cisco IOS version that is running on the device.

Implementing SSH via SDM

To configure and implement SSH via Cisco SDM, perform the following steps:

1. On the main configuration page, click on the **Additional Tasks** button
2. On the **Additional Tasks** page select **Router Properties** to configure the domain name

3. On the **Additional Tasks** page select **Router Access** > **SSH** to configure SSH parameters

4. Click on the **Generate RSA Key** radio button to generate RSA keys

5. Type in the size of the RSA key and click **OK**

Syslog Overview

- Syslog allows a host to send event notification messages across IP networks
- A Syslog solution is comprised of a Syslog server and a Syslog client
- A Syslog server is an entity that listens to the Syslog messages that are sent to it
- A Syslog client is an entity that generates Syslog messages
- Syslog uses UDP as the underlying transport mechanism, using a destination port of 514
- Syslog messages cannot exceed 1,024 bytes in size
- All Syslog messages contain three distinct parts. These parts are the:

1. Priority—this field represents both the Facility and Severity of the message
2. Header—this field contains the timestamp and the hostname or IP address of the device
3. Message—this field the text of the message and includes the TAG and CONTENT fields

Implementing Syslog via the CLI

To implement Syslog using the CLI, the following sequence of steps should be taken:

1. Enable logging globally by issuing the logging on global configuration command

2. Specify the location the router should send the logs using the logging command. For example, to send Syslog messages to the local buffer, the logging buffered command would be used; whereas to send Syslog messages to a Syslog server with the IP address 10.1.1.254, the logging 10.1.1.254 or logging host 10.1.1.254 global configuration commands would be used.

3. Specify the level of log messages to send to the Syslog server. For example, to send Level 7 (Debugging logs) to the local buffer, an administrator would use the logging buffered debugging global configuration command; however, to send Level 5 logs to a remote Syslog server, an administrator would use the logging trap notifications global configuration command.

4. Specify the facility for Syslog messages using the logging facility global configuration command. This step is optional and you are not required to implement this as part of the IINS requirements.

5. Verify logging by issuing the show logging command. This step is also optional.

Implementing Syslog via SDM

- To configure and implement Syslog via Cisco SDM, perform the following steps:
  1. On the main configuration page, click on the **Additional Tasks** button
  2. On the **Additional Tasks** page select **Router Properties** > **Logging** to configure Syslog
  3. Select **Edit** to edit default Syslog parameters
  4. Click **OK** when you are complete to have SDM issue the configuration on the router

- To view Syslog information via SDM, perform the following steps:
  1. Click on **Monitor**—next to the **Configure** main tab
  2. Select Logging on the main Monitor page

Commands Used in this Chapter

The following section is a summary of the commands used in this chapter:

Command	Description
ip domain-name [name]	Used to configure a domain name on the router
crypto key generate rsa	Used to generate public RSA keys for SSH
crypto key generate rsa general-keys	Performs the same function as the crypto key generate rsa command and generates a public key for SSH
ip ssh timeout	Used to configure the SSH timeout value in seconds
ip ssh authentication-retries	Used to specify the SSH authentication attempts
copy running-config startup-config	Used to save the running-config (RAM) to the startup-config (NVRAM)
copy system:running-config nvram: startup-config	Used to save the running-config (RAM) to the startup-config (NVRAM)
transport input ssh	Allows SSH access only for the specified VTY lines
crypto key zeroize rsa	Used to delete the existing RSA public key
show crypto key mypubkey rsa	Used to view the configured RSA public key
show ip ssh	Used to view the current version of SSH enabled
logging facility	Used to specify a logging facility
logging buffered	Used to specify local buffer logging parameters
logging trap	Used to specify Syslog server logging parameters
logging on	Used to globally enable logging (enabled by default)
clock set hh:mm:ss	Used to set the local router time
logging host	Used to specify the IP address of the Syslog server
show logging	Used to view the local router log (buffer)

CHAPTER 6

Implementing Local Area Network Security

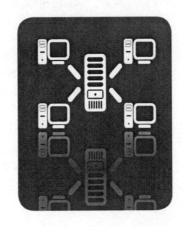

The Data Link Layer of the OSI Model provides the functional and procedural means to transfer data among network entities with interoperability and connectivity to other layers, but from a security perspective, it presents its own set of challenges. The IINS exam objective covered in this chapter is as follows:

- Describe how to prevent Layer 2 attacks by configuring basic Catalyst switch security features

This chapter is broken up into the following sections:

- LAN Switching Overview
- CAM Table Overflow Attacks
- MAC Spoofing Attacks
- ARP Spoofing Attacks
- VTP Attacks
- VLAN Hopping Attacks
- PVLAN Attacks
- Spanning-Tree Protocol Attacks
- DHCP Spoofing and Starvation Attacks
- Identity Based Networking Services
- IEEE 802.1x Attacks
- Other Cisco Catalyst Switch Security Features

IINS Exam Objective	Section(s) Covered
Describe how to prevent Layer 2 attacks by configuring basic Catalyst switch security features	• CAM Table Overflow Attacks • MAC Spoofing Attacks • ARP Spoofing Attacks • VTP Attacks • VLAN Hopping Attacks • PVLAN Attacks • Spanning-Tree Protocol Attacks • DHCP Spoofing and Starvation Attacks • IEEE 802.1x Attacks
Other related topics	• LAN Switching Overview • Identity Based Networking Services • Other Cisco Catalyst Switch Security Features

LAN Switching Overview

LAN switching is a core component of the CCNA certification, which is a prerequisite for the IINS certification, and as such is not described in detail in this section. Instead, this section provides basic details on LAN switch operation, functionality, and protocols.

Switches operate at the Data Link Layer of the OSI Model and send frames. These frames contain source and destination MAC addresses for the sending and receiving hosts. The MAC addresses are stored in the switch MAC address table. The MAC address table uses Content Addressable Memory (CAM) and is referred to as the CAM table.

CAM is a memory type used in high-speed searching applications. CAM is used on switches because they are hardware-based, unlike bridges, which are software-based. By using Application Specific Integrated Circuits, or ASICs, switches can perform faster hardware-based lookups and forwarding than bridges can.

When building their CAM tables, switches note the incoming port of any particular MAC address when the device connected to that port sends a frame. Initially, switches have no idea where the destination device is, and so they broadcast the frame they receive from a particular host out of every port, except for the port on which the frame was received.

After the switch has flooded the frame, it will wait for a device to respond. When a device responds to the broadcast frame, the switch will note the port the response was received on and place that address in the MAC address table. This process is repeated until the switch has learned the MAC addresses of all devices connected to all ports. The MAC address learning process used by switches is illustrated in Figure 6.1:

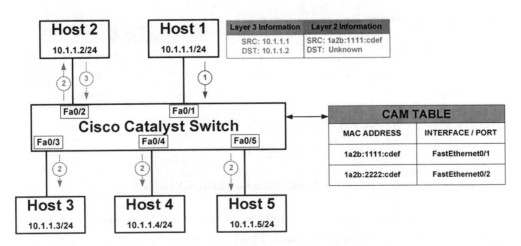

Figure 6.1. MAC Address Learning Process

Referencing the Figure 6.1 above, five devices are connected to a Cisco Catalyst switch: Host 1, Host 2, Host 3, Host 4, and Host 5. Host 1 wants to send data to Host 2. However, Host 1 only knows the IP address of Host 2, which is 10.1.1.2; it does not know the MAC address. In order to resolve the IP address of Host 2 to a MAC address, Host 1 will send out an ARP broadcast frame. ARP—Address Resolution Protocol—is used to resolve IP addresses to MAC addresses. This packet is sent to the Catalyst switch, as illustrated in step 1.

When the switch receives this frame from Host 1, it notes the incoming port, which is FastEthernet0/1, and because the switch does not currently know the MAC address of Host 2, it broadcasts the frame on all interfaces, except for FastEthernet0/1, as illustrated in step 2.

When Host 2 receives this broadcast frame, it responds to the broadcast with its MAC address. The switch then proceeds and notes the incoming port for the response from Host 2, which is FastEthernet0/2. This is illustrated in step 3. This received information is added to the switch CAM table. Subsequent frames from Host 1 to Host 2 will be switched between the FastEthernet interfaces the devices are connected to. This same process is repeated until the switch knows all the MAC addresses of all devices connected to it (e.g. Host 3, Host 4, and Host 5) as well.

Taking this concept one step further, switch CAM tables also reflect MAC addresses based on their VLAN allocations. A VLAN is a logical grouping of hosts, which can be restricted to a single switch or can span multiple physical switches. The concept of CAM table building for multiple VLANs is illustrated in Figure 6.2:

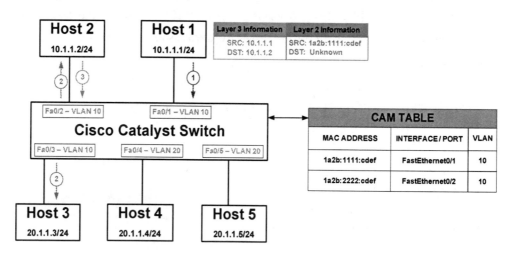

Figure 6.2. CAM Tables for Multiple VLANs

Referencing Figure 6.2 illustrated above, five devices are connected to a Cisco Catalyst switch: Host 1, Host 2, Host 3, Host 4, and Host 5. However, VLANs have been configured on the switch; Host 1, Host 2, and Host 3 reside in VLAN 10, and Host 4 and Host 5 reside in VLAN 20.

Host 1 wants to send data to Host 2. However, Host 1 only knows the IP address of Host 2, which is 10.1.1.2; it does not know the MAC address. In order to resolve the IP address of Host 2 to a MAC address, Host 1 will send out an ARP broadcast frame. This frame is sent to the Catalyst switch, as illustrated in step 1.

When the switch receives this frame from Host 1, it notes the incoming port, which is FastEthernet0/1, as well as the VLAN the port resides in, which is VLAN 10. Because the switch does not currently know the MAC address of Host 2, it sends out a broadcast on all interfaces in VLAN 10, except for the interface on which the frame was received. Given that FastEthernet0/1, FastEthernet0/2, and FastEthernet0/3 reside in VLAN 10, the broadcast will be sent only to those ports, as illustrated in step 2.

When Host 2 receives this broadcast frame, it responds to the broadcast with its MAC address. The switch then proceeds and notes the incoming port for the response from Host 2, which is FastEthernet0/2, as illustrated in step 3. This received information is added to the switch CAM table. Subsequent frames from Host 1 to Host 2 will be switched between the FastEthernet interfaces the devices are connected to. This same process is applicable to Host 4 and Host 5, which reside in VLAN 20. The switch CAM table is viewed by issuing the show mac-address-table command. The options available with this command are as follows:

```
Sw1#show mac-address-table ?
  address        address keyword
  aging-time     aging-time keyword
  count          count keyword
  dynamic        dynamic entry type
  interface      interface keyword
  multicast      multicast info for selected wildcard
  notification   MAC notification parameters and history table
  static         static entry type
  vlan           VLAN keyword
  |              Output modifiers
  <cr>
```

There are only a few keywords that you should be familiar with for the purposes of the IINS course requirements. The address keyword allows administrators to view the specific MAC addresses in the CAM table. The aging-time keyword prints out information on the time MAC entries stored in the CAM table will be valid for. The dynamic keyword prints out all learned dynamic MAC entries in the CAM table. And, finally, the vlan keyword prints out all learned dynamic or configured static MAC addresses for the specified VLAN.

For example, to view all dynamic MAC address entries in the CAM table, the show mac-address-table dynamic command would be issued, as illustrated in the following output:

```
Sw1#show mac-address-table dynamic
        Mac Address Table
-------------------------------------------

Vlan    Mac Address         Type        Ports
----    ----------------    --------    -----
  2     000c.cea7.f3a0      DYNAMIC     Fa0/1
  2     0013.1986.0a20      DYNAMIC     Fa0/2
  6     0004.c16f.8741      DYNAMIC     Fa0/3
  6     0030.803f.ea81      DYNAMIC     Fa0/4
  8     0004.c16f.8742      DYNAMIC     Fa0/5
  8     0030.803f.ea82      DYNAMIC     Fa0/6
Total Mac Addresses for this criterion: 6
```

When multiple switches are connected together via trunk links, they need to have some method to communicate VLAN information between them. This is accomplished by using the VLAN Trunking Protocol (VTP). VTP is a Cisco proprietary Layer 2 messaging protocol that manages the addition, deletion, and renaming of VLANs on a network-wide basis. Switches must reside within the same VTP domain in order to share VLAN information.

Trunk ports are used to carry traffic that belongs to multiple VLANs between switches, using the same link. By default, all VLANs are permitted to traverse a trunk port. However, the Cisco IOS software allows administrators to change this default behavior and manually specify which VLANs administrators want to traverse any given trunk link. VTP packets are sent across the trunk links either in Inter-Switch Link (ISL) or in IEEE 802.1Q (dot1Q) frames.

In switched networks with multiple, redundant trunk links between source and destination stations, the Spanning-Tree Protocol (STP) is used to prevent network loops. STP is defined in the IEEE 802.1d standard, and it uses the Spanning Tree Algorithm (STA) to determine which switch ports will be in a blocking state and which will be in a forwarding state. When all ports on all switches in the network are in either a blocking state or a forwarding state, the Layer 2 network is said to be converged.

CAM Table Overflow Attacks

As described in the previous section, CAM tables are storage locations that contain lists of MAC addresses known on physical ports of the switch, as well as their VLAN parameters. Switches, like all computing devices, do not have unlimited memory. This means that the CAM table has a fixed, allocated memory space.

Attackers can exploit the CAM table memory space limitation by flooding the switch with a large number of randomly generated invalid source and destination MAC addresses, until the CAM table fills up and the switch is no longer able to accept new entries. In such situations, the switch effectively turns into a hub and simply begins to broadcast all newly received frames to all ports (within the same VLAN) on the switch, essentially turning the VLAN into one big broadcast domain. CAM table attacks are easy to perform, and tools such as MACOF and DSNIFF are readily available to launch this type of attack.

While increasing the number of VLANs, which reduces the size of broadcast domains, can assist in reducing the effects of CAM table attacks, the recommended security solution is to enable and configure switch port security.

Port Security Overview

Port security is a dynamic Cisco Catalyst switch feature that secures switch ports, and ultimately the CAM table, by limiting the number of MAC addresses that can be learned on a particular port or interface. Port security can be implemented in the following three ways:

- Static Secure MAC Addresses
- Dynamic Secure MAC Addresses
- Sticky Secure MAC Addresses

Static secure MAC addresses are statically configured by network administrators and are stored in the MAC address table, as well as in the switch configuration. When static secure MAC addresses are assigned to a secure port, the switch will not forward frames that do not have a source MAC address that matches the configured static secure MAC address or addresses.

Dynamic secure MAC addresses are dynamically learned by the switch and are stored in the MAC address table. However, unlike static secure MAC addresses, dynamic secure MAC address entries are removed from the switch when the switch is reloaded or powered down.

Sticky secure MAC addresses are a combination of static secure MAC addresses and dynamic secure MAC addresses. These addresses can be learned dynamically or configured statically and are stored in the MAC address table, as well as in the switch configuration. This means that when the switch is powered down or rebooted, it will not need to dynamically discover the MAC addresses again because they will already be saved in the configuration file.

Once port security has been enabled, administrators can define the actions the switch will take in the event of a port security violation. Cisco IOS software allows administrators to specify three different actions to take when a violation occurs:

- Protect
- Shutdown
- Restrict

The protect option forces the port into a protected port mode. In this mode, all Unicast or Multicast frames with unknown source MAC addresses, i.e. MAC addresses not presently in the CAM table, are discarded by the switch. When the switch is configured to protect a port, it will not send out a notification when operating in protected port mode, meaning that administrators would never know when an attack was prevented in this mode.

The shutdown option places a port in an error-disabled state when a security violation occurs. The corresponding LED on the switch port is also turned off in this state. In shutdown mode, the switch sends out an SNMP trap and a Syslog message, and the violation counter is incremented.

The restrict option is used to drop packets with unknown MAC addresses, i.e. MAC addresses not presently in the CAM table, when the number of secure MAC addresses reaches the administrator-defined maximum limit for the port. In this mode, the switch will continue to restrict additional MAC addresses from sending frames until a sufficient number of secure MAC addresses is removed, or the number of maximum allowable addresses is increased. As is the case with the shutdown option, the switch sends out an SNMP trap and a Syslog message, and the violation counter is incremented.

Configuring Port Security

Port security is configured via the switchport port-security interface configuration command. The options available with this command are illustrated in the following output:

```
Sw1(config)#int faste 0/1
Sw1(config-if)#switchport port-security ?
  aging           Port-security aging commands
  mac-address     Secure mac address
  maximum         Max secure addrs
  violation       Security Violation Mode
  <cr>
```

The printed options are listed and described in Table 6.1:

Table 6.1. Port Security Options

Keyword	Description
aging	This keyword is used to specify the aging time for secure MAC addresses.
mac-address	This keyword is used to configure a static secure MAC address or to utilize sticky learning.

maximum	This keyword is used to specify the maximum number of secure MAC addresses that can be learned on an interface.
violation	This keyword is used to specify the action the switch will take in the event of a violation.

The following example illustrates how to enable port security on an interface using a static secure MAC address of 001f:3c59:d63b to be forwarded by the switch:

```
Sw1(config)#int fastethernet0/2
Sw1(config-if)#switchport port-security
Sw1(config-if)#switchport port-security mac-address 001f.3c59.d63b
```

Port security configuration can be validated by issuing the show port-security command, as illustrated in the following switch output:

```
Sw1#show port-security
Secure Port       MaxSecureAddr  CurrentAddr  SecurityViolation  Security Action
                    (Count)        (Count)        (Count)
------------------------------------------------------------------------------------
       Fa0/2           1              1              0             Shutdown
------------------------------------------------------------------------------------

Total Addresses in System : 1
Max Addresses limit in System : 1024
```

NOTE: Keep in mind that, as illustrated in the output above, the default action in the event of a violation is to shut down the port. This default behavior can be modified by using the switchport port-security violation interface configuration command.

The following example illustrates how to configure port security to dynamically learn no more than two secure MAC addresses on a particular switch port. In the event that this value is exceeded, the switch has been configured to restrict frames from any other MAC addresses:

```
Sw1(config)#int fastethernet0/2
Sw1(config-if)#switchport port-security
Sw1(config-if)#switchport port-security maximum 2
Sw1(config-if)#switchport port-security violation restrict
```

In the event of a security violation, and assuming that the switch has been configured for logging capabilities, the local switch log would reflect the following:

```
Sw1#show logging
Syslog logging: enabled (0 messages dropped, 0 messages rate-limited, 0 flushes, 0 overruns)
    Console logging:        disabled
```

Monitor logging:	level debugging, 0 messages logged
Buffer logging:	level informational, 243 messages logged
Exception Logging:	size (4096 bytes)
File logging:	disabled
Trap logging:	level informational, 247 message lines logged

Log Buffer (4096 bytes):

01:06:16: %PORT_SECURITY-2-PSECURE_VIOLATION: Security violation occurred, caused by MAC address 0013.1986.0a20 on port Fa0/2.

01:06:36: %PORT_SECURITY-2-PSECURE_VIOLATION: Security violation occurred, caused by MAC address 000c.cea7.f3a0 on port Fa0/2.

01:06:41: %PORT_SECURITY-2-PSECURE_VIOLATION: Security violation occurred, caused by MAC address 0004.c16f.8741 on port Fa0/2.

Additionally, a remote Syslog server would show the following port security messages:

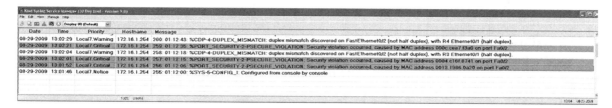

Figure 6.3. Syslog Security Messages

The increments in the port security violation counter can be viewed by using the show port-security command, as illustrated in the following output:

Sw1#**show port-security**

Secure Port	MaxSecureAddr (Count)	CurrentAddr (Count)	**SecurityViolation (Count)**	Security Action
Fa0/2	2	2	**16**	Restrict

Total Addresses in System : 2
Max Addresses limit in System : 1024

The following example illustrates how to enable sticky learning on a port for a maximum of ten MAC addresses. In the event that unknown MAC addresses are detected on the port, the port is configured to go into protected port mode:

```
Sw1(config)#int fastethernet0/2
Sw1(config-if)#switchport port-security
Sw1(config-if)#switchport port-security mac-address sticky
Sw1(config-if)#switchport port-security maximum 10
Sw1(config-if)#switchport port-security violation protect
```

The configuration is validated via the show port-security [options] command, as follows:

```
Sw1#show port-security
Secure Port    MaxSecureAddr  CurrentAddr  SecurityViolation  Security Action
               (Count)        (Count)      (Count)
--------------------------------------------------------------------------------------------
     Fa0/2         10              5              0                Protect
--------------------------------------------------------------------------------------------

Total Addresses in System : 5
Max Addresses limit in System : 1024
```

An important aspect to remember regarding sticky learning is that the learned addresses are automatically added to the switch configuration and this configuration is retained between reboots. The show running-config interface [name] command can be used to view the learned and saved sticky MAC addresses per interface, as illustrated in the following output:

```
Sw1#show running-config interface fastethernet 0/2
Building configuration...

Current configuration : 550 bytes
!
interface FastEthernet0/2
 switchport access vlan 2
 switchport mode access
 switchport port-security
 switchport port-security maximum 10
 switchport port-security violation protect
 switchport port-security mac-address sticky
 switchport port-security mac-address sticky 0004.c16f.8741
 switchport port-security mac-address sticky 000c.cea7.f3a0
 switchport port-security mac-address sticky 0013.1986.0a20
 switchport port-security mac-address sticky 001d.09d4.0238
 switchport port-security mac-address sticky 0030.803f.ea81
 no ip address
end
```

Additionally, the show port-security address command can be used to view sticky addresses on a per-interface basis, as illustrated in the following output:

```
Sw1#show port-security address
      Secure Mac Address Table
--------------------------------------------------------------------------------------------
Vlan   Mac Address       Type                    Ports   Remaining Age
                                                         (mins)
------  ----------------  -----                   ------  --------------------
```

```
2   0004.c16f.8741        SecureSticky        Fa0/2    -
2   000c.cea7.f3a0        SecureSticky        Fa0/2    -
2   0013.1986.0a20        SecureSticky        Fa0/2    -
2   001d.09d4.0238        SecureSticky        Fa0/2    -
2   0030.803f.ea81        SecureSticky        Fa0/2    -
-----------------------------------------------------------------------
Total Addresses in System : 5
Max Addresses limit in System : 1024
```

In addition to configuring the different port security parameters, it is important to completely understand the implications of port security on MAC address aging. By default, the secure MAC address will not be aged out and will remain in the switch MAC table until the switch is powered off. This means that even if a host with a secured MAC address is removed from the switch port, the MAC address entry will be retained in the switch CAM table. To address this issue, and the potential problems it may cause, the Cisco IOS software allows administrators to configure port security aging. There are two types of aging mechanisms that can be used:

- Absolute
- Inactivity

The absolute mechanism causes the secured MAC addresses on the port to age out after a fixed specified time, upon which all references are flushed from the secure address list. The inactivity mechanism, also referred to as the idle time mechanism, causes the secured MAC addresses on the port to age out if there is no activity (i.e. frames) during the specified time period.

The following example illustrates how to configure an aging time of two hours for inactive secured MAC addresses on FastEthernet0/2:

```
Sw1(config)#int fastethernet0/2
Sw1(config-if)#switchport port-security aging time 120
Sw1(config-if)#switchport port-security aging type inactivity
```

The following example illustrates how to configure a switch port so that all secured MAC addresses are flushed every eight hours:

```
Sw1(config)#int fastethernet0/2
Sw1(config-if)#switchport port-security aging time 480
Sw1(config-if)#switchport port-security aging type absolute
```

The remaining valid time for secure MAC addresses, based on the port security timer configuration, can be viewed by issuing the show port-security address command, as follows:

```
Sw1#show port-security address
        Secure Mac Address Table
-----------------------------------------------------------------------
Vlan   Mac Address        Type              Ports   Remaining Age
                                                     (mins)

------   ----------------   -----             ------   --------------------
   2    0004.c16f.8741     SecureDynamic     Fa0/2    479
   2    000c.cea7.f3a0     SecureDynamic     Fa0/2    479
   2    0013.1986.0a20     SecureDynamic     Fa0/2    478
   2    001d.09d4.0238     SecureDynamic     Fa0/2    478
   2    0030.803f.ea81     SecureDynamic     Fa0/2    479
-----------------------------------------------------------------------
```

Total Addresses in System : 5
Max Addresses limit in System : 1024

MAC Spoofing Attacks

Earlier in this guide, we learned that spoofing is masquerading or pretending to be someone you are not. In addition, we also learned that the most common types of spoofing attacks are IP spoofing attacks. In this section, we are going to be learning about spoofing at the Data Link Layer, specifically MAC address spoofing.

MAC spoofing is used to spoof a source MAC address to impersonate other hosts or devices in the network. The primary objective of MAC spoofing is to confuse the switch and cause it to believe that the same host is connected to two ports, which causes the switch to attempt to forward frames destined to the trusted host to the attacker as well. Figure 6.4 illustrates a switch with four connected hosts, as well as the current CAM table of the switch:

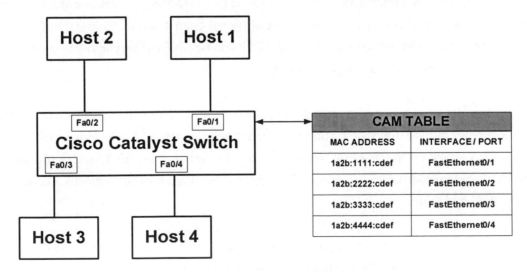

Figure 6.4. Switch CAM Table

In Figure 6.4 illustrated above, the switch is operating normally and, based on CAM table entries, knows the MAC addresses for all devices connected to its ports. Therefore, if Host 4 wanted to send a frame to Host 2, the switch would simply forward the frame out of its FastEthernet0/2 interface to Host 2.

Now, suppose Host 1 was compromised by an attacker who wanted to receive all traffic destined for Host 2. Using MAC spoofing, the attacker crafts an Ethernet frame using the source address of Host 2. When the switch receives this frame, it notes the source MAC address and overwrites the CAM table entry for the MAC address of Host 2, and points it to port FastEthernet0/1 instead of port FastEthernet0/2, where the real Host 2 is connected. This concept is illustrated in Figure 6.5:

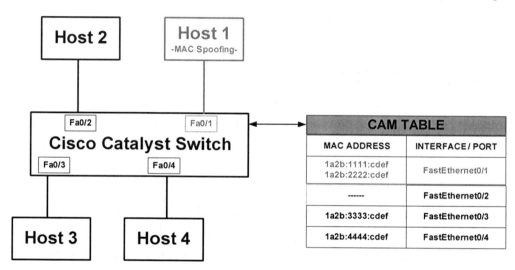

Figure 6.5. Compromised CAM Table

When Host 3 or Host 4 attempts to send frames destined to Host 2, the switch will forward them to the attacker on Host 1 because the CAM table entry has been poisoned. When Host 2 attempts to send frames, the switch relearns the same MAC address from FastEthernet0/2 and rewrites the CAM table entry once again to reflect this change.

The result is a tug-of-war between Host 2 and Host 1 as to which host owns this MAC address. In addition, this confuses the switch and causes repetitive rewrites of MAC address table entries, causing a DoS attack on the real host, i.e. Host 2. If the number of spoofed MAC addresses used is high, this attack could have serious performance consequences for the switch that is constantly rewriting its CAM table.

MAC spoofing attacks can be mitigated by implementing port security, which was described in detail in the previous section along with configuration examples.

ARP Spoofing Attacks

ARP spoofing attacks are used by attackers to disguise their source MAC address by the impersonation of another host on the network. It is important to understand that this is not the same thing as a MAC spoofing attack. In ARP spoofing attacks, the switch is misguided by poisoning the ARP cache. In MAC spoofing attacks, however, the switch is misguided into believing that two ports have the same MAC address, which effectively poisons the MAC address table.

ARP is used to resolve IP addresses to MAC addresses. For example, if a host has an IP address and needs to reach another host with a different IP address, it will use ARP to resolve that IP address to a MAC address so that the switch can forward the frames to the intended destination. Cisco routers and switches maintain ARP tables to show IP-to-MAC address mappings. Keep in mind that an ARP table is not the same as the switch CAM table. In Cisco IOS software, the ARP table can be viewed by issuing the show arp (for all IP and non-IP ARP mappings) or the show ip arp (for IP ARP mappings) commands. The following output illustrates an ARP table on a Cisco IOS router:

```
R1#show arp
Protocol  Address          Age (min)  Hardware Addr   Type   Interface
Internet  150.10.100.102    105       0000.a710.859b  ARPA   Ethernet0/0
Internet  150.10.100.102    115       0000.a710.68cd  ARPA   Ethernet0/0
```

On Windows-based machines, the arp –a command can also be used to view the ARP table:

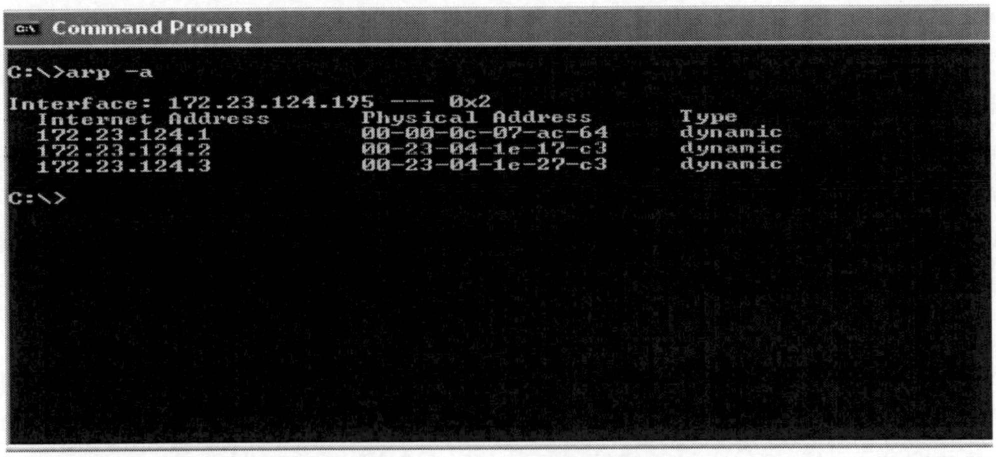

Figure 6.6. arp -a Command Output

ARP spoofing occurs during the ARP request and reply messaging between two or more legitimate host systems. It is during this exchange of messages that the attacker can inject a fake ARP reply message with his or her own MAC address masquerading as one of the legitimate hosts, as illustrated in Figure 6.7:

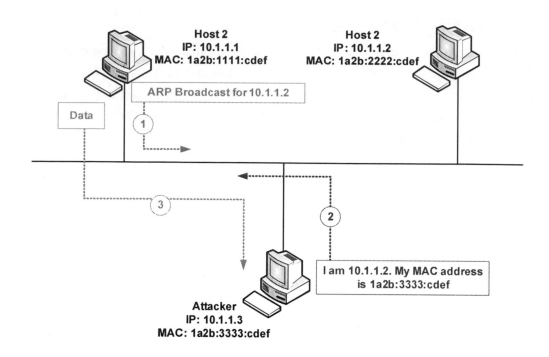

Figure 6.7. ARP Spoofing

In Figure 6.7 illustrated above, three hosts reside on a shared LAN segment. There are two legitimate hosts, Host 1 and Host 2, in addition to a machine that has been compromised and is now being operated by the attacker. When Host 1 wants to send data to Host 2, it sends out an ARP broadcast to resolve the IP address of Host 2 to a MAC address, as illustrated in step 1.

However, before Host 2 can respond to the ARP request from Host 1, the attacker crafts a packet and responds to Host 1, providing it with the MAC address of its machine instead. The ARP table on Host 1 is updated and incorrectly reflects an IP-to-MAC address mapping of 10.1.1.2 with the MAC address 1a2b.3333.cdef. This causes Host 1 to send all traffic that should be destined to Host 2 to the attacker's machine instead.

Another ARP function that can be used to steer traffic to the attacker's machine is accomplished using gratuitous ARP (GARP), which is an unsolicited ARP broadcast that contains the IP address of the target host and the attacker's MAC address. The GARP causes all hosts to update incorrectly their ARP tables with an ARP entry that pairs the target's IP address with the MAC address of the machine belonging to the attacker.

Similarly, GARP will also cause the switch to update incorrectly its CAM table, and when any host needs to send data to the target IP address, it will be forwarded to the machine belonging to the attacker instead. This concept is illustrated in Figure 6.8:

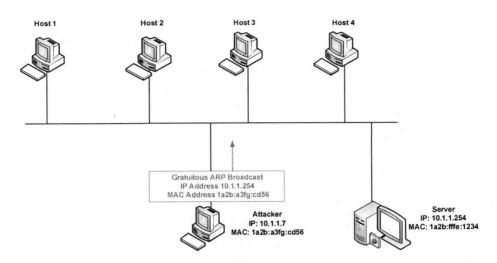

Figure 6.8. Attacker Using GARP

As illustrated in Figure 6.8 above, the attacker sends an unsolicited GARP to the LAN, causing all hosts to update their ARP tables with the MAC address 1a2b:a3fg:cd56 for the server 10.1.1.254. Therefore, all data sent to the server from Host 1, Host 2, Host 3, and Host 4, will actually be forwarded to the machine of the attacker.

ARP spoofing is very easy to perform and is commonly used in MITM attacks. In addition to this, readily available tools such as DSNIFF and ETTERCAP can be used to perform these attacks with relative ease. The recommended solution to prevent such attacks in Cisco Catalyst switches is to implement Dynamic ARP Inspection (DAI).

NOTE: DAI is only supported in medium-and-high-end Cisco Catalyst switches, such as the Cisco 4500 and Cisco 6500 series switches. It is not supported on lower-end switches, such as the Cisco Catalyst 2950 and 3750 series switches.

Dynamic ARP Inspection Overview

Dynamic ARP Inspection, or DAI, is a Cisco Catalyst switch security feature that validates ARP packets in a network. DAI determines the validity of packets by performing an IP-to-MAC address binding inspection, which is stored in a trusted DHCP snooping database on the switch. DHCP snooping will be described in detail later in this chapter.

Once this validity has been confirmed, packets are then forwarded to their destination; however, DAI will drop all packets with invalid IP-to-MAC address bindings that fail the inspection validation process. This capability protects the network from MITM attacks. Additionally, DAI ensures that only valid ARP requests and responses are relayed. When DAI is enabled, the switch performs the following activities:

1. It intercepts all ARP requests and responses on untrusted ports. However, it is important to keep in mind that it inspects only inbound packets; it does not inspect outbound packets.
2. It verifies that each of these intercepted packets has a valid IP-to-MAC address binding before updating the local ARP cache or before forwarding the packet to the its destination.
3. It drops invalid ARP packets. These are ARP packets that contain invalid or incorrect IP-to-MAC address bindings.

DAI can be used in both DHCP and non-DHCP environments. In non-DHCP environments, there is no DHCP snooping database, but DAI can validate ARP packets against a user-defined ARP ACL to map hosts with a statically configured IP address to their MAC address. Figure 6.9 illustrates basic DAI operation in a DHCP environment, on a Cisco Catalyst switch enabled for DAI in conjunction with DHCP snooping:

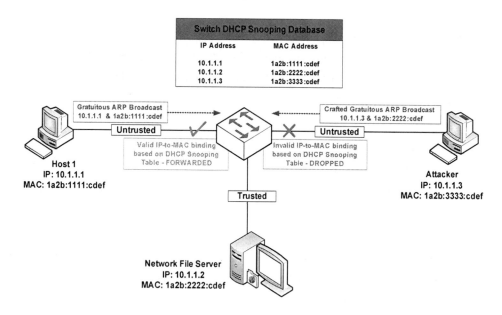

Figure 6.9. DAI With DHCP

Based on the Figure 6.9 illustrated above, DAI has been enabled on the switch to which Host 1, Host 2, and an attacker's machine are connected. The switch is showing the IP-to-MAC bindings in the DHCP snooping database. Therefore, if the attacker attempts to send a GARP with a spoofed MAC address, DAI will intercept the packet, and because it has an invalid IP-to-MAC address binding, the packet will be discarded.

DAI associates a trust state with each interface on the switch. Packets arriving on trusted interfaces bypass all DAI validation checks, and those arriving on untrusted interfaces undergo the DAI validation process. In a typical network configuration, you configure all switch ports connected to host ports as untrusted and configure all switch ports connected to switches (i.e. trunks) as trusted.

With this configuration, all ARP packets entering the network from a given switch bypass the security check, but because they have been validated on the host port, they pose no security threats. No other validation is needed at any other place in the VLAN or in the network. This concept is illustrated in Figure 6.10:

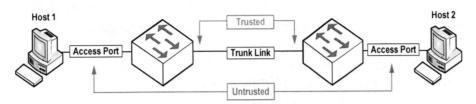

Figure 6.10. DAI Trusted Packets

As illustrated in Figure 6.10, the trunk link between the two switches is trusted. This means that ARP packets that traverse this link will not be subject to DAI validation. However, the access ports that connect Host 1 and Host 2 to the switches are untrusted, which means that ARP packets that traverse these links will be subject to DAI validation.

Configuring Dynamic ARP Inspection in a DHCP Environment

Configuring DAI in a DHCP environment is a relatively straightforward process. DAI is configured via the ip arp inspection vlan [vlan-range] global configuration command for either a specific VLAN or a range of VLANs. Once DAI has been configured for a specific VLAN or a range of VLANs, all ports are untrusted, by default. Therefore, to enable the DAI trusted state for ports, the ip arp inspection trust interface configuration command must be configured on the trusted interface.

You are not expected to perform advanced DAI configuration as part of the IINS course requirements. However, you are expected to know how to enable and verify a basic DAI implementation in Cisco IOS Catalyst switches. The following example illustrates how to enable and verify DAI for VLAN 5 on a switch:

```
Sw1(config)#ip arp inspection vlan 5
Sw1(config)#exit
Sw1#
Sw1#show ip arp inspection vlan 5
Source Mac Validation      : Disabled
Destination Mac Validation : Disabled
IP Address Validation      : Disabled
```

Vlan	Configuration	Operation	**ACL Match**	Static ACL
5	Enabled	Active		

Vlan	ACL Logging	DHCP Logging
5	Deny	Deny

The following example illustrates how to configure a port as a trusted port for DAI. This port either could be a trunk link or connected to a secure network server, for example:

```
Sw1(config)#int gigabitethernet5/1
Sw1(config-if)#description 'Trunk Link Connected To Sw2'
Sw1(config-if)#switchport trunk encapsulation dot1q
Sw1(config-if)#switchport mode trunk
Sw1(config-if)#ip arp inspection trust
Sw1(config-if)#exit
Sw1(config)#exit
Sw1#
Sw1#show ip arp inspection interfaces gigabitethernet5/1
```

Interface	Trust State	Rate (pps)
Gi5/1	Trusted	None

Configuring Dynamic ARP Inspection in a Non-DHCP Environment

While the configuration of DAI in a non-DHCP environment is beyond the scope of the IINS course requirements, this section is provided for the purposes of being thorough. In order to configure DAI in a non-DHCP environment, administrators must first configure ARP ACLs that DAI will use to validate ARP packets. This is performed via the arp access-list [name] global configuration command.

Next, administrators can configure DAI to validate packets against the ARP ACL(s) via the ip arp inspection filter [arp-acl-name] vlan [vlan-range] global configuration command. The following example illustrates how to configure an ARP ACL to permit ARP packets from host 10.1.1.1 with a MAC address of 1a2b.1111.cdef, and how to configure and verify DAI inspection of ARP packets in VLAN 5 based on this ACL:

```
Sw1(config)#arp access-list VLAN-5-ARP
Sw1(config-arp-nacl)#permit ip host 10.1.1.1 mac host 1a2b.1111.cdef
Sw1(config-arp-nacl)#exit
Sw1(config)#ip arp inspection filter VLAN-5-ARP vlan 5
Sw1(config)#exit
Sw1#
Sw1#show arp access-list
ARP access list VLAN-5-ARP
    permit ip host 10.1.1.1 mac host 1a2b.1111.cdef
```

The show ip arp inspection command is used to validate the DAI configuration, as follows:

Sw1#**show ip arp inspection vlan 5**

Source Mac Validation   : Disabled
Destination Mac Validation : Disabled
IP Address Validation   : Disabled

Vlan	Configuration	Operation	ACL Match	Static ACL
5	Enabled	Active	VLAN-5-ARP	No

Vlan	ACL Logging	DHCP Logging
5	Deny	Deny

VTP Attacks

VTP is a Cisco-proprietary Layer 2 protocol used to distribute VLAN configuration information between switches in the same VTP domain over trunk links. There is only one documented case of an actual VTP attack that exploits a well-known vulnerability in the following low-end Cisco IOS Catalyst switches (most of which are end-of-life products and are no longer sold by Cisco):

- Cisco 2900XL Series
- Cisco 2900XL LRE Series
- Cisco 2940 Series
- Cisco 2950 Series
- Cisco 2950-LRE Series
- Cisco 2955 Series
- Cisco 3500XL Series
- Cisco IGESM

This attack includes the sending of malformed VTP packets to these switches. Upon receiving a malformed VTP packet, the switches listed above may reboot. This attack could be executed repeatedly, causing an extended DoS attack.

In order to exploit successfully this vulnerability, the attacker must know the VTP domain name, as well as send the malformed VTP packet to a port on the switch configured for trunking using either ISL or 802.1Q. If these older switches are incorporated into networks, administrators should ensure that only known, trusted devices are connected to ports configured for ISL or 802.1q trunking to mitigate against this attack.

The remaining VTP attacks are theoretical and there are no practical or real-world cases demonstrating such attacks. The theory behind these VTP attacks is that an intruder could either impersonate a trunk link in order to receive all VLAN information via VTP or send falsified VTP messages across trunk links, pretending to be a VTP server, which would allow the intruder to add, delete, or modify VLAN information throughout the VTP domain, or even create Spanning-Tree loops in the network.

To prevent the possibility of VTP attacks, it is recommended that a VTP password should be configured for the VTP domain using the `vtp password [password]` global configuration command. In addition, if the switch platform supports it, administrators should also consider running VTP version 3. While going into the details pertaining to VTP version 3 is beyond the scope of the IINS course requirements, the following section lists the enhancements in VTPv3 over VTPv2 and VTPv1:

* Support for extended VLANs
* Support for the creation and advertising of private VLANs
* Support for VLAN instances and MST mapping propagation instances
* Improved server authentication
* Protection from the 'wrong' database accidentally being inserted into a VTP domain
* Interaction with VTP version 1 and VTP version 2
* Ability to be configured on a per-port basis

The most important enhancement in VTPv3, from a security perspective, is the enhanced authentication capabilities: it introduces an enhancement to the handling of VTP passwords; it allows the configuration of a primary server; and its server cannot make any configuration changes in the domain without first becoming the primary server for the domain. The VTPv3 authentication enhancements are as follows:

* If no password is configured, or if a password is configured the same way as in VTPv1 or VTPv2, the following occurs:
  1. A switch can become the primary server and configure the domain with no restriction;
  2. The password appears in the configuration; and
  3. This enhancement is equivalent to the existing VTPv1 and VTPv2 levels of security.

* If a password is configured as a hidden password, the following occurs:
  1. The password does not appear in plain text in the configuration; and
  2. If you try to configure the switch as a primary server, you are prompted for the password.

While delving into the specifics of VTPv3 or configuring and validating VTPv3 is beyond the scope of the IINS course requirements, the following example illustrates how to configure the VTPv1 and VTPv2 password in Cisco IOS Catalyst switches:

```
Sw1(config)#vtp password !in5s3cur!ty
Setting device VLAN database password to !in5s3cur!ty
Sw1(config)#exit
```

Once configured, the show vtp status command is used to validate configuration. However, it is important to remember that the password is automatically printed in encrypted form and is not legible. However, administrators can ensure that all switches have the same password by validating that the generated hash is consistent on all devices:

```
Sw1#show vtp status
VTP Version : 2
Configuration Revision : 4
Maximum VLANs supported locally : 250
Number of existing VLANs : 11
VTP Operating Mode : Server
VTP Domain Name : SECURITY
VTP Pruning Mode : Enabled
VTP V2 Mode : Enabled
VTP Traps Generation : Disabled
MD5 digest : 0x7C 0x00 0x6F 0x3D 0xCD 0x53 0xC5 0xE5
Configuration last modified by 0.0.0.0 at 3-1-93 00:30:52
Local updater ID is 172.16.1.254 on interface Vl2 (lowest numbered VLAN interface found)
```

VLAN Hopping Attacks

By default, in order for users in different VLANs to communicate, inter-VLAN routing must be employed. This can be done using a one-armed-router, also referred to as a router-on-a-stick, by using sub-interfaces on the router. Alternatively, and more commonly, multi-Layer switches, such as the Cisco Catalyst 3750, 4500, and 6500 series switches, are used in the network. These switches have the capability to both route and switch. Inter-VLAN routing is a core concept and requirement of the CCNA certification. It is explained, in detail, in the CCNA study guide available from www.howtonetwork.net.

VLAN hopping attacks are methods in which an attacker attempts to bypass a Layer 3 device to communicate directly between VLANs, with the main objective being to compromise a device residing on another VLAN. There are two primary methods used to perform VLAN hopping attacks:

- Switch spoofing
- Double-tagging

Switch Spoofing Attacks

In switch spoofing, the attacker impersonates a switch by emulating ISL or 802.1Q signaling, as well as Dynamic Trunking Protocol (DTP) signaling. DTP provides switches with the ability to negotiate the trunking method for the trunk link they will establish between themselves.

If an attacker can successfully emulate ISL, 802.1Q, or DTP signaling, the attacker's system becomes a member of all VLANs, since trunk links forward all VLAN information. Switch spoofing attacks exploit the default native VLAN, which is VLAN 1, that is used on Cisco Catalyst switches.

By default, when an access port sends a frame to a remote switch, and that packet is encapsulated into 802.1Q format with the native VLAN ID, it will be successfully forwarded to the remote switch without the need to cross a Layer 3 device. Network administrators can prevent switch spoofing attacks by performing the following actions:

- Disabling DTP on trunk ports
- Disabling trunking capabilities on ports that should not be configured as trunk links
- Preventing user data from traversing the native VLAN

The show interfaces [name] switchport command shows the default values for a switch port:

```
Sw1#show interfaces gigabitethernet 0/2 switchport
Name: Gi0/2
Switchport: Enabled
Administrative Mode: dynamic desirable
Operational Mode: down
Administrative Trunking Encapsulation: dot1q
Negotiation of Trunking: On
Access Mode VLAN: 1 (default)
Trunking Native Mode VLAN: 1 (default)
Voice VLAN: none
Administrative private-vlan host-association: none
Administrative private-vlan mapping: none
Operational private-vlan: none
Trunking VLANs Enabled: ALL
Pruning VLANs Enabled: 2-1001
Capture Mode Disabled
Capture VLANs Allowed: ALL

Protected: false
```

Voice VLAN: none (Inactive)
Appliance trust: none

The following example illustrates how a DTP can be disabled for a trunk port:

```
Sw1(config)#int gigabitethernet 0/1
Sw1(config-if)#description 'Trunk Link'
Sw1(config-if)#switchport trunk encapsulation dot1q
Sw1(config-if)#switchport nonegotiate
```

The operational status of the trunk can be validated by issuing the show interfaces [name] switch-port command, as illustrated in the following output:

```
Sw1#show interfaces gigabitethernet 0/1 switchport
Name: Gi0/1
Switchport: Enabled
Administrative Mode: trunk
Operational Mode: down
Administrative Trunking Encapsulation: dot1q
Negotiation of Trunking: Off
Access Mode VLAN: 1 (default)
Trunking Native Mode VLAN: 1 (default)
Voice VLAN: none
Administrative private-vlan host-association: none
Administrative private-vlan mapping: none
Operational private-vlan: none
Trunking VLANs Enabled: ALL
Pruning VLANs Enabled: 2-1001
Capture Mode Disabled
Capture VLANs Allowed: ALL

Protected: false

Voice VLAN: none (Inactive)
Appliance trust: none
```

The following example illustrates how to disable trunking capabilities on ports that should not be used to form trunk links on the switch:

```
Sw1(config)#int fastethernet 0/1
Sw1(config-if)#description 'Non-Trunk Access Link'
Sw1(config-if)#switchport
Sw1(config-if)#switchport mode access
Sw1(config-if)#switchport access vlan 2
```

This configuration can be validated via the show interfaces [name] switchport command:

```
Sw1#show interfaces fastethernet 0/1 switchport
Name: Fa0/1
Switchport: Enabled
Administrative Mode: static access
Operational Mode: down
Administrative Trunking Encapsulation: dot1q
Negotiation of Trunking: Off
Access Mode VLAN: 2 (VLAN0002)
Trunking Native Mode VLAN: 1 (default)
Voice VLAN: none
Administrative private-vlan host-association: none
Administrative private-vlan mapping: none
Operational private-vlan: none
Trunking VLANs Enabled: ALL
Pruning VLANs Enabled: 2-1001
Capture Mode Disabled
Capture VLANs Allowed: ALL

Protected: false

Voice VLAN: none (Inactive)
Appliance trust: none
```

Finally, the following example illustrates how administrators can prevent user data from being sent across the native VLAN by specifying a VLAN other than VLAN 1, which does not span the entire Layer 2 network. Remember, VLAN 1 cannot be deleted or modified, but all other VLANs can:

```
Sw1(config)#int giga0/1
Sw1(config-if)#switchport trunk native vlan 5
```

The following configuration can be validated via the show interfaces [name] switchport command:

```
Sw1#show interfaces gigabitethernet 0/1 switchport
Name: Gi0/1
Switchport: Enabled
Administrative Mode: trunk
Operational Mode: down
Administrative Trunking Encapsulation: dot1q
Negotiation of Trunking: Off
Access Mode VLAN: 1 (default)
Trunking Native Mode VLAN: 5 (My-Native-VLAN)
Voice VLAN: none
Administrative private-vlan host-association: none
Administrative private-vlan mapping: none
Operational private-vlan: none
```

Trunking VLANs Enabled: ALL
Pruning VLANs Enabled: 2-1001
Capture Mode Disabled
Capture VLANs Allowed: ALL

Protected: false

Voice VLAN: none (Inactive)
Appliance trust: none

Double-Tagging Attacks

By default, the traffic in the native VLAN used on 802.1Q trunks is not tagged, as frames travel between switches in the Layer 2-switched network. This default behavior means that if an attacker resides on the native VLAN used by the switches, he or she could successfully launch a double-tagging network attack.

Double-tagging or double encapsulated VLAN hopping attacks involve tagging frames with two 802.1Q tags to forward the frames to a different VLAN. The embedded hidden 802.1Q tag inside the frame allows the frame to traverse a VLAN that the outer 802.1Q tag did not specify. This is a particularly dangerous attack because it will work even if the trunk port is set to OFF.

The first switch that encounters the double-tagged frame strips off the first tag and forwards the frame, the result being that the frame is forwarded with the inner 802.1Q tag out to all ports on the switch, including the trunk ports configured with the native VLAN ID of the network attacker. The second switch then forwards the frame to the destination based on the VLAN identifier in the second 802.1Q header. This concept is illustrated in Figure 6.11:

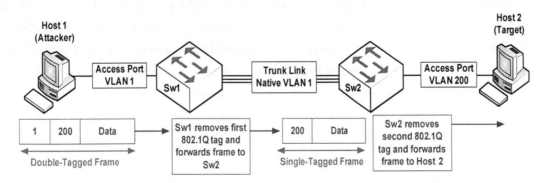

Figure 6.11. Double Tagging Attack

As illustrated in Figure 6.11 above, an attacker has compromised Host 1 and is trying to access Host 2. The attacker sends a double-tagged frame to Sw1, which includes the native VLAN (VLAN 1), and the VLAN Host 2 resides in, which is VLAN 200.

When Sw1 receives the frame, it strips off the first tag (1) and forwards the frame to Sw2. When Sw2 receives the frame, it only contains VLAN 200. The switch removes this tag and forwards the frame to Host 2, which resides in VLAN 200. Thus, the attacker has successfully managed to traverse different VLANs while bypassing any Layer 3 network devices.

To prevent double-tagging attacks, administrators should ensure that the native VLAN used on all the trunk ports is different from the VLAN ID of user access ports. It is best to use a dedicated VLAN that is specific for each pair of trunk ports and not the default VLAN, as illustrated in Figure 6.12:

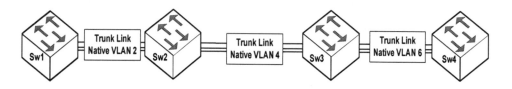

Figure 6.12. Preventing Double Tagging Attacks

Additionally, configuring the native VLAN to tag all traffic prevents the vulnerability of double-tagged 802.1Q frames hopping VLANs. This functionality can be enabled by issuing the vlan dot1q tag native global configuration command.

PVLAN Attacks

Private VLAN Basics

Private VLANs (PVLANs) prevent inter-host communication by providing port-specific security between adjacent ports within a VLAN across one or more switches. Access ports within PVLANs are allowed to communicate only with the certain designated router ports, which are typically those connected to the default gateway for the VLAN. Both normal VLANs and private VLANs can co-exist on the same switch; however, unlike normal VLANs, private VLANs allow for the segregation of traffic at Layer 2, thereby transforming a broadcast segment into a non-broadcast multi-access segment.

Private VLAN Ports

The PVLAN feature uses three different types of ports:

- Community
- Isolated
- Promiscuous

Community PVLAN ports are logically combined groups of ports in a common community that can pass traffic amongst themselves and with promiscuous ports. Ports are separated at Layer 2 from all other interfaces in other communities or isolated ports within their PVLAN.

Isolated PVLAN ports cannot communicate with any other ports within the PVLAN. However, isolated ports can communicate with promiscuous ports. Traffic from an isolated port can be forwarded only to a promiscuous port and no other port.

Promiscuous PVLAN ports can communicate with any other ports, including community and isolated PVLAN ports. The function of the promiscuous port is to allow traffic between ports in a community of isolated VLANs. Promiscuous ports can be configured with switch ACLs to define what traffic can pass between these VLANs. It is important to know that only one (1) promiscuous port is allowed per PVLAN, and that port serves the community and isolated VLANs within that PVLAN. Because promiscuous ports can communicate with all other ports, this is the recommended location to place switch ACLs to control traffic between the different types of ports and VLANs.

Isolated and community port traffic can enter or leave switches via trunk links, because trunks support VLANs carrying traffic among isolated community and promiscuous ports. Hence, PVLANs are associated with a separate set of VLANs that are used to enable PVLAN functionality in Cisco Catalyst switches. There are three types of VLANs used in PVLANs:

- Primary VLANs
- Isolated VLANs
- Community VLANs

Primary VLANs carry traffic from a promiscuous port to isolated, community, and other promiscuous ports within the same primary VLAN.

Isolated VLANs carry traffic from isolated ports to a promiscuous port. Ports in isolated VLANs cannot communicate with any other port in the private VLAN without going through the promiscuous port.

Community VLANs carry traffic between community ports within the same PVLAN, as well as to promiscuous ports. Ports within the same community VLAN can communicate with each other at Layer 2; however, they cannot communicate with ports in other community or isolated VLANs without going through a promiscuous port.

Isolated and community VLANs are typically referred to as secondary VLANs. Therefore, a private VLAN actually contains three elements: the PVLAN itself, the secondary VLANs, and the promiscuous port. This concept is illustrated in Figure 6.13:

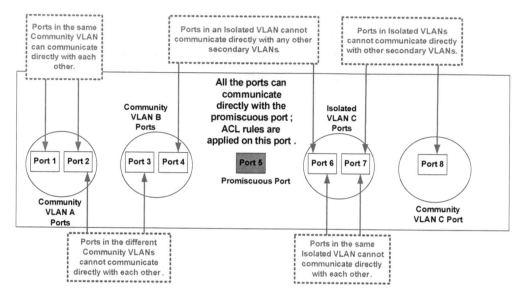

Figure 6.13. Private VLANs

NOTE: Complete PVLAN configuration is only supported in Cisco Catalyst switches 3750 switches and above. PVLAN configuration is not supported in Layer 2-only switches, such as the Cisco Catalyst 2950 series.

Configuring Private VLANs

NOTE: Before configuring PVLANs, it is important to remember to configure the switch in VTP Transparent mode before creating the PVLANs. Although PVLANs can be propagated between switches, they are created in the context of a single switch and cannot have member switches. The following configuration steps are required to configure private VLANs:

1. Configure the primary VLAN by issuing the `private-vlan primary` VLAN configuration mode command for the desired VLAN;

2. Configure the secondary VLAN(s) by issuing the `private-vlan [community|isolated]` VLAN configuration mode command for the desired VLAN(s);

3. Associate the secondary VLAN(s) to the primary VLAN via the `private-vlan association` VLAN configuration command under the primary VLAN created in step 1;

4. Map secondary VLANs to the Switch Virtual Interface (Layer 3 VLAN interface) of the primary VLAN via the `private-vlan mapping` interface configuration command;

5. Configure Layer 2 interfaces as isolated or community ports, and associate the Layer 2 interface with the primary VLAN and selected secondary VLAN pair via the `switchport mode private-vlan host` and the `switchport private-vlan host association [primary vlan] [secondary vlan]` interface configuration commands; and

6. Configure a Layer 2 interface as a promiscuous port and map the PVLAN promiscuous port to the private VLAN and to the selected VLAN pair via the `switchport mode private-vlan promiscuous` and the `switchport private-vlan mapping [primary vlan] [secondary vlans]` interface configuration commands.

To reinforce these six steps, the following example illustrates how to implement private VLANs. VLAN 111 will be configured as the primary VLAN; VLAN 222 will be configured as a community VLAN; and VLAN 333 will be configured as an isolated VLAN. Switch port FastEthenet0/1 will be assigned to VLAN 111; switch port FastEthenet0/2 will be assigned to VLAN 222; and switch port FastEthernet0/3 will be assigned to VLAN 333. These parameters are provided in Table 6.2:

Table 6.2. VLAN Parameters

VLAN Number	VLAN Type	VLAN Port
111	Primary	FastEthernet0/1
222	Community	FastEthernet0/2
333	Isolated	FastEthernet0/3

Configure the primary VLAN by issuing the `private-vlan primary` VLAN configuration mode command for the desired VLAN, as follows:

```
Sw1(config)#vlan 111
Sw1(config-vlan)#name 'My-Primary-VLAN'
Sw1(config-vlan)#private-vlan primary
Sw1(config-vlan)#exit
```

Configure the secondary VLAN(s) by issuing the `private-vlan [community|isolated]` VLAN configuration mode command for the desired VLAN(s), as follows:

```
Sw1(config)#vlan 222
Sw1(config-vlan)#name 'My-Community-VLAN'
Sw1(config-vlan)#private-vlan community
```

```
Sw1(config-vlan)#exit
Sw1(config)#vlan 333
Sw1(config-vlan)#name 'My-Isolated-VLAN'
Sw1(config-vlan)#private-vlan isolated
Sw1(config-vlan)#exit
```

Associate the secondary VLAN(s) to the primary VLAN via the private-vlan association VLAN configuration command under the primary VLAN created in step 1, as follows:

```
Sw1(config)#vlan 111
Sw1(config-vlan)#private-vlan association 222,333
Sw1(config-vlan)#exit
```

Map secondary VLANs to the Switch Virtual Interface (Layer 3 VLAN interface) of the primary VLAN via the private-vlan mapping interface configuration command, as follows:

```
Sw1(config-if)#int vlan 111
Sw1(config-if)#private-vlan mapping add 222,333
Sw1(config-if)#exit
```

Configure Layer 2 interfaces as isolated or community ports, and associate the Layer 2 interface with the primary VLAN and selected secondary VLAN pair via the switchport mode private-vlan host and the switchport private-vlan host association [primary vlan] [secondary vlan] interface configuration commands, as follows:

```
Sw1(config)#int fa0/2
Sw1(config-if)#switchport mode private-vlan host
Sw1(config-if)#switchport private-vlan host-association 111 222
Sw1(config-if)#exit
Sw1(config)#int fa0/3
Sw1(config-if)#switchport mode private-vlan host
Sw1(config-if)#switchport private-vlan host-association 111 333
Sw1(config-if)#exit
```

Configure a Layer 2 interface as a promiscuous port and map the PVLAN promiscuous port to the private VLAN and to the selected VLAN pair via the switchport mode private-vlan promiscuous and the switchport private-vlan mapping [primary vlan] [secondary vlans] interface configuration commands, as follows:

```
Sw1(config)#int fast0/1
Sw1(config-if)#switchport mode private-vlan promiscuous
Sw1(config-if)#switchport private-vlan mapping 111 222 333
Sw1(config-if)#exit
```

Private VLAN Attacks

Now that we have an understanding of PVLANs, this section describes a Proxy Attack, which can be used to bypass access restrictions that are enforced by PVLANs. During a Proxy Attack, frames are forwarded to a host on the network that is connected to a promiscuous port. In this attack, both the source (attacker) and the destination (victim) are on the same subnet, but their direct communication has been restricted via PVLAN implementation. This attack is performed by the attacker sending a crafted packet that contains the following three elements:

- The source IP and MAC address of the machine compromised by the attacker;
- The destination IP address of the victim; and
- The destination MAC address of the upstream router connected to the promiscuous port.

This concept is illustrated in Figure 6.14:

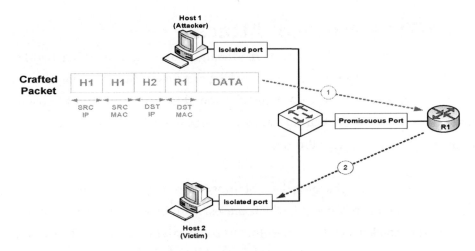

Figure 6.14. Private VLAN Attacks

Referencing Figure 6.14 above, the attacker crafts a packet that contains his or her (Host 1) source IP and MAC addresses, the IP address of the intended target (Host 2), and the destination MAC address of the host connected to the promiscuous port (R1).

In step 1, when the switch receives this packet, it forwards it using the MAC address, not the IP address, and so it forwards the frame to R1 based on the destination MAC address. R1 receives this frame successfully.

In step 2, having received the packet, R1 looks at the IP address and notes that it belongs to Host 2. The router then forwards the packet to Host 2 and rewrites the destination MAC address to that of Host 2. The attack is successful and Host 1 is able to communicate with Host 2, while bypassing PVLAN restrictions.

The recommended method to prevent PVLAN attacks is to implement ACLs on the gateway(s), which are typically connected to promiscuous ports. For example, referring to the diagram used in the previous example, if Host 1 and Host 2 were on the 172.16.1.0/24 subnet, the following ACL would be used to prevent the hosts on this subnet from communicating with each other, thus preventing a PVLAN attack:

```
R1(config)#access-list 100 remark 'Prevent PVLAN Attacks'
R1(config)#access-list 100 deny ip 172.16.1.0 0.0.0.255 172.16.1.0 0.0.0.255 log
R1(config)#access-list 100 permit ip any any
R1(config)#interface fas 0/0
R1(config-if)#description 'IINS PVLAN Gateway Connected to Sw1 FastEthernet0/1'
R1(config-if)#ip address 172.16.1.1 255.255.255.0
R1(config-if)#ip access-group 100 in
```

Spanning-Tree Protocol Attacks

The Spanning-Tree Protocol (STP) is used in redundantly connected Layer 2 networks to prevent loops by placing interfaces or ports in either a blocking or a forwarding state. Because STP is a core component and requirement of the CCNA certification, this section will not be covered in detail. Instead, this section will focus on security features that can be enabled to secure switched networks that are running the Spanning-Tree Protocol.

STP attacks typically center on changing the root bridge of the Layer 2 network by injecting falsified Bridge Protocol Data Units information, which causes Spanning-Tree Protocol recalculations and effectively allows the attacker's switch to become the root bridge of the Layer 2 network. When this happens, traffic is transmitted across the attacker's switch, allowing him or her to view any and all data by using simple tools such as packet captures.

Cisco IOS Catalyst switches can be configured to allow administrators to enforce the placement of the root bridge in the Layer 2 network, prevent rogue switch network extensions, and ultimately mitigate STP attacks using the following two features:

- BPDU Guard
- Root Guard

BPDU Guard

The BPDU Guard feature is designed to keep the STP active topology predictable and to enhance network reliability by enforcing the STP domain borders. This feature either can be enabled globally (i.e. for the entire switch) or on a per-interface basis. In a valid switch configuration, ports configured for PortFast, which is used immediately to transition an interface on the switch to the forwarding state and is implemented on access ports, do not receive BPDUs.

Receiving a BPDU on an interface enabled for PortFast indicates an invalid configuration or possible security condition, i.e. the connection of an unauthorized device. The BPDU Guard feature places all ports with PortFast enabled that receive a BPDU into an error-disabled state. Once the interface has been placed into an error-disabled state, it must be enabled manually by the administrator, providing an additional layer of security, as well as a secure response to invalid configurations or possible security conditions.

At the global level, BPDU Guard is enabled by issuing the spanning-tree portfast bpduguard default global configuration command; and at the interface level, BPDU Guard is enabled by issuing the spanning-tree bpduguard enable interface configuration command. These two configuration options are illustrated in the following output:

```
Sw1(config)#spanning-tree portfast bpduguard default
Sw1(config)#int fast0/1
Sw1(config-if)#spanning-tree bpduguard enable
Sw1(config-if)#exit
```

Once enabled, BPDU Guard can be validated by issuing the show spanning-tree summary. The information printed by this command is illustrated in the following output:

```
Sw1#show spanning-tree summary
Switch is in pvst mode
Root bridge for: VLAN0002
EtherChannel misconfiguration guard is enabled
Extended system ID         is enabled
Portfast                   is disabled by default
PortFast BPDU Guard        is enabled by default
Portfast BPDU Filter       is disabled by default
Loopguard                  is disabled by default
UplinkFast                 is disabled
BackboneFast               is disabled
Pathcost method used is short
```

Name	Blocking	Listening	Learning	Forwarding	STP Active
VLAN0002	0	0	0	1	1
1 vlan	0	0	0	1	1

To verify BPDU Guard on a per-interface basis, the show spanning-tree interface [name] detail command can be used, as illustrated in the following output:

Sw1#**show spanning-tree interface fastethernet 0/1 detail**
 Port 1 (FastEthernet0/1) of VLAN0002 is forwarding
   Port path cost 19, Port priority 128, Port Identifier 128.1.
   Designated root has priority 32770, address 000d.bd06.4100
   Designated bridge has priority 32770, address 000d.bd06.4100
   Designated port id is 128.1, designated path cost 0
   Timers: message age 0, forward delay 0, hold 0
   Number of transitions to forwarding state: 1
   Link type is point-to-point by default
   Bpdu guard is enabled
   BPDU: sent 43, received 0

Root Guard

Root Guard is a Cisco Catalyst switch feature that allows administrators to identify the correct placement of the root switch in a Layer 2 network. The Root Guard feature is configured on any and all interfaces that are non-root ports. A root port, in a Spanning-Tree Protocol implementation, is any port on the switch that is closest to the root bridge of the Spanning-Tree-switched domain. Figure 6.15 illustrates how the Root Guard feature would be implemented to prevent non-root ports from becoming root switches:

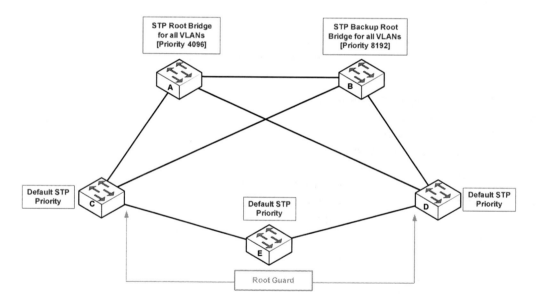

Figure 6.15. Root Guart on a Cisco Network

Figure 6.15 above illustrates a Layer 2-switched network consisting of five switches: Switch A through Switch E. The network administrators have decided to implement a predictable STP network and have configured Switch A as the STP root bridge by assigning a priority value of 4096 for all configured VLANs. For redundancy, the network administrators have configured Switch B with an STP priority value of 8192. Switches C, D, and E are all using default STP priority values of 32,768.

In this topology, there is no reason that Switch E should ever become the root bridge of the STP network. Therefore, the Root Guard feature can be enabled on the Switch C and Switch D interfaces that are connected to Switch E. This sets those interfaces as designated ports and if any device through those ports becomes the root bridge, perhaps through an incorrect configuration that results in superior BPDUs or via an STP attack, the interface will be placed into a root-inconsistent state. While the port is in this state, all traffic will be blocked by the switch. Additionally, the port will remain in this state until the superior BPDUs received on those ports are no longer being received.

Unlike the BPDU Guard feature, which can be enabled globally for the entire switch or on a per-interface basis, the Root Guard feature can only be enabled on a per-interface basis. This is performed via the spanning-tree guard root interface configuration command. The following configuration example illustrates how to configure the Root Guard feature on an interface:

```
Sw1(config)#int fas 0/1
Sw1(config-if)#spanning-tree guard root
Sw1(config-if)#exit
```

Once configured, administrators can use the show spanning-tree interface [name] detail command to view Root Guard status on a per-interface basis, as follows:

```
Sw1#show spanning-tree interface fastethernet 0/1 detail
 Port 1 (FastEthernet0/1) of VLAN0002 is forwarding
   Port path cost 19, Port priority 128, Port Identifier 128.1.
   Designated root has priority 32770, address 000d.bd06.4100
   Designated bridge has priority 32770, address 000d.bd06.4100
   Designated port id is 128.1, designated path cost 0
   Timers: message age 0, forward delay 0, hold 0
   Number of transitions to forwarding state: 1
   Link type is point-to-point by default
   Bpdu guard is enabled
   Root guard is enabled on the port
   BPDU: sent 4860, received 0
```

Finally, the show spanning-tree inconsistentports command can be used to view inconsistent Spanning-Tree Protocol ports, as illustrated in the following output:

```
Sw1#show spanning-tree inconsistentports

Name        Interface           Inconsistency
----------  ------------------  ---------------------
 VLAN1      FastEthernet0/1     Root Inconsistent

Number of inconsistent ports (segments) in the system :1
```

Because BPDU Guard and Root Guard are among the most misunderstood topics, it is important to ensure that you have a solid understanding of the differences between these two features and of what their purposes are. Table 6.3 summarizes the BPDU Guard and Root Guard feature and what kind of STP attacks they are used to mitigate:

Table 6.3. BPDU and Root Guard Features

STP Attack Type	STP Mitigation Technique	STP Mitigation Operation
Attacker attempts to connect an unauthorized network device, such as another switch, to an access port to gain access to the Layer 2-switched network	BPDU Guard, which is enabled globally or on a per-interface basis for all interfaces with PortFast enabled	BPDU Guard will error-disable an interface configured for PortFast that receives a BPDU
Attacker attempts to manipulate the STP root bridge so that all traffic is forwarded to his or her switch	Root Guard, which is enabled on a per-interface basis for all non-root ports on the switch	Root Guard will block all forwarding of packets on an interface that receives superior BPDUs that has this feature enabled

DHCP Spoofing and Starvation Attacks

DHCP spoofing and starvation attacks are methods used by intruders to exhaust the DHCP address pool on the DHCP sever, resulting in resource starvation where there are no DHCP addresses available to be assigned to legitimate users.

DHCP is used to dynamically assign hosts with IP addresses. A DHCP server can be configured to provide DHCP clients with a great deal of information, such as DNS servers, NTP servers, WINS information, and default gateway (router) information. DHCP uses UDP port 68. Cisco IOS routers and some switches can be configured as both DHCP clients and DHCP servers.

When using DHCP on a network, the DHCP client sends a DHCPDISCOVER message to locate a DHCP server. This is a Layer 2 broadcast, because the client has no Layer 3 address, and so the message is directed to the Layer 2 broadcast address FFFF:FFFF:FFFF. If the DHCP server is on the same Layer 2 broadcast domain as the DHCP client, no explicit configuration is needed from a network configuration standpoint.

Upon receiving the DHCPDISCOVER message, the DHCP server offers network configuration settings to the client via the DHCPOFFER message. This message is sent only to the requesting DHCP client.

The client then sends another DHCPREQUEST broadcast message so that any other servers that had responded to the initial DHCPDISCOVER message, after the first issuing DHCP server, can reclaim the IP addresses they had offered to that client. Finally, the issuing DHCP server then confirms that the IP address has been allocated to the client by issuing a DHCPACK message to the requesting DHCP client.

Figure 6.16 illustrates DHCP packet exchange between a DHCP client and server:

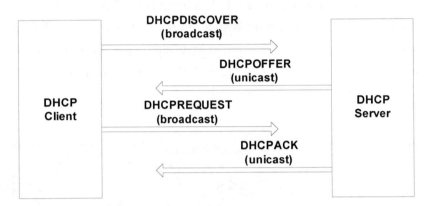

Figure 6.16. DHCP Packet Exchange

DHCP starvation attacks work on MAC address spoofing by flooding a large number of DHCP requests with randomly generated spoofed MAC addresses to the target DHCP server, thereby exhausting the address space available for a period of time. This prevents legitimate DHCP clients from being served by the DHCP server.

Once the legitimate DHCP server has been successfully flooded and can no longer service legitimate clients, the attacker then proceeds to introduce a rogue DHCP server, which then responds to the DHCP requests of legitimate clients with the intent of providing incorrect configuration information to the clients, such as default gateways and WINS or DNS servers. This forged information then allows the attacker to perform other types of attacks, such as MITM attacks. Common and readily available tools such as MACOF and GOBBLER can be used by attackers to perform DHCP starvation attacks.

There are several techniques that can be used to prevent such attacks from occurring. The first is port security, which can be used to limit the number of MAC addresses on a switch port and thus mitigate DHCP spoofing and starvation attacks. The second method is VLAN ACLs (VACLs), which are ACLs that are applied to entire VLANs and are used to control host communication within VLANs. VACLs are described later in this chapter. The third method, which is also the most recommended method, is to enable DHCP snooping.

DHCP Snooping Overview

The DHCP snooping feature provides network protection from rogue DHCP servers by creating a logical firewall between untrusted hosts and DHCP servers. When DHCP snooping is enabled, the switch builds and maintains a DHCP snooping table, which was described briefly in the section pertaining to DAI.

The DHCP snooping table is also referred to as the DHCP binding table, and it is used to prevent and filter untrusted messages from the network. In a manner similar to DAI, the DHCP snooping feature uses the concept of trusted and untrusted interfaces. For incoming packets received on untrusted ports, packets are dropped if the source MAC address of those packets does not match the MAC address in the binding table entry. Figure 6.17 serves to illustrate the basic operation of the DHCP snooping feature:

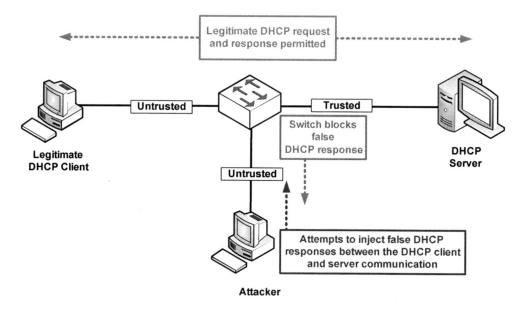

Figure 6.17. DHCP Snooping

As illustrated in Figure 6.17 above, an attacker attempts to inject false DHCP responses into the exchange of DHCP messages between the DHCP client and server. However, because DHCP snooping is enabled on the switch, these packets are dropped because they are originating from an untrusted interface, and the source MAC address does not match the MAC address in the binding table entry.

However, the exchange between the legitimate client, who is also on an untrusted interface, and the DHCP server, which is on the trusted interface, is permitted because the source address does match the MAC address in the binding table entry. Figure 6.18 illustrates the use of the DHCP snooping table that is used to filter untrusted DHCP messages from the network:

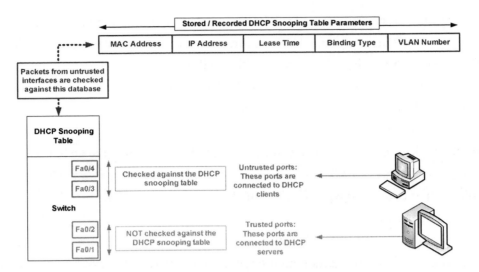

Figure 6.18. DCHP Snooping Table

In Figure 6.18 illustrated above, packets sourced from trusted ports are not subject to DHCP snooping checks. Trusted interfaces for DHCP snooping would be configured for ports directly connected to DHCP servers. However, all packets from untrusted interfaces are checked against the entries in the DHCP snooping table.

This means that if an attacker attempts to use randomly generated MAC addresses to initiate a DHCP snooping and starvation attack, all packets will be checked against the DHCP snooping table, and because there will be no matches for those specific MAC addresses, all packets will be discarded by the switch, effectively preventing this type of attack from occurring.

NOTE: The DHCP snooping feature is only supported in medium-and-high-end Cisco Catalyst switches, such as the Cisco 4500 and Cisco 6500 series switches. It is not supported on lower-end switches, such as the Cisco Catalyst 2950 and 3750 series switches.

Configuring DHCP Snooping

NOTE: The following section provides information on basic DHCP snooping configuration. You are not expected to perform advanced DHCP snooping configuration as part of the IINS course requirements. Configuring basic DHCP snooping involves three basic steps:

1. Globally enabling DHCP snooping on the switch by issuing the `ip dhcp snooping` global configuration command;
2. Enabling DHCP snooping for a VLAN or a range of VLANs by issuing the `ip dhcp snooping vlan [vlan-number|vlan-range]` global configuration command; and

3. Configuring trusted interfaces for DHCP snooping by issuing the ip dhcp snooping trust interface configuration command. It is extremely important to remember that in order for DHCP snooping to function properly, all DHCP servers must be connected to the switch through trusted interfaces. All untrusted DHCP messages (i.e. messages from untrusted ports) will be forwarded only to trusted interfaces.

Optionally, network administrators can configure the switch to support the DHCP Relay Agent Information Option, which is DHCP option 82, by issuing the ip dhcp snooping information option global configuration command when configuring DHCP snooping on the switch.

Once DHCP snooping has been enabled, administrators can use the show ip dhcp snooping configuration to validate their configuration. The following example illustrates how to enable DHCP snooping for VLAN 100 and to enable DHCP Option 82 insertion. Additionally, interface FastEthernet5/24 is connected to a DHCP server and is configured as a trusted interface:

```
Sw2(config)#ip dhcp snooping
Sw2(config)#ip dhcp snooping vlan 100
Sw2(config)#ip dhcp snooping information option
Sw2(config)#int fast 5/24
Sw2(config-if)#ip dhcp snooping trust
```

Once DHCP snooping has been enabled, the show ip dhcp snooping command can be used to validate DHCP snooping configuration, as illustrated in the following output:

```
Sw2#show ip dhcp snooping
Switch DHCP snooping is enabled.
DHCP Snooping is configured on the following VLANs:
100
Insertion of option 82 information is enabled.
Interface          Trusted       Rate limit (pps)
------------       ----------    ----------------
FastEthernet5/24   yes           none
```

Additionally, administrators can also use the show ip dhcp snooping binding command to view DHCP snooping binding entries that correspond to untrusted ports. The information printed by this command is illustrated in the following output:

```
Sw2#show ip dhcp snooping binding
MacAddress        IP Address      Lease (seconds)   Type      VLAN    Interface
----------------  --------------  -----------------  -----     -------  ------------
0021.8642.0b01    10.1.1.254      1600              dynamic   100     FastEthernet5/1
```

Identity Based Networking Services

The Cisco Identity Based Networking Services (IBNS) provides an important addition to the tools available for securing the network. The Cisco IBNS is an integrated solution combining several Cisco products that offer authentication, access control, and user policies to secure network access and resources. The IBNS solution extends network access security based on the 802.1x technology, Extensible Authentication Protocol (EAP) technologies, and the RADIUS security server service. IBNS provides identity-based network access control and policy enforcement at the port level.

Cisco IBNS offers scalable and flexible access control and policy enforcement services, as well as capabilities at the network edge (i.e. at switch access ports), by providing the following:

- Per-user or per-service authentication services
- Policies mapped to network identity
- Port-based network access control based on authentication and authorization policies
- Additional policy enforcement based on access level

Cisco Secure Access Control Server Basics

Cisco Secure Access Control Server (ACS) is a key component of IBNS. IBNS is primarily a security standard for port-based access control that combines IEEE 802.1x and Extensible Authentication Protocol (EAP), which will be described in detail later in this chapter, to extend AAA security inside the LAN. When the Cisco ACS server is used as the authentication server in IBNS, the following features are available for network security administrators:

- Time and day restrictions
- NAS restrictions
- MAC address filtering
- Per-user and per-group VLAN assignments
- Per-user and per-group ACL assignments

Additionally, the Cisco ACS RADIUS server supports internal and external user database sources such as Microsoft Active Directory, Novell NDS, and Lightweight Directory Access Protocol (LDAP). The external database support provides the flexibility and scalability of integrating into the existing user database structure, which simplifies its deployment.

IEEE 802.1x Basics

IEEE 802.1x is a protocol standard framework for both wired and wireless Local Area Networks that authenticates users or network devices and provides policy enforcement services at the port level to provide secure network access control. The 802.1x protocol provides the definition to encapsulate the transport of EAP messages at the Data Link Layer over any PPP or IEEE 802 media (e.g. Ethernet, FDDI, or Token Ring) through the implementation of a port-based network access control to a network device.

The 802.1x standard describes how the EAP messages are communicated between an end device, referred to as a supplicant, and an authenticator, which can be either a switch or a wireless access point. The authenticator relays the EAP information to the authentication server, e.g. a Cisco Secure ACS server, via the RADIUS security server protocol. There are three primary components (or roles) in the 802.1x authentication process:

- Supplicant or Client
- Authenticator
- Authentication Server

An IEEE 802.1x supplicant or client is simply an 802.1x-compliant device such as a workstation, a laptop, or even an IP phone with software that supports the 802.1x and EAP protocols. The supplicant client sends an authentication request to the access LAN via the connected authenticator device (e.g. the access switch) using EAP, as illustrated in Figure 6.19:

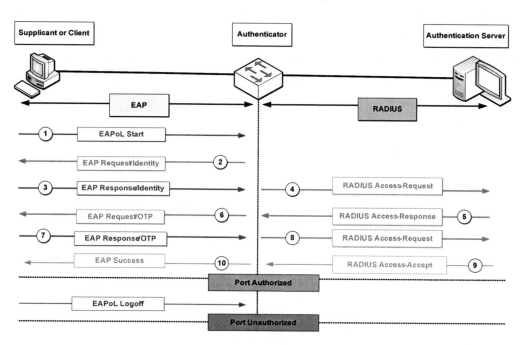

Figure 6.19. Authentication using EAP

Referring to Figure 6.19 above, the first step in the authentication process is the client or supplicant sending the authenticator an EAP over LAN (EAPoL) frame to start the authentication process. The switch responds to the EAPoL frame by sending the supplicant a login request, asking for the correct credentials (e.g. username and password pair) to gain network access, as illustrated in step 2.

In step 3, the supplicant provides the credentials to the authenticator, which then encapsulates them in RADIUS format and relays them to the RADIUS authentication server, as illustrated in step 4. When the RADIUS server receives the authentication request, it checks its database, which can be either internal or external, and then sends a response back, as illustrated in step 5. This response is relayed by the authenticator to the supplicant, as illustrated in step 6.

The supplicant provides the requested information, as illustrated in step 7, and the authenticator relays this information to the RADIUS server, as illustrated in step 8. Assuming that the check is successful and the credentials match and have been validated, the supplicant receives a permit access message, as illustrated in steps 9 and 10. The port then transitions to an authorized state and the supplicant is allowed to send packets onto the network. When the supplicant logs off the network, the port transitions to the unauthorized state and the login and authentication process will start over when the supplicant logs back on.

If the credentials are incorrect, the supplicant can also receive a deny message and will not be allowed access onto the LAN, and will also be blocked at the port level. The authorized and unauthorized port states are described, in detail, later in this chapter.

An 802.1x authenticator is a device that enforces physical access control to the network based on the authentication status (i.e. permit or deny) or the supplicant. An example of an authenticator would be the switch illustrated in the diagram in the previous example. The authenticator acts as a proxy and relays information between the supplicant and the authentication server.

The authenticator receives the identity information from the supplicant via EAPoL frames, which are verified and then encapsulated into RADIUS protocol format before being forwarded to the authentication server. It is important to remember that the EAP frames are not modified or examined during the encapsulation process, which means that the authentication server must support EAP within the native frame format. When the authenticator receives frames from the authentication server, the RADIUS header is removed, leaving only the EAP frame, which is then encapsulated in the 802.1x format. These frames are then sent back to the supplicant or client.

The authentication server is the database policy software, such as Cisco Secure ACS, that supports the RADIUS server protocol and performs authentication of the supplicant that is relayed by the authenticator via the RADIUS client-server model.

The authentication server validates the identity of the client and notifies the authenticator whether the client is allowed or denied access to the network. Based on the response from the authentication server, the authenticator relays this information back to the supplicant. It is important to remember that during the entire authentication process, the authentication server remains transparent to the client because the supplicant is communicating only to the authenticator. The RADIUS protocol with EAP extensions is the only supported authentication server; in other words, you cannot use TACACS+ or Kerberos as the authentication server.

EAP Technologies

While you are not expected to display advanced knowledge of the different types of EAP methods that are commonly used in the IBNS control solution, you should have a basic understanding of the different types of EAP technologies and their basic characteristics. This section provides a brief description of the following EAP technologies:

- EAP Message Digest 5 (MD5)
- EAP Transport Layer Security (TLS)
- EAP Flexible Authentication via Secure Tunneling (FAST)
- Protected EAP (PEAP)
- Cisco Lightweight Extensible Authentication Protocol (LEAP)
- EAP Tunneled TLS (EAP-TTLS)

EAP MD5 is a standards-based EAP type that uses an MD5 challenge, similar to that used by PPP CHAP authentication. EAP MD5 uses a series of EAP challenge request and response messages to validate supplicant credentials. In the event that the authentication process is successful, an EAP Success Notification message is sent from the authenticator to the client.

EAP TLS was designed by Microsoft to address weaknesses found in other EAP types. This EAP type is more complex than other EAP types and uses certificate-based (i.e. X.509) authentication. This means that both the supplicant and the authentication server must have a valid digital certificate in order to be able to perform mutual authentication. EAP TLS provides several advantages over other EAP types. These advantages include the following:

- It can provide encryption and authentication for each packet.
- Keys are exchanged using a standards-based approach.
- It supports the fragmentation and reassembly of packets (in a manner similar to PPP).
- It provides acknowledgements for both success and failure operations.

EAP FAST, which was developed by Cisco, protects authentication messages within a secure TLS tunnel. Transport Layer Security (TLS) and its predecessor, Secure Sockets Layer (SSL), are cryptographic protocols that provide security and data integrity for communications over networks such as the Internet. TLS and SSL encrypt the segments of network connections at the Transport Layer end-to-end. EAP FAST uses shared secret keys, which are unique to each user and are referred to as protected access credentials (PACs). These PACs allow authentication to happen much faster than when digital certificates are used.

PEAP comes in several different forms. PEAP version 0 uses Microsoft Challenge Handshake Authentication Protocol version 2 (MS-CHAPv2) and PEAP version 1 uses a Generic Token Card (GTC) for authentication. PEAP version 0 was co-developed by Cisco, Microsoft, and RSA and it increases the protection of authentication messages by creating a protected TLS tunnel, and then within this protected tunnel, an authentication protocol such as MS-CHAPv2 can then be used.

Cisco LEAP uses a username and password pair to perform authentication. This version of EAP is typically found in Cisco wireless LAN (WLAN) implementations. WLAN implementations are beyond the scope of the IINS course requirements.

EAP-TTLS uses a secured TLS tunnel to send other authentication messages. Like Cisco LEAP, EAP-TTLS is beyond the scope of the IINS course requirements.

802.1x Port States and Authentication Flowchart

When 802.1x is enabled on the authenticator, there are two port states in which the physical ports on the authenticator may be: the authorized and unauthorized states. Initially, all 802.1x-enabled ports start off in an unauthorized state. In this state, no traffic is allowed through the port except for 802.1x message exchange packets.

If a non-802.1x connects to an unauthorized port, the authenticator has no way of knowing that the client does not support 802.1x, and so it sends the client a login request asking for identity credentials. However, because the client does not support 802.1x, the client is unable to interpret the received packet and does not respond to the authenticator's request.

Based on this, the authenticator denies all packets on that port and the switch port remains in the unauthorized state. Administrators control the port authorization state by using the dot1x port-control interface configuration command and one of the following keywords:

- The force-authorized keyword—this disables 802.1X and causes the port to transition to the authorized state without any authentication exchange required. The port transmits and receives normal traffic without 802.1X-based authentication of the client. This is by default.
- The force-unauthorized keyword—this causes the port to remain in the unauthorized state, ignoring all attempts by the client to authenticate. The switch cannot provide authentication services to the client through the interface.

• The auto keyword—this enables 802.1X authentication and causes the port to begin in the unauthorized state, allowing only EAPoL frames to be sent and received through the port. The authentication process begins when the link state of the port transitions from down to up, or when an EAPoL-start frame is received. The switch requests the identity of the client and begins relaying authentication messages between the client and the authentication server. Each client attempting to access the network is uniquely identified by the switch by using the client's MAC address.

While this is by default, it is important to understand that if the authenticator is a Cisco Catalyst switch, the user may not necessarily be blocked but could instead be assigned to a guest or a restricted VLAN. Both VLAN types will be described in the next section.

Inversely, if an 802.1x-compliant device connects to a port that is not running 802.1x, the client initially begins to send EAPoL start packets, but because there is no response from the authenticator, the client assumes that 802.1x authentication is not required and continues to send packets as though the port were in an authorized state. The switch does not block access because there is no 802.1x enabled on that port, even though the client is an 802.1x-compliant client. Figure 6.20, provided by Cisco for the Catalyst 3560 switches, illustrates the 802.1x authentication flowchart:

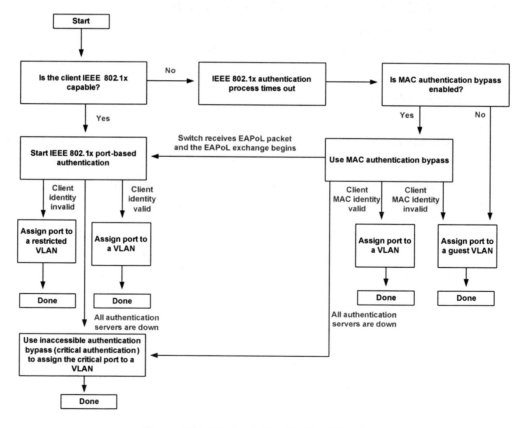

Figure 6.20. 802.1x Authentication Flowchart

802.1x VLAN Assignment and RADIUS Attributes

AAA Authorization must be enabled on the authenticator if network-related services such as per-user or per-group VLAN assignment on 802.1x authenticated ports are required. While Cisco Secure ACS configuration is beyond the scope of the IINS course requirements, it is important to know that there are two types of RADIUS server selections available in Cisco ACS that can be selected to achieve this purpose, and both options can be used when defining the authenticator as the AAA client in the network configuration on Cisco Secure ACS. These two options are:

- RADIUS (IETF)
- RADIUS (Cisco IOS/PIX 6.0)

When the RADIUS (IETF) server is selected as the NAS type in Cisco Secure ACS, the following three attributes must be returned to the switch for 802.1x authentication:

- [RADIUS Attribute 64] Tunnel-Type=VLAN. RADIUS attribute 64 must contain the value 'VLAN', which is type 13;
- [RADIUS Attribute 65] Tunnel-Medium-Type=802. RADIUS attribute 65 must contain the value '802', which is type 6; and
- [RADUIS Attribute 81] Tunnel-Private-Group-ID=VLAN NAME. RADIUS attribute 81 contains the VLAN name of VLAN ID assigned to the authenticated user.

When RADIUS (Cisco IOS/PIX 6.0) is selected as the NAS type in Cisco Secure ACS, the vendor-specific AV-Pair (Attribute 26) must be used to download attribute 64, 65, and 81 to be returned to the switch for 802.1x authentication, and the values are as follows:

- cisco-avpair='tunnel-type(#64)=VLAN(13)'
- cisco-avpair='tunnel-medium-type(#65)=802 media(6)'
- cisco-avpair='tunnel-private-group-ID(#81)=vlan_name or vlan_id'

In addition to standard VLANs, Cisco Catalyst switches (authenticators) also support guest VLANs. These VLANs are used for clients that do not support or are not enabled for 802.1x and are connected to a switch port configured for 802.1x authentication. Guest VLANs typically have limited access to network resources, such as the Internet, for example. As a network administrator, you can use the dot1x guest-vlan interface configuration command on the switch to specify an active VLAN as an IEEE 802.1x guest VLAN. However, in Cisco IOS Catalyst switches running IOS version 12.2(25)SE, administrators can use the dot1x guest-vlan supplicant global configuration command to enable this behavior

Restricted VLANs are also supported when Cisco Catalyst switches are authenticators in an 802.1x-enabled network. Unlike guest VLANs, which support clients that are not enabled for 802.1x authentication, a restricted VLAN can be used to provide limited network access to clients that are 802.1x-enabled but that have failed authentication. In a manner similar to that of guest VLANs, restricted VLANs also typically have limited access to network resources. If administrators choose to use the restricted VLAN feature, they must be aware of the following restrictions that pertain to these types of VLANs:

- Restricted VLANs are only supported on static access ports, i.e. not on trunk ports, etc.
- Restricted VLANs are compatible only when a switch is running in single-host mode.
- Restricted VLANs cannot be used for Remote SPAN (RSPAN).
- Restricted VLANs cannot be used as voice VLANs, sometimes called auxiliary VLANs.

NOTE: Remote SPAN (RSPAN) is beyond the scope of the IINS course requirements.

A switch can be configured to place a port in the configured restrictive VLAN after a connected client fails to successfully authenticate after a certain number of tries by issuing the dot1x auth-fail max-attempts interface configuration command on the switch port.

Configuring Basic 802.1x Port-Based Authentication

Configuring basic 802.1x port-based authentication is a relatively straightforward process that is comprised of the following four basic steps:

- Globally enable AAA services on the switch by issuing the aaa new-model global configuration command. AAA must be enabled before a switch can be configured for 802.1x port-based authentication services;
- Create or use the default 802.1X authentication method list and specify RADIUS server information by issuing the aaa authentication dot1x [method-list|default] group [name|radius] global configuration command;
- Configure RADIUS server parameters (e.g. keys and ports) via the radius-server host global configuration command for an individual server or the aaa group server radius global configuration command for a RADIUS server group; and
- Enable 802.1x port-based authentication on desired switch ports by issuing the dot1x port-control auto interface configuration command.

To reinforce these configuration steps and familiarize you with the configuration of 802.1x port-based authentication services, we will be going over a few configuration examples. The first configuration example illustrates the configuration of 802.1x port-based authentication on the FastEthernet0/23 and FastEthernet0/24 interfaces of a Cisco Catalyst switch. A RADIUS server with the IP address and secret key d0t!xauth will be configured to authentication 802.1x users. This RADIUS server will have the IP address 10.1.1.254 and will use UDP port 1812 for Authentication services:

```
Sw1(config)#aaa new-model
Sw1(config)#aaa authentication dot1x default group radius
Sw1(config)#radius-server host 10.1.1.254 auth-port 1812 key d0t!xauth
Sw1(config)#interface range fastethernet0/23 - 24
Sw1(config-if-range)#switchport mode access
Sw1(config-if-range)#dot1x port-control auto
Sw1(config-if-range)#exit
```

The second configuration example illustrates how to configure IEEE 802.1x port-based authentication against a RADUIS server group named DOT1X-RADIUS, which contains servers 10.1.1.254, 11.1.1.254, and 12.1.1.254. In addition to this, 802.1x port-based authentication will be configured to use the method list DOT1X-LIST for authentication. 802.1x port-based authentication will be enabled on the FastEthernet0/12 interface of the switch:

```
Sw1(config)#aaa new-model
Sw1(config)#aaa authentication dot1x DOT1X-LIST group DOT1X-RADIUS
Sw1(config)#aaa group server radius DOT1X-RADIUS
Sw1(config-sg-radius)#server 10.1.1.254
Sw1(config-sg-radius)#server 11.1.1.254
Sw1(config-sg-radius)#server 12.1.1.254
Sw1(config-sg-radius)#exit
Sw1(config)#int f0/12
Sw1(config-if)#switchport mode access
Sw1(config-if)#dot1x port-control auto
Sw1(config-if)#exit
```

The third and final configuration example illustrates how to enable 802.1x port-based authentication for port FastEthernet0/1 against a RADIUS server with the IP address 172.16.1.254, using default RADIUS port values. Additionally, FastEthernet0/2 will have 802.1x port-based authentication disabled so that the port can transition to the authorized state without any authentication exchange required; and FastEthernet0/3 will have 802.1x port-based authentication enabled but will be configured to remain in the unauthorized state:

```
Sw1(config)#aaa new-model
Sw1(config)#aaa authentication dot1x default group radius
Sw1(config)#radius-server host 172.16.1.254
Sw1(config)#int f0/1
```

```
Sw1(config-if)#switchport mode access
Sw1(config-if)#dot1x port-control auto
Sw1(config-if)#exit
Sw1(config)#int f0/2
Sw1(config-if)#switchport mode access
Sw1(config-if)#dot1x port-control force-authorized
Sw1(config-if)#exit
Sw1(config)#int f0/3
Sw1(config-if)#switchport mode access
Sw1(config-if)#dot1x port-control force-unauthorized
Sw1(config-if)#exit
```

It is important to remember to configure the switch port as a static access port before enabling 802.1x port-based authentication; otherwise, the following error message will be received:

```
Sw1(config)#int f0/15
Sw1(config-if)#dot1x port-control auto
% Error: 802.1X can not be configured on a dynamic port
```

Once 802.1x has been implemented and configured, administrators can use the show dot1x [options] command to view 802.1x configuration parameters and statistics on Cisco Catalyst switches. For example, to view the 802.1x configuration of an interface, administrators should issue the show dot1x interface [name] command, as illustrated in the following output:

```
Sw1#show dot1x interface fastethernet 0/1
802.1X is enabled on FastEthernet0/1
  Status            Unauthorized
  Port-control      Auto
  Supplicant        Not set
  Multiple Hosts    Disallowed
  Current Identifier 2

  Authenticator     State Machine
    State           CONNECTING
    Reauth Count    2

  Backend           State Machine
    State           IDLE
    Request Count   0
    Identifier (Server) 0

  Reauthentication State Machine
    State           INITIALIZE
```

For troubleshooting purposes, administrators can use the show dot1x statistics interface [name] command to view 802.1x statistics on a per-interface basis, as illustrated below:

Sw1#show dot1x statistics interface fastethernet 0/1

FastEthernet0/1

Rx:	EAPOL Start	EAPOL Logoff	EAPOL Invalid	EAPOL Total	EAP Resp/Id	EAP Resp/Oth	EAP LenError
	0	0	0	0	0	0	0

	Last EAPOLVer	Last EAPOLSrc
	0	0000.0000.0000

Tx:	EAPOL Total	EAP Req/Id	EAP Req/Oth
	23	13	0

IEEE 802.1x Attacks

As we learned in the previous section, the 802.1x framework defines the guidelines for packaging EAP messages by using the EAPoL protocol, which is Ethernet frames using the EAP encapsulation over Local Area Networks. While EAPoL is a relatively secure protocol, it is important to know that there are two critical vulnerabilities present in EAPoL:

- The injection of spoofed EAP-Success messages; and
- The ability of attackers to hijack the session.

The first critical vulnerability is the injection of a spoofed EAP-Success message towards the end of the EAPoL authentication sequence, resulting in an MITM attack. The EAP-Success message is sent from the authenticator to the supplicant, and this message does not have any integrity check to ensure that message has not been altered as it traversed from the authenticator to the supplicant. Attackers can take advantage of this and send an unsolicited forged EAP-Success message to the supplicant that appears to come from the authenticator, allowing the attacker passively to establish a path between the supplicant and the authenticator.

The second critical vulnerability that exists is that an intruder can hijack an existing session that is established. After the supplicant has successfully been authenticated, the authenticator and supplicant both move to the authenticated state. An intruder can take advantage of this and send a crafted dissociate frame to the supplicant, spoofing the MAC address of the authenticator. This causes the supplicant to assume the message is coming from the authenticator, and the supplicant terminates the session. However, because the authenticator did not send the message, it remains in the authenticated state and the attacker simply spoofs the source MAC address of the former legitimate supplicant and gains network access by assuming that supplicant's identity. The authenticator has no way to validate that the legitimate supplicant is still connected and the session is therefore considered hijacked.

Mitigating 802.1x Attacks

There is no integrity mechanism available in the EAPoL protocol that can mitigate against an 802.1x attack. Therefore, the recommended solution is to use PEAP instead. The PEAP authentication protocol was developed to address these and other concerns pertaining to 802.1x security. PEAP offers integrity by implementing the authentication sequence in two distinct parts:

- A TLS session is established between the supplicant and the PEAP authentication server; and
- The EAP exchange is carried out over the TLS session to authenticate the supplicant.

Other Cisco Catalyst Switch Security Features

The final section in this chapter describes some other Cisco Catalyst switch security features, as follows:

- Storm Control
- Protected Ports
- Port Blocking
- Port ACLs
- VLAN ACLs
- MAC ACLs
- IP Source Guard

Storm Control

The storm control feature, also referred to as the traffic suppression feature, prevents network traffic from being disrupted by a Broadcast, Multicast, or Unicast packet storm (i.e. flood) on any of the physical interfaces on the Cisco Catalyst switch. This feature monitors inbound packets on a physical interface over a 1-second interval and compares them to a configured storm control suppression level by using one of the following methods to measure the packet activity:

1. The percentage of total bandwidth available of the port allocated for Broadcast, Multicast, or Unicast traffic; or
2. The traffic rate over a 1-second interval in packets-per-second (pps) at which Broadcast, Multicast, or Unicast packets are received on the interface.

Regardless of the method used, packets are blocked until the traffic rate drops below the configured suppression level, at which point the port resumes normal forwarding. The storm control feature is enabled by issuing the storm-control interface configuration command. The options available with this command are as follows:

```
Sw1(config)#int fastethernet0/1
Sw1(config-if)#storm-control ?
  action     Action to take for storm-control
  broadcast  Broadcast address storm control
  multicast  Multicast address storm control
  unicast    Unicast address storm control
```

The action keyword is used to specify the action that the port will enforce in the event of a violation of the configured policy. There are two possible actions that can be defined, either shutdown the port or generate and send an SNMP trap, as illustrated below:

```
Sw1(config)#int fastethernet0/1
Sw1(config-if)#storm-control action ?
  shutdown Shutdown this interface if a storm occurs
  trap     Send SNMP trap if a storm occurs
```

The broadcast, multicast, and unicast keywords are used to define storm control parameters for Broadcast, Multicast, and Unicast traffic, respectively. For example, to block Broadcast traffic if it exceeds 50 per cent of the physical port bandwidth, the following configuration would be implemented on a switch port:

```
Sw1(config)#int fast 0/2
Sw1(config-if)#storm-control broadcast level 50
```

The following example illustrates how to block all Multicast traffic if it exceeds 80 per cent of the physical port bandwidth but resumes all normal forwarding when it falls below 40 per cent:

```
Sw1(config)#int fastethernet 0/2
Sw1(config-if)#storm-control multicast level 80 40
```

Storm control configuration can be validated by issuing the show storm-control [options] command. For example, to view configured storm control parameters for FastEthernet0/2 on a Cisco Catalyst switch, the following command would be issued:

```
Sw1#show storm-control fastethernet 0/2 broadcast
```

Interface	Filter State	Trap State	Upper	Lower	Current	Traps Sent
Fa0/2	Forwarding	inactive	50.00%	50.00%	0.00%	0

```
Sw1#
```

```
Sw1#show storm-control fastethernet 0/2 multicast
Interface    Filter State    Trap State      Upper     Lower     Current     Traps Sent
-----------  --------------  --------------  --------  --------  ----------  --------------
Fa0/2        Forwarding      inactive        80.00%    40.00%    0.00%       0
Sw1#
Sw1#show storm-control fastethernet 0/2 unicast
Interface    Filter State    Trap State      Upper     Lower     Current     Traps Sent
-----------  --------------  --------------  --------  --------  ----------  --------------
Fa0/2        inactive        inactive        100.00%   100.00%   N/A         0
```

Protected Ports

Protected ports operate in a similar manner to private VLANs. These ports have the following characteristics when enabled on Cisco Catalyst switches:

- The switch will not forward any traffic between ports that are configured as protected; any data must be routed via a Layer 3 device between the protected ports;
- Control traffic, such as routing protocol traffic, is considered an exception and will be forwarded between protected ports; and
- Forwarding between protected and non-protected ports proceeds normally, i.e. protected ports can communicate with non-protected ports without using a Layer 3 device.

By default, no ports are protected. However, administrators can enable this feature by issuing the switchport protected interface configuration command on all interfaces that they want to become protected ports. The following example illustrates how to configure a protected port:

```
Sw1(config)#int fastethernet 0/4
Sw1(config-if)#switchport protected
```

Once configured, administrators can validate protected port status by issuing the show interfaces [name] switchport command, as illustrated in the following output:

```
Sw1#show interfaces fastethernet 0/4 switchport
Name: Fa0/4
Switchport: Enabled
Administrative Mode: dynamic desirable
Operational Mode: down
Administrative Trunking Encapsulation: dot1q
Negotiation of Trunking: On
Access Mode VLAN: 2 (VLAN0002)
Trunking Native Mode VLAN: 1 (default)
Voice VLAN: none
Administrative private-vlan host-association: none
Administrative private-vlan mapping: none
Operational private-vlan: none
```

Trunking VLANs Enabled: ALL
Pruning VLANs Enabled: 2-1001
Capture Mode Disabled
Capture VLANs Allowed: ALL

Protected: true

Voice VLAN: none (Inactive)
Appliance trust: none

Port Blocking

NOTE: Port blocking is only supported in Cisco Catalyst 3750 switches and above. It is not supported on lower-end switches, such as the Cisco Catalyst 2950.

When a packet arrives at a switch port, the switch performs a CAM table lookup to determine the port that it will use to send the packet to its destination. If no entry is found for the destination MAC address, the switch will flood the packet out of all interfaces, except for the interface on which the packet was received, and wait for a response. While this default behavior is generally acceptable, it is important to understand that from a security perspective, the forwarding of unknown traffic to a protected port could raise security issues.

To address these concerns, Cisco Catalyst switches can be configured to block unknown Unicast and Multicast traffic from being forwarded on a per-interface basis. This is performed by using the switchport block [multicast|unicast] interface configuration command. The following example illustrates how to block unknown Unicast and Multicast packets on a particular port:

```
Sw1(config)#int fast 0/6
Sw1(config-if)#switchport block multicast
Sw1(config-if)#switchport block unicast
```

This configuration can be validated by issuing the show interfaces [name] switchport command, as illustrated in the following output:

```
Sw1#show interfaces fastethernet 0/6 switchport
Name: Fa0/6
Switchport: Enabled
Administrative Mode: dynamic auto
Operational Mode: down
Administrative Trunking Encapsulation: negotiate
Negotiation of Trunking: On
Access Mode VLAN: 1 (default)
Trunking Native Mode VLAN: 1 (default)
```

Trunking VLANs Enabled: ALL
Pruning VLANs Enabled: 2-1001

Protected: false
Unknown unicast blocked: enabled
Unknown multicast blocked: enabled

Port ACLs

NOTE: Complete PACLs are only supported in medium-and-high-end Cisco Catalyst switches, such as the Cisco 4500 and Cisco 6500 series switches. They are not supported on lower-end switches, such as the Cisco Catalyst 2950 and 3750 series switches

Port ACLs, or PACLs, are similar to router ACLs but are supported and configured on Layer 2 (i.e. non-routed) interfaces on a switch. PACLs are supported on physical interfaces and EtherChannel interfaces. The following access lists are supported on Layer 2 interfaces:

- Standard IP ACLs
- MAC extended ACLs
- Extended IP ACLs

The main advantage afforded by PACLs is that they can be used to filter both IP (i.e. IP standard and IP extended ACLs) and non-IP (i.e. MAC ACLs) traffic on a Layer 2 interface. The following output illustrates how to configure a PACL using an extended IP ACL:

```
Sw4(config)#ip access-list extended MY-IP-PACL
Sw4(config-ext-nacl)#permit ip any any
Sw4(config-ext-nacl)#exit
Sw4(config)#interface fastethernet 5/1
Sw4(config)#switchport mode access
Sw4(config)#switchport access vlan 15
Sw4(config-if)#ip access-group MY-IP-PACL in
```

The following example illustrates how a MAC ACL can be applied to a switch port:

```
Sw4(config)#mac access-list extended MY-MAC-PACL
Sw4(config-ext-macl)#permit host 1a2b.1111.cdef any
Sw4(config-ext-macl)#exit
Sw4(config)#interface fastethernet 6/1
Sw4(config)#switchport mode access
Sw4(config)#switchport access vlan 7
Sw4(config-if)#mac access-group MY-MAC-PACL out
```

Cisco IOS software allows administrators to use the access-group mode interface configuration command to change the way PACLs interact with other ACLs, such as VLAN ACLs (VACLs) that may be configured for the VLAN that the Layer 2 interface is also configured for. In a per-interface fashion, the access-group mode command can be implemented with one of the following keywords:

*   The prefer port keywords—If PACL is configured on a Layer 2 interface, then the PACL takes effect and overwrites the effect of other ACLs configured on the interface, or for the entire VLAN. However, if no PACL is configured on the Layer 2 interface, other features applicable to the interface are merged and applied on the interface. This is by default.
*   The prefer vlan keywords—When used, VLAN-based ACL features take effect on the port provided they have been applied on the port and no PACLs are in effect. If no VLAN-based ACL features are applicable to the Layer 2 interface, then the PACL feature already on the interface is applied.
*   The merge keyword—This command merges applicable ACL features before they are programmed into the switch hardware.

NOTE: You are not expected to perform any advanced PACL configurations, as they are beyond the scope of the IINS course requirements. Therefore, no configuration examples are provided on the access group mode feature.

VLAN ACLs

NOTE: VACLs are only supported in medium-and-high-end Cisco Catalyst switches, such as the Cisco 4500 and Cisco 6500 series switches. They are not supported on lower-end switches, such as the Cisco Catalyst 2950 and 3750 series switches.

VLAN ACLs, or VACLs, are also commonly referred to as VLAN maps. These ACLs provide filtering capabilities for all traffic types (i.e. IP and non-IP) that are bridged within a VLAN or routed into or out of the VLAN. Unlike traditional router ACLs, VACLs are not defined by an inbound or outbound direction. Instead, all packets entering or leaving the VLAN are checked against the configured VACL.

VACLs are processed in switch hardware and therefore do not cause any performance impact when implemented on switches. VACL configuration is a straightforward process that is performed in three steps:

1. Create the extended IP ACL that matches the desired packets using either the IP or MAC address against one or more standard or extended access lists;

2. Configure the VLAN access map, which is an ordered list of entries, that will be used to match the ACL(s) configured in step 1. This is performed via the vlan access-map global configuration command. In addition, the VLAN access map must be configured to drop or forward the packets matched in the ACL by using the action [drop|forward] VLAN access map configuration command; and

3. Apply a VLAN map to one or more VLANs by using the vlan filter [map-name] vlan-list [list-of-vlans] global configuration command.

While you are not expected to perform advanced VACL configurations, you are expected to be familiar with the configuration of simple VACLs. The following configuration example illustrates how to configure an extended IP ACL named ALLOW-TCP that permits all TCP traffic, match that ACL using a VLAN access map named MY-VACL-MAP, which allows this traffic to be forwarded, and apply the configuration to VLAN 22 via a VLAN map named VLAN-22-MAP:

```
Sw4(config)#ip access-list extended ALLOW-TCP
Sw4(config-ext-nacl)#permit tcp any any
Sw4(config-ext-nacl)#exit
Sw4(config)#vlan access-map MY-VACL-MAP
Sw4(config-access-map)#match ip address ALLOW-TCP
Sw4(config-access-map)#action forward
Sw4(config-access-map)#exit
Sw4(config)#vlan filter map VLAN-22-MAP vlan-list 22
```

The following configuration example illustrates how to configure an extended IP ACL named DENY-UDP that permits all UDP traffic, match that ACL using a VLAN access map named UDP-DROP-VACL-MAP, which allows this traffic to be dropped, and apply the configuration to VLANs 11-15 via a VLAN map named VLAN-11-To-15-MAP:

```
Sw4(config)#ip access-list extended DENY-UDP
Sw4(config-ext-nacl)#permit udp any any
Sw4(config-ext-nacl)#exit
Sw4(config)#vlan access-map UDP-DROP-VACL-MAP
Sw4(config-access-map)#match ip address DENY-UDP
Sw4(config-access-map)#action drop
Sw4(config-access-map)#exit
Sw4(config)#vlan filter map VLAN-11-To-15-MAP vlan-list 11-15
```

Administrators can then use the show vlan access-map command to view VACL configuration. The information printed by this command is provided in the following output:

```
Sw4#show vlan access-map

Vlan access-map " MY-VACL-MAP " 10
```

```
Match clauses:
  ip address: ALLOW-TCP
Action:
  drop

Vlan access-map " UDP-DROP-VACL-MAP " 10
  Match clauses:
   ip address: DENY-UDP
  Action:
   forward
```

The following restrictions should be kept in mind when configuring VACLs:

- VLAN maps do not filter IPv4 ARP packets.
- If there is no router ACL configured to deny traffic on a routed VLAN interface (input or output), and no VLAN map configured, all traffic is permitted.
- Each VLAN map consists of a series of entries. The order of entries in a VLAN map is important. A packet that comes into the switch is tested against the first entry in the VLAN map. If it matches, the action specified for that part of the VLAN map is taken. If there is no match, the packet is tested against the next entry in the map.
- If the VLAN map has at least one match clause for the type of packet (IP or MAC) and the packet does not match any of these match clauses, the default is to drop the packet. If there is no match clause for that type of packet in the VLAN map, the default is to forward the packet.
- The system might take longer to boot if you have configured a large number of ACLs.

MAC ACLs

MAC ACLs, also referred to as Ethernet ACLs, can filter non-IP traffic on a VLAN (i.e. be used in conjunction with VACLs) as well as on a port (i.e. be used as a PACL). The configuration logic of MACLs follows that of extended IP ACLs. While delving into advanced MACL configuration is beyond the requirements of the IINS course requirements, the following example illustrates how to configure and apply an MACL that permits DECNET Spanning-Tree Protocol and NETBOIS:

```
Sw1(config)#mac access-list extended MY-MAC-ACL
Sw1(config-ext-macl)#permit any any dec-spanning
Sw1(config-ext-macl)#permit any any netbios
Sw1(config-ext-macl)#exit
Sw1(config)#int fa 0/10
Sw1(config-if)#mac access-group MY-MAC-ACL in
Sw1(config-if)#exit
```

Once they have been configured and implemented, MACLs can be validated by issuing the show mac access-group [options] command. For example, to view the MACL configured on FastEthernet0/10, the following commands would be executed:

```
Sw1#show mac access-group interface fastethernet 0/10
Interface FastEthernet0/10:
   Inbound access-list is MY-MAC-ACL
```

IP Source Guard

NOTE: IP Source Guard is only supported in Cisco Catalyst 3750 switches and above. It is not supported on lower-end switches, such as the Cisco Catalyst 2950 series switches.

IP Source Guard is a feature that restricts IP traffic on untrusted Layer 2 ports by filtering the traffic based on the DHCP snooping binding database or manually configured IP source bindings. This feature is used to prevent IP spoofing attacks. Any traffic coming into the interface with a source IP address other than that assigned via DHCP or static configuration will be filtered out on the untrusted Layer 2 ports.

The IP Source Guard feature is typically enabled in combination with DHCP snooping on untrusted Layer 2 interfaces. IP Source Guard builds and maintains an IP source binding table that is learned by DHCP snooping or manually configured bindings. Entries in the IP source binding table contain the IP address and the associated MAC and VLAN numbers. The IP Source Guard feature is only supported on Layer 2 interfaces, which include access and trunk links. The IP Source Guard feature is enabled by issuing the ip verify source interface configuration command on Layer 2 interfaces.

Additionally, port security can be enabled by issuing the ip verify source port security interface configuration command. However, it is important to remember that this configuration command requires the global configuration command ip dhcp snooping information option, which allows the DHCP server to support DHCP option 82. DHCP option 82 is simply the DHCP Relay Agent Information Option. All other advanced DHCP options and IP Source Guard configuration are beyond the scope of the IINS course requirements.

Chapter Summary

The following section is a summary of the major points you should be aware of in this chapter:

LAN Switching Overview

- Switches operate at the Data Link Layer of the OSI Model and send frames
- Frames sent by switches contain source and destination MAC addresses
- The source and destination MAC addresses are stored in the switch MAC address table
- The MAC address table is commonly referred to as the CAM table
- Content Addressable Memory is a memory type used in high-speed searching applications
- The switch CAM table is viewed by issuing the show mac-address-table command
- A VLAN is a logical grouping of hosts
- VTP is a Cisco proprietary Layer 2 messaging protocol that manages VLANs network-wide
- VTP packets are sent across the trunk links in either ISL or in IEEE 802.1Q frames
- Trunk ports are used to carry traffic that belongs to multiple VLANs
- Spanning-Tree Protocol is used to prevent loops in switched networks

CAM Table Overflow Attacks

- Attackers can exploit CAM memory limitation with a large number of MAC addresses
- The recommended method to mitigate against such attacks is to implement port security
- Port security can be implemented in three ways:
  1. Static Secure MAC Addresses
  2. Dynamic Secure MAC Addresses
  3. Sticky Secure MAC Addresses

- When a port security violation is detected, switches can perform the following actions:
  1. Protect
  2. Shutdown
  3. Restrict

- The port security feature has two types of aging methods or mechanisms:
  1. Absolute
  2. Inactivity

MAC Spoofing Attacks

- MAC spoofing is used to spoof a source MAC address impersonate other hosts or devices
- MAC spoofing confuses the switch and it believes the same MAC is connected to two ports
- MAC spoofing attacks can be mitigated by implementing port security

ARP Spoofing Attacks

- ARP spoofing attacks are used by attackers to disguise their source MAC address
- ARP spoofing occurs during the ARP request and reply messaging between two hosts
- ARP spoofing attacks can be implemented by implementing Dynamic ARP Inspection
- DAI is a security feature that validates ARP packets in a network
- DAI validates ARP packets by performing an IP-to-MAC address binding inspection
- DAI can be implemented in DHCP or non-DHCP environments

VTP Attacks

- VTP attacks include the sending of malformed VTP packets to these switches
- To mitigate VTP attacks, administrators should configure a VTP password
- Additionally, administrators can also implement VTPv3, which has the following features:
  1. Support for extended VLANs
  2. Support for the creation and advertising of private VLANs
  3. Support for VLAN instances and MST mapping propagation instances
  4. Improved server authentication
  5. Protection from the "wrong" database accidentally being inserted into a VTP domain
  6. Interaction with VTP version 1 and VTP version 2
  7. Ability to be configured on a per-port basis

VLAN Hopping Attacks

- VLAN hopping attacks bypass a Layer 3 device to communicate directly between VLANs
- There are two primary methods used to perform VLAN hopping attacks:
  1. Switch spoofing
  2. Double-tagging

- In switch spoofing, the attacker impersonates a switch
- Double-tagging attacks involve tagging frames with two 802.1Q tags
- VTP attacks can be mitigated by performing the following:
  1. Disable DTP on trunk ports
  2. Disable trunking capabilities on ports that should not be configured as trunk links
  3. Prevent user data from traversing the native VLAN
  4. Ensuring the native VLAN on trunks is different from the VLAN ID of user VLANs

PVLAN Attacks

- Private VLANs prevent inter-host communication by providing port-specific security
- The private VLAN feature uses three different types of ports:
  1. Community
  2. Isolated
  3. Promiscuous

- The three types of VLANs used in PVLANs are:
  1. Primary VLANs
  2. Community VLANs
  3. Isolated VLANs

- PVLAN attacks are performed by r sending a crafted packet that contains the following:
  1. The source IP and MAC address of the machine compromised by the attacker
  2. The destination IP address of the victim
  3. The destination MAC address of the upstream router connected to the promiscuous port

- PVLAN attacks can be mitigated by implementing ACLs on the promiscuous port

Spanning-Tree Protocol Attacks

- STP is used in redundantly connected switched networks to prevent Layer 2 loops
- STP attacks typically center on changing the root bridge of the Layer 2 network
- STP attacks can be mitigated by implementing two features:
  1. BPDU Guard
  2. Root Guard

- The following table highlights the scenarios in which these features would be implemented:

STP Attack Type	STP Mitigation Technique	STP Mitigation Operation
Attacker attempts to connect an unauthorized network device, such as another switch to an access port to gain access to the Layer 2 switched network	BPDU Guard, which is enabled globally or on a per-interface basis for all interfaces with PortFast enabled	BPDU Guard will error-disable an interface configured for PortFast that receives a BPDU
Attacker attempts to manipulate the STP root bridge so that all traffic is forwarded to their switch	Root Guard, which is enabled on a per-interface basis for all non-root ports on the switch	Root Guard will block all forwarding of packets on an interface which receives superior BPDUs that has this feature enabled

DHCP Spoofing and Starvation Attacks

- These attacks are methods used by intruders to exhaust the DHCP address pool
- The following solutions can be implemented to mitigate against these attacks:
  1. Port Security
  2. VLAN ACLs, or VACLs
  3. DHCP Snooping

- DHCP snooping creates a logical firewall between untrusted hosts and DHCP servers
- This feature builds a DHCP snooping table which is used to validate packets

Identity Based Networking Services

- IBNS is an integrated solution that offers authentication, access control and user policies
- IBNS extends network access security based on the 802.1x, EAP, and RADIUS
- IBNS provides identity-based access control and policy enforcement at the port level
- Cisco IBNS provides the following:
  1. Per-user or per-service authentication services
  2. Policies mapped to network identity
  3. Port-based network access control based on authentication and authorization policies
  4. Additional policy enforcement based on access level

- IEEE 802.1x is a protocol standard framework that authenticates users or network devices
- IEEE 802.1x provides policy enforcement services at the port level
- IEEE 802.1x allows for the encapsulation of EAP messages at the Data Link Layer
- There are three primary components (or roles) in the 802.1x authentication process:
  1. Supplicant or Client
  2. Authenticator
  3. Authentication Server

- The most common types of EAP technologies are:
  1. EAP Message Digest 5 (MD5)
  2. EAP Transport Layer Security (TLS)
  3. EAP Flexible Authentication via Secure Tunneling (FAST)
  4. Protected EAP (PEAP)
  5. Cisco Lightweight Extensible Authentication Protocol (LEAP)
  6. EAP Tunneled TLS (EAP-TTLS)

- There are two port states in which the physical ports on the authenticator may be:
  1. Authorized
  2. Unauthorized

- There are two types of RADIUS server selections in Cisco ACS that are used for 802.1x:
  1. RADIUS (IETF)
  2. RADIUS (Cisco IOS/PIX 6.0)

- In addition to standard VLANs, 802.1x can use restricted and guest VLANs
- Guest VLANs typically have limited access to network resources
- Guest VLANs are used for clients that do not support or are not enabled for 802.1x
- Restricted VLANs can be used to provide limited network access to clients
- Restricted VLANs are used for 802.1x-enabled client that have failed authentication
- Restricted VLANs have the following restrictions:
  1. Restricted VLANs are only supported on static access ports, i.e. not on trunk ports, etc
  2. Restricted VLANs are compatible only when a switch is running in single-host mode
  3. Restricted VLANs cannot be used for Remote SPAN (RSPAN)
  4. Restricted VLANs cannot be used as voice VLANs, sometimes called auxiliary VLANs

IEEE 802.1x Attacks

- Two critical vulnerabilities that are present in EAPoL are:
  1. The injection of spoofed EAP-Success messages
  2. The ability of attackers to hijack the session

- The recommended method to mitigate EAPoL vulnerabilities is to use PEAP
- PEAP offers integrity by implementing the authentication sequence in two distinct parts:
  1. A TLS session is established between the supplicant and the PEAP authentication server
  2. EAP exchange is carried out over the TLS session to authenticate the supplicant

Other Cisco Catalyst Switch Security Features

- Other Cisco Catalyst switch features that can be used to enhance LAN security are:
  1. Storm Control
  2. Protected Ports
  3. Port Blocking
  4. Port ACLs
  5. VLAN ACLs
  6. MAC ACLs
  7. IP Source Guard

Commands Used in this Chapter

The following section is a summary of the commands used in this chapter:

Command	Description
show mac-address-table	Used to view the switch CAM table
switchport port-security	Used to enable port security
switchport port-security mac-address	Use to configure static secure MACs
switchport port-security maximum	Used to specify the maximum number of secure MACs
switchport port-security violation	Used to specify switch action in the event of violations
show logging	Used to view the local logs
show port-security	Used to verify port security configuration and statistics
switchport port-security aging	Used to configure port security aging parameters
ip arp inspection vlan	Used to enable DAI for a VLAN or range of VLANs
ip arp inspection trust	Used to configure a DAI trusted interface
show ip arp inspection	Used to verify DAI configuration and statistics
arp access-list	Used to create a static IP-to-MAC binding
ip arp inspection filter	Used to configure DAI based on a static ARP entry
vtp password	Used to configure a VTP password
show vtp status	Used to verify VTP configuration
show interfaces [name] switchport	Used to view interface switch port parameters
switchport nonegotiate	Used to disable DTP on trunk links
switchport trunk encapsulation	Used to specify the trunk encapsulation protocol
switchport mode access	Used to specify an interface as a static access port
switchport access vlan	Used to assign an interface to a VLAN
vlan dot1q tag native	Used to tag the 802.1Q native VLAN frames
private-vlan primary	Used to configure the primary PVLAN
private-vlan [community|isolated]	Used to configure the secondary PVLAN
private-vlan association	Used to associate primary and secondary PVLANs
private-vlan mapping	Used to map secondary PVLANs to the SVI
switchport mode private-vlan	Used to configure PVLAN parameters on interfaces
spanning-tree portfast bpduguard default	Used to enable the BPDU Guard feature globally on the entire switch
spanning-tree bpduguard enable	Used to enable the BPDU Guard feature per interface
show spanning-tree summary	Used to verify STP configuration parameters
show spanning-tree interface	Used to verify STP interface configuration parameters

Command	Description
spanning-tree guard root	Used to enable the Root Guard feature per interface
show spanning-tree inconsistentports	Used to view inconsistent STP ports
ip dhcp snooping	Used to globally enable DHCP snooping
ip dhcp snooping vlan	Used to enable DHCP snooping for a VLAN
ip dhcp snooping trust	Used to configure trusted DHCP snooping interfaces
show ip dhcp snooping	Used to view DHCP snooping configuration parameters
show ip dhcp snooping binding	Used to view the DHCP snooping binding table
dot1x port-control	Used to enable 802.1x on a switch port or ports
dot1x guest-vlan	Used to enable guest VLANs for newer IOS versions
dot1x guest-vlan supplicant	Used to enable guest VLANs for IOS 12.2(25)SE
dot1x auth-fail max-attempts	Used to specify the number of authentication attempts
aaa new-model	Used to enable AAA
aaa authentication dot1x	Used to configure Authentication parameters for 802.1x
show dot1x interface	Used to view interface 802.1x configuration
show dot1x statistics interface	Used to view interface 802.1x statistics
storm-control	Used to configure storm control parameters
switchport protected	Used to enable the protected port feature
switchport block	Used to configure switch port blocking
mac access-list extended	Used to configure an extended MAC ACL
mac access-group	Used to apply a MAC ACL to an interface
show mac access-group	Used to view MAC ACLs applied to an interface
ip verify source	Used to enable the IP Source Guard feature
ip verify source port security	Used to enable IP Source Guard and Port Security
ip dhcp snooping information option	Used to allow the DHCP server to support option 82
vlan access-map	Used to configure a VLAN access map
vlan filter map	Used to map a VLAN access map to a VLAN

CHAPTER 7

Cisco IOS Firewall and Security Appliances

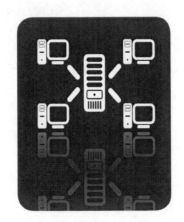

The Cisco IOS Firewall set feature provides a single point of protection at the network perimeter, making security policy enforcement an inherent component of the network. The IINS exam objectives covered in this chapter are as follows:

- Describe the operational strengths and weaknesses of the different firewall technologies
- Explain Stateful firewall operations and the function of the state table
- Implement Zone-Based Policy Firewall using SDM

This chapter is broken up into the following sections:

- Cisco IOS Firewall Overview
- Types of Firewalls
- Hardware versus Software Firewalls
- Cisco Security Appliances
- Context-Based Access Control
- Cisco Zone-Based Policy Firewall

IINS Exam Objective	Section(s) Covered
Describe the operational strengths and weaknesses of the different firewall technologies	• Cisco IOS Firewall Overview • Types of Firewalls • Hardware versus Software Firewalls
Explain Stateful firewall operations and the function of the state table	• Types of Firewalls • Cisco Security Appliances
Implement Zone-Based Policy Firewall using SDM	• Cisco Zone-Based Policy Firewall
Other related topics	• Context-Based Access Control

Cisco IOS Firewall Overview

The Cisco IOS Firewall set feature provides network security with integrated, inline security solutions and comprises a suite of services that allow administrators to provision a single point of protection at the network perimeter. The Cisco IOS Firewall set feature is a Stateful inspection firewall engine with application-level inspection. This provides dynamic control to allow or deny traffic flows, thereby providing enhanced security. Stateful inspection will be described in detail later in this chapter.

In its most basic form, the principal function of any firewall is to filter and monitor traffic. Cisco IOS routers can be configured with the IOS Firewall feature set in the following scenarios:

- As a firewall router facing the Internet;
- As a firewall router to protect the internal network from external networks, e.g. partners;
- As a firewall router between groups of networks in the internal network; and
- As a firewall router that provides secure connection to remote offices or branches.

The Cisco IOS Firewall provides an extensive set of security features that allow administrators to design customized security solutions tailored to the specific needs of their organization. The Cisco IOS Firewall is comprised of the following functions and technologies:

- Cisco IOS Stateful Packet Inspection
- Context-Based Access Control
- Intrusion Prevention System
- Authentication Proxy
- Port-to-Application Mapping
- Network Address Translation
- Zone-Based Policy Firewall

Cisco IOS Stateful Packet Inspection

Cisco IOS Stateful Packet Inspection (SPI) provides firewall capabilities designed to protect networks against unauthorized traffic and to control legitimate business-critical data. Cisco IOS SPI maintains state information and counters of connections, as well as the total connection rate through the firewall and intrusion prevention software. SPI will be described in detail later in this chapter.

Context-Based Access Control

Context-Based Access Control (CBAC) is a Stateful inspection firewall engine that provides dynamic traffic filtering capabilities. CBAC, also known as the Classic Firewall, will be described in detail later in this chapter.

Intrusion Prevention System

The Cisco IOS Intrusion Prevention System (IPS) is an inline intrusion detection and prevention sensor that scans packets and sessions flowing through the router to identify any of the Cisco IPS signatures that protect the network from internal and external threats. Cisco IPS solutions will be described in detail in the following chapter.

Authentication Proxy

The Authentication Proxy feature, also known as Proxy Authentication, allows administrators to enforce security policy on a per-user basis. With this feature, administrators can authenticate and authorize users on a per-user policy with access control customized to an individual level. Authentication Proxy configuration and detailed knowledge is beyond the scope of the IINS course requirements and will not be described in detail in this guide.

Port-to-Application Mapping

Port-to-Application Mapping (PAM) allows administrators to customize TCP or UDP port numbers for network services or applications to non-standard ports. For example, administrators could use PAM to configure standard HTTP traffic, which uses TCP port 80 by default, to use TCP port 8080. PAM is also used by CBAC, which uses this information to examine non-standard Application Layer protocols. PAM configuration and detailed knowledge is beyond the scope of the IINS course requirements and will not be described in detail in this guide.

Network Address Translation

Network Address Translation (NAT) is used to hide internal addresses, which are typically private addresses (i.e. RFC 1918 addresses), from networks that are external to the firewall. The primary purpose of NAT is address conservation for networks that use RFC 1918 addressing due to the shortage of globally routable IP (i.e. public) address space. NAT provides a lower level of security by hiding the internal network from the outside world. NAT configuration and detailed knowledge is beyond the scope of the IINS course requirements and will not be described in detail in this guide.

Zone-Based Policy Firewall

Zone-Based Policy Firewall (ZPF) is a new Cisco IOS Firewall feature designed to replace and address some of the limitations of CBAC, the Classic Firewall. ZPF allows Stateful inspection to be applied on a zone-based model, which provides greater granularity, flexibility, scalability, and ease-of-use over the Classic Firewall. ZPF is described in detail later in this chapter.

Types of Firewalls

A firewall protects networked computers from intentional hostile intrusion that could compromise confidentiality or result in data corruption or denial of service. Firewalls may be dedicated hardware-based devices, or even software-based programs that run on a secure computer or server. Firewalls must have at least two network interfaces, one for the network it is intended to protect, and one for the network it is exposed to. Basic firewalls consist of two main mechanisms.

The first mechanism is designed to block traffic. This could be traffic originating from external networks, such as the Internet, or internally, such as from restricted users and hosts. The second mechanism is designed to allow traffic. This traffic could be internally originated traffic (e.g. internal users accessing the Internet) or external traffic (e.g. Internet users accessing a company-owned web server). Firewalls fall into four broad categories:

1. Static or Network-Level Packet Filters
2. Circuit-Level Gateways
3. Application-Level Firewalls or Gateways
4. Stateful Inspection Firewalls

As is the case with any technology, firewalling capabilities have evolved as the methods of attacks used by intruders have evolved. Currently, there are four generations of firewall technology. First-generation firewalls were the first types of firewalls used to secure computer networks. These firewalls provided basic filtering capabilities at Layer 3 and Layer 4 of the OSI Model. Second-generation firewalls were introduced to provide further firewalling capabilities into the network. These firewalls allowed network security administrators to provide network security by monitoring traffic at Layer 3, Layer 4, and Layer 5 of the OSI Model.

Third-generation firewalls superseded second-generation firewalls and provided firewalling capabilities at Layer 3, Layer 4, Layer 5, and Layer 7 of the OSI Model. And, finally, the most recent (or the latest generation of) firewalls are fourth-generation firewalls. These firewalls operate at Layer 3, Layer 4, Layer 5, and Layer 7 of the OSI Model and use a concept referred to as Stateful inspection, which allows them to offer greater security than that offered by third-generation firewalls. Stateful inspection is described in detail later in this chapter.

Despite their generational differences, it is important to understand and keep in mind that different generations of firewalls can be used in conjunction with each other, as is often the case, to enhance network security. For example, first-generation firewalls can be used in conjunction with fourth-generation firewalls to provide additional security within a network.

Static or Network-Level Packet Filters

Static or Network-Level Packet Filters are first-generation firewalls. These firewalls work at the Network Layer of the OSI Model by inspecting packet headers and filtering traffic based on the IP address of the source and the destination, the port, and the service. Static packet filters can also filter packets based on protocols, the domain name of the source, and a few other attributes, depending on the software capabilities of the platforms they are implemented on.

Static packet filters are fast and relatively easy to implement. Cisco IP extended ACLs are examples of static packet filters that are supported in Cisco IOS routers and switches, as well as Cisco PIX and ASA firewalls. While static packet filters provide relatively advanced capabilities, they provide limited security capabilities in that they do not understand languages such as HTML and XML, and they are not capable of decoding SSL-encrypted packets to examine their content, for example. As a result, static packet filters cannot validate user inputs or detect maliciously modified parameters in a URL request, which leaves the network vulnerable to threats.

Figure 7.1 illustrates how static packet filters (e.g. IP extended ACLs) can be used to protect internal networks from outside threats:

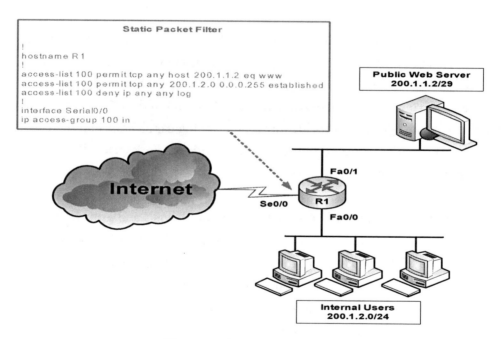

Figure 7.1. Static Packet Filters

The static packet filter illustrated in Figure 7.1 is an IP extended ACL configured and applied to the Serial0/0 interface of Internet-facing R1. This filter allows only WWW connections to the web server with the IP address 200.1.1.2/29 and allows only TCP packets that were originated by internal hosts on the 200.1.2.0/24 subnet to be permitted inbound on the Serial0/0 interface.

Network administrators could also configure network-level filters to control the flow of traffic between the internal user subnet (200.1.2.0/24) and the company web server, for example. The advantages of packet filtering firewalls are their low cost, in monetary terms, and their relatively low impact on network performance. Most routers support packet filtering. Even if other firewalls are used within the network, implementing packet filtering at the router level provides networks with an additional level of security, albeit a relatively low one.

Circuit-Level Gateways

Circuit-level gateways are second-generation firewalls. These firewalls work at the Session Layer of the OSI Model or the TCP layer of the TCP/IP Model. Circuit-level gateways monitor TCP handshaking between hosts to make sure a session is legitimate and are used to validate whether a packet is either a connection request or a data packet belonging to an established connection or virtual circuit.

Information passed to a remote computer through a circuit-level gateway appears to have originated from the gateway and not from the actual internal host. This is useful for hiding information about internal (protected) networks. While circuit-level gateways are relatively inexpensive and have the advantage of hiding information about the private network they protect, it is important to know that they provide relatively limited enhanced network security capabilities due to the fact that they do not filter individual packets. Circuit-level gateways are considered obsolete and have all but disappeared from the networks of today.

Application-Level Firewalls or Gateways

Application-Level Gateways (ALG) are third-generation firewalls. These firewalls evaluate packets for valid data at the Application Layer before allowing a connection. ALGs, which are also referred to as proxies, have the ability to looking more deeply into the Application Layer data going through their filters and, as such, can also filter at Layers 3, 4, and 5, in addition to their Layer 7 filtering capabilities. The two main functions of Application-Level Firewalls are to keep machines behind them anonymous and to speed up access to a resource via caching. Keep in mind that Application-Level Gateway and Application-Level Firewall are interchangeable terms; either can be used and they both refer to the same thing.

By considering the context of client requests and application responses, these firewalls attempt to enforce correct application behavior, block malicious activity, and help organizations ensure the safety of sensitive information and systems. They can also log user activity. Application-level filtering may include protection against spam and viruses as well, and may be able to block undesirable websites based on content rather than just their IP addresses. Figure 7.2 illustrates the basic operation of an ALG:

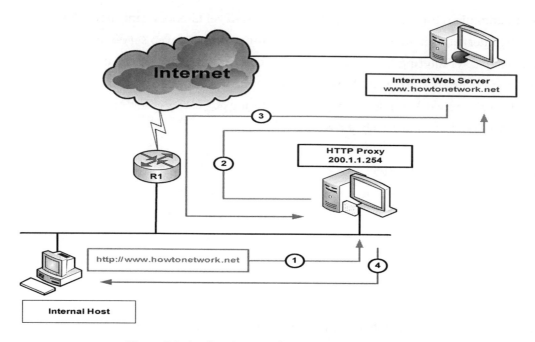

Figure 7.2. Application-Level Gateways in Operation

In Figure 7.2 above, the internal host is attempting to connect to the web server belonging to www. howtonetwork.net. Because the host has been configured to use a proxy, this request is forwarded to 200.1.1.254, as illustrated in step 1. The ALG, or proxy, receives the request from the internal host and in turn contacts the Internet server on behalf of the host, as illustrated in step 2.

The Internet server receives a request from 200.1.1.254 (the ALG) and, assuming all defaults, sends the web page to the proxy, as illustrated in step 3. Finally, in step 4, the proxy then proceeds and forwards the page to the computer on the intranet, i.e. the internal host. The user is now connected to www.howtonetwork.net via the ALG.

There are many different types of proxies. Some of the most common ones are as follows:

- File Transfer Protocol (FTP) proxies
- SOCKS proxies
- Hypertext Transfer Protocol (HTTP) proxies
- Network Address Translation (NAT) proxies
- Secure Sockets Layer (SSL) proxies

NOTE: You are not required to demonstrate detailed knowledge on each of these different types of proxies. However, the following section provides a brief description of each type.

FTP proxies are used to relay and cache FTP traffic. SOCKS proxies allow for the relaying of far more different types of data, which could be TCP or UDP data. SOCKS is an Internet protocol that facilitates the routing of network packets between client-server applications via a proxy and performs at Layer 5 of the OSI Model. SOCKS uses a handshake protocol to inform the proxy software about the connection that the client is trying to make.

HTTP proxies are used to provide a one-way request to retrieve web pages. An HTTP proxy analyses the HTTP headers sent through it in order to deduce the address of the server and therefore may only be used for HTTP traffic. NAT proxies allow for the redirection of all packets without a program having to support a proxy server.

And, finally, SSL proxies are an extension that was created to enhance the HTTP proxy server, which allows for the relaying of TCP data similar to a SOCKS proxy server. This is performed mainly to allow encryption of web page requests. SSL is a cryptographic protocol that provides security and data integrity for communications over networks such as the Internet. SSL encrypts the segments of network connections at the Transport Layer end-to-end.

Furthermore, a Proxy Server can be split into anonymous and transparent proxy servers. Anonymous proxy servers block the remote computer from knowing the identity of the computer using the proxy server to make requests. This is similar to the operation of Network Address Translation, which hides internal IP addresses from external users; however, it is important to keep in mind that these two technologies are distinctly different.

A transparent proxy server tells the remote computer the IP address of your computer. This provides no privacy as internal addresses are exposed to external users. Anonymous proxies can further be broken down into two more categories, which are elite and disguised.

An elite proxy is not identifiable to the remote computer as a proxy in any way. In other words, the remote host does not know that the originating host is using a proxy server. A disguised proxy gives the remote host enough information to let it know that it is a proxy; however, it is still considered secure because it does not give away the IP of the host that it is relaying information for. The destination host knows that it is talking to a proxy server; however, it does not know the IP address of the originating host.

Application- Level Firewalls provide the following advantages:

- They enhance network security by hiding internal networks. Proxies make connection requests on behalf of their clients, masking or hiding the IP addresses of those clients to external networks and devices.

- They authenticate individuals and not devices. Application-Level Firewalls allow connection requests to be authenticated before traffic is passed to internal or external resources. This allows administrators to authenticate the user making the connection request instead of the device on which the connection request is made.

- They make it more difficult for attackers to perform IP spoofing attacks. By performing NAT-like functions, and breaking up the end-to-end IP connection, proxies can prevent most spoofing attacks.

- They can be used to mitigate against DoS attacks. Application-Level Firewalls can detect DoS attacks and reduce the burden on internal resources, such as routers, etc. However, it should be noted that the proxy itself could fall victim to a DoS attack.

- They can monitor and filter application data, such as web addresses. Proxies have the ability to detect attacks such as malformed URLs, buffer overflow attempts, and unauthorized access. A Uniform Resource Locator (URL) is a subset of the Uniform Resource Identifier (URI) that specifies where an identified resource is available and the mechanism for retrieving it. A URI is commonly referred to as a web address. For example, JPEG files could be blocked based on matches, or language filters could dynamically detect unwanted programming language. If the content is rejected, the proxy returns an HTTP fetch error.

- They can provide detailed logging for security audits. ALGs have the capability to produce detailed logging information, as well as allow administrators to monitor the actual data an individual is sending across the connection.

However, despite these advantages, Application-Level Firewalls also have several disadvantages, which must be weighed during consideration. These disadvantages are as follows:

- They are not as efficient because more operations take place to inspect a packet. Proxies use up a lot of CPU cycles to handle many connections. Advanced filtering capabilities only add to this overhead.

- They come at a higher cost because of higher complexity. Cost is a factor when considering ALGs. Additional hardware such as memory and hard disk space may be needed to handle more connections and provide greater caching capabilities. These add to the proxy cost.

- They require manual updates for new or modified application protocols. Administrators must update proxies to filter modified protocols or applications. This increases the administration overhead.

- Attacks can still occur if there is a weakness in the application itself. For example, there could be a Java script buffer overrun, even though the underlying HTTP protocol has valid headers. This introduces potential security risks.

- Every protocol must have a proxy in order for the firewall to be completely effective. If administrators must allow the use of a protocol that the proxy does not specifically support, they are reduced to using a generic proxy. Generic proxies do not have any in-depth knowledge of the protocols they proxy, so they can only provide basic security checks based on the information contained within the headers of the packets.

- They improve performance reduction since application services have to go through a proxy. ALGs are slower at passing information than other firewalls because of the proxy applications.

- They are not transparent to end users and require manual configuration of each client computer. Client computers on a network with an ALG firewall need to be configured to be able to use the proxies to access resources outside the network.

Stateful Inspection Firewalls

Stateful firewalls are fourth-generation dynamic packet filtering firewalls and are the most common firewall technology used in modern-day networks. These firewalls operate at Layers 3, 4, and 5 of the OSI Model. Stateful firewalls differ significantly from Stateless firewalls, which were the norm in the networks of yesteryear. A Stateless firewall is a firewall that treats each packet in isolation. Because of this, Stateless firewalls have no way of knowing whether any given packet is part of an existing connection, is trying to establish a new connection, or is just a rogue packet. These limitations are addressed in Stateful firewalls.

Stateful firewalls perform Stateful Packet Inspection (SPI), or Stateful Inspection, and keep track of the state of network connections, such as TCP and UDP streams traveling across them. The Cisco IOS Firewall is a Stateful firewall that uses the inherent Stateful inspection engine of Cisco IOS Software for maintaining the detailed session database, which is referred to as the state table.

Stateful firewalls are able to hold a significant amount of attributes of each connection in memory, from start to finish. These attributes, which are known as connection states, may include such details as the IP addresses and port numbers involved in the connection, as well as the sequence numbers of the packets traversing the connection.

Once the initial connection request has been processed and screened, which is usually the most processor-intensive process, all packets after that, for that particular session, can then be processed rapidly because the firewall can determine whether they belong to an existing, pre-screened session. Once the session has ended, the entry for that connection is removed from the state table. Figure 7.3 illustrates a basic Stateful firewall and state table operation:

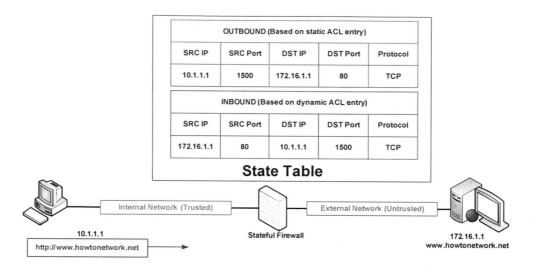

Figure 7.3. Basic Stateful Firewall and State Table

Based on Figure 7.3 above, the internal host (10.1.1.1) initiates an HTTP connection to www.how-tonetwork.net. Using DNS, the web address is translated to the IP address 172.16.1.1 and the packet is forwarded to the Stateful firewall. The Stateful firewall receives this packet and because it was originated internally, notes the TCP SYN and creates outbound session information that includes the source and destination IP addresses and ports, as well as the Transport Layer protocol, i.e. TCP.

The external web server receives this packet and sends back a SYN + ACK packet. The Stateful firewall receives this response and checks that either the ACK or the RST bit is set. In this case, the ACK bit is set in the SYN + ACK sent by the external web server. This check is performed to ensure that only internal hosts can initiate a TCP session to an external location, while preventing any external TCP sessions to the internal network. The check succeeds and a dynamic entry is created in the ACL to permit the return traffic.

The internal host acknowledges the SYN + ACK from the external server with an ACK packet and the TCP session is established. The session is then monitored in the state table. Once the session is terminated, the entry is removed from the state table.

As is the case with any other computing resources, the state table is not finite. In other words, it can be exhausted depending on the number of connections and the platform the Stateful firewall has been implemented on. Therefore, in order to prevent the state table from filling up, sessions will time out if no traffic has passed for a certain period, i.e. if they are idle for a certain amount of time. These stale connections are then removed from the state table to prevent it from being filled up by these sessions. To prevent application timeout due to this firewall behavior, many applications send keepalive messages periodically in order to stop a firewall from dropping the connection during periods of no user activity. Additionally, some firewalls can be configured to send these messages for applications.

Because Stateful firewalls maintain state information, they are susceptible to DoS attacks, with the most common type of attack being TCP SYN floods. These attacks aim to fill up the state tables of these firewalls by sending many SYN packets and not completing the TCP three-way handshake. These connections are referred to as embryonic or half-open connections. However, most firewalls, such as the Cisco IOS firewall and Cisco Adaptive Security Appliance, which will be described later in this chapter, can be configured to time out embryonic connections and clear them from the state table based on administrator-defined time thresholds.

Stateful firewalls provide the following advantages over packet filtering firewalls:

*   They are aware of the state of a connection. Stateful firewalls build and maintain a state table to allow only return traffic from connections currently listed in the state table.

*   They do not have to open up a large range of ports to allow returning traffic back into the network. Stateful firewalls use the state table to determine whether this is returning traffic (i.e. traffic originated on the internal network and destined to an external network or host), and if so, the connection is permitted; however, if this is not return traffic, the firewall's filtering table is used to filter the traffic.

*   They prevent more kinds of DoS attacks (e.g. TCP SYN attacks) than packet filtering firewalls. This is performed by using the state table to allow only legitimate connections into the network.

*   They provide more-detailed logging capabilities than packet filter firewalls. Stateful firewalls can provide detailed logging information on when a connection was established, how long it was up for, and when it was disconnected, for example.

*   They can dynamically open ports for certain applications, such as UDP ports used by Real-Time Protocol (RTP) for delivering audio and video over the IP networks, as well as for other audio and video standards, such as H.323.

However, despite their advantages, it is also imperative to know that Stateful firewalls are not infallible. Stateful firewalls have the following disadvantages:

- They can be very complex to configure. Some features in the Cisco ASA, which are described later in this chapter, are extremely complex to configure.

- They cannot prevent Application Layer attacks because they operate at Layers 3, 4, and 5 of the OSI Model. However, it should be noted that some Stateful firewalls, such as the Cisco ASA, can provide Application Layer inspection and filtering.

- They do not support the user authentication of connections. That is, Stateful firewalls do not authenticate sessions originated internally, destined to external networks or hosts.

- Some applications open up multiple connections and some use dynamic port numbers for the additional connections. FTP is a classic example of this.

- Stateful firewalls increase overhead due to the need to maintain state tables. This makes Stateful firewalls slower than packet filtering firewalls.

- Not all protocols contain state information. Examples of protocols that do not support state information are UDP and ICMP. However, it should be noted that Stateful firewalls can perform pseudo-Stateful tracking for UDP. Pseudo-Stateful tracking simply tracks IP addresses and port numbers for UDP because UDP does not use flags or sequence numbers as used by TCP. Additionally, even though TCP does support state information, certain aspects of it are not supported by Stateful firewalls. For example, Microsoft Windows Vista and Windows 7, uses TCP window scaling for non-HTT connections; however, this behavior is incompatible with some firewalls that use Stateful Packet Inspection.

Hardware versus Software Firewalls

The primary difference between a hardware-based firewall and a software-based firewall is the underlying dependency on the operating system on which the firewall is running. Hardware firewalls provide a strong degree of protection from most forms of attack coming from the outside to the internal network. Hardware firewalls can protect computers on a LAN and they can be implemented without much configuration difficulty.

Hardware firewalls are robust and built specifically for the purposes of firewalling. These dedicated devices are also less vulnerable to attack than software firewalls. Examples of hardware firewalls are the Cisco Packet Internetwork Exchange (PIX) firewall and the Cisco Adaptive Security Algorithm (ASA) firewall.

Software firewalls are installed on individual computers and they need sufficient configuration to be effective. Software firewalls contain a set of related programs, usually located at a network gateway server, that protect the resources of a private network from users on other networks or from internal users. Software firewalls allow application screening to verify the interaction between the requesting client and the requested resource.

An example of a software firewall is the Cisco IOS Firewall technology. This is integrated into the Cisco IOS software, providing a Stateful inspection firewall engine with application-level intelligence. Both hardware and software firewalls each have their own advantages and disadvantages. The advantages of hardware firewalls over software firewall are as follows:

- They can operate at greater speeds. Hardware firewalls are dedicated hardware designed for faster response times, and they can handle more traffic.

- They provide greater security than software firewalls. A firewall with its own dedicated operating system (proprietary) is less prone to attacks. This in turn reduces the security risk. For example, the Cisco PIX uses the Finesse Operating System.

- They have enhanced security controls. Because they are designed for a dedicated purpose, hardware firewalls typically provider greater controls.

- They provide less network interference. A physical box that is separated from other network components can be managed better and does not load or slowdown other applications. The box can be moved, shutdown, or reconfigured with minimal interference to the network.

However, despite their advantages, hardware firewalls also have the following disadvantages:

- They cost more. Pricing is a big concern because these are dedicated devices. Therefore, a dedicated hardware firewall typically is more expensive than a software firewall.

- They are difficult to install and upgrade. These dedicated devices are built to be secure and typically use proprietary operating systems. This makes it that much harder to implement, configure, and operate hardware firewalls.

- They typically take up physical space and involve wiring for network connectivity. While software firewalls can be integrated into existing servers, for example, hardware firewalls are standalone physical appliances that must be racked, stacked, and cabled to be integrated into the network.

The best preparation is to have a combination of both hardware and software firewalls. This allows you to have a well-protected system.

Cisco Security Appliances

NOTE: When reading this section, it is important to keep in mind that the emphasis of the IINS course is on the Cisco IOS Firewall feature set. You are not expected to perform any configuration or troubleshoot any Cisco hardware firewall technologies as a requirement.

The Cisco firewall technology provides a wealth of advanced security and networking services for small- to medium-sized enterprises, as well as service provider networks, in a modular, purpose-built solution. Cisco hardware firewall technologies come in three different forms:

- The Cisco PIX 500 Series Security Appliances
- The Cisco ASA 5500 Series Adaptive Security Appliances
- The Cisco Firewall Services Module

The Cisco PIX 500 Series Security Appliances

The Cisco PIX 500 Series Security Appliances use a dedicated software engine that incorporates the Cisco Adaptive Security Algorithm (ASA), which will be described in the following section. The Cisco PIX 500 Series Security Appliances provide robust integrated network security services, including Stateful inspection, firewalling capabilities, Virtual Private Network (VPN) capabilities, and inline Intrusion Detection System capabilities. Intrusion Detection Systems (ISDs) will be described in detail later in this guide. Table 7.1 lists and provides a description of the Cisco PIX 500 Series devices:

Table 7.1. Cisco PIX 500 Series Models

Device Type	Description
Cisco PIX 501	The Cisco PIX 501 Security Appliance is a compact, plug-and-play security appliance for small office/home office (SOHO) environments. PIX 501 security appliances provide an integrated 4-port 10/100 FastEthernet switch and a dedicated 10/100 FastEthernet uplink.
Cisco PIX 506E	The Cisco PIX 506E Security Appliance is for remote office/branch office (ROBO) environments. The PIX 506E Security Appliance provides two auto-sensing 10/100 FastEthernet interfaces.
Cisco PIX 515E	The Cisco PIX 515E Security Appliance is a modular, high-performance security appliance for small- to medium-sized and enterprise network environments. The Cisco PIX 515E Security Appliance can support up to six 10/100 FastEthernet interfaces.

Cisco PIX 525	The Cisco PIX 525 Security Appliance provides GigabitEthernet connectivity for medium- to large-sized and enterprise network environments. The Cisco PIX 525 is capable of supporting up to eight 10/100 FastEthernet interfaces or three GigabitEthernet interfaces.
Cisco PIX 535	The Cisco PIX 535 Security Appliance is a modular, high-performance GigabitEthernet security appliance for service provider network environments. The Cisco PIX 535 can support up to ten 10/100 FastEthernet interfaces or nine GigabitEthernet interfaces, as well as redundant power supplies.

NOTE: The Cisco PIX 500 Series Security Appliances are End-of-Sale (EoS) and can no longer be ordered from Cisco. The recommended replacement, the Cisco ASA 5500 Series Security Appliance, is described in the following section.

The Cisco ASA 5500 Series Adaptive Security Appliances

The Cisco ASA security appliances deliver converged firewall, Intrusion Prevention System (IPS), advanced adaptive threat defense services (which include Anti-X defenses), application security, and VPN services. At the heart of the ASA 5500 Series design is the Adaptive Identification and Mitigation (AIM) architecture that provides proactive threat mitigation. The Cisco ASA 5500 Series Adaptive Security Appliance is an innovative appliance that builds on the depth and breadth of security features, combining the following three technologies:

- Firewall Technology
- Intrusion Prevention System (IPS) Technology
- VPN Technology

The Cisco ASA 5500 Series offers five high-performance, purpose-built (i.e. dedicated) appliances that span small- to medium-sized to large enterprises and service provider environments. Table 7.2 lists and describes the different ASA 5500 Series models:

Table 7.2. Cisco ASA 5500 Series Models

Device Type	Description
Cisco ASA 5505	The Cisco ASA 5505 Adaptive Security Appliance is a cost-effective, easy-to-deploy appliance for small business, branch office, and enterprise teleworker environments. This mode offers an integrated 8-port 10/100 FastEthernet switch, with two Power over Ethernet (PoE) ports.
Cisco ASA 5510	The Cisco ASA 5510 Adaptive Security Appliance is a cost-effective, easy-to-deploy appliance with advanced security and networking services for medium-sized businesses, remote office/branch office (ROBO), and enterprise environments.

Cisco ASA 5520	The Cisco ASA 5520 Adaptive Security Appliance provides high-availability services and GigabitEthernet connectivity. This model is suitable for medium-sized enterprise networks.
Cisco ASA 5540	The Cisco ASA 5540 Adaptive Security Appliance is a high-density, high-availability appliance that provides GigabitEthernet connectivity. This model is recommended for medium- to large-sized enterprise and service provider network environments.
Cisco ASA 5550	The Cisco ASA 5550 Adaptive Security Appliance is a Gigabit-class security appliance that offers up to 1.2Gbps of firewall throughput, with high-availability services, as well as GigabitEthernet and Fiber connectivity. This model is recommended for large enterprise and service provider network environments.

The Cisco Firewall Services Module

The Cisco Firewall Services Module (FWSM) is a high-speed, high-performance integrated firewall module that is installed in Cisco Catalyst 6500 Series switches or Cisco 7600 Series routers. The key features of the FWSM are:

- It is an integrated module. Because the module is installed into Cisco Catalyst 6500 Series switches or Cisco 7600 Series routers, it has the ability to provide advanced security services inside the network infrastructure.

- It provides superior performance and scalability. The FWSM offers the fastest firewall solution in the industry and has unprecedented rates. The FWSM can handle up to 5 Gbps of traffic, 100,000 connections per second, and 1 million concurrent connections. With the capacity to install up to four FWSMs in a single chassis, throughput can be increased up to 20 Gbps to meet growing demands.

- It is a proven technology. The FWSM software is based on the Cisco PIX technology and uses the same tried-and-tested Cisco PIX Operating System.

- It provides a lower Total Cost of Ownership (TCO). The FWSM can be used in virtualized firewall deployments, which allow for multiple firewalls on a single physical platform. Virtualization reduces the number of physical devices required in the network, minimizing complexity, enhancing operational efficiency, and reducing overall costs.

- It has a higher Return on Investment (ROI) than other firewall technologies. The FWSM provides higher ROI due to its flexible deployment, which leverages existing network infrastructure investments, e.g. the Cisco Catalyst 6500 Series switches.

Firewall Modes

Cisco security appliances can run in either routed firewall mode, which is the default, or in transparent firewall mode, which is essentially a Layer 2 firewall.

When running in routed firewall mode, the security appliance is considered to be a router hop in the network. For example, if you perform a Traceroute from an internal workstation to an external IP address, the Traceroute will show the firewall as one of the hops in the path from the source to the destination. This is illustrated in Figure 7.4:

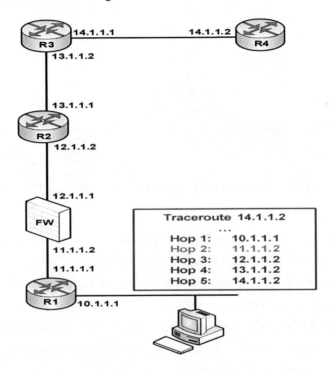

Figure 7.4. IP Routed Firewalls are Counted as a Hop

As illustrated in Figure 7.4 above, a user performs a Traceroute from Host 1 to the IP address 14.1.1.2. Assuming that all routing is correctly configured, the packet traverses R1 and is then forwarded to the FW. Because the FW is running in routed mode (default), and assuming that the firewall is configured to allow Traceroute, the IP address of the firewall (which is in red font in the diagram above) is printed in the Traceroute from the source to the destination. However, for security purposes, firewalls in routed mode typically do not provide their IP address information, and in most Traceroutes, users will simple see a * (wildcard) in the Traceroute from source to destination.

Firewall software version 7.0 allows administrators to deploy Cisco security appliances in a secured bridging mode, referred to as the transparent firewall, or even the stealth firewall. In transparent mode, security appliances simply appear as a 'bump in the wire' and not as an actual router hop, as would be the case in routed firewall mode. In essence, the network is simply split into two Layer 2 segments and the appliance is placed in between these two segments, while Layer 3 remains unchanged. This is illustrated in Figure 7.5:

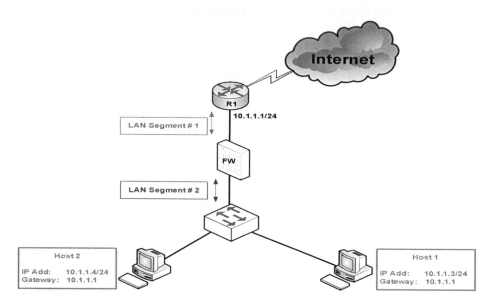

Figure 7.5. In Secured Bridging Mode Firewall not a Hop

In Figure 7.5 above, the Cisco security appliance is placed in between the switch and the Internet-facing router, effectively creating two LAN segments: one between the switch and the firewall, and the other between the firewall and the router. However, from a Layer 3 (Network) perspective, the two hosts connected to the switch reside on the same IP subnet as the router. These hosts both have their default gateway pointing to R1. Taking this concept an additional step further, the Traceroute example that was used in the routed firewall section would show the following when the security appliance was operating in transparent mode:

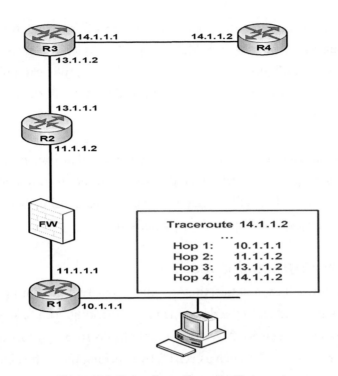

Figure 7.6. Firewall not Shown in Traceroute

As illustrated in Figure 7.6 above, even though the security appliance is physically present and is segmenting the network at the Data Link Layer, it is invisible at the Network Layer in the Traceroute. The user is unaware that there is even a firewall in the path.

While it is commonly thought that transparent firewalls are unable to provide the same functionality as routed firewalls, this belief is incorrect. In fact, the Cisco security appliance deployed in transparent mode continues to perform Stateful inspection with Application Layer intelligence and still possesses regular firewalling capabilities. Additionally, the security appliance in transparent mode can also perform Network Address Translation (NAT).

In transparent mode, the egress interface of the security appliance is determined by performing a MAC address lookup instead of a route lookup. The only Layer 3 addressing required on a transparent firewall is the management IP address, which is used as the source IP address for packets originating from the security appliance, such as AAA and Syslog messages. The management IP address, however, must reside on the same connected subnet.

While transparent mode is a good technique to protect the network passively, i.e. without an intruder or attacker detecting the existence of a firewall (e.g. via Traceroutes), there are some restrictions that should be taken into consideration.

The first restriction is that transparent firewalls do not support IP routing protocols, such as OSPF, RIP, and EIGRP, because they operate in bridged (Layer 2) mode. The second restriction is that while static routes may be configured on the transparent firewall, they can only be used for traffic that originates from the security appliance and not for traffic that will traverse the security appliance. This is a common misconception.

However, despite these restrictions, it is important to remember that transparent firewalls do allow IP routing protocols through the firewall, as long as ACLs on the firewall permit these protocols through. For example, an EIGRP neighbor relationship can be established between two EIGRP-enabled routers separated by a security appliance in stealth mode.

Application Layer Protocol Inspection

In addition to Stateful firewall capabilities, the Adaptive Security Algorithm provides built-in Application Layer intelligence that assists in detecting and preventing both protocol and Application Layer attacks. The Adaptive Security Algorithm is able to do so by performing deep packet inspection of Application Layer traffic, such as HTTP, by checking the IP header and payload (data) contents. This differs from conventional Stateful firewalls that can only maintain session state information details.

Application awareness allows the security appliance to perform deep packet inspection in the data for any malicious activity. Advanced network attacks that tunnel viruses or worms in HTTP traffic, for example, cannot be detected by traditional Stateful firewalls. However, the security appliance, armed with application inspection, which is enabled by default for most standard well-known protocols with specific TCP and UDP port numbers (e.g. HTTP, DNS, and FTP), provides protection from these attacks that attempt to use embedding techniques to pass malicious traffic encapsulated in other well-known Application Layer protocols.

Adaptive Security Algorithm Operation

There are three basic operational functions that form the basis of the Adaptive Security Algorithm (ASA) in Cisco security appliances:

- Access Control Lists
- Xlate and Conn Tables
- Inspection Engine

ACLs are used to control network access based on specific networks, hosts, and services, such as TCP and UDP port numbers.

Cisco security appliances utilize xlate and conn tables (i.e. translation and connection tables) to maintain state information for each connection. This state information can then be used by the ASA and cut-through proxy to forward traffic effectively within established connections.

The inspection engine is used by security appliances to perform Stateful inspection as well as Application Layer inspection functions. These inspection rule sets are predefined to validate application compliance, as mandated in RFCs and other standards, and cannot be modified in any manner by administrators or other users.

Figure 7.7 illustrates how these three functions work together with security appliances:

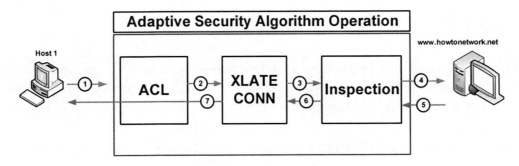

Figure 7.7. ASA Operation

Going by Figure 7.7 illustrated above, in step 1, Host 1 initiates an HTTP connection to the www. howtonetwork.net address, and a TCP SYN packet destined to the server is sent and then received by the security appliance. The security appliance receives the packet and checks the ACL database to determine whether the connection is permitted. For simplicity's sake, we will assume that it is.

The security appliance creates a new entry in the connection database (xlate and conn tables), as illustrated in step 2, using the necessary session information, i.e. source and destination IP address pair, protocol type, and the source and destination port number pair.

The security appliance then proceeds and checks the predefined rule sets in the inspection engine, as illustrated in step 3, and performs further Application Layer inspection. Based on these predefined rule sets, and the outcome of the check, the security appliance can either forward or drop the packet. In this example, we will assume that all checks succeed and the packet is forwarded to the www.howtonetwork.net server, as illustrated in step 4.

When the server receives the SYN packet from Host 1, it responds by sending a SYN + ACK back to the host, as illustrated in step 5.

The security appliance receives the server's response, performs the inspection, and then looks up the connection information in the connection table (xlate and conn tables) to determine whether the session information matches an existing session, as illustrated in step 6.

Once the connection table has been verified, and the security appliance has matched the response from the server to an existing connection, the packet is forwarded to Host 1, as illustrated in step 7, because it belongs to an existing session, i.e. a session that was originated by an internal host to an external network or destination. Host 1 then sends an ACK packet to the server and the HTTP session is established.

Context-Based Access Control

NOTE: CBAC is described in this section for the purposes of being thorough. However, CBAC is being replaced by the Zone-Based Policy Firewall (ZPF). ZPF is a mandatory requirement of the IINS course, while CBAC is viewed as a related topic.

Context-Based Access Control (CBAC) is also commonly referred to as the Classic Firewall. CBAC is a part of the Cisco IOS Firewall set and it provides an advanced firewall engine, which provides advanced traffic-filtering functionality to Cisco IOS routers. The main features of Context-Based Access Control are as follows:

- It protects internal networks from external intrusion;
- It provides DoS protection;
- It provides per-application control mechanisms;
- It examines Layer 3 and Layer 4, as well as Application Layer, information;
- It maintains state information for every connection;
- It generates real-time event alert failures and log messages; and
- It provides enhanced audit trail features.

CBAC provides network protection by offering traffic filtering and traffic inspection capabilities, as well as alerts and audit trails.

Traffic Filtering

CBAC is a software-based firewall feature that offers dynamic traffic filtering capabilities to filter TCP and UDP packets based on Application Layer protocols, such as HTTP. In order for CBAC to work, the network must be divided into trusted (internal) and untrusted (external) logical segments. The principle of CBAC traffic filtering is that it allows any and all traffic originated from the trusted (internal) network to go out to the untrusted (external) network.

Traffic Inspection

CBAC inspects all traffic that traverses the firewall and maintains state information for all TCP and UDP sessions. This state information is then used to create temporary (dynamic) openings through the firewall to allow access to returning traffic that was originated internally.

CBAC also provides deep packet inspection capabilities that look into the payload (data) of Application Layer protocols for malicious activity, e.g. viruses and worms. This prevents attacks that use embedding techniques to pass malicious traffic by encapsulating it into well-known protocols, such as HTTP and SMTP (E-Mail).

Alerts and Audit Trails

CBAC can generate real-time event alerts and audit trails for all session information maintained in the state table. The enhanced audit trail feature uses Syslog to track all network transactions, recording information such as source and destination address pairs, port information, bytes transmitted, and connection duration, for example. For any suspicious activity, CBAC can be configured to send real-time event alerts using Syslog notification messages. CBAC inspection rules can be configured for reporting event alerts and audit trail information on a per-application-protocol basis.

Understanding CBAC Operation

This section describes the basic operation of CBAC, i.e. how it inspects packets and maintains state table information for all connections, allowing it to provide intelligent packet filtering.

CBAC performs per-protocol inspection. Each protocol that requires inspection is individually enabled and an interface and interface direction (i.e. inbound or outbound) is specified to determine where the inspection occurs. Only the protocols specified by the administrator will be inspected by CBAC. All other protocols that are not specified continue uninterrupted, although they may be subject to other router functions, such as NAT or ACL restrictions, etc.

Packets that enter the firewall are subject to inspection only if they first pass the inbound ACL at the input interface and outbound ACL at the output ACL. If a packet is denied by the ACL, the router will simply drop it without CBAC inspection. For TCP inspection, CBAC will keep track of TCP sequence numbers, and any packets with sequence numbers that are not in the expected ranges will be dropped.

CBAC uses several timeout and threshold values to manage session state information. These values help determine when to drop sessions that do not become fully established, which allows CBAC to free up system resources, e.g. memory and CPU. CBAC sends a reset message for all dropped sessions, sending one message to the source and another to the destination. CBAC monitors these thresholds as follows:

- The number of embryonic (half-open) sessions based on time
- The total number of half-open (embryonic) TCP or UDP sessions
- The number of per-host embryonic TCP sessions

As is the case with Stateful firewalls, CBAC maintains a session state table and for every incoming packet, the state table is updated with information pertaining to the session, which typically includes source and destination address pairs, protocol information, and port information for the session. For UDP, CBAC does not maintain state information because of the fact that UDP is a connectionless protocol; however, all returning UDP packets are checked with the idle timeout period to ensure that they have the corresponding source and destination IP addresses and port numbers.

Finally, CBAC uses the connection information in the state table to open dynamic holes in the firewall access list to allow returning traffic that would normally be blocked. CBAC performs this action by dynamically adding and removing ACL entries at the firewall interfaces. However, it is important to remember that these dynamically created ACL entries are temporary and are not saved into NVRAM; that is, if the router is reloaded, the dynamic ACL entries created by CBAC are not retained.

Configuring and Verifying CBAC

NOTE: You are not required to perform any CBAC configuration for the IINS course; however, because you may be called upon to answer questions based on provided configurations, this section has been included.

CBAC configuration and verification is a straightforward process that involves six basic steps:

1. Select an internal and external interface. An internal interface refers to the internal or trusted side where sessions must originate for traffic to be allowed through the firewall. The internal interface is also referred to as the trusted interface and is typically the router LAN interface. The external interface, on the other hand, refers to the untrusted and unprotected side where sessions should not originate, e.g. the Internet. Sessions originating from the external side should be blocked unless explicitly permitted. The concept of internal and external interfaces is illustrated in Figure 7.8:

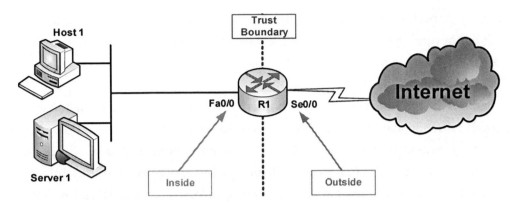

Figure 7.8. CBAC Internal and External Interfaces

As illustrated in Figure 7.8 above, R1 has been enabled for CBAC and has two defined trust boundaries. The FastEthernet0/0 interface resides on the inside and everything behind it (i.e. Host 1 and Server 1) is trusted. The Serial0/0 interface resides on the outside and everything in front of it (i.e. the Internet) is untrusted. Traffic from inside hosts to the Internet is permitted by default; however, traffic from the Internet (untrusted) will be denied by default, unless explicitly permitted.

2. Configure an IP extended ACL. For CBAC to work, an ACL must be configured and implemented in order to create temporary openings through the firewall to allow return traffic. You cannot use a standard ACL; only named or numbered IP extended ACLs can be used in conjunction with CBAC. As a general rule, explicitly permit network traffic that originates from untrusted networks or hosts (e.g. the Internet) and is destined for the trusted network (e.g. company-owned web servers); all other traffic from untrusted networks or hosts to the trusted network or hosts should be denied. IP extended ACLs are configured using the access-list [100-199|2000-2699] or ip access-list extended [name] global configuration commands for numbered and named IP extended ACLs, respectively.

3. Define an inspection rule. This rule is created to specify which IP traffic, i.e. Application Layer protocols, will be inspected by the firewall engine. Inspection rules should specify each desired Application Layer protocol, as well as the generic TCP or UDP protocols. The inspection rule consists of a series of statements, each listing a protocol, which specifies the same inspection rule name. Inspection rule statements can include other options, such as controlling alert and audit trail messages, as well as checking IP fragmentation. Inspection rules are configured using the ip inspect name [name] [protocol] global configuration command. The same name is used for all protocols to be inspected.

4. Configure global timeouts and thresholds. This step is optional and presents advanced options, which are beyond the scope of the IINS course requirements. Global timeout and threshold configuration will not be described in this guide.

5. Apply the ACL and inspection rule to an interface. CBAC inspection should be applied to the external (outbound) interface when configuring CBAC for outbound traffic. This is performed by using the ip inspect [name] out interface configuration command. CBAC should be applied to the internal interface (inbound) when configuring CBAC for inbound traffic. This is performed by using the ip inspect [name] in interface configuration command. ACLs are applied to interfaces using the ip access-group [name|number] [in|out] interface configuration command.

6. Verify CBAC configuration and operation by using the show ip inspect [options] command to view configuration and statistical information for CBAC.

The following section provides CBAC configuration examples based on Figure 7.9:

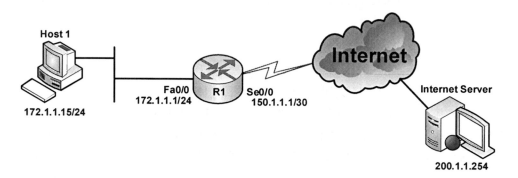

Figure 7.9. CBAC Network

In the following configuration example, CBAC is configured on R1 as follows:

*   The ACL is configured to deny all traffic; CBAC will create dynamic entries as needed.
*   CBAC is configured to use an inspection rule named IINS-CBAC.
*   CBAC is configured to inspect all HTTP (TCP) traffic.
*   The CBAC inspection rule will be applied to the Se0/0 interface of R1 for outbound traffic.
*   The CBAC inspection rule will be applied to the Fa0/0 interface of R1 for inbound traffic.

```
R1(config)#access-list 100 deny ip any any
R1(config)#ip inspect name IINS-CBAC http
R1(config)#ip inspect name IINS-CBAC tcp
R1(config)#int se0/0
R1(config-if)#ip inspect IINS-CBAC out
```

```
R1(config-if)#ip access-group 100 in
R1(config-if)#exit
R1(config)#int fa0/0
R1(config-if)#ip inspect IINS-CBAC in
R1(config-if)#ip access-group 100 out
R1(config-if)#exit
```

Once configured, administrators can validate CBAC operation by using the show ip inspect [options] command. The options available with this command are illustrated below:

```
R1#show ip inspect ?
  all             Inspection all available information
  config          Inspection configuration
  interfaces      Inspection interfaces
  mib             FW MIB specific show commands
  name            Inspection name
  sessions        Inspection sessions
  sis             Inspection sessions (debug version)
  statistics      Inspection statistics
  tech-support    Inspection technical support
```

The options printed by this command that you should be aware of are in Table 7.3:

Table 7.3. 'ip inspect' Options

Keyword	Description
name [name]	Used to view the configuration for the rule specified
config	Used to view the complete CBAC inspection configuration
interfaces	Used to view the interface configuration, i.e. inspection rules and ACLs
session [detail]	Used to view sessions currently being tracked and inspected by CBAC
all	Used to view all CBAC configuration and all existing sessions

The following output illustrates an HTTP session on R1, from Host 1 to the Internet server:

```
R1#show ip inspect sessions
Established Sessions
  Session 84362E94 (172.1.1.15:3624)=>(200.1.1.254:80) http SIS_OPEN
```

The show ip inspect sessions detail provides detailed session information as follows:

```
R1#show ip inspect sessions detail
Established Sessions
  Session 84362E94 (172.1.1.15:3624)=>(200.1.1.254:80) http SIS_OPEN
```

```
Created 00:01:59, Last heard 00:01:57
Bytes sent (initiator:responder) [425:200]
Out SID 200.1.1.254[80:80]=>172.1.1.15[3624:3624] on ACL 100
In  SID 200.1.1.254[80:80]=>172.1.1.15[3624:3624] on ACL 100  (4 matches)
```

In the following configuration example, CBAC is configured on R1 as follows:

- The ACL is configured to explicitly permit TCP WWW traffic to internal server 172.16.1.254.
- The ACL is configured to deny all other IP traffic.
- CBAC is configured to use an inspection rule named IINS-CBAC.
- CBAC is configured to inspect all ICMP and SMTP (UDP) traffic.
- The CBAC inspection rule will be applied to the Se0/0 interface of R1 for outbound traffic.
- The CBAC inspection rule will be applied to the Fa0/0 interface of R1 for inbound traffic.

```
R1(config)#ip access-list extended CBAC-ACL
R1(config-ext-nacl)#permit tcp any host 172.16.1.254 eq 80
R1(config-ext-nacl)#deny ip any any
R1(config-ext-nacl)#exit
R1(config)#ip inspect name IINS-CBAC icmp
R1(config)#ip inspect name IINS-CBAC smtp
R1(config)#ip inspect name IINS-CBAC udp
R1(config)#int s0/0
R1(config-if)#ip inspect IINS-CBAC out
R1(config-if)#ip access-group CBAC-ACL in
R1(config-if)#exit
R1(config)#int f0/0
R1(config-if)#ip inspect IINS-CBAC in
R1(config-if)#ip access-group CBAC-ACL out
R1(config-if)#exit
```

To view detailed session information for CBAC for a ping from Host 1 to the Internet server, for example, the show ip inspect sessions detail command is used, as illustrated below:

```
R1#show ip inspect sessions detail
Established Sessions
 Session 84362BCC (172.1.1.15:8)=>(200.1.1.254:0) icmp SIS_OPEN
  Created 00:00:09, Last heard 00:00:06
  ECHO request
  Bytes sent (initiator:responder) [128:128]
  Out SID 200.1.1.254[0:0]=>172.1.1.15[0:0] on ACL CBAC-ACL
  In  SID 200.1.1.254[0:0]=>172.1.1.15[0:0] on ACL CBAC-ACL  (4 matches)
  Out SID 0.0.0.0[0:0]=>172.1.1.15[3:3] on ACL CBAC-ACL
  In  SID 0.0.0.0[0:0]=>172.1.1.15[3:3] on ACL CBAC-ACL
  Out SID 0.0.0.0[0:0]=>172.1.1.15[11:11] on ACL CBAC-ACL
  In  SID 0.0.0.0[0:0]=>172.1.1.15[11:11] on ACL CBAC-ACL
```

To view all CBAC configuration parameters, the show ip inspect config command is used as follows:

```
R1#show ip inspect config
Session audit trail is disabled
Session alert is enabled
one-minute (sampling period) thresholds are [unlimited : unlimited] connections
max-incomplete sessions thresholds are [unlimited : unlimited]
max-incomplete tcp connections per host is unlimited. Block-time 0 minute.
tcp synwait-time is 30 sec -- tcp finwait-time is 5 sec
tcp idle-time is 3600 sec -- udp idle-time is 30 sec
tcp reassembly queue length 16; timeout 5 sec; memory-limit 1024 kilo bytes
dns-timeout is 5 sec
Inspection Rule Configuration
 Inspection name IINS-CBAC
    icmp alert is on audit-trail is off timeout 10
    smtp max-data 20000000 alert is on audit-trail is off timeout 3600
    udp alert is on audit-trail is off timeout 30
```

Alternatively, the show ip inspect interfaces command can also be issued. This command allows administrators to view interface CBAC configuration, as illustrated in the output below:

```
R1#show ip inspect interfaces
Interface Configuration
 Interface Serial0/0
 Inbound inspection rule is not set
 Outgoing inspection rule is IINS-CBAC
   icmp alert is on audit-trail is off timeout 10
   smtp max-data 20000000 alert is on audit-trail is off timeout 3600
   udp alert is on audit-trail is off timeout 30
 Inbound access list is CBAC-ACL
 Outgoing access list is not set
 Interface FastEthernet0/0
 Inbound inspection rule is IINS-CBAC
   icmp alert is on audit-trail is off timeout 10
   smtp max-data 20000000 alert is on audit-trail is off timeout 3600
   udp alert is on audit-trail is off timeout 30
 Outgoing inspection rule is not set
 Inbound access list is not set
 Outgoing access list is CBAC-ACL
```

Before we move on to the next section of this chapter, there are several Cisco IOS Firewall enhancements that were introduced in Cisco IOS software 12.3(T) and 12.4 Mainline. While going into configuration detail on each of these features is beyond the scope of the IINS course requirements, the features are described briefly. These features are as follows:

- HTTP Inspection Engine
- E-Mail Inspection Engine
- Inspection of Router-Generated Traffic
- Firewall ACL Bypass
- Transparent IOS Firewall

The HTTP Inspection Engine in the Cisco IOS Firewall has been enhanced with the introduction of Advanced Application Inspection and Control. This allows for deep packet inspection of HTTP traffic, which may be used by attackers to embed malicious traffic, such as worms and Trojans, for example. Any HTTP packets that do not conform to standards in HTTP are dropped and a reset message is sent out to both source and destination. Additionally, the router also sends out a Syslog message.

The E-Mail Inspection Engine in the Cisco IOS Firewall adds support for ESMTP, Post Office Protocol (POP) 3, and Internet Message Access Protocol (IMAP). ESMTP, which stands for Enhanced Simple Mail Transport Protocol, is similar to the basic SMTP and provides a basic method for exchanging e-mail messages. However, ESMTP specifies service extensions to the original SMTP standard that support graphics, audio and video files, and text in various national languages. ESMTP also uses the EHLO command, which is not used in SMTP. An ESMTP client starts a connection by using the EHLO command, instead of the HELO command that is used in SMTP. Advanced application inspection in the Cisco IOS Firewall prevents protocol masquerading and enforces strict RFC standards.

The inspection of router-generated traffic allows CBAC to inspect TCP, UDP, and H.323 (which is used in voice communications) connections that may have the firewall as one of the connection endpoints. For example, CBAC now has the ability to inspect Telnet sessions originated from the router, which negates the need to explicitly permit the traffic in the IP extended ACL used in conjunction with CBAC.

The Firewall ACL Bypass feature allows a packet to avoid redundant ACL checks by allowing the firewall to permit the packet on the basis of existing inspection sessions instead of dynamic ACLs. Thus, input and output dynamic ACL searches are eliminated, improving the overall throughput performance of the base engine. Because input and output dynamic ACLs are no longer necessary, the need for CBAC to create dynamic ACLs on the interface is eliminated. This results in improved connections-per-second performance of the firewall, as well as reduced run-time memory consumption of the firewall. Additionally, this feature is transparent to the user and no additional commands are required to enable or disable it.

The Transparent IOS Firewall feature acts as a Layer 2 transparent bridge using CBAC. Transparent firewalls were described in detail earlier in this chapter. This enhancement allows a Cisco IOS Firewall to be implemented concurrently as a Layer 2 and a Layer 3 firewall.

Cisco Zone-Based Policy Firewall

The Cisco Zone-Based Policy Firewall (ZPF) was designed to overcome the interface-based model limitation of CBAC, also known as the Classic Firewall. This limitation was that all traffic passing through the interface was subject to the same inspection policy, which in turn limited granularity and policy enforcement, especially in scenarios where multiple interfaces existed. This concept is illustrated in Figure 7.10:

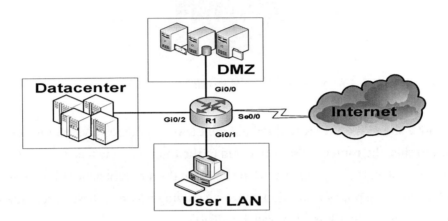

Figure 7.10. Cisco CBAC Firewall with Network Segments

Figure 7.10 above illustrates a Cisco IOS Firewall-enabled router (CBAC) with three different network segments and an external connection to the Internet, via Serial0/0. While CBAC could be used to inspect traffic from the internal (trusted) networks to the external (untrusted) networks, the same CBAC inspection rules would also then apply for traffic between internal network segments, which may not be desirable in some cases.

When using CBAC, it is not possible to configure it to inspect HTTP and SMTP traffic from the User LAN to the Internet and vice-versa, to inspect HTTP traffic from the User LAN to the DMZ and vice-versa, and to inspect FTP traffic from the User LAN to the Datacenter, for example, because only one CBAC rule can be applied inbound or outbound per interface.

With ZFW, Stateful inspection can now be applied in a zone-based model. Interfaces are assigned to zones and policy inspection is applied to traffic moving between zones. This concept is illustrated in Figure 7.11:

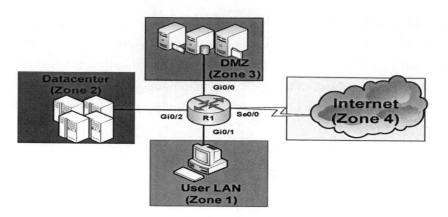

Figure 7.11. ZFW Stateful Inspecton on a Network

Figure 7.11 above shows a router with three different LAN segments, divided into Zones 1, 2, and 3. In addition to this, the router is also connected to the Internet, which is Zone 4. Using ZPF, administrators can control the inspection of traffic between the different zones by assigning interfaces to zones and performing policy inspection on traffic moving between these different zones. This is not possible when using the Classic Firewall, i.e. CBAC.

ZPF provides greater granularity, flexibility, and scalability, as well as an easy-to-use zone-based security approach. With a zone-based inspection model, varying policies can be applied to multiple groups of hosts connected to the same interface. The security zones used in ZPF establish the security boundaries of the network where traffic is subjected to policy restrictions as it crosses to another zone within the network.

Rules for Implementing and Applying Zones

There are certain rules that you must be familiar with when implementing ZPF. These rules are applicable to the configuration and implementation of ZPF in Cisco IOS routers as follows:

- A zone must be configured before interfaces can be assigned to the zone. In other words, an interface cannot be assigned to a zone that does not exist.

- An interface can be assigned to only one security zone. This same concept is applicable in CBAC. Assigning an interface to multiple zones would result in confusing the router.

- All traffic to and from a given interface is implicitly blocked when the interface is assigned to a zone, except traffic to and from other interfaces in the same zone and traffic to any interface on the router, e.g. Loopback interfaces.

- Traffic is implicitly allowed to flow by default among interfaces that are members of the same zone. In other words, if two or more interfaces are in the same zone, all hosts connected to those interfaces can communicate with each other by default.

- In order to permit traffic to and from a zone member interface, a policy allowing or inspecting traffic must be configured between that zone and any other zone.

- The self zone is the only exception to the default 'deny all' policy. The self zone controls traffic sent to the router itself or originated by the router. Therefore, all traffic to any router interface or traffic originated by the router is allowed until explicitly denied.

- Traffic cannot flow between a zone member interface and any interface that is not a zone member, by default. Pass, inspect, and drop actions can only be applied between two configured zones. For example, if interface FastEthernet0/0 is a member of Zone A and interface FastEthernet0/1 is not affiliated with any zones, traffic from FastEthernet0/0 cannot flow to FastEthernet0/1, and vice-versa.

- Interfaces that have not been assigned to a zone function as classical router ports and can still use classic Stateful inspection/CBAC configuration. However, interfaces that have been configured for zones cannot be configured for CBAC.

- If it is required that an interface on the router not be part of the zone-based firewall policy, it might still be necessary to put that interface in a zone and configure a pass all policy, which is sort of a dummy policy, between that zone and any other zone to which traffic flow is desired. Otherwise, that interface will not be able to communicate with other interfaces that have been assigned to zones, and vice-versa, as described earlier.

Configuring ZPF Using Cisco Policy Language

NOTE: You are not required to configure ZPF using CPL, as the only requirement of the IINS course is ZPF configuration using Cisco SDM; however, it is important to be familiar with the terminology, as well as the configuration format used in CPL.

ZFW is configured using the new Cisco Policy Language (CPL). CPL is a new format of configuration integrated into Cisco IOS versions 12.3(T) and 12.4 Mainline that is used to configure ZPF from the CLI. While there are several steps that need to be completed, they do not necessarily have to be implemented in the order that is illustrated below:

1. Define zones. CPL allows administrators to define their own zone names. For example, administrators can create an INTERNAL zone for all internal users and a DMZ zone for all DMZ devices. A DMZ is a firewall configuration for securing LANs. Typically, company-owned public-facing servers, such as web servers, are found in a DMZ.

2. Define zone-pairs; for example the INTERNAL zone and the DMZ zone could be paired together so that a policy can be applied for traffic between these two zones. It is important to remember that this action must be performed for both directions. For example, for the INTERNAL and DMZ zones to communicate in a bi-directional manner, traffic must be permitted to go from the INTERNAL zone to the DMZ zone and from the DMZ zone to the INTERNAL zone.

3. Define class-maps that describe traffic that must have policy applied as it crosses a zone-pair. Class-maps are commonly used in Modular QoS CLI (MQC), and they can be used to match ACLs, protocols, and other criteria. Class-map configuration is beyond the scope of the IINS course requirements.

4. Define policy-maps to apply action to your class-map traffic. Policy-maps contain one or more class-maps. The policy-map is the inspection policy. As is the case with class-map configuration, policy-map configuration is beyond the scope of the IINS course requirements.

5. Apply policy-maps (inspection policy) to the zone-pair(s). This allows for inspection between the different zones based on the traffic specified in the policy-maps. For example, a policy-map could contain a class-map that matches all TCP traffic and another class-map that matches all UDP traffic. This policy-map is then assigned to a zone-pair (e.g. the INTERNAL and DMZ zone) and it will inspect all TCP and UDP traffic for that zone-pair.

6. Assign interfaces to zones. As previously stated, interfaces can only belong to a single zone. It is therefore important to pay close attention to what you are doing; otherwise, if the configuration is incorrect, traffic will be denied by default.

Configuring ZPF Using Cisco Router and Security Device Manager

It is important that you understand how to configure ZPF using Cisco SDM, as this is a mandatory requirement of the IINS course. In this section, ZPF configuration using Cisco SDM will be illustrated using the following network diagram as a reference:

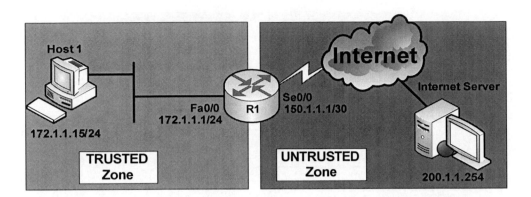

Figure 7.12. ZPF Network

The first task in configuring ZPF using SDM is to select the **Firewall and ACL** option on the main configuration page in Cisco SDM and then click on the **Basic Firewall** radio button, as illustrated in the Figure 7.13:

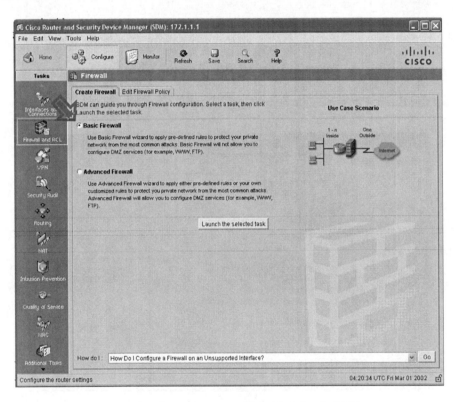

Figure 7.13. Choose 'Firewall and ACL' with SDM

Next, click on the **Launch the selected task** button, as illustrated in Figure 7.14:

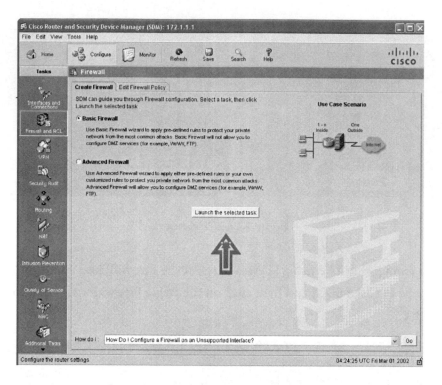

Figure 7.14. Launch Basic Firewall Wizard

This brings up the **Basic Firewall Configuration Wizard**. Click on **Next** to continue:

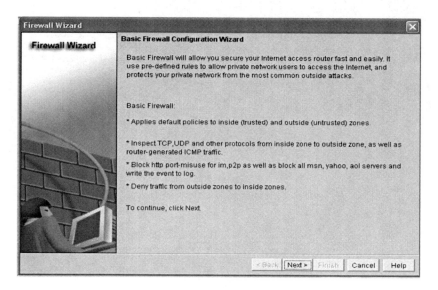

Figure 7.15. Click 'Next'

On the following screen, select the outside (untrusted) and inside (trusted) interfaces. Based on the network topology used in this configuration example, the outside interface is Serial0/0 and the inside interface is FastEthernet0/0. Select these interfaces by checking the appropriate checkboxes next to the interface, as illustrated in Figure 7.16:

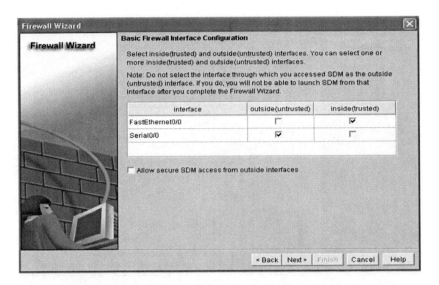

Figure 7.16. Select the Outside and Inside Interfaces

NOTE: The **Allow secure SDM access from outside interfaces** checkbox allows administrators to allow external networks to communicate with internal networks; for example, allowing external networks to communicate with an internal company-owned web server. By default, all traffic from external networks to internal networks is blocked, unless it is return traffic that has been originated by an internal host. This is beyond the scope of the IINS course requirements. Administrators are warned of this default action (i.e. all external traffic to internal networks and to the router is blocked) by the following pop-up box. Simply click **OK** to continue:

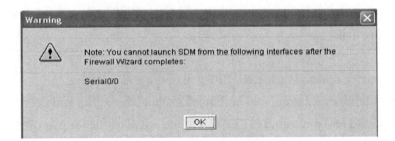

Figure 7.17. Click 'OK'

Once you have clicked **OK**, SDM transitions to the **Basic Firewall Security Configuration** page, which is illustrated in Figure 7.18:

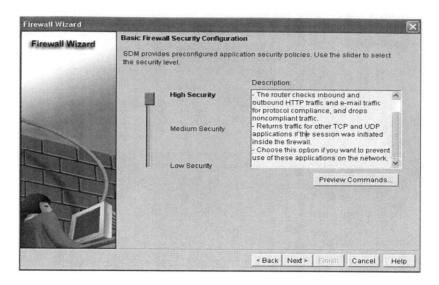

Figure 7.18. Basic Firewall Security Configuration Page

On the **Basic Firewall Security Configuration** page, three different security levels can be selected: **High Security, Medium Security,** or **Low Security.** It is important to understand ZPF operation when any one of these options is selected.

If the **High Security** option is selected, ZPF will operate as follows:
1. The router checks inbound and outbound HTTP traffic and email traffic for protocol compliance, and drops noncompliant traffic; and
2. The router returns traffic for other TCP and UDP applications if the session was initiated inside the firewall.

If the **Medium Security** option is selected, ZPF will operate as follows:
1. The router identifies inbound and outbound Instant Messaging and Peer-to-Peer traffic, and checks inbound and outbound HTTP traffic and email traffic for protocol compliance; and
2. The router returns TCP and UDP traffic on sessions initiated inside the firewall.

If the **Low Security** option is selected, ZPF will operate as follows:
1. The router does not identify application-specific traffic; and
2. The router returns TCP and UDP traffic on sessions initiated inside the firewall.

Unless absolutely justified, it is recommended that the **High Security** option, which is the default, be selected. Click on the **Next** button. This will bring you to the **Basic Firewall Domain Name Server Configuration** page, as illustrated in Figure 7.19:

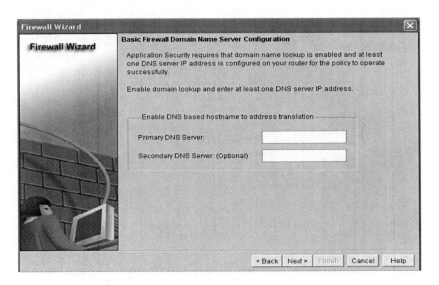

Figure 7.19. Basic Firewall Domain Name Server Page

Enter the desired DNS credentials and click on **Next,** as illustrated in Figure 7.20:

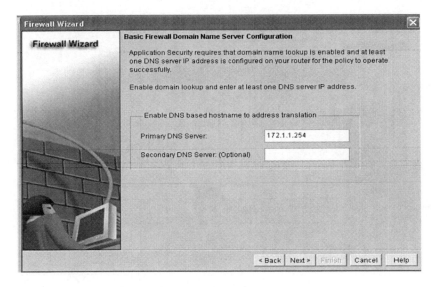

Figure 7.20. Enter the DNS Credentials

After clicking on the **Next** button, SDM transitions to the **Firewall Configuration Summary** page, which provides a summary of the selected options. The **Firewall Configuration Summary** page is illustrated in Figure 7.21:

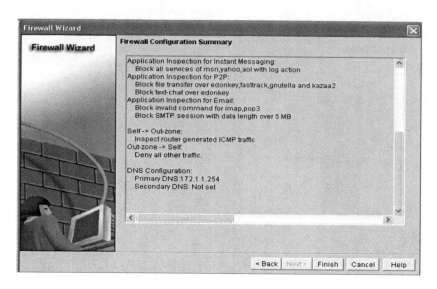

Figure 7.21. Summary Page

To complete the configuration, click on the **Finish** button. Cisco SDM then prepares the commands that it will send to the IOS router, as illustrated in Figure 7.22:

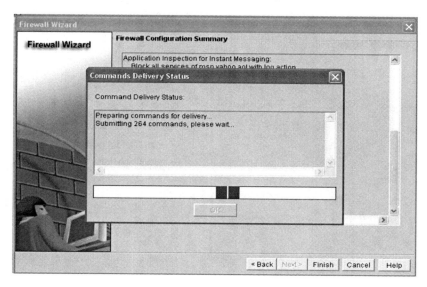

Figure 7.22. Command Preparation

Once Cisco SDM has prepared the commands it will use to configure the router, click on the **OK** button for these commands to be delivered to the router, i.e. for Cisco SDM to configure the router. Cisco SDM then brings up a pop-up box indicating the router has been configured for ZPF as designed by the administrator. This is illustrated in Figure 7.23:

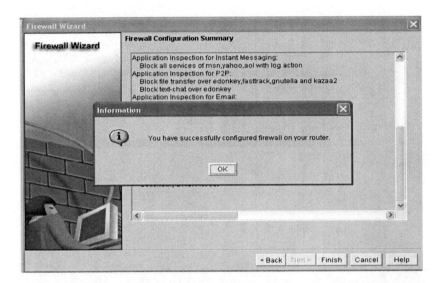

Figure 7.23. Click 'OK'

Finally, click on the **OK** button to confirm and complete ZPF configuration. By default, SDM then brings up the **Edit Firewall Policy** page, as illustrated in Figure 7.24:

Figure 7.24. Edit Firewall Policy Page

The headings with the minus (-) signs next to them represent the default policy-maps created by SDM and applied to a zone pair. By default, these are presented in an expanded format in SDM, which allows administrators to view their applicable class-maps. Clicking on the minus signs hides all associated class-maps, as illustrated in Figure 7.25:

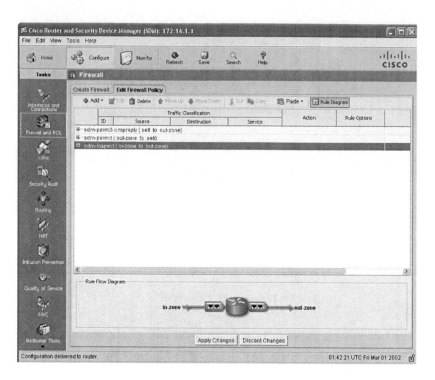

Figure 7.25. Hiding the Class-Maps

While the policy-map names cannot be edited, new rules (i.e. class-maps) can be added to each policy-map by right-clicking the selected option, as illustrated in Figure 7.26:

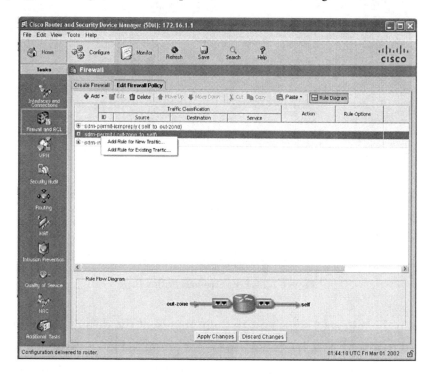

Figure 7.26. New Rules can be Added

To view (and edit) the contents of each class-map (i.e. the traffic matched), double-click on the class-map. For example, to view the traffic matched by the **sdm-cls-protocol-p2p** class-map, double-click on it, as illustrated in Figure 7.27:

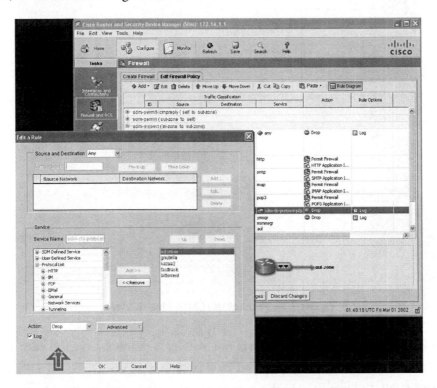

Figure 7.27. Double Click 'Class-Map' to View and Edit

From the output illustrated Figure 7.27 above, the **sdm-cls-protocol-p2p** class-map matches edonkey, gnutella, kazaa2, fasttrack, and bittorrent traffic. The **Action:** drop-down menu shows that this traffic will be dropped. Additionally, this information will be logged, as indicated by the checked **Log** checkbox.

The traffic matched by class-maps can also be viewed by simply pointing the mouse over the desired class-map, under the desired policy-map, as illustrated in Figure 7.28:

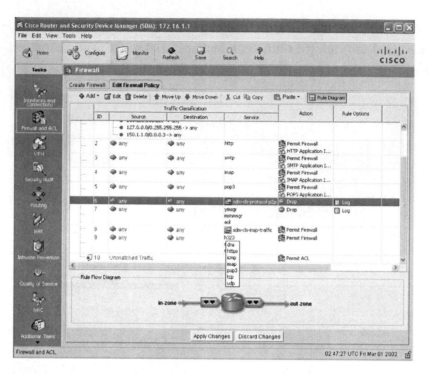

Figure 7.28. Point at the Class-Map to View

In the Figure 7.28 above, the mouse (which is not visible) is pointed over the **sdm-cls-insp-traf-fic** class-map. The traffic (protocols) matched by this class-map are DNS, HTTPS, ICMP, IMAP, POP3, TCP, and UDP. As illustrated in the screenshot, this traffic is permitted by the firewall.

Once ZPF has been configured, administrators can monitor and view traffic statistics by navigating to the **Monitor** page (on the top toolbar) in SDM and navigating to and selecting the **Firewall Status** option, as illustrated in Figure 7.29:

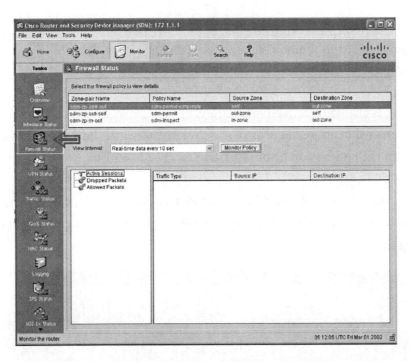

Figure 7.29. 'Firewall Status' Tab Shows Statistics

To view traffic statistics, select the zone-pair name and click on the **Monitor Policy** button. For example, to monitor traffic from the in-zone (LAN) to the out-zone (Internet), select the **sdm-zp-in-out** zone-pair and click on the **Monitor Policy** button. This operation is illustrated in Figure 7.30:

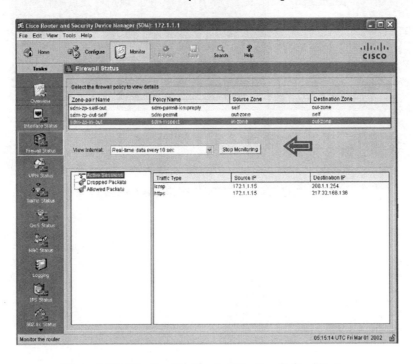

Figure 7.30. Monitor Traffic via 'Monitor Policy' Button

NOTE: Once you click on the **Monitor Policy** button, Cisco SDM enables monitoring for the selected zone-pair. To stop monitoring a zone-pair, click on the **Stop Monitoring** button, as illustrated in Figure 7.30 above.

When monitoring is enabled, the **Active Sessions** option allows administrators to view all active sessions. In the screenshot above, there are two active sessions: an ICMP session from 172.1.1.25 to 200.1.1.254 and an HTTPS session from 172.1.1.15 to 217.32.166.136.

The **Dropped Packets** option allows administrators to view packet loss information. Finally, the **Allowed Packets** option provides administrators with a graph on traffic throughput statistics, as illustrated in Figure 7.31:

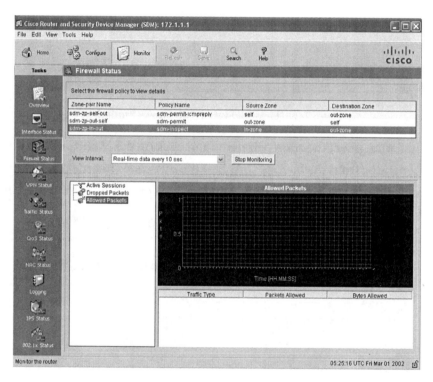

Figure 7.31. 'Dropped Packets' Shows Packet Loss

Chapter Summary

The following section is a summary of the major points you should be aware of in this chapter:

Cisco IOS Firewall Overview

- Cisco IOS Firewall set provides network security with integrated, inline security solutions
- The Cisco IOS Firewall set is a Stateful inspection firewall engine
- The Cisco IOS Firewall suite also includes application-level inspection
- Cisco IOS routers can be configured with the IOS Firewall feature set as follows:
    1. As a firewall router facing the Internet
    2. As a firewall router to protect the internal network from external networks, e.g. partners
    3. As a firewall router between groups of networks in the internal network
    4. As a firewall router that provides secure connection to remote offices or branches

- The Cisco IOS Firewall is comprised of the following functions and technologies:
    1. Cisco IOS Stateful Packet Inspection
    2. Context-Based Access Control
    3. Intrusion Prevention System
    4. Authentication Proxy
    5. Port-to-Application Mapping
    6. Network Address Translation
    7. Zone-Based Policy Firewall

Types of Firewalls

- A firewall protects networked computers from intentional hostile intrusion
- Firewalls must have at least two network interfaces: internal and external
- Basic firewalls consist of two main mechanisms:
    1. The first mechanism is designed to block traffic
    2. The second mechanism is designed to allow traffic

- Firewalls fall into five broad categories:
    1. Static or Network-Level Packet Filters
    2. Circuit Level Gateways
    3. Application Level Firewalls or Gateways
    4. Stateful Inspection Firewalls

- Static or Network-Level Packet Filters are first-generation firewalls
- ACLs used in Cisco IOS routers are considered static or Network-Level packet filters
- Circuit level gateways are second-generation firewalls

- Circuit level gateways work at the Session Layer of the OSI Model
- Circuit level gateways monitor TCP handshaking between packets
- Application Level Gateways, or ALGs, are third-generation firewalls
- ALGs evaluate packets for valid data at the Application Layer
- ALGs filter at Layers 3, 4, and 5, and 7
- ALGs are also referred to as Proxies
- There are many different types of proxies. Some of the most common ones are:
  1. File Transfer Protocol (FTP) proxies
  2. SOCKS proxies
  3. Hypertext Transfer Protocol (HTTP) proxies
  4. Network Address Translation (NAT) proxies
  5. Secure Sockets Layer (SSL) proxies

- Stateful firewalls are fourth-generation dynamic packet filtering firewalls
- Stateful firewalls operate at Layers 3, 4, 5, and 7 of the OSI Model
- Stateful firewalls perform Stateful Packet Inspection (SPI)
- Stateful firewalls maintain detailed session database, referred to as the state table

Hardware versus Software Firewalls

- Hardware firewalls are robust and built specifically for the purposes of firewalling
- Examples of hardware firewalls are the Cisco PIX and ASA firewalls
- Software firewalls are installed on individual computers
- An example of a software firewall is the Cisco IOS Firewall technology

Cisco Security Appliances

- Cisco hardware firewall technologies come in three different forms:
  1. The Cisco PIX 500 Series Security Appliances
  2. The Cisco ASA 5500 Series Adaptive Security Appliances
  3. The Cisco Firewall Services Module

- The following table lists and provides a description of the Cisco PIX 500 series devices:

Device Type	Description
Cisco PIX 501	The Cisco PIX 501 is a compact, plug-and-play security appliance for small office/home office (SOHO) environments. PIX 501 security appliances provide an integrated 4-port 10/100 FastEthernet switch and a dedicated 10/100 FastEthernet uplink

Cisco PIX 506E	The Cisco PIX 506E is a security appliance for remote office/branch office (ROBO) environments. The PIX 506E security appliance provides two auto-sensing 10/100 FastEthernet interfaces
Cisco PIX 515E	The Cisco PIX 515E security appliance is a modular, high-performance security appliance for small-to-medium and enterprise network environments. The Cisco PIX 515E security appliance can support up to six 10/100 FastEthernet interfaces
Cisco PIX 525	The Cisco PIX 525 security appliance provides GigabitEthernet connectivity for medium-to-large enterprise network environments. The Cisco PIX 525 is capable of supporting up to eight 10/100 FastEthernet interfaces or three GigabitEthernet interfaces
Cisco PIX 535	The Cisco PIX 535 security appliance is a modular, high-performance GigabitEthernet security appliance for service provider network environments. The Cisco PIX 535 can support up to ten 10/100 FastEthernet interfaces, or nine GigabitEthernet interfaces, as well as redundant power supplies

- The following table lists and describes the different ASA 5500 series models:

Device Type	Description
Cisco ASA 5505	The Cisco ASA 5505 security appliance is a cost-effective, easy-to-deploy appliance for small business, branch office, and enterprise teleworkers environments. This mode offers and integrated 8-port 10/100 FastEthernet switch, with two Power over Ethernet (PoE) ports
Cisco ASA 5510	The Cisco ASA 5510 security appliance is a cost-effective, easy-to-deploy appliance for medium-sized businesses, remote office/branch office (ROBO) and enterprise environments with advanced security and networking services
Cisco ASA 5520	The Cisco ASA 5520 security appliance provides high-availability services and GigabitEthernet connectivity. This model is suitable for medium-sized enterprise networks
Cisco ASA 5540	The Cisco ASA 5540 security appliance is a high-density, high-availability appliance that provides GigabitEthernet connectivity. This model is recommended for medium-to-large enterprises and service provider network environments
Cisco ASA 5550	The Cisco ASA 5550 security appliance is a Gigabit-class security appliance that offers up to 1.2Gbps of firewall throughput, with high-availability services, as well as GigabitEthernet and Fiber connectivity. This model is recommended for large enterprise and service provider network environments

- The FWSM is a high-speed, high-performance integrated firewall module
- The FWSM is supported in Cisco Catalyst 6500 switches, or Cisco 7600 routers
- Cisco security appliances can run in routed or in transparent firewall mode
- Routed firewall mode is the default for any Cisco firewall
- In routed firewall mode, the security appliance is a router hop in the network
- Transparent firewalls are also referred to as stealth firewalls
- In transparent mode, security appliances simply appear as a 'bump in the wire'
- There are three basic operational functions that form the basis of the ASA:
  1. Access Control Lists
  2. Xlate and Conn Tables
  3. Inspection Engine

Context-Based Access Control

- CBAC is being replaced by the Zone-Based Policy Firewall (ZPF)
- CBAC is also commonly referred to as the Classic Firewall
- CBAC is a part of the Cisco IOS Firewall set and it provides and advanced firewall engine
- The main features of Context-Based Access Control are:
  1. It protects internal networks from external intrusion
  2. It provides DoS protection
  3. It provides per-application control mechanisms
  4. It examines Layer 3 and Layer 4, as well as Application Layer information
  5. It maintains state information for every connection
  6. It generates real-time event alert failures and log messages
  7. It provides enhanced audit trail features

Cisco Zone-Based Policy Firewall

- ZPF was designed mainly to overcome the interface-based model limitation of CBAC
- ZPF uses a zone-based model, where interfaces are assigned to different zones
- The following rules must be acknowledged when implementing ZPF:
  1. A zone must be configured before interfaces can be assigned to the zone
  2. An interface can be assigned to only one security zone
  3. All traffic to and from a given interface is implicitly blocked when the interface is assigned to a zone, except traffic to and from other interfaces in the same zone, and traffic to any interface on the router, e.g. Loopback interfaces.
  4. Traffic is implicitly allowed to flow by default among interfaces that are members of the same zone.
  5. In order to permit traffic to and from a zone member interface, a policy allowing or inspecting traffic must be configured between that zone and any other zone.

6. The self zone is the only exception to the default "deny all" policy. The self zone controls traffic sent to the router itself or originated by the router. Therefore, all traffic to any router interface or traffic originated by the router allowed until explicitly denied.

7. Traffic cannot flow between a zone member interface and any interface that is not a zone member, by default. Pass, inspect, and drop actions can only be applied between two configured zones.

8. Interfaces that have not been assigned to a zone function as classical router ports and can still use classic Stateful inspection/CBAC configuration. However, interfaces that have been configured for zones cannot be configured for CBAC.

9. If it is required that an interface on the router not be part of the zone-based firewall policy, it might still be necessary to put that interface in a zone and configure a pass all policy, which is sort of a dummy policy, between that zone and any other zone to which traffic flow is desired

Commands Used in this Chapter

The following section is a summary of the commands used in this chapter:

Command	Description
ip inspect name [name] [prot]	Used to enabled CBAC inspection for a protocol
ip inspect [name] [in|out]	Used to apply CBAC inspection policies to interfaces
access-list [100-199|2600-2699]	Used to create a numbered IP extended ACL
ip access-list extended [name]	Used to create a named IP extended ACL
ip access-group	Used to apply an ACL to an interface
show ip inspect [options]	Used to view CBAC statistics and configuration

CHAPTER 8

Intrusion Detection and Prevention

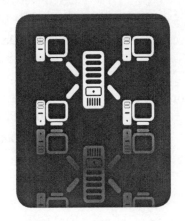

The rapid growth of the Internet has resulted in the vast proliferation of viruses, worms, Trojans, and other malicious codes and programs. This makes modern-day networks easy targets because infection can spread across the network rapidly. Due to this growing threat, networks need to be designed and equipped with solid intelligence to diagnose and mitigate threats in real-time. Intrusion Detection Systems and Intrusion Prevention Systems protect networks from unauthorized access by detecting and, if capable, preventing unauthorized access to network resources or hosts. The IINS exam objectives covered in this chapter are as follows:

- Define network-based vs. host-based intrusion detection and prevention
- Explain IPS technologies, attack responses, and monitoring options
- Enable and verify Cisco IOS IPS operations using SDM

This chapter is broken up into the following sections:

- Intrusion Detection and Prevention Systems
- IDS and IPS Signatures
- IDS and IPS System Types
- Cisco Network Intrusion Prevention Systems
- Cisco Host Intrusion Prevention Systems
- Cisco IOS IPS Overview and Implementation
- Anomaly Detection and Mitigation

IINS Exam Objective	Section(s) Covered
Define network-based vs. host-based intrusion detection and prevention	• Intrusion Detection and Prevention Systems • Cisco Network Intrusion Prevention Systems • Cisco Host Intrusion Prevention Solution
Explain IPS technologies, attack responses, and monitoring options	• Intrusion Detection and Prevention Systems • IDS and IPS Signatures • IDS and IPS System Types
Enable and verify Cisco IOS IPS operations using SDM	• Cisco IOS IPS Overview and Implementation
Other related topics	• Anomaly Detection and Mitigation

Intrusion Detection and Prevention Systems

The terms Intrusion Detection System (IDS) and Intrusion Prevention System (IPS) are commonly, but incorrectly, used interchangeably. While IDS and IPS devices perform the same basic functions, there are significant differences in their capabilities, functionality, and implementation, as we will learn through this chapter. It is imperative that you are able to differentiate between an IDS device and an IPS device, as well as their operation, functionality, and implementation within networks and on endpoints.

Intrusion Detection Systems

An Intrusion Detection System is used to detect malicious behavior that can compromise the security and trust of a computer system or network. This includes, but is not limited to, network attacks against vulnerable services, data-driven attacks on applications, host-based attacks such as privilege escalation, unauthorized logins, and access to sensitive files, as well as malware.

Although there are different types of IDS implementations, as we will learn later in this chapter, from a networking standpoint, the term IDS is typically limited to sensors (which refers to the software that runs on the physical appliance and is used to detect threats) that use only promiscuous monitoring based on an out-of-packet stream. Promiscuous monitoring refers to the monitoring of data from anywhere within the network, while the term out-of-packet implies that the IDS is not directly in the physical path of the traffic that it is monitoring. These concepts are illustrated in Figure 8.1:

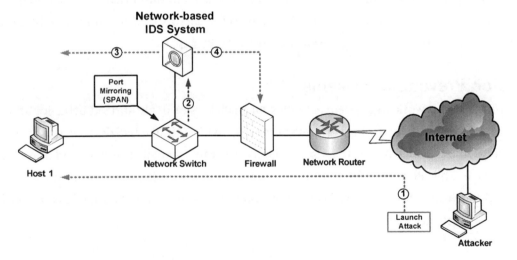

Figure 8.1. Network IDS Placement

Figure 8.1 illustrated above shows the placement of a Network-based IDS device. In step 1, an attack is initiated by the attacker to Host 1. Although the IDS is not directly in the physical traffic path between the attacker and Host 1, by using promiscuous monitoring, the Intrusion Detection

System is able to see this attack because a copy of all network traffic between the host and the attacker is sent to it via the port mirroring configuration on the network switch it is connected to, as illustrated in step 2.

> **NOTE:** In Cisco Catalyst switches, administrators can configure the Switched Port Analyzer feature, which allows administrators to mirror traffic received from a port, a group of ports, a VLAN, or a group of VLANs to a destination port where this information can be viewed by the device connected to the port, such as an IDS, for example. Although SPAN configuration is beyond the scope of the IINS course requirements, the following example illustrates how a Cisco IOS Catalyst switch can be configured to mirror all transmit and receive traffic on port FastEthernet1/1 to port FastEthernet5/5, which is connected to an Intrusion Prevention System:

```
Sw1(config)#monitor session 1 source interface fastethernet 1/1
Sw1(config)#monitor session 1 destination interface fastethernet 5/5
```

Additionally, SPAN can be used to mirror traffic received from an entire VLAN. The following configuration example illustrates how to mirror all traffic in VLAN 55 to port FastEthernet12/1, which is connected to an Intrusion Prevention System:

```
Sw1(config)#monitor session 1 source vlan 55
Sw1(config)#monitor session 1 destination interface fastethernet 12/1
```

Continuing with the IDS example, upon viewing this attack, the IDS will log the information and signal an alert, as illustrated in step 3. It is important to keep in mind that an IDS system cannot prevent the attack from happening on its own; however, it can instruct the firewall to block (shun) this traffic via dynamic ACL configuration, as illustrated in step 4.

Intrusion Prevention Systems

An IPS monitors network and system activities for malicious or unauthorized behavior and reacts in real-time (i.e. is reactive) to block or prevent those activities. Unlike IDS devices, IPS devices typically resides inline, which means that user and network traffic actually traverses and flows through the IPS device. This allows an IPS to drop malicious packets or traffic flows while still allowing all other legitimate traffic flows and packets to pass through. The implementation of a Network-based IPS device is illustrated in Figure 8.2:

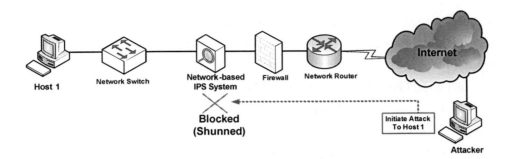

Figure 8.2. IPS Device Implementation

As illustrated in Figure 8.2 above, the Network-based IPS is in the actual physical path of traffic flow between Host 1 and the Internet, and vice-versa. By residing inline, i.e. in the actual physical traffic path, IPS devices have the capability to respond to suspicious activity by resetting connections themselves. Additionally, IPS devices can reprogram other infrastructure devices (e.g. routers and firewalls) to block network traffic (which is referred to as shunning) from the suspected malicious source. These actions can be performed automatically by the IPS itself or manually by the network security administrator.

While an IPS is typically implemented inline, it is important to remember that it can also be implemented in promiscuous mode, i.e. in a manner similar to an IDS. Additionally, an IPS can also be implemented in both an inline and a promiscuous mode, depending on the number of physical interfaces the device has, as illustrated in Figure 8.3:

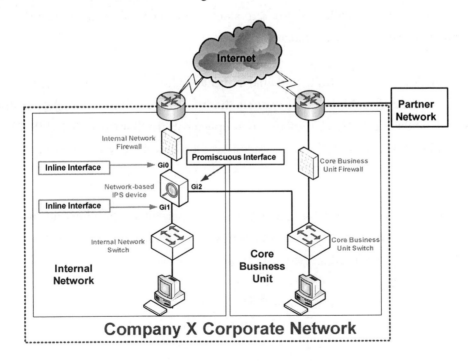

Figure 8.3. Inline and Promiscuous Modes

Figure 8.3 above illustrates two separate networks within the Company X corporate network: the internal network and the core business unit network. For the purposes of this example, assume that these two networks are separate physical entities. An IPS has been deployed inline within the internal network, using the Gi0 and Gi1 interfaces. This allows the IPS to monitor and block all traffic from internal network hosts to the Internet, and vice-versa.

In addition to this, the IPS is also deployed in a promiscuous manner using the Gi2 interface. This allows the IPS to monitor all traffic from the core business unit to the partner network. However, because this interface is not inline (i.e. is operating in promiscuous mode), the IPS cannot block (shun) traffic between these two networks by itself, but it can instruct the core business unit firewall to shun the traffic using dynamic ACLs and filtering.

IDS and IPS System Architecture

IDS and IPS devices typically use protocol analyzers to decode Application Layer protocols, such as HTTP or FTP, which allows them to evaluate different parts of the protocol for anomalous behavior or exploits, such as embedding techniques used by attackers.

At a very basic level, IDS and IPS appliances are composed of three core components. These components are a console, an engine, and a sensor. The console is used to monitor generated events and alerts, and is also used to control and configure the sensors.

The engine uses a system of rules to generate alerts from received security events and records events logged by the sensor into a database.

The sensor provides packet capturing and analyzing capabilities when monitoring the traffic. This is achieved via the use of multiple micro-engines that the sensor will use to analyze traffic to see if it matches a particular signature. A signature is simply a pattern that the IDS and IPS devices look for in traffic and match against. IDS and IPS signatures are described in detail in the following section.

Although going into specific detail on IDS and IPS system architecture is beyond the scope of the IINS certification requirements, Figure 8.4 illustrates the basic design and architecture of the Cisco IPS Sensor Software system used in Cisco IPS appliances:

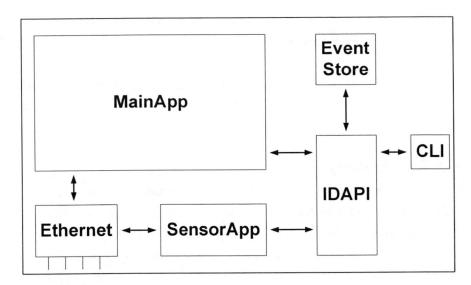

Figure 8.4. IPS Sensor—Basic Design and Architecture

The following section provides a brief description of the components illustrated in Figure 8.4:

- The MainApp is the core engine of the sensor operating system. It is responsible for all major functions, including, but not limited to, managing the system processes, configuring the system, starting or stopping other applications, and performing routine maintenance.

- The Event Store is the placeholder for storing all the sensor events, which include system messages, alerts, and errors.

- The SensorApp, which is also referred to as the Analysis Engine, provides packet capturing and analyzing capabilities when monitoring the traffic.

- The CLI is the Command Line Interface that allows network security administrators to manage and configure the sensor. The CLI can be accessed using various methods, which include a direct sensor console connection, Telnet, and Secure Shell (SSH). This is also referred to as the command and control interface.

- IDAPI stands for Integrated Database Application Program Interface or Independent Database Application Program Interface. The sensor operating system applications communicate with each other using IDAPI.

- The Ethernet port is used to connect to the monitored network. This can be placed inline or used to view traffic in a promiscuous operating mode. It is important to know that at a minimum, IPS systems must have two interfaces so that they can be placed inline. IDS devices, on the other hand, can have only a single interface.

The Cisco IPS Sensor OS runs on a Linux platform, which is secured and hardened by removing unnecessary software packages from the OS, disabling unused services, restricting network access, and removing access to the shell.

IDS and IPS Terminology

Before we move on to specific IDS and IPS topics, it is important to understand the terminology that is used when talking about Intrusion Detection Systems and Intrusion Prevention Systems. The following section lists and describes terminology relating to these two technologies that you should be familiar with and are expected to know. These terms are as follows:

- Alert or Alarm
- True attack stimulus
- False attack stimulus
- False positive
- False negative
- Noise
- Site policy
- Site policy awareness
- Confidence value
- Alarm filtering

An alert or alarm is a signal that is sent by an IDS or IPS suggesting a system has been or is being attacked. IDS and IPS devices can send alerts or alarms via numerous communication protocols, all of which will be described in detail later in this chapter.

A true attack stimulus is an IDS or IPS event that triggers the system to produce an alarm and react as though a real attack were in progress. In other words, the system believes an attack is happening, based on configured thresholds or detected signatures in monitored traffic.

A false attack stimulus is an IDS or IPS event that signals the system to produce an alarm when no attack has taken place. This typically occurs when a flow is mistakenly identified as an attack when it is not, in fact, an actual attack.

A false positive is an IDS or IPS alert or alarm that is triggered when no actual attack has taken place. A false positive is basically an incorrect positive alert or alarm. The IDS or IPS incorrectly believes that an attack is occurring and triggers a false alarm.

A false negative is defined as a failure of the system to detect an actual attack. In other words, the IDS or IPS fails to identify an actual attack as a true, legitimate attack, allowing the attacker to access the network or network hosts as though he or she were a legitimate user.

Noise is the data or interference that can cause the IDS or IPS device to trigger a false positive. It is important to keep in mind that noise is based on the interpretation of the vendor manufacturing the IDS or IPS device. For example, the IDS or IPS of one vendor might view a certain application stream as an attack, based on the pattern, while that of another might not.

A site policy provides the guidelines within an organization that control the rules and configurations of the system.

Site policy awareness is the ability the IDS or IPS device has to change its rules and configurations dynamically in response to changing environmental activity.

The confidence value is a value an organization places on itself based on past performance and analysis to help determine its ability to effectively identify an attack.

And, finally, alarm filtering is the process of categorizing attack alerts produced by the system in order to distinguish false positives from actual attacks.

IDS and IPS Detection Methods

Now that we have an understanding of the differences between an IDS and an IPS, as well as the terminology used when discussing IDS and IPS technologies, the following section describes the methods used by an IDS or IPS system to detect attacks. The following four methods are used by IDS and IPS devices to detect attacks:

* Policy-based Detection
* Anomaly-based Detection
* Honey Pot Detection
* Signature-based Detection

The policy-based detection method is dependent on an administrator's definition of normal and acceptable behavior of the network. For example, the administrator could define normal or acceptable communication between specific types of hosts, such as a web server and its clients, and the IDS or IPS device could then identify any traffic that is considered out-of-profile and generate an alarm or notification to report that activity.

An anomaly-based detection method is a system for detecting computer intrusions and misuse by monitoring system or network activity and classifying it as either normal or abnormal. This classification method is based on rules and will detect any type of misuse that falls out of what is considered normal system or network operation. Anomaly-based detection may be implemented using either statistical or non-statistical anomaly-based detection methods.

- A statistical anomaly-based system establishes a performance baseline based on what the IDS or IPS considers as normal network traffic. It will then sample current network traffic activity to this baseline in order to detect whether it is within baseline parameters. If the sampled traffic is outside baseline parameters, an alarm will be triggered.

  For example, assume that there is usually an average of 100 connections to a web server every hour, and all of a sudden the server receives 5000 connections within an hour, the system will consider this an anomaly and generate or trigger an alarm. However, it is important to know that this could actually be legitimate traffic, which means the alarm would be a false positive.

- A non-statistical anomaly-based system allows network security administrators to define what traffic patterns are supposed to look like, and is somewhat similar to a policy-based detection method. As is the case with statistical and policy-based detection methods, a non-statistical anomaly-based method is prone to a significant amount of false positives.

  As an example, assume that a company with several thousand employees is using Trend Micro anti-virus software, and the license has expired and needs to be renewed. Based on this, thousands of clients begin to renew and download their licenses and updates, respectively, at the same time. If the IDS or IPS system is using non-statistical anomaly-based detection, it would easily think that this was some kind of attack and generate or trigger an alarm. However, given that this is actually legitimate user traffic, even though it is out-of-profile from what the network security administrators have defined, this would be considered a false positive.

A honey pot is a trap set to lure attackers away from legitimate targets. The system that is designated as the honey pot acts as an attractive attack target, and attackers attack it, instead of other legitimate network servers and devices, because it appears to be more valuable. Honey pot detection monitors the honey pot and allows network security administrators to gather valuable information and knowledge, such as what the attacker is typing, what programs he or she is running, etc., which can then be used to protect legitimate systems.

Signature-based detection examines network traffic for preconfigured and predetermined attack patterns, which are known as signatures. Many attacks today have distinct signatures. Once a known signature is identified by the system, an alarm will be triggered or the traffic will be blocked. Because attackers are constantly changing and updating methods of attack to avoid detection, it is important to remember that a signature-based system must have its signature database constantly updated to ensure that it can mitigate emerging threats. Signature-based detection is the primary method used by IDS and IPS devices.

IDS and IPS Signatures

As stated in the previous section, signature-based detection is the primary method used by IDS and IPS devices. Signatures are at the heart of signature-based detection solutions. A good set of signatures should be flexible enough to detect known attacks and, in some cases, newer attacks that are being developed by attackers. Signatures can be grouped into two general classes: attack and informational.

Attack signatures are used to indicate that an attack is occurring against your network and other network resources, such as hosts and servers, for example. An informational signature doesn't necessarily indicate an attack. Instead, informational signatures are typically used to gather information about traffic flowing through the network, as well as to validate certain kinds of attacks. Each of these signature classes is then further divided into other subclasses.

Signature Implementations

The design of signatures involves two main components: implementations and structures. Additionally, there are two implementation methods for signatures, which are context and content. With a context implementation, a signature looks only at the packet header of captured packets, but it does not look at the actual contents (payload) within the packet. The information that these signatures look for in the packet header may include source and destination IP addresses, TCP and UDP port numbers, IP fragment parameters, and IP, TCP, and UDP checksum information, for example.

With a content signature implementation, the signature looks at the actual contents of the packet (i.e. the payload) for information that could indicate an attack. For example, a content signature may inspect an FTP session and look for commands executed during the session.

Signature Structures

The structure of the signature is used to determine how many packets the IDS or IPS device has to examine for a particular signature when looking for attacks. There are two basic signature structures: atomic and stateful.

Atomic signatures represent the simplest signature type. An atomic structure looks at a single packet for a match on a signature. An example would be looking for the SYN flag in a TCP packet header. Because atomic signatures trigger on a single event, the IDS or IPS does not have to maintain connection state information or maintain a state table. The entire inspection can be accomplished in an operation that does not require any knowledge of past or future activities.

Because of their basic nature, atomic structures have the following advantages:

- The first advantage is that an atomic structure uses minimal system resources, such as CPU and memory, on the IDS or IPS system on which they are being used. This allows network security administrators to implement a significant amount of these signatures.

- The second advantage to an atomic structure is that the signatures are easy for network security administrators to understand because they only search for a specific event, e.g. the presence of a particular TCP flag in a TCP-based connection.

- The third advantage offered by atomic structures is that due to their simple nature, network security administrators can perform traffic analysis very quickly and efficiently.

Despite their advantages, atomic structures also have some disadvantages, which are as follows:

- When using atomic structures, network security administrators have to know all the atomic events that they want to look for, and then, for each of these events, they have to create the appropriate signature. As the number of atomic signatures increases, just managing the different signatures significantly increases overhead and can become overwhelming.

- The second disadvantage is that these signatures can be applied only to situations in which the context of the event is not important. For example, a signature can be configured to trigger an alert action whenever any traffic being analyzed contains the .exe extension to prevent executable files from being downloaded by users. However, because atomic structures do not contain state information, an alarm is triggered each time the .exe string is seen, even though an actual session may not have been established.

Unlike atomic signatures, stateful signatures are triggered on a sequence of specific events that requires the system to maintain connection state information. The length of time that the signatures must maintain state, or the maximum amount of time over which an attack signature can successfully be detected, is known as the event horizon.

Because of the fact that stateful structures require a specific event to be detected in a known context, their implementation increases the likelihood that the activity represents legitimate attack traffic. This, in turn, reduces the number of false positives that may be generated by stateful signatures. However, despite this significant advantage over atomic structures, stateful structures also have the following disadvantages that must be taken into consideration:

- The main disadvantage to stateful signatures is that maintaining connection state information requires significant amounts of memory and physical disk space, which increases the monetary cost of these devices.

- The second disadvantage is that stateful structures consume a large amount of resources, e.g. memory and CPU, which can lead to a slow response time, dropped packets, missed signatures, and so on, and this adversely impacts the effectiveness of the system.

Signature Triggers

The most important part of any signature is the mechanism that causes the signature to trigger. Different vendors use different triggering mechanisms. The triggering mechanism refers to the condition, or conditions, that cause the system to generate a signature action, which can be an alert, notification, or both, for example.

Some devices use basic triggering mechanisms, while others use advanced, complex triggering mechanisms. Regardless of the simplicity or complexity of the mechanism used, most IDS and IPS implementations incorporate various triggering mechanisms when developing signatures, the most common being pattern-based, anomaly-based, and behavior-based.

Pattern-based signature triggering is the most common and one of the simplest triggering mechanisms because its main function is to identify a specific pattern. Once the pattern is matched, the signature is triggered. This pattern may be as simple as text or a binary string, or it may be relatively advanced and use regular expressions or de-obfuscation techniques.

A regular expression is simply a pattern-matching language that enables you to define a flexible search pattern. For example, in Cisco IOS software, the regular expression (also referred to as regexp) ^123 matches all patterns that begin with the numbers 123. This would match 1234 and 123123, but it would not match 01234, for example. Going into detail on regular expressions is beyond the scope of the IINS course requirements.

Obfuscation is the concealment of the intended meaning in communication, which results in the communication being confusing, intentionally ambiguous, and more difficult to interpret. This technique is used by attackers to attempt to confuse the IDS or IPS system so that it will miss valid strings that have been obfuscated. This technique is commonly used when requesting web pages from a server. Going into detail on the various obfuscation techniques used by attackers is beyond the scope of the IINS course requirements.

In anomaly-based detection, which is also known as profile-based detection, signatures are triggered when certain activities deviate from what is considered normal. As described earlier in this chapter, anomaly-based detection may be implemented using either statistical or non-statistical anomaly-based detection methods.

Behavior-based signatures are triggered when any behaviors that do not occur normally are observed, as this may be an indication of a network attack or other malicious activity. Before they can be used, behavior-based signatures must be manually defined. However, the drawback to this is that it takes much research to determine behaviors that do not occur normally and that can accurately indicate suspicious behavior.

An example of behavior-based signatures would be a signature that is triggered when a user attempts to download and install an executable file or program from an external web site when company policy clearly forbids such activities.

Signature Actions

Up to this point, we have learned about the different types of signatures and all of their characteristics. In this section on IDS and IPS signatures, we are going to learn about the different actions that the device can take once a signature has been triggered. When a signature observes the activity that it is configured to detect, the signature triggers one or more actions, which can include, but are not limited to, the following:

- Generating an alert
- Dropping or preventing the activity
- Logging the activity
- Resetting a TCP connection
- Blocking future activity
- Allowing the activity

IDS and IPS devices can generate atomic alerts, summary alerts, or a combination of both. An atomic alert is generated every time a signature triggers. These are the most common alerts generated by IDS and IPS devices. A summary alert is a single alert that indicates multiple occurrences of the same signature from the same source address and/or port. This reduces the overall number of individual alerts that are generated for the same incident.

For example, if an IDS or IPS system signature is triggered by 100 occurrences of the same event, say from a host with the IP address 172.16.1.254, it would send out 100 alerts for each occurrence. Naturally, this would be redundant information, as it indicated the same event. Therefore, using summary alerts, network security administrators could configure a signature summary interval so that when the length of time specified by the summary interval has elapsed, a summary alarm is sent, indicating the number of alarms that occurred during the time interval specified by the summary interval parameter. This would reduce the overall number of alarms but still capture the same information.

One of the greatest advantages of an IPS device over an IDS device is the capability to directly drop packets when implemented inline. This action enables the device to stop an attack before it has the chance to perform malicious activity. Besides dropping individual packets, the drop action can be expanded to drop all packets for a specific session or even all packets from a specific host for a certain amount of time. This flexibility allows the IPS to conserve resources, such as processor and memory, by dropping traffic without having to analyze each packet separately.

Logging capabilities allow the IDS and IPS systems to log the actions or packets that are seen so that network security administrators can analyze this information in greater detail. The log information is typically stored locally on the device itself, in a specific file. Because the signature also generates an alert, administrators can observe the alert on the management console and then retrieve the log data from the IPS device, so as to analyze the activity that the attacker performed on the network after triggering the initial alarm.

The majority of IPS devices that are implemented inline have the capability to terminate TCP connections that are performing unwanted or unauthorized operations by generating a packet for the connection with the TCP RST flag set. This resets the session for the attacker as well as for the victim (target) systems.

As we learned earlier in this chapter, IDS and IPS devices operating in promiscuous mode can be configured automatically to configure another infrastructure device, such as a firewall, when they detect an attack in the traffic they are monitoring. This ACL stops traffic from an attacking system without requiring the IDS or IPS to consume resources analyzing the traffic. After a configured period of time, the IDS or IPS device can be configured to remove the ACL or leave it in place, preventing similar future activity from occurring.

Finally, allowing the activity refers to the process of defining exceptions to configured signatures. Configuring exceptions enables you to take a more restrictive approach to security because you first deny everything and then allow only the activities that are needed. For example, an exception might be that no other department except for the IT department is allowed to download .exe files from external web servers. If someone who is not in the IT department attempts to download an .exe file, an alert is generated.

IDS and IPS System Types

Now that we have a solid understanding of IDS and IPS systems and their capabilities, operation, and characteristics, we are going to be learning about the different types of IDS and IPS solutions available. Because the IINS exam requirements explicitly state host-based and network-based IDS and IPS types, this section provides a description of both of these, as well as other common IDS and IPS types.

Intrusion Detection System Types

There are several different kinds of IDS types, and the following section provides a brief overview of each of these, including:

- Network-based Intrusion Detection System (NIDS)
- Protocol-based Intrusion Detection System (PIDS)
- Application Protocol-based Intrusion Detection System (APIDS)
- Host-based Intrusion Detection System (HIDS)
- Hybrid Intrusion Detection System

A Network-based Intrusion Detection System (NIDS) is an independent, standalone platform used to identify intrusions by examining network traffic and monitoring multiple hosts. A NIDS is typically connected to a network switch and relies on Switched Port Analyzer (SPAN) or other similar port mirroring implementation to view network traffic. Cisco Secure IDS 4200 Series Sensors available from Cisco are an example of a Network-based IDS solution. However, the Cisco product range of Network-based IDS solutions is End-of-Life and is no longer sold and, in some cases, no longer supported by Cisco. Instead, Cisco recommends that their Network-based IPS solutions be implemented. NIPS will be described later in this chapter.

A Protocol-based Intrusion Detection System (PIDS) is a system or agent that monitors and analyzes the communication between a server and the devices connected to it. For example, a PIDS would monitor the HTTP protocol on a web server. Going into detail on PIDS is beyond the scope of the IINS course requirements, and it will not be described any further in this guide.

An Application Protocol-based Intrusion Detection System (APIDS) is somewhat similar to a PIDS; however, instead of monitoring a specific protocol, an APIDS is used to monitor and analyze the communication for specific application protocols. For example, an APIDS could be used to monitor the SQL protocol on an Oracle database server. Going into detail on APIDS is beyond the scope of the IINS course requirements, and it will not be described any further in this guide.

A Host-based Intrusion Detection System (HIDS) is an agent that resides on a network host, e.g. a PC, laptop, or server, which is used to identify intrusions by analyzing system calls, application logs, file-system modifications, and other host activities and state. An example of a HIDS is the Cisco Security Agent (CSA). However, it should be noted that while the CSA provides HIDS capabilities, the latest versions of this software are truly a Host-based IPS solution and are marketed as such. HIPS will be described later in this chapter.

A Hybrid Intrusion Detection System is simply an IDS solution that combines two or more of the other IDS characteristics. For example, a Hybrid IDS could provide both HIDS and APIDS capabilities. Going into detail on Hybrid Intrusion Detection Systems is beyond the scope of the IINS course requirements, and it will not be described any further in this guide.

Intrusion Prevention System Types

As is the case with IDS systems, there are several different types of IPS solutions, as follows:

- Host-based Intrusion Prevention System (HIPS)
- Network-based Intrusion Prevention System (NIPS)
- Content-based Intrusion Prevention System (CIPS)
- Rate-based Intrusion Prevention System (RBIPS)

A Host-based Intrusion Prevention System (HIPS) is an IPS system that resides on a network host, such as a computer, laptop, or server. A Host-based Intrusion Prevention System is typically implemented on these endpoints in conjunction with other security software, such as anti-virus software. The primary function of the HIPS is to prevent malicious code from modifying the system or other software on the system. This is performed by an integrated firewall, system-level action control, sandboxing, or whitelisting.

Sandboxing is simply a security mechanism for separating running programs that is used to execute untested code or untrusted programs. The sandbox on the host provides a tightly controlled set of resources for guest programs to run in, such as free space on disk and memory.

A whitelist is the opposite of a blacklist. In other words, a whitelist is a list or compilation that identifies entities or programs that are permitted, recognized, or provided a particular privilege, service, mobility, access, or recognition. For example, on a Windows-based machine, Microsoft Outlook, which is used for email communication, may be whitelisted, which means that the HIPS on the host will allow this program to execute if initiated by the user. An example of a Host-based IPS is the Cisco Security Agent. HIPS is a core topic and a requirement of the IINS course, and CSA will be described in greater detail later in this chapter.

A Network-based Intrusion Prevention System (NIPS) is an IPS system-dedicated hardware or software platform designed to analyze, detect, and report on network security events. NIPS are designed to inspect traffic and, based on their configuration or security policy, they can drop malicious traffic. Unlike Host-based IPS systems, a Network-based IPS system can detect potential security events all over the network and react to each of them, whereas a HIPS can detect and react to potential security events only on the host on which it resides. An example of a Network-based IPS is the Cisco IPS 4200 Sensors. NIPS is a core topic and a requirement of the IINS course, and Cisco NIPS solutions will be described in greater detail later in this chapter.

A Content-based Intrusion Prevention System (CIPS) is used to inspect the content (i.e. payload or data) of network packets for signatures, which allows it to detect and prevent known types of attacks, such as worm infections and hacks. While there are dedicated CIPS systems, it is important to know that this functionality is typically integrated into other IPS systems. Going into detail on CIPS is beyond the scope of the IINS course requirements, and it will not be described any further in this guide.

A Rate-based Intrusion Prevention System (RBIPS) is primarily used to prevent DoS and DDoS attacks. A Rate-based IPS is similar to a statistical anomaly-based IDS in that it monitors and baselines normal network behavior. Through real-time traffic monitoring and comparison with stored statistics, RBIPS can identify abnormal rates for certain types of traffic. Once an attack is detected, various prevention techniques may be used such as rate-limiting, which is basically slowing down the speed of specific attack-related traffic types, source, or connection tracking, and source-address, blacklisting, or whitelisting.

Although going into detail on RBIPS is technically beyond the scope of the IINS course requirements, the Cisco Traffic Anomaly Detector and the Cisco Guard DDoS Mitigation, which provide RBIPS services as part of the Cisco Anomaly Detection and Mitigation solution, are described later in this chapter, as a related topic.

Cisco Network Intrusion Prevention Systems

The Cisco Network-based Intrusion Prevention solutions are an integral part of the Cisco Self-Defending Network strategy that provides network intelligence to identify and prevent malicious traffic including, but not limited to, network viruses, worms, spyware, adware, and application abuse. The Cisco Network-based Intrusion Prevention solution protects the network from policy violations, vulnerability exploitations, and anomalous activity through detailed inspection of traffic at Layers 2 though 7, throughout the entire network. The Network-based Intrusion Prevention solutions available from Cisco are as follows:

- The Cisco IPS 4200 Series Appliance Sensors
- The Cisco IDS Services Module 2 (IDSM-2)
- The Cisco Advanced Inspection and Protection Security Services Module
- The Cisco IPS Advanced Integration Module (IPS-AIM)
- The Cisco Internetwork Operating System (IOS) IPS

The Cisco IPS 4200 Series Appliance Sensors

The Cisco IPS 4200 Series Appliance Sensors offer a broad range of solutions, providing easy integration into enterprise and service provider networks. The following section describes the five purpose-built appliances that encompass the IPS 4200 Series Appliance Sensor offerings manufactured by Cisco:

- The IPS 4215 Appliance Sensor can deliver up to 80Mbps of transactional performance and is suitable for multiple T1/E1 and T3/E3 environments. The 4215 supports up to five monitoring interfaces per appliance.

- The IPS 4240 Appliance Sensor can deliver up to 250Mbps of transactional performance, providing protection in switched environments on multiple T3/E3 subnets. The 4240 can support multiple 10/100/1000 interfaces and can be deployed on partially utilized GigabitEthernet links or fully saturated FastEthernet links.

- The IPS 4255 Appliance Sensor supports transactional performance at 600Mbps and can be used to protect partially utilized GigabitEthernet links and traffic traversing switches that are being used to aggregate traffic from numerous subnets.

- The IPS 4260 Appliance Sensor can be deployed to deliver transactional performance of up to 1Gbps of dedicated intrusion prevention protection. The 4260 can also be used to protect both GigabitEthernet subnets and aggregated traffic that is traversing switches from multiple subnets.

- The IPS 4270 Appliance Sensor supports unparalleled performance and can be deployed to deliver transactional performance of up to 2Gbps of dedicated intrusion prevention protection. It can also be used to protect both GigabitEthernet subnets and aggregated traffic that is traversing switches from multiple subnets.

The Cisco IDS Services Module 2 (IDSM-2)

The Cisco IDS Services Module 2 (IDSM-2) is a high-speed, high-performance integrated IPS module that can be installed into Cisco Catalyst 6500 switches or Cisco 7600 Series routers. The IDSM-2 can deliver up to 600Mbps of intrusion prevention protection in passive mode and up to 500Mbps in inline mode.

Amongst many other features, the IDSM-2 offers Cisco IPS Device Manager (IDM), which is a GUI-based, Java-enabled, built-in web-based tool for sensor configuration and management. IDM can be accessed through any web browser and is enabled to use Secure Sockets Layer (SSL) by default. Additionally, IDSM-2 provides event monitoring for up to five IPS sensors through the Cisco IPS Event Viewer (IEV).

The Cisco Advanced Inspection and Protection Security Services Module

The Cisco Advanced Inspection and Protection Security Services Module, or AIP-SSM, as it is more commonly referred to as, is designed for the Cisco ASA 5500 Series Security Appliances. The AIP-SSM provides a full-featured intrusion prevention solution to protect against malicious traffic, including network viruses and worms.

Using Cisco IPS sensor software, the AIP-SSM combines inline prevention services that offer all the major functions available in the traditional Cisco IPS sensor solutions. Cisco ASA 5500 Series Security Appliances coupled with AIP-SSM provide the best in-class firewall and intrusion prevention capabilities in a single, easy-to-deploy platform.

The Cisco IPS Advanced Integration Module (IPS-AIM)

The Cisco IPS Advanced Integration Module (IPS-AIM) is part of the Cisco integrated IDS/IPS sensor family portfolio and is an integral part of the Cisco Self-Defending Network. The IPS-AIM can be used with Cisco Integrated Services Routers (ISRs), such as the Cisco 2800 and 3800 Series platforms.

The Cisco IPS-AIM has dedicated processors and Dynamic Random Access Memory (DRAM). Although the IPS-AIM does not provide dedicated command and control (management) interfaces, administrators can use the internal GigabitEthernet port for in-band management.

The Cisco Internetwork Operating System (IOS) IPS

The Cisco Internetwork Operating System (IOS) IPS feature set provides an integrated inline deep-packet inspection solution with router software architecture. This solution is available on all Cisco Integrated Services Routers (ISRs) and offers an integrated security and policy enforcement solution. The Cisco IOS IPS will be described in detail later in this chapter.

> **NOTE:** It is important to know that prior to the Cisco IPS 4200 Series Appliance Sensors, Cisco offered the Cisco IDS 4200 Series Appliance Sensors that were truly only IDS-capable devices. The appliances offered included the Cisco IDS 4250 Sensor, the IDS 4235 Sensor, the IDS 4230 Sensor, the IDS 4220 Sensor, and the IDS 4210 Sensor. These products are no longer being sold and might not be supported. Therefore, we will not be describing them or their capabilities and functionality in any detail in this guide.

Deploying an IPS into the traffic stream (i.e. inline) introduces a new device into the data path that has the potential to fail and prevent traffic from flowing. Fortunately, with Cisco IPS solutions, a failed IPS can be prevented from interrupting the flow of network traffic via a fail-open mechanism, a failover mechanism, or by performing load balancing. While going into detail on these mechanisms is beyond the scope of the IINS course requirements, it is important to have a basic understanding of what they mean.

Cisco NIPS solutions can use a hardware-based or software-based fail-open mechanism to allow traffic to go through uninterrupted in the event of any hardware (e.g. power failure) or software (e.g. signature failure) issues. Cisco IOS software also allows administrators to implement various failover mechanisms, such as HSRP and Spanning-Tree Protocol, in order to provide NIPS redundancy. HSRP stands for Hot Standby Router Protocol; however, it is beyond the scope of the IINS course requirements. And, finally, network security administrators can use load-balancing techniques in conjunction with Cisco NIPS solutions to prevent a single NIPS failure from preventing the flow of traffic.

Sensor Communication Protocols

As we learned earlier in this chapter, the sensor OS applications communicate with each other using IDAPI. However, it is also important to understand the other different communication protocols used by the Cisco IPS sensor software, and they are as follows:

- RDEP2
- IDIOM
- IDCONF
- SDEE
- CIDEE

RDEP stands for Remote Data Exchange Protocol and is a Cisco proprietary Application-level protocol used by Cisco IDS Sensors that uses both a subset of the HTTP/1.1 protocol and a client request/server response model. RDEP2 is used primarily for external communications; specifically, it is used to exchange IDS events, IP logs, configurations, and control messages between IPS clients and IPS servers. RDEP2 is no longer used and has been replaced by Security Device Event Exchange (SDEE) in the current Cisco IPS Sensor software versions. SDEE will be described later in this section.

IDIOM, which stands for Intrusion Detection Interchange and Operations Messages, is a data format standard that defines the event messages that are reported by the IPS, as well as the operational messages that are used to configure control intrusion-detection systems. These messages consist of XML (Extensible Markup Language) documents that conform to the IDIOM XML schema. IDIOM supports two types of interactions: the event and control transactions. Event transactions are used to exchange IPS events, such as IPS alerts. Control transactions utilize four types of IDIOM messages: request, response, configuration, and error messages. Event and control transactions that are communicated between application instances within a host are known as local events or local control transactions, or, collectively, as local IDIOM messages. Events and control transactions that are communicated between different hosts using the RDEP2 protocol are known as remote events and remote control transactions, or, collectively, as remote IDIOM messages. It is important to know that in the latest sensor software OS, IDIOM has for the most part been superseded by IDCONF, SDEE, and CIDEE, all of which are described later in this section.

IDCONF, which stands for Intrusion Detection Configuration, specifies the XML schema including IPS control transactions. Cisco IPS sensor software manages its configuration by using XML. However, it is important to know that the IDCONF schema does not specify the contents of the configuration documents but, rather, the framework from which the configuration documents are developed. IDCONF messages are exchanged over RDEP2 and are wrapped inside IDIOM request and response messages.

SDEE, which stands for Security Device Event Exchange, is a new standard proposed by the International Computer Security Association (ICSA) that specifies the format of messages and protocol used to communicate events generated by security devices. SDEE is an enhancement to the current version of RDEP2 that adds extensibility features that are needed for communicating events generated by various types of security devices. Systems that use SDEE to communicate events to clients are referred to as SDEE providers. SDEE specifies that events can be transported using the HTTP or HTTP over SSL and TLS protocols. When HTTP or HTTPS is used, SDEE providers act as HTTP servers, while SDEE clients are the initiators of HTTP requests.

IPS includes Web Server, which processes HTTP or HTTPS requests. Web Server uses run-time loadable servlets to process the different types of HTTP requests. Each servlet handles HTTP requests that are directed to the URL associated with the servlet. The SDEE server is implemented as a web server servlet and processes only authorized requests. A request is authorized if it originates from a web server to authenticate the identity and determine the privilege level of the client.

CIDEE, which stands for Cisco Intrusion Detection Event Exchange, specifies the extensions to SDEE that are used by the Cisco IPS. The CIDEE standard specifies all possible extensions that are supported by IPS systems. However, it is mandatory that any extension that is designated as being required be supported by all systems. CIDEE supports the following events:

- evError (error event)—this is generated by the CIDEE provider when the provider detects an error or warning condition. The evError event contains error code and textual description of the error.

- evStatus (status message event)—this is generated by CIDEE providers to indicate that something of potential interest occurred on the host. Different types of status messages can be reported in the status event—one message per event. Each type of status message contains a set of data elements that are specific to the type of occurrence that the status message is describing. The information in many of the status messages is useful for audit purposes. Errors and warnings are not considered status information and are reported using evError rather than evStatus.

- evShunRqst (block request event)—this is generated to indicate that a block action is to be initiated by the service that handles network blocking.

NOTE: SDEE is the default protocol used by Cisco IPS Sensor software, as well as by the Cisco IOS IPS feature set used on Cisco IOS routers.

Cisco Host Intrusion Prevention Systems

This section provides details on the Cisco Host-based Intrusion Prevention solution that uses Cisco Security Agent (CSA). This section describes core concepts pertaining to CSA, such as CSA architecture, components, policies, rules, and rule modules, as well as basic details on managing and deploying CSA using CSA Management Center (CSA MC).

CSA provides proactive HIDS and HIPS solutions for endpoint systems, such as desktops, laptops, and servers, for known and unknown (day-zero) threats. CSA does not rely on a signature-based architecture. Instead, CSA uses a flexible policy-based and behavior-based architecture, which allows it to offer defense against targeted attacks, viruses, worms, spyware, adware, rookits, and day-zero attacks that have not been discovered, as well as new exploits and variants taking advantage of known and unknown vulnerabilities.

CSA also has the capability to provide policy compliance controls, offering protection to sensitive information on the system. For example, CSA can use granular controls that restrict the removal of USB keys, prevent copy-and-paste operations between applications, and restrict peer-to-peer applications such as instant messaging, amongst many other things. The following list highlights the characteristics and benefits offered by CSA:

- Endpoint system protection
- Host-based intrusion prevention
- Policy-based and behavior-based architecture
- Personal firewall protection
- Day-zero attack protection
- Regulatory policy compliance enforcement
- Acceptable corporate use policy compliance
- Preventative protection against targeted attacks
- Stability and protection of the underlying operating system
- File and directory protection
- Host application visibility
- Application control
- Correlation of system calls and application functions

CSA Architecture

The architecture of CSA software is unique in that the host agent resides between the applications and the OS kernel, as illustrated in Figure 8.5:

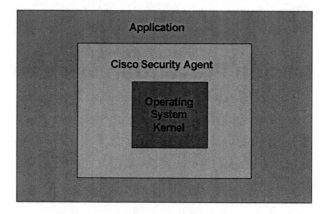

Figure 8.5. CSA Architecture

The placement of the CSA agent, as illustrated in Figure 8.5 above, provides application visibility with minimal impact to the stability and performance of the underlying OS. CSA works at the kernel level by controlling file system and network actions, as well as other components of the OS.

CSA architecture intercepts all OS and application-related calls when access is requested for certain resources, such as file access, device access, registry access, and application execution calls. CSA is also capable of intercepting dynamic runtime resources requested, such as memory pages, services, and shared library modules. This means that when an application attempts an operation or requests access, CSA checks the operation against the security policy, which allows it to make real-time decisions on whether to allow or deny the operation.

CSA Components

CSA has three basic components: CSA endpoints, the CSA Management Server, and the CSA Management Console (CSA MC).

CSA endpoints are computing desktops, servers, laptops, and point-of-sale (POS) terminals. The CSA is responsible for enforcing security policies received from the management server, sending events, and interacting with the user.

The CSA management server is the core component in the CSA deployment. The management server is a repository of the configuration database, and is responsible for deploying the security policies to the endpoints, receiving and storing all events, sending alerts to the network security administrator, and deploying software to the endpoints.

The CSA MC is an administrative web-based user interface and policy configuration tool that provides network security administrators with event views. All communication between the CSA MC and the management server are secured using SSL. The CSA MC binds with the server database, which holds all the policies. All CSA endpoint agents then register with the CSA MC to receive the policy. The CSA MC validates the host and deploys the respective policy pertaining to that host or group of hosts.

Managing CSA Groups

Groups are a logical collection of hosts. The grouping system used in CSA deployment provides several advantages, which include:

* Policy consistency through the application of the same set of policies on multiple hosts across the network;
* The capability to apply alternative mechanisms and set parameters based on group configurations; and
* A test mode feature that can be used to validate policies on groups of hosts before they are actively enforced on production systems.

The CSA group feature simplifies configuration management by associating policy controls and other parameters into group settings. When a user is associated with a group, the host will inherit all of the parameters configured within the group. This ensures consistency across the entire CSA deployment because all hosts have uniform settings when associated to the same group. This scalable approach of grouping hosts allows network security administrators to perform large-scale CSA deployments with great ease and reduced complexity.

Another advantage of having groups is that it makes the creation of agent kits, which are the CSA installation executable files that are installed onto the endpoint system, much easier because the group parameter is the only element required to build agent kits.

CSA MC has several built-in, predefined groups that can be used according to the requirements. Additionally, network security administrators can create custom groups using the CSA MC. Groups in CSA MC are divided into the following three categories:

- Mandatory groups
- Predefined groups
- Custom groups

NOTE: You are not required to demonstrate detailed knowledge on the CSA MC groups.

By default, CSA MC provides three auto-enrollment mandatory groups as follows:

- All Windows
- All Solaris
- All Linux

One of these mandatory groups will be associated with each endpoint host according to its OS architecture upon registration. For example, when Windows-based hosts are registered to the CSA MC, they are automatically enrolled into the All Windows group, in addition to any other custom groups that are mapped to the particular host. Given this, it is important to know that hosts cannot be removed from the mandatory groups, because mandatory groups are used to enforce some of the compulsory security policies that are utilized to prevent critical services from being inadvertently disturbed. For example, a mandatory policy can dictate that a user cannot disable the DNS or DHCP service.

Because hosts can belong to one or more groups, which means that they will inherit multiple policies from these groups, in the event of a rule conflict, the combined rule set will follow the rule precedence process when deciding which rules to override.

CSA Policies, Rule Modules, and Rules

In CSA terminology, a policy is a collection of rule modules, and a rule module is a collection of multiple rules. The rule module acts as the container for rules, whereas the policy serves as the unit of attachment to groups. Rules provide control access to system or network resources.

Multiple rule policies can be attached to a single policy, and multiple policies can be attached to a single group. Different types of rules in a rule module can coexist, and different types of rules within a single policy can also coexist. CSA MC allows for the creation of several types of policies in addition to the default, built-in policies (e.g. the Windows, Solaris, and Linux policies). It is imperative to remember that policies, rule modules, and rules are the enforcement tools that are used in the CSA architecture.

NOTE: You are not required to perform any configuration tasks using CSA in the IINS exam.

CSA Access Control Process

This next section on CSA outlines, in order, the access process that the CSA performs:

1. Identify the resource being accessed. This may be a network resource, a memory function call, an application execution, files access, a system configuration, or any other OS kernel system calls, for example.

2. Gather data about the operation. For example, if a file access operation is requested, CSA will identify and gather the process name, file path, file name, and file operation, such as read, write, or erase.

3. Determine the state of the system. This includes the current IP address, MAC address, DNS suffix, VPN client status (if applicable), NAC (if application), and virus or worm detection.

4. Consult the security policy by analyzing rules and consulting the local policies. For example, anomaly-based, atomic, pattern-based, or behavioral-based rules, or another type of access control matrix.

5. Take action as per policy defined in the rules. For example, depending on the rule configuration, CSA may permit, deny, query, change the internal state, or monitor.

CSA Interceptor and Correlation

At the core of CSA architecture is the interceptor and correlation mechanism. The interceptor is used to intercept key actions that are attempted on the system and to check the action in question against the rule correlation engine to determine whether a rule set allows or denies it. Based on the information the interceptors receive, either they allow the action to take place or they stop it. Interceptors intercept application-related and system-related functions to enforce policy-based and behavior-based rules. There are five different interceptors used by CSA, depending on the platform on which it is installed, i.e. Windows or UNIX. These interceptors are as follows:

- The network application interceptor is applicable to both Windows- and UNIX-based platforms. It is used to regulate and control which applications are allowed to communicate with the network.
- The network traffic interceptor provides system-hardening features such as SYN flood protection and port scan detection. This interceptor is used on both Windows- and UNIX-based platforms.
- The file interceptor, which is used in UNIX- and Windows-based platforms, controls which applications can read and/or write to specified system files and directories.
- The registry interceptor controls system behavior, preventing applications from writing to particular registry keys. This interceptor is used only for Windows-based platforms.
- The system call interceptor is the UNIX-equivalent of the Windows platform registry interceptor. This interceptor protects the UNIX kernel in the same manner the registry interceptor protects the Windows registry.

As the interceptors are allowing or denying actions, they produce an event each time a rule set is triggered by a system action. These events are stored in the event correlation engine, which forwards them on to the local event manager and global event manager.

> NOTE: Before we move on to correlation, it is important to know that some documentation refers to only four interceptors, which are the file system interceptor, the network interceptor, the configuration interceptor, and the execution space interceptor.
>
> The file system interceptor is the same as the file interceptor, and the network interceptor is the same as the network traffic interceptor. The configuration interceptor is responsible for intercepting read/write requests to the Windows registry or rc files in UNIX-based systems. This single interceptor performs the same actions as the current system called interceptor and registry interceptor for both UNIX- and Windows-based platforms, respectively. And, finally, the execution space interceptor maintains the integrity of the dynamic runtime environment of individual applications. The execution space interceptor also blocks attempts by any application to inject code into other applications.

Correlation is the enforcement engine for CSA, where relationships between events are established to determine whether the behavior is acceptable and whether the event should be allowed or denied. CSA correlation maintains the state of all system calls and application activities on the host system. In addition to this, CSA correlation enhances interoperability between applications, such as protecting the usage of the command shell from unauthorized access and ensuring that legitimate applications can invoke this without interruption. CSA can correlate numerous activities to increase the accuracy of its rules and policies, as well as to enhance its capability to make accurate decisions about what is dangerous.

While going into the details pertaining to the CSA interceptor and correlation mechanism is beyond the scope of requirements of the IINS course, the following diagram illustrates the core architecture of the CSA correlation system and shows how it intercepts various system and application-related functions or calls:

Cisco IOS IPS Overview and Implementation

Deploying the Cisco IOS IPS inline provides network security administrators with unique filtering capabilities that enable them to stop the attack at the point of origin. The IOS IPS solution can be deployed at various points within the network and can be ideally situated at the network edge to protect the network from malicious and offending traffic entering into the network. As of the time of the writing of this section, Cisco is the only vendor that delivers this integrated functionality on a router.

Cisco IOS IPS Basics

The Cisco IOS IPS feature is a suite of intrusion prevention solutions provisioning a single point of protection at the network perimeter. The IOS IPS offers unparalleled intrusion security, reliability, scalability, and multilevel performance. Some of the key features of the IOS IPS are as follows:

- It protects the network from viruses, worms, and a large variety of threats and exploits;
- It eliminates the need for a standalone IPS device;
- It provides integrated inline deep-packet inspection;
- It complements the Cisco IOS Firewall and VPN solutions for superior threat protection;
- It supports about 2000 attack signatures;
- It uses Cisco IOS routing capabilities to deliver integrated functionality;
- It enables distributed network-wide threat mitigation; and
- It sends a Syslog message or an alarm in SDEE format when a threat is detected.

When a Cisco IOS router will be acting as an IPS device, it needs to have a place to store the signature files, referred to as Signature Definition Files (SDFs), that it will use to identify malicious traffic. A Signature Definition File is a file, usually in XML format, that contains signature definitions that can be used to load signatures on the Cisco IOS router. In most cases, the SDF is located in the router Flash Memory; however, Cisco IOS routers also have the capability to reference multiple SDFs located on network servers (e.g. TFTP servers) for increased signature coverage.

In order to ensure that the Signature Definition Files are up-to-date, which allows them to be effective against ever-changing and evolving threats, network security administrators need to manually update the SDFs periodically by downloading the latest files from the Cisco website. SDFs have a .sdf file extension name, for example, 128MB.sdf, 256MB.sdf, and attack-drop.sdf.

However, it is important to know and remember that in Cisco IOS 12.4(11)T and later, Cisco IOS IPS uses the Cisco IPS 5.x signature format, which is a version-based signature-definition XML format also used by other Cisco appliance-based IPS products. Support for signatures and SDFs in Cisco IPS Version 4.x are discontinued in this and further Cisco IOS T-Train Software releases. Additionally, it is important to remember that IPS 4.x uses a version format of 2.xxx.xxx while IPS 5.x uses a version format of 3.xxx.xxx.

Configuring Cisco IOS IPS Using SDM

IMPORTANT NOTE:

Before you can enable Cisco IOS IPS on a Cisco IOS router, you must first do the following:

1. Download the signature package from the Cisco website. This file uses a .pkg file name extension and contains all the SDFs. An example would be IOS-S360-CLI.pkg.
2. Download the Public Crypto Key from the Cisco website. By default, the public key is named realm-cisco.pub. This key is downloaded as a simple text file (.txt) that administrators can paste into SDM when configuring and enabling Cisco IOS IPS.

The configuration exercise in this section is based on the following Figure 8.6:

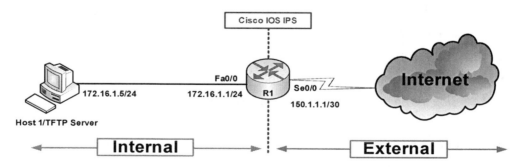

Figure 8.6. IOS IPS Network Topology

Configuring the Cisco IOS IPS feature using SDM is a relatively straightforward process. The first configuration step is to navigate to the main configuration page and click on the **Intrusion Prevention** task, as illustrated in Figure 8.7:

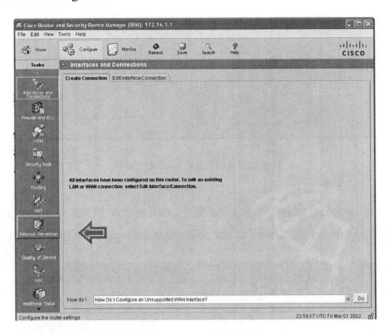

Figure 8.7. Select 'Intrusion Prevention'

This will bring up the **Intrusion Prevention System (IPS)** page. On the **Create IPS** tab, click on the **Launch IPS Rule Wizard** button, as illustrated in Figure 8.8:

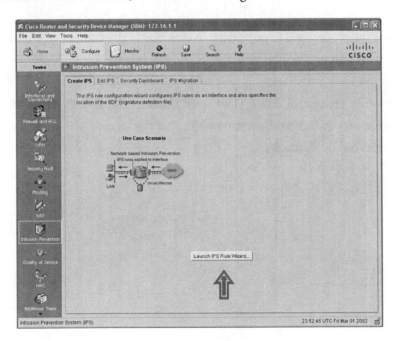

Figure 8.8. Launch the Wizard

Once you have clicked on the **Launch IPS Rule Wizard** button, SDM presents the following warning pop-up box stating that SDEE, which is the default and recommended communication protocol for sending IPS events, is not enabled. Click **OK** to enable SDEE:

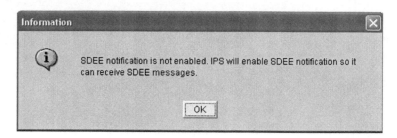

Figure 8.9. OK the Warning Box

Another pop-up box appears, advising that the SDM will enable SDEE to allow the Cisco IOS IPS to send event notifications, as illustrated in the following screenshot. Click **OK** to accept:

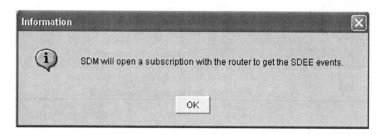

Figure 8.10. OK the Event Notification

SDM then prompts for credentials to perform this task. Enter the correct administrator credentials and click on **OK** to continue.

Once authentication is successful, SDM then transitions to the **IPS Policies Wizard** page. This page provides a summary of the configuration tasks that the wizard will assist with. Click on **Next** to continue, as illustrated in Figure 8.11:

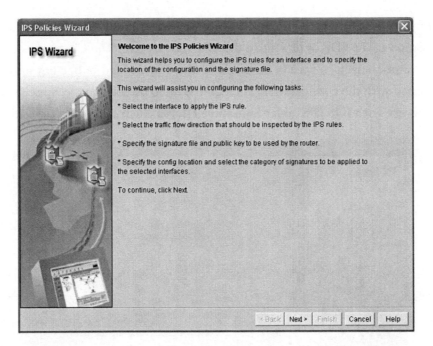

Figure 8.11. Click 'Next'

The next page allows you to specify the interfaces on which the IPS policy should be applied and the direction the policy should be applied in, i.e. inbound, outbound, or both. In this example, the IPS policy will be applied inbound on FastEthernet0/0 and outbound on Serial0/0. Once the relevant boxes have been checked, click on **Next** to proceed:

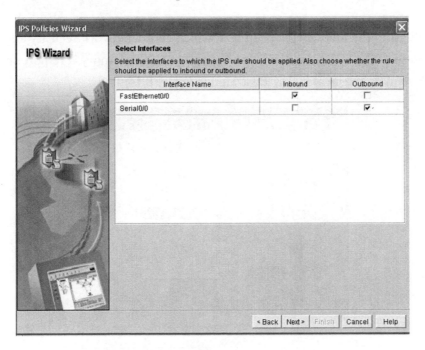

Figure 8.12. Select Interfaces and Direction

SDM transitions to the **Signature File and Public Key** page. From this page, administrators can specify the location of the SDF or download the SDF directly from the Cisco website. Network security administrators must also specify the name of the downloaded public key and input the key string. To proceed with the configuration, click on the radio button next to **Specify the signature file you want to use with IOS IPS** under **Signature File**, as illustrated in Figure 8.13:

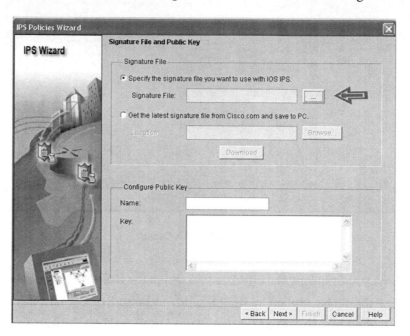

Figure 8.13. Specify the Signature File

This action brings up the following pop-up box, which allows network security administrators to select the location of the SDFs; this can be on the router Flash Memory, a remote server (e.g. FTP, TFTP, etc.), or even on the local PC, as illustrated in Figure 8.14:

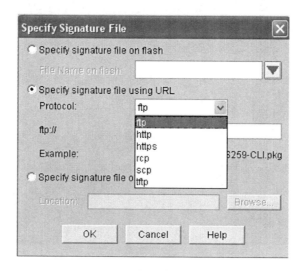

Figure 8.14. Browse to the file

In this example, the SDF that will be used is located on a TFTP server (which also happens to be the local PC in the network diagram). Therefore, the **Specify signature file using URL** option is selected and the valid path for the SDF is specified. Additionally, the public key downloaded from the Cisco website is also entered. Click on **Next** to proceed:

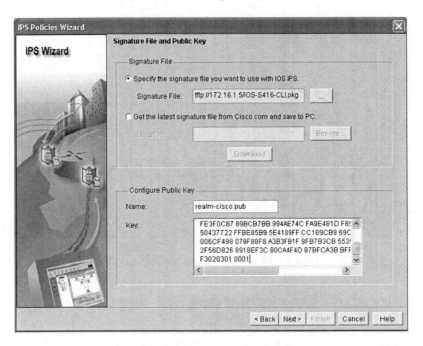

Figure 8.15. Example Using TFTP

SDM transitions to the **Config Location and Category** page. Delving into the specifics of the **Config Location** is beyond the scope of the IINS course requirements; therefore, simply use Flash Memory as the location and type in **flash:/** for the **Config Location**.

Additionally, depending on the memory on the router that Cisco IOS IPS is being implemented on, network security administrators can select either the **advanced** or the **basic** signature category. In this example, the router being used has 128MB of memory and so the **basic** signature category option is selected, as illustrated in Figure 8.16:

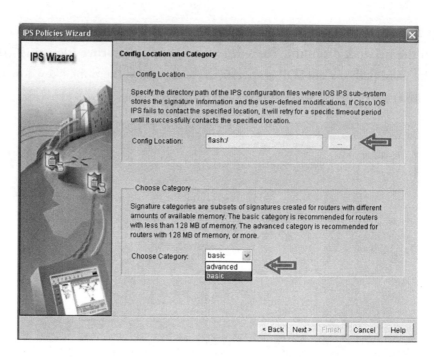

Figure 8.16. Choose 'Basic' or 'Advanced'

Once the desired category has been selected, click on **Next** to continue.

The next page displayed is the **Summary** page, illustrated in Figure 8.17:

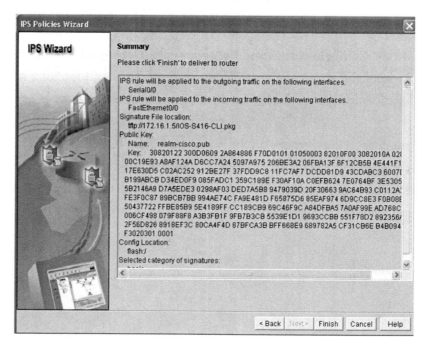

Figure 8.17. Summary Page

Click **Finish** to complete the implementation of Cisco IOS IPS. SDM then prepares the configuration commands and configures the router. Click **OK** to complete the process:

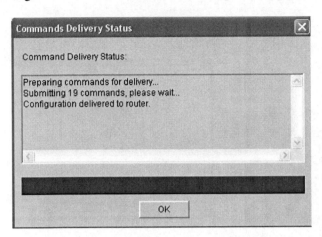

Figure 8.18. Configuration Files Prepared

SDM then configures the signatures on the router, as illustrated in Figure 8.19:

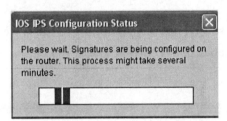

Figure 8.19. Signatures Prepared

NOTE: Depending on the size of the signature file, this process could take anywhere from a couple of minutes to around ten minutes. It is important that you understand this and allow SDM to complete this process. Do NOT reboot the router or close SDM during this process.

Once the configuration process is complete, SDM transitions to the **Intrusion Prevention System (IPS)** page, which is illustrated in Figure 8.20:

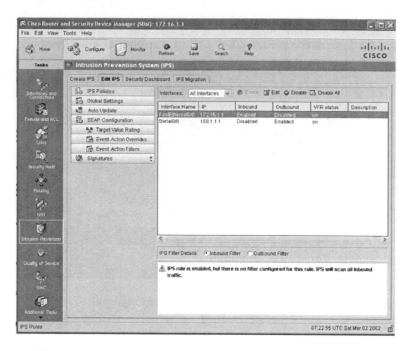

Figure 8.20. IPS Page

From this page, you can select several options pertaining to the IPS configuration. The **Global Settings** tab under the **Edit IPS** tab displays current global IPS configuration, as illustrated in Figure 8.21:

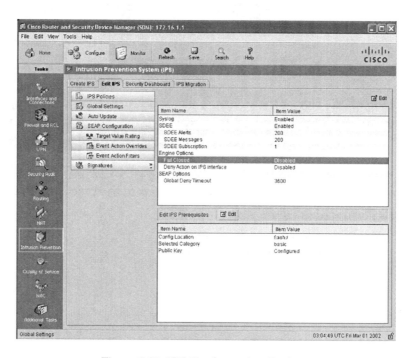

Figure 8.21. IPS Configuration Options

In Figure 8.21 above, we can see that **Syslog** and **SDEE** are enabled. However, the most important consideration on this screen is the **Fail Closed** option under **Engine Options**, which is highlighted above. If the **Fail Closed** option is enabled, the Cisco IOS IPS will drop packets if they are received while it is compiling a new signature for a particular engine.

Because the IOS IPS is co-resident with the router, it is typically not desirable for traffic to be blocked or dropped. Therefore, this option is disabled by default. However, if it is acceptable to drop packets during signature compilation, click on the **Edit** button in the top right-hand corner of the page to bring up the **Edit Global Settings** pop-up box. From the **Edit Global Settings** pop-up box, select the **Global Engine** tab and check the **Enable Engine Fail Closed** checkbox, as illustrated in Figure 8.22:

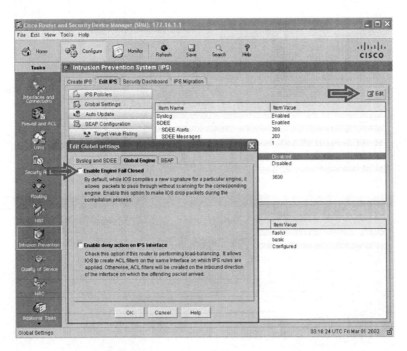

Figure 8.22. 'Edit Global Sessions' Options

In addition to **Global Settings**, the **Signatures** tab under the **Edit IPS** tab allows network security administrators to view all the signatures that have been loaded, as illustrated in Figure 8.23:

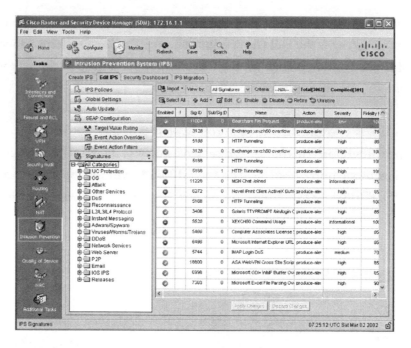

Figure 8.23. View Signatures

Finally, to monitor the Cisco IOS IPS, navigate to the **Monitor** page and select the **IPS Status** task, as illustrated in Figure 8.24:

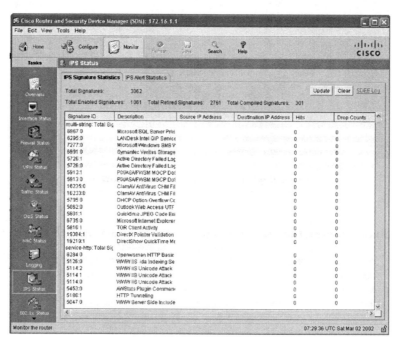

Figure 8.24. Monitor the IPS Status

From this page, you can also view the SDEE log by clicking on the blue **SDEE Log** link in the top right-hand corner of the page, as illustrated in Figure 8.25:

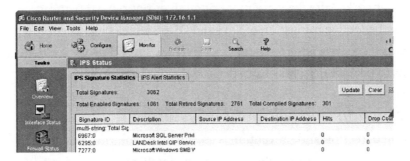

Figure 8.25. SDEE Log View

Alternatively, the same result can be obtained by navigating to the **Monitor** page, selecting the **Logging** task, and then clicking on the **SDEE Message Log** tab, as illustrated in Figure 8.26:

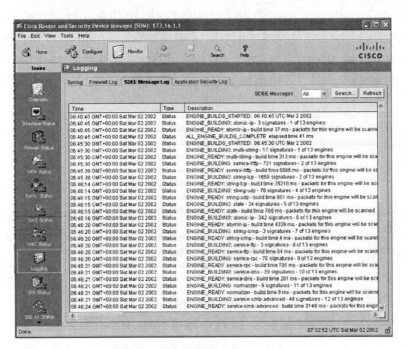

Figure 8.26. Alternative Option to View Log

Anomaly Detection and Mitigation

DoS and DDoS attacks have become more sophisticated and prevalent over the years. In today's rapidly evolving networks, attackers are more often than not one step ahead of network security administrators, and effective mitigation of DoS and DDoS attacks has become a pressing problem. Fortunately, network security administrators can leverage several proactive detection and prevention mechanisms to protect networks from these malicious techniques.

Anomaly Detection and Mitigation Systems

Anomaly intrusion detection and prevention is an enhanced solution designed to combat DoS and DDoS attacks. Anomaly detection solutions provide intelligence-based intrusion prevention by monitoring system activity and categorizing the traffic as either normal or anomalous (abnormal). The classification is based on heuristics or rules rather than traditional patterns or signatures used by other Intrusion Prevention Systems.

Anomaly detection systems are initially in learning mode so that they can characterize normal activity and establish a baseline for normal traffic and network conditions. Anomaly detection involves defining or learning normal activity and looking for deviations from the various baseline profiles that have been created. This can be performed using the following methods:

- Protocol anomaly detection
- Behavioral anomaly detection
- Network anomaly detection

Protocol anomaly detection involves looking for deviations from a standard protocol. This method is useful for identifying deviations from normal protocol behavior. For example, this method can be used to detect HTTP embedding methods used by attackers.

Behavioral anomaly detection involves learning normal user behavior and detecting the relational traffic pattern activities of individual hosts or a group of hosts. If a change occurs, an alarm is generated. This method is most useful in a very tightly controlled environment. For example, if company policy mandates that no executable files are to be downloaded, and this has been clearly communicated to all employees, but someone downloaded or attempted to download an executable file, an alarm would be triggered.

Network anomaly detection involves watching or learning the normal network traffic levels, for example, using a time-based classification of normal traffic activity. If deviation from normal traffic activity is detected, an alarm is generated. However, it is important to understand that network conditions change constantly, and so this method can result in many false positives.

Anomaly Detection Operation and Characteristics

Once baselines have been established, anomaly detection compares all traffic with the baseline profile, and any deviation from the profile is considered a potential attack. However, the issue is that on many occasions, legitimate traffic is integrated with the attack traffic; therefore, network security administrators must examine traffic patterns in real-time so that valid traffic can be processed and still be passed without interruption. Attack traffic can then be diverted to a mitigation device.

Anomaly detection and mitigation algorithms can detect all kinds of attacks, including day-zero attacks. This differs significantly from signature-based systems, which can only detect attacks for which a static signature has been defined. The following section lists the characteristics of anomaly detection techniques:

- They do not require the use of signatures or patterns;
- They are granular and are based on observed traffic pattern behavior;
- They can perform relational and behavioral anomaly detection;
- They detect in real-time, i.e. anything they report is actually happening at that time;
- They support dynamic filtering;
- They include sophisticated anti-spoofing techniques;
- They can detect day-zero and minute-zero attacks;
- They can highlight behaviors that do not indicate an attack but are of some interest; and
- They include a traffic diversion architecture.

Cisco Anomaly Detection and Mitigation Solution

The Cisco Anomaly Detection and Mitigation solution is used to combat complex and sophisticated DDoS attacks. This solution can be used in both enterprise and service provider networks and provides the following capabilities:

- It can detect and mitigate a wide range of DDoS attacks;
- It can classify legitimate traffic and attack traffic in real-time;
- It can block large botnet and zombie attacks;
- It can block attack traffic by using source-based dynamic filters; and
- It delivers multi-gigabit performance at line rate.

Figure 8.27 illustrates packet flow through the defense modules that provide advanced DDoS protection using the Cisco Anomaly Detection and Mitigation solution:

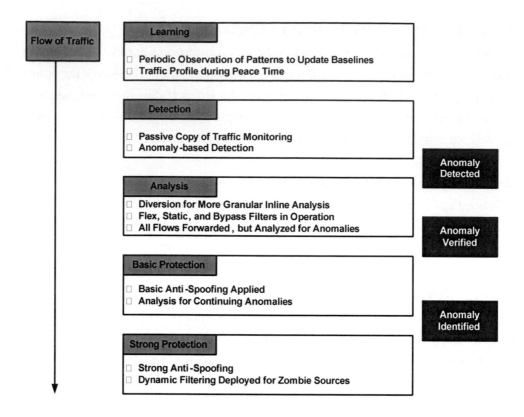

Figure 8.27. Packet Flow Through for Cisco Anomaly Detection

The Cisco DDoS Anomaly Detection and Mitigation solution consists of two core components:

- Cisco Traffic Anomaly Detector
- Cisco Guard DDoS Mitigation

NOTE: While going into detail on both of these solutions is beyond the scope of the IINS course requirements, the following section provides a brief description of each component.

The Cisco Traffic Anomaly Detector

The Cisco Traffic Anomaly Detector devices work in conjunction with the Cisco Guard DDoS Mitigation devices. These devices identify potential DDoS attacks and divert traffic destined to the target device(s) to the Cisco Guard to screen, identify, and block (in real-time), without affecting legitimate traffic flows. When anomalous traffic is detected, the Cisco Traffic Anomaly Detector performs one or more of the following actions:

- It sends an alert to initiate a manual response from network security administrators;
- It triggers an existing management system; and/or
- It launches the Cisco Guard DDoS Mitigation device to begin mitigation.

The Cisco Traffic Anomaly Detector performs the following tasks:

- Traffic learning—the Cisco Traffic Anomaly Detector classifies and categorizes the normal zone traffic pattern by using an algorithm-based process to establish a baseline. During the learning process, the Cisco Traffic Anomaly Detector modifies the default traffic policies and policy thresholds to match the characteristics of normal traffic. The traffic policies and thresholds define the reference points that the Cisco Traffic Anomaly Detector uses to determine when the traffic is normal or when it is abnormal, which indicates an attack.

- Traffic anomaly detection—the Cisco Traffic Anomaly Detector detects anomalies in protected zone traffic based on normal traffic characteristics.

The Cisco Guard DDoS Mitigation

The Cisco Guard DDoS Mitigation is a unique Multi-Verification (MVP) architecture that subjects diverted traffic (from the Cisco Traffic Anomaly Detector) to the most advanced anomaly recognition, protocol analysis, source verification, and anti-spoofing technologies. The Cisco Guard DDoS Mitigation device can identify a broad range of DDoS attacks, such as:

- TCP-based attacks
- UDP-based attacks
- HTTP attacks
- Botnet and zombie attacks
- DNS attacks
- Voice-over-IP attacks

The Cisco Guard DDoS Mitigation performs the following tasks:

- Traffic learning—the Cisco Guard DDoS Mitigation classifies and categorizes the normal zone traffic pattern by using an algorithm-based process to establish a baseline. During the learning process, the Cisco Guard DDoS Mitigation modifies default traffic policies and policy thresholds to match the characteristics of normal traffic. The traffic policies and thresholds define the reference points that the Cisco Guard DDoS Mitigation uses to determine when the traffic is normal or when it is abnormal, which indicates an attack.

- Traffic protection—the Cisco Guard DDoS Mitigation distinguishes between legitimate and malicious traffic and filters the malicious traffic so that only the legitimate traffic is allowed to pass on to the protected zone.

- Traffic diversion—the Cisco Guard DDoS Mitigation diverts the zone traffic from its normal network path to the Guard learning and protection processes and then returns legitimate zone traffic back to the network.

Because the Cisco Anomaly Detection and Mitigation solution is typically hard to understand, Figure 8.28 illustrates how these two components complement each other:

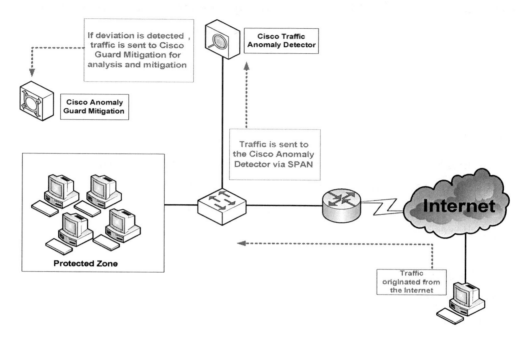

Figure 8.28. Cisco Anomaly Detection Example

NOTE: As previously stated, you are not expected to answer questions on specific details pertaining to the Cisco DDoS Anomaly Detection and Mitigation solution. Additionally, you do not need to know intricate details about the communication between the two components.

Chapter Summary

The following section is a summary of the major points you should be aware of in this chapter:

Intrusion Detection and Prevention Systems

- An Intrusion Detection System is used to detect malicious behavior
- IDS devices can only perform promiscuous monitoring based on an out-of-packet stream
- In order to allow an IDS to view traffic, the switch must be configured for SPAN
- SPAN can be configured to monitor all traffic from a port, ports, VLAN or group of VLANs
- An IDS cannot block traffic on its own
- An IDS can notify another infrastructure device (e.g. firewall or router) to shun an attack
- An IPS monitors traffic in the same way as an IDS
- An IPS can be implemented inline, in promiscuous mode, or a combination of both
- Unlike an IDS, an IPS is reactive, and can block traffic on its own
- In promiscuous mode, an IPS can notify other devices to shun an attack
- IDS /IPS devices use protocol analyzers to decode Application Layer protocols
- IDS /IPS devices are composed of a sensor, a console and an engine
- The IDS/IPS console monitors events and controls the sensors
- The IDS/IPS engine uses rules to generate alerts
- The IDS/IPS sensor provides packet capturing and analyzing capabilities
- The IDS/IPS sensor uses multiple micro-engines to analyze traffic against signatures
- The following table lists and describes IDS and IPS you are expected to know:

Term	Description
Alert or Alarm	A signal suggesting a system has been or is being attacked
True attack stimulus	An event that triggers an system to produce an alarm and react as though a real attack were in progress
False attack stimulus	The event signaling the system to produce an alarm when no attack has taken place
False Positive	An alert or alarm that is triggered when no actual attack has taken place; i.e. an incorrect positive alert or alarm
False negative	A failure of the system to detect an actual attack
Noise	Data or interference that can trigger a false positive
Site policy	Guidelines within an organization that control the rules and configurations of the system
Site policy awareness	The ability the system has to dynamically change its rules and configurations in response to changing environmental activity
Confidence value	A value an organization places based on past performance and analysis to help determine its ability to effectively identify an attack
Alarm filtering	The process of categorizing attack alerts produced by the system in order to distinguish false positives from actual attacks

- The four methods used by IDS and IPS devices to detect attacks are:
  1. Policy-based Detection
  2. Anomaly-based Detection
  3. Honey Pot Detection
  4. Signature-based Detection

- Policy-based detection is based on administrator definition of normal network behavior
- Anomaly-based detection uses either statistical or non-statistical anomaly-based detection
- A honey pot is a trap set to lure attackers away from legitimate targets
- Signature-based detection examines network traffic for defined attack patterns
- Signature-based detection is the primary method used by IDS/IPS devices

IDS and IPS Signatures

- Signatures are at the heart of signature-based detection solutions
- Signatures can be grouped into two general classes: attack and informational
- Attack signatures are used to indicate that an attack is occurring
- Informational signatures are used to gather information about traffic
- The design of signatures involves implementations and structures
- There are two implementation methods for signatures: context and content
- With context implementation, a signature looks only at the packet header
- With content implementation, the signature looks at the packet payload
- Signature structure determines how many packets the IDS/IPS device has to examine
- There are two basic signature structures: atomic and stateful
- An atomic structure looks at a single packet for a match on a signature
- Stateful signatures are triggered on a sequence of specific events
- The most important part of a signature is the mechanism that causes it to trigger
- The most common triggering mechanisms are pattern, anomaly, and behavior-based
- When a signature is triggered, it can perform one of the following activities:
  1. Generating an alert
  2. Dropping or preventing the activity
  3. Logging the activity
  4. Resetting a TCP connection
  5. Blocking future activity
  6. Allowing the activity

- IDS and IPS devices can generate atomic alerts, summary alerts or a combination of both
- Atomic alerts are the most common; they are generated every time a signature triggers
- A summary alert is a single alert that indicates multiple occurrences of the same signature

IDS and IPS System Types

- There are several different types of IDS types, which are:
    1. Network-based Intrusion Detection System (NIDS)
    2. Protocol-based Intrusion Detection System (PIDS)
    3. Application Protocol-based Intrusion Detection System (APIDS)
    4. Host-based Intrusion Detection System (HIDS)
    5. Hybrid Intrusion Detection System

- There are several different types of IPS solutions. These are:
    1. Host-based Intrusion Prevention Systems (HIPS)
    2. Network-based Intrusion Prevention Systems (NIPS)
    3. Content-based Intrusion Prevention Systems (CIPS)
    4. Rate-based Intrusion Prevention Systems (RBIPS)

Cisco Network Intrusion Prevention Systems

- The Network-based Intrusion Prevention solutions available from Cisco are:
    1. The Cisco IPS 4200 Series Appliance Sensors
    2. The Cisco IDS Services Module 2 (IDSM-2)
    3. The Cisco Advanced Inspection and Protection Security Services Module
    4. The Cisco IPS Advanced Integration Module (IPS-AIM)
    5. The Cisco Internetwork Operating System (IOS) IPS

- The Cisco IPS 4200 Series sensors are purpose-built appliances manufactured by Cisco
- The Cisco IDSM-2 can be installed into Catalyst 6500 switches or 7600 series routers
- The Cisco AIP-SSM is designed for the Cisco ASA 5500 series security appliances
- The Cisco IPS-AIM can be used with Cisco Integrated Services Routers, such as the 2800
- The Cisco IOS IPS provides an integrated solution with the router software architecture
- Cisco IPS Sensor software can use the following protocols to exchange IPS events:
    1. RDEP2
    2. IDIOM
    3. IDCONF
    4. SDEE
    5. CIDEE

Cisco Host Intrusion Prevention Systems

- The Cisco Security Agent is the Cisco Host-based Intrusion Prevention solution
- CSA provides proactive HIDS and HIPS solutions for endpoint systems
- Unlike other IPS solutions, CSA does not rely on a signature-based architecture
- CSA uses a flexible policy-based and behavior-based architecture

- CSA also has the capability to provide policy compliance controls
- The following list highlights the characteristics and benefits offered by CSA:
  1. Endpoint system protection
  2. Host-based intrusion prevention
  3. Policy-based and behavior-based architecture
  4. Personal firewall protection
  5. Day-zero attack protection
  6. Regulatory policy compliance enforcement
  7. Acceptable corporate use policy compliance
  8. Preventative protection against targeted attacks
  9. Stability and protection of the underlying Operating System
  10. File and directory protection
  11. Host application visibility
  12. Application control
  13. Correlation of system calls and application functions

- The CSA software is unique in that the host agent resides between the applications and OS
- CSA architecture intercepts all OS and application-related calls
- CSA is also capable of intercepting dynamic runtime resources requested
- CSA has three basic components:
  1. CSA endpoints—e.g. computing desktops, servers, laptops, and POS terminals
  2. CSA Management Server—which is the core component of the CSA architecture
  3. CSA Management Console—an administrative web-based user interface

- CSA architecture uses a grouping system
- Groups are a logical collection of hosts
- Groups in CSA MC are divided into the following three categories:
  1. Mandatory groups
  2. Predefined groups
  3. Custom groups

- By default, CSA MC provides three auto-enrollment mandatory groups, which are:
  1. All Windows
  2. All Solaris
  3. All Linux

- In CSA terminology, policy is a collection of rule modules
- In CSA terminology, a rule module is a collection of multiple rules
- Rules provide control access to system or network resources
- At the core of CSA architecture is the interceptor and correlation mechanism
- Correlation is the enforcement engine for CSA

Cisco IOS IPS Overview and Implementation

- Cisco is the only vendor that delivers integrated IPS functionality on a router
- The IOS IPS feature is a suite of intrusion prevention solutions
- Some of the key features of the IOS IPS are:
    1. It protects the network from viruses, worms and a large variety of threats and exploits
    2. It eliminates the need for a standalone IPS device
    3. It provides integrated inline deep-packet inspection
    4. It complements the Cisco IOS Firewall and VPN solutions for superior threat protection
    5. It supports about 2000 attack signatures
    6. It uses Cisco IOS routing capabilities to deliver integrated functionality
    7. It enables distributed network-wide threat mitigation
    8. It sends a Syslog message or an alarm in SDEE format when a threat is detected

- Cisco IOS IPS routers use Signature Definition Files (SDFs) to identify malicious traffic
- An SDF is a file, usually in XML format, that contains signature definitions
- In most cases, the SDF is located in the router Flash Memory
- Signature Definition Files use an .sdf file extension, for example 128MB.sdf
- Before configuring Cisco IOS IPS, the following two prerequisites must be satisfied:
    1. Download the signature package from the Cisco website
    2. Download the Public Crypto Key from the Cisco website

Anomaly Detection and Mitigation

- Anomaly intrusion detection and prevention is used to combat DoS and DDoS attacks
- Anomaly detection solutions categorize traffic as either normal or anomalous (abnormal)
- Anomaly detection classification is based on heuristics, rather than traditional signatures
- Anomaly detection defines or learns normal activity using the following methods:
    1. Protocol anomaly detection
    2. Behavioral anomaly detection
    3. Network anomaly detection

- Protocol anomaly detection involves looking for deviations from a standard protocol
- Behavioral anomaly detection involves learning normal user behavior
- Network anomaly detection involves watching or learning the normal network traffic levels
- The following section lists the characteristics of anomaly detection techniques:
    1. They do not require the use of signatures or patterns
    2. They are granular and are based on observed traffic pattern behavior
    3. They can perform relational and behavioral anomaly detection
    4. They detect in real-time; i.e. anything they report is actually happening at that time
    5. They support dynamic filtering

6. They include sophisticated anti-spoofing techniques
7. They can detect day-zero and minute-zero attacks
8. They can highlight behaviors that do not indicate an attack, but are of some interest
9. They include a traffic diversion architecture

- The Cisco Anomaly Detection and Mitigation solution provides the following capabilities:
  1. It can detect and mitigate a wide range of DDoS attacks
  2. It can classify legitimate traffic and attack traffic in real-time
  3. It can block large botnet and zombie attacks
  4. It can block attack traffic by using source-based dynamic filters
  5. It delivers multi-gigabit performance at line rate

- The Cisco DDoS Anomaly Detection and Mitigation solution consists of two components:
  1. Cisco Traffic Anomaly Detector
  2. Cisco Guard DDoS Mitigation

- The Cisco Traffic Anomaly Detector identifies potential DDoS attacks
- When anomalous traffic is detected, the Cisco Traffic Anomaly Detector does the following:
  1. It sends an alert to initiate a manual response from network security administrators
  2. It triggers and existing management system
  3. It launches the Cisco Guard DDoS Mitigation device to begin mitigation

- The Cisco Traffic Anomaly Detector performs the following tasks:
  1. Traffic learning
  2. Traffic anomaly detection

- The Cisco Guard DDoS Mitigation is a unique Multi-Verification (MVP) architecture
- The Cisco Guard DDoS Mitigation can identify a broad range of DDoS attacks, such as:
  1. TCP-based attacks
  2. UDP-based attacks
  3. HTTP attacks
  4. Botnet and Zombie attacks
  5. DNS attacks
  6. Voice over IP attacks

- The Cisco Guard DDoS Mitigation performs the following tasks:
  1. Traffic learning
  2. Traffic protection
  3. Traffic diversion

CHAPTER 9

Data Privacy and Secure Communications

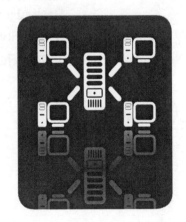

With the exponential growth in popularity of the Internet, and millions of people using it as a communications highway, data privacy and secure communications have become extremely important. From the Physical Layer to the Application Layer, cryptography is the first of many steps that are necessary to provide a secure communications solution. The IINS exam objectives covered in this chapter are as follows:

- Explain the different methods used in cryptography
- Explain IKE protocol functionality and phases
- Describe the building blocks of IPsec and the security functions it provides
- Configure and verify IPsec site-to-site VPN with pre-shared key authentication using SDM

This chapter is broken up into the following sections:

- Cryptography Overview
- Symmetric Key Cryptography
- Asymmetric Key Cryptography
- Hash Algorithms
- VPN Technologies
- IP Security
- IPsec VPN Configuration in SDM

IINS Exam Objective	Section(s) Covered
Explain the different methods used in cryptography	• Cryptography Overview • Symmetric Key Cryptography • Asymmetric Key Cryptography • Hash Algorithms
Explain IKE protocol functionality and phases	• IP Security
Describe the building blocks of IPsec and the security functions it provides	• VPN Technologies • IP Security
Configure and verify IPsec site-to-site VPN with pre-shared key authentication using SDM	• IPsec VPN Configuration in SDM

Cryptography Overview

Cryptography is the art of protecting information by encrypting, or translating it into an unreadable format, which is then referred to as ciphertext. In order to view ciphertext, users must possess a secret key that can decipher, or decrypt, the message back into plaintext. Cryptographic technologies and solutions help address issues related to information confidentiality, integrity, and access control, which are the three core reasons for security solutions. Cryptography solutions also provide techniques that allow network security administrators to identify unauthorized data modifications and alterations.

A cryptosystem, or cryptographic system, is a framework that involves the application of cryptography to provide secure communications. In essence, a cryptosystem is a collection of protocols, procedures, and algorithms that are required to implement an encoding and decoding system using cryptography. By implementing a cryptosystem, the confidentiality and integrity of information can be achieved by using various methods that employ cryptography, such as encryption and decryption techniques, hash functions, digital signatures, and key management techniques, which will all be described in detail in this chapter.

Cryptographic Terminology

Before delving into the specifics of cryptosystems and related technologies, it is imperative to have a sound understanding of the jargon or terminology used in cryptography. This section describes the following cryptographic terminologies that will be used throughout this chapter and that you should be familiar with:

- Encryption
- Decryption
- Plaintext
- Ciphertext
- Hash
- Virtual Private Network

Encryption is the process of obscuring information to make it unreadable to unauthorized recipients. Encryption employs the use of algorithmic processes that use secret keys to transform plain data into a secret code. Encryption is used to provide data confidentiality.

Decryption is the reverse of encryption. This process is used to make the encrypted information readable by converting the data back into its original form.

Plaintext is information a sender wishes to transmit to a receiver. In other words, it is the original, unencrypted data. Plaintext is used as input to an encryption algorithm.

Ciphertext is the product of the encryption process. This is simply the plaintext data that has been encrypted. It is therefore considered the output of an encryption algorithm.

A hash, also referred to as a message digest, is a unique number from a sequence of text that is generated by applying a mathematical formula. The basic function of a hash is to take a random-length block of data and return a fixed-size bit string, which is then referred to as the hash value or message digest. Any accidental or intentional changes to the data will also result in a change of the hash value. Hashing is used to provide data integrity. For example, Table 9.1 lists four different phrases and their corresponding hash values:

Table 9.1. Hash Values

Phase (Random-length Block of Data)	Hash (Fixed-size Bit String)
Cryptography is fun!	690f76027b02363393535937e1e12a44
IINS Security	589ab55fc5929b8fdb5c10bea26a1a18
CCNA	3d645983387566a4af67b11ff5f6bc1d
Howtonetwork is great!	cbb34c101e51142e808dbfd6c6c71a2b

As illustrated in Table 9.1 above, even though the four phrases contain different numbers of letters (i.e. are different lengths) the hash value for all four values contains exactly the same number of alphanumeric digits (i.e. is a fixed-size bit string).

A Virtual Private Network (VPN) is used to carry private traffic over a public transport, such as the Internet. In all cases, a VPN consists of two endpoints, which may be routers, firewalls, servers, or even individual client workstations. While a VPN can use both cryptographic and non-cryptographic approaches to create a secure communication channel, this chapter focuses exclusively on cryptographic VPN technologies—specifically IP Security, also called IPsec.

Figure 9.1 provides a basic illustration of these components within a cryptosystem:

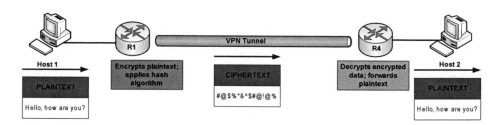

Figure 9.1. Hash Values Through a VPN

In Figure 9.1 illustrated above, Host 1 sends a plaintext message to Host 2. This plaintext is encrypted by R1, which scrambles the data using a hash algorithm. The ciphertext is then forwarded to R4 across the VPN tunnel between R1 and R4. R4 receives the encrypted data and then decrypts it. The plaintext is forwarded to Host 2 and appears as was originally sent by Host 1. Keep in mind that this diagram serves only as a basic representation of the entire process. We will go into detail on these and other terms as we progress through this chapter.

Cryptographic Algorithms

Cryptographic techniques can be classified as either traditional or modern. Traditional techniques use transposition and substitution mechanisms and are sometimes referred to as classical cryptographic techniques.

A transposition mechanism is an encryption method that simply reorders plaintext such that the derived ciphertext represents a variation of the original plaintext. In layman's terms, transposition simply reorders plaintext, making it illegible.

A substitution cipher is a method of encryption by which units of plaintext are replaced with ciphertext according to a regular system. The receiver deciphers the text by performing an inverse substitution. A substitution cipher that operates on single letters is referred to as a simple substitution cipher, while a substitution cipher that operates on larger groups of letters is referred to as a polygraphic cipher. Additionally, a monoalphabetic cipher uses fixed substitution over the entire message, whereas a polyalphabetic cipher uses a number of substitutions at different times in the message.

The current IINS certification exam focuses primarily on modern ciphers. Therefore, traditional or classical cryptographic techniques will not be described in any further detail in this chapter. You are only expected to demonstrate detailed knowledge of modern cryptographic techniques.

Modern cryptographic techniques, which will be described in detail in this chapter, rely on sophisticated protocols and algorithms to ensure the security of information. There are three types of cryptographic algorithms:

- Symmetric Key Cryptography
- Asymmetric Key Cryptography
- Hash Algorithms

Symmetric key cryptography uses a single key for the encryption and decryption process. It is also commonly referred to as secret key or pre-shared key cryptography. Symmetric key cryptography will be described in detail later in this chapter.

Asymmetric key cryptography uses two keys for the encryption and decryption process; that is, one key for encryption and another key for decryption. Asymmetric key cryptography is also commonly referred to as public-key cryptography. Asymmetric key cryptography will be described in detail later in this chapter.

Hash algorithms, or hash functions, use a one-way mathematical function to produce an algorithmically randomized unique hash value to identify data. Because of the one-way process, the original message cannot be reconstituted, even with knowledge of the hash algorithm. Hash algorithms will also be described in detail later in this chapter.

Symmetric Key Cryptography

Symmetric key cryptography is used to encrypt the contents of a message to provide data confidentiality. Symmetric key cryptography uses a single shared secret key for the encryption and decryption process. This key is referred to as a symmetric key. Due to the fact that the symmetric key is shared, it must be known to the entity that encrypts the message as well as the entity that is going to eventually decrypt the message. There are two categories of symmetric key cryptography:

- Block ciphers
- Stream ciphers

Block Ciphers

Block ciphers encrypt plaintext in chunks. These ciphers are used to encrypt plaintext on a fixed-length group of bits, with an unvarying transformation during the encryption cycle. A block cipher encrypts blocks of data by using the same key on each block. The block size is typically 64 or 128 bits in length, with the latter being the most commonly used in modern cryptography. However, some ciphers, which will be described later in this chapter, have the ability to use a variable block size.

A block cipher consists of two paired algorithms, one for encryption and another for decryption. Both algorithms accept two inputs. The first is an input block of a particular size, and the second input is the shared secret key, also of a particular size. This allows the block cipher to produce a corresponding 128-bit block of ciphertext. For example, a block cipher encryption algorithm might take a 128-bit block of plaintext as input and produce a corresponding 128-bit block of ciphertext. However, the exact transformation is controlled using a second input, which is the shared secret key. Additionally, it is important to understand that with block ciphers, if the input changes even in the slightest manner (e.g. if a plaintext bit or the secret key is changed), the resultant ciphertext is completely changed. This characteristic is referred to as the avalanche effect.

Most block ciphers are constructed by repeatedly applying a simpler function. These ciphers are known as iterated block ciphers. Iterated block ciphers increase the effectiveness of the encryption algorithm by repeatedly applying the same algorithm. This means that with each repetition, the message is further encrypted. Each single repetition, or iteration, is referred to as a round, and the repeated function is referred to as the round function. The number of rounds selected is usually determined by the computational power available and the security level desired. In general terms, anywhere between four and thirty-two rounds are typical.

Feistel ciphers are a special class of iterated block ciphers, where the ciphertext is calculated from the plaintext by repeated application of the encryption process. The Feistel structure uses similar encryption and decryption operations, which can also be identical.

Block ciphers have several modes of operation. Currently, the National Institute of Standards and Technology (NIST) has approved eight block cipher modes. There are five confidentiality modes, which are ECB, CBC, CFB, OFB, and CTR; one authentication mode, which is CMAC; and two combined modes for confidentiality and authentication, which are CCM and GCM. These modes are defined as follows:

- ECB, which stands for Electronic Code Book, is only as secure as the underlying block cipher. However, plaintext patterns are not concealed. Each identical block of plaintext gives an identical block of ciphertext. The plaintext can be easily manipulated by removing, repeating, or inter-changing blocks. The speed of each encryption operation is identical to that of the block cipher. ECB allows easy parallelization to yield higher performance.

- CBC stands for Cipher Block Chaining. In this mode, the initial block is encrypted using an initialization vector that is randomly generated, and then, for additional blocks, the cipher text of an encoded block is simply XORed (i.e. an either-or operation is performed) with the next plaintext block that is to be encoded. This means that the resulting ciphertext not only is a function of the key and the encryption algorithm but also depends on the blocks that were previously encoded.

- CFB, which stands for Cipher Feedback Mode, is only as secure as the underlying cipher and plaintext patterns that are concealed in the ciphertext by the use of the XOR operation. In CFB, the previous ciphertext block is encrypted and the output produced is combined with the plain-text block using XOR to produce the current ciphertext block. An initialization vector is used as a seed for the process. With CFB and full feedback, when two ciphertext blocks are identical, the outputs from the block cipher operation at the next step are also identical. However, it is possible to define CFB so it uses feedback that is less than one full data block. It is important to keep in mind that a block cipher in CFB is essentially a self-synchronizing stream cipher. Stream ciphers are described in the following section.

- OFB, which stands for Output Feedback Mode, is similar to CFB, except that the quantity XORed with each plaintext block is generated independently of both the plaintext and the ciphertext. An initialization vector is used as a seed for a sequence of data blocks, and each data block is derived from the encryption of the previous data block. The encryption of a plaintext block is derived by taking the XOR of the plaintext block with the relevant data block. OFB makes a block cipher into a synchronous stream cipher because it generates keystream blocks. Stream ciphers are described in detail in the following section.

- CTR stands for Counter. This mode is similar to OFB in that it turns a block cipher into a stream cipher. It generates the next keystream block by encrypting successive values of a counter. The counter can be any function that produces a sequence that is guaranteed not to repeat for a long time, although an actual counter is the simplest and most popular.

- CMAC stands for Cipher Block Chaining Message Authentication Code and can also be abbreviated as CBC-MAC. The message is encrypted with some block cipher algorithm in CBC mode to create a chain of blocks such that each block depends on the proper encryption of the previous block. This interdependence ensures that a change to any of the plaintext bits will cause the final encrypted block to change in a way that cannot be predicted or counteracted without knowing the key to the block cipher.

- CCM, which stands for Counter with CBC-MAC, is a modern construction, building on traditional mechanisms developed by RSA. CCM was designed initially for use with packet-oriented security protocols. As such, it includes provisions to authenticate the packet header and the payload while encrypting only the payload. However, CCM can also be used for encrypting files, messages, and other data. CCM uses a single cryptographic key to provide authentication and encryption. The primary advantages offered by CCM are its smaller implementation size, packet header authentication, use of a single key for all cryptographic operations, and solid cryptographic confidence backed by mathematical proof.

- GCM, which stands for Galois/Counter Mode, is an authenticated encryption algorithm designed to provide both authentication and privacy. GCM is defined for block ciphers with a block size of 128 bits. GMAC is an authentication-only variant of the GCM.

An XOR or EOR algorithm, which was described in Chapter 3, is an algorithm that basically means either one or the other, but not both. This concept is illustrated in Table 9.2:

Table 9.2. XOR/EOR Algorithms

First Color Selected	Second Color Selected	Does this make the color green?
Yellow	Blue	Yes
Yellow	Yellow	No
Blue	Yellow	Yes
Blue	Blue	No

In Table 9.2 above, one of the second colors selected to make the color green must be either yellow or blue, depending on the first color selected. If the first and second color selected is blue, the end result will never be the color green. Likewise, if the first and second color selected is yellow, the end result will never be the color green. The XOR operator would only create the color green if the colors selected were either [yellow + blue] or [blue + yellow], not if they were either [blue + blue] or [yellow + yellow].

Stream Ciphers

Unlike block ciphers, stream or state ciphers encrypt plaintext digits (bits or bytes) one by one. This means that the transformation of encrypted output varies during the encryption cycle. In stream ciphers, plaintext bits are combined with a pseudo-random cipher bit stream, referred to as a keystream. The keystream is combined with the plaintext digits one at a time to form the ciphertext, typically via an XOR operation.

There are two categories of stream ciphers: synchronous and self-synchronizing. In a synchronous stream cipher, a stream of pseudo-random digits is generated independently of the plaintext and ciphertext messages and then combined with the plaintext (to encrypt the data) or the ciphertext (to decrypt the data). In the most common form, binary digits (bits) are used, and the keystream is combined with the plaintext using the XOR operation. This is referred to as a binary additive stream cipher.

In addition to this, when using a synchronous stream cipher, it is important to remember that the sender and the receiver must be exactly in sync for decryption to be successful. If digits are added or removed from the message during transmission, synchronization is lost. To restore synchronization, various offsets can be tried systematically to obtain the correct decryption. Alternatively, another approach that is commonly used is to tag the ciphertext with markers at regular points in the output.

If, however, a digit is corrupted in transmission, rather than added or lost, only a single digit in the plaintext is affected and the error does not propagate to other parts of the message. This property is useful when the transmission error rate is high; however, it makes it less likely the error would be detected without further mechanisms. Moreover, because of this property, synchronous stream ciphers are very susceptible to active attacks whereby an attacker changes a digit in the ciphertext, allowing him or her to make predictable changes to the corresponding plaintext bit; for example, flipping or changing a single bit or byte in the ciphertext causes the same bit or byte to be flipped or changed in the plaintext.

Self-synchronizing stream ciphers use several of the previous ciphertext digits to compute the key-stream. These stream ciphers are also commonly referred to as self-synchronizing stream ciphers, asynchronous stream ciphers, or ciphertext autokey (CTAK). Self-synchronizing stream ciphers allow the receiver automatically to synchronize with the keystream generator after receiving ci-phertext digits, making it easier to recover if digits are dropped or added to the message stream. This limits the effects of single-digit errors. An example of a self-synchronizing stream cipher is a block cipher in cipher-feedback mode.

Because these terms are relatively confusing, keep in mind that the generation of the keystream in stream ciphers can be independent of the plaintext and ciphertext, resulting in a synchronous stream cipher. Alternatively, the generation of the keystream can also depend on the data and its encryption, in which case the stream cipher is self-synchronizing. Additionally, also remember that the majority of stream cipher designs are for synchronous stream ciphers.

Binary stream ciphers are often constructed using linear feedback shift registers (LFSRs) because they can easily be implemented in hardware and can readily be analyzed mathematically. LFSR is a mechanism for generating a sequence of binary bits. Delving into further details on LSFRs is beyond the scope of the IINS course requirements.

Stream ciphers attempt to operate in the same manner as the one-time pad, or OTP, which is also referred to as the Vernam cipher. OTP uses a string of bits that is generated completely at random. Because of this, OTP is said to offer perfect secrecy, and the analysis of the OTP is seen as one of the cornerstones of modern cryptography. OTP has proven, in theory, to be an unbreakable cipher; however, it must be noted that while perfectly secure, the OTP is, in general, impractical.

Because the information covered in this section may be quite overwhelming at first glance, keep in mind that a block cipher mode yields the same ciphertext from a block of plaintext when using the same key; however, a stream cipher mode yields different ciphertext from the same plaintext. Use this as a baseline to remember the different modes of operation and algorithms that are used for block ciphers and stream ciphers. We will conclude this section by describing some of the most common symmetric cryptographic algorithms, which are as follows:

- Digital Encryption Standard
- Triple-Digital Encryption Standard
- Advanced Encryption Standard
- RC4
- International Data Encryption Algorithm
- Blowfish

Data Encryption Standard

The Data Encryption Standard (DES) is a block cipher algorithm and is the name of the Federal Information Processing Standards (FIPS), which describes the data encryption algorithm (DEA). DEA is also defined in the ANSI standard X3.92. DES was adopted by the NIST in 1977 for commercial and unclassified government documents. DEA, often called DES, has been extensively studied since its initial publication and is perhaps the best-known and most commonly used symmetric algorithm in the world.

DEA has a 64-bit block size and uses a 56-bit key during execution because parity bits are stripped off from the full 64-bit key. DEA is a symmetric cryptosystem, specifically a 16-round Feistel cipher, which was originally designed for implementation in hardware. When used for communication, both sender and receiver must know the same secret key, which can be used to encrypt and decrypt the message or to generate and verify a message authentication code (MAC). DEA can also be used for single-user encryption, such as to store files on a hard disk in encrypted form. In a multi-user environment, secure key distribution may be difficult; however, public-key cryptography provides an ideal solution to this problem. Public-key cryptography will be described in detail later in this chapter.

DES uses both block and stream cipher modes to encrypt or decrypt more than 64 bits of data. For block cipher mode, DES uses Electronic Code Book (ECB) or Cipher Block Chaining (CBC) to provide data confidentiality. However, for stream cipher mode, DES uses Cipher Feedback Mode (CFB) or Output Feedback Mode (OFB) to provide data confidentiality. Figure 9.2 illustrates the basic DES encryption process:

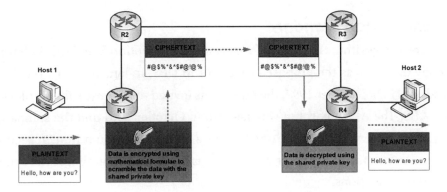

Figure 9.2. Basic DES Encryption

In Figure 9.2 illustrated above, Host 1 wants to send a plaintext message to Host 2. This data is sent to R1, where it is encrypted with a shared key and sent over the IP network in an unreadable format until it is received by R4. R4, in turn, decrypts the ciphertext using the shared key and the resulting plaintext is forwarded on to Host 2.

In modern-day networks, DES is no longer considered very secure, primarily because the inherent 56-bit key size is too small. DES has been known to be compromised in less than 24 hours. However, in the case of Triple DES, the documented key-breaking times are approximately 10 billion years when one million PC 3 computers are used. As a result, Triple DES, which is described next, is recommended instead of DES.

Triple-Digital Encryption Standard

Triple-DES is a block cipher and is a variant of DES that encrypts the plaintext with the DES algorithm three times. Three keys are used to encrypt data, resulting in a 168-bit key, which is calculated by multiplying the original DES key size of 56 by 3. The following six steps serve to illustrate the manner in which Triple-DES, or 3DES, operates:

1. The sending device encrypts the data with the first 56-bit key.
2. The sending device decrypts the data with the second key, also 56-bits long.
3. The sending device encrypts the data for a final time with another 56-bit key.
4. The receiving device decrypts the data with the first 56-bit key.
5. The receiving device then encrypts the data with the second key, also 56-bits long.
6. Finally, the receiving device decrypts the data with the third and final 56-bit key.

The end goal of DES and 3DES is to provide data confidentiality by hiding secret data. The data must have integrity to ensure that it has not been modified in any manner or form, and it must be authenticated by ensuring that the source or destination endpoint is indeed what it professes to be. Data integrity and authentication mechanisms will be described later in this chapter.

Advanced Encryption Standard

AES is a block cipher algorithm that stands for Advanced Encryption Standard. AES was issued as FIPS PUB 197 by the NIST as the proposed successor to DES. In January 1997, the AES initiative was announced, and in September 1997, the public was invited to propose suitable block ciphers as candidates for AES. The AES algorithm was selected in October 2001 and the standard was published in November 2002. NIST's intent was to have a cipher that would remain secure well into the next century. AES is one of the most commonly used algorithms amongst the symmetric key cryptography implementations.

The AES algorithm can use a variable block and key length. AES supports key sizes of 128 bits, 192 bits, and 256 bits, in contrast to the 56-bit keys offered by DES. The AES algorithm resulted from a multi-year evaluation process led by the NIST with submissions and review by an international community of cryptography experts. The Rijndael algorithm, invented by Joan Daemen and Vincent Rijmen, was selected as the standard. Over time, many implementations are expected to upgrade to AES, both because it offers a 128-bit key size, and because it is a federal standard.

Unlike its predecessor, DES, AES does not use a Feistel network. Instead, AES encryption is an algorithm based on permutations. For the mathematically inclined, AES is based on a design principle known as a Substitution-Permutation Network (SPN). This makes AES very fast in both software and hardware. Additionally, this means that AES is relatively easy to implement and requires little memory. Going into the details pertaining to the algorithm used is beyond the scope of the IINS course requirements; however, at a very high level, AES operates as follows:

- AES encryption receives the message or information (plaintext) that needs to be sent as an input.
- This information is then scrambled using the shared key during the encryption process. The bigger the key used, the larger the scrambled output. For example, a 512-bit shared key will produce larger ciphertext output than a 128-bit shared key.
- Finally, the generated ciphertext is then sent to the recipient, as illustrated in Figure 9.3:

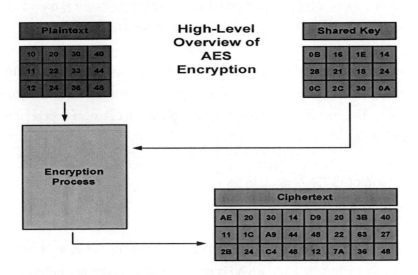

Figure 9.3. Overview of AES Encryption

The recipient then uses the shared secret key to decrypt the ciphertext and read the message. This process makes AES very secure. You are not required to demonstrate knowledge of the AES encryption algorithm(s). However, ensure that you have a basic understanding of the overall process used in AES encryption.

AES is so secure that up until May 2009, the only successful published attacks against the full AES were side-channel attacks on specific implementations. A side-channel attack is any attack that is based on information gained from the physical implementation of a cryptosystem, rather than brute force or theoretical weaknesses in the algorithms used by the method of encryption. For example, in April 2005, D.J. Bernstein announced a cache-timing attack that he used to break a custom server that used OpenSSL's AES encryption. The custom server was designed to give out as much timing information as possible, and the attack required over 200 million chosen plaintexts in order to be successful.

RC4

RC4 is the most widely-used software stream cipher. This cipher was designed by Rivest for RSA Data Security, now RSA Security. RC4 is also known as ARC4 or ARCFOUR. RC4 is used in popular protocols such as Secure Sockets Layer (SSL) and Wired Equivalent Privacy (WEP), which is used to secure wireless networks.

RC4 is a variable-key-size stream cipher with byte-oriented operations. The algorithm is based on the use of a random permutation. Although independent analysts have scrutinized the algorithm and it is considered secure, RC4 has weaknesses that argue against its use in new systems. For example, it is especially vulnerable when the beginning of the output keystream is not discarded, when nonrandom or related keys are used, or when a single keystream is used twice. As a result, some ways of using RC4 can lead to very insecure cryptosystems, such as WEP.

RC4 generates a pseudo-random keystream that, for encryption, is combined with the plaintext using bit-wise XOR. Because RC4 is a symmetric cryptographic algorithm, decryption is also performed the same way. To generate the keystream, the cipher makes use of a secret internal state that consists of two parts:

- A permutation of all 256 possible bytes
- Two 8-bit index-pointers

The permutation is initialized with a variable-length key, typically between 40 and 256 bits, using the key-scheduling algorithm, or KSA, which is used to initialize the permutation. Upon completion, the stream of bits is generated using the pseudo-random generation algorithm, which is abbreviated as PRGA. For as many iterations as are needed, the PRGA modifies the state and outputs a byte of the keystream. The design of RC4 avoids the use of LFSRs and is ideal for software implementation, as it requires only byte manipulations. The algorithm used in RC4 is extremely complex and is beyond the scope of the IINS course requirements.

International Data Encryption Algorithm

IDEA, which stands for International Data Encryption Algorithm, is a block cipher designed and presented by Lai and Massey. IDEA is a 64-bit iterative block cipher with a 128-bit key. The encryption process requires eight complex rounds. In other words, the data is encrypted eight times over. While the cipher does not have a Feistel structure, because it is a symmetric cryptographic algorithm, the decryption process is carried out in the same manner as encryption once the decryption subkeys have been calculated from the encryption subkeys.

The cipher structure was designed to be easily implemented in both software and hardware, and the security of IDEA relies on the use of three incompatible types of arithmetic operations on 16-bit words. However some of the arithmetic operations used in IDEA are not particularly fast in software. As a result the speed of IDEA in software is similar to that of DES. IDEA is generally considered to be a very secure cipher, and both the cipher development and its theoretical basis have been openly and widely discussed. Going into specific detail on the IDEA algorithm is beyond the scope of the IINS course requirements.

Blowfish

Blowfish is a 64-bit block cipher developed by Bruce Schneier. While Blowfish provides a good encryption rate in software and has yet to be cracked, it is not as popular as AES. Blowfish is a Feistel cipher and each round consists of a key-dependent permutation and a key-and-data-dependent substitution. All operations are based on XORs and additions on 32-bit words. The key that is used has a variable length, with a maximum length of 448 bits, and is used to generate several subkey arrays. This cipher was designed specifically for 32-bit machines and is significantly faster than DES.

While going into specific details on Blowfish is beyond the scope of the IINS course requirements, it is important to remember that it was designed as a general-purpose algorithm, intended as a replacement for the aging DES. In other words, Blowfish is unpatented and can be used by anyone, anywhere in the world.

Asymmetric Key Cryptography

Now that we have a solid understanding of symmetric key cryptography, we are going to be learning about asymmetric key cryptography, which is also referred to as public-key cryptography. In this section, we are going to learn about asymmetric key cryptography and conclude with the most common public-key algorithms. It is important to remember that in this section, and throughout this guide, asymmetric key cryptography and public-key cryptography mean the same thing and are used interchangeably.

Public-Key Cryptography Overview

Asymmetric key cryptography design uses a two-key pair. One key is used to encrypt the plaintext and the other key is used to decrypt the ciphertext. Unlike symmetric key cryptography, two parties using public-key cryptography can communicate securely over an insecure channel without having to share a secret key.

Public-key cryptography is typically used in digital certification and key management, both of which will be described later in this chapter. However, in theory, asymmetric key cryptography could also be used to actually encrypt data, although this is rarely done because symmetric key cryptography is much more efficient and much less computationally intensive than asymmetric key cryptography. Figure 9.4 provides a basic illustration of the operation of asymmetric key cryptography:

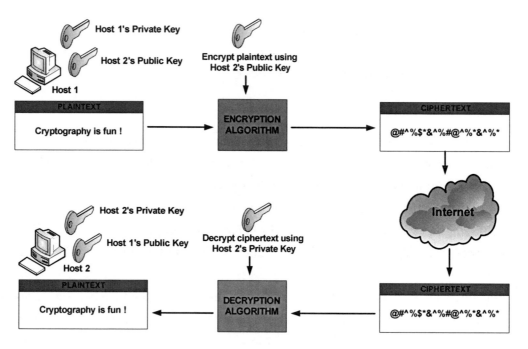

Figure 9.4. Asymmetric Key Cryptography

In Figure 9.4 above, Host 1 wants to send a message to Host 2. Using public-key cryptography, the plaintext is encrypted using the public key of Host 2. The cipher text is then sent over an insecure communications channel, such as the Internet, which is used in this example. In order for Host 2 to view the message, it must decrypt the ciphertext using its private key. Once decrypted, the plaintext message is legible. The same process would be applicable if Host 2 sent data to Host 1.

In asymmetric key cryptography, it is important to know that the public key is widely distributed to all users; however, the private key is never exchanged or revealed to any other party. Another variation of the asymmetric key approach is used to validate the identity of the sender by having the sender encrypt the message using their private key and the receiver decrypt the message using the public key of the sender. If the key pairs match, then the process will work; if not, the message will not be decrypted. This method is typically used to provide non-repudiation, which simply means that the sender cannot deny, or repudiate, that he or she sent the message. This concept is analogous to being captured on camera in broad daylight. Once you view the tape, you cannot deny that it was in fact you.

The two types of asymmetric key cryptography are public key encryption and digital signatures. When public key encryption is employed, a message encrypted with a recipient's public key cannot be decrypted by anyone except a possessor of the matching private key. Referencing the diagram used in the previous example, because the plaintext is encrypted using Host 2s public key, only Host 2 can decrypt the message using the corresponding private key. This method is used for data confidentiality.

When digital signatures are employed, a message signed with a sender's private key can be verified by anyone who has access to the sender's public key, thereby proving that the sender had access to the private key and that the message has not been tampered with. This is used to ensure the authentication of messages, i.e. authenticity.

Public Key Infrastructure (PKI) schemes may employ a trusted third party that issues digital certificates for use by other parties. This trusted third party is referred to as a Certificate Authority or Certification Authority (CA). The CA issues digital certificates that contain a public key and the identity of the owner; however, the private key is never disclosed. The CA signs the public keys of entities in PKI-based systems. If the entity trusts the CA and can verify the CA's signature, then it can also verify that a certain public key does indeed belong to the person identified in the certificate.

The asymmetric key cryptography algorithms that will be described in this section are:

- Rivest, Shamir, and Adleman
- Diffie-Hellman
- Digital Signature Algorithm and Digital Signature Standard
- Public-Key Cryptography Standards

Rivest, Shamir, and Adleman

The RSA algorithm was invented by Ronald L. Rivest, Adi Shamir, and Leonard Adleman in 1977. RSA is an asymmetric cipher and is the first greatest advancement that used the asymmetric cryptography mechanism, suitable for both digital signing and encryption. RSA is one of the most popular and widely implemented asymmetric algorithms that can be used for key exchange, digital signatures, and message encryption. The RSA algorithm involves key generation, encryption, and decryption.

The RSA key generation process is used to generate the public and the private keys. The public key is typically known to everyone (i.e. is non-secret) and is used for encrypting messages. Messages encrypted with the public key can only be decrypted using the private key, which is secret. The details pertaining to the computation of the RSA algorithm are beyond the scope of the IINS course requirements. They will not be described in this chapter.

RSA encryption and decryption processes use both public and private keys. Public keys are used to encrypt messages and create ciphertext from plaintext, while private keys are used to decrypt messages and create plaintext from ciphertext. When used in practice, RSA is generally combined with some padding scheme, which further secures RSA. Padding is the process of preparing a message for encryption or signing with a low-level cryptographic algorithm, such as a one-way hash function. Standards such as PKCS #1 have been carefully designed to securely pad messages prior to RSA encryption. PKCS is described in detail later in this section.

RSA has proven to have several disadvantages and flaws from a security perspective. One of the main weaknesses of RSA is that it is significantly slower to compute when compared to other secret-key algorithms, such as DES and Triple-DES. Additionally, RSA has some security implications that should be considered. For example, Cisco's IKE implementation uses a Diffie-Hellman exchange to get the secret keys. With the Diffie-Hellman exchange, if DES is used, the key never crosses the network, which is not the case with RSA encryption and signing. IKE and Diffie-Hellman will be described later in this chapter.

Another disadvantage that is important to know is that RSA is not public domain. In other words, you must be licensed by RSA Data Security to use RSA. From a security perspective, Branch Prediction Analysis (BPA) attacks, which use a spy process running alongside the RSA process, allow attackers to collect almost all the secret bits used in an RSA signing operation by monitoring the states of a CPU. This information allows attackers successfully to extract almost all secret key bits used by RSA—effectively cracking it. Additionally, RSA has also effectively been cracked by using an Adaptive Chosen Ciphertext Attack (CCA2), which is an attack where an attacker sends a number of ciphertexts to be decrypted and then proceeds to use the results of these decryptions to select subsequent ciphertexts.

RSA algorithms are available in varying standards, such as RC1, RC2, RC3, RC4, RC5, and RC6. All RC ciphers were named after Ronald Rivest (the abbreviation RC stands for Ron's Code). RC4 has already been described earlier in this chapter; RC3 was broken at RSA Security during development and was never published; and RC1 was also never published. The following section provides a brief description of RC2, RC5, and RC6:

- RC2 is a block cipher designed by Ron Rivest. RC2 has a block size of 64 bits and is about two to three times faster than DES in software. An additional string, between 40 to 88 bits long, referred to as salt, can be used to thwart attackers who try to pre-compute a large look-up table of possible encryptions.

- RC5 is a fast block cipher also designed by Ronald Rivest. The RC5 algorithm uses a variable block size, a variable key size, and a variable number of rounds. Block sizes can be 32 bits, 64 bits, or 128 bits in length. The number of rounds can range from 0 to 255, while the key can range from 0 bits to 2040 bits in size. There are three routines in RC5: key expansion, encryption, and decryption. Going into detail on these is beyond the scope of the IINS course requirements.

- RC6 is a block cipher based on RC5 and was designed by Rivest, Sidney, and Yin. Like RC5, RC6 uses a variable block size, key size, and number of rounds; again, the upper limit on the key size is 2040 bits.

Diffie-Hellman

The Diffie-Hellman algorithm, abbreviated as DH, was introduced shortly after the RSA algorithm was published. DH allows two parties to establish a shared secret over insecure communications channels, such as the Internet. Diffie-Hellman is a public-key distributing system, also known as a key-exchange protocol, which uses asymmetric key cryptography. Contrary to the RSA algorithm, DH is not used for authentication or digital signatures. Instead, it is used only for secret key exchange.

DH ensures that by exchanging just the public keys, both devices can generate a session and ensure that data is encrypted and decrypted by valid sources only. It is imperative to keep in mind that only public keys are exchanged (in clear text) over the public network. Private keys will never be exchanged over the network. By using each device's public key, and running the key through the DH algorithm, a common session key is generated, which can then be used to encrypt subsequent messages using a symmetric key algorithm.

The DH protocol has two system parameters: p and g. They are both public and may be used by all the users in a system. Parameter p is a prime number and parameter g, which is usually called a generator, is an integer less than p. These two non-secret (public) numbers must be agreed upon by both parties before the DH exchange process can begin. If the two parties do not agree on these two non-secret numbers, the DH exchange will not proceed.

Figure 9.5 illustrates a basic Diffie-Hellman exchange between two hosts that want to agree on a shared secret key:

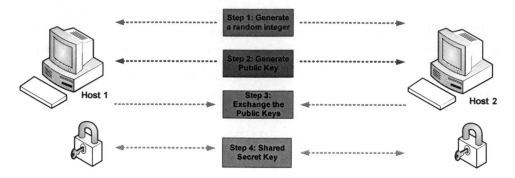

Figure 9.5. Diffe-Hellman Exchange

In Figure 9.5 above, Host 1 and Host 2 want to agree on a shared secret key using the Diffie-Hellman key agreement protocol. The first thing that happens is that both Host 1 and Host 2 generate a random private value drawn from the set of integers, as illustrated in step 1. Next, Host 1 and Host 2 derive their public values using parameters p and g and their private keys, as illustrated in step 2.

In the third step of the process, Host 1 and Host 2 exchange their public values. Finally, as illustrated in step 4, Host 1 and Host 2 compute the shared secret key. This symmetric shared key is then used to facilitate the secure exchange of data between Host 1 and Host 2.

While the DH protocol depends on the discrete logarithm problem, which assumes that it is computationally infeasible to calculate the shared secret key, its security is still susceptible to other attacks, with the most common being MITM attacks. For example, referencing the diagram used in the explanation of the protocol operation, an attacker intercepts Host 1's public key and sends his or her own public key to Host 2, and when Host 2 transmits its public value, the attacker substitutes it with his or her own public value and sends it to Host 1. Thus, the attacker and Host 1 agree on one shared key and the attacker and Host 2 agree on another shared key.

After this exchange, the attacker simply decrypts any messages sent out by Host 1 or Host 2, and then reads and possibly modifies them before re-encrypting with the appropriate key and transmitting them to the other party. This vulnerability is present because Diffie-Hellman key exchange does not authenticate the participants. However, this can be mitigated by including the use of digital signatures and the authenticated Diffie-Hellman key agreement protocol.

The authenticated Diffie-Hellman key agreement protocol, or Station-to-Station (STS) protocol, was developed in 1992 to defeat the MITM attack on the Diffie-Hellman key agreement protocol.

The immunity is achieved by allowing the two parties to authenticate themselves to each other by the use of digital signatures and public-key certificates, both of which will be described in the following sections in this chapter.

The basic idea behind STS is that prior to execution of the protocol, the two parties (e.g. Host 1 and Host 2) each obtain a public and private key pair, as well as a certificate for the public key. During the protocol, Host 1, for example, computes a signature on certain messages, covering the public value. Host 2 proceeds in a similar way. Even though an attacker is still able to intercept messages between Host 1 and Host 2, the attacker cannot forge signatures without Host 1's private key and Host 2's private key. Hence, the enhanced protocol defeats the MITM attack.

Digital Signature Algorithm and Digital Signature Standard

Digital Signature Algorithm (DSA) is an asymmetric key algorithm proposed by the NIST in 1991 for their use in Digital Signature Standard. DSA is also a Federal Information Processing Standards (FIPS) standard for digital signatures.

DSA is based on the discrete logarithm problem, which is also used by the DH protocol. Unlike RSA, which can be used for both encryption and digital signatures, the DSA can only be used to provide digital signatures, which ensures the authentication of messages. Additionally, in DSA, signature generation is faster than signature verification, whereas with the RSA algorithm, signature verification is very much faster than signature generation.

The use of digital signatures protects data from undetected changes while traversing the network. This is typically accomplished by using a hashing algorithm in conjunction with DSS. Hashing algorithms, such as MD5, will be described in the following section in this chapter. Figure 9.6 provides an illustration of the DSS signature generation used in conjunction with a keyed-hash algorithm that ensures that data is protected over an insecure channel:

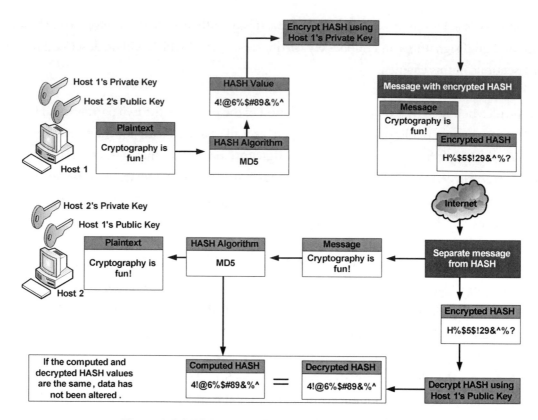

Figure 9.6. DES Signature Generation with Keyed-Hash

Given that Figure 9.6 above is self-explanatory, and to avoid being redundant, we will not describe the step-by-step process illustrated above. However, it is worth pointing out the fact that it is imperative that the computed and decrypted hash values are the same. If they are not, this indicates that the data has been modified along the way.

Public-Key Cryptography Standards

Public-Key Cryptography Standards (or PKCS) is a set of interoperable public-key cryptography standards and guidelines designed and published by RSA Data Security. There are numerous PKCS standards; and while going into detail on them is beyond the IINS course requirements, Table 9.3 lists and describes these standards:

Table 9.3. PKCS Standards

Standard	Description
PKCS # 1	RSA Cryptography Standard. Defines the mathematical properties and format of RSA public and private keys and the basic algorithms and encoding/padding schemes for performing RSA encryption, decryption, and producing and verifying signatures. Standardized in RFC 3447.
PKCS # 2	This standard was withdrawn and merged into PKCS # 1. It covered RSA encryption of message digests. This standard is no longer active.
PKCS # 3	This specifies the Diffie-Hellman Key Agreement Standard.
PKCS # 4	This standard was withdrawn and merged into PKCS # 1. It covered RSA key syntax. This standard is no longer active.
PKCS # 5	This specifies the Password-based Encryption Standard. It was standardized in RFC 2898.
PKCS # 6	This specifies the Extended-Certificate Syntax Standard. It defines extensions to the old X.509v1 certificate specification, which was made obsolete by X.509v3.
PKCS # 7	This specifies the Cryptographic Message Syntax Standard. It is used to sign or encrypt messages under a Public Key Infrastructure, or PKI. It is standardized in RFC 2315. This standard describes general syntax for encrypted messages and messages with digital signatures.
PKCS # 8	This specifies the Private-Key Information Syntax Standard. Used to carry private certificate keypairs, which may be encrypted or unencrypted.
PKCS # 9	This specifies the Selected Attribute Types and defines these types for use in PKCS #6 extended certificates, PKCS #7 digitally signed messages, PKCS #8 private-key information, and PKCS #10 certificate-signing requests. It is standardized in RFC 2985.
PKCS # 10	This specifies the Certification Request Syntax Standard, as specified in RFC 2986. It defines the format of messages sent to a Certification Authority to request certification of a public key.
PKCS # 11	This specifies the Cryptographic Token Interface, or cryptoki. It is an API that defines a generic interface to cryptographic tokens. It is often used for single sign-on and smart card authentication.
PKCS # 12	This specifies the Personal Information Exchange Syntax Standard. It defines a file forma commonly used to store private keys with accompanying public-key certificates protected with a password-based symmetric system. This standard can be used as a format for the Java key store.
PKCS # 13	This specifies the Elliptic Curve Cryptography (ECC) Standard. This is still under development.
PKCS # 14	This specifies the Pseudo-Random Number Generation (PRNG) Standard. PRNG is an algorithm that is used to generate a sequence of numbers that is not truly random.
PKCS # 15	This specifies the Cryptographic Token Information Format Standard. It defines a standard allowing users or cryptographic tokens to identify themselves to applications, independent of the application's cryptoki (PKCS # 11) implementation or other Application Programming Interface (API).

Hash Algorithms

Hash algorithms are referred to by many various names. They may be referred to as a hash function, a message digest, or one-way encryption. Hash algorithms use a mathematical formula to compute a fixed-length hash value based on the original plaintext. One significant advantage to hashing plaintext is that the original message cannot be reconstituted, even with knowledge of the hash algorithm.

Hash functions are generally faster than encryption algorithms and are typically used to provide a digital fingerprint of any type of data to ensure that information has not been modified or altered during transmission, which provides information integrity. Additionally, hash algorithms are commonly used for both data integrity and digital certificates. In a manner similar to block ciphers, hash algorithms are also susceptible to the avalanche effect, which results in completely different ciphertext, if even a single bit in the plaintext is changed. For example, the MD5 hash for the word Test is 0cbc6611f5540bd0809a388dc95a615b; but if the entire word was written in lower-caps (i.e. test) the resulting MD5 hash would be 098f6bcd4621d373cade4e832627b4f6.

The following two hash algorithms will be described in detail in the next two sections:

- Message Digest
- Secure Hash Algorithm

Message Digest

Message Digest (MD) algorithms are a series of byte-oriented cryptographic hash functions that take variable-length data and produce a mathematically computed 128-bit fixed-length hash value. This hash is commonly referred to as the fingerprint, message digest, or simply just as the digest. There are three message digest algorithms, all developed by Rivest, which are:

- MD2
- MD4
- MD5

MD2 is standardized in RFC 1319. This algorithm was developed by Rivest in 1989, and was designed and optimized for 8-bit machines, or machines with limited memory, such as smart cards.

MD4 was developed by Rivest in 1989 and standardized in RFC 1320. MD4 was designed and optimized for 32-bit machines. MD4 is similar to MD2 but was designed specifically for faster processing in software.

Because MD2 and MD4 are considered broken—i.e. have been cracked—Rivest designed MD5 in 1991. MD5 is standardized in RFC 1321 and is similar to MD4, although additional enhancements have been added to provide better security. For example, salt—an additional string of bits (which was described earlier in this chapter)—can be used with MD5 to enhance security. MD5 remains popular and is widely used in various products and applications.

For example, the `enable secret` command used in Cisco IOS software uses an MD5 hashing algorithm. However, it should be noted that MD5 is no longer considered very secure because it has been documented that it can be broken. Figure 9.7 provides a basic illustration of the MD5 hashing algorithm:

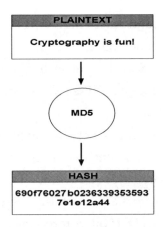

Figure 9.7. MD5 Hashing

Secure Hash Algorithm

Secure Hash Algorithm (SHA) is another series of popular cryptographic hash algorithms. SHA is the newer, more secure version of MD5, and Hash-based Message Authentication (HMAC) provides further security with the inclusion of a key exchange. HMAC, which can be used in conjunction with SHA, is a type of message authentication code (MAC) that may be used to verify data integrity and the authenticity of a message. The cryptographic strength of the HMAC depends on the cryptographic strength of the underlying hash function, on the size and quality of the key, and on the size of the hash output length in bits. Going into detail on the algorithms used in HMAC is beyond the scope of the IINS course requirements.

SHA produces a 160-bit output and was developed by the National Security Agency (NSA) and published as a US government standard. The SHA algorithm is also used in NIST's Secure Hash Standard (SHS). While SHA is computationally slower than MD5, it is much more secure. As is the case with MD, there are several versions of the SHA hash algorithm, which are:

- SHA-0
- SHA-1
- SHA-2
- SHA-3

SHA-0 was the original specification of the algorithm published in 1993. At that time, it was published as the Secure Hash Standard. SHA-0 did not have a long lifespan and was withdrawn by the NSA shortly after publication to be superseded by SHA-1. Due to the sensitive nature of the algorithm, the only information provided by the NSA on the migration to SHA-1 was that there was a need to correct a flaw in the SHA-0 algorithm that reduced its cryptographic security.

SHA-1 was introduced in 1995 and standardized in RFC 3147. SHA-1 is used in a variety of applications and protocols, including, but not limited to, Transport Layer Security (TLS), Pretty Good Privacy (PGP), Secure Sockets Layer (SSL), Secure Shell (SSH), and IP Security (IPsec). SSL and SSH have already been described in this guide. IPsec will be described later in this chapter.

TLS is the successor of SSL. Like SSL, TLS is a cryptographic protocol that provides security for communications over networks such as the Internet. Both TLS and SSL encrypt the segments of network connections at the Transport Layer end-to-end. TLS provides endpoint authentication and communications confidentiality over the Internet using cryptography. TLS provides RSA security with 1024 and 2048 bit strengths. TLS involves three basic phases, which are peer negotiation for algorithm support, key exchange and authentication, and symmetric cipher encryption and message authentication.

PGP is a software package developed by Philip Zimmermann that provides cryptographic routines for email and file storage applications. PGP is most commonly used for signing, encrypting, and decrypting emails to increase the security of email communications.

SHA-1 is based on principles similar to those used by Rivest in the design of the MD4 and MD5 message digest algorithms.

Four additional variants of SHA have also been introduced. These variants, which are collectively referred to as SHA-2, are SHA-224, SHA-256, SHA-384, and SHA-512. These variants are described in RFC 4634. SHA-256 and SHA-512 are novel hash functions computed with 32- and 64-bit words, respectively. They use different shift amounts and additive constants, but their structures are otherwise virtually identical, differing only in the number of rounds. SHA-224 and SHA-384 are simply truncated versions of SHA-256 and SHA-512, computed with different initial values. However, it should be noted that these hash functions are not as widely used as SHA-1, even though they provide much better security, because protocols like SSL do not make it easy to introduce new hash functions without breaking backwards compatibility.

SHA-3 is still in the development phase and has yet to be standardized. As of the time of this writing, the publication of the new standard is scheduled to take place in the year 2012.

VPN Technologies

As defined in RFC 2828, a Virtual Private Network (VPN) is:

A restricted-use, logical (i.e., artificial or simulated) computer network that is constructed from the system resources of a relatively public, physical (i.e., real) network (such as the Internet), often by using encryption (located at hosts or gateways), and often by tunneling links of the virtual network across the real network.

There are three distinct types of VPN technologies that are available today, as follows:

- Secure Virtual Private Networks
- Trusted Virtual Private Networks
- Hybrid Virtual Private Networks

Secure Virtual Private Networks

Secure VPNs are also referred to as Cryptographic VPNs. These VPN types use cryptographic technologies and protocols to ensure the confidentiality, integrity, and authenticity of data. Secure VPNs are often deployed over insecure communication channels, such as the Internet. These VPN types are commonly used to replace or augment existing point-to-point networks that utilize dedicated leased lines (e.g. T1/E1 and T3/E3 circuits) or even WAN networks over common technologies such as Frame Relay. Secure VPN technologies include:

- IP Security (IPsec)
- Layer 2 Tunneling Protocol (L2TP) over IPsec
- Point-to-Point Tunneling Protocol (PPTP)
- SSL Encryption (SSL VPN)

The only secure VPN technology that you are required to demonstrate detailed knowledge of, as well as configure and troubleshoot, as a requirement of the IINS certification is IPsec VPNs. However, it is important that you demonstrate some basic knowledge on the other secure VPN technologies listed above. IPsec will be described in the next section in this chapter.

The Layer 2 Tunnel Protocol (L2TP) is an emerging Internet Engineering Task Force (IETF) standard that combines the best features of two existing tunneling protocols: Cisco's Layer 2 Forwarding (L2F) and Microsoft's Point-to-Point Tunneling Protocol (PPTP). L2F is beyond the scope of the IINS course requirements. L2TP is one of the key building blocks for virtual private networks in the dial access space. It does not provide any encryption on its own but can be deployed in conjunction with IPsec to provide encryption services and data confidentiality.

The Point-to-Point Tunneling Protocol (PPTP) is a method for implementing virtual private networks. In a manner similar to L2TP, PPTP does not provide confidentiality or encryption by itself and, as such, is typically deployed in conjunction with IPsec to provide encryption services and data confidentiality. PPTP has been made obsolete by L2TP and IPSec.

The SSL VPN solution offers a flexible and highly secure way to extend network resources to virtually any remote user with access to the Internet and a web browser. Unlike traditional VPNs that require software programs to allow client machines to connect to the VPN, the SSL VPN is accessible via HTTP over almost all web browsers. This flexibility allows SSL VPN technology to be customized for special applications, for example.

SSL VPNs support asymmetric algorithms, such as RSA and the Diffie-Hellman protocol, for authentication and key exchange. Additionally, SSL VPNs use symmetric algorithms, such as DES, Triple-DES, and AES, for encryption. SSL VPNs are becoming very popular and are perceived by many as a solid alternative and possible replacement for all IPsec VPNs. However, it should be noted that SSL VPNs can be deployed on routers in conjunction with IPsec VPNs (although this does have some performance impact), allowing greater secure VPN flexibility.

The three most common secure VPN deployment scenarios are:

- Intranet-based VPNs
- Internet-based VPNs
- Extranet-based VPNs

An Intranet-based VPN is used to provide protection for private communications within an enterprise or organization that may or may not involve traffic traversing a WAN. An Intranet-based VPN connection takes advantage of IP connectivity in an organization intranet. Figure 9.8 illustrates an Intranet-based VPN. This VPN type is used to allow secure communication between users and hosts in the Sales and Finance departments of Company Z:

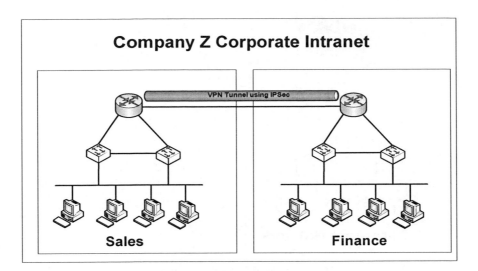

Figure 9.8. Intranet VPN

Internet-based VPNs are the most common types of VPNs. These VPNs protect private communications over the public network, or Internet. Internet-based VPNs can take several forms. Although there are numerous types of secure Internet-based VPNs, the only type that falls within the confinements of the IINS course requirements is a site-to-site VPN using IPsec. Figure 9.9 serves to illustrate a typical site-to-site Internet-based VPN between two different office locations of the same company:

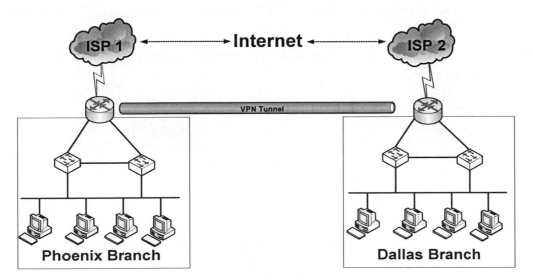

Figure 9.9. Internet VPN

Another common Internet-based VPN is a remote access VPN. A remote access VPN is used to establish a secure connection to a trusted network over unsecure communications channels, such as the Internet. A remote access VPN is illustrated in Figure 9.10:

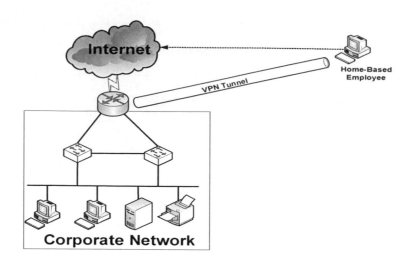

Figure 9.10. Remote Access VPN

In Figure 9.10 illustrated above, the home-based employee uses a remote VPN to establish a secure connection to the corporate network. The home-based employee uses software installed onto his or her PC to establish a connection to the VPN termination device, also referred to as the headend VPN device. Once a secure connection has been established, the home-based employee is able to access internal network resources in the same manner as employees physically located at the corporate office.

Extranet-based VPNs provide private communications between two or more separate entities. For example, a company can deploy an extranet VPN between its headquarters to certain business partner networks. The business partner is given access only to the headquarters' public server to perform various IP-based network tasks, such as placing and managing product orders, as illustrated in Figure 9.11:

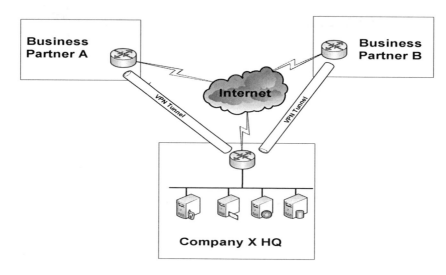

Figure 9.11. Extranet VPN

Trusted Virtual Private Networks

Trusted VPNs are also referred to as non-cryptographic VPNs. These VPN technologies are usually provided by a dedicated service provider. Trusted VPNs allow service providers to offer a dedicated or leased circuit or channel to a customer, which allows pseudo point-to-point communication for different customer locations.

Unlike secure VPNs, the security and integrity of trusted VPN traffic relies on the fact that the circuit is not shared because each circuit is dedicated to a single site. Trusted VPN technologies are beyond the scope of the IINS course requirements and will not be described further.

Hybrid Virtual Private Networks

A hybrid VPN is a combination of both a trusted VPN and a secure VPN. Hybrid VPNs are an emerging technology that is slowly gaining momentum. While going into detail on the hybrid VPN technologies is beyond the scope of the IINS course requirements, it is important to note that a hybrid VPN is only secure in the parts that are based on secure VPNs. That is, adding a secure VPN to a trusted VPN does not increase the security for the entire trusted VPN, only to the part that was directly secured. The secure VPN only acquires the advantages of the trusted VPN.

IP Security

As stated in RFC 2401:

IPsec provides security services at the IP layer by enabling a system to select required security protocols, determine the algorithm(s) to use for the service(s), and put in place any cryptographic keys required to provide the requested services. IPsec can be used to protect one or more "paths" between a pair of hosts, between a pair of security gateways, or between a security gateway and a host. (The term "security gateway" is used throughout the IPsec documents to refer to an intermediate system that implements IPsec protocols. For example, a router or a firewall implementing IPsec is a security gateway.)

The IPsec framework is a set of open standards developed by the Internet Engineering Task Force (IETF). IPsec is implemented by a set of cryptographic protocols for securing IP datagrams. The IPsec framework secures IP traffic operating at the Network Layer of the OSI Model, thus securing all network applications and communications that use the IP network.

While IPsec is defined in a number of RFCs, it is not a mandatory requirement for IPv4. However, IPsec is a mandatory requirement for IPv6. IPv6 is beyond the scope of the requirements of the IINS course and will not be described in this guide. Using a combination of hashing, symmetric key, and asymmetric key cryptographic algorithms, the IPsec framework offers the following security services:

- Peer Authentication
- Data Confidentiality
- Data Integrity
- Data Origin Authentication
- Replay Detection
- Access Control
- Traffic Flow Confidentiality

IPsec Modes

IPsec can use two different modes to propagate data across networks. These modes, which are commonly referred to as Security Association, or SA, are used to provide security to a given IP connection. The two modes used by IPsec are transport mode and tunnel mode.

Transport mode protects the payload (data) of the original IP datagram. This mode is typically used for host-to-host and end-to-end sessions, for example, protecting data between Host 1 in Site 1 and Host 2 in Site 2, as illustrated in Figure 9.12:

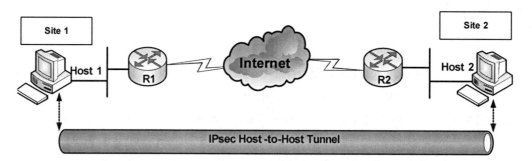

Figure 9.12. Transport Mode for Host-to-Host Comms

In transport mode, the original IP header is retained, while the IPsec header is inserted between the original IP header and the payload. Figure 9.13 shown below illustrates the insertion of the IPsec header between the original IP header and the data, or payload, when using transport mode:

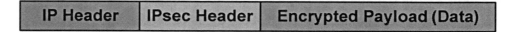

Figure 9.13. IPSec Header Inside IP Packet

Transport mode can be used only when two different IPsec endpoints are the source and destination (respectively) of the original IP datagram, or packet. Transport mode is commonly used by end systems (i.e. hosts) to protect individual sockets or by intermediate systems (i.e. routers) to protect traffic that is already tunneled.

Tunnel mode is used to protect data in network-to-network (i.e. between networks or subnets) or site-to-site scenarios; for example, tunnel mode would be used to protect data between the 10.1.1.0/24 subnet in Site 1 and the 192.168.1.0/24 subnet in Site 2. When operating in tunnel mode, IPsec encrypts traffic through IPsec peers, as illustrated in Figure 9.14:

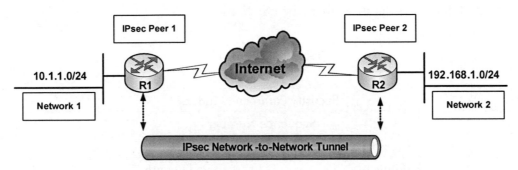

Figure 9.14. Tunnel Mode for Network-to-Network Comms

Tunnel mode allows IPsec to encapsulate the entire IP packet (i.e. the IP header as well as the payload or data) in a new IP packet, as illustrated in Figure 9.15:

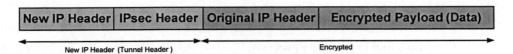

Figure 9.15. New IP Packet Generated

It is important to understand that IPsec is unidirectional. In other words, SA is required for both inbound and outbound connections. Internet Key Exchange (IKE), which will be described in detail later in this chapter, allows for bidirectional SAs. In both transport and tunnel mode, IPsec adds a new header to all IP packets to provide information for securing the data within the original IP datagram. This header may be either an Encapsulating Security Payload or an Authentication Header. These two types of headers are described in the next two sections.

Encapsulating Security Payload

Encapsulating Security Payload (ESP) is an IP-based protocol that uses IP port 50 for communication between IPsec peers. ESP is documented in RFC 4303 and is used to provide the confidentiality, integrity, and authenticity of the data. Additionally, ESP also provides anti-replay protection services. The IPsec anti-replay service is described later in this chapter.

ESP does not provide any kind of protection for the outer IP header. In other words, ESP does not encrypt the original IP header. When used for data integrity, ESP does not include the invariant field in the IP header, which means that ESP is unable to detect any alternations during packet delivery. Table 9.4 illustrates the structure of the ESP header:

Table 9.4. ESP Header

0	7	15	23	31
Security Parameters Index				
Sequence Number				
Payload Data				
Padding			Pad Length	Next Header
Authentication Data				

The information contained in each field is as follows:

- Security Parameters Index

  The Security Parameters Index (SPI) is an arbitrary 32-bit value that, in conjunction with the destination IP address and the security protocol (ESP), uniquely identifies the Security Association for this datagram. A reserved SPI value will not normally be assigned by IANA unless the use of the assigned SPI value is specified in an RFC. The SPI is typically selected by the destination system upon establishment of an SA. This field is mandatory. The value of zero is reserved for local, implementation-specific use and must never be sent across the wire.

- Sequence Number

  The Sequence Number field is an unsigned 32-bit field that contains a consistently increasing counter. As is the case with the SPI, the sequence number is mandatory and must always be sent by the sender, even if the receiver does not elect to enable the anti-replay service for a specific SA. The sender's counter and the receiver's counter are initialized to 0 when an SA is established. The first packet sent using a given SA will have a sequence number of 1. If anti-replay is enabled, which is the default, the transmitted sequence number must never be allowed to cycle. Thus, the sender's counter and the receiver's counter must be reset by establishing a new SA and thus a new key prior to the transmission of the second packet on an SA.

- Payload Data

  This 32-bit field contains the data described by the Next Header field. This field is mandatory and is an integral number of bytes in length. If the algorithm used to encrypt the payload requires cryptographic synchronization data, e.g. an Initialization Vector, then this data may be carried explicitly in the Payload Data field. Any encryption algorithm that requires such explicit, per-packet synchronization data must indicate the length, any structure for such data, and the location of this data as part of an RFC specifying how the algorithm is used with ESP. If such synchronization data is implicit, the algorithm for deriving the data MUST be part of the RFC.

- Padding

  The Padding field is a variable-length field. Padding is used when the frame needs to meet minimum frame size formats. Padding is used, irrespective of encryption algorithm requirements, to ensure that the resulting ciphertext terminates on a 4-byte boundary. Specifically, the Pad Length and Next Header fields must be right-aligned within a 4-byte word to ensure that the Authentication Data field, if present, is aligned on a 4-byte boundary.

- Pad Length

  This 8-bit field is used to define the length of padding used. In other words, this field specifies the size of the Padding field, in bytes.

- Next Header

  The Next Header field is an 8-bit field that identifies the type of data contained in the Payload Data field. It is simply an IPv4 protocol number describing the format of the Payload Data field.

- Authentication Data

  The Authentication Data field is a variable-length field that contains the Integrity Check Value (ICV) computed over the ESP packet minus the Authentication Data. The ICV is a checksum capable of detecting modification of an information system and is the result of the integrity process. In other words, the ICV is used to ensure data integrity. The length of the Authentication Data field is specified by the authentication function selected. This field is optional and is included only if the authentication service has been selected for the SA in question. The authentication algorithm specification must specify the length of the ICV, as well as the comparison rules and the processing steps for validation.

Figure 9.16 illustrates the ESP header when using IPsec in transport mode:

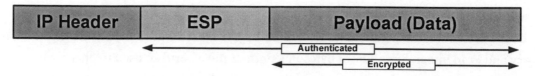

Figure 9.16. ESP Header Using Transport Mode

As illustrated in Figure 9.16 above, both ESP and the payload are authenticated; however, only the payload is actually encrypted. Figure 9.17 illustrates the ESP header when using IPsec in tunnel mode:

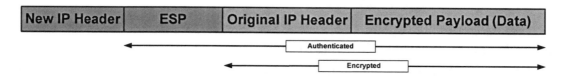

Figure 9.17. ESP Header Using Tunnel Mode

In tunnel mode, the ESP header, original IP header, and payload are authenticated; however, only the original IP header and payload are actually encrypted, as illustrated above.

Authentication Header

Authentication Header (AH) is an IP-based protocol that uses IP port 51 for communication between IPsec peers. AH is used to protect the integrity and authenticity of data, and also offers anti-replay protection; however, AH does not provide confidentiality protection. Unlike ESP, AH provides protection to the IP header; however, not all fields in the IP header are encrypted. For example, the TTL field is not encrypted. AH is described in RFC 2402.

When using AH, authentication is performed by applying a one-way hash to create a message digest of the packet. Replay detection can be implemented using the sequence number in the IP packet header. Table 9.5 illustrates the AH header structure:

Table 9.5. Authentication Header Structure

0	7	15	23	31
Next Header		Length	0	
Security Parameters Index				
Sequence Number				
Authentication Data				

The Next Header, SPI, Sequence Number, and Authentication Data fields contained in the AH header are the same as those contained in the ESP header. To avoid being redundant, they will not be described again. The Length field is an 8-bit field specifying the length of the AH header in 32-bit words, minus 2.

AH can operate in transport or tunnel mode. Unlike ESP, AH also protects the fields in the outer IP header (i.e. the original IP header in transport mode) or the newly added IP header in tunnel mode, which are normally considered invariable. AH ensures that if the original IP header has been altered, the packet is rejected.

IPsec Anti-Replay Service

Both ESP and AH provide an anti-replay mechanism, which is used to defeat replay attacks and is mainly based on sequence numbers combined with authentication. The sender increments the sequence number after each transmission, and the receiver can check the sequence number and reject the packet if it is out of sequence. However, as stated previously, checking and using the sequence numbers is optional for the receiver. Without the anti-replay mechanism, an attacker could replay intercepted encrypted packets.

Before delving into the configuration of IPsec on Cisco IOS routers, it is important to understand how keys are exchanged between secure devices to ensure that data is not compromised. IPsec ensures that once an IPsec tunnel is created, the keys are not modified, which prevents attackers from replicating the keys and creating IPsec tunnels to insecure locations. Internet Security Association and Key Management Protocol (ISAKMP) and IKE provide the framework that allows for secure key determination and distribution mechanisms in IPsec.

Internet Security Association and Key Management Protocol

ISAKMP describes the framework for key management and defines the procedure and packet format necessary to establish, negotiate, modify, and delete Security Association. ISAKMP offers the identification of the peers only; it does not offer a key exchange mechanism. ISAKAMP is documented in RFC 2408 but was made obsolete by RFC 4306, which standardized Internet Key Exchange version 2.

Internet Key Exchange

IKE is a hybrid protocol. It is basically a combination of ISAKMP, Oakley key exchange, and the SKEME protocol. Oakley describes a series of key exchanges, called modes, and details the services provided by each. These services include perfect forward secrecy for keys, identity protection, and authentication. SKEME describes a versatile key exchange technique that provides anonymity, non-repudiation, and quick key refreshment. Both Oakley and SKEME are beyond the scope of requirements for the IINS course.

IKE defines the mechanism for exchanging keys. IKE derives authenticated keying material and negotiates SAs that are used for the ESP and AH protocols. IKE uses UDP port 500 and is documented in RFC 2409, and updated in RFC 4306, which is IKEv2 (the current IKE standard).

> **NOTE:** The terms ISAKMP and IKE are often used interchangeably in many texts. While we will only be using the term IKE in this chapter, you should be aware of this fact if you encounter a question on ISAKMP or IKE during the IINS certification exam.

IKE is a two-phase, multimode protocol that offers the following three methods of authenticating a remote peer:

- The pre-shared key method uses statically defined keys and is the most common method because of its ease of deployment; however, this method is not scalable or secure.
- The public key signature method, also referred to as the RSA-Signature method, is the most secure method and requires Public Key Infrastructure (PKI).
- The public key encryption, commonly referred to as the RSA-Nonce, is similar to the public key signature method but requires prior knowledge of the peer's public key. However, it is important to know that this method has limited support.

IKE phase 1 verifies the identity of a remote peer and the two peers establish a secure authentication communications channel. This phase is primarily concerned with the protection suite for IKE messages. IKE phase 1 also protects the negotiation of phase 2 communication. Phase 1 operations are required infrequently and can use either main or aggressive mode.

Main mode is the default method used in most implementations. Main mode defines six message exchanges to establish SA. Messages 1 and 2 are used to negotiate IKE policy, messages 3 and 4 are used to perform an authenticated Diffie-Hellman exchange, and messages 5 and 6 are used to protect the identities of the IKE peers. This exchange is illustrated in Figure 9.18:

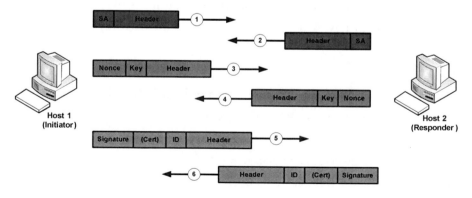

Figure 9.18. Main Mode in Operation

Figure 9.18 illustrated above shows the messages exchanged between Host 1, the initiator, and Host 2, the responder, during IKE phase 1.

Messages 1 and 2 are used to negotiate the IKE policy. Message 1, sent by the initiator, offers acceptable encryption, authentication algorithms, and proposals, such as 3DES, MD5, RSA, and the DH group number. The DH group number, also referred to as the prime modulus group, is used to specify the size, in bits, of the DH key. Currently, Cisco IOS supports three groups, which are listed and described in Table 9.6:

Table 9.6. DH Groups

DH Group Number	Description
1	This specifies the 768-bit Diffie-Hellman group.
2	This specifies the 1024-bit Diffie-Hellman group.
3	This specifies the 1536-bit Diffie-Hellman group.

Message 2, sent by the responder, states whether the proposals are accepted, and if not, then what proposals Host 2 is prepared to accept. All messages are carried in UDP packets with a destination port of 500. The UDP data comprises a header, the SA payload, and one or more proposals. Message 1 offers many proposals, while message 2 contains only a single proposal.

Messages 3 and 4 carry out the DH exchange. Message 3 contains the DH key and nonce, or bit string. The key value is usually 1024 bits in length. Message 4, from the responder, also contains the DH key and bit string. Message types 3 and 4 also contain the remote peer's IP public key and hashing algorithm. A common session key is created on both ends and the remaining IKE messages exchanged from this point are encrypted. If perfect forward secrecy (PFS) is enabled, then another DH exchange will be completed. PFS is the property that ensures that a session key derived from a set of long-term public and private keys will not be compromised if one of the (long-term) private keys is compromised in the future.

Messages 5 and 6 are used to protect the identities of the IKE peers. Message 5 contains the initiator signature, cert (if used for authentication data, for example), and ID. Message 6, received from the responder, provides the same information. Messages 5 and 6 are the last stage before traffic is sent over the IPsec tunnel. In essence, message 5 allows the initiator to authenticate the responder and message 6 allows the responder to authenticate the initiator. These messages are not sent in clear text; rather, they are encrypted using the agreed upon encryption methods in messages 1 and 2.

Aggressive mode is faster than main mode because it uses three message exchanges to establish phase 1. However, this means that aggressive mode is not as secure as main mode. Aggressive mode uses a three-way packet exchange, while main mode uses a six-way packet exchange. Figure 9.19 illustrates message exchange when using aggressive mode:

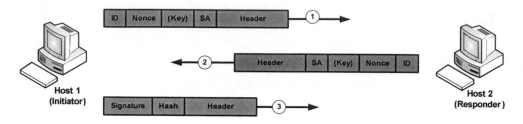

Figure 9.19. Aggressive Mode Exchange

In aggressive mode, the first message from the initiator is used to perform the key exchange, ID, and nonce, as well as for parameter proposals, e.g. hashing algorithms.

The responder uses message 2 for its key exchange and ID, as well as to specify whether the parameters presented are acceptable.

Finally, in message 3, the initiator provides its signature, hash, and ID. IKE phase 1 is considered complete after this exchange.

IKE phase 2 is used to protect the data and establish SA for IPsec. IKE phase 2 is used to negotiate the protection suite (i.e. ESP and AH), the algorithms that will be used within the protection suite (e.g. DES, 3DES, AES, or SHA-1), the networks or traffic that is being encrypted, which is sometimes referred to as proxy identities or phase 2 identities, and any optional keying material for negotiated protocols.

Unlike IKE phase 1, IKE phase 2 has one mode, which is quick mode. Quick mode uses message exchanges to establish the phase 2 IPsec SA. Phase 2 SA is negotiated for a given proxy or phase 2 identities and a given IPsec protocol (ESP). Multiple phase 2 SAs can be established under the same phase 1 SA. Phase 2 contains three messages, as illustrated in Figure 9.20:

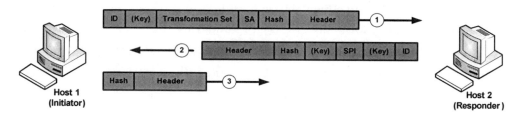

Figure 9.20. Phase 2 Messages

IKE phase 2 datagrams are also exchanged using UDP, with a destination port of 500. Phase 2 negotiations occur in Oakley quick mode, which can be without key exchange (no PFS enabled) or with key exchange (with PFS enabled); this requires the DH algorithm to be run twice to generate the shared secret key.

In IKE phase 2, message 1 allows the initiator to authenticate itself and select a random nonce, as well as propose an SA to the remote peer. Additionally, a public key can be provided. This public key can be different from that exchanged in IKE phase 1.

Message 2 is sent by the responder and it allows the responding peer to generate the hash. This message is used by the responding peer to authenticate itself, as well as to select a random number and accept the SA offered by the initiating peer. Message 3 acknowledges information sent from quick mode message 2 so that the phase 2 tunnel can be established.

At the end of phase 2 negotiations, two unidirectional IPsec SAs are established for user data. One SA is for sending data and the other SA is for receiving encrypted data. The concept of an SA is that two devices have agreed on certain policy parameters to be used during their communication session. In other words, an SA is an agreement between two entities on a method to communicate securely. Each IKE phase has its own SA. Phase 1 has ISAKMP/IKE SA and phase 2 has IPsec SA. This concept is illustrated in Figure 9.21:

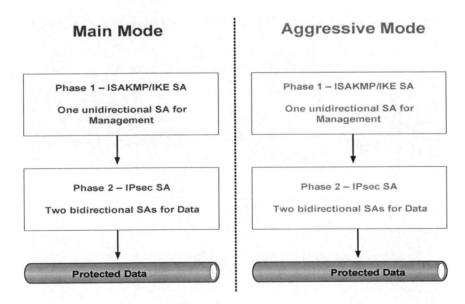

Figure 9.21. IKE Phases

IPsec VPN Configuration in SDM

While IPsec VPN configuration can be performed using CLI or SDM, the requirement of the IINS course is that you have a solid understanding of IPsec VPN configuration using SDM. This section walks through the configuration tasks required in order to enable IPsec VPN using Cisco SDM. The example used in this section will be based on Figure 9.22:

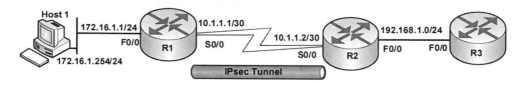

Figure 9.22. Ipsec VPN Example

> **NOTE:** As illustrated in Figure 9.22 above, a network-to-network IPsec tunnel will be created to encrypt data between the 172.16.1.0/24 and 192.168.1.0/24 subnets. Because the configuration tasks on R1 and R2 will be similar, only the configuration of R1 will be illustrated. In addition, it is also assumed that R2 has already been configured for an IPsec tunnel to its peer (R1), and routing for R1, R2, and R3 has already been configured to allow for end-to-end IP connectivity.

The first configuration step required to enable the IPsec VPN is to select **VPN** under the **Tasks** menu on the main configuration page, as illustrated in Figure 9.23:

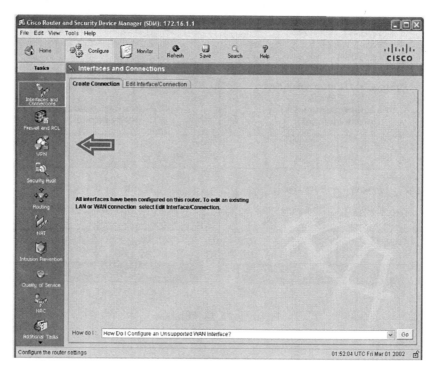

Figure 9.23. Select 'VPN' Under 'Tasks'

On the VPN page, ensure that **Site-to-Site VPN** is highlighted and click on the **Launch the selected task** button, as illustrated in Figure 9.24:

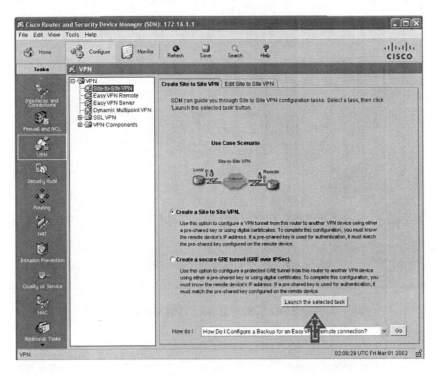

Figure 9.24. Launch the Slected Task

> NOTE: The **Create a secure GRE tunnel (GRE over IPSec)** option allows network security administrators to configure a Generic Routing Encapsulation tunnel between the two peer routers to enable IPsec over this tunnel. This configuration is beyond the scope of the IINS course requirements.

The next page is the **Site-to-Site VPN Wizard** page. From this page, network security administrators can configure IPsec using **Quick setup** (default option) or customize their configuration by using the **Step by step wizard**. Because we are only concerned with basic IPsec implementation, click on **Next** to accept the default option and continue, as illustrated in Figure 9.25:

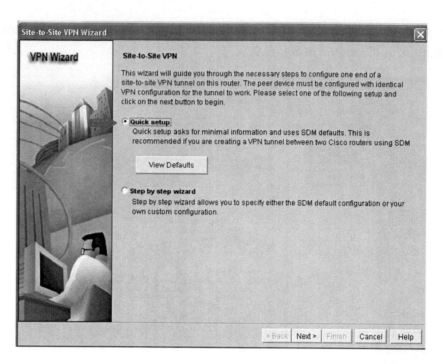

Figure 9.25. Site-to-Site VPN Wizard

This action brings up the **Site-to-Site VPN Wizard**. This page asks for several inputs. The **VPN Connection Information** option asks for the interface on which the IPsec configuration will be applied. In this example, this will be the **Serial0/0** interface.

The **Peer Identity** section asks for the type of IPsec peer, as well as the IP address of that peer. Based on the network topology used in this example, a **Peer with a static IPsec** is being configured (R2) and the IP address is **10.1.1.2**.

The **Authentication** section is used to specify whether pre-shared keys or digital certificates are to be used. Adhering to the requirements of the IINS course requirements, **Pre-shared keys** should be selected. Manually specify the pre-shared key, which should be the same as that configured on R2.

The **Traffic to encrypt** section asks for the **Source** and **Destination** subnets. In this example, the source will be the 172.16.1.0/24 subnet (the **FastEthernet0/0** interface on R1) and the destination will be the **192.168.1.0/24** subnet (the FastEthernet0/0 interface on R2).

Once these parameters have been entered, click on **Next** to proceed. This configuration is illustrated in Figure 9.26:

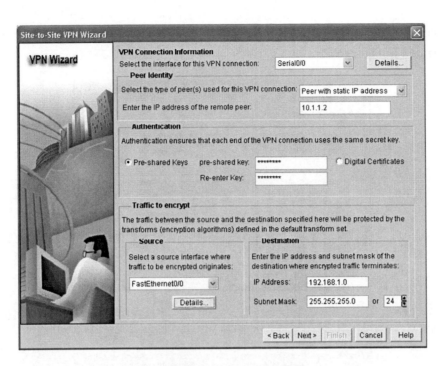

Figure 9.26. Select the Correct Inputs

This action brings up the **Summary of the Configuration page**. From this page, it is highly recommended that network security administrators check the **Test VPN connectivity after configuring** checkbox so that SDM can ensure that the IPsec VPN is up. This is illustrated in Figure 9.27:

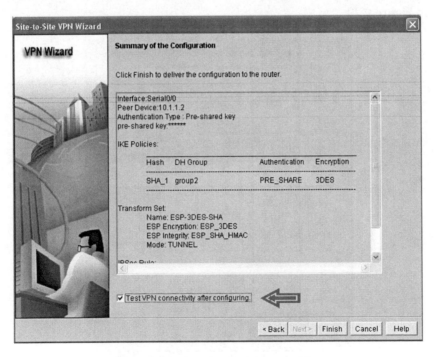

Figure 9.27. Test the VPN Connectivity

Once SDM has configured the router, it will perform VPN troubleshooting to ensure that the VPN is up, as illustrated in Figure 9.28:

Figure 9.28. VPN Testing

Enter the destination IP address of a host on the remote subnet and click on **Continue** to proceed, as illustrated in Figure 9.29:

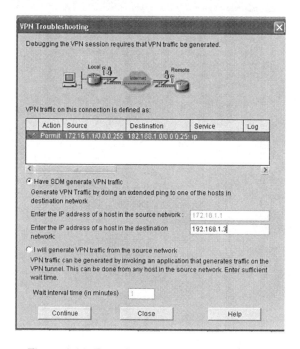

Figure 9.29. Enter Remote Host IP and Subnet

If there are any issues, SDM will advise the administrator of the problem. However, assuming there are no configuration issues, the VPN tunnel will come up and SDM will advise of this status, as illustrated in Figure 9.30:

Figure 9.30. VPN Status Report

To monitor VPN statistics, select **Monitor** and click on **VPN**. This brings up the **VPN Status** page, as illustrated in Figure 9.31:

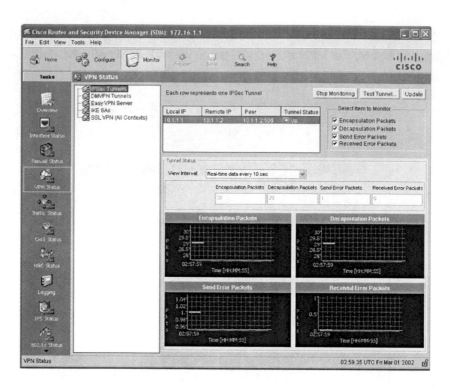

Figure 9.31. Monitor VPN Page

For example to view real-time traffic statistics, a continuous ping from Host 1 to R3 is initiated via the **ping 192.168.1.3 −t** command, as illustrated in Figure 9.32:

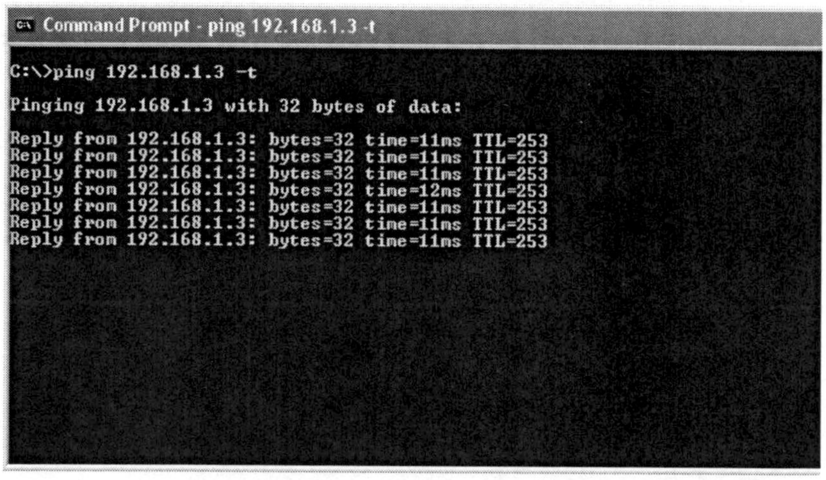

```
Command Prompt - ping 192.168.1.3 -t

C:\>ping 192.168.1.3 -t

Pinging 192.168.1.3 with 32 bytes of data:

Reply from 192.168.1.3: bytes=32 time=11ms TTL=253
Reply from 192.168.1.3: bytes=32 time=11ms TTL=253
Reply from 192.168.1.3: bytes=32 time=11ms TTL=253
Reply from 192.168.1.3: bytes=32 time=12ms TTL=253
Reply from 192.168.1.3: bytes=32 time=11ms TTL=253
Reply from 192.168.1.3: bytes=32 time=11ms TTL=253
Reply from 192.168.1.3: bytes=32 time=11ms TTL=253
```

Figure 9.32. Test With Continuous Ping

Based on the continuous ping, the **VPN Status** page shows the spike on the charts depicting **Encapsulation Packets** and **Decapsulation Packets**, as illustrated in Figure 9.33:

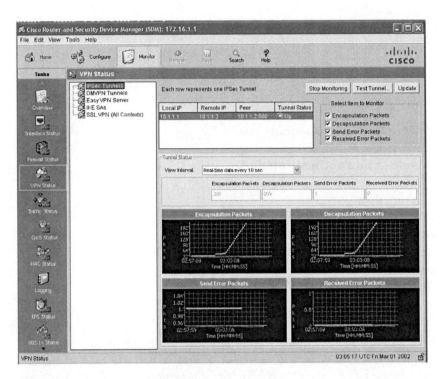

Figure 9.33. VPN Status Page

While you are not required to perform CLI configuration for IPsec VPNs, the following output shows the configuration commands implemented by SDM based on the previous configuration example. The IPsec VPN configuration is illustrated in bold font:

R1#**show running-config**
Building configuration...

Current configuration : 3219 bytes
!
version 12.4
service timestamps debug datetime msec
service timestamps log datetime msec
no service password-encryption
!
hostname R1
!
boot-start-marker
boot-end-marker
!
no logging buffered
no logging console
!
no aaa new-model
no network-clock-participate slot 1

```
no network-clock-participate wic 0
ip cef
!
!
!
!
ip domain name howtonetwork.net
!
multilink bundle-name authenticated
!
!
crypto pki trustpoint TP-self-signed-533650306
 enrollment selfsigned
 subject-name cn=IOS-Self-Signed-Certificate-533650306
 revocation-check none
 rsakeypair TP-self-signed-533650306
!
!
crypto pki certificate chain TP-self-signed-533650306
 certificate self-signed 01
  30820249 308201B2 A0030201 02020101 300D0609 2A864886 F70D0101 04050030
  30312E30 2C060355 04031325 494F532D 53656C66 2D536967 6E65642D 43657274
  69666963 6174652D 35333336 35303330 36301E17 0D303230 33303130 31303335
  315A170D 32303031 30313030 30303030 5A303031 2E302C06 03550403 1325494F
  532D5365 6C662D53 69676E65 642D4365 72746966 69636174 652D3533 33363530
  33303630 819F300D 06092A86 4886F70D 01010105 0003818D 00308189 02818100
  A10043E2 FB10C1D1 BA18F3AD 554F081C ACA14F4C EA48E0C1 4739653D B7759EE7
  8EB29881 7F391723 E2BB7EC6 54EB6F25 B4E94520 DF8DA15C 3B9E6F7C 3AA57549
  80AB643F A9427071 965DD56A 2D3E60CE 775F2ED5 C9014FCD F313F3EB B5189F62
  09F461BC 32E3E78F F93C8B07 0740DDA8 7B880D1B A3185787 CE621B35 3511A9D5
  02030100 01A37330 71300F06 03551D13 0101FF04 05300301 01FF301E 0603551D
  11041730 15821352 312E686F 77746F6E 6574776F 726B2E6E 6574301F 0603551D
  23041830 168014CD 63D2C471 B7ABA4AC F9C2B602 0D4A8954 71C7F930 1D060355
  1D0E0416 0414CD63 D2C471B7 ABA4ACF9 C2B6020D 4A895471 C7F9300D 06092A86
  4886F70D 01010405 00038181 002A76D9 7EB68101 CC23FE4F DD2F0D1F C952DC42
  A7AC65A8 74D21FB0 577DF998 79B86023 239F8E5E AFD09B29 E87B777D 079642DB
  3B629E27 803E28F9 1987544F 40F2DC8F 700EBAA2 C8833DD1 7BE366F0 D8ADD696
  BD57262E F0C4A5AC 516D6A46 AC593CC6 AA0E71C3 D45557B3 C88BFC09 046D3D8D
  EA605BF6 E0AF1DDD 27D64C91 A8
    quit
!
!
username secadmin privilege 15 secret 5 $1$LE94$AOOi72zIa5fPxRcubcQU1.
archive
```

```
log config
 hidekeys
!
!
crypto isakmp policy 1
 encr 3des
 authentication pre-share
 group 2
crypto isakmp key security address 10.1.1.2
!
!
crypto ipsec transform-set ESP-3DES-SHA esp-3des esp-sha-hmac
!
crypto map SDM_CMAP_1 1 ipsec-isakmp
 description Tunnel to10.1.1.2
 set peer 10.1.1.2
 set transform-set ESP-3DES-SHA
 match address 100
!
!
!
ip ssh time-out 30
ip ssh authentication-retries 2
!
!
!
interface Loopback0
 ip address 1.1.1.1 255.255.255.255
!
interface FastEthernet0/0
 ip address 172.16.1.1 255.255.255.0
 duplex auto
 speed auto
!
interface Serial0/0
 ip address 10.1.1.1 255.255.255.252
 crypto map SDM_CMAP_1
!
router eigrp 1
 network 0.0.0.0
 no auto-summary
!
ip forward-protocol nd
!
!
ip http server
ip http authentication local
ip http secure-server
!
```

```
access-list 100 remark SDM_ACL Category=4
access-list 100 remark IPSec Rule
access-list 100 permit ip 172.16.1.0 0.0.0.255 192.168.1.0 0.0.0.255
!
!
!
!
control-plane
!
!
!
line con 0
line aux 0
line vty 0 4
 privilege level 15
 password cisco
 login
!
!
end

R1#
```

Chapter Summary

The following section is a summary of the major points you should be aware of in this chapter:

Cryptography Overview

- Cryptography is the art of protecting information by encrypting it
- Users must possess a secret key can decrypt ciphertext into plaintext
- A cryptosystem is a framework that involves the application of cryptography
- Encryption is the process of obscuring information to make it unreadable
- Decryption is the reverse of encryption
- Plaintext is information a sender wishes to transmit to a receiver
- Ciphertext is the product of the encryption process
- A hash is a unique generated by applying a mathematical formula
- A VPN, is used to carry private traffic over a public transport, such as the Internet
- Cryptographic techniques can be classified as either traditional or modern
- Traditional techniques use transposition and substitution mechanisms
- Modern cryptographic techniques rely on sophisticated protocols and algorithms
- There are three types of cryptographic algorithms, which are:
  1. Symmetric Key Cryptography

2. Asymmetric Key Cryptography
3. Hash Algorithms

- Symmetric key cryptography uses a single key for encryption and decryption
- Asymmetric key cryptography uses two keys for encryption and decryption
- Hash algorithms use a one-way function to produce a randomized unique hash value

Symmetric Key Cryptography

- Symmetric key cryptography uses a single shared secret key for encryption and decryption
- The two categories of symmetric key cryptography are stream ciphers and block ciphers
- Block ciphers encrypt plaintext in chunks, or blocks
- Block ciphers have several modes of operation, which are:
    1. ECB—Electronic Code Book
    2. CBC—Cipher Block Chaining
    3. CFB—Cipher Feedback Mode
    4. OFB—Output Feedback Mode
    5. CTR—Counter
    6. CMAC—Cipher Block Chaining Message Authentication Code
    7. CCM—Counter with CBC MAC
    8. GCM—Galois/Counter Mode

- Stream or state ciphers encrypt plaintext digits (bits or bytes) one by one
- There are two categories of stream ciphers: synchronous and self-synchronizing
- Stream ciphers attempt to operate in the same manner as OTP
- Some of the most common symmetric cryptographic algorithms, which are:
    1. Digital Encryption Standard
    2. Triple-Digital Encryption Standard
    3. Advanced Encryption Standard
    4. RC4
    5. International Data Encryption Algorithm
    6. Blowfish

Asymmetric Key Cryptography

- Asymmetric key cryptography is commonly referred to as public key cryptography
- Asymmetric key cryptography design uses a two-key pair
- Public key cryptography is typically used in digital certification and key management
- The two types of public key cryptography are public key encryption and digital signatures
- Some of the most common asymmetric key cryptography algorithms are:

1. Rivest, Shamir, and Adleman
2. Diffie-Hellman
3. Digital Signature Algorithm and Digital Signature Standard
4. Public-Key Cryptography Standards

Hash Algorithms

- Hash algorithms use a mathematical formula to compute a fixed-length hash value
- With hashing, the original message cannot be reconstituted
- Hash functions are generally faster than encryption algorithms
- Hash algorithms are commonly used for both data integrity and digital certificates
- The most common hash algorithms are:
  1. Message Digest
  2. Secure Hash Algorithm

VPN Technologies

- VPN technology is described in RFC 2828
- The three types of VPN technologies that are available today are:
  1. Secure Virtual Private Networks
  2. Trusted Virtual Private Networks
  3. Hybrid Virtual Private Networks

- Secure VPNs are also referred to as Cryptographic VPNs
- Secure VPN technologies include:
  1. IP Security (IPsec)
  2. Layer 2 Tunneling Protocol (L2TP) over IPsec
  3. Point-to-Point Tunneling Protocol (PPTP)
  4. SSL Encryption (SSL VPN)

- The three most common secure VPN deployment scenarios are:
  1. Intranet-based VPNs
  2. Internet-based VPNs
  3. Extranet-based VPNs

- Trusted VPNs are also referred to as non-cryptographic VPNs
- Trusted VPN technologies are usually provided by a dedicated service provider
- A hybrid VPN is a combination of both a trusted VPN and a secure VPN

IP Security

- IP Security is standardized in RFC 2401
- The IPsec framework is a set of open standards developed by the IETF
- IPsec is implemented by a set of cryptographic protocols
- The IPsec framework secures IP traffic operating at the Network Layer of the OSI Model
- The IPsec framework offers the following security services:
  1. Peer Authentication
  2. Data Confidentiality
  3. Data Integrity
  4. Data Origin Authentication
  5. Replay Detection
  6. Access Control
  7. Traffic Flow Confidentiality

- IPsec can use transport mode and tunnel mode propagate data across networks.
- IPsec modes are commonly referred to as Security Association, or SA
- Transport mode protects the payload (data) of the original IP datagram
- Transport mode is used host-to-host and end-to-end sessions
- Tunnel mode allows IPsec to encapsulate the entire IP packet
- Tunnel mode is used to protect data in network-to-network or site-to-site scenarios
- IPsec is unidirectional and SA is required for both inbound and outbound connections
- IKE allows for bidirectional SAs within the IPsec framework
- The IPsec header may either be Encapsulating Security Payload or Authentication Header
- ESP is an IP-based protocol that uses IP port 50
- ESP is documented in RFC 4303
- ESP is used to provide confidentiality, integrity, and authenticity of the data
- ESP does not provide any kind of protection for the outer IP header
- AH is an IP-based protocol that uses IP port 51
- AH is used to protect the integrity and authenticity of data
- AH provides protection to the IP header
- AH is described in RFC 2402
- Both ESP and AH provide an anti-replay mechanism
- Anti-replay services are possible by using the sequence numbers in the ESP and AH headers
- ISAKMP is used to establish, negotiate, modify, and delete Security Association
- ISAKAMP is documented in RFC 2408, but was made obsolete by RFC 4306 (IKEv2)
- IKE is a combination of ISAKMP, Oakley key exchange, and the SKEME protocol
- IKE defines the mechanism for exchanging keys
- IKE uses UDP port 500 and is documented in RFC 2409, and updated in RFC 4306

- The terms ISAKMP and IKE are often used interchangeably in many texts
- IKE is a two-phase, multimode protocol
- IKE uses pre-shared keys, public key signature, and public key encryption
- IKE phase 1 operations can use either main or aggressive mode
- IKE phase 1 main mode uses a six message exchange process
- IKE phase 1 aggressive mode uses a three message exchange process
- IKE phase 2 operates in quick mode
- IKE phase 2 uses a three message exchange process
- A single SA is created in IKE phase 1
- Two SAs are created in IKE phase 2: one for sending and the other for receiving data

PART 2

Labs

LAB 1

Cisco IOS User and Command Privilege Levels

Lab Objective:

The objective of this lab exercise is for you to learn and understand how implement different privilege levels for users and commands within the Cisco IOS software.

Lab Purpose:

It is important to understand that the Cisco IOS software provides the capability to restrict certain commands from being executed by different users based on their privilege levels.

Lab Difficulty:

This lab has a difficulty rating of 7/10.

Readiness Assessment:

When you are ready for your certification exam, you should complete this lab in no more than 15 minutes.

Lab Topology:

Please use the following topology to complete this lab exercise:

Lab 1 Configuration Tasks

Task 1:

Configure the hostnames and IP addresses on R1 and R2 as illustrated in the network diagram. Configure R2 to send R1 clocking information at a rate of 512Kbps. Ping between R1 and R2 to verify your configuration and ensure that the two routers have IP connectivity.

Task 2:

Configure R2 with the following command restrictions:

Command	Privilege Level
ping	15
traceroute	15
show ip route	15
show version	15
show	1
show ip	1

Task 3:

Configure the following users and corresponding privilege levels on R2:

Username	Privilege Level	Secret
beginner	1	Cisco123
intermediate	7	Cisco456
expert	15	Cisco789

Task 4:

Configure Telnet access to R2 so that the router authenticates users based on locally configured usernames and passwords.

Task 5:

Configure R2 so that when the user named **intermediate** logs into the router, R2 immediately issues the output of the **show ip interface brief** command and logs them out automatically.

Task 6:

Telnet into R2 from R1 using username **beginner** and validate the following:
* You cannot issue the ping command
* You cannot issue the show version command
* You cannot issue the traceroute command
* You cannot issue the show ip route command

Telnet into R2 from R1 using username **intermediate** and validate the following:
* The router prints the output of the show ip interface brief command and logs you out

Telnet into R2 from R1 using username **expert** and validate the following:
* You can issue the ping command
* You can issue the show version command

Lab 1 Configuration and Verification

Task 1:

```
Router(config)#hostname R1
R1(config)#interface serial0/0
R1(config-if)#no shutdown
R1(config-if)#ip address 10.1.1.1 255.255.255.0
R1(config-if)#end
R1#
```

```
Router(config)#hostname R2
R2(config)#interface serial0/0
R2(config-if)#no shutdown
R2(config-if)#clock rate 512000
R2(config-if)#ip address 10.1.1.2 255.255.255.252
R2(config-if)#exit
R2(config)#exit
R2#
R2#ping 10.1.1.1
```

```
Type escape sequence to abort.
Sending 5, 100-byte ICMP Echos to 10.1.1.1, timeout is 2 seconds:
!!!!!
Success rate is 100 percent (5/5), round-trip min/avg/max = 4/4/8 ms
```

Task 2:

```
R2(config)#privilege exec level 1 show ip
R2(config)#privilege exec level 1 show
R2(config)#privilege exec level 15 ping
R2(config)#privilege exec level 15 traceroute
R2(config)#privilege exec level 15 show ip route
R2(config)#privilege exec level 15 show version
R2(config)#exit
R2#
```

Task 3:

```
R2(config)#username beginner privilege 1 secret cisco123
R2(config)#username intermediate privilege 7 secret cisco456
R2(config)#username expert privilege 15 secret cisco789
R2(config)#exit
R2#
```

Task 4:

```
R2(config)#line vty 0 4
R2(config-line)#login local
R2(config-line)#exit
R2(config)#exit
R2#
```

Task 5:

```
R2(config)#username intermediate autocommand show ip interface brief
R2(config)#exit
R2#
```

Task 6:

Because the default privilege level of these commands has been changed from 0 to 15, the user beginner—who has restricted only to level 0 commands—will be unable to execute these commands. However, any other commands (that have a privilege level of 0) will still work.

```
R1#telnet 10.1.1.2
Trying 10.1.1.2 ... Open

User Access Verification

Username: beginner
Password:
R2>ping 10.1.1.1
     ^
% Invalid input detected at '^' marker.

R2>show version
     ^
% Invalid input detected at '^' marker.

R2>traceroute 10.1.1.1
     ^
% Invalid input detected at '^' marker.

R2>show ip route
     ^
% Invalid input detected at '^' marker.
```

The **username [name] autocommand [line]** command is used to execute the specified command immediately after the user logs in and then automatically disconnect the user session. This security mechanism can be used to restrict the information certain users can get from routers.

```
R1#telnet 10.1.1.2
Trying 10.1.1.2 ... Open


User Access Verification

Username: intermediate
Password:
```

```
Interface          IP-Address      OK?    Method       Status       Protocol
FastEthernet0/0    172.16.1.2      YES    NVRAM        up           up
Serial0/0          10.1.1.2        YES    manual       up           up
[Connection to 10.1.1.2 closed by foreign host]
R1#
```

Level 15 users have complete access to the entire suite of Cisco IOS commands.

```
R1#telnet 10.1.1.2
Trying 10.1.1.2 ... Open


User Access Verification
Username: expert
Password:


R2#ping 10.1.1.1


Type escape sequence to abort.
Sending 5, 100-byte ICMP Echos to 10.1.1.1, timeout is 2 seconds:
!!!!!
Success rate is 100 percent (5/5), round-trip min/avg/max = 4/5/8 ms
R2#
R2#show version
Cisco IOS Software, C2600 Software (C2600-ADVSECURITYK9-M), Version 12.4(15)T9, RE-
LEASE SOFTWARE (fc5)
Technical Support: http://www.cisco.com/techsupport
Copyright (c) 1986-2009 by Cisco Systems, Inc.
Compiled Tue 28-Apr-09 11:35 by prod_rel_team

ROM: System Bootstrap, Version 12.2(7r) [cmong 7r], RELEASE SOFTWARE (fc1)

R2 uptime is 11 hours, 48 minutes
System returned to ROM by power-on
System image file is "flash:c2600-advsecurityk9-mz.124-15.T9.bin"
```

This product contains cryptographic features and is subject to United
States and local country laws governing import, export, transfer and
use. Delivery of Cisco cryptographic products does not imply
third-party authority to import, export, distribute or use encryption.
Importers, exporters, distributors and users are responsible for
compliance with U.S. and local country laws. By using this product you
agree to comply with applicable laws and regulations. If you are unable
to comply with U.S. and local laws, return this product immediately.

A summary of U.S. laws governing Cisco cryptographic products may be found at:
http://www.cisco.com/wwl/export/crypto/tool/stqrg.html

If you require further assistance please contact us by sending email to export@cisco.com.

Cisco 2650XM (MPC860P) processor (revision 1.0) with 127627K/3445K bytes of memory.
Processor board ID JAE07170JUQ
M860 processor: part number 5, mask 2
1 FastEthernet interface
1 Serial interface
32K bytes of NVRAM.
32768K bytes of processor board System flash (Read/Write)

Configuration register is 0x2102

R2#
R2#**exit**

[Connection to 10.1.1.2 closed by foreign host]

Lab 1 Configurations

R1 Configuration

R1#show run
Building configuration...

Current configuration : 2421 bytes
!
version 12.4
service timestamps debug datetime msec
service timestamps log datetime msec
no service password-encryption
!
hostname R1
!
boot-start-marker
boot-end-marker
!
no logging console
!
no aaa new-model
no network-clock-participate slot 1
no network-clock-participate wic 0
ip cef
!
multilink bundle-name authenticated
!

```
crypto pki trustpoint TP-self-signed-533650306
 enrollment selfsigned
 subject-name cn=IOS-Self-Signed-Certificate-533650306
 revocation-check none
 rsakeypair TP-self-signed-533650306
!
crypto pki certificate chain TP-self-signed-533650306
 certificate self-signed 02
  30820238 308201A1 A0030201 02020102 300D0609 2A864886 F70D0101 04050030
  30312E30 2C060355 04031325 494F532D 53656C66 2D536967 6E65642D 43657274
  69666963 6174652D 35333336 35303330 36301E17 0D303230 33303130 31343234
  395A170D 32303031 30313030 30303030 5A303031 2E302C06 03550403 1325494F
  532D5365 6C662D53 69676E65 642D4365 72746966 69636174 652D3533 33363530
  33303630 819F300D 06092A86 4886F70D 01010105 0003818D 00308189 02818100
  BFA77FF5 5DA56F31 10110D3C 4FD35D6D 73FCECF4 4CA7C9E3 9D74F273 32C32446
  5037C8DF 3E8C9E91 8BDB70A4 777D4123 5EE29FAF 0B242DE0 90CAAD02 3511FC48
  60F48E39 9F2CBA37 FE3D3A7F 0840F41E DB785FE7 1F45FF1F 58E93C0B D443E328
  D8C0E8C2 7896916E 0B094B2E EBEC9368 C89FC2E1 02468E00 B9B6E9A1 0D4778DB
  02030100 01A36230 60300F06 03551D13 0101FF04 05300301 01FF300D 0603551D
  11040630 04820252 31301F06 03551D23 04183016 80146187 D2B080E6 4CA4B596
  C026BA5E 13E1EA03 A064301D 0603551D 0E041604 146187D2 B080E64C A4B596C0
  26BA5E13 E1EA03A0 64300D06 092A8648 86F70D01 01040500 03818100 1643A58E
  DD5E53CC 19252661 1958B313 5E658456 13686B9E 46EF2D9E DB273F0A AAB16242
  FA41F7DD CF4B006A 86C93C42 33DF5494 9269A702 1515EA22 71F36292 FDFBF0CA
  2DAA158D 94759BF0 96BE918C 598A936D 73F743D0 A0B2C415 B5220ECC 720BD0D2
  C9AD4DA1 72201C52 C7011ECF 1B5CF261 31AE28E8 86A6C8DD 9E2B87AD
    quit
!
archive
 log config
  hidekeys
!
interface FastEthernet0/0
 no ip address
 duplex auto
 speed auto
!
interface Serial0/0
 ip address 10.1.1.1 255.255.255.0
!
ip forward-protocol nd
!
ip http server
ip http authentication local
```

```
ip http secure-server
!
control-plane
!
line con 0
line aux 0
line vty 0 4
 password cisco
 login local
!
end
```

R2 Configuration

```
R2#show run
Building configuration...

Current configuration : 2924 bytes
!
version 12.4
service timestamps debug datetime msec
service timestamps log datetime msec
no service password-encryption
!
hostname R2
!
boot-start-marker
boot-end-marker
!
no logging console
!
no aaa new-model
no network-clock-participate slot 1
no network-clock-participate wic 0
ip cef
!
no ip domain lookup
!
multilink bundle-name authenticated
!
crypto pki trustpoint TP-self-signed-3473940174
 enrollment selfsigned
 subject-name cn=IOS-Self-Signed-Certificate-3473940174
 revocation-check none
 rsakeypair TP-self-signed-3473940174
!
crypto pki certificate chain TP-self-signed-3473940174
 certificate self-signed 03
```

```
3082023A  308201A3  A0030201  02020103  300D0609  2A864886  F70D0101  04050030
31312F30  2D060355  04031326  494F532D  53656C66  2D536967  6E65642D  43657274
69666963  6174652D  33343733  39343031  3734301E  170D3032  30333031  30313436
30345A17  0D323030  31303130  30303030  305A3031  312F302D  06035504  03132649
4F532D53  656C662D  5369676E  65642D43  65727469  66696361  74652D33  34373339
34303137  3430819F  300D0609  2A864886  F70D0101  01050003  818D0030  81890281
8100C824  4F0BABB6  A557E3A3  3EE6D399  5A495CF6  8F7E131A  62670291  9710DF0F
CB6918CB  D3B817C8  51D4648C  79B882A8  637804CB  8984FB80  D9F1D86B  E79C8292
E1617724  252490F4  BE0322C0  5C984515  3E0A4550  75E9BCC7  7A19900C  0084F632
19643491  5C0E821D  5442E1C8  FB4BE8A3  034E2954  01B4377C  DC14AF72  0F4C92DC
70A90203  010001A3  62306030  0F060355  1D130101  FF040530  030101FF  300D0603
551D1104  06300482  02523230  1F060355  1D230418  30168014  4020A082  2373EFEF
CD379B8C  2A1A4D13  43842D59  301D0603  551D0E04  16041440  20A08223  73EFEFCD
379B8C2A  1A4D1343  842D5930  0D06092A  864886F7  0D010104  05000381  81001AAA
E85188C2  E95DE2CF  D61FA051  5E1D4C7D  C0BC58CB  CB80016D  658BBD4B  B686C4B2
1B843186  2D80A25E  345FBFF9  B9976FE3  415FDA67  822C640D  D01E1890  6E127888
5CF59396  BA35884D  1713DE91  6F3EA49C  2BA819FF  80B2861B  04E25605  C10FCC78
B42586D5  34259EA9  82A1662E  62A5BDD8  8AB52BA4  B9721200  795E512B  9559
      quit
```

```
!
username beginner privilege 1 secret 5 $1$Yeha$jl.KYeF5h5MTK7UH7LOtN1
username intermediate privilege 7 secret 5 $1$5sxC$SDQbUDJIpKfHbST8wsPcf.
username intermediate autocommand show ip interface brief
username expert privilege 15 secret 5 $1$KW5c$2aN9EWbsUpfY.FchBr2df1
archive
 log config
  hidekeys
!
interface FastEthernet0/0
 no ip address
 duplex auto
 speed auto
!
interface Serial0/0
 ip address 10.1.1.2 255.255.255.252
 clock rate 512000
!
ip forward-protocol nd
!
!
ip http server
ip http authentication local
ip http secure-server
!
```

```
control-plane
!
privilege exec level 15 traceroute
privilege exec level 15 ping
privilege exec level 15 show ip route
privilege exec level 1 show ip
privilege exec level 15 show version
privilege exec level 1 show
!
line con 0
line aux 0
line vty 0 4
 login local
!
end
```

LAB 2

Cisco IOS Login Block

Lab Objective:

The objective of this lab exercise is for you to learn and understand how implement the Cisco IOS Login Block feature.

Lab Purpose:

The Cisco IOS Login Enhancements (Login Block) feature allows users to enhance the security of a router by configuring options to automatically block further login attempts when a possible Denial-of-Service (DoS) attack is detected.

Lab Difficulty:

This lab has a difficulty rating of 8/10.

Readiness Assessment:

When you are ready for your certification exam, you should complete this lab in no more than 15 minutes.

Lab Topology:

Please use the following topology to complete this lab exercise:

Lab 2 Configuration Tasks

Task 1:

Configure the hostnames and IP addresses on R1 and R2 as illustrated in the network diagram. Configure R2 to send R1 clocking information at a rate of 512Kbps. Ping between R1 and R2 to verify your configuration and ensure that the two routers have IP connectivity.

Task 2:

Configure the following interfaces on R2:

Interface	Address/Mask
Loopback10	10.10.10.2/26
Loopback20	20.20.20.2/28

Task 3:

Configure a static default route on R1 via Serial0/0. Ping R1 from the Loopback10 and Loopback20 interfaces of R2 and validate IP connectivity.

Task 4:

Configure Cisco IOS Login Block on R1 as follows:
- If there are more than 2 failed login attempts within 20 seconds of each other, the router should block login access for a period of 40 seconds.
- However, during the blocking time, the router should allow only TELNET connections from the Loopback20 subnet on R2 to attempt to log in.
- In addition to this, the router should log every single successful and failed login attempt.

Task 5:

Configure a user with the username **ccna** and password **security** on R1. This user should have Level 15 privileges. In addition, configure R1 to allow Telnet access while authenticating users based on the local router database. Finally, configure R1 to log ALL messages to the buffer.

Task 6:

Test your login configuration as follows:
- Telnet to R1 from the Loopback10 interface of R2, purposely using an incorrect password for user **ccna**. For example, use the password **security1** instead. Repeat this activity at least two times in 20 seconds. If your configuration is correct, the router should activate the quiet period and a subsequent connection attempt to R1 should be denied. Validate this.

- Telnet to R1 from the Loopback20 interface of R2 while the router is in the quiet period. Despite this, the exception configured in Task 4 should allow user **ccna** to log in—using the correct password. Verify that this is the case.
- Issue the **show log** on R1 command. You should observe some SYSLOG messages pertaining to all failed and successful login attempts on the router.

Lab 2 Configuration and Verification

Task 1:
```
Router(config)#hostname R1
R1(config)#interface serial0/0
R1(config-if)#no shutdown
R1(config-if)#ip address 10.1.1.1 255.255.255.0
R1(config-if)#end
```

```
R1#
Router(config)#hostname R2
R2(config)#interface serial0/0
R2(config-if)#no shutdown
R2(config-if)#clock rate 512000
R2(config-if)#ip address 10.1.1.2 255.255.255.252
R2(config-if)#exit
R2(config)#exit
R2#
R2#ping 10.1.1.1

Type escape sequence to abort.
Sending 5, 100-byte ICMP Echos to 10.1.1.1, timeout is 2 seconds:
!!!!!
Success rate is 100 percent (5/5), round-trip min/avg/max = 4/4/8 ms
```

Task 2:

```
R2(config)#interface loopback 10
R2(config-if)#ip address 10.10.10.2 255.255.255.192
R2(config-if)#exit
R2(config)# interface loopback 20
R2(config-if)#ip address 20.20.20.2 255.255.255.240
R2(config-if)#exit
R2(config)#exit
R2#
```

Task 3:

```
R1(config)#ip route 0.0.0.0 0.0.0.0 serial0/0
R1(config)#exit
R1#
R1#ping 10.10.10.2

Type escape sequence to abort.
Sending 5, 100-byte ICMP Echos to 10.10.10.2, timeout is 2 seconds:
!!!!!
Success rate is 100 percent (5/5), round-trip min/avg/max = 4/4/8 ms
R1#
R1#ping 20.20.20.2

Type escape sequence to abort.
Sending 5, 100-byte ICMP Echos to 20.20.20.2, timeout is 2 seconds:
!!!!!
Success rate is 100 percent (5/5), round-trip min/avg/max = 4/6/8 ms
```

Task 4:

```
R1(config)#login block-for 40 attempts 2 within 20
R1(config)#ip access-list extended R2-LPBK-20-TELNET
R1(config-ext-nacl)#permit tcp 20.20.20.0 0.0.0.15 any eq telnet
R1(config-ext-nacl)#exit
R1(config)#login quiet-mode access-class R2-LPBK-20-TELNET
R1(config)#login on-success log every 1
R1(config)#login on-failure log every 1
R1(config)#exit
R1#
```

Task 5:

```
R1(config)#username ccna privilege 15 secret security
R1(config)#line vty 0 4
R1(config-line)#login local
R1(config-line)#exit
R1(config)#exit
R1#
```

Task 6:

```
R2#telnet 10.1.1.1
Trying 10.1.1.1 ... Open


User Access Verification

Username: ccna
Password:
% Login invalid

Username: ccna
Password:
% Login invalid

[Connection to 10.1.1.1 closed by foreign host]

R2#telnet 10.1.1.1
Trying 10.1.1.1 ...
% Connection refused by remote host
```

The following message should be visible on R1 when this happens:

```
R1#show log
Syslog logging:     enabled (1 messages dropped, 0 messages rate-limited,
                    0 flushes, 0 overruns, xml disabled, filtering disabled)
```

No Active Message Discriminator.

No Inactive Message Discriminator.

    Console logging: disabled
    Monitor logging: level debugging, 0 messages logged, xml disabled,
                 filtering disabled
    Buffer logging: level debugging, 5 messages logged, xml disabled,
                 filtering disabled
    Logging Exception size (4096 bytes)
    Count and timestamp logging messages: disabled
    Persistent logging: disabled
    Trap logging: level informational, 32 message lines logged

Log Buffer (4096 bytes):

*Mar 1 00:20:02.078: %SYS-5-CONFIG_I: Configured from console by ccna on vty0 (10.1.1.2)
*Mar 1 00:20:10.300: %SEC_LOGIN-4-LOGIN_FAILED: Login failed [user: ccna] [Source: 10.1.1.2] [localport: 23] [Reason: Login Authentication Failed - BadPassword] at 00:20:10 UTC Fri Mar 1 2002
*Mar 1 00:20:14.422: %SEC_LOGIN-4-LOGIN_FAILED: Login failed [user: ccna] [Source: 10.1.1.2] [localport: 23] [Reason: Login Authentication Failed - BadPassword] at 00:20:14 UTC Fri Mar 1 2002
Mar 1 00:20:14.422: %SEC_LOGIN-1-QUIET_MODE_ON: Still timeleft for watching failures is 6 secs, [user: ccna] [Source: 10.1.1.2] [localport: 23] [Reason: Login Authentication Failed - BadPassword] [ACL: R2-LPBK-20-TELNET] at 00:20:14 UTC Fri Mar 1 2002
*Mar 1 00:20:54.424: %SEC_LOGIN-5-QUIET_MODE_OFF: Quiet Mode is OFF, because block period timed out at 00:20:54 UTC Fri Mar 1 2002

To validate the second requirement of the Task, Telnet to R1 during the quiet period and the connection from ONLY the Loopback20 subnet of R2 should be permitted.

R2#**telnet 10.1.1.1**
Trying 10.1.1.1 ...
% Connection refused by remote host

R2#**telnet 10.1.1.1 /source loopback 10**
Trying 10.1.1.1 ...
% Connection refused by remote host

R2#**telnet 10.1.1.1 /source loopback 20**
Trying 10.1.1.1 ... Open

User Access Verification

Username: **ccna**
Password:
R1#

Because all login attempts are being logged, you should see quite a few logs. Make sure that you have enabled logging by using the logging buffered command on R1.

R1#**show log**
Syslog logging: enabled (1 messages dropped, 0 messages rate-limited, 0 flushes, 0 overruns, xml disabled, filtering disabled)

No Active Message Discriminator.

No Inactive Message Discriminator.

   Console logging: disabled
   Monitor logging: level debugging, 0 messages logged, xml disabled, filtering disabled
   Buffer logging: level debugging, 14 messages logged, xml disabled, filtering disabled
   Logging Exception size (4096 bytes)
   Count and timestamp logging messages: disabled
   Persistent logging: disabled
   Trap logging: level informational, 41 message lines logged

Log Buffer (4096 bytes):

*Mar 1 00:20:02.078: %SYS-5-CONFIG_I: Configured from console by ccna on vty0 (10.1.1.2)
*Mar 1 00:20:10.300: %SEC_LOGIN-4-LOGIN_FAILED: Login failed [user: ccna] [Source: 10.1.1.2] [localport: 23] [Reason: Login Authentication Failed - BadPassword] at 00:20:10 UTC Fri Mar 1 2002
*Mar 1 00:20:14.422: %SEC_LOGIN-4-LOGIN_FAILED: Login failed [user: ccna] [Source: 10.1.1.2] [localport: 23] [Reason: Login Authentication Failed - BadPassword] at 00:20:14 UTC Fri Mar 1 2002
*Mar 1 00:20:14.422: %SEC_LOGIN-1-QUIET_MODE_ON: Still timeleft for watching failures is 6 secs, [user: ccna] [Source: 10.1.1.2] [localport: 23] [Reason: Login Authentication Failed - BadPassword] [ACL: R2-LPBK-20-TELNET] at 00:20:14 UTC Fri Mar 1 2002
*Mar 1 00:20:54.424: %SEC_LOGIN-5-QUIET_MODE_OFF: Quiet Mode is OFF, because block period timed out at 00:20:54 UTC Fri Mar 1 2002
*Mar 1 00:23:49.663: %SEC_LOGIN-4-LOGIN_FAILED: Login failed [user: ccns] [Source: 10.1.1.2] [localport: 23] [Reason: Login Authentication Failed - BadUser] at 00:23:49 UTC Fri Mar 1 2002

```
*Mar  1 00:23:54.062: %SEC_LOGIN-4-LOGIN_FAILED: Login failed [user: ccna] [Source:
10.1.1.2] [localport: 23] [Reason: Login Authentication Failed - BadPassword] at 00:23:54
UTC Fri Mar 1 2002
*Mar  1 00:23:54.062: %SEC_LOGIN-1-QUIET_MODE_ON: Still timeleft for watching fail-
ures is 0 secs, [user: ccna] [Source: 10.1.1.2] [localport: 23] [Reason: Login Authentication
Failed - BadPassword] [ACL: R2-LPBK-20-TELNET] at 00:23:54 UTC Fri Mar 1 2002
*Mar  1 00:24:10.409: %SEC_LOGIN-4-LOGIN_FAILED: Login failed [user: ccna] [Source:
20.20.20.2] [localport: 23] [Reason: Login Authentication Failed - BadPassword] at
00:24:10 UTC Fri Mar 1 2002
*Mar  1 00:24:10.409: %SEC_LOGIN-1-QUIET_MODE_ON: Still timeleft for watching fail-
ures is 0 secs, [user: ccna] [Source: 20.20.20.2] [localport: 23] [Reason: Login Authentica-
tion Failed - BadPassword] [ACL: R2-LPBK-20-TELNET] at 00:24:10 UTC Fri Mar 1 2002
*Mar  1 00:24:21.411: %SEC_LOGIN-4-LOGIN_FAILED: Login failed [user: ccna] [Source:
20.20.20.2] [localport: 23] [Reason: Login Authentication Failed - BadPassword] at
00:24:21 UTC Fri Mar 1 2002
*Mar  1 00:24:21.411: %SEC_LOGIN-1-QUIET_MODE_ON: Still timeleft for watching fail-
ures is 0 secs, [user: ccna] [Source: 20.20.20.2] [localport: 23] [Reason: Login Authentica-
tion Failed - BadPassword] [ACL: R2-LPBK-20-TELNET] at 00:24:21 UTC Fri Mar 1 2002
*Mar  1 00:24:41.897: %SEC_LOGIN-5-LOGIN_SUCCESS: Login Success [user: ccna]
[Source: 20.20.20.2] [localport: 23] at 00:24:41 UTC Fri Mar 1 2002
*Mar  1 00:25:01.413: %SEC_LOGIN-5-QUIET_MODE_OFF: Quiet Mode is OFF, because
block period timed out at 00:25:01 UTC Fri Mar 1 2002
```

Lab 2 Configurations

R1 Configuration

```
R1#show run
Building configuration...

Current configuration : 1077 bytes
!
version 12.4
service timestamps debug datetime msec
service timestamps log datetime msec
no service password-encryption
!
hostname R1
!
boot-start-marker
boot-end-marker
!
logging buffered 4096
no logging console
!
no aaa new-model
no network-clock-participate slot 1
no network-clock-participate wic 0
```

```
ip cef
!
login block-for 40 attempts 2 within 20
login quiet-mode access-class R2-LPBK-20-TELNET
login on-failure log
login on-success log
!
multilink bundle-name authenticated
!
username ccna privilege 15 secret 5 $1$LlaJ$13RVZPlzHe1KOhx6nYq9s1
archive
 log config
  hidekeys
!
interface FastEthernet0/0
 ip address 172.16.1.1 255.255.255.0
 duplex auto
 speed auto
!
interface Serial0/0
 ip address 10.1.1.1 255.255.255.252
!
ip forward-protocol nd
ip route 0.0.0.0 0.0.0.0 Serial0/0
!
ip http server
no ip http secure-server
!
ip access-list extended R2-LPBK-20-TELNET
 permit tcp 20.20.20.0 0.0.0.15 any eq telnet
!
control-plane
!
line con 0
line aux 0
line vty 0 4
 password cisco
 login local
!
end
```

R2 Configuration

```
R2#show run
Building configuration...

Current configuration : 919 bytes
!
version 12.4
service timestamps debug datetime msec
service timestamps log datetime msec
```

```
no service password-encryption
!
hostname R2
!
boot-start-marker
boot-end-marker
!
no logging console
!
no aaa new-model
no network-clock-participate slot 1
no network-clock-participate wic 0
ip cef
!
no ip domain lookup
!
multilink bundle-name authenticated
!
archive
 log config
  hidekeys
!
interface Loopback10
 ip address 10.10.10.2 255.255.255.192
!
interface Loopback20
 ip address 20.20.20.2 255.255.255.240
!
interface FastEthernet0/0
 ip address 172.16.1.2 255.255.255.0
 duplex auto
 speed auto
!
interface Serial0/0
 ip address 10.1.1.2 255.255.255.252
 clock rate 512000
!
ip forward-protocol nd
!
ip http server
ip http authentication local
no ip http secure-server
!
control-plane
!
line con 0
line aux 0
line vty 0 4
 password cisco
 login
!
end
```

LAB 3

Context-Based Access Control

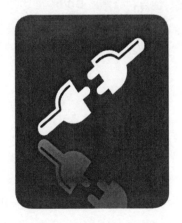

Lab Objective:

The objective of this lab exercise is for you to learn and understand how implement the Cisco Context-based Access Control.

Lab Purpose:

CBAC intelligently filters TCP and UDP packets based on application-layer protocol session information. You can configure CBAC to permit specified TCP and UDP traffic through a firewall only when the connection is initiated from within the network you want to protect. CBAC can inspect traffic for sessions that originate from either side of the firewall, and CBAC can be used for intranet, extranet, and Internet perimeters of your network.

Lab Difficulty:

This lab has a difficulty rating of 7/10.

Readiness Assessment:

When you are ready for your certification exam, you should complete this lab in no more than 15 minutes.

Lab Topology:

Please use the following topology to complete this lab exercise:

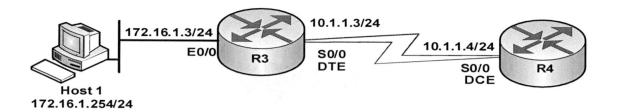

Lab 3 Configuration Tasks

Task 1:

Configure the hostnames and IP addresses on R3 and R4 as illustrated in the network diagram. Configure R4 to send R3 clocking information at a rate of 768Kbps. Ping between R3 and R4 to verify your configuration and ensure that the two routers have IP connectivity.

Task 2:

Configure Host 1 with the IP address illustrated in the diagram and a default gateway of the Ethernet0/0 interface of R3, which is 172.16.1.3.

NOTE: If you do not have a Host in your lab, you can simply substitute Host 1 for another router with an Ethernet interface and a default static route pointing to 172.16.1.3.

Task 3:

Configure R4 with a default static route pointing to R3. Configure the username **cisco** with a password of **cisco** and privilege level of 15 on R4. Finally, configure R4 to allow Telnet and HTTP access while authenticating using the local database.

Verify that Host 1 and R4 can ping each other and have complete network connectivity.

Task 4:

Configure CBAC on R3 as follows:
- Use the name MY-CBAC for the inspection policy
- Configure CBAC to inspect ICMP traffic
- Configure CBAC to inspect TCP traffic
- Configure CBAC to inspect HTTP traffic
- Use ACL 150 for CBAC and explicitly deny all traffic
- The Ethernet0/0 interface of R3 should be considered the private/trusted interface
- The Serial0/0 interface of R3 should be considered the public/untrusted interface

Task 5:

Test your configuration as follows:
- Ping from Host 1 to R4 and verify that CBAC works as configured
- Telnet from Host 1 to R4 and verify that CBAC works as configured

Lab 3 Configuration and Verification

Task 1:
```
Router(config)#hostname R3
R3(config)#interface ethernet0/0
R3(config-if)#ip address 172.16.1.3 255.255.255.0
R3(config-if)#no shutdown
R3(config-if)#exit
R3(config)#interface serial0/0
```

R3(config-if)#**ip address 10.1.1.3 255.255.255.0**
R3(config-if)#**no shutdown**
R3(config-if)#**exit**
R3(config)#**exit**
R3#

Router(config)#**hostname R4**
R4(config)#**interface serial0/0**
R4(config-if)#**ip address 10.1.1.4 255.255.255.0**
R4(config-if)#**clock rate 768000**
R4(config-if)#**no shut**
R4(config-if)#**exit**
R4(config)#**exit**
R4#
R4#**ping 10.1.1.3**

Type escape sequence to abort.
Sending 5, 100-byte ICMP Echos to 10.1.1.3, timeout is 2 seconds:
!!!!!
Success rate is 100 percent (5/5), round-trip min/avg/max = 4/4/4 ms

Task 2:

```
Command Prompt                                                    _ □ ×

C:\>ipconfig

Windows IP Configuration

Ethernet adapter Local Area Connection 2:

        Connection-specific DNS Suffix  . :
        IP Address. . . . . . . . . . . . : 172.16.1.254
        Subnet Mask . . . . . . . . . . . : 255.255.255.0
        Default Gateway . . . . . . . . . : 172.16.1.3

Ethernet adapter Wireless Network Connection:

        Media State . . . . . . . . . . . : Media disconnected

C:\>
```

Task 3:

R4(config)#**ip route 0.0.0.0 0.0.0.0 serial0/0**
R4(config)#**username cisco privilege 15 secret cisco**
R4(config)#**ip http server**
R4(config)#**ip http authentication local**
R4(config)#**line vty 0 4**
R4(config-line)#**login local**
R4(config-line)#**exit**
R4(config)#**exit**
R4#

```
Command Prompt                                           _ □ ×

C:\>ping 10.1.1.4

Pinging 10.1.1.4 with 32 bytes of data:

Reply from 10.1.1.4: bytes=32 time=3ms TTL=254
Reply from 10.1.1.4: bytes=32 time=3ms TTL=254
Reply from 10.1.1.4: bytes=32 time=3ms TTL=254
Reply from 10.1.1.4: bytes=32 time=3ms TTL=254

Ping statistics for 10.1.1.4:
    Packets: Sent = 4, Received = 4, Lost = 0 (0% loss),
Approximate round trip times in milli-seconds:
    Minimum = 3ms, Maximum = 3ms, Average = 3ms

C:\>
```

Task 4:

```
R3(config)#ip inspect name MY-CBAC icmp
R3(config)#ip inspect name MY-CBAC tcp
R3(config)#ip inspect name MY-CBAC http
R3(config)#access-list 150 deny ip any any
R3(config)#int e0/0
R3(config-if)#ip inspect MY-CBAC in
R3(config-if)#ip access-group 150 out
R3(config-if)#exit
R3(config)#int s0/0
R3(config-if)#ip access-group 150 in
R3(config-if)#ip inspect MY-CBAC out
R3(config-if)#exit
R3(config)#exit
R3#
```

Task 5:

```
Command Prompt                                           _ □ ×

C:\>ping 10.1.1.4

Pinging 10.1.1.4 with 32 bytes of data:

Reply from 10.1.1.4: bytes=32 time=3ms TTL=254
Reply from 10.1.1.4: bytes=32 time=3ms TTL=254
Reply from 10.1.1.4: bytes=32 time=3ms TTL=254
Reply from 10.1.1.4: bytes=32 time=3ms TTL=254

Ping statistics for 10.1.1.4:
    Packets: Sent = 4, Received = 4, Lost = 0 (0% loss),
Approximate round trip times in milli-seconds:
    Minimum = 3ms, Maximum = 3ms, Average = 3ms

C:\>
```

```
R3#show ip inspect sessions detail
Established Sessions
 Session 646642E0 (172.16.1.254:8)=>(10.1.1.4:0) icmp SIS_OPEN
  Created 00:00:09, Last heard 00:00:06
   ECHO request
```

Bytes sent (initiator:responder) [128:128]
Out SID 10.1.1.4[0:0]=>172.16.1.254[0:0] on ACL 150
In SID 10.1.1.4[0:0]=>172.16.1.254[0:0] on ACL 150 (4 matches)
Out SID 0.0.0.0[0:0]=>172.16.1.254[3:3] on ACL 150
In SID 0.0.0.0[0:0]=>172.16.1.254[3:3] on ACL 150
Out SID 0.0.0.0[0:0]=>172.16.1.254[11:11] on ACL 150
In SID 0.0.0.0[0:0]=>172.16.1.254[11:11] on ACL 150

R3#**show ip inspect sessions detail**
Established Sessions
 Session 646642E0 (172.16.1.254:2075)=>(10.1.1.4:23) tcp SIS_OPEN
 Created 00:00:07, Last heard 00:00:04
 Bytes sent (initiator:responder) [45:82]
 Out SID 10.1.1.4[23:23]=>172.16.1.254[2075:2075] on ACL 150
 In SID 10.1.1.4[23:23]=>172.16.1.254[2075:2075] on ACL 150 (16 matches)

Lab 3 Configurations

R3 Configuration
R3#show run
Building configuration...

Current configuration : 1019 bytes
!
version 12.4
service timestamps debug datetime msec
service timestamps log datetime msec
no service password-encryption
!
hostname R3
!
boot-start-marker
boot-end-marker
!
no logging console

```
!
no aaa new-model
!
ip cef
!
ip inspect name MY-CBAC icmp
ip inspect name MY-CBAC tcp
ip inspect name MY-CBAC http
ip auth-proxy max-nodata-conns 3
ip admission max-nodata-conns 3
!
interface Ethernet0/0
 ip address 172.16.1.3 255.255.255.0
 ip access-group 150 out
 ip inspect MY-CBAC in
 full-duplex
!
interface Serial0/0
 ip address 10.1.1.3 255.255.255.0
 ip access-group 150 in
 ip inspect MY-CBAC out
!
interface Ethernet0/1
 no ip address
 shutdown
 half-duplex
!
ip http server
ip http authentication local
ip http secure-server
!
ip forward-protocol nd
!

access-list 150 deny   ip any any
!
control-plane
!
line con 0
line aux 0
line vty 0 4
 password cisco
 login local
!
end
```

R4 Configuration

```
R4#show run
Building configuration...

Current configuration : 876 bytes
```

```
!
version 12.4
service timestamps debug datetime msec
service timestamps log datetime msec
no service password-encryption
!
hostname R4
!
boot-start-marker
boot-end-marker
!
no logging console
!
no aaa new-model
!
ip cef
!
ip auth-proxy max-nodata-conns 3
ip admission max-nodata-conns 3
!
username cisco privilege 15 secret 5 $1$5xfY$qduHuWEcucGng94cEg6q7/
!
interface Ethernet0/0
 no ip address
 full-duplex
!
interface Serial0/0
 ip address 10.1.1.4 255.255.255.0
 clock rate 768000
 no fair-queue
!
interface Ethernet0/1
 no ip address
 shutdown
 half-duplex
!
ip http server
ip http authentication local
no ip http secure-server
!
ip forward-protocol nd
ip route 0.0.0.0 0.0.0.0 Serial0/0
!
control-plane
!
line con 0
line aux 0
line vty 0 4
 login local
!
end
```

LAB 4

Authentication and Authorization

Lab Objective:

The objective of this lab exercise is for you to learn and understand how configure Authentication and Authorization in Cisco IOS software.

Lab Purpose:

Authentication and Authorization are two of the three components of AAA services. These two components secure access to Cisco IOS routers and dictate who can access these devices and what they can do on these devices.

Lab Difficulty:

This lab has a difficulty rating of 6/10.

Readiness Assessment:

When you are ready for your certification exam, you should complete this lab in no more than 10 minutes.

Lab Topology:

Please use the following topology to complete this lab exercise:

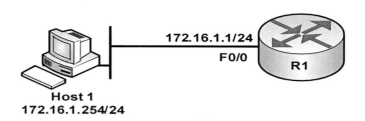

Lab 4 Configuration Tasks

Task 1:

Configure the hostname on R1 and IP addressing as illustrated in the diagram. In addition, configure Host 1 with the IP address specified and a default gateway of 172.16.1.1.

NOTE: If you do not have a Host in your lab, you can simply substitute Host 1 for another router with an Ethernet interface and a default static route pointing to 172.16.1.1.

Task 2:

Configure Authentication as follows on R1:

- Users should first attempt to be authenticated against TACACS+ server 172.16.1.192
- If the TACACS+ server is unavailable, users should be authenticated locally
- If the local database is corrupted, users should be authenticated using the enable password
- The Authentication username prompt should read: "Please Enter The Correct Username:"
- The Authentication password prompt should read: "Please Enter The Correct Password:"
- The TACACS+ server should use the password securetacacs+ for security

Task 3:

Configure Authorization as follows on R1:

- Users should be allowed to execute EXEC commands once successfully authenticated
- Network connections to R1 should be authenticated via TACACS+
- Authorization should NOT be used for configuration commands

Task 4:

Configure user **ccna** with a password of **security** on R1. In addition to this, configure an enable secret of **aaasecret** on R1. Finally, configure R1 so that AAA is used for Telnet/SSH connections.

Task 5:

Verify that your Authentication and Authorization configuration works as expected using the appropriate debugging commands while you Telnet from Host 1 to R1.

Lab 4 Configuration and Verification

Task 1:
```
Router(config)#hostname R1
R1(config)#int f0/0
R1(config-if)#ip address 172.16.1.1 255.255.255.0
R1(config-if)#no shutdown
R1(config-if)#exit
R1(config)#exit
R1#
```

```
Command Prompt                                                    _ □ ×
C:\>ipconfig

Windows IP Configuration

Ethernet adapter Local Area Connection 2:

        Connection-specific DNS Suffix  . :
        IP Address. . . . . . . . . . . : 172.16.1.254
        Subnet Mask . . . . . . . . . . : 255.255.255.0
        Default Gateway . . . . . . . . : 172.16.1.1

Ethernet adapter Wireless Network Connection:

        Media State . . . . . . . . . . : Media disconnected

C:\>_
```

Task 2:

R1(config)#**aaa new-model**
R1(config)#**aaa authentication login default group tacacs+ local enable**
R1(config)#**aaa authentication username-prompt "Please Enter The Correct Username:"**
R1(config)#**aaa authentication password-prompt "Please Enter The Correct Password:"**
R1(config)#**tacacs-server host 172.16.1.192 key securetacacs+**

Task 3:

R1(config)#**aaa authorization exec default if-authenticated**
R1(config)#**aaa authorization network default group tacacs+**
R1(config)#**no aaa authorization config-commands**

Task 4:

R1(config)#**username ccna secret security**
R1(config)#**enable secret aaasecret**
R1(config)#**line vty 0 4**
R1(config-line)#**login authentication default**
R1(config-line)#**exit**
R1(config)#**exit**
R1#

Task 5:

```
Telnet 172.16.1.1                                    - □ ×

User Access Verification

Please Enter The Correct Username:ccna
Please Enter The Correct Password:

R1>enable
Please Enter The Correct Password:
R1#
R1#show run int f0/0
Building configuration...

Current configuration : 95 bytes
!
interface FastEthernet0/0
 ip address 172.16.1.1 255.255.255.0
 duplex auto
 speed auto
end

R1#
```

R1#**debug aaa authentication**

AAA Authentication debugging is on

R1#

R1#**debug aaa authorization**

AAA Authorization debugging is on

R1#

R1#**debug tacacs authentication**

TACACS+ authentication debugging is on

R1#

R1#**show debugging**

General OS:

 TACACS+ authentication debugging is on

 AAA Authentication debugging is on

 AAA Authorization debugging is on

R1#

R1#

*Mar 1 01:33:11.428: AAA/BIND(00000006): Bind i/f

*Mar 1 01:33:11.428: AAA/AUTHEN/LOGIN (00000006): Pick method list 'default'

*Mar 1 01:33:11.432: TPLUS: Queuing AAA Authentication request 6 for processing

*Mar 1 01:33:11.432: TPLUS: processing authentication start request id 6

*Mar 1 01:33:11.436: TPLUS: Authentication start packet created for 6()

*Mar 1 01:33:11.436: TPLUS: Using server 172.16.1.192

*Mar 1 01:33:11.440: TPLUS(00000006)/0/NB_WAIT/83C593B4: Started 5 sec timeout

*Mar 1 01:33:16.440: TPLUS(00000006)/0/NB_WAIT/83C593B4: timed out

*Mar 1 01:33:16.440: TPLUS(00000006)/0/NB_WAIT/83C593B4: timed out, clean up

*Mar 1 01:33:16.440: TPLUS(00000006)/0/83C593B4: Processing the reply packet

*Mar 1 01:33:23.471: AAA/AUTHOR (00000006): Method=If-authen for method list id=00000000Skip author

*Mar 1 01:33:25.298: AAA: parse name=tty66 idb type=-1 tty=-1

*Mar 1 01:33:25.302: AAA: name=tty66 flags=0x11 type=5 shelf=0 slot=0 adapter=0 port=66 channel=0

*Mar 1 01:33:25.302: AAA/MEMORY: create_user (0x83FE0350) user='ccna' ruser='NULL' ds0=0 port='tty66' rem_addr='172.16.1.254' authen_type=ASCII service=ENABLE priv=15 initial_task_id='0', vrf= (id=0)
*Mar 1 01:33:25.302: AAA/AUTHEN/START (103502052): port='tty66' list='' action=LOGIN service=ENABLE
*Mar 1 01:33:25.302: AAA/AUTHEN/START (103502052): non-console enable - default to enable password
*Mar 1 01:33:25.302: AAA/AUTHEN/START (103502052): Method=ENABLE
*Mar 1 01:33:25.302: AAA/AUTHEN(103502052): Status=GETPASS
*Mar 1 01:33:29.000: AAA/AUTHEN/CONT (103502052): continue_login (user='(undef)')
*Mar 1 01:33:29.000: AAA/AUTHEN(103502052): Status=GETPASS
*Mar 1 01:33:29.000: AAA/AUTHEN/CONT (103502052): Method=ENABLE
*Mar 1 01:33:29.032: AAA/AUTHEN(103502052): Status=PASS
*Mar 1 01:33:29.032: AAA/MEMORY: free_user (0x83FE0350) user='NULL' ruser='NULL' port='tty66' rem_addr='172.16.1.254' authen_type=ASCII service=ENABLE priv=15 vrf= (id=0)

Lab 4 Configurations

R1 Configuration

```
R1#show run
Building configuration...

Current configuration : 1145 bytes
!
version 12.4
service timestamps debug datetime msec
service timestamps log datetime msec
no service password-encryption
!
hostname R1
!
boot-start-marker
boot-end-marker
!
enable secret 5 $1$y8wu$AFbDAxFJykgN55jMYOICo0
!
aaa new-model
!
aaa authentication password-prompt "Please Enter The Correct Password:"
aaa authentication username-prompt "Please Enter The Correct Username:"
aaa authentication login default group tacacs+ local enable
aaa authorization exec default if-authenticated
aaa authorization network default group tacacs+
!
```

```
aaa session-id common
no network-clock-participate slot 1
no network-clock-participate wic 0
ip cef
!
multilink bundle-name authenticated
!
username ccna secret 5 $1$Fzrf$K2Ek3GaOj49kbylSrbjJh1
archive
 log config
  hidekeys
!
interface FastEthernet0/0
 ip address 172.16.1.1 255.255.255.0
 duplex auto
 speed auto
!
interface Serial0/0
 no ip address
!
ip forward-protocol nd
!
ip http server
no ip http secure-server
!
tacacs-server host 172.16.1.192 key securetacacs+
!
control-plane
!
line con 0
line aux 0
line vty 0 4
!
end
```

LAB 5

Accounting

Lab Objective:

The objective of this lab exercise is for you to learn and understand how configure Accounting in Cisco IOS software.

Lab Purpose:

Accounting is one of the three components of AAA services. Accounting allows administrators to configure Cisco IOS routers to send information on the commands or other actions taken by Authenticated and Authorized users on those devices.

Lab Difficulty:

This lab has a difficulty rating of 6/10.

Readiness Assessment:

When you are ready for your certification exam, you should complete this lab in no more than 10 minutes.

Lab Topology:

Please use the following topology to complete this lab exercise:

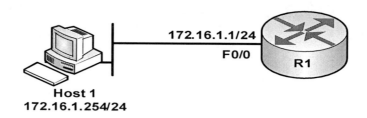

Host 1
172.16.1.254/24

Lab 5 Configuration Tasks

Task 1:

Configure the hostname on R1 and IP addressing as illustrated in the diagram. In addition, configure Host 1 with the IP address specified and a default gateway of 172.16.1.1.

NOTE: If you do not have a Host in your lab, you can simply substitute Host 1 for another router with an Ethernet interface and a default static route pointing to 172.16.1.1.

Task 2:

Configure Authentication as follows on R1:

- The Authentication username prompt should read: "Enter Username:"

- The Authentication password prompt should read: "Enter Password:"
- Users should be Authenticated only against the local database

Task 3:

Configure Authorization as follows on R1:

- Level 15 commands should be Authorized based on the local database
- Level 1 commands should be Authorized if the user is successfully Authenticated
- The local database should be used to Authorize configuration commands

Task 4:

Configure Accounting as follows on R1:

- R1 should record start and stop without waiting for Level 15 commands
- R1 should record stop when service terminates for Level 1 commands
- Accounting information should be sent to RADUIS server 172.16.1.192

Task 5:

Configure the following username/password pairs on R1:

Username	Secret	Privilege Level
super	cisco123	15
basic	cisco456	1

In addition, ensure that R1 uses AAA for inbound connection.

Task 6:

Verify that your Accounting configuration works as expected using the appropriate debugging commands while you Telnet from Host 1 to R1.

Lab 5 Configuration and Verification

Task 1:
```
Router(config)#hostname R1
R1(config)#int f0/0
R1(config-if)#ip address 172.16.1.1 255.255.255.0
R1(config-if)#no shutdown
R1(config-if)#exit
R1(config)#exit
R1#
```

```
Command Prompt                                                    _ □ ×

C:\>ipconfig

Windows IP Configuration

Ethernet adapter Local Area Connection 2:

        Connection-specific DNS Suffix  . :
        IP Address. . . . . . . . . . . : 172.16.1.254
        Subnet Mask . . . . . . . . . . : 255.255.255.0
        Default Gateway . . . . . . . . : 172.16.1.1

Ethernet adapter Wireless Network Connection:

        Media State . . . . . . . . . . : Media disconnected

C:\>_
```

Task 2:

R1(config)#aaa new-model
R1(config)#aaa authentication username-prompt "Enter Username:"
R1(config)#aaa authentication password-prompt "Enter Password:"
R1(config)#aaa authentication login default local

Task 3:

R1(config)#aaa authorization commands 15 default local
R1(config)#aaa authorization commands 1 default if-authenticated
R1(config)#aaa authorization exec default local
R1(config)#aaa authorization config-commands

Task 4:

R1(config)#aaa accounting commands 15 default start-stop group AAA-RADIUS
R1(config)#aaa accounting commands 1 default stop-only group AAA-RADIUS
R1(config)#aaa group server radius AAA-RADIUS
R1(config-sg-radius)#server 172.16.1.192
R1(config-sg-radius)#exit
R1(config)#exit
R1#

Task 5:

R1(config)#username super privilege 15 secret cisco123
R1(config)#username basic privilege 1 secret cisco456
R1(config)#line vty 0 4
R1(config-line)#login authentication default
R1(config-line)#exit
R1(config)#exit
R1#

Task 6:

```
User Access Verification

Enter Username:super
Enter Password:

R1#conf
Configuring from terminal, memory, or network [terminal]?
Enter configuration commands, one per line.  End with CNTL/Z.
R1(config)#ip routing
R1(config)#exit
R1#
R1#_
```

R1#**debug aaa accounting**
AAA Accounting debugging is on
R1#
R1#
R1#
*Mar 1 01:10:24.351: AAA/ACCT/EVENT/(00000007): CALL START
*Mar 1 01:10:24.351: Getting session id for NET(00000007) : db=84461164
*Mar 1 01:10:24.351: AAA/ACCT(00000000): add node, session 5
*Mar 1 01:10:24.355: AAA/ACCT/NET(00000007): add, count 1
*Mar 1 01:10:24.355: Getting session id for NONE(00000007) : db=84461164
*Mar 1 01:10:30.396: AAA: parse name=tty66 idb type=-1 tty=-1
*Mar 1 01:10:30.396: AAA: name=tty66 flags=0x11 type=5 shelf=0 slot=0 adapter=0
port=66 channel=0
*Mar 1 01:10:30.396: AAA/MEMORY: create_user (0x844A52A4) user='super' ruser='R1'
ds0=0 port='tty66' rem_addr='172.16.1.254' authen_type=ASCII service=NONE priv=15 ini-
tial_task_id='0', vrf= (id=0)
*Mar 1 01:10:30.396: AAA/MEMORY: free_user (0x844A52A4) user='super' ruser='R1'
port='tty66' rem_addr='172.16.1.254' authen_type=ASCII service=NONE priv=15 vrf= (id=0)
*Mar 1 01:10:33.445: AAA: parse name=tty66 idb type=-1 tty=-1
*Mar 1 01:10:33.445: AAA: name=tty66 flags=0x11 type=5 shelf=0 slot=0 adapter=0
port=66 channel=0
*Mar 1 01:10:33.445: AAA/MEMORY: create_user (0x835307CC) user='super' ruser='R1'
ds0=0 port='tty66' rem_addr='172.16.1.254' authen_type=ASCII service=NONE priv=15
initial_task_id='0', vrf= (id=0)
*Mar 1 01:10:33.445: AAA/MEMORY: free_user (0x835307CC) user='super' ruser='R1'
port='tty66' rem_addr='172.16.1.254' authen_type=ASCII service=NONE priv=15 vrf=
(id=0)
*Mar 1 01:10:34.575: %SYS-5-CONFIG_I: Configured from console by super on vty0
(172.16.1.254)
*Mar 1 01:11:57.824: unknown AAA/DISC: 1/"User Request"
*Mar 1 01:11:57.824: unknown AAA/DISC/EXT: 1020/"User Request"
*Mar 1 01:11:57.828: AAA/ACCT/EVENT/(00000007): CALL STOP
*Mar 1 01:11:57.828: AAA/ACCT/CALL STOP(00000007): Sending stop requests

*Mar 1 01:11:57.828: AAA/ACCT(00000007): Send all stops
*Mar 1 01:11:57.828: AAA/ACCT/NET(00000007): STOP
*Mar 1 01:11:57.828: AAA/ACCT/NET(00000007): Method list not found
*Mar 1 01:11:57.828: AAA/ACCT(00000007): del node, session 5
*Mar 1 01:11:57.828: AAA/ACCT/NET(00000007): free_rec, count 0
*Mar 1 01:11:57.828: AAA/ACCT/NET(00000007) reccnt 0, csr TRUE, osr 0
*Mar 1 01:11:57.828: AAA/ACCT/NET(00000007): Last rec in db, intf not enqueued

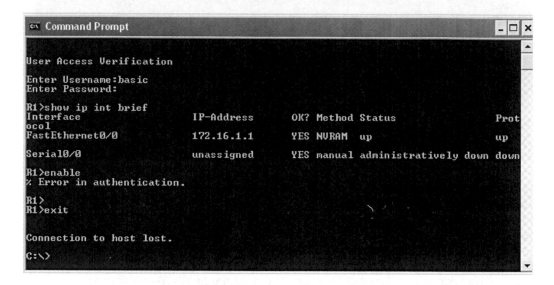

R1#**debug aaa accounting**
AAA Accounting debugging is on
R1#
*Mar 1 01:13:55.372: AAA/ACCT/EVENT/(00000009): CALL START
*Mar 1 01:13:55.372: Getting session id for NET(00000009) : db=83678F6C
*Mar 1 01:13:55.372: AAA/ACCT(00000000): add node, session 7
*Mar 1 01:13:55.372: AAA/ACCT/NET(00000009): add, count 1
*Mar 1 01:13:55.372: Getting session id for NONE(00000009) : db=83678F6C
*Mar 1 01:14:03.999: AAA: parse name=tty66 idb type=-1 tty=-1
*Mar 1 01:14:03.999: AAA: name=tty66 flags=0x11 type=5 shelf=0 slot=0 adapter=0 port=66 channel=0
*Mar 1 01:14:03.999: AAA/MEMORY: create_user (0x84460E48) user='basic' ruser='R1' ds0=0 port='tty66' rem_addr='172.16.1.254' authen_type=ASCII service=NONE priv=1 initial_task_id='0', vrf= (id=0)
*Mar 1 01:14:03.999: AAA/MEMORY: free_user (0x84460E48) user='basic' ruser='R1' port='tty66' rem_addr='172.16.1.254' authen_type=ASCII service=NONE priv=1 vrf= (id=0)
*Mar 1 01:14:06.150: AAA: parse name=tty66 idb type=-1 tty=-1
*Mar 1 01:14:06.150: AAA: name=tty66 flags=0x11 type=5 shelf=0 slot=0 adapter=0 port=66 channel=0
*Mar 1 01:14:06.150: AAA/MEMORY: create_user (0x8446107C) user='basic' ruser='NULL' ds0=0 port='tty66' rem_addr='172.16.1.254' authen_type=ASCII service=ENABLE priv=15 initial_task_id='0', vrf= (id=0)
*Mar 1 01:14:06.154: AAA/MEMORY: free_user (0x8446107C) user='basic' ruser='NULL' port='tty66' rem_addr='172.16.1.254' authen_type=ASCII service=ENABLE priv=15 vrf= (id=0)

```
*Mar  1 01:14:09.820: unknown AAA/DISC: 1/"User Request"
*Mar  1 01:14:09.820: unknown AAA/DISC/EXT: 1020/"User Request"
*Mar  1 01:14:09.824: AAA/ACCT/EVENT/(00000009): CALL STOP
*Mar  1 01:14:09.824: AAA/ACCT/CALL STOP(00000009): Sending stop requests
*Mar  1 01:14:09.824: AAA/ACCT(00000009): Send all stops
*Mar  1 01:14:09.824: AAA/ACCT/NET(00000009): STOP
*Mar  1 01:14:09.824: AAA/ACCT/NET(00000009): Method list not found
*Mar  1 01:14:09.824: AAA/ACCT(00000009): del node, session 7
*Mar  1 01:14:09.824: AAA/ACCT/NET(00000009): free_rec, count 0
*Mar  1 01:14:09.828: AAA/ACCT/NET(00000009) reccnt 0, csr TRUE, osr 0
*Mar  1 01:14:09.828: AAA/ACCT/NET(00000009): Last rec in db, intf not enqueued
```

Lab 5 Configurations

R1 Configuration

```
R1#show run
Building configuration...

Current configuration : 1208 bytes
!
version 12.4
service timestamps debug datetime msec
service timestamps log datetime msec
no service password-encryption
!
hostname R1
!
boot-start-marker
boot-end-marker
!
aaa new-model
!
aaa group server radius AAA-RADIUS
 server 172.16.1.192 auth-port 1645 acct-port 1646
!
aaa authentication password-prompt "Enter Password:"
aaa authentication username-prompt "Enter Username:"
aaa authentication login default local
aaa authorization config-commands
aaa authorization exec default local
aaa authorization commands 1 default if-authenticated
aaa authorization commands 15 default local
!
aaa session-id common
no network-clock-participate slot 1
no network-clock-participate wic 0
ip cef
!
multilink bundle-name authenticated
```

```
!
username super privilege 15 secret 5 $1$pvqx$JttbM.xHYFDzzfiBnS89.1
username basic secret 5 $1$ffy6$/cFBje9BqMb1Te64Gwdja0
archive
 log config
  hidekeys
!
interface FastEthernet0/0
 ip address 172.16.1.1 255.255.255.0
 duplex auto
 speed auto
!
interface Serial0/0
 no ip address
 shutdown
!
ip forward-protocol nd
!
ip http server
no ip http secure-server
!
control-plane
!
line con 0
line aux 0
line vty 0 4
!
end
```

LAB 6

Unicast Reverse Path Forwarding

Lab Objective:

The objective of this lab exercise is for you to learn and understand how implement Unicast Reverse Path Forwarding in Cisco IOS routers.

Lab Purpose:

The Unicast RPF feature helps to mitigate problems that are caused by the introduction of malformed or forged (spoofed) IP source addresses into a network by discarding IP packets that lack a verifiable IP source address.

Lab Difficulty:

This lab has a difficulty rating of 5/10.

Readiness Assessment:

When you are ready for your certification exam, you should complete this lab in no more than 10 minutes.

Lab Topology:

Please use the following topology to complete this lab exercise:

NOTE: The purpose of this lab is to understand the configuration commands. You are not required to test the configuration as the complexity is beyond the scope of the CCNA Security.

Lab 6 Configuration Tasks

Task 1:

Configure the hostnames and IP addresses on R1 and R2 as illustrated in the network diagram. Configure R2 to send R1 clocking information at a rate of 512Kbps. Ping between R1 and R2 to verify your configuration and ensure that the two routers have IP connectivity.

Task 2:

Configure uRPF on R1, while adhering to the following guidelines:

- Deny all traffic sourced from the 127.0.0.0/8 subnet. This traffic should be logged in detail.
- Deny all traffic sourced from any RFC 1918 subnet. This traffic should be logged in detail.
- Permit all other traffic. This traffic should not be logged.
- Use an ACL of your liking, but do not apply the ACL to the interface.

In addition, configure R1 to allow Telnet access using a password of **cisco**. Ensure that users that log in are automatically assigned Level 15 access without using an enable password.

Task 3:

Verify your uRPF configuration by using the appropriate show commands. Keep in mind that the objective of this lab is to validate your configuration knowledge. You are not expected to spoof IP addresses to test uRPF configuration as this is beyond the scope of this course.

Lab 6 Configuration and Verification

Task 1:
```
Router(config)#hostname R1
R1(config)#int s0/0
R1(config-if)#ip add 150.1.1.1 255.255.255.0
R1(config-if)#no shutdown
R1(config-if)#exit
R1(config)#exit
R1#


Router(config)#hostname R2
R2(config)#int s0/0
R2(config-if)#clock rate 512000
R2(config-if)#ip address 150.1.1.2 255.255.255.252
R2(config-if)#no shutdown
R2(config-if)#exit
R2(config)#exit
R2#
R2#ping 150.1.1.1

Type escape sequence to abort.
Sending 5, 100-byte ICMP Echos to 150.1.1.1, timeout is 2 seconds:
!!!!!
Success rate is 100 percent (5/5), round-trip min/avg/max = 4/4/8 ms
```

Task 3:

```
R1(config)#ip cef
R1(config)#access-list 111 remark "This is my uRPF ACL"
R1(config)#access-list 111 deny ip 127.0.0.0 0.255.255.255 any log-input
R1(config)#access-list 111 deny ip 10.0.0.0 0.255.255.255 any log-input
R1(config)#access-list 111 deny ip 172.16.0.0 0.15.255.255 any log-input
R1(config)#access-list 111 deny ip 192.168.0.0 0.0.255.255 any log-input
R1(config)#access-list 111 permit ip any any
R1(config)#int s0/0
R1(config-if)#ip verify unicast reverse-path 111
R1(config-if)#exit
R1(config)#line vty 0 4
R1(config-line)#password cisco
R1(config-line)#login
R1(config-line)#privilege level 15
R1(config-line)#exit
R1(config)#exit
R1#
```

Task 4:

The show cef interface [name] command is used to verify if uRPF is configured on an interface:

```
R1#show cef interface serial 0/0
Serial0/0 is up (if_number 4)
  Corresponding hwidb fast_if_number 4
  Corresponding hwidb firstsw->if_number 4
  Internet address is 150.1.1.1/24
  ICMP redirects are always sent
  Per packet load-sharing is disabled
  IP unicast RPF check is enabled
  Inbound access list is not set
  Outbound access list is not set
  Interface is marked as point to point interface
  Hardware idb is Serial0/0
  Fast switching type 4, interface type 63
  IP CEF switching enabled
  IP CEF Feature Fast switching turbo vector
  Input fast flags 0x4000, Input fast flags2 0x0, Output fast flags 0x0, Output fast flags2
0x0
  ifindex 2(2)
  Slot 0 Slot unit 0 Unit 0 VC -1
  Transmit limit accumulator 0x0 (0x0)
  IP MTU 1500
R1#
```

In a production environment, if uRPF is configured, the **show ip interfaces [name]** command can be used to view the packets dropped by the uRPF feature in Cisco IOS software:

R1#**show ip interface serial 0/0**
Serial0/0 is up, line protocol is up
  Internet address is 150.1.1.1/24
  Broadcast address is 255.255.255.255
  Address determined by setup command
  MTU is 1500 bytes
  Helper address is not set
  Directed broadcast forwarding is disabled
  Outgoing access list is not set
  Inbound access list is not set
  -----[Truncated Output]-----
  WCCP Redirect outbound is disabled
  WCCP Redirect inbound is disabled
  WCCP Redirect exclude is disabled
  IP verify source reachable-via RX, allow default, ACL 111
  34 verification drops
  31 suppressed verification drops

Lab 6 Configurations

R1 Configuration

R1#show run
Building configuration...

Current configuration : 1116 bytes
!
version 12.4
service timestamps debug datetime msec
service timestamps log datetime msec
no service password-encryption
!
hostname R1
!
boot-start-marker
boot-end-marker
!
logging buffered 4096
no logging console
!
no aaa new-model
no network-clock-participate slot 1
no network-clock-participate wic 0
ip cef
!
multilink bundle-name authenticated
!

```
archive
 log config
  hidekeys
!
interface FastEthernet0/0
 no ip address
 duplex auto
 speed auto
!
interface Serial0/0
 ip address 150.1.1.1 255.255.255.0
 ip verify unicast reverse-path 111
!
ip forward-protocol nd
!
ip http server
no ip http secure-server
!
access-list 111 deny      ip 127.0.0.0 0.255.255.255 any log-input
access-list 111 deny      ip 10.0.0.0 0.255.255.255 any log-input
access-list 111 deny      ip 172.16.0.0 0.15.255.255 any log-input
access-list 111 deny      ip 192.168.0.0 0.0.255.255 any log-input
access-list 111 permit    ip any any
access-list 111 remark    "This is my uRPF ACL"
!
control-plane
!
line con 0
line aux 0
line vty 0 4
 privilege level 15
 password cisco
 login
!
end
```

R2 Configuration

```
R2#show run
Building configuration...

Current configuration : 774 bytes
!
version 12.4
service timestamps debug datetime msec
service timestamps log datetime msec
no service password-encryption
!
```

```
hostname R2
!
boot-start-marker
boot-end-marker
!
no logging console
!
no aaa new-model
no network-clock-participate slot 1
no network-clock-participate wic 0
ip cef
!
no ip domain lookup
!
multilink bundle-name authenticated
!
archive
 log config
  hidekeys
!
interface FastEthernet0/0
 no ip address
 duplex auto
 speed auto
!
interface Serial0/0
 ip address 150.1.1.2 255.255.255.252
 clock rate 512000
!
ip forward-protocol nd
!
ip http server
ip http authentication local
no ip http secure-server
!
control-plane
!
line con 0
line aux 0
line vty 0 4
 privilege level 15
 password cisco
 login
!
end
```

LAB 7

Using ACLs to Secure Access to Cisco IOS Routers

Lab Objective:

The objective of this lab exercise is for you to learn and understand how implement ACLs to secure access to Cisco IOS routers.

Lab Purpose:

ACLs can be used to prevent unauthorized hosts and subnets from gaining access to Cisco IOS routers in numerous methods.

Lab Difficulty:

This lab has a difficulty rating of 5/10.

Readiness Assessment:

When you are ready for your certification exam, you should complete this lab in no more than 15 minutes.

Lab Topology:

Please use the following topology to complete this lab exercise:

NOTE: The purpose of this lab is to understand the configuration commands. You are not required to test the configuration as the complexity is beyond the scope of the CCNA Security.

Lab 7 Configuration Tasks

Task 1:

Configure the hostnames and IP addresses on R1 and R2 as illustrated in the network diagram. Configure R2 to send R1 clocking information at a rate of 512Kbps. Ping between R1 and R2 to verify your configuration and ensure that the two routers have IP connectivity.

Task 2:

On R1, configure an ACL for the VTY lines that performs the following:

- Denies Telnet and SSH traffic from the RFC 1918 subnets to R1
- Denies Telnet and SSH traffic from the 127.0.0.0/8 subnet to R1
- Permits Telnet and SSH traffic from all other subnets. This permit must be logged in detail.

The VTY lines should be secured by the password **cisco** and provide Level 15 access by default.

Task 3:

Configure the following interfaces on R2:

Interface	Address	Mask
Loopback160	160.1.1.2	/27
Loopback170	170.1.1.2	/22
Loopback180	180.1.1.2	/19

Task 4:

Configure anti-spoofing ACLs on R2 that performs the following:

Inbound
- Denies the 127.0.0.0/8 address space and provides detailed logging
- Denies the Loopback160, Loopback170 and Loopback180 address space without logging
- Permits all other IP traffic

Outbound
- Permits the Loopback160, Loopback170 and Loopback180 address space
- Denies the RFC 1918 address space and provides detailed logging

Task 5:

Configure an ACL on R1 to restrict HTTP and HTTPS access as follows:
- Allow HTTP from the 192.168.0.0/24 subnet
- Deny HTTP from the 192.168.1.0/24 subnet
- Deny HTTP from the 127.0.0.0/8 subnet
- Allow HTTP from all other subnets

Lab 7 Configuration and Verification

Task 1:

```
Router(config)#hostname R1
R1(config)#int s0/0
R1(config-if)#ip add 150.1.1.1 255.255.255.0
R1(config-if)#no shutdown
R1(config-if)#exit
R1(config)#exit
R1#


Router(config)#hostname R2
R2(config)#int s0/0
R2(config-if)#clock rate 512000
R2(config-if)#ip address 150.1.1.2 255.255.255.252
R2(config-if)#no shutdown
R2(config-if)#exit
R2(config)#exit
R2#
R2#ping 150.1.1.1

Type escape sequence to abort.
Sending 5, 100-byte ICMP Echos to 150.1.1.1, timeout is 2 seconds:
!!!!!
Success rate is 100 percent (5/5), round-trip min/avg/max = 4/4/8 ms
```

Task 2:

```
R1(config)#ip access-list extended VTY-SECURITY
R1(config-ext-nacl)#deny tcp 10.0.0.0 0.255.255.255 any eq telnet
R1(config-ext-nacl)#deny tcp 10.0.0.0 0.255.255.255 any eq 22
R1(config-ext-nacl)# deny tcp 172.16.0.0 0.15.255.255 any eq telnet
R1(config-ext-nacl)# deny tcp 172.16.0.0 0.15.255.255 any eq 22
R1(config-ext-nacl)#deny tcp 192.168.0.0 0.0.255.255 any eq telnet
R1(config-ext-nacl)#deny tcp 192.168.0.0 0.0.255.255 any eq 22
R1(config-ext-nacl)#deny tcp 127.0.0.0 0.255.255.255 any eq telnet
R1(config-ext-nacl)#deny tcp 127.0.0.0 0.255.255.255 any eq 22
R1(config-ext-nacl)#permit tcp any any eq telnet log-input
R1(config-ext-nacl)#permit tcp any any eq 22 log-input
R1(config-ext-nacl)#exit
R1(config)#line vty 0 4
R1(config-line)#access-class VTY-SECURITY in
R1(config-line)#password cisco
R1(config-line)#privilege level 15
R1(config-line)#login
R1(config-line)#exit
R1(config)#exit
R1#
```

Task 3:
```
R2(config)#int loopback 160
R2(config-if)#ip address 160.1.1.2 255.255.255.224
R2(config-if)#exit
R2(config)#int loopback 170
R2(config-if)#ip address 170.1.1.2 255.255.252.0
R2(config-if)#exit
R2(config)#int loopback 180
R2(config-if)#ip address 180.1.1.2 255.255.224.0
R2(config-if)#exit
R2(config)#exit
R2#
```

Task 4:
```
R2(config)#ip access-list extended ANTI-SPOOF-IN
R2(config-ext-nacl)#deny ip 127.0.0.0 0.255.255.255 any log-input
R2(config-ext-nacl)#deny ip 160.1.1.0 0.0.0.31 any
R2(config-ext-nacl)#deny ip 170.1.0.0 0.0.3.255 any
R2(config-ext-nacl)#deny ip 180.1.0.0 0.0.31.255 any
R2(config-ext-nacl)#permit ip any any
R2(config-ext-nacl)#exit
R2(config)#ip access-list extended ANTI-SPOOF-OUT
R2(config-ext-nacl)#permit ip 160.1.1.0 0.0.0.31 any
R2(config-ext-nacl)#permit ip 170.1.0.0 0.0.3.255 any
R2(config-ext-nacl)#permit ip 180.1.0.0 0.0.31.255 any
R2(config-ext-nacl)#deny ip 10.0.0.0 0.255.255.255 any log-input
R2(config-ext-nacl)#deny ip 172.16.0.0 0.0.15.255 any log-input
R2(config-ext-nacl)#no deny ip 172.16.0.0 0.0.15.255 any log-input
R2(config-ext-nacl)#deny ip 172.16.0.0 0.15.255.255 any log-input
R2(config-ext-nacl)#exit
R2(config)#int s0/0
R2(config-if)#ip access-group ANTI-SPOOF-IN in
R2(config-if)#ip access-group ANTI-SPOOF-OUT out
R2(config-if)#exit
R2(config)#exit
R2#
R2#show ip interface serial 0/0
Serial0/0 is up, line protocol is up
  Internet address is 150.1.1.1/30
  Broadcast address is 255.255.255.255
  Address determined by setup command
  MTU is 1500 bytes
  Helper address is not set
  Directed broadcast forwarding is disabled
  Outgoing access list is ANTI-SPOOF-OUT
  Inbound  access list is ANTI-SPOOF-IN
  Proxy ARP is enabled
----[Truncated Output]-----
```

Task 5:

```
R1(config)#access-list 50 remark "This is my HTTP/HTTPS ACL"
R1(config)#access-list 50 permit 192.168.0.0 0.0.0.255
R1(config)#access-list 50 deny 192.168.1.0 0.0.0.255
R1(config)#access-list 50 deny 127.0.0.0 0.255.255.255
R1(config)#access-list 50 permit any
R1(config)#ip http server
R1(config)#ip http secure-server
R1(config)#ip http access-class 50
R1(config)#exit
R1#
```

Lab 7 Configurations

R1 Configuration

```
R1#show run
Building configuration...

Current configuration : 1494 bytes
!
version 12.4
service timestamps debug datetime msec
service timestamps log datetime msec
no service password-encryption
!
hostname R1
!
boot-start-marker
boot-end-marker
!
no logging console
!
no aaa new-model
no network-clock-participate slot 1
no network-clock-participate wic 0
ip cef
!
multilink bundle-name authenticated
!
crypto pki trustpoint TP-self-signed-3473940174
 enrollment selfsigned
 subject-name cn=IOS-Self-Signed-Certificate-3473940174
 revocation-check none
 rsakeypair TP-self-signed-3473940174
!
```

```
crypto pki certificate chain TP-self-signed-3473940174
certificate self-signed 01
  3082023A 308201A3 A0030201 02020101 300D0609 2A864886 F70D0101 04050030
  31312F30 2D060355 04031326 494F532D 53656C66 2D536967 6E65642D 43657274
  69666963 6174652D 33343733 39343031 3734301E 170D3032 30333031 30343433
  31305A17 0D323030 31303130 30303030 305A3031 312F302D 06035504 03132649
  4F532D53 656C662D 5369676E 65642D43 65727469 66696361 74652D33 34373339
  34303137 3430819F 300D0609 2A864886 F70D0101 01050003 818D0030 81890281
  8100C824 4F0BABB6 A557E3A3 3EE6D399 5A495CF6 8F7E131A 62670291 9710DF0F
  CB6918CB D3B817C8 51D4648C 79B882A8 637804CB 8984FB80 D9F1D86B E79C8292
  E1617724 252490F4 BE0322C0 5C984515 3E0A4550 75E9BCC7 7A19900C 0084F632
  19643491 5C0E821D 5442E1C8 FB4BE8A3 034E2954 01B4377C DC14AF72 0F4C92DC
  70A90203 010001A3 62306030 0F060355 1D130101 FF040530 030101FF 300D0603
  551D1104 06300482 02523230 1F060355 1D230418 30168014 4020A082 2373EFEF
  CD379B8C 2A1A4D13 43842D59 301D0603 551D0E04 16041440 20A08223 73EFEFCD
  379B8C2A 1A4D1343 842D5930 0D06092A 864886F7 0D010104 05000381 81003F41
  884FE500 E8EBCBF8 9711C10F 6A1F4110 B850B68D A84DDFDD D14EC73A 06B47781
  3B4CAB5E 05FE96F9 AEEFD074 A49AD426 D830B3E4 468D5D98 1ADAC3C5 04958145
  E99C3B0C 218EFD94 6780FE45 5AA6E608 19E067B7 A582601C 280AE0A1 135ADF47
  35016D1C 6F6A7252 A054845B BF16FCA8 7873C9B3 62E09894 AC5C4375 FADB
    quit
!
archive
 log config
  hidekeys
!
interface FastEthernet0/0
 no ip address
 duplex auto
 speed auto
!
interface Serial0/0
 ip address 150.1.1.1 255.255.255.252
!
ip forward-protocol nd
!
ip http server
ip http access-class 50
ip http secure-server
!
ip access-list extended VTY-SECURITY
 deny     tcp 10.0.0.0 0.255.255.255 any eq telnet
 deny     tcp 10.0.0.0 0.255.255.255 any eq 22
 deny     tcp 172.16.0.0 0.15.255.255 any eq telnet
 deny     tcp 172.16.0.0 0.15.255.255 any eq 22
 deny     tcp 192.168.0.0 0.0.255.255 any eq telnet
```

```
 deny      tcp 192.168.0.0 0.0.255.255 any eq 22
 deny      tcp 127.0.0.0 0.255.255.255 any eq telnet
 deny      tcp 127.0.0.0 0.255.255.255 any eq 22
 permit    tcp any any eq telnet log-input
 permit    tcp any any eq 443 log-input
!
access-list 50 remark      "This is my HTTP/HTTPS ACL"
access-list 50 permit      192.168.0.0 0.0.0.255
access-list 50 deny        192.168.1.0 0.0.0.255
access-list 50 deny        127.0.0.0 0.255.255.255
access-list 50 permit      any
!
control-plane
!
line con 0
line aux 0
line vty 0 4
 access-class VTY-SECURITY in
 privilege level 15
 password cisco
 login
!
end
```

R2 Configuration

```
R2#sh run
Building configuration...

Current configuration : 1502 bytes
!
version 12.4
service timestamps debug datetime msec
service timestamps log datetime msec
no service password-encryption
!
hostname R2
!
boot-start-marker
boot-end-marker
!
no logging console
!
no aaa new-model
no network-clock-participate slot 1
no network-clock-participate wic 0
ip cef
!
no ip domain lookup
!
multilink bundle-name authenticated
!
```

```
archive
 log config
  hidekeys
!
interface Loopback160
 ip address 160.1.1.2 255.255.255.224
!
interface Loopback170
 ip address 170.1.1.2 255.255.252.0
!
interface Loopback180
 ip address 180.1.1.2 255.255.224.0
!
interface FastEthernet0/0
 no ip address
 duplex auto
 speed auto
!
interface Serial0/0
 ip address 150.1.1.1 255.255.255.252
 ip access-group ANTI-SPOOF-IN in
 ip access-group ANTI-SPOOF-OUT out
 clock rate 512000
!
ip forward-protocol nd
!
ip http server
ip http authentication local
no ip http secure-server
!
ip access-list extended ANTI-SPOOF-IN
 deny      ip 127.0.0.0 0.255.255.255 any log-input
 deny      ip 160.1.1.0 0.0.0.31 any
 deny      ip 170.1.0.0 0.0.3.255 any
 deny      ip 180.1.0.0 0.0.31.255 any
 permit    ip any any
ip access-list extended ANTI-SPOOF-OUT
 permit    ip 160.1.1.0 0.0.0.31 any
 permit    ip 170.1.0.0 0.0.3.255 any
 permit    ip 180.1.0.0 0.0.31.255 any
 deny      ip 10.0.0.0 0.255.255.255 any log-input
 deny      ip 172.16.0.0 0.15.255.255 any log-input
!
control-plane
!
line con 0
line aux 0
line vty 0 4
 password cisco
 login
!
end
```

LAB 8

Role-Based CLI Access

Lab Objective:

The objective of this lab exercise is for you to learn and understand how implement Role Based CLI access on Cisco IOS routers.

Lab Purpose:

The Role-Based CLI Access feature allows the network administrator to define "views," which are a set of operational commands and configuration capabilities that provide selective or partial access to EXEC and configuration mode commands. This allows administrators to exercise better control over access to Cisco networking devices.

Lab Difficulty:

This lab has a difficulty rating of 8/10.

Readiness Assessment:

When you are ready for your certification exam, you should complete this lab in no more than 15 minutes.

Lab Topology:

Please use any single router to complete this lab

Lab 8 Configuration Tasks

Task 1:

Configure the hostname of the router as illustrated in the following diagram.

Task 2:

Configure an enable secret of **c?sco** on R1.

Task 3:

Configure the IOS Role-Based CLI Access on R1 as follows:

View Name	View Password	View Commands
BASIC	basic	1. The show hardware command 2. The show version command 3. The show inventory command
EXPERT	expert	1. All show commands
CONFIG	config	1. All configure commands

Task 4:

Create a view named SUPER. This View should contain all possible **show** and **configure** commands contained in all other views that were previously created.

Task 5:

Verify your configuration by logging into the router using different credentials.

Lab 8 Configuration and Verification

Task 1:
```
Router(config)#hostname R1
R1(config)#end
R1#
```

Task 2:

To complete this Task, it is important that you remember that you must use the **CTRL/V** keystrokes to be able to use the question mark in a password on Cisco IOS devices.

```
R1(config)#enable secret c?sco
R1(config)#exit
R1#
```

Task 3:
```
R1(config)#aaa new-model
R1(config)#exit
R1#disable
R1>enable view
Password:

R1#
R1#show parser view
Current view is 'root'
R1#
```

```
R1#
R1#config t
Enter configuration commands, one per line.  End with CNTL/Z.
R1(config)#parser view BASIC
R1(config-view)#secret basic
R1(config-view)#commands exec include show hardware
R1(config-view)#commands exec include show version
R1(config-view)#commands exec include show inventory
R1(config-view)#exit
R1(config)#parser view EXPERT
R1(config-view)#secret expert
R1(config-view)#commands exec include all show
R1(config-view)#exit
R1(config)#parser view CONFIG
R1(config-view)#secret config
R1(config-view)#commands exec include all configure
R1(config-view)#exit
R1(config)#exit
R1#
```

Task 4:

```
R1(config)#parser view SUPER superview
R1(config-view)#secret super
R1(config-view)#view BASIC
R1(config-view)#view EXPERT
R1(config-view)#view CONFIG
R1(config-view)#exit
R1(config)#exit
R1#
```

Task 5:

The first view we will validate is the **BASIC** view as configured on R1. This view will be limited to just a select few **show** commands.

```
R1#disable
R1>
R1>
R1>enable view BASIC
Password:

R1#
R1#
R1#?
Exec commands:
  enable    Turn on privileged commands
  exit      Exit from the EXEC
  show      Show running system information
```

```
R1#
R1#show ?
  flash:    display information about flash: file system
  hardware  Hardware specific information
  inventory Show the physical inventory
  parser    Show parser commands
  version   System hardware and software status
R1#
R1#show parser view
Current view is 'BASIC'
```

The second view we will validate is the **EXPERT** view as configured on R1. This view will have access to the entire range of **show** commands.

```
R1>enable view EXPERT
Password:

R1#
R1#
R1#show parser view
Current view is 'EXPERT'
R1#
R1#?
Exec commands:
  enable   Turn on privileged commands
  exit     Exit from the EXEC
  show     Show running system information
R1#
R1#show ?
  aaa               Show AAA values
  accounting        Accounting data for active sessions
  alarm-interface   Display information about a specific Alarm Interface
                Card
  alignment         Show alignment information
  appfw             Application Firewall information
  archive           Archive of the running configuration information
  arp               ARP table
  auto              Show Automation Template
  backup            Backup status
----[Truncated Output]----
```

The third view we will validate is the **CONFIG** view as configured on R1. This view will have only configuration commands.

```
R1>enable view CONFIG
Password:
```

```
R1#?
Exec commands:
  configure Enter configuration mode
  enable    Turn on privileged commands
  exit      Exit from the EXEC
  show      Show running system information

R1#show ip int brie
       ^
% Invalid input detected at '^' marker.

R1#configure
Configuring from terminal, memory, or network [terminal]? terminal
Enter configuration commands, one per line.  End with CNTL/Z.
R1(config)#
R1(config)#exit
R1#
R1#show parser view
Current view is 'CONFIG'
```

The final view we will validate is the **SUPER** view as configured on R1. This view will have all possible show and configure commands that are supported in the Cisco IOS software. However, this view will not have any debug commands available!! Those will be available to the ROOT.

```
R1>enable view SUPER
Password:

R1#?
Exec commands:
  configure Enter configuration mode
  enable    Turn on privileged commands
  exit      Exit from the EXEC
  show      Show running system information
R1#
R1#show ip interface brief
Interface        IP-Address    OK?   Method     Status      Protocol
FastEthernet0/0  unassigned    YES   manual     up          up
Serial0/0        unassigned    YES   manual     up          up
R1#
R1#configure
Configuring from terminal, memory, or network [terminal]? terminal
Enter configuration commands, one per line.  End with CNTL/Z.
R1(config)#exit
R1#
R1#show parser view
Current view is 'SUPER
```

Lab 8 Configurations

R1 Configuration

```
R1#show run
Building configuration...

Current configuration : 1295 bytes
!
version 12.4
service timestamps debug datetime msec
service timestamps log datetime msec
no service password-encryption
!
hostname R1
!
boot-start-marker
boot-end-marker
!
no logging console
enable secret 5 $1$bj1Q$6UA5t8qk8xaXVH0vZC3WB/
!
aaa new-model
!
aaa session-id common
no network-clock-participate slot 1
no network-clock-participate wic 0
ip cef
!
multilink bundle-name authenticated
!
archive
 log config
  hidekeys
!
interface FastEthernet0/0
 no ip address
 duplex auto
 speed auto
!
interface Serial0/0
 no ip address
!
ip forward-protocol nd
!
ip http server
no ip http secure-server
!
control-plane
!
line con 0
line aux 0
```

```
line vty 0 3
line vty 4
parser view BASIC
 secret 5 $1$oi7H$u4u8IrhImpWVXHs2nfDKp0
 commands exec include show inventory
 commands exec include show version
 commands exec include show hardware
 commands exec include show
!
parser view EXPERT
 secret 5 $1$aPyv$Oq/IUadCBjEG5HyNo09Qu1
 commands exec include all show
!
parser view CONFIG
 secret 5 $1$g/3P$kazl6S9zkjDNV.Fsc4AWe/
 commands exec include configure
!
parser view SUPER superview
 secret 5 $1$tZZI$UW/C0ZeJ/rn6C3ntutJo01
 view BASIC
 view EXPERT
 view CONFIG
!
end
```

LAB 9

Enabling SSH and HTTPS access to Cisco IOS Routers

Lab Objective:

The objective of this lab exercise is for you to learn and understand how enable SSH and HTTPS access to Cisco IOS routers.

Lab Purpose:

SSH and HTTPS are secure management protocols that are recommended for remotely accessing and managing Cisco IOS devices. It is imperative to understand the configuration tasks required to enable SSH access in the Cisco IOS software suite.

Lab Difficulty:

This lab has a difficulty rating of 5/10.

Readiness Assessment:

When you are ready for your certification exam, you should complete this lab in no more than 10 minutes.

Lab Topology:

Please use the following topology to complete this lab:

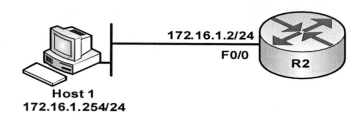

Host 1
172.16.1.254/24

NOTE: If you do not have a Host in your lab, you can simply substitute Host 1 for another router with an Ethernet interface and a default static route pointing to 172.16.1.2.

Lab 9 Configuration Tasks

Task 1:

Configure the hostname on R2 and IP addressing as illustrated in the diagram. In addition, configure Host 1 with the IP address specified and a default gateway of 172.16.1.2. Verify that Host 1 can ping R2 successfully.

Task 2:

Configure R2 with the domain name **howtonetwork.net**. In addition to this, configure R2 so that is generates a 2048-bit RSA key for maximum security.

Task 3:

Enable HTTPS support on R2. Ensure that only the 172.16.1.0/24 subnet can access the router via HTTPS. All attempts from any other subnet should be logged. In addition to this, configure R2 to only allow SSH connections without using an ACL.

Task 4:

Configure a username of **ccna** with a password of **security** on R2. This user should have Level 15 access to the router. In addition, R2 should authenticate all HTTPS and SSH sessions using the local router database.

Task 5:

Verify your configuration by accessing R2 via HTTPS and SSH.

Lab 9 Configuration and Verification

Task 1:
```
Router(config)#hostname R2
R2(config)#interface fastethernet0/0
R2(config-if)#ip address 172.16.1.2 255.255.255.0
R2(config-if)#no shutdown
R2(config-if)#exlt
R2(config)#exit
R2#
```

```
Command Prompt                                                  - □ x

C:\>ipconfig

Windows IP Configuration

Ethernet adapter Local Area Connection 2:

        Connection-specific DNS Suffix  . :
        IP Address. . . . . . . . . . . : 172.16.1.254
        Subnet Mask . . . . . . . . . . : 255.255.255.0
        Default Gateway . . . . . . . . : 172.16.1.2

Ethernet adapter Wireless Network Connection:

        Media State . . . . . . . . . . : Media disconnected

C:\>ping 172.16.1.2

Pinging 172.16.1.2 with 32 bytes of data:

Reply from 172.16.1.2: bytes=32 time=1ms TTL=255
Reply from 172.16.1.2: bytes=32 time=1ms TTL=255
Reply from 172.16.1.2: bytes=32 time=1ms TTL=255
Reply from 172.16.1.2: bytes=32 time=1ms TTL=255

Ping statistics for 172.16.1.2:
    Packets: Sent = 4, Received = 4, Lost = 0 (0% loss),
Approximate round trip times in milli-seconds:
    Minimum = 1ms, Maximum = 1ms, Average = 1ms

C:\>_
```

Task 2:

R2(config)#**ip domain-name howtonetwork.net**
R2(config)#**crypto key generate rsa**
The name for the keys will be: R2.howtonetwork.net
Choose the size of the key modulus in the range of 360 to 2048 for your
 General Purpose Keys. Choosing a key modulus greater than 512 may take
 a few minutes.

How many bits in the modulus [512]: **2048**
% Generating 2048 bit RSA keys, keys will be non-exportable...

R2(config)#**exit**
R2#
R2#**show crypto key mypubkey rsa**
% Key pair was generated at: 01:40:01 UTC Mar 1 2002
Key name: TP-self-signed-3473940174
 Storage Device: private-config
 Usage: General Purpose Key
 Key is not exportable.
 Key Data:

30819F30 0D06092A 864886F7 0D010101 05000381 8D003081 89028181 00C8244F
0BABB6A5 57E3A33E E6D3995A 495CF68F 7E131A62 67029197 10DF0FCB 6918CBD3
B817C851 D4648C79 B882A863 7804CB89 84FB80D9 F1D86BE7 9C8292E1 61772425
2490F4BE 0322C05C 9845153E 0A455075 E9BCC77A 19900C00 84F63219 6434915C
0E821D54 42E1C8FB 4BE8A303 4E295401 B4377CDC 14AF720F 4C92DC70 A9020301
0001

% Key pair was generated at: 08:01:11 UTC Mar 1 2002
Key name: TP-self-signed-3473940174.server
Temporary key
 Usage: Encryption Key
 Key is not exportable.
 Key Data:
 307C300D 06092A86 4886F70D 01010105 00036B00 30680261 00D77959 F38BD5A2
 8584B71C 05919DC2 B33C3B3F 7024C5C2 45672D12 E3271AEE 763D42ED 3D7501E5
 2A335EEE 1E3591E1 72FF256A 04E488D0 F2ECEFA4 78240955 C0CA1BB0 04BC39F1
 6C915A7F 27833169 48F06FAA AA6F9278 40335603 260B5C0B 8B020301 0001

% Key pair was generated at: 08:27:21 UTC Mar 1 2002
Key name: R2.howtonetwork.net
 Storage Device: not specified
 Usage: General Purpose Key
 Key is not exportable.
 Key Data:
 30820122 300D0609 2A864886 F70D0101 01050003 82010F00 3082010A 02820101
 00CE0214 97E827CC E6BAE894 ECD5E4BE 11172513 BDCA271E 79132E55 CE24C58C
 05D76DD5 3C675C8A 4CAE8DD6 3BD5BE9A 4EAC74D1 165DE340 5334A797 0B4FB5C6
 5654E0B8 5827EEEB 256C495C CCDA3E41 F8E2FB1C F81C3124 61F7C7F3 051FD914
 A1CEF9DA 38352EEC 0850E3F2 498DA640 1510D929 00556458 C49A42C2 9A15692D
 BB9B7BA6 C946B1DE AFB6151C 22CEAACE AAE3A56D 28676D2A C1227F88 394204AF
 827E7486 131E5E90 D3C8FA5A 7CFB2A3C E6E2645E 5347047F 28EAC93C 902D0CA7
 93BBA7F1 E8904054 73AC4AAC D408F729 927CADD2 0BCAF6D9 F54FFC96 9BF80FE6
 60805FE2 CDE1140D 2A33B883 E2537641 5B631CD4 0E42CDFB 90013487 EDA587F8
 29020301 0001

Task 3:
    R2(config)#access-list 10 remark "This is my HTTPS ACL"
    R2(config)#access-list 10 permit 172.16.1.0 0.0.0.255
    R2(config)#access-list 10 deny any log
    R2(config)#ip http secure-server
    R2(config)#ip http access-class 10
    R2(config)#line vty 0 4
    R2(config-line)#transport input ssh
    R2(config-line)#exit
    R2(config)#exit
    R2#

Task 4:

R2(config)#**username ccna privilege 15 secret security**
R2(config)#**ip http authentication local**
R2(config)#**line vty 0 4**
R2(config-line)#**login local**
R2(config-line)#**exit**
R2(config)#**exit**
R2#

Task 5:

To verify SSH, you need an SSH client, such as Putty—for example:

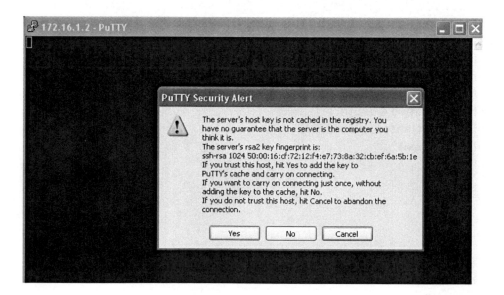

To verify HTTPS access, all you need is a simple Web Browser:

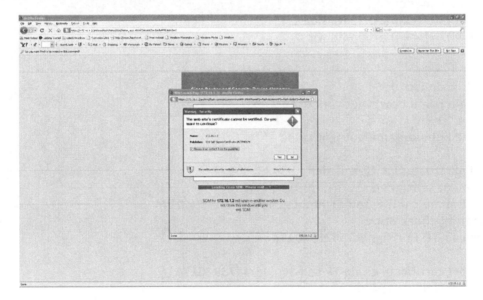

Lab 9 Configurations

R2 Configuration

```
R2#show run
Building configuration...

Current configuration : 2666 bytes
!
version 12.4
service timestamps debug datetime msec
service timestamps log datetime msec
no service password-encryption
!
hostname R2
!
boot-start-marker
boot-end-marker
!
no logging console
!
no aaa new-model
no network-clock-participate slot 1
no network-clock-participate wic 0
ip cef
!
no ip domain lookup
ip domain name howtonetwork.net
!
multilink bundle-name authenticated
!
crypto pki trustpoint TP-self-signed-3473940174
 enrollment selfsigned
 subject-name cn=IOS-Self-Signed-Certificate-3473940174
 revocation-check none
 rsakeypair TP-self-signed-3473940174
!
crypto pki certificate chain TP-self-signed-3473940174
 certificate self-signed 03
  3082024B 308201B4 A0030201 02020103 300D0609 2A864886 F70D0101 04050030
  31312F30 2D060355 04031326 494F532D 53656C66 2D536967 6E65642D 43657274
  69666963 6174652D 33343733 39343031 3734301E 170D3032 30333031 30383330
  32395A17 0D323030 31303130 30303030 305A3031 312F302D 06035504 03132649
  4F532D53 656C662D 5369676E 65642D43 65727469 66696361 74652D33 34373339
  34303137 3430819F 300D0609 2A864886 F70D0101 01050003 818D0030 81890281
  8100C824 4F0BABB6 A557E3A3 3EE6D399 5A495CF6 8F7E131A 62670291 9710DF0F
  CB6918CB D3B817C8 51D4648C 79B882A8 637804CB 8984FB80 D9F1D86B E79C8292
```

```
E1617724 252490F4 BE0322C0 5C984515 3E0A4550 75E9BCC7 7A19900C 0084F632
19643491 5C0E821D 5442E1C8 FB4BE8A3 034E2954 01B4377C DC14AF72 0F4C92DC
70A90203 010001A3 73307130 0F060355 1D130101 FF040530 030101FF 301E0603
551D1104 17301582 1352322E 686F7774 6F6E6574 776F726B 2E6E6574 301F0603
551D2304 18301680 144020A0 822373EF EFCD379B 8C2A1A4D 1343842D 59301D06
03551D0E 04160414 4020A082 2373EFEF CD379B8C 2A1A4D13 43842D59 300D0609
2A864886 F70D0101 04050003 81810018 BD971958 6D275769 5ADFF84C 566F8F39
857E730C 27B0E083 7DCF3C01 67BBEEAF 3CA291EF B92A711D C4D4AE49 A0C521CD
2A09AC35 C1D0A813 86B326AD E4EBE346 50F79E63 D35A47AF F1C54CB1 74C0F6D1
72547F28 EAE15C2C B7EB4944 C40B2FD8 050DF971 CE10C8DA 171E6161 FE0AAB91
FCCFBFA0 8ACC608A C7D9799A 73F95A
  quit
!
username ccna privilege 15 secret 5 $1$AMJ7$Jhs/IcLaJsecnzlaKZCl91
archive
 log config
  hidekeys
!
interface FastEthernet0/0
 ip address 172.16.1.2 255.255.255.0
 duplex auto
 speed auto
!
interface Serial0/0
 no ip address
!
ip forward-protocol nd
!
ip http server
ip http access-class 10
ip http authentication local
ip http secure-server
!
access-list 10 remark "This is my HTTPS ACL"
access-list 10 permit 172.16.1.0 0.0.0.255
access-list 10 deny   any log
!
control-plane
!
line con 0
line aux 0
line vty 0 4
 password cisco
 login local
 transport input ssh
!
end
```

LAB 10

Catalyst Switch Port Security

Lab Objective:

The objective of this lab exercise is for you to learn and understand how enable the Port Security feature on Cisco IOS Catalyst switches.

Lab Purpose:

Port Security is a fundamental component of Catalyst switch security. This feature is used to provide security against CAM overflow attacks on switched networks.

Lab Difficulty:

This lab has a difficulty rating of 7/10.

Readiness Assessment:

When you are ready for your certification exam, you should complete this lab in no more than 15 minutes.

Lab Topology:

Please use the following topology to complete this lab:

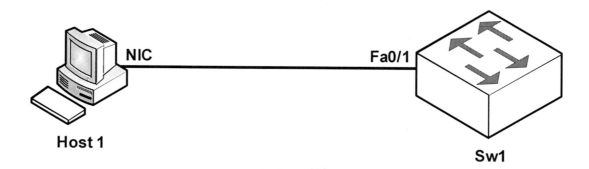

NOTE: This lab is based on a Cisco Catalyst switch with 24-10/100 FastEthernet ports and 2-1000Mbs GigabitEthernet ports. If you do NOT have a similar switch, substitute the port numbers or port ranges used in this lab with those available on your switch. For example, if you only have 12-10/100 FastEthernet ports and a Task refers to Ports 1-24, simply adjust the question to Ports 1-12 so that you can complete the lab on your switch. In a similar manner, if a Task asks for configuration on the GigabitEthernet ports, and you only have a 12-port 10/100 FastEthernet switch, simply substitute GigabitEthernet0/1 and GigabitEthernet0/2 with FastEthernet0/11 and FastEthernet0/12, for example.

Lab 10 Configuration Tasks

Task 1:

Configure the hostname on Sw1 as illustrated in the diagram. In addition to this, configure the following VLANs on Sw1:

VLAN Number	VLAN Name	VLAN Ports
10	VLAN_10_SECURITY	FastEthernet0/1 – FastEthernet0/12
20	VLAN_20_SECURITY	FastEthernet0/13 – FastEthernet0/24

Task 2:

Configure Port Security for VLAN 10 so that all learned MAC addresses are saved to the NVRAM of Sw1. In addition to this, ensure that only 1 MAC address per port is learned and if more than one is detected, the switch port(s) should be shut down. Verify your configuration.

Task 3:

Configure Port Security for VLAN 20 so that a maximum of 5 MAC addresses can be learned dynamically. If the event that more than 5 MAC addresses are detected, the switch port(s) should restrict the port(s). These dynamically learned entries should be flushed every 24 hours. Verify your configuration using the appropriate Catalyst switch **show** commands.

Lab 10 Configuration and Verification

Task 1:
```
Switch#config t
Enter configuration commands, one per line.  End with CNTL/Z.
Switch(config)#hostname Sw1
Sw1(config)#vlan 10
Sw1(config-vlan)#name VLAN_10_SECURITY
Sw1(config-vlan)#exit
Sw1(config)#vlan 20
Sw1(config-vlan)#name VLAN_20_SECURITY
Sw1(config-vlan)#exit
Sw1(config)#interface range fastethernet0/1 - 12
Sw1(config-if-range)#switchport mode access
Sw1(config-if-range)#switchport access vlan 10
Sw1(config-if-range)#no shutdown
Sw1(config-if-range)#exit
Sw1(config)#interface range fastethernet0/13 - 24
Sw1(config-if-range)#switchport mode access
```

```
Sw1(config-if-range)#switchport access vlan 20
Sw1(config-if-range)#no shutdown
Sw1(config-if-range)#exit
Sw1(config)#exit
Sw1#
Sw1#show vlan brief
```

VLAN	Name	Status	Ports
1	default	active	Gi0/1, Gi0/2
10	VLAN_10_SECURITY	active	Fa0/1, Fa0/2, Fa0/3, Fa0/4
			Fa0/5, Fa0/6, Fa0/7, Fa0/8
			Fa0/9, Fa0/10, Fa0/11, Fa0/12
20	VLAN_20_SECURITY	active	Fa0/13, Fa0/14, Fa0/15, Fa0/16
			Fa0/17, Fa0/18, Fa0/19, Fa0/20
			Fa0/21, Fa0/22, Fa0/23, Fa0/24
1002	fddi-default	active	
1003	trcrf-default	active	
1004	fddinet-default	active	
1005	trbrf-default	active	

Task 2:

This Task requires the use of Host 1 for accurate validation. By configuring dynamic sticky learning, you can validate that the switch has written the learned MAC address of Host 1 to NVRAM. This means that the entry will not be flushed if the switch is rebooted.

```
Sw1(config)#interface range fastethernet0/1 - 12
Sw1(config-if-range)#switchport port-security maximum 1
Sw1(config-if-range)#switchport port-security mac-address sticky
Sw1(config-if-range)#switchport port-security violation shutdown
Sw1(config-if-range)#exit
Sw1(config)#exit
Sw1#
Sw1#copy run start
Destination filename [startup-config]?
Building configuration...
[OK]
Sw1#
Sw1#show port-security
```

Secure Port	MaxSecureAddr (Count)	CurrentAddr (Count)	SecurityViolation (Count)	Security Action
Fa0/1	**1**	**1**	**0**	**Shutdown**
Fa0/2	1	0	0	Shutdown
Fa0/3	1	0	0	Shutdown
Fa0/4	1	0	0	Shutdown
Fa0/5	1	0	0	Shutdown

Fa0/6	1	0	0	Shutdown
Fa0/7	1	0	0	Shutdown
Fa0/8	1	0	0	Shutdown
Fa0/9	1	0	0	Shutdown
Fa0/10	1	0	0	Shutdown
Fa0/11	1	0	0	Shutdown
Fa0/12	1	0	0	Shutdown

Total Addresses in System : 1
Max Addresses limit in System : 1024
Sw1#
Sw1#**show port-security interface fastethernet 0/1 address**
    Secure Mac Address Table

Vlan	Mac Address	Type	Ports	Remaining Age (mins)
------	-----------------	------	-------	--------------------
10	**001d.09d4.0238**	**SecureSticky**	**Fa0/1**	**-**

Total Addresses: 1

Sw1#
Sw1#**show running-config interface fastethernet 0/1**
Building configuration...

Current configuration : 230 bytes
!
interface FastEthernet0/1
 switchport access vlan 10
 switchport mode access
 switchport port-security
 switchport port-security mac-address sticky
 switchport port-security mac-address sticky 001d.09d4.0238
 no ip address
end

Task 3:

Sw1(config)#**interface range fastethernet0/12 - 24**
Sw1(config-if-range)#**switchport port-security**
Sw1(config-if-range)#**switchport port-security maximum 5**
Sw1(config-if-range)#**switchport port-security violation restrict**
Sw1(config-if-range)#**switchport port-security aging time 1440**
Sw1(config-if-range)#**exit**
Sw1(config)#**exit**
Sw1#
Sw1#**show port-security | begin Fa0/13**
    Fa0/13   5   0   0   Restrict

Fa0/14	5	0	0	Restrict
Fa0/15	5	0	0	Restrict
Fa0/16	5	0	0	Restrict
Fa0/17	5	0	0	Restrict
Fa0/18	5	0	0	Restrict
Fa0/19	5	0	0	Restrict
Fa0/20	5	0	0	Restrict
Fa0/21	5	0	0	Restrict
Fa0/22	5	0	0	Restrict
Fa0/23	5	0	0	Restrict
Fa0/24	5	0	0	Restrict

Total Addresses in System : 1
Max Addresses limit in System : 1024
Sw1#
Sw1#
Sw1#**show port-security interface fastethernet 0/13**
Port Security : Enabled
Port status : SecureUp
Violation mode : Restrict
Maximum MAC Addresses : 5
Total MAC Addresses : 0
Configured MAC Addresses : 0
Sticky MAC Addresses : 0
Aging time : 1440 mins
Aging type : Absolute
SecureStatic address aging : Disabled
Security Violation count : **0**

Lab 10 Configurations

Sw1 Configuration

Sw1#show running-config
Building configuration...

Current configuration : 5684 bytes
!
version 12.1
no service pad
service timestamps debug uptime
service timestamps log uptime
no service password-encryption
!
hostname Sw1
!

```
no logging console
!
ip subnet-zero
!
spanning-tree mode pvst
no spanning-tree optimize bpdu transmission
spanning-tree extend system-id
!
vlan 10
 name VLAN_10_SECURITY
!
vlan 20
 name VLAN_20_SECURITY
!
interface FastEthernet0/1
 switchport access vlan 10
 switchport mode access
 switchport port-security
 switchport port-security mac-address sticky
 switchport port-security mac-address sticky 001d.09d4.0238
 no ip address
!
interface FastEthernet0/2
 switchport access vlan 10
 switchport mode access
 switchport port-security
 switchport port-security mac-address sticky
 no ip address
!
interface FastEthernet0/3
 switchport access vlan 10
 switchport mode access
 switchport port-security
 switchport port-security mac-address sticky
 no ip address
!
interface FastEthernet0/4
 switchport access vlan 10
 switchport mode access
 switchport port-security
 switchport port-security mac-address sticky
 no ip address
!
interface FastEthernet0/5
 switchport access vlan 10
 switchport mode access
 switchport port-security
 switchport port-security mac-address sticky
```

```
 no ip address
!
interface FastEthernet0/6
 switchport access vlan 10
 switchport mode access
 switchport port-security
 switchport port-security mac-address sticky
 no ip address
!
interface FastEthernet0/7
 switchport access vlan 10
 switchport mode access
 switchport port-security
 switchport port-security mac-address sticky
 no ip address
!
interface FastEthernet0/8
 switchport access vlan 10
 switchport mode access
 switchport port-security
 switchport port-security mac-address sticky
 no ip address
!
interface FastEthernet0/9
 switchport access vlan 10
 switchport mode access
 switchport port-security
 switchport port-security mac-address sticky
 no ip address
!
interface FastEthernet0/10
 switchport access vlan 10
 switchport mode access
 switchport port-security
 switchport port-security mac-address sticky
 no ip address
!
interface FastEthernet0/11
 switchport access vlan 10
 switchport mode access
 switchport port-security
 switchport port-security mac-address sticky
 no ip address
!
interface FastEthernet0/12
 switchport access vlan 10
 switchport mode access
 switchport port-security
```

```
 switchport port-security maximum 5
 switchport port-security violation restrict
 switchport port-security aging time 1440
 switchport port-security mac-address sticky
 no ip address
!
interface FastEthernet0/13
 switchport access vlan 20
 switchport mode access
 switchport port-security
 switchport port-security maximum 5
 switchport port-security violation restrict
 switchport port-security aging time 1440
 no ip address
!
interface FastEthernet0/14
 switchport access vlan 20
 switchport mode access
 switchport port-security
 switchport port-security maximum 5
 switchport port-security violation restrict
 switchport port-security aging time 1440
 no ip address
!
interface FastEthernet0/15
 switchport access vlan 20
 switchport mode access
 switchport port-security
 switchport port-security maximum 5
 switchport port-security violation restrict
 switchport port-security aging time 1440
 no ip address
!
interface FastEthernet0/16
 switchport access vlan 20
 switchport mode access
 switchport port-security
 switchport port-security maximum 5
 switchport port-security violation restrict
 switchport port-security aging time 1440
 no ip address
!
interface FastEthernet0/17
 switchport access vlan 20
 switchport mode access
 switchport port-security
 switchport port-security maximum 5
 switchport port-security violation restrict
```

```
 switchport port-security aging time 1440
 no ip address
!
interface FastEthernet0/18
 switchport access vlan 20
 switchport mode access
 switchport port-security
 switchport port-security maximum 5
 switchport port-security violation restrict
 switchport port-security aging time 1440
 no ip address
!
interface FastEthernet0/19
 switchport access vlan 20
 switchport mode access
 switchport port-security
 switchport port-security maximum 5
 switchport port-security violation restrict
 switchport port-security aging time 1440
 no ip address
!
interface FastEthernet0/20
 switchport access vlan 20
 switchport mode access
 switchport port-security
 switchport port-security maximum 5
 switchport port-security violation restrict
 switchport port-security aging time 1440
 no ip address
!
interface FastEthernet0/21
 switchport access vlan 20
 switchport mode access
 switchport port-security
 switchport port-security maximum 5
 switchport port-security violation restrict
 switchport port-security aging time 1440
 no ip address
!
interface FastEthernet0/22
 switchport access vlan 20
 switchport mode access
 switchport port-security
 switchport port-security maximum 5
 switchport port-security violation restrict
 switchport port-security aging time 1440
 no ip address
!
```

```
interface FastEthernet0/23
 switchport access vlan 20
 switchport mode access
 switchport port-security
 switchport port-security maximum 5
 switchport port-security violation restrict
 switchport port-security aging time 1440
 no ip address
!
interface FastEthernet0/24
 switchport access vlan 20
 switchport mode access
 switchport port-security
 switchport port-security maximum 5
 switchport port-security violation restrict
 switchport port-security aging time 1440
 no ip address
!
interface GigabitEthernet0/1
 no ip address
!
interface GigabitEthernet0/2
 no ip address
!
interface Vlan1
 no ip address
 no ip route-cache
 shutdown
!
ip http server
!
!
line con 0
line vty 5 15
!
end
```

LAB 11

Catalyst Switch 802.1x Security

Lab Objective:

The objective of this lab exercise is for you to learn and understand how enable 802.1x authentication on Cisco IOS Catalyst switches.

Lab Purpose:

802.1x is used to provide Catalyst switch access port security by authenticating users before allowing them to pass traffic through ports on Cisco IOS Catalyst switches.

Lab Difficulty:

This lab has a difficulty rating of 7/10.

Readiness Assessment:

When you are ready for your certification exam, you should complete this lab in no more than 15 minutes.

Lab Topology:

Please use any single switch to complete this lab:

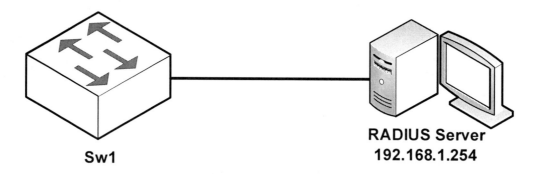

Sw1

RADIUS Server
192.168.1.254

NOTE: This lab is based on a Cisco Catalyst switch with 24-10/100 FastEthernet ports and 2-1000Mbs GigabitEthernet ports. If you do NOT have a similar switch, substitute the port numbers or port ranges used in this lab with those available on your switch. For example, if you only have 12-10/100 FastEthernet ports and a Task refers to Ports 1-24, simply adjust the question to Ports 1-12 so that you can complete the lab on your switch. In a similar manner, if a Task asks for configuration on the GigabitEthernet ports, and you only have a 12-port 10/100 FastEthernet switch, simply substitute GigabitEthernet0/1 and GigabitEthernet0/2 with FastEthernet0/11 and FastEthernet0/12, for example.

In addition to this, the RADIUS server is not required. It is depicted here for the purposes of being thorough! RADIUS server configuration is beyond the scope of this course.

Lab 11 Configuration Tasks

Task 1:

Configure the hostname on Sw1 as illustrated in the diagram. In addition to this, configure the following VLANs on Sw1:

VLAN Number	VLAN Name	VLAN Ports
2020	802-1X-VLAN	FastEthernet0/1 – FastEthernet0/24

In addition to this, configure interface VLAN 2020 on Sw1 and assign the interface and IP address of 192.168.1.1/24. Verify your configuration.

Task 2:

Configure user **catalyst** with a password of **security** on Sw1. This user should have Level 15 access privileges on the switch. Configure a secret password on Sw1 of **security**.

Task 3:

Configure Authentication on Sw1 so that all users are authenticated against the local database. In addition to this, enable access should use the enable secret for authentication.

Task 4:

Configure 802.1x authentication on ports FastEthernet0/1—24 on Sw1. 802.1x authentication will be performed by a RADUIS server with the IP address 192.168.1.254. This RADIUS server should use the password **dot1x** for authentication. Verify your configuration.

Lab 11 Configuration and Verification

Task 1:

To complete this Task, you will need to enable VTP Transparent mode so that you can configure extended range VLANs on the switch.

```
Switch(config)#hostname Sw1
Sw1(config)#vtp mode transparent
Setting device to VTP TRANSPARENT mode.
Sw1(config)#vlan 2020
Sw1(config-vlan)#name 802-1X-VLAN
Sw1(config-vlan)#exit
Sw1(config)#interface range fastethernet0/1 - 24
Sw1(config-if-range)#switchport mode access
```

```
Sw1(config-if-range)#switchport access vlan 2020
Sw1(config-if-range)#no shutdown
Sw1(config-if-range)#exit
Sw1(config)#interface vlan 1
Sw1(config-if)#shutdown
Sw1(config-if)#exit
Sw1(config)#interface vlan 2020
Sw1(config-if)#no shutdown
Sw1(config-if)#ip address 192.168.1.1 255.255.255.0
Sw1(config-if)#exit
Sw1(config)#exit
Sw1#
Sw1#
Sw1#show vlan brief
```

VLAN Name	Status	Ports
1 default	active	Gi0/1, Gi0/2
1002 fddi-default	active	
1003 trcrf-default	active	
1004 fddinet-default	active	
1005 trbrf-default	active	
2020 802-1X-VLAN	active	Fa0/1, Fa0/2, Fa0/3, Fa0/4
		Fa0/5, Fa0/6, Fa0/7, Fa0/8
		Fa0/9, Fa0/10, Fa0/11, Fa0/12
		Fa0/13, Fa0/14, Fa0/15, Fa0/16
		Fa0/17, Fa0/18, Fa0/19, Fa0/20
		Fa0/21, Fa0/22, Fa0/23, Fa0/24

```
Sw1#
Sw1#show interface vlan 2020
Vlan2020 is up, line protocol is up
  Hardware is CPU Interface, address is 000d.bd06.4100 (bia 000d.bd06.4100)
  Internet address is 192.168.1.1/24
  MTU 1500 bytes, BW 1000000 Kbit, DLY 10 usec,
    reliability 255/255, txload 1/255, rxload 1/255
  Encapsulation ARPA, loopback not set
----[Truncated Output]----
```

NOTE: Keep in mind that if you have no active ports in VLAN2020 that are up, interface VLAN2020 will show a down/down status. This is normal behavior.

Task 2:

To successfully complete this Task, keep in mind that switches have 16 VTY lines.

```
Sw1(config)#username catalyst privilege 15 secret security
Sw1(config)#enable secret security
Sw1(config)#exit
Sw1#
```

Task 3:

```
Sw1(config)#aaa new-model
Sw1(config)#aaa authentication login default local
Sw1(config)#aaa authentication enable default enable
Sw1(config)#line vty 0 15
Sw1(config-line)#login authentication default
Sw1(config-line)#exit
Sw1(config)#exit
Sw1#
```

Task 4:

Keep in mind that because there is no actual RADIUS server and any hosts you may have connected to your switch are not configured for 802.1x authentication, we will not see any authenticated host information on the switch.

```
Sw1(config)#aaa authentication dot1x default group radius
Sw1(config)#aaa authorization network default group radius
Sw1(config)#radius-server host 192.168.1.254 key dot1x
Sw1(config)#interface range fastethernet0/1 - 24
Sw1(config-if-range)#dot1x port-control auto
Sw1(config-if-range)#exit
Sw1(config)#exit
Sw1#
Sw1#show dot1x interface fastethernet0/1
802.1X is enabled on FastEthernet0/1
    Status                  Unauthorized
    Port-control            Auto
    Supplicant              Not set
    Multiple Hosts          Disallowed
    Current Identifier      0

    Authenticator State     Machine
     State                  INITIALIZE
     Reauth Count           0

    Backend State           Machine
     State                  INITIALIZE
     Request Count          0
     Identifier (Server)    0

    Reauthentication State  Machine
     State          INITIALIZE
Sw1#
Sw1#
Sw1#show dot1x statistics interface fastethernet 0/1

FastEthernet0/1
```

Rx:	EAPOL Start	EAPOL Logoff	EAPOL Invalid	EAPOL Total	EAP Resp/Id	EAP Resp/Oth	EAP LenError
	0	0	0	0	0	0	0

	Last EAPOLVer	Last EAPOLSrc
	0	0000.0000.0000

Tx:	EAPOL Total	EAP Req/Id	EAP Req/Oth
	2	0	0

Lab 11 Configurations

Sw1 Configuration

```
Sw1#show running-config
Building configuration...

Current configuration : 3956 bytes
!
version 12.1
no service pad
service timestamps debug uptime
service timestamps log uptime
no service password-encryption
!
hostname Sw1
!
no logging console
aaa new-model
aaa authentication login default local
aaa authentication enable default enable
aaa authentication dot1x default group radius
aaa authorization network default group radius
enable secret 5 $1$3Dc3$/wfLheMTaIRMjokszyF8K/
!
username catalyst privilege 15 secret 5 $1$r5Rt$WSspCtMNiorq8cx65fGqi0
ip subnet-zero
vtp domain CISCO
vtp mode transparent
!
spanning-tree mode pvst
no spanning-tree optimize bpdu transmission
spanning-tree extend system-id
!
```

```
!
vlan 2020
 name 802-1X-VLAN
!
interface FastEthernet0/1
 switchport access vlan 2020
 switchport mode access
 no ip address
 dot1x port-control auto
!
interface FastEthernet0/2
 switchport access vlan 2020
 switchport mode access
 no ip address
 dot1x port-control auto
!
interface FastEthernet0/3
 switchport access vlan 2020
 switchport mode access
 no ip address
 dot1x port-control auto
!
interface FastEthernet0/4
 switchport access vlan 2020
 switchport mode access
 no ip address
 dot1x port-control auto
!
interface FastEthernet0/5
 switchport access vlan 2020
 switchport mode access
 no ip address
 dot1x port-control auto
!
interface FastEthernet0/6
 switchport access vlan 2020
 switchport mode access
 no ip address
 dot1x port-control auto
!
interface FastEthernet0/7
 switchport access vlan 2020
 switchport mode access
 no ip address
 dot1x port-control auto
!
interface FastEthernet0/8
 switchport access vlan 2020
```

```
 switchport mode access
 no ip address
 dot1x port-control auto
!
interface FastEthernet0/9
 switchport access vlan 2020
 switchport mode access
 no ip address
 dot1x port-control auto
!
interface FastEthernet0/10
 switchport access vlan 2020
 switchport mode access
 no ip address
 dot1x port-control auto
!
interface FastEthernet0/11
 switchport access vlan 2020
 switchport mode access
 no ip address
 dot1x port-control auto
!
interface FastEthernet0/12
 switchport access vlan 2020
 switchport mode access
 no ip address
 dot1x port-control auto
!
interface FastEthernet0/13
 switchport access vlan 2020
 switchport mode access
 no ip address
 dot1x port-control auto
!
interface FastEthernet0/14
 switchport access vlan 2020
 switchport mode access
 no ip address
 dot1x port-control auto
!
interface FastEthernet0/15
 switchport access vlan 2020
 switchport mode access
 no ip address
 dot1x port-control auto
!
interface FastEthernet0/16
 switchport access vlan 2020
```

```
 switchport mode access
 no ip address
 dot1x port-control auto
!
interface FastEthernet0/17
 switchport access vlan 2020
 switchport mode access
 no ip address
 dot1x port-control auto
!
interface FastEthernet0/18
 switchport access vlan 2020
 switchport mode access
 no ip address
 dot1x port-control auto
!
interface FastEthernet0/19
 switchport access vlan 2020
 switchport mode access
 no ip address
 dot1x port-control auto
!
interface FastEthernet0/20
 switchport access vlan 2020
 switchport mode access
 no ip address
 dot1x port-control auto
!
interface FastEthernet0/21
 switchport access vlan 2020
 switchport mode access
 no ip address
 dot1x port-control auto
!
interface FastEthernet0/22
 switchport access vlan 2020
 switchport mode access
 no ip address
 dot1x port-control auto
!
interface FastEthernet0/23
 switchport access vlan 2020
 switchport mode access
 no ip address
 dot1x port-control auto
!
interface FastEthernet0/24
 switchport access vlan 2020
```

```
 switchport mode access
 no ip address
 dot1x port-control auto
!
interface GigabitEthernet0/1
 no ip address
!
interface GigabitEthernet0/2
 no ip address
!
interface Vlan1
 no ip address
 no ip route-cache
 shutdown
!
interface Vlan2020
 ip address 192.168.1.1 255.255.255.0
 no ip route-cache
!
ip http server
!
radius-server host 192.168.1.254 auth-port 1812 acct-port 1813 key dot1x
radius-server retransmit 3
!
line con 0
line vty 5 15
!
end
```

LAB 12

Catalyst Switch STP and DTP Security

Lab Objective:

The objective of this lab exercise is for you to learn and understand how enable other Catalyst switch security features that can be used in conjunction with STP and DTP.

Lab Purpose:

While there are a plethora of security features that can be configured on Catalyst switches, it is important to understand and have practical knowledge of those that pertain to the CCNA Security course and how they are implemented and validated.

Lab Difficulty:

This lab has a difficulty rating of 7/10.

Readiness Assessment:

When you are ready for your certification exam, you should complete this lab in no more than 15 minutes.

Lab Topology:

Please use any single switch to complete this lab:

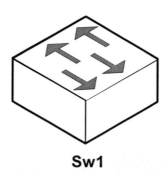

Sw1

NOTE: This lab is based on a Cisco Catalyst switch with 24-10/100 FastEthernet ports and 2-1000Mbs GigabitEthernet ports. If you do NOT have a similar switch, substitute the port numbers or port ranges used in this lab with those available on your switch. For example, if you only have 12-10/100 FastEthernet ports and a Task refers to Ports 1-24, simply adjust the question to Ports 1-12 so that you can complete the lab on your switch. In a similar manner, if a Task asks for configuration on the GigabitEthernet ports, and you only have a 12-port 10/100 FastEthernet switch, simply substitute GigabitEthernet0/1 and GigabitEthernet0/2 with FastEthernet0/11 and FastEthernet0/12, for example.

Lab 12 Configuration Tasks

Task 1:

Configure the hostname on Sw1 as illustrated in the diagram. In addition to this configure the following VLANs on Sw1 and assign the ports specified to those VLANs:

VLAN Number	VLAN Name	VLAN Ports
100	CATALYST_VLAN_100	FastEthernet0/1 – FastEthernet0/9
200	CATALYST_VLAN_200	FastEthernet0/10 – FastEthernet0/19

Task 2:

Configure all ports in VLAN 100 as static Access ports that also use Port Fast. These ports will always be connected to end hosts (i.e. PCs), therefore, configure these ports so that if a BPDU is received, the ports will be immediately shut down.

Task 3:

Configure all ports in VLAN 200 as static Access ports that also use Port Fast. These ports will also be connected to end hosts (i.e. PCs); however, Sw1 should never send BPDUs on these ports, as is the default behavior of all switches.

Task 4:

Ports FastEthernet0/20 to FastEthernet0/24 are currently not being used and should be shut down. However, in order to prevent an STP topology change in the event that someone plugs in a switch with superior BPDUs on any one of these ports and brings them up, configure these ports so that the placement of the root bridge in the network is not changed.

Task 5:

Configure the GigabitEthernet0/1 and GigabitEthernet0/2 interfaces of Sw1 as Trunk ports that will never use the Dynamic Trunking Protocol.

Lab 12 Configuration and Verification

Task 1:
```
Switch(config)#hostname Sw1
Sw1(config)#vlan 100
Sw1(config-vlan)#name CATALYST_VLAN_100
Sw1(config-vlan)#exit
Sw1(config)#vlan 200
```

```
Sw1(config-vlan)#name CATALYST_VLAN_200
Sw1(config-vlan)#exit
Sw1(config)#interface range fast 0/1 - 9
Sw1(config-if-range)#switchport access vlan 100
Sw1(config-if-range)#exit
Sw1(config)#interface range fast 0/10 - 19
Sw1(config-if-range)#switchport access vlan 200
Sw1(config-if-range)#exit
Sw1(config)#exit
Sw1#
Sw1#show vlan brief
```

VLAN Name	Status	Ports
1 default	active	Fa0/20, Fa0/21, Fa0/22, Fa0/23 Fa0/24, Gi0/1, Gi0/2
100 CATALYST_VLAN_100	active	Fa0/1, Fa0/2, Fa0/3, Fa0/4 Fa0/5, Fa0/6, Fa0/7, Fa0/8 Fa0/9
200 CATALYST_VLAN_200	active	Fa0/10, Fa0/11, Fa0/12, Fa0/13 Fa0/14, Fa0/15, Fa0/16, Fa0/17 Fa0/18, Fa0/19
1002 fddi-default	active	
1003 trcrf-default	active	
1004 fddinet-default	active	
1005 trbrf-default	active	

Task 2:

```
Sw1(config)#spanning-tree portfast bpduguard default
Sw1(config)#interface range fast 0/1 - 9
Sw1(config-if-range)#switchport mode access
Sw1(config-if-range)#spanning-tree portfast
%Warning: portfast should only be enabled on ports connected to a single
 host. Connecting hubs, concentrators, switches, bridges, etc... to this
 interface  when portfast is enabled, can cause temporary bridging loops.
 Use with CAUTION

%Portfast will be configured in 9 interfaces due to the range command
 but will only have effect when the interfaces are in a non-trunking mode.
Sw1(config-if-range)#spanning-tree bpduguard enable
Sw1(config-if-range)#exit
Sw1(config)#exit
Sw1#
Sw1#show spanning-tree summary
Switch is in pvst mode
Root bridge for: none
EtherChannel misconfiguration guard is enabled
```

Extended system ID	is enabled
Portfast	is disabled by default
PortFast BPDU Guard	**is enabled by default**
Portfast BPDU Filter	is disabled by default
Loopguard	is disabled by default
UplinkFast	is disabled
BackboneFast	is disabled
Pathcost method used	is short

Name	Blocking	Listening	Learning	Forwarding	STP Active
Total	0	0	0	0	0

To further verify your configuration, you can enable a port in VLAN 100 - that has a device connected to it—and issue the **show spanning-tree interface** command as follows:

```
Sw1#show spanning-tree interface f0/1 detail
 Port 1 (FastEthernet0/1) of VLAN0100 is forwarding
   Port path cost 19, Port priority 128, Port Identifier 128.1.
   Designated root has priority 32868, address 000d.bd06.4100
   Designated bridge has priority 32868, address 000d.bd06.4100
   Designated port id is 128.1, designated path cost 0
   Timers: message age 0, forward delay 0, hold 0
   Number of transitions to forwarding state: 1
   The port is in the portfast mode
   Link type is point-to-point by default
   Bpdu guard is enabled
   Bpdu filter is disabled by default
   BPDU: sent 11, received 0
```

Task 3:

```
Sw1(config)#spanning-tree portfast bpdufilter default
Sw1(config)#interface range fast 0/10 - 19
Sw1(config-if-range)#switchport mode access
Sw1(config-if-range)#spanning-tree portfast
%Warning: portfast should only be enabled on ports connected to a single
 host. Connecting hubs, concentrators, switches, bridges, etc... to this
 interface  when portfast is enabled, can cause temporary bridging loops.
 Use with CAUTION

%Portfast will be configured in 10 interfaces due to the range command
 but will only have effect when the interfaces are in a non-trunking mode.
Sw1(config-if-range)#spanning-tree bpdufilter enable
Sw1(config-if-range)#exit
Sw1(config)#exit
Sw1#
```

```
Sw1#show spanning-tree summary
Switch is in pvst mode
Root bridge for: none
EtherChannel misconfiguration guard is enabled
Extended system ID        is enabled
Portfast                  is disabled by default
PortFast BPDU Guard       is enabled by default
Portfast BPDU Filter      is enabled by default
Loopguard                 is disabled by default
UplinkFast                is disabled
BackboneFast              is disabled
Pathcost method used      is short


Name             Blocking Listening Learning Forwarding STP Active
---------------- -------- --------- -------- ---------- ----------
Total            0        0         0        0          0
```

To further verify your configuration, you can enable a port in VLAN 100 - that has a device connected to it—and issue the **show spanning-tree interface** command as follows:

```
Sw1#show spanning-tree interface f0/12 detail
 Port 12 (FastEthernet0/12) of VLAN0200 is forwarding
   Port path cost 19, Port priority 128, Port Identifier 128.12.
   Designated root has priority 32968, address 000d.bd06.4100
   Designated bridge has priority 32968, address 000d.bd06.4100
   Designated port id is 128.12, designated path cost 0
   Timers: message age 0, forward delay 0, hold 0
   Number of transitions to forwarding state: 1
   The port is in the portfast mode
   Link type is point-to-point by default
   Bpdu guard is enabled by default
   Bpdu filter is enabled
   BPDU: sent 0, received 0
```

Task 4:
```
Sw1(config)#interface range f0/20 - 24
Sw1(config-if-range)#description 'Currently not being used'
Sw1(config-if-range)#shutdown
Sw1(config-if-range)#spanning-tree guard root
Sw1(config-if-range)#exit
Sw1(config)#exit
Sw1#
```

Task 5:

```
Sw1(config)#interface range g0/1 - 2
Sw1(config-if-range)#no shutdown
Sw1(config-if-range)#switchport mode trunk
Sw1(config-if-range)#switchport nonegotiate
Sw1(config-if-range)#exit
Sw1(config)#exit
Sw1#
Sw1#show interfaces gigabitethernet 0/1 switchport
Name: Gi0/1
Switchport: Enabled
Administrative Mode: trunk
Operational Mode: down
Administrative Trunking Encapsulation: dot1q
Negotiation of Trunking: Off
Access Mode VLAN: 1 (default)
Trunking Native Mode VLAN: 1 (default)
Voice VLAN: none
Administrative private-vlan host-association: none
Administrative private-vlan mapping: none
Operational private-vlan: none
Trunking VLANs Enabled: ALL
Pruning VLANs Enabled: 2-1001
Capture Mode Disabled
Capture VLANs Allowed: ALL

Protected: false

Voice VLAN: none (Inactive)
Appliance trust: none
```

Lab 12 Configurations

Sw1 Configuration

```
Sw1#show running-config
Building configuration...

Current configuration : 4260 bytes
!
version 12.1
no service pad
service timestamps debug uptime
service timestamps log uptime
no service password-encryption
!
```

```
hostname Sw1
!
no logging console
!
ip subnet-zero
vtp domain LAB12
vtp mode transparent
!
spanning-tree mode pvst
spanning-tree portfast bpduguard default
spanning-tree portfast bpdufilter default
no spanning-tree optimize bpdu transmission
spanning-tree extend system-id
!
vlan 100
 name CATALYST_VLAN_100
!
vlan 200
 name CATALYST_VLAN_200
!
interface FastEthernet0/1
 switchport access vlan 100
 switchport mode access
 no ip address
 spanning-tree portfast
 spanning-tree bpduguard enable
!
interface FastEthernet0/2
 switchport access vlan 100
 switchport mode access
 no ip address
 spanning-tree portfast
 spanning-tree bpduguard enable
!
interface FastEthernet0/3
 switchport access vlan 100
 switchport mode access
 no ip address
 spanning-tree portfast
 spanning-tree bpduguard enable
!
interface FastEthernet0/4
 switchport access vlan 100
 switchport mode access
 no ip address
 spanning-tree portfast
 spanning-tree bpduguard enable
!
```

```
interface FastEthernet0/5
 switchport access vlan 100
 switchport mode access
 no ip address
 spanning-tree portfast
 spanning-tree bpduguard enable
!
interface FastEthernet0/6
 switchport access vlan 100
 switchport mode access
 no ip address
 spanning-tree portfast
 spanning-tree bpduguard enable
!
interface FastEthernet0/7
 switchport access vlan 100
 switchport mode access
 no ip address
 spanning-tree portfast
 spanning-tree bpduguard enable
!
interface FastEthernet0/8
 switchport access vlan 100
 switchport mode access
 no ip address
 spanning-tree portfast
 spanning-tree bpduguard enable
!
interface FastEthernet0/9
 switchport access vlan 100
 switchport mode access
 no ip address
 spanning-tree portfast
 spanning-tree bpduguard enable
!
interface FastEthernet0/10
 switchport access vlan 200
 switchport mode access
 no ip address
 spanning-tree portfast
 spanning-tree bpdufilter enable
!
interface FastEthernet0/11
 switchport access vlan 200
 switchport mode access
 no ip address
 spanning-tree portfast
 spanning-tree bpdufilter enable
```

```
!
interface FastEthernet0/12
 switchport access vlan 200
 switchport mode access
 no ip address
 spanning-tree portfast
 spanning-tree bpdufilter enable
!
interface FastEthernet0/13
 switchport access vlan 200
 switchport mode access
 no ip address
 spanning-tree portfast
 spanning-tree bpdufilter enable
!
interface FastEthernet0/14
 switchport access vlan 200
 switchport mode access
 no ip address
 spanning-tree portfast
 spanning-tree bpdufilter enable
!
interface FastEthernet0/15
 switchport access vlan 200
 switchport mode access
 no ip address
 spanning-tree portfast
 spanning-tree bpdufilter enable
!
interface FastEthernet0/16
 switchport access vlan 200
 switchport mode access
 no ip address
 spanning-tree portfast
 spanning-tree bpdufilter enable
!
interface FastEthernet0/17
 switchport access vlan 200
 switchport mode access
 no ip address
 spanning-tree portfast
 spanning-tree bpdufilter enable
!
interface FastEthernet0/18
 switchport access vlan 200
 switchport mode access
 no ip address
 spanning-tree portfast
```

```
 spanning-tree bpdufilter enable
!
interface FastEthernet0/19
 switchport access vlan 200
 switchport mode access
 no ip address
 spanning-tree portfast
 spanning-tree bpdufilter enable
!
interface FastEthernet0/20
 description 'Currently not being used'
 no ip address
 shutdown
 spanning-tree guard root
!
interface FastEthernet0/21
 description 'Currently not being used'
 no ip address
 shutdown
 spanning-tree guard root
!
interface FastEthernet0/22
 description 'Currently not being used'
 no ip address
 shutdown
 spanning-tree guard root
!
interface FastEthernet0/23
 description 'Currently not being used'
 no ip address
 shutdown
 spanning-tree guard root
!
interface FastEthernet0/24
 description 'Currently not being used'
 no ip address
 shutdown
 spanning-tree guard root
!
interface GigabitEthernet0/1
 switchport mode trunk
 switchport nonegotiate
 no ip address
!
interface GigabitEthernet0/2
 switchport mode trunk
 switchport nonegotiate
 no ip address
```

```
!
interface Vlan1
 no ip address
 no ip route-cache
 shutdown
!
ip http server
!
line con 0
line vty 5 15
!
end
```

LAB 13

Catalyst Switch Port-Based Traffic Control

Lab Objective:

The objective of this lab exercise is for you to learn and understand how enable port-based traffic control features on Cisco IOS Catalyst switches.

Lab Purpose:

Catalyst switch port-based traffic control features are implemented at the port-level on Cisco IOS Catalyst switches and provide per-port security on these devices.

Lab Difficulty:

This lab has a difficulty rating of 8/10.

Readiness Assessment:

When you are ready for your certification exam, you should complete this lab in no more than 15 minutes.

Lab Topology:

Please use any single switch to complete this lab:

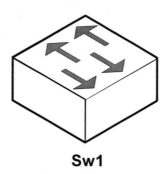

Sw1

NOTE: This lab is based on a Cisco Catalyst switch with 24-10/100 FastEthernet ports and 2-1000Mbs GigabitEthernet ports. If you do NOT have a similar switch, substitute the port numbers or port ranges used in this lab with those available on your switch. For example, if you only have 12-10/100 FastEthernet ports and a Task refers to Ports 1-24, simply adjust the question to Ports 1-12 so that you can complete the lab on your switch. In a similar manner, if a Task asks for configuration on the GigabitEthernet ports, and you only have a 12-port 10/100 FastEthernet switch, simply substitute GigabitEthernet0/1 and GigabitEthernet0/2 with FastEthernet0/11 and FastEthernet0/12, for example.

Lab 13 Configuration Tasks

Task 1:

Configure the hostname on Sw1 as illustrated in the diagram. In addition to this configure Sw1 so that it operates in Transparent mode switch in VTP domain **SECURITY**. This domain should be secured by the password **secure** for security purposes.

Task 2:

Configure storm control on ports FastEthernet0/1—FastEthernet0/8 as follows:

Traffic Type	Suppress when exceeds (%)	Forward when below (%)
Broadcast	15	10
Multicast	80	50
Unicast	95	75

When these thresholds are exceeded, Sw1 should send an SNMP Trap notification to server 192.168.1.254. This server uses the SNMP community **STRMCTRL** as a RO community.

Task 3:

Configure FastEthernet0/9—FastEthernet0/15 so that there is never an exchange of Unicast, Broadcast, or Multicast traffic between these ports on the switch.

Task 4:

Configure FastEthernet0/16—FastEthernet0/24 so that these ports send an SNMP trap when a MAC address is added to the entries already learned.

Lab 13 Configuration and Verification

Task 1:
```
Switch(config)#hostname Sw1
Sw1(config)#vtp mode transparent
Setting device to VTP TRANSPARENT mode.
Sw1(config)#vtp domain SECURITY
Changing VTP domain name from Null to SECURITY
Sw1(config)#vtp password secure
Setting device VLAN database password to secure
Sw1(config)#exit
Sw1#
Sw1#show vtp status
```

VTP Version   : 2
Configuration Revision   : 0
Maximum VLANs supported locally : 250
Number of existing VLANs   : 5
VTP Operating Mode   : Transparent
VTP Domain Name   : SECURITY
VTP Pruning Mode   : Enabled
VTP V2 Mode   : Enabled
VTP Traps Generation   : Disabled
MD5 digest   : 0x32 0xB2 0x45 0x18 0xB1 0x28 0x56 0x70
Configuration last modified by 0.0.0.0 at 3-1-93 00:17:41

Task 2:
Sw1(config)#**int range fastethernet0/1 - 8**
Sw1(config-if-range)#**storm-control broadcast level 15.00 10.00**
Sw1(config-if-range)#**storm-control multicast level 80.00 50.00**
Sw1(config-if-range)#**storm-control unicast level 95.00 75.00**
Sw1(config-if-range)#**storm-control action trap**
Sw1(config-if-range)#**exit**
Sw1(config)#**snmp-server host 192.168.1.254 traps STRMCTRL**
Sw1(config)#**snmp-server community STRMCTRL ro 10**
Sw1(config)#**access-list 10 permit 192.168.1.254**
Sw1(config)#**exit**
Sw1#
Sw1#**show snmp**
Chassis: FOC0730W239
0 SNMP packets input
    0 Bad SNMP version errors
    0 Unknown community name
    0 Illegal operation for community name supplied
    0 Encoding errors
    0 Number of requested variables
    0 Number of altered variables
    0 Get-request PDUs
    0 Get-next PDUs
    0 Set-request PDUs
0 SNMP packets output
    0 Too big errors (Maximum packet size 1500)
    0 No such name errors
    0 Bad values errors
    0 General errors
    0 Response PDUs
    0 Trap PDUs
SNMP global trap: disabled

SNMP logging: enabled
    Logging to 192.168.1.254.162, 0/10, 0 sent, 0 dropped.

```
SNMP agent enabled
Sw1#
Sw1#
Sw1#show storm-control broadcast
```

Interface	Filter State	Trap State	Upper	Lower	Current	Traps Sent
Fa0/1	Forwarding	Below rising	15.00%	10.00%	0.00%	0
Fa0/2	Forwarding	Below rising	15.00%	10.00%	0.00%	0
Fa0/3	Forwarding	Below rising	15.00%	10.00%	0.00%	0
Fa0/4	Forwarding	Below rising	15.00%	10.00%	0.00%	0
Fa0/5	Forwarding	Below rising	15.00%	10.00%	0.00%	0
Fa0/6	Forwarding	Below rising	15.00%	10.00%	0.00%	0
Fa0/7	Forwarding	Below rising	15.00%	10.00%	0.00%	0
Fa0/8	Forwarding	Below rising	15.00%	10.00%	0.00%	0

```
----[Truncated Output]----
Sw1#
Sw1#show storm-control multicast
```

Interface	Filter State	Trap State	Upper	Lower	Current	Traps Sent
Fa0/1	Forwarding	Below rising	80.00%	50.00%	0.00%	0
Fa0/2	Forwarding	Below rising	80.00%	50.00%	0.00%	0
Fa0/3	Forwarding	Below rising	80.00%	50.00%	0.00%	0
Fa0/4	Forwarding	Below rising	80.00%	50.00%	0.00%	0
Fa0/5	Forwarding	Below rising	80.00%	50.00%	0.00%	0
Fa0/6	Forwarding	Below rising	80.00%	50.00%	0.00%	0
Fa0/7	Forwarding	Below rising	80.00%	50.00%	0.00%	0
Fa0/8	Forwarding	Below rising	80.00%	50.00%	0.00%	0

```
----[Truncated Output]----
Sw1#
Sw1#show storm-control unicast
```

Interface	Filter State	Trap State	Upper	Lower	Current	Traps Sent
Fa0/1	Forwarding	Below rising	95.00%	75.00%	0.00%	0
Fa0/2	Forwarding	Below rising	95.00%	75.00%	0.00%	0
Fa0/3	Forwarding	Below rising	95.00%	75.00%	0.00%	0
Fa0/4	Forwarding	Below rising	95.00%	75.00%	0.00%	0
Fa0/5	Forwarding	Below rising	95.00%	75.00%	0.00%	0
Fa0/6	Forwarding	Below rising	95.00%	75.00%	0.00%	0
Fa0/7	Forwarding	Below rising	95.00%	75.00%	0.00%	0
Fa0/8	Forwarding	Below rising	95.00%	75.00%	0.00%	0

Task 3:

```
Sw1(config)#int range f0/9 - 15
Sw1(config-if-range)#switchport protected
Sw1(config-if-range)#exit
Sw1(config)#exit
Sw1#
Sw1#show interfaces fastethernet0/15 switchport
Name: Fa0/15
```

Switchport: Enabled
Administrative Mode: dynamic desirable
Operational Mode: down
Administrative Trunking Encapsulation: dot1q
Negotiation of Trunking: On
Access Mode VLAN: 1 (default)
Trunking Native Mode VLAN: 1 (default)
Voice VLAN: none
Administrative private-vlan host-association: none
Administrative private-vlan mapping: none
Operational private-vlan: none
Trunking VLANs Enabled: ALL
Pruning VLANs Enabled: 2-1001
Capture Mode Disabled
Capture VLANs Allowed: ALL

Protected: true

Voice VLAN: none (Inactive)
Appliance trust: none

Task 4:
Sw1(config)#**mac-address-table notification**
Sw1(config)#**snmp-server enable traps mac-notification**
Sw1(config)#**interface range f0/16 - 24**
Sw1(config-if-range)#**snmp trap mac-notification added**
Sw1(config-if-range)#**exit**
Sw1(config)#**exit**
Sw1#
Sw1#**show mac-address-table notification**
MAC Notification Feature is Enabled on the switch
Interval between Notification Traps : 1 secs
Number of MAC Addresses Added : 0
Number of MAC Addresses Removed : 0
Number of Notifications sent to NMS : 0
Maximum Number of entries configured in History Table : 1
Current History Table Length : 0
MAC Notification Traps are Enabled
History Table contents

Sw1#
Sw1#
Sw1#**show mac-address-table notification interface f0/24**
MAC Notification Feature is Enabled on the switch

Interface	MAC Added Trap	MAC Removed Trap
FastEthernet0/24	Enabled	Disabled

Lab 13 Configurations

Sw1 Configuration

```
Sw1#show run
Building configuration...

Current configuration : 3453 bytes
!
version 12.1
no service pad
service timestamps debug uptime
service timestamps log uptime
no service password-encryption
!
hostname Sw1
!
no logging console
!
ip subnet-zero
vtp domain SECURITY
vtp mode transparent
!
spanning-tree mode pvst
no spanning-tree optimize bpdu transmission
spanning-tree extend system-id
!
interface FastEthernet0/1
 no ip address
 storm-control broadcast level 15.00 10.00
 storm-control multicast level 80.00 50.00
 storm-control unicast level 95.00 75.00
 storm-control action trap
!
interface FastEthernet0/2
 no ip address
 storm-control broadcast level 15.00 10.00
 storm-control multicast level 80.00 50.00
 storm-control unicast level 95.00 75.00
 storm-control action trap
!
interface FastEthernet0/3
 no ip address
 storm-control broadcast level 15.00 10.00
 storm-control multicast level 80.00 50.00
 storm-control unicast level 95.00 75.00
 storm-control action trap
!
```

```
interface FastEthernet0/4
 no ip address
 storm-control broadcast level 15.00 10.00
 storm-control multicast level 80.00 50.00
 storm-control unicast level 95.00 75.00
 storm-control action trap
!
interface FastEthernet0/5
 no ip address
 storm-control broadcast level 15.00 10.00
 storm-control multicast level 80.00 50.00
 storm-control unicast level 95.00 75.00
 storm-control action trap
!
interface FastEthernet0/6
 no ip address
 storm-control broadcast level 15.00 10.00
 storm-control multicast level 80.00 50.00
 storm-control unicast level 95.00 75.00
 storm-control action trap
!
interface FastEthernet0/7
 no ip address
 storm-control broadcast level 15.00 10.00
 storm-control multicast level 80.00 50.00
 storm-control unicast level 95.00 75.00
 storm-control action trap
!
interface FastEthernet0/8
 no ip address
 storm-control broadcast level 15.00 10.00
 storm-control multicast level 80.00 50.00
 storm-control unicast level 95.00 75.00
 storm-control action trap
!
interface FastEthernet0/9
 switchport protected
 no ip address
!
interface FastEthernet0/10
 switchport protected
 no ip address
!
interface FastEthernet0/11
 switchport protected
 no ip address
!
interface FastEthernet0/12
```

```
 switchport protected
 no ip address
!
interface FastEthernet0/13
 switchport protected
 no ip address
!
interface FastEthernet0/14
 switchport protected
 no ip address
!
interface FastEthernet0/15
 switchport protected
 no ip address
!
interface FastEthernet0/16
 no ip address
 snmp trap mac-notification added
!
interface FastEthernet0/17
 no ip address
 snmp trap mac-notification added
!
interface FastEthernet0/18
 no ip address
 snmp trap mac-notification added
!
interface FastEthernet0/19
 no ip address
 snmp trap mac-notification added
!
interface FastEthernet0/20
 no ip address
 snmp trap mac-notification added
!
interface FastEthernet0/21
 no ip address
 snmp trap mac-notification added
!
interface FastEthernet0/22
 no ip address
 snmp trap mac-notification added
!
interface FastEthernet0/23
 no ip address
 snmp trap mac-notification added
!
interface FastEthernet0/24
```

```
 no ip address
 snmp trap mac-notification added
!
interface GigabitEthernet0/1
 no ip address
!
interface GigabitEthernet0/2
 no ip address
!
interface Vlan1
 no ip address
 no ip route-cache
 shutdown
!
ip http server
!
access-list 10 permit 192.168.1.254
snmp-server community STRMCTRL RO 10
snmp-server enable traps MAC-Notification
snmp-server host 192.168.1.254 STRMCTRL
!
line con 0
line vty 5 15
!
mac-address-table notification
end
```

LAB 14

Cisco IOS Syslog and SNMP Configuration

Lab Objective:

The objective of this lab exercise is for you to learn and understand how configure Syslog and SNMP reporting on Cisco IOS routers.

Lab Purpose:

Syslog and SNMP are tools that can be used to provide security-related information, such as access breaches, configuration changes and high processor utilization, for example. As a CCNA Security administrator, you are expected to demonstrate a solid understanding of the basic Syslog and SNMP configuration in Cisco IOS routers.

Lab Difficulty:

This lab has a difficulty rating of 7/10.

Readiness Assessment:

When you are ready for your certification exam, you should complete this lab in no more than 15 minutes.

Lab Topology:

Please use any single switch to complete this lab:

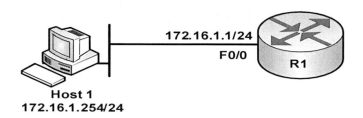

Host 1
172.16.1.254/24

Lab 14 Configuration Tasks

Task 1:

Configure the hostname on R1 and IP addressing as illustrated in the diagram. In addition, configure Host 1 with the IP address specified and a default gateway of 172.16.1.1.

NOTE: If you do not have a Host in your lab, you can simply substitute Host 1 for another router with an Ethernet interface and a default static route pointing to 172.16.1.1.

Task 2:

Configure the following Loopback interfaces on R1:

Interface	Address	Mask
Loopback 10	10.1.1.1	/24
Loopback 20	20.1.1.1	/28
Loopback 30	30.1.1.1	/20

Task 3:

Configure an extended ACL on R1 that provides the most detailed logging on all traffic to the Loopback10, Loopback20 and Loopback30 subnets. This ACL should deny all IP traffic to these subnets. Apply this ACL inbound on the FastEthernet0/0 interface of R1.

Task 4:

Configure the local time on R1 as 20:00 GMT/UTC using today's date for the clock date.

Task 5:

Configure Syslog on R1 as follows:
- Log all debugging messages to the local router buffer
- Configure a buffer size of 10,000
- Log all informational messages to SYSLOG server 172.16.1.254

In addition to this, configure the logs to show the date and time, as well as the time zone. And, finally, configure R1 so that all logs include sequence numbers for easier identification.

Task 6:

Configure SNMP on R1 as follows:
- Configure R1 to send all configuration traps to server 172.16.1.254
- Configure R1 so that server 172.16.1.254 has read and write access to the router
- Server 172.16.1.254 will use the SNMP Community string secret to manage R1

Task 7:

Clear your logs and verify your configuration by pinging from Host 1 to any of the Loopback interfaces on R1. There should be entries that provided detailed information in the local router buffer. You can also Telnet from Host 1 to any of the Loopback interfaces on R1.

Verify your SNMP configuration by entering/exiting configuration mode on R1. If you have configured this correctly, you will see SNMP traps being sent by R1.

Lab 14 Configuration and Verification

Task 1:
```
Router(config)#hostname R1
R1(config)#interface f0/0
R1(config-if)#ip address 172.16.1.1 255.255.255.0
R1(config-if)#no shut
R1(config-if)#exit
R1(config)#exit
R1#show ip interface brief
```

Interface	IP-Address	OK?	Method	Status	Protocol
FastEthernet0/0	172.16.1.1	YES	NVRAM	up	up
Serial0/0	unassigned	YES	manual	administratively down	down

```
Command Prompt                                              _ □ ×

C:\>ipconfig

Windows IP Configuration


Ethernet adapter Local Area Connection 2:

        Connection-specific DNS Suffix  . :
        IP Address. . . . . . . . . . . . : 172.16.1.254
        Subnet Mask . . . . . . . . . . . : 255.255.255.0
        Default Gateway . . . . . . . . . : 172.16.1.1

Ethernet adapter Wireless Network Connection:

        Media State . . . . . . . . . . . : Media disconnected

C:\>ping 172.16.1.1

Pinging 172.16.1.1 with 32 bytes of data:

Reply from 172.16.1.1: bytes=32 time=5ms TTL=255
Reply from 172.16.1.1: bytes=32 time=1ms TTL=255
Reply from 172.16.1.1: bytes=32 time=1ms TTL=255
Reply from 172.16.1.1: bytes=32 time=1ms TTL=255

Ping statistics for 172.16.1.1:
    Packets: Sent = 4, Received = 4, Lost = 0 (0% loss),
Approximate round trip times in milli-seconds:
    Minimum = 1ms, Maximum = 5ms, Average = 2ms

C:\>
```

Task 2:
```
R1(config)#int lo 10
R1(config-if)#ip address 10.1.1.1 255.255.255.0
R1(config-if)#exit
R1(config)#int lo 20
R1(config-if)#ip address 20.1.1.1 255.255.255.240
R1(config-if)#exit
R1(config)#int lo 30
R1(config-if)#ip address 30.1.1.1 255.255.240.0
R1(config-if)#exit
R1(config)#exit
R1#
```

```
R1#
R1#show ip interface brief
Interface        IP-Address    OK?   Method    Status                  Protocol
FastEthernet0/0  172.16.1.1    YES   NVRAM     up                      up
Serial0/0        unassigned    YES   manual    administratively down   down
Loopback10       10.1.1.1      YES   manual    up                      up
Loopback20       20.1.1.1      YES   manual    up                      up
Loopback30       30.1.1.1      YES   manual    up                      up
```

Task 3:

To complete this Task, do not forget that there is an implicit deny all statement at the end of ACLS; therefore ensure that you permit all other traffic once your deny statements are done.

```
R1(config)#ip access-list extended DETAILED-LOGGING
R1(config-ext-nacl)#deny ip any 10.1.1.0 0.0.0.255 log-input
R1(config-ext-nacl)#deny ip any 20.1.1.0 0.0.0.15 log-input
R1(config-ext-nacl)#deny ip any 30.1.1.0 0.0.15.255 log-input
R1(config-ext-nacl)#permit ip any any
R1(config-ext-nacl)#exit
R1(config)#int fast0/0
R1(config-if)#ip access-group DETAILED-LOGGING in
R1(config-if)#exit
R1(config)#exit
R1#
R1#show ip interface fast0/0
FastEthernet0/0 is up, line protocol is up
  Internet address is 172.16.1.1/24
  Broadcast address is 255.255.255.255
  Address determined by non-volatile memory
  MTU is 1500 bytes
  Helper address is not set
  Directed broadcast forwarding is disabled
  Outgoing access list is not set
  Inbound  access list is DETAILED-LOGGING
  Proxy ARP is enabled
----[Truncated Output]----
```

Task 4:

```
R1(config)#clock timezone UTC -0
R1(config)#exit
R1#clock set 20:00:00 28 July 2009
R1#
R1#show clock
20:00:03.545 UTC Tue Jul 28 2009
```

Task 5:

R1(config)#**logging on**
R1(config)#**logging buffered debugging**
R1(config)#**logging buffered 10000**
R1(config)#**logging trap informational**
R1(config)#**logging host 172.16.1.254**
R1(config)#**service timestamps log datetime show-timezone**
R1(config)#**service sequence-numbers**
R1(config)#**exit**
R1#
R1#**show logging**
Syslog logging: enabled (1 messages dropped, 0 messages rate-limited,
                      0 flushes, 0 overruns, xml disabled, filtering disabled)

No Active Message Discriminator.

No Inactive Message Discriminator.

    Console logging: disabled
    Monitor logging: level debugging, 0 messages logged, xml disabled,
                     filtering disabled
    **Buffer logging: level debugging, 3 messages logged, xml disabled,
                     filtering disabled**
    Logging Exception size (4096 bytes)
    Count and timestamp logging messages: disabled
    Persistent logging: disabled
    Trap logging: level informational, 38 message lines logged
       Logging to 172.16.1.254 (udp port 514, audit disabled,
           authentication disabled, encryption disabled, link up),
           3 message lines logged,
           0 message lines rate-limited,
           0 message lines dropped-by-MD,
           xml disabled, sequence number disabled
           filtering disabled

Log Buffer (10000 bytes):

000035: Jul 28 20:03:17 UTC: %SYS-5-CONFIG_I: Configured from console by console
000036: Jul 28 20:13:17 UTC: %SYS-5-CONFIG_I: Configured from console by console
000037: Jul 28 20:14:07 UTC: %SYS-5-CONFIG_I: Configured from console by console

Task 6:

```
R1(config)#access-list 5 permit host 172.16.1.254
R1(config)#snmp-server community secret RW 5
R1(config)#snmp-server host 172.16.1.254 traps secret config
R1(config)#snmp-server enable traps config
R1(config)#exit
R1#
R1#
R1#show snmp
Chassis: FTX0915A2V4
0 SNMP packets input
    0 Bad SNMP version errors
    0 Unknown community name
    0 Illegal operation for community name supplied
    0 Encoding errors
    0 Number of requested variables
    0 Number of altered variables
    0 Get-request PDUs
    0 Get-next PDUs
    0 Set-request PDUs
    0 Input queue packet drops (Maximum queue size 1000)
2 SNMP packets output
    0 Too big errors (Maximum packet size 1500)
    0 No such name errors
    0 Bad values errors
    0 General errors
    0 Response PDUs
    2 Trap PDUs

SNMP logging: enabled
    Logging to 172.16.1.254.162, 2/10, 0 sent, 0 dropped.
```

Task 7:

```
R1#clear log
Clear logging buffer [confirm]
R1#
R1#show logging
Syslog logging:     enabled (1 messages dropped, 0 messages rate-limited,
                    0 flushes, 0 overruns, xml disabled, filtering disabled)


No Active Message Discriminator.



No Inactive Message Discriminator.
```

Console logging: level debugging, 1 messages logged, xml disabled,
    filtering disabled
Monitor logging: level debugging, 0 messages logged, xml disabled,
    filtering disabled
Buffer logging: level debugging, 7 messages logged, xml disabled,
    filtering disabled
Logging Exception size (4096 bytes)
Count and timestamp logging messages: disabled
Persistent logging: disabled
Trap logging: level informational, 42 message lines logged
   Logging to 172.16.1.254 (udp port 514, audit disabled,
     authentication disabled, encryption disabled, link up),
     7 message lines logged,
     0 message lines rate-limited,
     0 message lines dropped-by-MD,
     xml disabled, sequence number disabled
     filtering disabled

Log Buffer (10000 bytes):
R1#

Now, perform a ping from Host 1 to any Loopback interface on R1 and verify the logs:

R1#show logging
Syslog logging: enabled (1 messages dropped, 0 messages rate-limited,
     0 flushes, 0 overruns, xml disabled, filtering disabled)

No Active Message Discriminator.

No Inactive Message Discriminator.

Console logging: level debugging, 126 messages logged, xml disabled,
    filtering disabled
Monitor logging: level debugging, 0 messages logged, xml disabled,
    filtering disabled
Buffer logging: level debugging, 132 messages logged, xml disabled,
    filtering disabled
Logging Exception size (4096 bytes)
Count and timestamp logging messages: disabled
Persistent logging: disabled
Trap logging: level informational, 44 message lines logged
   Logging to 172.16.1.254 (udp port 514, audit disabled,
     authentication disabled, encryption disabled, link up),
     9 message lines logged,
     0 message lines rate-limited,

            0 message lines dropped-by-MD,
            xml disabled, sequence number disabled
            filtering disabled

Log Buffer (10000 bytes):

000116: Jul 28 20:30:40 UTC: %SEC-6-IPACCESSLOGDP: list DETAILED-LOGGING denied icmp 172.16.1.254 (FastEthernet0/0 001d.09d4.0238) -> 20.1.1.1 (0/0), 1 packet

To validate SNMP, use the **debug snmp packets** command and then access configuration mode. You will see SNMP traps being sent by R1 to the SNMP server 172.16.1.254

```
R1#debug snmp packets
SNMP packet debugging is on
R1#
R1#config t
Enter configuration commands, one per line.  End with CNTL/Z.
R1(config)#
R1(config)#
000119: Jul 28 20:33:22.727: SNMP: Queuing packet to 172.16.1.254
000120: Jul 28 20:33:22.727: SNMP: V1 Trap, ent ciscoConfigManMIB.2, addr 172.16.1.1,
gentrap 6, spectrap 1
 ccmHistoryEventEntry.3.32 = 1
 ccmHistoryEventEntry.4.32 = 2
 ccmHistoryEventEntry.5.32 = 3
000121: Jul 28 20:33:22.979: SNMP: Packet sent via UDP to 172.16.1.254
R1(config)#exit
R1#
R1#conf
000122: Jul 28 20:33:31 UTC: %SYS-5-CONFIG_I: Configured from console by console
Configuring from terminal, memory, or network [terminal]?
Enter configuration commands, one per line.  End with CNTL/Z.
R1(config)#
000123: Jul 28 20:33:39.975: SNMP: Queuing packet to 172.16.1.254
000124: Jul 28 20:33:39.975: SNMP: V1 Trap, ent ciscoConfigManMIB.2, addr 172.16.1.1,
gentrap 6, spectrap 1
 ccmHistoryEventEntry.3.33 = 1
 ccmHistoryEventEntry.4.33 = 2
 ccmHistoryEventEntry.5.33 = 3
000125: Jul 28 20:33:40.227: SNMP: Packet sent via UDP to 172.16.1.254
R1(config)#exit
R1#
000126: Jul 28 20:33:44 UTC: %SYS-5-CONFIG_I: Configured from console by console
R1#undebug all
All possible debugging has been turned off
```

Lab 14 Configurations

R1 Configuration

```
R1#show running-config
Building configuration...

Current configuration : 1458 bytes
!
! Last configuration change at 20:33:44 UTC Tue Jul 28 2009
!
version 12.4
service timestamps debug datetime msec
service timestamps log datetime show-timezone
no service password-encryption
service sequence-numbers
!
hostname R1
!
boot-start-marker
boot-end-marker
!
no logging message-counter syslog
logging buffered 10000
!
no aaa new-model
no network-clock-participate slot 1
no network-clock-participate wic 0
ip cef
!
multilink bundle-name authenticated
!
archive
 log config
  hidekeys
!
interface Loopback10
 ip address 10.1.1.1 255.255.255.0
!
interface Loopback20
 ip address 20.1.1.1 255.255.255.240
!
interface Loopback30
 ip address 30.1.1.1 255.255.240.0
!
interface FastEthernet0/0
 ip address 172.16.1.1 255.255.255.0
 ip access-group DETAILED-LOGGING in
```

```
 duplex auto
 speed auto
!
interface Serial0/0
 no ip address
 shutdown
!
ip forward-protocol nd
!
ip http server
ip http secure-server
!
ip access-list extended DETAILED-LOGGING
 deny   ip any 10.1.1.0 0.0.0.255 log-input
 deny   ip any 20.1.1.0 0.0.0.15 log-input
 deny   ip any 30.1.0.0 0.0.15.255 log-input
 permit ip any any
!
logging 172.16.1.254
access-list 5 permit 172.16.1.254
snmp-server community secret RW 5
snmp-server enable traps config
snmp-server enable traps cpu threshold
snmp-server host 172.16.1.254 secret  config
!
control-plane
!
line con 0
line aux 0
line vty 0 4
 privilege level 15
 password cisco
 login
!
end
```

LAB 15

Cisco IOS Secure Copy

Lab Objective:

The objective of this lab exercise is for you to learn and understand how configure the Cisco IOS Secure Copy feature on Cisco IOS routers.

Lab Purpose:

The Secure Copy (SCP) feature relies on Secure Shell (SSH) and provides a secure and authenticated method for copying router configuration or router image files.

Lab Difficulty:

This lab has a difficulty rating of 7/10.

Readiness Assessment:

When you are ready for your certification exam, you should complete this lab in no more than 15 minutes.

Lab Topology:

Please use the following topology to complete this lab exercise:

Lab 15 Configuration Tasks

Task 1:

Configure the hostnames and IP addresses on R1 and R2 as illustrated in the network diagram. Configure R2 to send R1 clocking information at a rate of 512Kbps. Ping between R1 and R2 to verify your configuration and ensure that the two routers have IP connectivity.

Task 2:

Configure R1 as an SCP server as follows:
- Configure a domain name of **howtonetwork.net**
- Use an RSA key size of 1024
- The SSH session should time out after 30 seconds of inactivity
- SSH users can only attempt to log in 2 times

Task 3:

Configure a user with the name **admin**, a privilege level of 15 and a secret of **cisco** on R1.

Task 4:

Configure Authentication and Authorization on R1 as follows:
- Authentication for inbound connections should be performed against the local database
- Authorization for EXEC access should be granted based on local user privileges

Task 5:

Save the running configuration of R1 to Flash memory using the file name **TEST**. In addition to this, configure R1 as a TFTP server so that remote users can download this file.

Task 6:

Securely copy the file **TEST** from R1 to the Flash memory of R2 and verify your work.

Lab 15 Configuration and Verification

Task 1:
```
Router(config)#hostname R1
R1(config)#interface serial0/0
R1(config-if)#no shutdown
R1(config-if)#ip address 10.1.1.1 255.255.255.0
R1(config-if)#end
R1#


Router(config)#hostname R2
R2(config)#int serial0/0
R2(config-if)#no shutdown
R2(config-if)#ip address 10.1.1.2 255.255.255.252
R2(config-if)#clock rate 512000
R2(config-if)#exit
R2(config)#exit
R2#
R2#ping 10.1.1.1

Type escape sequence to abort.
Sending 5, 100-byte ICMP Echos to 10.1.1.1, timeout is 2 seconds:
!!!!!
Success rate is 100 percent (5/5), round-trip min/avg/max = 4/5/8 ms
```

Task 2:

R1(config)#**ip domain-name howtonetwork.net**
R1(config)#**crypto key generate rsa**
The name for the keys will be: R1.howtonetwork.net
Choose the size of the key modulus in the range of 360 to 2048 for your
  General Purpose Keys. Choosing a key modulus greater than 512 may take
  a few minutes.

How many bits in the modulus [512]: 1024
% Generating 1024 bit RSA keys, keys will be non-exportable...[OK]

R1(config)#**ip ssh time-out 30**
R1(config)#**ip ssh authentication-retries 2**
R1(config)#**ip scp server enable**
R1(config)#**exit**
R1#

Task 3:

R1(config)#**username admin privilege 15 secret cisco**
R1(config)#**exit**
R1#

Task 4:

R1(config)#**aaa new-model**
R1(config)#**aaa authentication login default local**
R1(config)#**aaa authorization exec default local**
R1(config)#**exit**
R1#

Task 5:

R1#**copy running-config flash:**
Destination filename [r1-confg]? **TEST**
Erase flash: before copying? [confirm]**n**
Verifying checksum... OK (0x9A6B)
2746 bytes copied in 10.681 secs (257 bytes/sec)
R1(config)#**tftp-server flash:TEST**
R1(config)#**exit**
R1#
R1#**show flash:**

System flash directory:
File Length   Name/status
  1   19615064   c2600-advsecurityk9-mz.124-15.T9.bin
  2   1038   home.shtml
  3   2754   sdmconfig-26xx.cfg
  4   112640   home.tar

```
5  1505280        common.tar
6  6389760        sdm.tar
7  931840         es.tar
8  2766           TEST
[28567284 bytes used, 4462856 available, 33030140 total]
32768K bytes of processor board System flash (Read/Write)
```

Task 6:

```
R2#copy scp: flash:
Address or name of remote host []? 10.1.1.1
Source username [R2]? admin
Source filename []? TEST
Destination filename [TEST]?
Erase flash: before copying? [confirm]n
Password:
!
Verifying checksum...  OK (0x6C6)
2766 bytes copied in 3.843 secs (720 bytes/sec)
R2#
```

Lab 15 Configurations

R1 Configuration

```
R1#show running-config
Building configuration...

Current configuration : 2789 bytes
!
version 12.4
service timestamps debug datetime msec
service timestamps log datetime msec
no service password-encryption
!
hostname R1
!
boot-start-marker
boot-end-marker
!
no logging console
!
aaa new-model
!
aaa authentication login default local
aaa authorization exec default local
```

```
!
aaa session-id common
no network-clock-participate slot 1
no network-clock-participate wic 0
ip cef
!
no ip domain lookup
ip domain name howtonetwork.net
!
multilink bundle-name authenticated
!
crypto pki trustpoint TP-self-signed-533650306
 enrollment selfsigned
 subject-name cn=IOS-Self-Signed-Certificate-533650306
 revocation-check none
 rsakeypair TP-self-signed-533650306
!
crypto pki certificate chain TP-self-signed-533650306
 certificate self-signed 01
  30820238 308201A1 A0030201 02020101 300D0609 2A864886 F70D0101 04050030
  30312E30 2C060355 04031325 494F532D 53656C66 2D536967 6E65642D 43657274
  69666963 6174652D 35333336 35303330 36301E17 0D303230 33303130 31303335
  315A170D 32303031 30313030 30303030 5A303031 2E302C06 03550403 1325494F
  532D5365 6C662D53 69676E65 642D4365 72746966 69636174 652D3533 33363530
  33303630 819F300D 06092A86 4886F70D 01010105 0003818D 00308189 02818100
  A10043E2 FB10C1D1 BA18F3AD 554F081C ACA14F4C EA48E0C1 4739653D B7759EE7
  8EB29881 7F391723 E2BB7EC6 54EB6F25 B4E94520 DF8DA15C 3B9E6F7C 3AA57549
  80AB643F A9427071 965DD56A 2D3E60CE 775F2ED5 C9014FCD F313F3EB B5189F62
  09F461BC 32E3E78F F93C8B07 0740DDA8 7B880D1B A3185787 CE621B35 3511A9D5
  02030100 01A36230 60300F06 03551D13 0101FF04 05300301 01FF300D 0603551D
  11040630 04820252 31301F06 03551D23 04183016 8014CD63 D2C471B7 ABA4ACF9
  C2B6020D 4A895471 C7F9301D 0603551D 0E041604 14CD63D2 C471B7AB A4ACF9C2
  B6020D4A 895471C7 F9300D06 092A8648 86F70D01 01040500 03818100 6BE0FD98
  BEC0DCDD AA6E3059 44434A63 DECC9224 22D81B23 35A29E70 74C17E92 14001495
  9E01FEA1 373EB386 9A046E56 14910BC5 05671798 869B8753 96E711EA E51B8908
  130D9B62 52F21D30 02B4C8AE FBB2919E 14815B80 E1C2FB39 97FEC0C2 190CAC10
  DD5CB1E3 EE8724A7 9A256D79 11855629 06428889 E237A7B9 D2808A50
        quit
!
username admin privilege 15 secret 5 $1$qMaz$S4.GkUbxDSA4iWn7CBQuU.
archive
 log config
  hidekeys
!
```

```
ip ssh time-out 30
ip ssh authentication-retries 2
ip scp server enable
!
interface FastEthernet0/0
 ip address 172.16.1.1 255.255.255.0
 duplex auto
 speed auto
!
interface Serial0/0
 ip address 10.1.1.1 255.255.255.252
!
ip forward-protocol nd
!
ip http server
ip http secure-server
!
tftp-server flash:TEST
!
control-plane
!
line con 0
line aux 0
line vty 0 4
 privilege level 15
 password cisco
!
end
```

R2 Configuration

```
R2#show running-config
Building configuration...

Current configuration : 795 bytes
!
version 12.4
service timestamps debug datetime msec
service timestamps log datetime msec
no service password-encryption
!
hostname R2
!
boot-start-marker
boot-end-marker
!
no logging console
!
no aaa new-model
```

```
no network-clock-participate slot 1
no network-clock-participate wic 0
ip cef
!
no ip domain lookup
!
multilink bundle-name authenticated
!
archive
 log config
  hidekeys
!
interface FastEthernet0/0
 ip address 172.16.1.2 255.255.255.0
 duplex auto
 speed auto
!
interface Serial0/0
 ip address 10.1.1.2 255.255.255.252
 clock rate 512000
!
ip forward-protocol nd
!
ip http server
ip http authentication local
no ip http secure-server
!
control-plane
!
line con 0
line aux 0
line vty 0 4
 privilege level 15
 password cisco
 login
!
end
```

LAB 16

Cisco IOS Auto Secure

Lab Objective:

The objective of this lab exercise is for you to learn and understand how use the Auto Secure feature available in Cisco IOS software.

Lab Purpose:

The Cisco IOS Auto Secure feature simplifies the security configuration of a router and hardens the router configuration.

Lab Difficulty:

This lab has a difficulty rating of 5/10.

Readiness Assessment:

When you are ready for your certification exam, you should complete this lab in no more than 15 minutes.

Lab Topology:

Please use any single router to complete this lab:

Lab 16 Configuration Tasks

Task 1:

Configure the hostname on R1 as illustrated in the diagram.

Task 2:

Enable the Auto Secure feature on R1 and secure the router Management plane only. Configure parameters of your choice. The objective here is to familiarize you with this feature.

Task 3:

Configure R1 so that all passwords (i.e. enable password, enable secret, VTY, etc) entered on the router must be at least 8 characters in length. In addition to this, configure R1 so that only 2 unsuccessful login attempts are permitted, and if this threshold is exceed a log message should be generated and stored in the local router buffer.

Lab 16 Configuration and Verification

Task 1:

```
Router(config)#hostname R1
R1(config)#exit
R1#
```

Task 2:

```
R1#auto secure management
          --- AutoSecure Configuration ---

*** AutoSecure configuration enhances the security of
the router, but it will not make it absolutely resistant
to all security attacks ***

AutoSecure will modify the configuration of your device.
All configuration changes will be shown. For a detailed
explanation of how the configuration changes enhance security
and any possible side effects, please refer to Cisco.com for
Autosecure documentation.
At any prompt you may enter '?' for help.
Use ctrl-c to abort this session at any prompt.

Gathering information about the router for AutoSecure

Is this router connected to internet? [no]: no

Securing Management plane services...

Disabling service finger
Disabling service pad
Disabling udp & tcp small servers
Enabling service password encryption
Enabling service tcp-keepalives-in
Enabling service tcp-keepalives-out
Disabling the cdp protocol

Disabling the bootp server
Disabling the http server
Disabling the finger service
Disabling source routing
Disabling gratuitous arp

Here is a sample Security Banner to be shown
at every access to device. Modify it to suit your
enterprise requirements.

Authorized Access only
  This system is the property of So-&-So-Enterprise.
```

UNAUTHORIZED ACCESS TO THIS DEVICE IS PROHIBITED.
You must have explicit permission to access this
device. All activities performed on this device
are logged. Any violations of access policy will result
in disciplinary action.

Enter the security banner {Put the banner between
k and k, where k is any character}:
#
This is the CCNA Security Auto Secure Lab
#
Enable secret is either not configured or
 is the same as enable password
Enter the new enable secret: ********
Confirm the enable secret : ********
Enter the new enable password: ********
Confirm the enable password: ********
Configuring AAA local authentication
Configuring Console, Aux and VTY lines for
local authentication, exec-timeout, and transport
Securing device against Login Attacks
Configure the following parameters

Blocking Period when Login Attack detected: **60**

Maximum Login failures with the device: **2**

Maximum time period for crossing the failed login attempts: **30**

Configure SSH server? [yes]: **no**

Configuring interface specific AutoSecure services
Disabling the following ip services on all interfaces:

 no ip redirects
 no ip proxy-arp
 no ip unreachables
 no ip directed-broadcast
 no ip mask-reply
Disabling mop on Ethernet interfaces

This is the configuration generated:

no service finger
no service pad
no service udp-small-servers
no service tcp-small-servers
service password-encryption
service tcp-keepalives-in
service tcp-keepalives-out

```
no cdp run
no ip bootp server
no ip http server
no ip finger
no ip source-route
no ip gratuitous-arps
no ip identd
banner motd ^C
This is the CCNA Security Auto Secure Lab
^C
security passwords min-length 6
security authentication failure rate 10 log
enable secret 5 $1$KqCV$PKI46q2v5RLX6tj19aaxE1
enable password 7 094F471A1A0A14110209
aaa new-model
aaa authentication login local_auth local
line con 0
 login authentication local_auth
 exec-timeout 5 0
 transport output telnet
line aux 0
 login authentication local_auth
 exec-timeout 10 0
 transport output telnet
line vty 0 4
 login authentication local_auth
 transport input telnet
login block-for 60 attempts 2 within 30
service timestamps debug datetime msec localtime show-timezone
service timestamps log datetime msec localtime show-timezone
logging facility local2
logging trap debugging
service sequence-numbers
logging console critical
logging buffered
interface FastEthernet0/0
 no ip redirects
 no ip proxy-arp
 no ip unreachables
 no ip directed-broadcast
 no ip mask-reply
 no mop enabled
interface Serial0/0
 no ip redirects
 no ip proxy-arp
 no ip unreachables
 no ip directed-broadcast
 no ip mask-reply
!
end
```

Apply this configuration to running-config? [yes]: **yes**

Applying the config generated to running-config

R1#

Task 3:
R1(config)#**security passwords min-length 8**
R1(config)#**security authentication failure rate 2 log**
R1(config)#**exit**
R1#

Lab 16 Configurations

R1 Configuration

R1#show running-config
Building configuration...

Current configuration : 3406 bytes
!
version 12.4
no service pad
service tcp-keepalives-in
service tcp-keepalives-out
service timestamps debug datetime msec localtime show-timezone
service timestamps log datetime msec localtime show-timezone
service password-encryption
service sequence-numbers
!
hostname R1
!
boot-start-marker
boot-end-marker
!
security authentication failure rate 2 log
security passwords min-length 8
logging buffered 4096
logging console critical
enable secret 5 1KqCV$PKI46q2v5RLX6tj19aaxE1
enable password 7 094F471A1A0A14110209
!
aaa new-model
!
aaa authentication login local_auth local
!

```
aaa session-id common
no network-clock-participate slot 1
no network-clock-participate wic 0
no ip source-route
no ip gratuitous-arps
ip cef
!
no ip bootp server
login block-for 60 attempts 2 within 30
!
multilink bundle-name authenticated
!
crypto pki trustpoint TP-self-signed-533650306
 enrollment selfsigned
 subject-name cn=IOS-Self-Signed-Certificate-533650306
 revocation-check none
 rsakeypair TP-self-signed-533650306
!
crypto pki certificate chain TP-self-signed-533650306
 certificate self-signed 01
  30820238 308201A1 A0030201 02020101 300D0609 2A864886 F70D0101 04050030
  30312E30 2C060355 04031325 494F532D 53656C66 2D536967 6E65642D 43657274
  69666963 6174652D 35333336 35303330 36301E17 0D303230 33303130 31303335
  315A170D 32303031 30313030 30303030 5A303031 2E302C06 03550403 1325494F
  532D5365 6C662D53 69676E65 642D4365 72746966 69636174 652D3533 33363530
  33303630 819F300D 06092A86 4886F70D 01010105 0003818D 00308189 02818100
  A10043E2 FB10C1D1 BA18F3AD 554F081C ACA14F4C EA48E0C1 4739653D B7759EE7
  8EB29881 7F391723 E2BB7EC6 54EB6F25 B4E94520 DF8DA15C 3B9E6F7C 3AA57549
  80AB643F A9427071 965DD56A 2D3E60CE 775F2ED5 C9014FCD F313F3EB B5189F62
  09F461BC 32E3E78F F93C8B07 0740DDA8 7B880D1B A3185787 CE621B35 3511A9D5
  02030100 01A36230 60300F06 03551D13 0101FF04 05300301 01FF300D 0603551D
  11040630 04820252 31301F06 03551D23 04183016 8014CD63 D2C471B7 ABA4ACF9
  C2B6020D 4A895471 C7F9301D 0603551D 0E041604 14CD63D2 C471B7AB A4ACF9C2
  B6020D4A 895471C7 F9300D06 092A8648 86F70D01 01040500 03818100 6BE0FD98
  BEC0DCDD AA6E3059 44434A63 DECC9224 22D81B23 35A29E70 74C17E92 14001495
  9E01FEA1 373EB386 9A046E56 14910BC5 05671798 869B8753 96E711EA E51B8908
  130D9B62 52F21D30 02B4C8AE FBB2919E 14815B80 E1C2FB39 97FEC0C2 190CAC10
  DD5CB1E3 EE8724A7 9A256D79 11855629 06428889 E237A7B9 D2808A50
    quit
!
archive
 log config
  logging enable
  hidekeys
```

```
!
interface FastEthernet0/0
 no ip address
 no ip redirects
 no ip unreachables
 no ip proxy-arp
 duplex auto
 speed auto
 no mop enabled
!
interface Serial0/0
 ip address 10.1.1.1 255.255.255.252
 no ip redirects
 no ip unreachables
 no ip proxy-arp
!
ip forward-protocol nd
!
no ip http server
ip http secure-server
!
logging trap debugging
logging facility local2
no cdp run
!
control-plane
!
banner motd ^C
This is the CCNA Security Auto Secure Lab
^C
!
line con 0
 exec-timeout 5 0
 login authentication local_auth
 transport output telnet
line aux 0
 login authentication local_auth
 transport output telnet
line vty 0 4
 privilege level 15
 password 7 094F471A1A0A
 login authentication local_auth
 transport input telnet
!
end
```

LAB 17

Cisco SDM One-Step Lockdown

Lab Objective:

The objective of this lab exercise is for you to learn and understand how use the Cisco SDM One-Step Lockdown feature.

Lab Purpose:

The Cisco SDM One-Step Lockdown feature tests your router configuration for any potential security problems and automatically makes any necessary configuration changes to correct any problems found. This is similar to the Cisco IOS Auto Secure feature.

Lab Difficulty:

This lab has a difficulty rating of 5/10.

Readiness Assessment:

When you are ready for your certification exam, you should complete this lab in no more than 15 minutes.

Lab Topology:

Please use the following topology to complete this lab exercise:

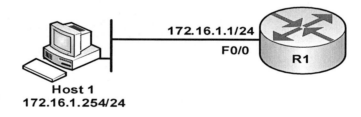

Lab 17 Configuration Tasks

Task 1:

Configure the hostname on R1 as illustrated in the diagram. In addition to this, configure Host 1 with the IP address illustrated. Because Host 1 and R1 are on the same subnet, you do not need to configure a default gateway on Host 1. However, ensure that Host 1 can ping R1.

Task 2:

Configure the username **sdmadmin** with a privilege level of 15 and a password of **security** on R1. In addition to this, enable SSH using default parameters, as well as HTTPS on R1. HTTPS users should be authenticated using the local router database. Configure **howtonetwork.net** as the domain name on R1.

Task 3:

Access R1 via SDM from Host 1 and navigate to the SDM One-Step Lockdown feature. Initiate this feature and familiarize yourself with navigating SDM to implement One-Step Lockdown.

Lab 17 Configuration and Verification

Task 1:

```
Router(config)#hostname R1
R1(config)#int fastethernet0/0
R1(config-if)#ip address 172.16.1.1 255.255.255.0
R1(config-if)#no shutdown
R1(config-if)#exit
R1(config)#exit
R1#
```

```
Command Prompt                                           _ □ ×

C:\>ipconfig

Windows IP Configuration

Ethernet adapter Local Area Connection 2:

        Connection-specific DNS Suffix  . :
        IP Address. . . . . . . . . . . : 172.16.1.254
        Subnet Mask . . . . . . . . . . : 255.255.255.0
        Default Gateway . . . . . . . . :

Ethernet adapter Wireless Network Connection:

        Media State . . . . . . . . . . : Media disconnected

C:\>ping 172.16.1.1

Pinging 172.16.1.1 with 32 bytes of data:

Reply from 172.16.1.1: bytes=32 time=5ms TTL=255
Reply from 172.16.1.1: bytes=32 time=1ms TTL=255
Reply from 172.16.1.1: bytes=32 time=1ms TTL=255
Reply from 172.16.1.1: bytes=32 time=19ms TTL=255

Ping statistics for 172.16.1.1:
        Packets: Sent = 4, Received = 4, Lost = 0 (0% loss),
Approximate round trip times in milli-seconds:
        Minimum = 1ms, Maximum = 19ms, Average = 6ms

C:\>_
```

Task 2:

```
R1(config)#username sdmadmin privilege 15 secret security
R1(config)#ip domain-name howtonetwork.net
R1(config)#crypto key generate rsa
```
The name for the keys will be: R1.howtonetwork.net
Choose the size of the key modulus in the range of 360 to 2048 for your
  General Purpose Keys. Choosing a key modulus greater than 512 may take
  a few minutes.

How many bits in the modulus [512]:
% Generating 512 bit RSA keys, keys will be non-exportable...[OK]

```
R1(config)#ip http secure-server
R1(config)#ip http authentication local
R1(config)#exit
R1#
```

Task 3:

To access a Cisco IOS router using SDM, you either need SDM installed on the local machine or you can simply use any web browser and connect to the router using the format https:// x.x.x.x to reach the device. Either method works in the same manner. This example will be based on SDM installed on the local computer:

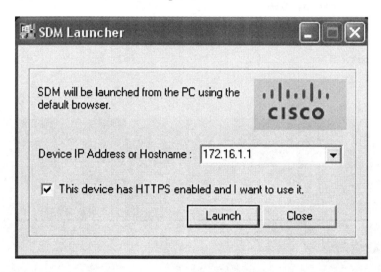

Next, log into SDM using the username and password pair configured on R1 and click **OK**:

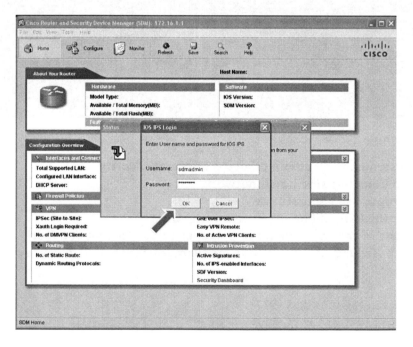

Once you have successfully logged into SDM, navigate to the **Configure** radio button – next to the **Home** button—in the top LEFT hand corner:

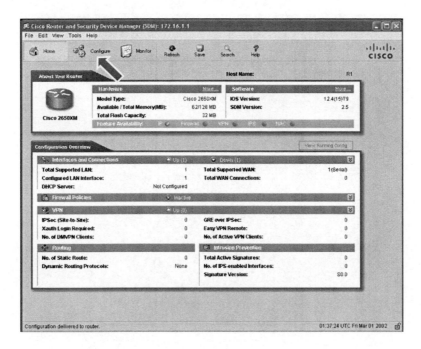

Next, click on the **Security Audit** button to take you to the next screen:

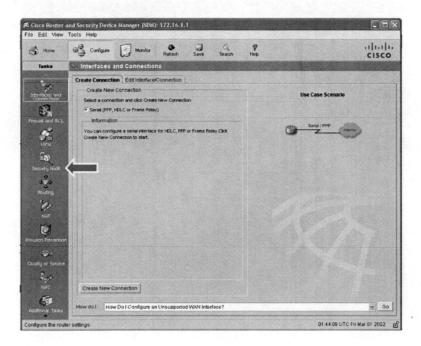

Once you are on the Security Audit page, click on the **One-step lockdown** radio button on the very bottom of the page:

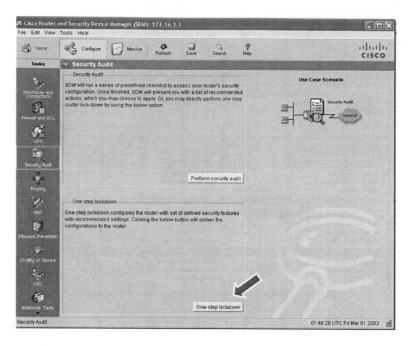

This will bring up a warning; click on **Yes** to initialize the Security Audit:

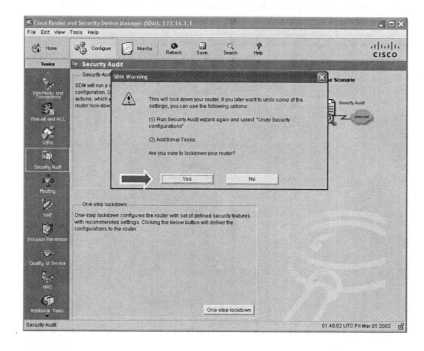

When the Wizard has run, click on the **Deliver** radio button:

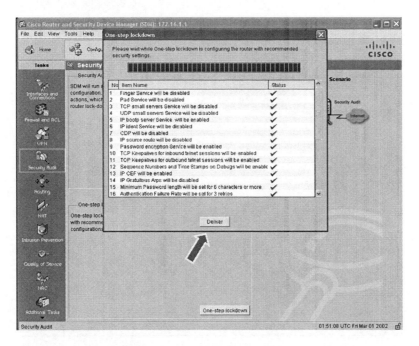

Once SDM has configured the router with the recommendations, click on **Ok** to accept:

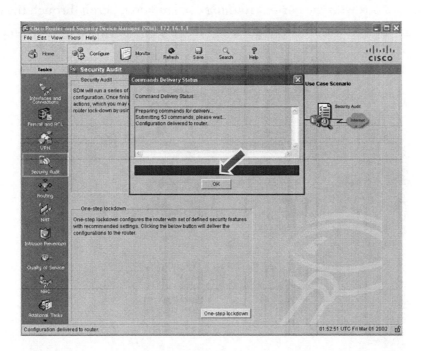

To verify your work, click on View—at the top of the Taskbar—and select **Running Config...**

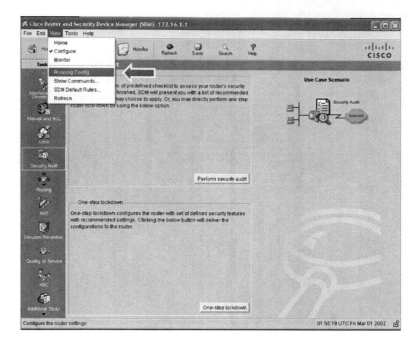

This opens up a box with the current running configuration. Scroll through the configuration an familiarize yourself with the configurations that are implemented by One-Step Lockdown:

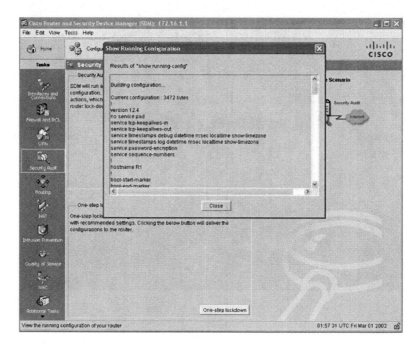

Lab 17 Configurations

R1 Configuration

```
R1#show running-config
Building configuration...

Current configuration : 3566 bytes
!
version 12.4
no service pad
service tcp-keepalives-in
service tcp-keepalives-out
service timestamps debug datetime msec localtime show-timezone
service timestamps log datetime msec localtime show-timezone
service password-encryption
service sequence-numbers
!
hostname R1
!
boot-start-marker
boot-end-marker
!
security authentication failure rate 3 log
security passwords min-length 6
logging buffered 51200
logging console critical
!
aaa new-model
!
aaa authentication login local_authen local
aaa authorization exec local_author local
!
aaa session-id common
no network-clock-participate slot 1
no network-clock-participate wic 0
no ip source-route
ip cef
!
no ip bootp server
ip domain name howtonetwork.net
!
multilink bundle-name authenticated
!
crypto pki trustpoint TP-self-signed-533650306
 enrollment selfsigned
 subject-name cn=IOS-Self-Signed-Certificate-533650306
 revocation-check none
```

```
 rsakeypair TP-self-signed-533650306
!
crypto pki certificate chain TP-self-signed-533650306
 certificate self-signed 02
  30820249 308201B2 A0030201 02020102 300D0609 2A864886 F70D0101 04050030
  30312E30 2C060355 04031325 494F532D 53656C66 2D536967 6E65642D 43657274
  69666963 6174652D 35333336 35303330 36301E17 0D303230 33303130 31323931
  385A170D 32303031 30313030 30303030 5A303031 2E302C06 03550403 1325494F
  532D5365 6C662D53 69676E65 642D4365 72746966 69636174 652D3533 33363530
  33303630 819F300D 06092A86 4886F70D 01010105 0003818D 00308189 02818100
  A10043E2 FB10C1D1 BA18F3AD 554F081C ACA14F4C EA48E0C1 4739653D B7759EE7
  8EB29881 7F391723 E2BB7EC6 54EB6F25 B4E94520 DF8DA15C 3B9E6F7C 3AA57549
  80AB643F A9427071 965DD56A 2D3E60CE 775F2ED5 C9014FCD F313F3EB B5189F62
  09F461BC 32E3E78F F93C8B07 0740DDA8 7B880D1B A3185787 CE621B35 3511A9D5
  02030100 01A37330 71300F06 03551D13 0101FF04 05300301 01FF301E 0603551D
  11041730 15821352 312E686F 77746F6E 6574776F 726B2E6E 6574301F 0603551D
  23041830 168014CD 63D2C471 B7ABA4AC F9C2B602 0D4A8954 71C7F930 1D060355
  1D0E0416 0414CD63 D2C471B7 ABA4ACF9 C2B6020D 4A895471 C7F9300D 06092A86
  4886F70D 01010405 00038181 0099F99A BE0C1D81 E0A31811 9FA6698A 7D703A20
  7A5CA49E 61A7FB5C FB0168D9 82064939 C0304B8B F1FA8654 DF2823CD D73C2664
  3B2B0C33 C1F6778C 4E3F59CB 08C11522 6BBC783C 6668E63C 7F6323EA F7E5FC8D
  42036432 34ACE605 AF94F67D A963A77F 7DF221AD 98772A67 4E08D7BF 6558FF99
  F5FA081C EC555DFC 49B89A6A 2E
        quit
!
username farai privilege 15 secret 5 $1$Eieg$ylhjr3td1Em4j/2K261Pm/
username sdmadmin privilege 15 secret 5 $1$Qfwn$rxYBRsMieBo4YDasMAI8B1
archive
 log config
  hidekeys
!
ip tcp synwait-time 10
ip ssh time-out 60
ip ssh authentication-retries 2
!
interface Null0
 no ip unreachables
!
interface FastEthernet0/0
 ip address 172.16.1.1 255.255.255.0
 no ip redirects
 no ip unreachables
 no ip proxy-arp
 ip route-cache flow
```

```
 duplex auto
 speed auto
 no mop enabled
!
interface Serial0/0
 no ip address
 no ip redirects
 no ip unreachables
 no ip proxy-arp
 ip route-cache flow
 shutdown
!
ip forward-protocol nd
!
ip http server
ip http authentication local
ip http secure-server
!
logging trap debugging
no cdp run
!
control-plane
!
banner login ^CAuthorized access only!
 Disconnect IMMEDIATELY if you are not an authorized user!
^C
!
line con 0
 login authentication local_authen
line aux 0
 login authentication local_authen
line vty 0 4
 privilege level 15
 password 7 13061E010803
 authorization exec local_author
 login authentication local_authen
 transport input ssh
!
scheduler allocate 4000 1000
!
end
```

LAB 18

Cisco Zone-Based Policy Firewall

Lab Objective:

The objective of this lab exercise is for you to learn and understand how use Cisco SDM to configure the Zone-Based Policy Firewall in Cisco IOS router.

Lab Purpose:

The Cisco SDM One-Step Lockdown feature tests your router configuration for any potential security problems and automatically makes any necessary configuration changes to correct any problems found. This is similar to the Cisco IOS Auto Secure feature.

Lab Difficulty:

This lab has a difficulty rating of 7/10.

Readiness Assessment:

When you are ready for your certification exam, you should complete this lab in no more than 15 minutes.

Lab Topology:

Please use the following topology to complete this lab exercise:

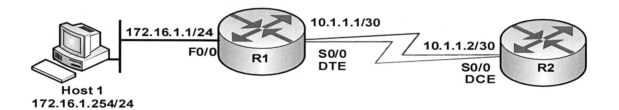

Lab 18 Configuration Tasks

Task 1:

Configure the hostnames and IP addresses on R1 and R2 as illustrated in the network diagram. Configure R2 to send R1 clocking information at a rate of 768Kbps. In addition, configure a static default route on R2 via its Serial0/0 interface. Ping between R1 and R2 to verify your configuration and ensure that the two routers have IP connectivity.

Task 2:

Configure Host 1 with the IP address illustrated in the diagram and a default gateway pointing to R1. Verify that Host 1 can ping R1 and R2.

Task 3:

Configure a username of **sdmadmin** with a privilege level of 15 and a password of **security** on R1. In addition to this, enable HTTPS and SSH on R1 using the domain name **howtonetwork. net**. Configure R1 to authenticate HTTPS users based on the local username and password pair configured on the router.

Task 4:

Using SDM (from Host 1), configure ZPF on R1 using the following parameters:
- FastEthernet0/0 should be the inside/trusted interface
- Serial0/0 should be outside/untrusted interface
- Configure ZPF for Medium security
- Use the DNS server 172.16.1.254

Test your configuration by pinging from Host 1 to R2 and validate that this works. However, a ping from R2 to Host 1 should not work.

Lab 18 Configuration and Verification

Task 1:
```
Router(config)#hostname R1
R1(config)#int f0/0
R1(config-if)#ip address 172.16.1.1 255.255.255.0
R1(config-if)#no shutdown
R1(config-if)#exit
R1(config)#int s0/0
R1(config-if)#ip address 10.1.1.1 255.255.255.252
R1(config-if)#no shut
R1(config-if)#exit
R1(config)#exit
R1#

Router(config)#hostname R2
R2(config)#int s0/0
R2(config-if)#ip address 10.1.1.2 255.255.255.252
R2(config-if)#clock rate 768000
R2(config-if)#no shut
R2(config-if)#exit
R2(config)#ip route 0.0.0.0 0.0.0.0 se0/0
R2(config)#exit
R2#

R2#ping 10.1.1.1
```

Type escape sequence to abort.
Sending 5, 100-byte ICMP Echos to 10.1.1.1, timeout is 2 seconds:
!!!!!
Success rate is 100 percent (5/5), round-trip min/avg/max = 4/5/9 ms

Task 2:

```
Command Prompt                                                    _ □ ×

C:\>ipconfig

Windows IP Configuration

Ethernet adapter Local Area Connection 2:

        Connection-specific DNS Suffix  . :
        IP Address. . . . . . . . . . . : 172.16.1.254
        Subnet Mask . . . . . . . . . . : 255.255.255.0
        Default Gateway . . . . . . . . : 172.16.1.1

Ethernet adapter Wireless Network Connection:

        Media State . . . . . . . . . . : Media disconnected

C:\>
C:\>ping 172.16.1.1

Pinging 172.16.1.1 with 32 bytes of data:

Reply from 172.16.1.1: bytes=32 time=1ms TTL=255
Reply from 172.16.1.1: bytes=32 time=1ms TTL=255
Reply from 172.16.1.1: bytes=32 time=1ms TTL=255
Reply from 172.16.1.1: bytes=32 time=1ms TTL=255

Ping statistics for 172.16.1.1:
        Packets: Sent = 4, Received = 4, Lost = 0 (0% loss),
Approximate round trip times in milli-seconds:
        Minimum = 1ms, Maximum = 1ms, Average = 1ms

C:\>
C:\>ping 10.1.1.2

Pinging 10.1.1.2 with 32 bytes of data:

Reply from 10.1.1.2: bytes=32 time=2ms TTL=255
Reply from 10.1.1.2: bytes=32 time=2ms TTL=255
Reply from 10.1.1.2: bytes=32 time=2ms TTL=255
Reply from 10.1.1.2: bytes=32 time=2ms TTL=255

Ping statistics for 10.1.1.2:
        Packets: Sent = 4, Received = 4, Lost = 0 (0% loss),
Approximate round trip times in milli-seconds:
        Minimum = 2ms, Maximum = 2ms, Average = 2ms

C:\>
```

Task 3:

R1(config)#**username sdmadmin privilege 15 secret security**
R1(config)#**ip domain-name howtonetwork.net**
R1(config)#**crypto key generate rsa**
The name for the keys will be: R1.howtonetwork.net
Choose the size of the key modulus in the range of 360 to 2048 for your
  General Purpose Keys. Choosing a key modulus greater than 512 may take
  a few minutes.

How many bits in the modulus [512]:
% Generating 512 bit RSA keys, keys will be non-exportable...[OK]

R1(config)#**ip http secure-server**
R1(config)#**ip http authentication local**
R1(config)#**exit**
R1#

Task 4:

For a reference on how to initialize and access SDM, please refer to the solutions in Lab 17.

From the **Firewall** screen, select the **Basic Firewall** radio button and then click the **Launch selected task** radio button at the bottom of the screen:

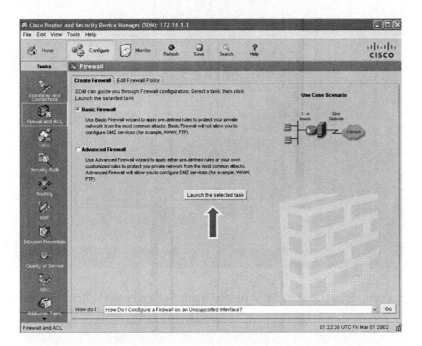

On the **Basic Firewall Configuration Wizard** screen, click on **Next** to continue:

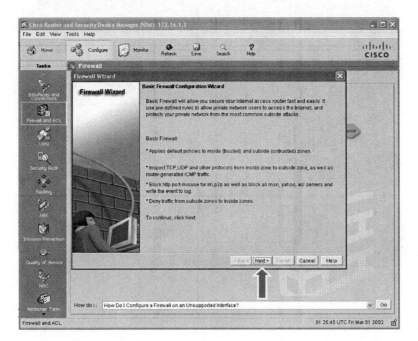

Click on the relevant checkboxes to ensure that Fa0/0 is the inside/trusted interface and Se0/0 is the outside/untrusted interface as illustrated below and click on **Next** to continue:

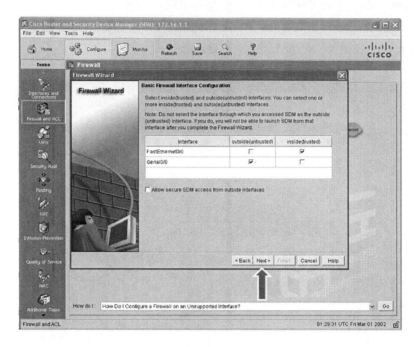

On the next screen, drag the scroll bar to **Medium Security** and click **Next** to continue:

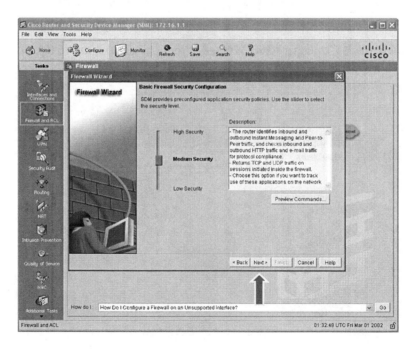

On the **Basic Firewall Domain Name Server Configuration** screen, enter the IP address of the DNS server and click on **Next** to continue:

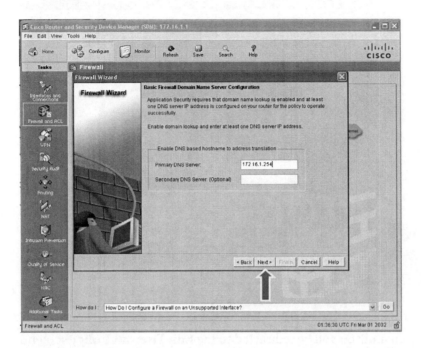

On the Firewall Configuration Summary screen, click on Finish to continue:

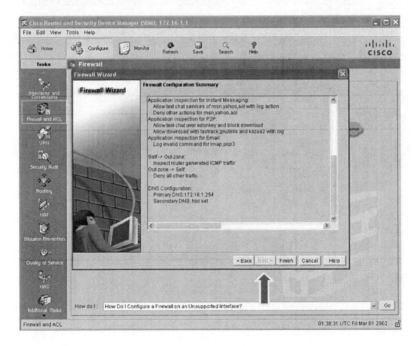

Once SDM has configured the router, click on **Ok** to complete your configuration:

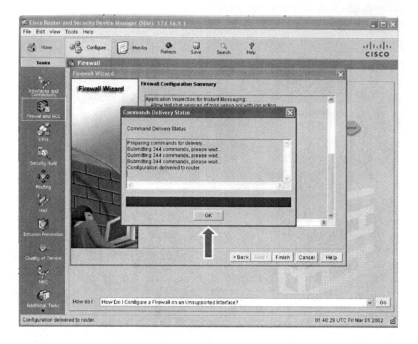

Click Ok again and you will be redirected to the **Edit Firewall Policy** screen as follows:

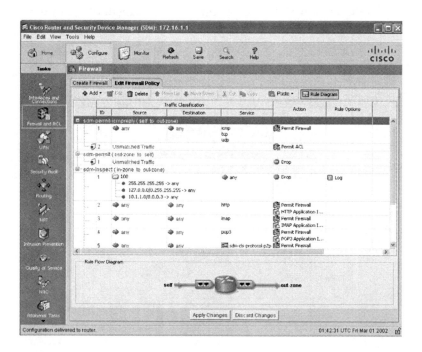

To validate your configuration, click on **Monitor**—on the top Taskbar next to **Configure**. This will bring you to the Firewall Status screen. Select the **sdm-zp-in-out** policy and click on the **Monitor Policy** radio button to start monitoring ZPF:

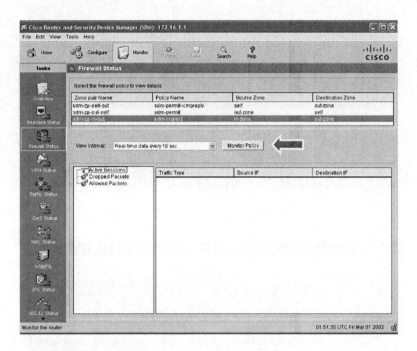

Send a continuous ping from Host 1 to R2 using the **ping –t 10.1.1.2** command—on Windows-based workstations. In addition to this, open up another window and Telnet from Host 1 to R2. If your SDM configuration is correct, you will see the following sessions:

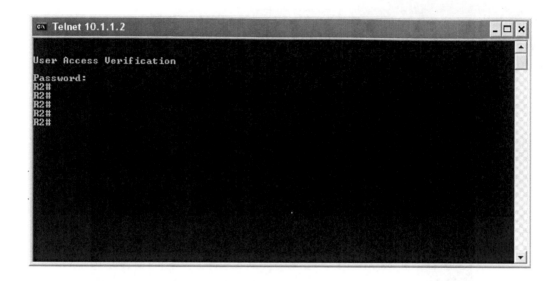

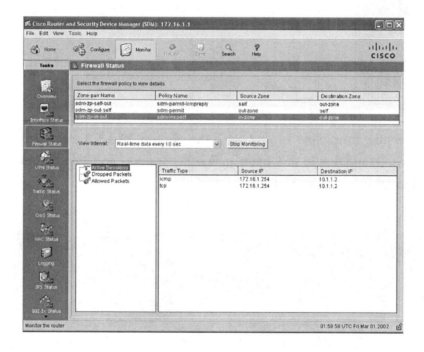

Lab 18 Configurations

R1 Configuration

```
R1#show run
Building configuration...

Current configuration : 10919 bytes
!
version 12.4
service timestamps debug datetime msec
service timestamps log datetime msec
no service password-encryption
!
hostname R1
!
boot-start-marker
boot-end-marker
!
no logging buffered
no logging console
!
no aaa new-model
no network-clock-participate slot 1
no network-clock-participate wic 0
ip cef
!
ip domain name howtonetwork.net
ip name-server 172.16.1.254
!
multilink bundle-name authenticated
parameter-map type protocol-info msn-servers
 server name messenger.hotmail.com
 server name gateway.messenger.hotmail.com
 server name webmessenger.msn.com

parameter-map type protocol-info aol-servers
 server name login.oscar.aol.com
 server name toc.oscar.aol.com
 server name oam-d09a.blue.aol.com

parameter-map type protocol-info yahoo-servers
 server name scs.msg.yahoo.com
 server name scsa.msg.yahoo.com
 server name scsb.msg.yahoo.com
 server name scsc.msg.yahoo.com
 server name scsd.msg.yahoo.com
 server name cs16.msg.dcn.yahoo.com
 server name cs19.msg.dcn.yahoo.com
 server name cs42.msg.dcn.yahoo.com
```

```
server name cs53.msg.dcn.yahoo.com
server name cs54.msg.dcn.yahoo.com
server name ads1.vip.scd.yahoo.com
server name radio1.launch.vip.dal.yahoo.com
server name in1.msg.vip.re2.yahoo.com
server name data1.my.vip.sc5.yahoo.com
server name address1.pim.vip.mud.yahoo.com
server name edit.messenger.yahoo.com
server name messenger.yahoo.com
server name http.pager.yahoo.com
server name privacy.yahoo.com
server name csa.yahoo.com
server name csb.yahoo.com
server name csc.yahoo.com

!
crypto pki trustpoint TP-self-signed-533650306
 enrollment selfsigned
 subject-name cn=IOS-Self-Signed-Certificate-533650306
 revocation-check none
 rsakeypair TP-self-signed-533650306
!
crypto pki certificate chain TP-self-signed-533650306
 certificate self-signed 02
  30820249 308201B2 A0030201 02020102 300D0609 2A864886 F70D0101 04050030
  30312E30 2C060355 04031325 494F532D 53656C66 2D536967 6E65642D 43657274
  69666963 6174652D 35333336 35303330 36301E17 0D303230 33303130 31313730
  335A170D 32303031 30313130 30303030 5A303031 2E302C06 03550403 1325494F
  532D5365 6C662D53 69676E65 642D4365 72746966 69636174 652D3533 33363530
  33303630 819F300D 06092A86 4886F70D 01010105 0003818D 00308189 02818100
  A10043E2 FB10C1D1 BA18F3AD 554F081C ACA14F4C EA48E0C1 4739653D B7759EE7
  8EB29881 7F391723 E2BB7EC6 54EB6F25 B4E94520 DF8DA15C 3B9E6F7C 3AA57549
  80AB643F A9427071 965DD56A 2D3E60CE 775F2ED5 C9014FCD F313F3EB B5189F62
  09F461BC 32E3E78F F93C8B07 0740DDA8 7B880D1B A3185787 CE621B35 3511A9D5
  02030100 01A37330 71300F06 03551D13 0101FF04 05300301 01FF301E 0603551D
  11041730 15821352 312E686F 77746F6E 6574776F 726B2E6E 6574301F 0603551D
  23041830 168014CD 63D2C471 B7ABA4AC F9C2B602 0D4A8954 71C7F930 1D060355
  1D0E0416 0414CD63 D2C471B7 ABA4ACF9 C2B6020D 4A895471 C7F9300D 06092A86
  4886F70D 01010405 00038181 000421F1 1957D29B D8DE3CC5 F7C72CC6 F9113BFE
  7E0D2AB0 73603E37 E385EA4D EAE0C148 1DBCB188 37A39B5F CF2DBEE5 75C81687
  5E9F80A3 5DE7C965 32B6DD69 149A9F8B D1714D7E C33FBAC2 2A9E05BD 610F7CBA
  F78912D6 117F4462 7E72FC42 3248CAB0 D77D0E01 23D65CC6 CA67EEEE 178E34DD
  261D7EB6 EB6B7217 C4DCEE69 F1
   quit
!
```

```
username sdmadmin privilege 15 secret 5 $1$PkTA$zhgv4R2GZy0KJHXGHahyL1
archive
 log config
  hidekeys
!
class-map type inspect imap match-any sdm-app-imap
 match  invalid-command
class-map type inspect match-any sdm-cls-protocol-p2p
 match protocol edonkey signature
 match protocol gnutella signature
 match protocol kazaa2 signature
 match protocol fasttrack signature
 match protocol bittorrent signature
class-map type inspect match-any sdm-cls-insp-traffic
 match protocol cuseeme
 match protocol dns
 match protocol ftp
 match protocol h323
 match protocol https
 match protocol icmp
 match protocol imap
 match protocol pop3
 match protocol netshow
 match protocol shell
 match protocol realmedia
 match protocol rtsp
 match protocol smtp extended
 match protocol sql-net
 match protocol streamworks
 match protocol tftp
 match protocol vdolive
 match protocol tcp
 match protocol udp
class-map type inspect match-all sdm-insp-traffic
 match class-map sdm-cls-insp-traffic
class-map type inspect gnutella match-any sdm-app-gnutella
 match  file-transfer
class-map type inspect match-any SDM-Voice-permit
 match protocol h323
 match protocol skinny
 match protocol sip
class-map type inspect msnmsgr match-any sdm-app-msn-otherservices
 match  service any
class-map type inspect ymsgr match-any sdm-app-yahoo-otherservices
 match  service any
class-map type inspect match-all sdm-protocol-pop3
 match protocol pop3
class-map type inspect match-any sdm-cls-icmp-access
 match protocol icmp
 match protocol tcp
```

```
 match protocol udp
class-map type inspect match-any sdm-cls-protocol-im
 match protocol ymsgr yahoo-servers
 match protocol msnmsgr msn-servers
 match protocol aol aol-servers
class-map type inspect aol match-any sdm-app-aol-otherservices
 match  service any
class-map type inspect pop3 match-any sdm-app-pop3
 match  invalid-command
class-map type inspect kazaa2 match-any sdm-app-kazaa2
 match  file-transfer
class-map type inspect match-all sdm-protocol-p2p
 match class-map sdm-cls-protocol-p2p
class-map type inspect http match-any sdm-http-blockparam
 match  request port-misuse im
 match  request port-misuse p2p
 match  req-resp protocol-violation
class-map type inspect match-all sdm-protocol-im
 match class-map sdm-cls-protocol-im
class-map type inspect match-all sdm-icmp-access
 match class-map sdm-cls-icmp-access
class-map type inspect match-all sdm-invalid-src
 match access-group 100
class-map type inspect ymsgr match-any sdm-app-yahoo
 match  service text-chat
class-map type inspect msnmsgr match-any sdm-app-msn
 match  service text-chat
class-map type inspect edonkey match-any sdm-app-edonkey
 match  file-transfer
 match  text-chat
 match  search-file-name
class-map type inspect http match-any sdm-app-httpmethods
 match  request method bcopy
 match  request method bdelete
 match  request method bmove
 match  request method bpropfind
 match  request method bproppatch
 match  request method connect
 match  request method copy
 match  request method delete
 match  request method edit
 match  request method getattribute
 match  request method getattributenames
 match  request method getproperties
 match  request method index
 match  request method lock
 match  request method mkcol
 match  request method mkdir
 match  request method move
 match  request method notify
```

```
match  request method options
match  request method poll
match  request method propfind
match  request method proppatch
match  request method put
match  request method revadd
match  request method revlabel
match  request method revlog
match  request method revnum
match  request method save
match  request method search
match  request method setattribute
match  request method startrev
match  request method stoprev
match  request method subscribe
match  request method trace
match  request method unedit
match  request method unlock
match  request method unsubscribe
class-map type inspect edonkey match-any sdm-app-edonkeychat
 match  search-file-name
 match  text-chat
class-map type inspect fasttrack match-any sdm-app-fasttrack
 match  file-transfer
class-map type inspect http match-any sdm-http-allowparam
 match  request port-misuse tunneling
class-map type inspect match-all sdm-protocol-http
 match protocol http
class-map type inspect edonkey match-any sdm-app-edonkeydownload
 match  file-transfer
class-map type inspect match-all sdm-protocol-imap
 match protocol imap
class-map type inspect aol match-any sdm-app-aol
 match  service text-chat
!
!
policy-map type inspect sdm-permit-icmpreply
 class type inspect sdm-icmp-access
  inspect
 class class-default
  pass
policy-map type inspect p2p sdm-action-app-p2p
 class type inspect edonkey sdm-app-edonkeychat
  log
  allow
 class type inspect edonkey sdm-app-edonkeydownload
  log
  allow
 class type inspect fasttrack sdm-app-fasttrack
  log
```

```
  allow
 class type inspect gnutella sdm-app-gnutella
  log
  allow
 class type inspect kazaa2 sdm-app-kazaa2
  log
  allow
 class class-default
policy-map type inspect http sdm-action-app-http
 class type inspect http sdm-http-blockparam
  log
  reset
 class type inspect http sdm-app-httpmethods
  log
  reset
 class type inspect http sdm-http-allowparam
  log
  allow
 class class-default
policy-map type inspect imap sdm-action-imap
 class type inspect imap sdm-app-imap
  log
 class class-default
policy-map type inspect pop3 sdm-action-pop3
 class type inspect pop3 sdm-app-pop3
  log
 class class-default
policy-map type inspect im sdm-action-app-im
 class type inspect aol sdm-app-aol
  log
  allow
 class type inspect msnmsgr sdm-app-msn
  log
  allow
 class type inspect ymsgr sdm-app-yahoo
  log
  allow
 class type inspect aol sdm-app-aol-otherservices
  log
  reset
 class type inspect msnmsgr sdm-app-msn-otherservices
  log
  reset
 class type inspect ymsgr sdm-app-yahoo-otherservices
  log
  reset
 class class-default
policy-map type inspect sdm-inspect
 class type inspect sdm-invalid-src
  drop log
```

```
class type inspect sdm-protocol-http
 inspect
 service-policy http sdm-action-app-http
class type inspect sdm-protocol-imap
 inspect
 service-policy imap sdm-action-imap
class type inspect sdm-protocol-pop3
 inspect
 service-policy pop3 sdm-action-pop3
class type inspect sdm-protocol-p2p
 inspect
 service-policy p2p sdm-action-app-p2p
class type inspect sdm-protocol-im
 inspect
 service-policy im sdm-action-app-im
class type inspect sdm-insp-traffic
 inspect
class type inspect SDM-Voice-permit
 inspect
class class-default
 pass
policy-map type inspect sdm-permit
 class class-default
 !
zone security out-zone
zone security in-zone
zone-pair security sdm-zp-self-out source self destination out-zone
 service-policy type inspect sdm-permit-icmpreply
zone-pair security sdm-zp-out-self source out-zone destination self
 service-policy type inspect sdm-permit
zone-pair security sdm-zp-in-out source in-zone destination out-zone
 service-policy type inspect sdm-inspect
 !
interface FastEthernet0/0
 description $FW_INSIDE$
 ip address 172.16.1.1 255.255.255.0
 zone-member security in-zone
 duplex auto
 speed auto
 !
interface Serial0/0
 description $FW_OUTSIDE$
 ip address 10.1.1.1 255.255.255.252
 zone-member security out-zone
 !
ip forward-protocol nd
 !
ip http server
ip http authentication local
ip http secure-server
```

```
!
access-list 100 remark SDM_ACL Category=128
access-list 100 permit ip host 255.255.255.255 any
access-list 100 permit ip 127.0.0.0 0.255.255.255 any
access-list 100 permit ip 10.1.1.0 0.0.0.3 any
!
control-plane
!
line con 0
line aux 0
line vty 0 4
 privilege level 15
 password cisco
 login
!
end
```

R2 Configuration

```
R2#show running-config
Building configuration...

Current configuration : 818 bytes
!
version 12.4
service timestamps debug datetime msec
service timestamps log datetime msec
no service password-encryption
!
hostname R2
!
boot-start-marker
boot-end-marker
!
no logging console
!
no aaa new-model
no network-clock-participate slot 1
no network-clock-participate wic 0
ip cef
!
no ip domain lookup
!
multilink bundle-name authenticated
!
archive
 log config
  hidekeys
!
```

```
interface FastEthernet0/0
 no ip address
 shutdown
 duplex auto
 speed auto
!
interface Serial0/0
 ip address 10.1.1.2 255.255.255.252
 clock rate 768000
!
ip forward-protocol nd
ip route 0.0.0.0 0.0.0.0 Serial0/0
!
ip http server
ip http authentication local
no ip http secure-server
!
control-plane
!
line con 0
line aux 0
line vty 0 4
 privilege level 15
 password cisco
 login
!
end
```

LAB 19

Cisco IOS Intrusion Prevention System

Lab Objective:

The objective of this lab exercise is for you to learn and understand how use Cisco SDM to configure the Cisco IOS Intrusion Prevention System.

Lab Purpose:

Cisco IOS IPS lets you monitor and prevents intrusions by comparing traffic against signatures of known threats and blocking the traffic when a threat is detected

Lab Difficulty:

This lab has a difficulty rating of 7/10.

Readiness Assessment:

When you are ready for your certification exam, you should complete this lab in no more than 15 minutes.

Lab Topology:

Please use the following topology to complete this lab exercise:

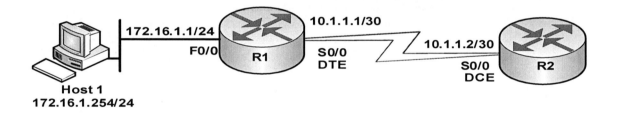

Lab 19 Configuration Tasks

Task 1:

Configure the hostnames and IP addresses on R1 and R2 as illustrated in the network diagram. Configure R2 to send R1 clocking information at a rate of 768Kbps. In addition, configure a static default route on R2 via its Serial0/0 interface. Ping between R1 and R2 to verify your configuration and ensure that the two routers have IP connectivity.

Task 2:

Configure Host 1 with the IP address illustrated in the diagram and a default gateway pointing to R1. Verify that Host 1 can ping R1 and R2.

Task 3:

Configure a username of **sdmadmin** with a privilege level of 15 and a password of **security** on R1. In addition to this, enable HTTPS and SSH on R1 using the domain name **howtonetwork. net**. Configure R1 to authenticate HTTPS users based on the local username and password pair configured on the router.

Task 4:

Using SDM (from Host 1), configure Cisco IOS IPS on R1 using the following parameters:
- Use FastEthernet0/0 as the inbound interface
- Use Serial0/0 as the outbound interface
- Use an SDF located on your PC/workstation/router (the file will have a .SDF extension)
- Configure a Public Key of your choice, using **security** as the password
- Store IPS files on the router Flash memory
- Use a Basic signature category

Lab 19 Configuration and Verification

Task 1:
```
Router(config)#hostname R1
R1(config)#int f0/0
R1(config-if)#ip address 172.16.1.1 255.255.255.0
R1(config-if)#no shutdown
R1(config-if)#exit
R1(config)#int s0/0
R1(config-if)#ip address 10.1.1.1 255.255.255.252
R1(config-if)#no shut
R1(config-if)#exit
R1(config)#exit
R1#


Router(config)#hostname R2
R2(config)#int s0/0
R2(config-if)#ip address 10.1.1.2 255.255.255.252
R2(config-if)#clock rate 768000
R2(config-if)#no shut
R2(config-if)#exit
R2(config)#ip route 0.0.0.0 0.0.0.0 se0/0
R2(config)#exit
R2#

R2#ping 10.1.1.1
```

Type escape sequence to abort.
Sending 5, 100-byte ICMP Echos to 10.1.1.1, timeout is 2 seconds:
!!!!!
Success rate is 100 percent (5/5), round-trip min/avg/max = 4/5/9 ms

Task 2:

```
Command Prompt                                                  - □ ×

C:\>ipconfig

Windows IP Configuration

Ethernet adapter Local Area Connection 2:

        Connection-specific DNS Suffix  . :
        IP Address. . . . . . . . . . . : 172.16.1.254
        Subnet Mask . . . . . . . . . . : 255.255.255.0
        Default Gateway . . . . . . . . : 172.16.1.1

Ethernet adapter Wireless Network Connection:

        Media State . . . . . . . . . . : Media disconnected

C:\>
C:\>ping 172.16.1.1

Pinging 172.16.1.1 with 32 bytes of data:

Reply from 172.16.1.1: bytes=32 time=1ms TTL=255
Reply from 172.16.1.1: bytes=32 time=1ms TTL=255
Reply from 172.16.1.1: bytes=32 time=1ms TTL=255
Reply from 172.16.1.1: bytes=32 time=1ms TTL=255

Ping statistics for 172.16.1.1:
    Packets: Sent = 4, Received = 4, Lost = 0 (0% loss),
Approximate round trip times in milli-seconds:
    Minimum = 1ms, Maximum = 1ms, Average = 1ms

C:\>
C:\>ping 10.1.1.2

Pinging 10.1.1.2 with 32 bytes of data:

Reply from 10.1.1.2: bytes=32 time=2ms TTL=255
Reply from 10.1.1.2: bytes=32 time=2ms TTL=255
Reply from 10.1.1.2: bytes=32 time=2ms TTL=255
Reply from 10.1.1.2: bytes=32 time=2ms TTL=255

Ping statistics for 10.1.1.2:
    Packets: Sent = 4, Received = 4, Lost = 0 (0% loss),
Approximate round trip times in milli-seconds:
    Minimum = 2ms, Maximum = 2ms, Average = 2ms

C:\>
```

Task 3:
R1(config)#**username sdmadmin privilege 15 secret security**
R1(config)#**ip domain-name howtonetwork.net**
R1(config)#**crypto key generate rsa**
The name for the keys will be: R1.howtonetwork.net
Choose the size of the key modulus in the range of 360 to 2048 for your
  General Purpose Keys. Choosing a key modulus greater than 512 may take
  a few minutes.

How many bits in the modulus [512]:
% Generating 512 bit RSA keys, keys will be non-exportable...[OK]

R1(config)#**ip http secure-server**
R1(config)#**ip http authentication local**
R1(config)#**exit**
R1#

Task 4:

For a reference on how to initialize and access SDM, please refer to the solutions in Lab 17.

From the **Intrusion Prevention System** screen click on the **Launch IPS Rule Wizard** button:

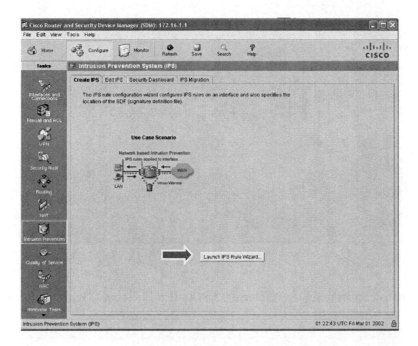

Click **Ok** to acknowledge the enabling of SDEE:

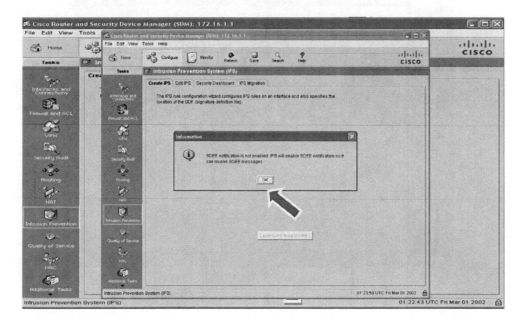

Click **Ok** to acknowledge the second pop-up window:

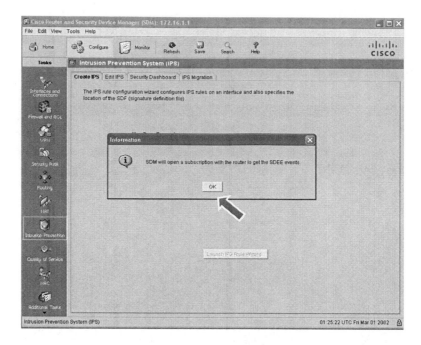

Click on **Next** to continue on the **Welcome to the IPS Policies Wizard** window:

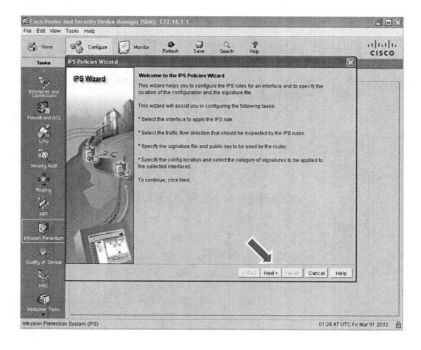

Check the appropriate boxes to configure Fa0/0 as the inbound interface and Se0/0 as the outbound interface and click **Next** to continue:

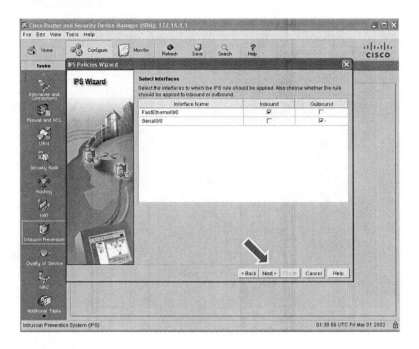

Select the location of your desired SDF file and click **Ok** to continue:

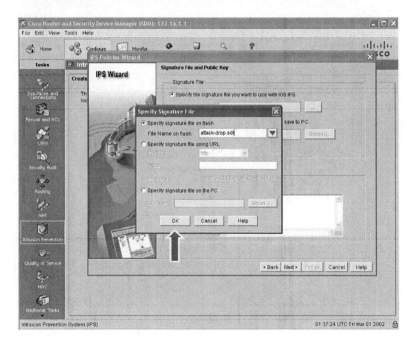

Click **Yes** to create the file:

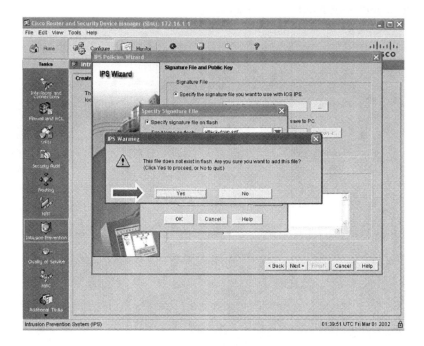

Click on **Next** to continue:

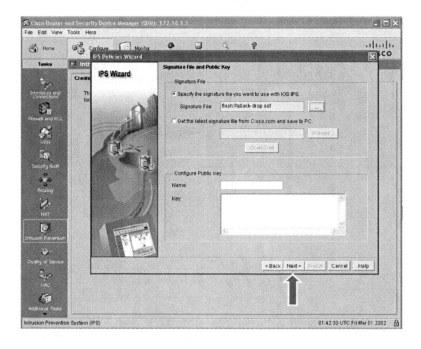

Configure your Public Key and the key string and click **Next** to continue:

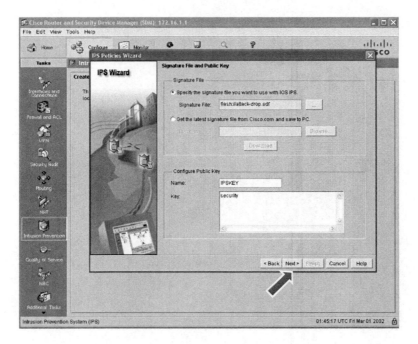

Specify the router Flash as the configuration location and click on **Next** to continue:

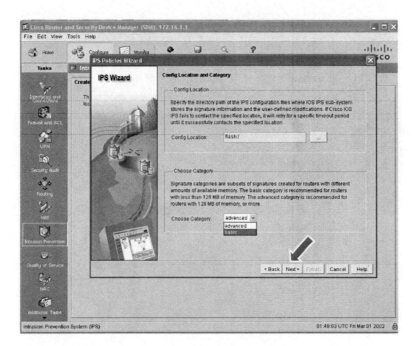

Click on the Finish radio button to complete your configuration:

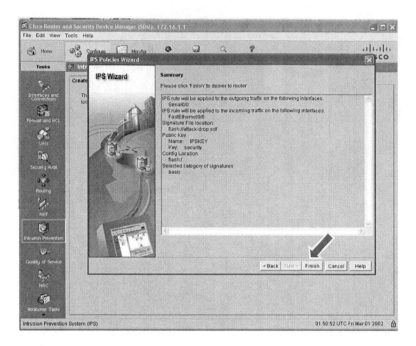

Click on **Ok** to complete your Cisco IOS IPS configuration:

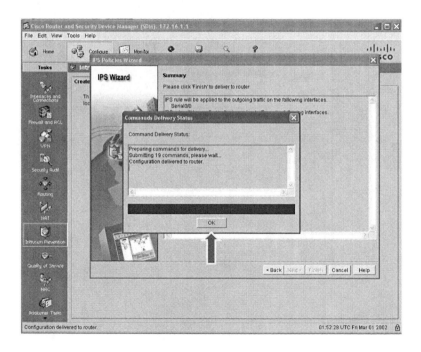

Once complete, you will be taken to the **Intrusion Prevention System** page. From **Edit IPS** tab you can click on **Signatures** to view IPS signatures:

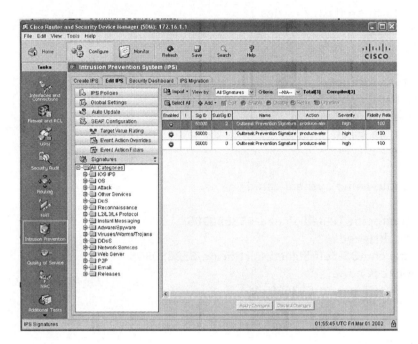

Lab 19 Configurations

R1 Configuration

```
R1#show run
Building configuration...

Current configuration : 2792 bytes
!
version 12.4
service timestamps debug datetime msec
service timestamps log datetime msec
no service password-encryption
!
hostname R1
!
boot-start-marker
boot-end-marker
!
no logging console
!
no aaa new-model
no network-clock-participate slot 1
```

```
no network-clock-participate wic 0
ip cef
!
ip ips config location flash:/ retries 1
ip ips notify SDEE
ip ips name sdm_ips_rule
!
ip ips signature-category
  category all
   retired true
  category ios_ips basic
   retired false
!
multilink bundle-name authenticated
!
crypto pki trustpoint TP-self-signed-533650306
 enrollment selfsigned
 subject-name cn=IOS-Self-Signed-Certificate-533650306
 revocation-check none
 rsakeypair TP-self-signed-533650306
!
crypto pki certificate chain TP-self-signed-533650306
 certificate self-signed 02
  30820238 308201A1 A0030201 02020102 300D0609 2A864886 F70D0101 04050030
  30312E30 2C060355 04031325 494F532D 53656C66 2D536967 6E65642D 43657274
  69666963 6174652D 35333336 35303330 36301E17 0D303230 33303130 31313834
  305A170D 32303031 30313030 30303030 5A303031 2E302C06 03550403 1325494F
  532D5365 6C662D53 69676E65 642D4365 72746966 69636174 652D3533 33363530
  33303630 819F300D 06092A86 4886F70D 01010105 0003818D 00308189 02818100
  A10043E2 FB10C1D1 BA18F3AD 554F081C ACA14F4C EA48E0C1 4739653D B7759EE7
  8EB29881 7F391723 E2BB7EC6 54EB6F25 B4E94520 DF8DA15C 3B9E6F7C 3AA57549
  80AB643F A9427071 965DD56A 2D3E60CE 775F2ED5 C9014FCD F313F3EB B5189F62
  09F461BC 32E3E78F F93C8B07 0740DDA8 7B880D1B A3185787 CE621B35 3511A9D5
  02030100 01A36230 60300F06 03551D13 0101FF04 05300301 01FF300D 0603551D
  11040630 04820252 31301F06 03551D23 04183016 8014CD63 D2C471B7 ABA4ACF9
  C2B6020D 4A895471 C7F9301D 0603551D 0E041604 14CD63D2 C471B7AB A4ACF9C2
  B6020D4A 895471C7 F9300D06 092A8648 86F70D01 01040500 03818100 506DD62A
  3B2BD8F7 9A48B649 FFA06BDF C0799E33 C6396BD8 EAB01D87 2E13E0B7 BF85BF1A
  0D35DBB7 0B8B52FF 2C7CA886 06677477 A0C1AEB0 EAB1E964 0E5BA4B0 C8B91456
  1BFA09D0 DDFC8D9A AF2BF871 BAF62DB0 066D082C 9EC9D36E 422F97D3 35CE049E
  01EECDB0 0FCF64E1 AE95ACD6 FADE74B8 950F7F41 09509770 CEEF7F30
        quit
!
username sdmadmin privilege 15 secret 5 $1$SJy7$VwV0NFQX7XpEIoAFSoekT1
```

```
archive
 log config
  hidekeys
!
crypto key pubkey-chain rsa
 named-key IPSKEY
  key-string
  quit
!
interface FastEthernet0/0
 ip address 172.16.1.1 255.255.255.0
 ip ips sdm_ips_rule in
 ip virtual-reassembly
 duplex auto
 speed auto
!
interface Serial0/0
 ip address 10.1.1.1 255.255.255.252
 ip ips sdm_ips_rule out
 ip virtual-reassembly
!
ip forward-protocol nd
!
ip http server
ip http authentication local
ip http secure-server
!
control-plane
!
line con 0
line aux 0
line vty 0 4
 privilege level 15
 password cisco
 login
!
end
```

R2 Configuration

```
R2#show running-config
Building configuration...

Current configuration : 818 bytes
!
version 12.4
service timestamps debug datetime msec
service timestamps log datetime msec
no service password-encryption
```

```
!
hostname R2
!
boot-start-marker
boot-end-marker
!
no logging console
!
no aaa new-model
no network-clock-participate slot 1
no network-clock-participate wic 0
ip cef
!
no ip domain lookup
!
multilink bundle-name authenticated
!
archive
 log config
  hidekeys
!
interface FastEthernet0/0
 no ip address
 shutdown
 duplex auto
 speed auto
!
interface Serial0/0
 ip address 10.1.1.2 255.255.255.252
 clock rate 768000
!
ip forward-protocol nd
ip route 0.0.0.0 0.0.0.0 Serial0/0
!
ip http server
ip http authentication local
no ip http secure-server
!
control-plane
!
line con 0
line aux 0
line vty 0 4
 privilege level 15
 password cisco
 login
!
end
```

LAB 20

Cisco IOS Site-to-Site VPN

Lab Objective:

The objective of this lab exercise is for you to learn and understand how use Cisco SDM to configure the Cisco IOS Site-to-Site VPN.

Lab Purpose:

A Virtual Private Network (VPN) lets you protect traffic that travels over lines that your organization may not own or control. VPNs can encrypt traffic sent over these lines and authenticate peers before any traffic is sent.

Lab Difficulty:

This lab has a difficulty rating of 8/10.

Readiness Assessment:

When you are ready for your certification exam, you should complete this lab in no more than 15 minutes.

Lab Topology:

Please use the following topology to complete this lab exercise:

Lab 20 Configuration Tasks

Task 1:

Configure the hostnames and IP addresses on R1 and R2 as illustrated in the network diagram. Configure R2 to send R1 clocking information at a rate of 512Kbps. Configure a static default route on R2 via its Serial0/0 interface. In addition, configure a static route to the 172.17.1.0/24 subnet on R1 via its Serial0/0 interface. Ping between R1 and R2 to verify your configuration and ensure that the two routers have IP connectivity.

Task 2:

Configure Host 1 with the IP address illustrated in the diagram and a default gateway pointing to R1. Verify that Host 1 can ping R1 and R2.

Task 3:

Configure a username of **sdmadmin** with a privilege level of 15 and a password of **security** on R1 and R2. In addition to this, enable HTTPS and SSH on R1 and R2 using the domain name **howtonetwork.net**. Configure R1 and R2 to authenticate HTTPS users based on the local username and password pair configured on the router.

Task 4:

Using SDM (from Host 1), configure Cisco IOS Site-to-Site VPN on R1 and R2 using the following parameters:

*   Use the pre-shared keys **security** between the routers
*   Encrypt traffic from the LAN subnet on R1 to the LAN subnet on R2 and vice versa
*   Use static peers using the Serial0/0 IP addresses of the routers
*   Use default encryption, hash and DH group information and Transform set

Lab 20 Configuration and Verification

Task 1:

```
Router(config)#hostname R1
R1(config)#int f0/0
R1(config-if)#ip address 172.16.1.1 255.255.255.0
R1(config-if)#no shut
R1(config-if)#exit
R1(config)#int s0/0
R1(config-if)#ip address 10.1.1.1 255.255.255.252
R1(config-if)#no shut
R1(config-if)#exit
R1(config)#ip route 172.17.1.0 255.255.255.0 serial0/0
R1(config)#exit
R1#

R2(config)#int s0/0
R2(config-if)#ip address 10.1.1.2 255.255.255.252
R2(config-if)#clock rate 512000
R2(config-if)#no shut
R2(config-if)#exit
R2(config)#int f0/0
R2(config-if)#ip address 172.17.1.2 255.255.255.0
R2(config-if)#no shut
R2(config-if)#exit
R2(config)#ip route 0.0.0.0 0.0.0.0 s0/0
R2(config)#exit
R2#
R2#ping 10.1.1.1
```

Type escape sequence to abort.
Sending 5, 100-byte ICMP Echos to 10.1.1.1, timeout is 2 seconds:
!!!!!
Success rate is 100 percent (5/5), round-trip min/avg/max = 4/5/8 ms

Task 2:

```
Command Prompt

C:\>ipconfig

Windows IP Configuration

Ethernet adapter Local Area Connection 2:

        Connection-specific DNS Suffix  . :
        IP Address. . . . . . . . . . . . : 172.16.1.254
        Subnet Mask . . . . . . . . . . . : 255.255.255.0
        Default Gateway . . . . . . . . . : 172.16.1.1

Ethernet adapter Wireless Network Connection:

        Media State . . . . . . . . . . . : Media disconnected

C:\>
C:\>
C:\>ping 172.16.1.1

Pinging 172.16.1.1 with 32 bytes of data:

Reply from 172.16.1.1: bytes=32 time=1ms TTL=255
Reply from 172.16.1.1: bytes=32 time=1ms TTL=255
Reply from 172.16.1.1: bytes=32 time=1ms TTL=255
Reply from 172.16.1.1: bytes=32 time=1ms TTL=255

Ping statistics for 172.16.1.1:
    Packets: Sent = 4, Received = 4, Lost = 0 (0% loss),
Approximate round trip times in milli-seconds:
    Minimum = 1ms, Maximum = 1ms, Average = 1ms

C:\>
C:\>
C:\>
C:\>ping 172.17.1.2

Pinging 172.17.1.2 with 32 bytes of data:

Reply from 172.17.1.2: bytes=32 time=3ms TTL=254
Reply from 172.17.1.2: bytes=32 time=3ms TTL=254
Reply from 172.17.1.2: bytes=32 time=3ms TTL=254
Reply from 172.17.1.2: bytes=32 time=3ms TTL=254

Ping statistics for 172.17.1.2:
    Packets: Sent = 4, Received = 4, Lost = 0 (0% loss),
Approximate round trip times in milli-seconds:
    Minimum = 3ms, Maximum = 3ms, Average = 3ms

C:\>_
```

Task 3:

R1(config)#**ip domain-name howtonetwork.net**
R1(config)#**crypto key generate rsa**
The name for the keys will be: R1.howtonetwork.net
Choose the size of the key modulus in the range of 360 to 2048 for your
 General Purpose Keys. Choosing a key modulus greater than 512 may take
 a few minutes.

How many bits in the modulus [512]:
% Generating 512 bit RSA keys, keys will be non-exportable...[OK]

R1(config)#**ip http secure-server**
R1(config)#**ip http authentication local**
R1(config)#**username sdmadmin privilege 15 secret security**
R1(config)#**exit**
R1#

R2(config)#**ip domain-name howtonetwork.net**
R2(config)#**crypto key generate rsa**
The name for the keys will be: R2.howtonetwork.net
Choose the size of the key modulus in the range of 360 to 2048 for your
  General Purpose Keys. Choosing a key modulus greater than 512 may take
  a few minutes.

How many bits in the modulus [512]:
% Generating 512 bit RSA keys, keys will be non-exportable...[OK]

R2(config)#**ip http secure-server**
R2(config)#**ip http authentication local**
R2(config)#**username sdmadmin privilege 15 secret security**
R2(config)#**exit**
R2#

Task 4:

For a reference on how to initialize and access SDM, please refer to the solutions in Lab 17.

On the **VPN** page, select **Site-to-Site VPN** and ensure that the **Create a Site to Site VPN** radio button is enabled and then click on **Launch the selected task** button to proceed:

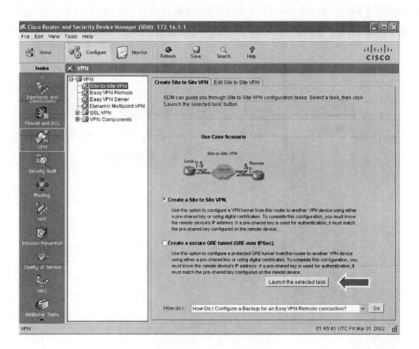

Select the **Step by step wizard** radio box and click on **Next** to continue:

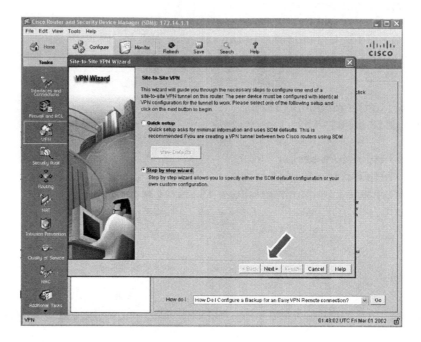

Click on the drop-down menu and select **Serial0/0** as the interface for the VPN. Enter the IP address of the Serial0/0 interface of R2 (or R1, depending on which router you decided to do first) as the static peer and ensure that the **Pre-Shared Keys** radio box is highlighted. Type in the key, which should be **security**, and click on **Next** to continue:

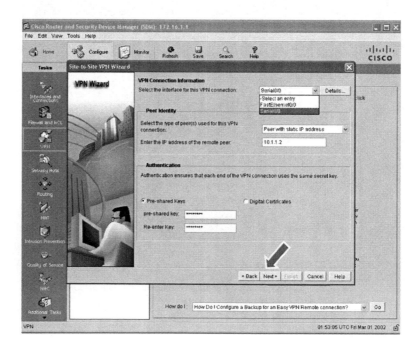

On the IKE properties page, accept the default values and click **Next** to continue:

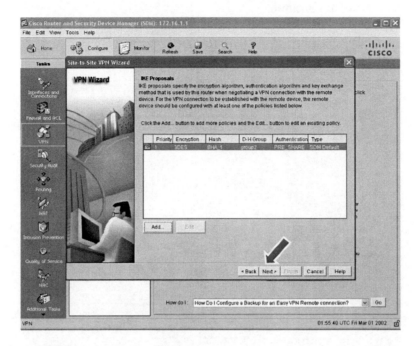

On the Transform Set page, accept the default values and click on **Next** to continue:

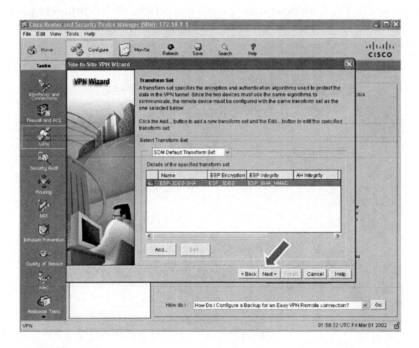

On the **Traffic to protect** page, enter the source and destination networks for encrypted traffic and then click on **Next** to continue:

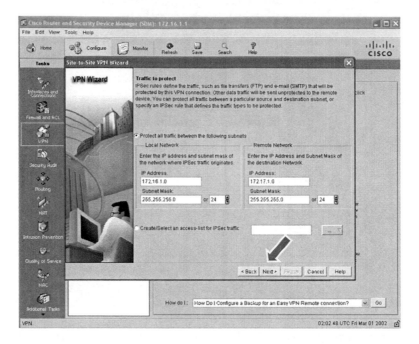

On the **Summary of the Configuration** page, click on **Finish** to complete your configuration:

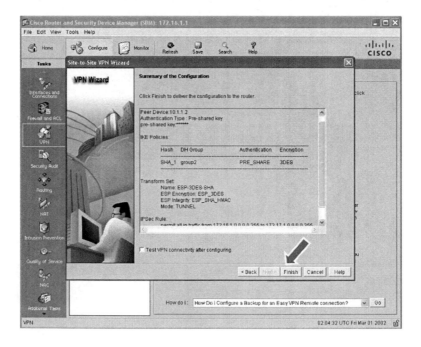

Using the same sequence of steps, perform the same configuration on the other router (i.e. either R1 or R2, depending on which router you decided to start with). In addition, click on the **Test VPN connectivity after configuring** check box before clicking on the **Finish** button on the second router to validate your configuration as follows:

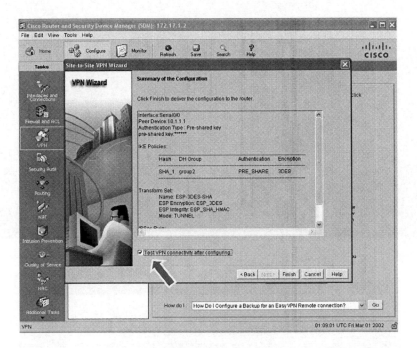

After you click **Finish** to complete your configuration and then **Ok** for SDM to configure the router, SDM will test the VPN for you as follows and advise you if it is up:

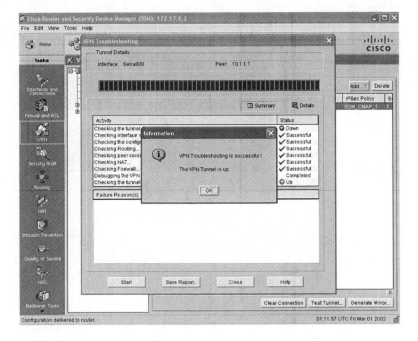

Next, click on **Monitor** and select VPN Status. To view incrementing statistics, perform a continuous ping from Host 1 to 172.17.1.2 (the FastEthernet0/0 interface of R2) as follows:

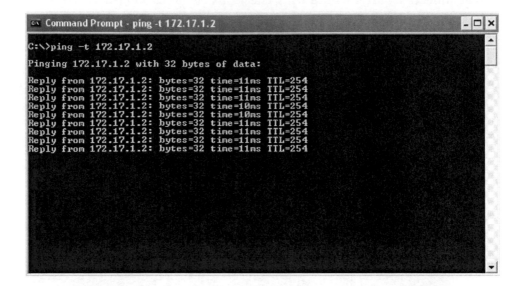

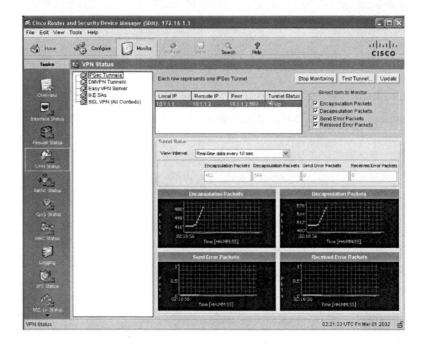

Lab 20 Configurations

R1 Configuration

```
R1#show running-config
Building configuration...

Current configuration : 3050 bytes
!
version 12.4
service timestamps debug datetime msec
service timestamps log datetime msec
no service password-encryption
!
hostname R1
!
boot-start-marker
boot-end-marker
!
no logging console
!
no aaa new-model
no network-clock-participate slot 1
no network-clock-participate wic 0
ip cef
!
ip domain name howtonetwork.net
!
multilink bundle-name authenticated
!
crypto pki trustpoint TP-self-signed-533650306
 enrollment selfsigned
 subject-name cn=IOS-Self-Signed-Certificate-533650306
 revocation-check none
 rsakeypair TP-self-signed-533650306
!
crypto pki certificate chain TP-self-signed-533650306
 certificate self-signed 02
  30820249 308201B2 A0030201 02020102 300D0609 2A864886 F70D0101 04050030
  30312E30 2C060355 04031325 494F532D 53656C66 2D536967 6E65642D 43657274
  69666963 6174652D 35333336 35303330 36301E17 0D303230 33303130 31333332
  365A170D 32303031 30313030 30303030 5A303031 2E302C06 03550403 1325494F
  532D5365 6C662D53 69676E65 642D4365 72746966 69636174 652D3533 33363530
  33303630 819F300D 06092A86 4886F70D 01010105 0003818D 00308189 02818100
  A10043E2 FB10C1D1 BA18F3AD 554F081C ACA14F4C EA48E0C1 4739653D B7759EE7
  8EB29881 7F391723 E2BB7EC6 54EB6F25 B4E94520 DF8DA15C 3B9E6F7C 3AA57549
```

```
80AB643F  A9427071  965DD56A  2D3E60CE  775F2ED5  C9014FCD  F313F3EB  B5189F62
09F461BC  32E3E78F  F93C8B07  0740DDA8  7B880D1B  A3185787  CE621B35  3511A9D5
02030100  01A37330  71300F06  03551D13  0101FF04  05300301  01FF301E  0603551D
11041730  15821352  312E686F  77746F6E  6574776F  726B2E6E  6574301F  0603551D
23041830  168014CD  63D2C471  B7ABA4AC  F9C2B602  0D4A8954  71C7F930  1D060355
1D0E0416  0414CD63  D2C471B7  ABA4ACF9  C2B6020D  4A895471  C7F9300D  06092A86
4886F70D  01010405  00038181  00675D26  40082389  498F83B1  2F6B6D2C  5C8B4242
6BA41413  22CA95FA  AE8F9CA3  3B07D8DD  1BB89FA9  75906C0A  DFC81504  44BC786A
EAB3F7A5  DE3EFDCC  88D1F90B  5A53ECE1  AB8DA8D2  F92D2C5A  B658474E  1DE7CF3A
74F8FCDA  35F26694  483A3B44  1D14D0FA  31B926F6  69662CD2  672A02F8  9FE2B68B
F4B8E1FD  09B91B84  26CCCBD0  81
      quit
!
username sdmadmin privilege 15 secret 5 $1$kNO5$fqVBJq4mH98ElG5LFRbHD/
archive
 log config
  hidekeys
!
crypto isakmp policy 1
 encr 3des
 authentication pre-share
 group 2
crypto isakmp key security address 10.1.1.2
!
crypto ipsec transform-set ESP-3DES-SHA esp-3des esp-sha-hmac
!
crypto map SDM_CMAP_1 1 ipsec-isakmp
 description Tunnel to10.1.1.2
 set peer 10.1.1.2
 set transform-set ESP-3DES-SHA
 match address 100
!
interface FastEthernet0/0
 ip address 172.16.1.1 255.255.255.0
 duplex auto
 speed auto
!
interface Serial0/0
 ip address 10.1.1.1 255.255.255.252
 crypto map SDM_CMAP_1
!
ip forward-protocol nd
ip route 172.17.1.0 255.255.255.0 Serial0/0
!
ip http server
ip http authentication local
```

```
ip http secure-server
!
access-list 100 remark SDM_ACL Category=4
access-list 100 remark IPSec Rule
access-list 100 permit ip 172.16.1.0 0.0.0.255 172.17.1.0 0.0.0.255
!
control-plane
!
line con 0
line aux 0
line vty 0 4
 privilege level 15
 password cisco
 login
!
end
```

R2 Configuration

```
R2#show run
Building configuration...

Current configuration : 3108 bytes
!
version 12.4
service timestamps debug datetime msec
service timestamps log datetime msec
no service password-encryption
!
hostname R2
!
boot-start-marker
boot-end-marker
!
no logging buffered
no logging console
!
no aaa new-model
no network-clock-participate slot 1
no network-clock-participate wic 0
ip cef
!
no ip domain lookup
ip domain name howtonetwork.net
!
multilink bundle-name authenticated
!
crypto pki trustpoint TP-self-signed-3473940174
```

```
enrollment selfsigned
subject-name cn=IOS-Self-Signed-Certificate-3473940174
revocation-check none
rsakeypair TP-self-signed-3473940174
!
crypto pki certificate chain TP-self-signed-3473940174
certificate self-signed 01
  3082024B 308201B4 A0030201 02020101 300D0609 2A864886 F70D0101 04050030
  31312F30 2D060355 04031326 494F532D 53656C66 2D536967 6E65642D 43657274
  69666963 6174652D 33343733 39343031 3734301E 170D3032 30333031 30303331
  32355A17 0D323030 31303130 30303030 305A3031 312F302D 06035504 03132649
  4F532D53 656C662D 5369676E 65642D43 65727469 66696361 74652D33 34373339
  34303137 3430819F 300D0609 2A864886 F70D0101 01050003 818D0030 81890281
  8100C824 4F0BABB6 A557E3A3 3EE6D399 5A495CF6 8F7E131A 62670291 9710DF0F
  CB6918CB D3B817C8 51D4648C 79B882A8 637804CB 8984FB80 D9F1D86B E79C8292
  E1617724 252490F4 BE0322C0 5C984515 3E0A4550 75E9BCC7 7A19900C 0084F632
  19643491 5C0E821D 5442E1C8 FB4BE8A3 034E2954 01B4377C DC14AF72 0F4C92DC
  70A90203 010001A3 73307130 0F060355 1D130101 FF040530 030101FF 301E0603
  551D1104 17301582 1352322E 686F7774 6F6E6574 776F726B 2E6E6574 301F0603
  551D2304 18301680 144020A0 822373EF EFCD379B 8C2A1A4D 1343842D 59301D06
  03551D0E 04160414 4020A082 2373EFEF CD379B8C 2A1A4D13 43842D59 300D0609
  2A864886 F70D0101 04050003 81810032 3B62EC00 A169C25C 4F7D6B20 C52D5A71
  02C7B7CF 792B6A90 1AEACA7F 5A0D76EB 0C251A25 7E1B53E7 0047652C CB5E0D45
  15578DDD 9A3BC3CC 228F5216 9157651B BC9BF57B F4217458 AF80DBB1 E0F169F7
  DC0B0867 70C21D71 6D8D0A7C 9A683BBF B3171051 E38F9D67 8798AC0C 396684F8
  31C7DF05 21569B49 B39D8FA6 9B5770
    quit
!
username sdmadmin privilege 15 secret 5 $1$/rkS$68SmNHyIaHIme1jQXwrIW1
archive
 log config
  hidekeys
!
crypto isakmp policy 1
 encr 3des
 authentication pre-share
 group 2
crypto isakmp key security address 10.1.1.1
!
crypto ipsec transform-set ESP-3DES-SHA esp-3des esp-sha-hmac
!
crypto map SDM_CMAP_1 1 ipsec-isakmp
 description Tunnel to10.1.1.1
```

```
 set peer 10.1.1.1
 set transform-set ESP-3DES-SHA
 match address 100
!
interface FastEthernet0/0
 ip address 172.17.1.2 255.255.255.0
 duplex auto
 speed auto
!
interface Serial0/0
 ip address 10.1.1.2 255.255.255.252
 clock rate 512000
 crypto map SDM_CMAP_1
!
ip forward-protocol nd
ip route 0.0.0.0 0.0.0.0 Serial0/0
!
ip http server
ip http authentication local
ip http secure-server
!
access-list 100 remark SDM_ACL Category=4
access-list 100 remark IPSec Rule
access-list 100 permit ip 172.17.1.0 0.0.0.255 172.16.1.0 0.0.0.255
!
control-plane
!
line con 0
line aux 0
line vty 0 4
 privilege level 15
 password cisco
 login
!
end
```

Lightning Source UK Ltd.
Milton Keynes UK
UKOW010436050512

192042UK00002B/13/P